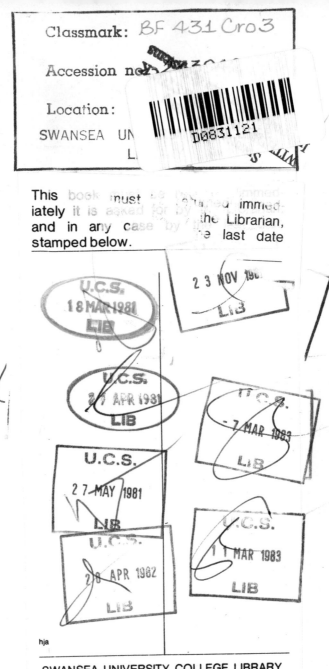

Essentials of Psychological Testing

Essentials of Psychological Testing

Third Edition

Lee J. Cronbach

Stanford University

HARPER INTERNATIONAL EDITION
Harper & Row, Publishers
New York, Evanston, and London

Essentials of Psychology Testing, Third Edition

Library of Congress Catalog Card Number: 73-86989

AINT-35-31217   EINT-35-61263   INT-35-02515

4th printing

Printed in Singapore by Times Printers Sdn. Bhd.

To My Parents

Contents

Figures

Tables

COMPUTING GUIDES

Preface to the Third Edition

A *grandfather clause* is one that begins "I remember when . . . ." Well, a preface to a third edition is entitled to a few grandfather clauses.

The first edition (1949) came when everybody who was anybody in psychology had recently been a full-time applied psychologist with the military, as a clinician, or in some interesting but less-talked-about job. There followed a decade of sorting-out, of getting back to theory on the one hand and of critically comparing means of applied service on the other. The 1960 edition came as new trends were emerging. The 1960s are too close for evaluation, but one can be sure that they will be noted for the revitalization of developmental psychology, for the discovery of education as a lively field for inquiry by the kind of research psychologist who had previously shunned it, and for the breakaway growth of psychotherapy separate from medical institutions. Forces like these leave their mark on the study of tests.

At the end of the 1940s my story was overwhelmingly applied. The books to be highlighted as major recent achievements were the 5-foot shelf of Air Force publications, the OSS story in *Assessment of men,* the 8-year study (Progressive Education Association) reported by Smith and Tyler, Rogers' *Counseling and psychotherapy,* and Klopfer and Beck on the Rorschach. (Strangely, not one of these had an influential sequel, though each has left its mark, indeed its deep grooves, in today's thought and practice.) On the basic-research side, in 1949, one could report seminal inquiries from Murray, from Bayley, and from the Fels group, for example. These lines of investigation have been continually renewed by students, disciples, critics, and the authors themselves. But as of 1949, theory in the differential areas was either aged and arthritic, or inchoately speculative.

The 1950s were a period of constructive disillusionment. We had a chance to put color-dimming distance between us and the "triumphs" hailed in wartime enthusiasm. Projective techniques, impressionistic assessment, factorial batteries, MMPI, Wechsler scatter analysis, and the other brave new ideas came under the critic's lash; some collapsed, and some emerged the better for the chastisement. Critical monographs loomed larger than new findings or integrative books: Meehl on clinical judgment, the *Technical recommendations*, Kelly and Fiske on assessment, something on decision theory—plus, of course, the superbooks edited by Oscar Buros. Important new batches of data enhanced test-interpretation—notably the GATB manual and revised DAT manual—but there were few new tests. This was not the decade of the innovator. Theory entered the second edition more than the first. Janet Taylor's work, McClelland's, and Piaget's were demonstrating ways to ask new types of questions about individuals. Two of my pet concepts, construct validation and aptitude-treatment interaction, had forced themselves upon us but we did not quite know what to do with them (nor do we know fully yet). The measurement field was beginning to polarize between dustier-than-ever empiricism and a methodologically permissive but soberly reasoned attempt to explain personal characteristics rather than merely to describe them.

The 1960s saw a flowering of research on personality theory, cognition, child development, and even on such remote matters as behavior genetics and brain chemistry. We have more findings than accepted theory at present, but there are less-promising states to be in. As for the practical side, new facts flood over us. Technical reporting on tests far surpasses that of 1950 or even 1960. But my overall impression of today's practical tests, as the reader will see, is that they are obsolescent. Tests that saw the light of day before 1949, with new norms and new scoring procedures, are in many areas the best we have today. Only the strict empiricists, those who eschew theory as entanglement, have been marketing practical new products and procedures. I cannot escape the feeling that the things actuarially scored tests cannot do are more important than the things they can do. Is the time not ripe for a wholly fresh effort to construct a new generation of tests? Or must testing based on theory wait until theoretic and metatheoric problems are better resolved?

In the last decade most of the creative thought on individual characteristics has looked toward theoretical understanding rather than practical contributions. This research accepts, consciously or not, the maxim of Campbell and Fiske that there is little use in establishing a generalization about a trait or intervening variable unless one can measure it (and, in experiments, manipulate it) by two or more distinctly different operations. An investigator used to spend his life investigating data from one operation; while no one would decry the contribution of Terman, Porteus, or Strong, that strategy is too little generalizable. Today's mainstream researcher grapples persistently with a single construct, matching protean operations to the protean elusiveness of the construct. The style is not new; Hartshorne-May and Piaget adopted it long ago. The current popularity of the style is promising for the progress of theory. While I doubt that any broad theory is now ready to set forth blueprints for test construction, my treatment of ability tests will make it evident that I see possible convergences between views put forward quite separately by Piaget, Cattell, Witkin, Guttman, Porteus, Vernon, and an army of cognitive simulators. Someone should be able to distill from this, and the literature in the older traditions of Wechsler and Thurstone-Guilford, a guide to the next generation of tests. Perhaps there are similar possibilities in the current career-development studies, the concept of personality as a set of coping strategies, and elsewhere.

Practical testing has thrived in this decade. Renewed interest in education increased the use of tests manyfold. Counselor training was advanced by the Federal government's interest in talent. Hunt's book managed to get across to the world what had never been listened to before: the message that intelligence develops and is not predetermined. Test publishers have raised their standards. They have put funds, energy, and skill into the updating, restandardization, and extension to new age levels of many tried-and-true tests. (But perhaps these very standards are making it difficult for a good new test to gain a foothold.)

On the other side of the ledger are the slings and arrows that accompany prominence: the attacks on ability tests as unfair to minority groups and on personality tests as invasions of privacy, the intensified skepticism about complex multiscore batteries, and the growing uneasiness about the effects of selection mechanisms on society. It seems to me that the profession should accept in a sober fashion most of the criticisms made of tests. Present tests, in the hands of qualified users, make valuable social and personal contributions. The task now is to extend the value of the enterprise.

I am more convinced than ever that the solution for most of the ills of testing is to develop sound knowledge of aptitude-treatment interactions. Then we can shift from a selection model or a prediction model to an allocation model, and use test procedures to pick the educational, therapeutic, or other approach that promises best results for the individual. This is both socially and logically right. Each year now, half-a-dozen pleas for this type of thinking come from *Annual Review* authors speaking for diverse branches of psychology. And the once-trickling evidence that there are such interactions is now at least a babbling brook. The evidence is so turbulent and sometimes bubbly that we cannot draw off any power. When we have crossvalidated evidence as to what *person* variables and *treatment* variables interact, we will be in a position to generate a new kind of practical testing.

Having read these remarks about the evolution of the field, past and to come, the reader may wonder to find so much on past work and on traditional tests in this book. But the book is first of all an account of the essentials: the methods of inquiry, the critical standards, and the key concepts of the field. Radically new thinking is going to build on these predecessors, not be started anew. Moreover, practicing testers are going to be using the established tests and their close relatives for a long time. While basically different tests will be needed for new functions, revisions of older tests will continue to serve traditional functions. The reader should expect to learn a great deal more, this year, next year, and every year, as the research literature unfolds. This book is intended to establish a base from which his knowledge can grow.

The chapter on Proficiency Tests from the second edition is not included this time, for the paradoxical reason that there is just too much to say on that subject. The old chapter provided a few leads for the personnel psychologist who might use tests of trade knowledge in hiring, and a few suggestions about school testing programs (together with some technical content that I have relocated in this addition). With recent developments on the national and international scene, psychologists have been plunged neckdeep in educational activities, all of which have their own special measurement problems: compensatory education, individualized instruction, linguistically oriented instruction in second languages, large-scale assessment of educational effectiveness, and curriculum evaluation, to name a few. The issues and techniques require book-length treatment which I hope will be provided in the ACE–AERA volume *Educational Measurement*, soon to appear under the editorship of R. L. Thorndike. (The complexity of the educational field today is suggested in that the chapter on validity I am contributing to that volume is about four times the length of the chapter here.) For those who wish to supplement the present book with a brief study of classroom achievement tests, a number of suitable paperback treatments can be considered.

It is a pleasure to thank the many who have contributed to this edition, in particular my editor Wayne Holtzman, numerous publishing firms and test authors, instructors who made suggestions for change, and a small army of typists and librarians. (A number of tables, figures, and extended quotations are reproduced from publications of the American Psychological Association, are copyrighted, and have been reproduced by permission.) Harper & Row has been a valued collaborator for more than 20 years, thanks to the understanding of George Middendorf, and Ed Tyler before him.

LEE J. CRONBACH

September, 1969
Stanford, California

part I

Basic Concepts

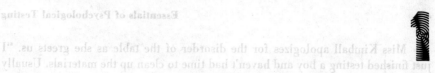

Who Uses Tests?

The testing movement stands as a prime example of social science in action, since it touches on vital questions in all phases of our life. What is character, and what sorts of children have good character? What personality makeup promises that an adolescent will be a stable, effective adult? How can we tell when a child is ready to begin learning to read? Is this young man a good prospect for training in watchmaking, or should he go into a different vocation— say steamfitting or patternmaking? Such are the problems toward which testing and research on individual differences are directed. In this book, we shall survey the methods that have been and are being developed to solve these problems.

Typical Test Users

One way to get a quick overview is to find out what testers do. By meeting a few of the people who work with tests we can get an impression of the variety of services tests perform and of the way they fit into a psychological career. The people to be described are imaginary, each one being a composite portrait of many psychologists such as can be found in every part of the country.

Let's begin by calling on Helen Kimball. At about 11:00 on a January morning, we find her at her desk in the central administration building of the school system of Riverton, population 17,000. Miss Kimball is dark, attractive, 35ish. Her position bears the title School Psychologist. The office in which we find her is unusually bright, with decorative pictures, drapes, and a table low enough to accommodate a child. On the table are spread several objects: blocks, a cutout puzzle, a folder of pictures.

Miss Kimball apologizes for the disorder of the table as she greets us. "I just finished testing a boy and haven't had time to clean up the materials. Usually I keep only a toy or two on the table, to attract the interest of any child sent down to see me. These test materials are from the Wechsler intelligence scale and a picture technique for studying personality called the Thematic Apperception Test." When we express interest in her case, and inquire about the reason for testing the boy, she outlines his background as follows.

Charles, in the fourth grade, suddenly is causing trouble after having been known as a friendly, successful pupil in other grades. His teacher reports that he has made almost no progress in school subjects since the start of the year, that he refuses her attempts to give extra help, and that he has begun to disturb the class by hitting other boys, taking objects from the girls to annoy them, and similar misdemeanors. A check with the files showed that his home is a stable one, but not well-to-do. His parents were born outside the United States, moving here before Charles was born. Charles' previous teachers had recorded many favorable remarks: "A fine worker. Does everything a little better than most other boys." "Learns new ideas quickly. Good at number work." But the objective tests given at the end of the third grade showed that he was not superior. In reading comprehension Charles was behind the average pupil of his class, and in arithmetic, his best score, he just reached the average. Probably his cheerfulness and industry led teachers to overrate his past learning.

"Now," says Miss Kimball, "they have asked me to try to determine the causes of his problem. Teachers in each school check most of the cases; for instance, they give intelligence tests and reading tests, and make studies of the children the school needs to know more about. Charles was sent to me because the teacher felt his behavior presented an especially serious problem. The school did have a mental-test record, because Charles' class took the Kuhlmann-Anderson group intelligence test two months ago. Charles' IQ was only 65. But his teacher said Charles wouldn't work on the test. He did a few items, then stopped and looked out the window; when she urged him to go ahead, he worked slowly, and seemed not to be trying.

"So my first problem was to try to find out how bright Charles is, to learn what he can be expected to accomplish in the usual school program. The Wechsler or the Stanford-Binet is our usual measure. Since we give these tests individually, most children cooperate well. When I gave the Wechsler this morning, Charles did about as well as most 10-year-olds; I haven't computed his IQ yet, but from the impression I formed as I gave the test, it will come out about 90 to 100—perhaps a trifle below average. The score might be affected by his schooling, as many of the questions use language. The Performance section of the test, though, uses blocks, picture puzzles, and other tasks not likely to be affected by schooling, and he did about the same as on the Verbal section; apparently language difficulties aren't his big problem. I was pleased that he cooperated, since he'd balked on the group test. He was eager to work, cheerful, and seemed pleased with his accomplishment. But of course we started out slowly, and I made a great effort to interest him in the 'games.'

"I did two other things with Charles. Usually we don't test so much in one day, but the school wants to make some decisions about Charles at midyear. So we broke off the testing and chatted awhile; then I gave him a vision test. I chose that because I noticed some squinting during the intelligence test, and the teacher had noted a few complaints of headaches. My vision tests aren't as precise as an oculist's, but they showed a little deficiency in one eye. Worse, though, is his coordination; the eyes don't work together, but instead look at slightly different parts of the page when he is reading. This probably can be corrected, but we'll need further visual tests to be sure. Poor visual coordination would cause trouble in reading and lead to fatigue.

"Since the emotional problem seemed to be severe, judging from the reports of Charles' social behavior, I used the picture-interpretation test. The child makes up stories about each picture, and the stories often reveal his worries and wishes. Here's one picture, for example, showing a boy huddled up in a corner. Charles made up a story that the boy was playing with the others and they made him stop and go home. The other boys said he had a different way of playing that wasn't right. Several stories like that suggest that Charles is greatly worried about losing his friends, and about 'being different.' The test gives many other suggestions about Charles' problems, but I need to study the record before I form definite conclusions.

"Our next steps will be to check on the vision problem and to clarify the emotional difficulties. I'll have several conferences with Charles, helping him talk out his difficulties. Then we will see what can be done to help him solve them. The fact that he has normal mental ability is encouraging, since we know he can do well if his adjustment improves. It will help to know that he is average rather than superior, as past teachers suggested. Perhaps he has had to live up to too high a reputation. We may use further tests later; the ones used so far have narrowed our field of investigation, so that I will learn more from my conferences with Charles."

No two of Miss Kimball's cases are just alike, nor are the same tests appropriate for every case. In contrast to her "clinical," individualized approach is the work of a personnel manager for a department store. This is a store with about 350 employees, ranging from roustabouts to buyers and office personnel. Edward Blake, the personnel manager, is a heavy-set, graying man of 45, who seems interested in whatever we have to say. But there is also a briskness, a sticking-to-a-schedule. "The routines of the job? I don't do much testing myself; but I do interview everybody we hire. That helps the store, because every employee knows there's someone here in the office who has met him and to whom he can take his problems.

"When an applicant comes in, he fills out a personal-history blank, and my assistant, Miss Field, gives him a set of tests. The tests aren't quite the same for everybody. We give all applicants a short intellectual screening test, since different jobs in the store call for employees of different caliber. The test items are in multiple-choice form, and require ability to follow directions and to do simple reasoning. Most applicants get a test of simple arithmetic—addition, percentages, discounts, and so on. For package wrappers and merchandise handlers, we use a test in which they place wooden cubes in a box as rapidly as possible. It doesn't predict who will be the best employee, but it saves us from some lemons. For a few departments, we have tests of information about the job. Some men claim to be shoe salesmen when they don't know a last from a counter. These tests check on the experience the applicant claims in his application blank.

"Whatever tests Miss Field gives are scored and recorded on the application blank. Then, when there is a vacancy, we pull out the names of people who have the qualifications that job requires. I call in one or more of these people, interview them, and if I think they'll do, I hire them. The tests are most useful to sort out the good from the poor prospects. Miss Field can give the tests very easily, and it saves us a lot of time we'd spend interviewing people who wouldn't be good workers. Of course, Miss Field does a nice job, encouraging each applicant to do his best and sending him away with a feeling that he's had fair consideration."

Mr. Blake, of course, is a little different from some other personnel manager we might have talked to. But his work is fairly typical of that in businesses having substantial turnover.

Unlike Miss Kimball and Mr. Blake, Max Samuels and Paul Sheridan are using tests for research which will have only distant practical applications. We find them in the psychology laboratory of Atherton University on a July day, surrounded by piles of test booklets. Samuels gets up from a tape recorder to which he has been listening and offers to show us around the project.

"We're studying how people solve problems. When we give an ordinary intelligence test, we see that people have many difficulties that seem to have nothing to do with their brightness. Sometimes a person becomes confused and makes the same mistake three or four times, even though he has already done harder problems. Another person may plan a solution to a problem and carry out several steps in an orderly way, but when he makes one error he loses his sense of direction and slips back into random trial and error. We are trying to develop exact methods of measuring these habitual ways of reacting to difficulties. They are important elements in problem solving, affecting scores on mental tests and also performance in practical situations. Intelligence tests, which measure the person's general level of success, do not give accurate data on his manner of problem solving.

"Sheridan and I are just beginning to explore what the important variables in problem solving may be. We will spend a couple of years refining our observation techniques before we are ready to carry out formal studies. Both of us teach during the school year, but we spend about a quarter of our time giving tests to students. During the summer we analyze the records, revise the tests for the next tryout, and take a few more steps toward a theory of problem solving."

The first test Samuels shows us uses the same blocks Miss Kimball had on her table. The person tested is shown a mosaic design and asked to make the same design out of blocks. "In the intelligence test," Samuels says, "the score reports the number of designs completed within certain time limits. The tester may record casual observations of the kinds of error the person makes, but he does not score them. We are trying to obtain dependable scores indicating how systematically the person attacks the problem, how often he repeats a mistake, and how long a time passes before he notices a mistake. Sheridan gives the test in a room with a large mirror set in the wall. The mirror is fixed so that one can see through from the back; I sit on that side and observe every detail of what the subject does. I dictate a record into the tape recorder. We can listen to the tapes whenever we wish, and work out the nature and time of each error. We have developed new designs that make certain types of error more likely, and later we hope to develop a simpler scoring method that will not require a tape recorder."

Samuels shows several other tests using mazes, anagrams, and designs made by building up layers of cutout colored stencils. "Our main purpose," he says, "is to identify consistent patterns the person shows on many different problems. These patterns are the ones we expect him to carry over when he writes a theme in English or tries to identify an unknown substance in chemistry."

We inquire about a piece of apparatus with a ring of lights and a few pushbuttons. "This experimental test," he says, "permits us to present much longer and more complex tasks than the usual puzzle. It is intended to measure abilities of high-level scientific and technical workers; one needs very difficult tasks to separate the best men in such a group. We are using it with average students because they make many errors, and our main concern is to study the types of error made by different persons. The apparatus is wired so that it follows some simple rules. These rules change with every problem. Three pushbuttons turn on and off various lights. The person's task may be to turn on light number 3 only. He presses the buttons in turn to find out what lights each button controls. For instance, when he presses button 1, lights 3, 4, and 5 go on. He must find a sequence of actions that will leave only light 3 lit. A problem of this type can be made very complicated; even a bright person takes thirty minutes on some of our problems. One interesting feature of this apparatus is its automatic recording. Every time the person presses a button, a record is made on tape. This tape can later be decoded to show just what the person did and when."

Sheridan comes in at this moment with an armload of boxes that turn out to contain cards for use in a computer. His role in the project, he explains, is to analyze the data after all the tests and records have been scored. "The electronic computer has been a blessing to research like this. We obtain about 200 scores on every student we test, and it would take forever to work out the relations by older methods. The electronic machine gives us the answers in just a few minutes of running time. The catch is that every observation has to be reduced to numerical form before it can be treated statistically.

"Our main statistical method is factor analysis. This helps us to separate variables that affect only a single task from the more central ones that show up consistently throughout the person's performance. We also find out which test scores give the best measures of each variable. We hope eventually to have dependable measures of how persistent, how systematic, and how adaptable the person is.

"We are not primarily interested in practical applications. If we can classify people according to the way they solve problems, then we want to study how they get that way. Anxiety appears to be an important cause of errors, but we want to learn why one anxious person's errors habitually differ from those of another. We will eventually do experiments in which we apply various sorts of pressure to see if different kinds of stress or risk produce different errors. Before we can do such research we have to be able to distinguish and measure these errors."

It is easy to think of applications for such tests as Sheridan and Samuels are developing. The tests might diagnose mental patients, select students for specialized training, or analyze students whose school performance is below their ability level. Very often, tests developed for laboratory investigations are applied later.

Our three examples represent only a few of the many ways in which tests are used. We might also describe the clinical psychologist in a hospital, the tester preparing standardized tests for school use, the vocational counselor, and many other highly qualified testers. We might pay more attention to the Miss Fields who give most of the tests in offices, clinics, schools, and industries. From the portraits presented we can draw these generalizations that warrant learning about tests:

Tests play an important part in making decisions about people and in psychological research. There are a great variety of tests, covering many sorts of characteristics. Even for a single characteristic such as mental ability, there are many tests which have different uses. The significance of test scores is greatest when they are combined with a full study of the person by means of interview, case-history records, application blanks, and other methods. Tests provide facts that help us understand people; the test is almost never a mechanical tool that makes decisions automatic.

As we go on, shortly, to talk of the testing industry, you may find yourself condemning testing as a handmaiden of the Establishment. To be sure, testing serves conservative forces: it was military testing in World War I that first brought testing into prominence, and employment managers, schools, and mental hospitals use tests to keep their institutions going smoothly. But do not be misled by the fact that the largest sales of tests are for essentially conservative purposes. Tests can also serve—indeed, are sometimes of great value to—the reformer. The pioneering tests of Galton, a hundred years ago, were inspired by, and did much to advance, the idea that a man's place should depend on what he can do and not on the social position of his parents. Precisely the same philosophy animates the pioneers, not too different from Miss Kimball, who are trying to provide disadvantaged children with fitting educational activities. Tests have been used in recent years to document the extent to which the schools fail the Negro. Tests have also demonstrated that a near-fascist personality can be found in many a person the community calls well-adjusted and successful (Adorno *et al.*, 1950). Tests are neutral; they serve those who want to maintain society without change, and they are a weapon available to those who want to criticize present institutions and create a society based fully on merit and self-determination.

Evolution of the Testing Enterprise

What amounts to an industry today had informal, even casual, beginnings. A psychologist or physician wanted to observe some type of motor, intellectual, or emotional behavior and chose a stimulus or task he thought gave a good opportunity for observation. As he mentioned his findings to others, they copied his technique in their own clinics and laboratories. Soon there was a small market for equipment (tachistoscopes for studying flash perception, formboards for testing perception and reasoning, etc.). Around 1910 a few books were written, each describing one investigator's procedures, but there was no large-scale manufacture of tests. Test publication in the modern sense resulted from the great interest in clinical and educational testing following successful mass testing of soldiers in World War I. The view then prevalent was that a test score can be interpreted adequately only by comparison with national norms based on thousands of cases. Users all over the country wished to purchase the same tests, packaged in a form that ensured uniform procedure, and accompanied by national norms.

What is still called "test publishing" was at the outset that and nothing more. A psychologist who had prepared a test printed copies for general sale, perhaps through a firm selling apparatus to psychology laboratories. As the demand for tests grew, particularly after World War I, some textbook publishers began to handle tests, and some firms specializing in school tests were established. Until about 1945, the typical test was developed by an author or team of authors who completed the test and then offered it to the publisher. The publisher gave some assistance in the final stages of research and in editing the test manual, but the main scientific responsibility was the author's.

Testing was entirely decentralized in those days. Every institution—college, business, clinic, or whatever—planned and administered its own program. Each school system was free to adopt tests or not, and to choose whichever ones it preferred. Different counseling agencies purchased different tests, and sometimes each psychologist within the agency chose the tests he preferred. This decentralization, combined with a demand for carefully developed instruments, provided a competitive market that encouraged publication of tests in great number and great variety. With these tests available, the industrial psychologist no longer thought it necessary to make up new tests for his own factory. Even a great national agency such as the Veterans Administration relies on published tests for its psychological and psychiatric clinics.

This picture of decentralization and variety is still largely valid, but an increasing centralization has to be recognized. States pass laws requiring tests at certain stages in the school program to encourage guidance programs and to get reports on the effectiveness of the schools; the law may not prescribe precisely the tests to be used, but it limits the choice. The day when each college could administer its own set of tests to applicants has passed. The number of tests an ambitious high-school senior had to take, to compete for admission and scholarships at various places, became a burden on students and high schools. Hence today almost every college admissions office relies on one or the other of two nationwide testing programs. A counselor could choose the test he preferred, in days when he saw an average of two new clients a day. Nowadays the counseling load is so great that the high school or college typically tests all entering students at once, sends the tests to the computer for scoring, and files them for use as occasion arises. There is nothing to prevent choosing supplementary tests for special cases, but the practice is less common. Centralizing and unifying influences give prominence to a few popular tests and sometimes crowd out worthy competitors. The big get bigger, the also-rans give up the struggle.

The market for a successful test is greater than ever. The publisher of the established test fights to hold on to its prominence, and the publisher of a new test must make a major effort if he is to break in. The publishing of tests is now a publishing enterprise in name only. To accept a test some professor has assembled in his spare time, almost as a hobby, and make it available to interested purchasers—that is traditional publishing. For a staff of professionals to identify a kind of instrument that could be sold, to design and construct such an instrument (perhaps with help from teachers or psychologists outside the staff), to carry out a three-year program of research before releasing the test, to promote the test by means of displays at professional meetings and seminars to train interpreters, to provide a scoring-and-reporting service—that is test production, which is the source of nearly all recent tests. It requires capital and a skilled, experienced staff. It has created a testing industry, whose dominant firms are sometimes subsidiaries of giants like IBM, sometimes large nonprofit institutions.

This industrialization is fully as beneficial as centralization has been in the drug industry. Quality standards have been greatly improved. Services are rapid and efficient. The test user can call on the firm for a high grade of advice, and can get numerous aids such as booklets for explaining test results to pupils. Money is set aside for research from which new and better tests eventually come.

Conservatism comes with centralization. Just as the Big Three compete by producing automobiles that are nearly indistinguishable, so the testing industry puts most of its effort on a few tried-and-true designs. The huge market of every-pupil testing programs is well served. Individual tests and tests to be applied to a fractional market are still left pretty much to a "cottage industry." Even in the main product line, there is a regrettable tendency to keep old titles and designs in production, with only minor improvements, when modern ideas suggest radically different designs. But an industry with a large investment cannot move far ahead of its customers. Only if the next generation of test purchasers understands the possibility of better tests will someone be enterprising enough to supply them.

Some sense of the life-history of a test is given by Figures 1.1 and 1.2, drawn from records of the Strong Vocational Interest Blank. This test was originally developed by E. K. Strong, Jr., in the 1920s, and published by the Stanford University Press in 1927. Its popularity grew slowly, as counselors developed interest in this kind of service and as more universities added counseling agencies. Immediately after World War II there was an enormous bulge of demand stemming from the counseling services provided for veterans, who were making educational and vocational decisions to which the Strong is highly relevant. The rather flat trend in sales after 1950 is very likely a composite of two tendencies. There was a marked rise in test use during this period—all tests considered—as a function of rising enrollments and demand for counseling services. There was a decline in the proportion of testers using the Strong, which was suspected of being out-of-date, which was being pushed aside by competitors to some extent, and which was cumbersome to score. The Strong has been "renewed" by a recent republication based on substantial research; the availability of computerized scoring services and simplification of its hand scoring also make use of the test more likely. Hence one can forecast a new climb in the usage curve, if users are satisfied with the validity of the new version and do not shift to some newborn competitor.

The Strong history is not representative of all tests. Some attract so many competitors that they are unable to command the attention of test users and researchers. Some are forced out by radical new conceptualizations—in the psychology of interests new concepts are as yet only being hinted at. A test produced directly for a publishing firm is sometimes killed within a few years if it does not reach a satisfactory level of sales. The firm will, in many such cases,

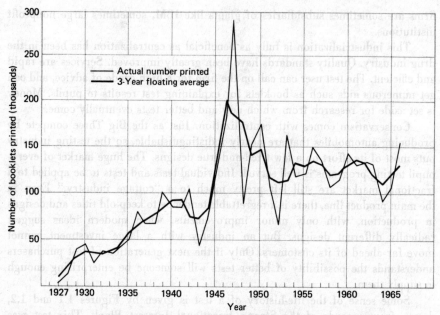

Figure 1.1.   Trends in demand for a psychological test over four decades.
Data are for the Strong Vocational Interest Blank. *D. P. Campbell, 1968.*

replace the test with one of different design that promises to have greater appeal. Even so, the history of the Strong argues that knowledge about today's tests is likely to be relevant for decades to come.

1. *Most American tests for use in counseling are distributed through publishers to anyone who is qualified and wishes to buy them. Another system is found in various national employment services and youth agencies, especially in Europe. Each counseling service devises a special set of aptitude tests for its own use. Only the counselors employed by this agency are allowed to use the tests. What are the advantages and disadvantages of this type of control, compared with the usual type of distribution?*

Questions like this are part of the text, capitalizing on the fact that the mind profits most when it works as it reads. By thinking through the questions on each section, the reader sees how the principles apply and becomes aware of topics that require further thought. The questions do not always have specific answers. Frequently they are deliberately controversial, or can be answered only by a qualified "Yes, but—." The student who sees two sides to any of the questions can have considerable confidence that he is doing good thinking.

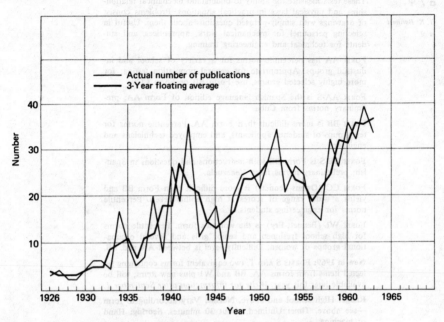

Figure 1.2. Trends in research publications on a single test.
Data are for the Strong Vocational Interest Blank. *D. P. Campbell, 1968.*

Purchasing Tests

Sources of Information About Tests

A first step in looking for tests is to consult catalogs of test distributors. With some important exceptions, the prominent tests in the United States are handled by these test-development companies: California Test Bureau, Educational Testing Service, Harcourt, Brace & World, Inc., The Psychological Corporation, and Science Research Associates. Major firms that emphasize publishing rather than development of tests by their own staffs include Consulting Psychologists Press, Houghton Mifflin, and Personnel Press. The person interested in purchasing tests should obtain the current catalogs of these firms and of any other publisher likely to have tests in his field of interest. Addresses of firms are given in the Appendix.

The catalog lists and describes tests. Most of the catalogs indicate clearly what level of training is required to use each test, and who may purchase it. The publisher's recommendation should be viewed conservatively; in some instances the publisher indicates that a purchaser with limited training can use a test for which testing authorities would favor a stricter standard.

Mechanical Comprehension Test

a / Ψ

G. K. Bennett et al.

These tests measure the ability to understand mechanical relationships and physical laws in practical situations. Problems consist of drawings with simply-phrased questions about them. Useful in selecting personnel for mechanical work, apprentices, and students for technical and engineering training.

FORM AA has percentile norms for a variety of school and industrial groups. Appropriate for general population testing; for more highly selected groups, use Form BB or Form CC.

FORM AA-S is the Spanish language edition of Form AA; preliminary norms from Cuba.

FORM BB is more difficult than Form AA. Percentile norms for ten groups of students, applicants, and employed technicians and engineers.

FORM BB-S is Form BB with instructions and questions in Spanish; preliminary norms from Venezuela.

FORM CC (Owens-Bennett) is more difficult than Form BB and yields a wider range of scores at high ability levels. Percentile norms for engineering students.

FORM W1 (Bennett-Fry) is the women's form. Percentile norms for high school freshmen and senior girls and several occupational groups of women. Difficulty level is between AA and BB.

New in 1969: FORMS S AND T, two equivalent forms containing selected items from forms AA, BB and W1 plus new items, will be available later this year. *Write for information after September 1.*

Range: High school and above. **Norms:** Vary according to form —see above. **Time:** Untimed, about 30 minutes. **Scoring:** Hand or machine.

Order each item separately
Answer sheet needed for each person tested

Reusable Booklets *Specify form and catalog number*

3C029	Form AA, pkg of 25....	5.50	10 or more pkgs, each..	4.90
3C081	Form BB, pkg of 25......	5.50	10 or more pkgs, each..	4.90
7Z613	Form CC, pkg of 25....	5.50	10 or more pkgs, each..	4.90
3C146	Form W1, pkg of 25....	5.50	10 or more pkgs, each..	4.90
7Z510	Form AA-S, pkg of 25....	6.30	10 or more pkgs, each..	5.60
3C108	Form BB-S, pkg of 25....	6.30	10 or more pkgs, each..	5.60

Answer Sheets, IBM 805 *Specify form and catalog number*

Form AA	3C213	Pkg of 50....	2.50	3C225 Pkg of 500....	20.00
Form BB	3C275	Pkg of 50....	2.50	3C287 Pkg of 500....	20.00
Form CC	7Z637	Pkg of 50....	2.50	7Z649 Pkg of 500....	20.00
Form W1	3C366	Pkg of 50....	2.50	3C378 Pkg of 500....	20.00
Form AA-S	7Z534	Pkg of 50....	2.50	7Z546 Pkg of 500....	20.00
Form BB-S	3C304	Pkg of 50....	2.50	3C316 Pkg of 500....	20.00

	Manual		Scoring Key		Specimen Set
Form AA	3C407	.30	3C457	.40	3C809 .60
Form BB	3C419	.30	3C471	.40	3C823 .60
Form CC	7Z651	.30	7Z663	.40	7Z675 .60
Form W1	3C433	.30	3C500	.40	3C847 .60
Form AA-S	7Z558	.50	7Z560	.60	7Z572 1.90
Form BB-S			3C483	.60	

Figure 1.3.   Catalog information on the Mechanical Comprehension Test.
This exhibit comes from the 1969 catalog of The Psychological Corporation. The code symbol *a* indicates that this test falls in the least restricted category; a business firm may purchase the test even if there is no qualified psychologist on the staff. The symbol *ψ* indicates that the test is published by The Psychological Corporation rather than an independent author. *Reproduced by permission.*

What information the catalog itself can provide is illustrated by Figure 1.3, describing the Bennett tests, which we shall discuss fully in Chapter 3 and subsequently. Tests may be suggested by several additional sources, particularly the *Mental Measurements Yearbook* (see p. 121) and the compilation in Appendix C of Anastasi's textbook (1968).

Before a decision to purchase the test for use is made, a detailed study of its manual is needed. Whereas the catalog description is only a few paragraphs long, the manual offers several pages of information on the purposes to which the test is best suited, methods of administering and interpreting it, and its limitations. Sometimes the information that describes the research basis of the test is placed in a technical handbook, leaving the less technical description for the examiner's manual. If the manual is divided in this way, both parts should be consulted. A "specimen set" of a test is a package including a manual, test booklet, and scoring key. Most universities and many school systems and counseling centers maintain collections of specimen sets for the use of the professional staff and persons in training. Publishers sell specimen sets to students and professional workers.

Who May Obtain Tests?

Tests are useful, but in the hands of persons with inadequate training they do a great deal of harm. An untrained user may administer a test incorrectly. He may place undue reliance on inaccurate measurements. He may misunderstand what the test measures and reach unsound conclusions. It is therefore important for the user to confine himself to tests that he can handle properly.

To see the implications of this remark, consider industrial personnel testing. To a manager it may appear simple to give a group intelligence test, score it with a punched-out key, tabulate the scores, and hire the best man. A personnel psychologist, however, knows that on some routine jobs average men make better employees than highly intelligent men, who become bored and quit. He knows that a general mental test does not measure the abilities most important in many factory jobs. He knows that even experts make errors when they try to guess which tests will predict success in a given job; a scientifically designed tryout is essential to make sure that the tests actually pick better employees.

Introducing and operating an industrial testing program requires many different abilities:

1. Analyzing the job to identify abilities that could be relevant.
2. Selecting promising tests for tryout.
3. Constructing new tests when no published test is suitable.
4. Planning and carrying out an experimental trial; choosing the final set of tests.
5. Deciding how test results are to be used in selection.

6. Routinely administering tests to applicants.
7. Scoring.
8. Interpreting the test and making hiring decisions within the general plan.
9. Periodically making follow-up studies to check the soundness of the program.

Advanced training is required to perform steps 1 through 5, and step 9. For most tests used in industry, step 6 can be performed by an intelligent clerk, and step 7 by a clerk or a machine. Step 8 may be a routine operation or may call for a decision by an executive who considers a psychologist's recommendation along with other facts.

Levels of qualification.   Industrial personnel workers in the United States are qualified at various levels:

• Diploma in industrial psychology. A diploma is awarded by the American Board of Professional Psychology to an applicant who possesses (among other qualifications) the training and experience required for carrying out all phases of an industrial testing program.[1]

• Doctoral degree in personnel psychology. A psychologist at this level (who may have received his training in a university department of psychology, education, or business management) should be able to perform all the functions listed above. If he has limited experience, he may need to consult a better-qualified person, especially in planning the program. Numerous consulting firms provide assistance in planning.

• Limited specialized training. Workers who have training in personnel methods equivalent to a master's degree can carry out specialized functions within a general plan. They can administer complicated tests, collect data on the performance of employees, and make some decisions about individuals. A psychologist can train an intelligent assistant to perform such functions, although he must then provide close supervision.[2]

• Intelligent workers without psychological training. A person without psychological training can learn to administer many group tests, take charge of the scoring of objective tests, and apply mechanical rules for selection on the basis of scores.

• Ordinary clerical workers. These workers should be used only for routine scoring under competent supervision, and for assisting in test administration.

If we were to consider use of tests in a vocational counseling service, a school testing program, or a diagnostic service in a mental hospital, we would observe similarly varied roles to be played. In each of these services there is need for some routine handling of tests and test data, for responsible supervision, and for

[1] The Board also grants diplomas in clinical psychology, in school psychology, and in counseling.
[2] One psychologist (D. Wilson, 1951) has described how he trained convicts (including a safecracker, a dope peddler, and a counterfeiter) to give even fairly complicated tests to other prisoners.

high-level planning of the total program. A testing program involves far more than a package of tests and a stopwatch.

The amount of specialized training required depends upon the tests to be used. Some tests can be administered and interpreted by responsible persons who have no specialized training. Other tests serving the same general purpose can be used only by well-qualified psychologists. For example, two tests that might have some value in selecting men for training as junior executives are the Concept Mastery Test and the Thematic Apperception Test (TAT). The former is a difficult test of word knowledge. The directions for administering it and the scoring procedure are so simple that a high-school graduate can follow them. An employer with no psychological training can easily understand what the results mean. To administer and interpret TAT, a person must have graduate training in the psychology of personality and should have supervised experience with this particular test. It is used to investigate the motives of the subject and his feelings about other persons. The conclusions it suggests are not highly dependable. Serious errors would result if the test were interpreted by anyone save a cautious and able psychologist.

Test distribution. Distributors of tests try to restrict sales to qualified persons, just as the sale of medicines is restricted. Test distributors check the qualifications of purchasers to determine whether they are competent to use whatever tests they order. Severe restrictions are placed on the tests that are most difficult to interpret and the misinterpretation of which would be most serious.

Security is a further reason for restriction. Copies of questions must not fall into the hands of persons who will later take the test. Students would like to become familiar with a college entrance examination in advance. Parents sometimes try to help their child by coaching him on intelligence test items, but to the extent that their coaching succeeds, it distorts decisions. The control system protects legitimate users of published tests.

The guiding principles of the control system are set down in the official *Ethical Standards of Psychologists* (American Psychological Association, 1968, p. 360):

> Psychological tests and other assessment devices, the value of which depends in part on the naïveté of the subject, are not reproduced or described in popular publications in ways that might invalidate the techniques. Access to such devices is limited to persons with professional interests who will safeguard their use.
> a. . . . Scorable tests and actual test items are not reproduced except in professional publications.
> b. The psychologist is responsible for the control of psychological tests and other devices and procedures used for instruction when their value might be damaged by revealing to the general public their specific contents and underlying principles.

Test scores, like test materials, are released only to persons who are qualified to interpret and use them properly.

    a. Materials for reporting test scores to parents, or which are designed for self-appraisal purposes in schools, social agencies, or industry are closely supervised by qualified psychologists or counselors. . . .

    b. Test results or other assessment data used for evaluation or classification are communicated to employers, relatives, and other appropriate persons in such a manner as to guard against misinterpretation or misuse. In the usual case, an interpretation of the test result rather than the score is communicated.

An earlier document amplified these *Standards* by suggesting a classification of tests into levels of complexity (American Psychological Association, 1953, pp. 146–148; the statement below is a slightly simplified version):

Level A. Tests or aids which can be adequately administered, scored and interpreted with the aid of the manual and a general orientation to the kind of organization in which one is working. (Examples: educational achievement, trade, and vocational proficiency tests.) Such tests and aids may be given and interpreted by responsible nonpsychologists such as school principals and business executives.

Level B. Tests or aids which require some technical knowledge of test construction and use, and of supporting subjects such as statistics, individual differences, the psychology of adjustment, personnel psychology, and guidance. (Examples: general intelligence and special aptitude tests, interest inventories and personality screening inventories.)

These tests and aids can be used by persons who have had suitable psychological training; or are employed and authorized to use them in their employment by an established school, government agency, or business enterprise; or use them in connection with a course for the study of such instruments.

Level C. Tests and aids which require substantial understanding of testing and supporting psychological topics, together with supervised experience in the use of these devices. (Examples: clinical tests of intelligence, and personality tests.)

Such tests and aids should be used only by Diplomates of the American Board of Examiners in Professional Psychology; or persons with at least a master's degree in psychology and at least one year of properly supervised experience; or other psychologists who are using tests for research or self-training purposes *with suitable precautions;* or graduate students enrolled in courses requiring the use of such devices under the supervision of a qualified psychologist; or members of kindred professions with adequate training in clincial psychological testing; or graduate students and other professional persons who have had training and supervised experience in administering and scoring the test in question, and who are working with a person who is qualified to interpret the test results.

Being a trained psychologist does not automatically make one a qualified user of all types of psychological tests. Being qualified as a user of tests in a specialty such as personnel selection, remedial reading, vocational and educational counseling, or psychodiagnosis does not necessarily qualify one in other specialties. Being a psychiatrist, social worker, teacher, or school administrator does not *ipso facto* qualify one to use projective techniques, intelligence tests, standardized achievement tests, etc.

The system for controlling distribution varies somewhat with the publisher. The major distributing firms check the name of each purchaser[3] against the directory of diplomates and similar sources to determine whether his qualifications are sufficient for the tests he has ordered. If there is doubt, the purchaser is asked to give information about his training. The distributor may ask some qualified psychologist who knows the purchaser (e.g., one of his former professors, or his clinical supervisor) to endorse his request. The publisher evaluates this information and authorizes the person to purchase tests up to a certain level. Because such investigations are costly, some of the smaller publishers have made no effective effort to control sales of their tests.

The ethical responsibility for restricting tests rests on the purchaser as much as on the distributor. A person who uses a test for which his training is insufficient risks making serious errors. It is essential that every tester evaluate his own qualifications (discussing them with a better-trained person if he is in doubt) and decide what tests he is ready to use. Ideally, professional workers would restrict their own testing by self-control, so that the publisher would have to concern himself only with nonprofessionals such as employers who believe that anyone can use a personality test, parents who want to test their children's intelligence, or job applicants who want to practice for tests they may be asked to take.

2. *An employer without psychological training decides to buy personality tests and use them on applicants. What is gained by refusing to sell him the tests, in view of the fact that without them he will base his judgments entirely on superficial impressions gained through an interview?*
3. *Examine two or three publishers' catalogs to see what statements are made about restriction of sale. Are the restrictions uniform? Do they follow exactly the levels stated in the text?*
4. *Classify the following tests according to the levels stated in the text:*
   a. *A mechanical aptitude test requires the person to assemble simple objects (e.g., a mousetrap) as fast as possible.*
   b. *The Strong Vocational Interest Blank is an objectively scored questionnaire.*
   c. *A test of arithmetic computation is intended for screening store clerks, cashiers, and similar employees.*
   d. *A diagnostic oral reading test calls for careful observation of the pupil's errors, self-confidence, method of attacking unfamiliar words, etc.*
5. *Sometimes a tester relies on the distributor's judgment, thinking like this: "I'm not sure whether I'm qualified to use this test. I'll order it, describing my training honestly; then if the publisher sells it to me, I will know that I'm qualified." What is wrong with this attitude?*
6. *What restrictions do the* Ethical Standards *imply regarding the behavior of college students studying from this book?*

[3] Such a check is not necessarily made if the purchase order comes from an institution such as a school system or mental hospital. Professional control should be exercised within such institutions.

7. *Psychologists do not favor distributing tests to people who wish to assess their own aptitudes, skills, or personality characteristics. Why?*

SUGGESTED READINGS

Anastasi, Anne. Nature and use of psychological tests. In *Psychological testing* (3d ed.). New York: Macmillan, 1968. Pp. 21–38.

> Pages 30–34 amplify our discussion of test distribution. The remainder of the chapter introduces topics to which we turn in later chapters.

Bauernfeind, R. H. An informal study of one school testing program. In *Building a school testing program* (2d ed.). Boston: Houghton Mifflin, 1969. Pp. 15–21. See also pp. 271–279.

> The first of these selections is a verbatim account of the reasoning behind a program of aptitude, achievement, and interest tests actually used by the school in a small community. The program is somewhat topheavy because the staff have some misconceptions about tests. The passage from later in the book represents Bauernfeind's suggested improvements in the program; while other specialists would recommend other tests, the way Bauernfeind reasons is an example of sophisticated planning.

Goldman, Leo. The case of Kathy Musgrove. In *Using tests in counseling*. New York: Appleton-Century-Crofts, 1961. Pp. 237–245.

> An example of effective use of tests in counseling a superior college student about vocational choice. Tests used include two measures of interests, several measures of ability, and a personality questionnaire. It is particularly to be noted that the tests did not "solve" Kathy's problem, but helped to raise more basic questions about her life plans that had to be worked out through discussion with the counselor.

Kelly, E. Lowell. Assessment: Present status and outlook. In *Assessment of human characteristics*. San Francisco: Brooks-Cole, 1967. Pp. 87–101.

> Kelly emphasizes the need for objective appraisals of individuals in view of the errors that enter into judgments, even those of professional psychologists. He considers the role the psychologist who studies individual differences may play in developing the science of psychology and its applications. For him, the psychologist's expertise lies not in his "insight" into other persons but in his skill in validating proposed decision rules.

Kirk, Samuel A. Amelioration of mental disabilities through psychodiagnostic and remedial procedures. In G. A. Jervis (Ed.), *Mental retardation*. Springfield, Ill.: Thomas, 1967. Pp. 186–219.

> Professor Kirk analyzes several cases, relying primarily on his recently developed Test of Psycholinguistic Abilities, but also using conventional intelligence tests and drawing tests. He demonstrates that merely to study a child's level of performance is quite inadequate; the pattern of strong and weak points indicates possible causes and remedies. The tests also are used to demonstrate the extent to which children improve under treatment.

Lawson, Douglas E. Need for safeguarding the field of intelligence testing. *Journal of Educational Psychology*, 1944, *35*, 240–247.

> Discusses errors made when teachers with inadequate training administer or interpret tests of mental ability.

Parkinson, C. Northcote. The short list, or principles of selection. In *Parkinson's law*. Boston: Houghton Mifflin, 1957. Pp. 45–58. (Reprinted in Jackson & Messick, 1967.)

> This account of the way talent is *really* identified will help the reader to not take tests too seriously.

Purposes and Types of Tests

Decisions for Which Tests Are Used

When one works with people he continually makes decisions. A personnel manager decides whom to hire; a teacher decides whether each pupil is ready to take up long division; a physician decides how a patient should be treated. The decision maker who obtains better information before making his decision will get better results.

All decisions involve prediction. Any test tells about some difference among people's performances at this moment. That fact would not be worth knowing if one could not then predict that these people will differ in some other performance, or in the same performance at some other time.

Consider a test of visual recognition. We flash a row of letters on the screen for an instant, and the person reports what he has seen. Some people recognize four letters; others grasp seven in the same brief interval. This difference is intriguing, but it is unimportant until it can be related to other behavior. The applied psychologist sees that this task possibly has something in common with airplane recognition and with perception in reading. He investigates whether the flash-recognition test will predict success in these practical activities. If so, it can assist the armed forces to select lookouts, or help the primary grade teacher to plan reading instruction.

Prediction is involved in clinical use of tests also. A clinician might use the flash technique to see whether a person has especial difficulty in perceiving emotionally toned words like *guilt* and *failure*, that being a possible indicator of emotional conflict. Such a test is useful only if the unusual score indicates a probability of deviant behavior or a serious emotional upset at some time in the future. The significance of the clinical test is that it predicts behavior that should be forestalled, or forecasts whether a certain treatment method will bring improvement.

The scientific investigator may not care whether the tests he uses help in practical decisions. He may not even be interested in individual differences. But he too must have tests that predict. The flash test is a good laboratory instrument because its scores are stable. If conditions are not altered, a person makes about the same score each time he is tested; thus today's test predicts tomorrow's score. If the score changes when the experimenter changes the illumination, we know that the change resulted from the illumination and not from chance variation. The experimenter therefore can study systematically how flash perception is related to illumination. When this relation is fully understood, he has a general law that predicts what changes in perception will accompany changes in illumination.

1. *Demonstrate that prediction is intended in each of the following situations:*
   a. *A foreman is asked to rate probationary workers on quality of work.*
   b. *Airlines require a periodic physical examination of pilots.*
   c. *A psychologist investigates whether students are more "liberal" in their attitudes toward birth control after two years of college study.*
   d. *A teacher gives James a grade of C in algebra and Harry a grade of A.*
2. *Tests are used to obtain information that will permit sounder decisions. Does this statement apply to the Gallup public opinion poll?*

Selection and Classification of Persons

Tests aid in making many sorts of decisions, including selection and classification of individuals, evaluation of educational or treatment procedures, and acceptance or rejection of scientific hypotheses. We shall consider briefly each of these types of decision, beginning with selection.

In a selection decision, an institution decides to accept some men and to reject others. Hiring an employee is such a selection decision. The distinguishing feature of the selection decision is that some men are rejected, and their future performance is of no direct concern to the institution. A person may be "selected" and "classified" at the same time.

Classification determines which of several possible assignments or treatments a person shall receive. Examples: The college student asks a counselor to help him choose the best curriculum. The Navy tests a recruit to determine whether he should be assigned to the engine room, the chartroom, or the gun turret. The schoolboy who reads poorly is tested to determine what remedial instruction he needs. One important classification problem is diagnosis of mental conditions. This may appear to be merely an attempt to find the right name for a patient's disorder, but it really is a choice among treatments, since the patient's label determines what treatment he gets.

Where people are assigned to different levels of work (rather than to distinctly different types of work) we have a placement decision. Placement is a kind of classification. "Placement tests" are used to allocate college freshmen to the proper section of English, i.e., to the appropriate instructional treatment. Choosing officer candidates from among enlisted men is a placement decision rather than a selection decision, since the men not chosen as officers remain in the army and are used in a different way.

A distinction between classification and selection is required because a test useful in making one type of decision may not help with the other (Cronbach & Gleser, 1965). A test that detects serious emotional disturbances would be useful in keeping unstable men out of the Army (selection). The test might not help at all in deciding how to treat men who break down in the service (classification). As we shall see in Chapter 13, one interprets validity data differently for classification and selection purposes.

A description of the person can be far more individualized than a simple classification. For instance, a test battery plus other facts might classify a student as a promising engineer, and this would lead him to a decision to enroll in engineering. A description would report in addition the assets and liabilities that distinguish this student from other prospective engineers. He is especially interested in aviation; he has a rather immature and uncooperative attitude toward superiors; he works energetically in short bursts, with no long-range scheduling. All these facts are useful to the counselor. Each one bears on a different decision about course planning, about disciplinary treatment, about advice on study, and so on. When a test is used descriptively, we do not confine ourselves to one definite question. Rather, we try to record all important facts so that they will be available when questions about treatment arise. A description may catalog a student's interests, describe his personality pattern, or inventory his knowledge about his major field. The description is multidimensional and helps resolve many different questions about how to treat the person.

Evaluation of Treatments

So far we have considered only decisions about persons. Tests are equally important as an aid in evaluating treatments and maintaining their effectiveness. When the teacher gives an arithmetic test, he is testing his instruction as much as he is testing the students' effort and ability. If the results are poor, he should probably alter his method.

In industry, the effectiveness of training is judged by performance tests, and supervision and personnel policies can be judged by tests of attitudes and morale.

Checking on Scientific Hypotheses

The functions discussed above illustrate the usefulness of tests in making decisions of immediate practical importance. Tests are also used extensively to measure outcomes of scientific experiments, as was illustrated in our discussion of the measurement of flash perception. The experimenter is not making decisions about particular individuals or the practices of an institution. He is trying to decide how much credence to place in an hypothesis such as, "The change of perceptual span with change in illumination is greater when a subject is under stress." If he finds such a relation he will try to express it as a numerical law. Tests provide a more objective and dependable basis for evaluating hypotheses than rough impressions do, and a careful measurement is essential to arrive at a numerical relationship.

Sometimes a scientific investigator uses tests published for practical purposes, but a test tailor-made to fit the experiment will often work better. In one study, for example, the experimenter played sound recordings of words backwards, in order to study how people learn to recognize strange stimuli. Such a task, just because it is novel, makes a good experimental test.

3. *Show that a reading test might sometimes be used by college counselors or administrators for each of the four types of decision listed above.*
4. *Classify each of the following according to the type of decision represented:*
   a. *A foundling home measures intelligence of a child and uses this as a basis for deciding which home to place the child in.*
   b. *An instructor rides with a pilot at the end of his training, and fills out a checklist to show which maneuvers he performs correctly.*
   c. *A psychologist compares the average vocabulary size of only children with that of children from larger families of similar social background.*
   d. *All applicants for a driver's license are tested.*
   e. *A school tests adolescents to identify those likely to become delinquent.*
   f. *A university class is divided in two parts, one of which sees the lectures and demonstrations by television while the other hears and sees the instructor directly. Both groups are given the same examination.*
5. *Describe one circumstance where tests might be used descriptively by:*
   a. *An employment manager.*
   b. *An assistant in a preschool.*
   c. *A teacher of typewriting.*

What Is a Test?

There is no fully satisfactory definition for the word *test*. The word usually calls to mind a procedure in which a standard series of questions is presented, and the subject gives written or oral answers. But the road test for a driver's license is a test having neither questions nor answers, and the procedure varies from one examiner to the next. Indeed, if the State of California tried to standardize the task set for the driver it would not be able to, since the traffic through which drivers are asked to maneuver will vary from one hour to another. Perhaps the following definition is broad enough to cover the procedures with which this book will be concerned: *A test is a systematic procedure for observing a person's behavior and describing it with the aid of a numerical scale or a category-system.* A numerical scale is used when a person is described as having 20/100 vision; a category system is used when he is said to have red-green color blindness. This definition includes questionnaires for obtaining reports on personality, procedures for observing social behavior, apparatus tests measuring coordination, and even systematic records of output on a production line.

Tests need not focus on a single person. A test may be applied to a group, in a social-psychological study evaluating a tactic of leadership. In the mammoth National Assessment of the educational system, questions are applied to young persons according to a random-sampling design so that different persons receive different questions. No description of single individuals or single schools is possible; a description of the results produced by the system as a whole is the intended result. The principles we develop in later chapters apply, with some fairly obvious modifications, to these and other instruments used in behavioral science. Indeed, they apply to procedures used in animal research as well as to those used with humans.

There are many terms used to characterize tests. The meaning of *pencil-and-paper test, apparatus test, oral test,* etc., should be obvious. Although all tests call for performance of some sort, the name *performance test* is usually applied to a task requiring a nonverbal response. Among the performance tests that have been used for various purposes are repairing a piece of electronic apparatus, drawing a picture of a man, stringing beads, and "inventing" a hatrack when given two long sticks and a C-clamp.

Group tests differ from *individual* tests in that the former permit many subjects to be tested at once. Group tests can be given to a single individual if that is desirable. Many individual tests require careful oral questioning or observation of reactions. Some individual tests can be modified and simplified to permit group administration. An example is the inkblot test of personality. In the individual form, a subject looks at a card bearing an inkblot and tells what he thinks the blot looks like. He is questioned about each response until the tester is sure just what the subject sees. A group form of the test may use printed booklets or may project the blots onto a screen. The subject writes his responses, and individual questioning is omitted. Information is less complete, but the cost of testing is much less.

Standardization and Objectivity

A distinction between standardized and unstandardized procedures grew up in the early days of testing. Every laboratory in those days had its own method of measuring memory span, reaction time, and so on, and it was difficult to compare results from different laboratories. It was difficult also for school officials to answer such practical questions as whether pupils were learning to spell as well as could be expected, when every teacher used a different test. Standardization attempts to overcome these problems. A *standardized test* is one in which the procedure, apparatus, and scoring have been fixed so that precisely the same testing procedures can be followed at different times and places.

Some tests are provided with tables of norms stating what scores are usually earned by representative subjects. Tests having such norms are sometimes called "standardized tests," and the process of gathering norm data is called "standardization." We are not using the word *standardized* in that sense, because we wish to emphasize standardization *of procedure*. A test may have a table of norms even though its procedures are not clearly specified, and a test with well-standardized procedures may not have norms. Obviously, collecting norms is not very profitable until procedures are well standardized.

The first major step toward standardization of psychological testing came in 1905, when a committee of the American Psychological Association defined procedures (e.g., for testing memory) that could be followed in all laboratories. Today, most published tests are carefully standardized, but a number of unstandardized procedures are in general use for personality assessment.

Standardization has a place in all research. In experimental psychology, standardization is not yet as well accepted as in testing, but the need for standardized procedures is much the same. These remarks regarding concept-formation experiments (Underwood & Richardson, 1956, p. 84) give arguments for standardization that apply equally well to tests:

. . . tasks or materials which have been used are quite diverse in nature. With few exceptions (e.g., Weigl-type card sorting) no systematic series of experiments has been built around a single task. While this lack of task standardization attests to the ingenuity of individual workers in constructing new materials, the situation may not be entirely satisfactory for efficient development of laws and theories. In the more highly-developed areas in psychology only a few basic tasks, procedures, or materials have been used. Thus, classical conditioning, the Skinner box, nonsense syllables, the pursuit rotor (to mention a few) all have had widespread use. While some may justifiably raise questions concerning generality of findings based on such a limited number of procedures and tasks, it cannot be doubted that interlaboratory communication and continuity is greatly facilitated by the use of common basic tasks and procedures.

Tests vary in the completeness with which they are standardized. Printing the questions and mass-producing the equipment assures a physical uniformity, but the directions to the subject are not always worked out in complete detail. Every condition that affects performance must be specified if the test is to be truly standardized. For a test of color-matching ability, one needs to use uniform color specimens, to follow uniform directions for administration and scoring, and also to use a certain amount and kind of illumination. If standardization of the test is fully effective, a man will earn very nearly the same score no matter who tests him or where. There are, however, many difficulties in completely standardizing the tester's procedure and the subject's attitude, some of which will be discussed in Chapter 3.

Tests vary in objectivity. If a test is objective, every observer or judge seeing a performance arrives at precisely the same report. To do this, he must pay attention to the same aspects of the performance, record his observations to eliminate errors of recall, and score the record by the same rules. Objectivity may be judged by comparing the final scores assigned by two independent observers. The more subjective the observation and evaluation, the less the two judges agree.

Tests in which the subject selects the best of several alternative answers (e.g., true-false, multiple-choice) are referred to as "objective tests" because all scorers can apply a scoring key and agree perfectly on the result. In contrast, an ordinary essay test allows room for great disagreement among scorers. By careful instructions to the observer or scorer, free-response tests and observations can be made fairly objective.

6. *Judge each of these statements true or false and defend your answer:*
   a. *Batting averages are objectively determined.*
   b. *The 220-yard low hurdle race is a standardized test.*
   c. *A teacher has each member of the class read the same article in a current magazine. Time is called at the end of three minutes, and each pupil marks the place where he is reading. He then counts the number of words read and computes his reading rate in words-per-minute. This score is compared with a table of average reading speeds for typical magazine articles. This test is highly objective.*
   d. *The test described in c is standardized.*

7. *Psychological tests often start from very crude procedures. Psychologist X thinks that he obtains useful information by laying a sheet of paper on the table at arm's length from his subject and asking him to touch with his pencil exactly in the center of a circle printed on the paper. The subject is told to withdraw his hand and repeat the movement, as rapidly and accurately as possible, until he is told to stop. Psychologist X gives the man a mark from 1 to 10 on each of the following qualities: speed, carefulness, and persistence.*
   a. *What changes would improve the objectivity of the test?*
   b. *What aspects of the procedure would need to be taken into account in standardizing the test?*

8. *Industrial morale surveys often use questions made up by the plant personnel office or its consultants. What advantages and disadvantages would there be in using the same standardized questions in many different plants?*

9. *The Kohs Block Design Test (See Figure 3.2, p. 49) is one of the most popular testing procedures. The subject is required to construct a pattern from colored blocks to match a printed sample. The test is chiefly used in child guidance, clinical diagnosis, and measurement of intelligence of persons who do poorly on verbal tests. It is also used for research on frustration and on cultural differences. At least twenty versions of the test (different items, different scoring rules, etc.) are used in different clinics and different countries. What are the possible advantages and disadvantages of this diversity?*

10. *The Kohs test was first published as a long series of carefully chosen items. Why do you think so many different versions now exist in different countries, even though the test is used for the same purpose in these places?*

Psychometric vs. Impressionistic Testing

There are two philosophies of testing, growing from different historical roots and fostering different types of test procedure and interpretation; both are mingled in contemporary practice. While we cannot discuss their differences exhaustively, especially in this introductory chapter, we can survey the main characteristics of each approach.

Psychometric testing obtains a numerical estimate of some aspect of performance at a time. Its ideal is expressed in two famous old pronouncements: that "If a thing exists, it exists in some amount," and "If it exists in some amount, it can be measured." One discerns an assumption that the psychologist is concerned with "things," i.e., with distinct elements or traits that somehow "exist." All people are considered to possess the same traits (e.g., intelligence, or mechanical experience), but in different amounts. This view of psychological investigation takes its cue from physical science, which identifies common aspects of dissimilar objects and describes any object by numbers representing such abstract dimensions as weight, volume, and intensity of energy of a certain wave length.

The second approach leads to a comprehensive descriptive picture of the individual. We shall refer to this style of investigation as impressionistic. Impressionistic psychologists think that understanding can be achieved only by a sensitive observer who looks for significant cues by any available means and integrates them into a total impression. Studying one trait or element at a time is, in their view, no substitute for considering the person as a whole. The impressionist is not satisfied with knowing "how much" of some ability the person has; he asks how the subject expresses his ability, what kinds of errors he makes, and why.

To evaluate a subject's background, for example, a psychometric tester would have him respond to a biographical checklist covering experiences that many people have and that are likely to be important in their development. (For example: "Were you a Boy Scout patrol leader?") He would score responses objectively by counting items checked in such categories as "Interest in sports" and "Leadership experience." The impressionist, on the other hand, would ask for an autobiographical essay, perhaps setting no more definite task than "Please write your life story in 2500 words." He could see what the subject considers important about himself, what emotional tone he uses to decribe his past, and what unique experiences he has had—experiences the checklist would not cover. The free response gives scant information on important areas covered thoroughly by the checklist, but it covers matters the checklist ignores.

Each approach has merit, and each has its limitations. Both have contributed to the development of present practice, and neither style can be adopted to the exclusion of the other. The measurer must fall back upon judgment whenever he applies score information in teaching, therapy, or supervision of employees. The portraitist, on the other hand, cannot afford to ignore the accurate facts psychometric instruments provide. The psychometric and impressionistic styles differ with respect to definiteness of tasks employed, control of response, objective recording of basic data, formal numerical scoring and numerical combination of data to reach decisions, and critical validation of interpretations. Most procedures are psychometric in some of these respects and impressionistic in others.

Definiteness of task.   The test designer decides how definitely the task is to be explained to the subject. In some tests, such as the biographical essay mentioned above, the subject is free to employ any style and any content he chooses. On the other hand, a questionnaire in which the subject is to check each activity he has engaged in during the past five years leaves little or no room for individual interpretation.

A test is said to be structured when all subjects interpret the task in the same way. The more latitude allowed, the less structured the test is. Of special interest are projective tests, which ask the subject to interpret a stimulus that has no obvious meaning. For instance, he may be shown an inkblot and told to report what it looks like to him. If he asks how many ideas to report, whether to use the same portion of the blot in two ideas, or any other such question, he is told, "That's up to you."

Structuring the task controls the performance so that all subjects are judged on very much the same basis. It therefore permits a definite answer to a question formulated in advance (e.g., How much experience with small boats has the subject had?). The less structured technique allows greater variation in responses and in that sense reveals more individualized response patterns. (The subject's essay may, for example, give information on some unusual interest, such as training dogs for show, but may tell nothing about boating experience.)

 Constructed response vs. response choice.   An open-end question asks the subject to construct a suitable response orally or in writing, or sometimes by manipulating objects. The subject gives whatever response seems fitting, within the range allowed by the test directions. Another form of test requires the subject to select a best answer from among choices provided by the tester. In a mental test, series-completion items (7 5 8 6 9 . . .) and verbal analogies (*wolf* is to *cub* as *cat* is to _____) may be left in free-response form, or the subject may be offered alternative answers from which to choose. An interviewer concerned with personality may ask "Are you ill-at-ease in social gatherings?", and wait for a reply. The tester provides the alternatives "Yes" and "No" or "Always," "Often," "Sometimes," etc.

The choice format makes scoring easier and more dependable, but it constrains the response so that the subject cannot display himself freely. Even on the number-series item, differences can appear. One subject says "Seven" directly; another hesitantly says "Well, it might be 7. I guess that's right." The psychometric tester generally prefers the choice format because it can be more objectively scored, does not depend on fluency or expressive skill, and is less open to misinterpretation of questions. Those who prefer free response value the supplementary observations.

A major issue in educational testing is whether constructed-response tests and choice-response tests on the same content measure the same ability. The emphasis on multiple-choice in standardized testing has been a source of concern to teachers who feel that only tests requiring free responses can measure adequately what they teach. Especially when the purpose of teaching is to produce ability to recall or invent new solutions, teachers tend to prefer free-response tests. The English teacher prefers to judge a student from a sample of his free writing, rather than from tests in which he merely identifies errors. The mathematics teacher contends that his students should be required to solve problems, rather than merely to select alternatives in "place-your-bet" questions.

One way to evaluate this argument is to determine whether the free-response and choice tests rank pupils in the same way. The result depends on the ability measured. In arithmetic, the two rankings correspond closely; but penmanship performance has negligible correlation with ability to recognize good handwriting. In college mathematics, multiple-choice questions had correlations with grades in later mathematics essentially the same as those for free-answer questions (College Entrance Examination Board, 1946). One might think that ability to generalize from data could be tested only by requiring that the student form his own generalizations. But a test requiring undergraduates to identify the best and poorest generalizations from a set of data correlated 0.85 with ability to form generalizations directly from the data. Planning an experiment is a creative function, yet a recognition test calling for choice among alternative plans correlated 0.79 with a free-response test of ability to make plans (R. Tyler, 1934, pp. 27–30).

There is still room, however, for the assumption that the two kinds of tests measure different things. In present schooling the student who learns to recognize good answers can also produce them best, according to findings of the studies noted above. But this does not apply to the comparison of present schooling with an experimental teaching procedure. That method might do wonders for improving choice responses beyond the present level, and not free responses, or vice versa. Hence when the validity of a multiple-choice test in evaluation of a curriculum is open to doubt, the tester ought to apply both kinds of test to the curriculum.

The most serious charge against choice-response tests in education is that they have often been confined to measurement of simple, even trivial knowledge of facts. It is possible, as many examining bodies in universities have demonstrated, to devise objective questions that call for deep comprehension. Even the standard multiple-choice format can require high-level reasoning, as is illustrated

Three of the following are essential to the operation of a private enterprise economy. Which one might such an economy operate without?

    A.   Profit motive
    B.   Markets
    C.   Corporations
    D.   Prices

Of the following, the principle of diminishing returns is best illustrated by

    A.   small firms being driven out of business by large firms
    B.   any decline in the average rate of profits
    C.   a slowing rate of increase in output as a farmer adds increasing amounts of fertilizer to his land
    D.   the decline in personal income as workers age

"Americans are a mixed-up people with no sense of ethical values. Everyone knows that baseball is far less necessary than food and steel, yet they pay ball players a lot more than farmers and steelworkers." Why?

    A.   Ball players are really entertainers rather than producers.
    B.   Ball players are more skilled than persons who get less pay.
    C.   Excellent baseball players are scarcer relative to the demand for their services.
    D.   There are fewer professional ball players than farmers or steelworkers.

Figure 2.1   Items from Test of Economic Understanding.
Reprinted from Test of Economic Understanding prepared by the Committee for Measurement of Economic Understanding of the Joint Council on Economic Education, by courtesy of the publisher, Science Research Associates, Inc. © 1963, the Joint Council on Economic Education.

in Figure 2.1, which presents some of the items from a test for high-school students. Even though the students have not studied economics specifically, it is expected that they will show some degree of competence as a result of their exposure through history courses and mass media. The only fundamental criticism of the test that can be made is the high level of verbal skill that is required; but in a theoretical subject, main ideas cannot be expressed except in a complex verbal form.

Product vs. process. Psychometric testing concerns itself with the tangible product of the performance—the answer given, the block tower constructed, or the essay written—and only rarely with the process. When a psychometric tester does pay attention to the process of performance, he arms himself with a record sheet for tabulating what the subject does. The impressionistic tester, however, watches the subject at work in order to form a general opinion; this general impression is indeed the basic datum with which he works. In describing their military testing during World War II, "German psychologists [who at that time carried the impressionistic style to extremes] stated repeatedly that observations of the candidate's behavior during a test were more important than the actual score which he earned. . . . One man . . . said that the chief fault of inexperienced military psychologists was that they attached too much weight to objective scores and did not pay enough attention to the formation of an intuitive impression from observation of the candidate's reactions and expressions. Individual examiners were permitted and often encouraged to vary testing procedures and to emphasize their favorite tests" (Fitts, 1946).

Analysis of results. It follows that formal scoring plays a large part in the psychometric test and a minor part in the work of the impressionistic tester. American devotion to the numerical score sometimes goes to such extremes that a tester reports nothing about a child but the IQ calculated for him, discarding all the other information obtained in an hour of close observation. The thoroughly impressionistic tester may in his turn translate a test performance into a character description without ever counting up a score. Preferably, in individual testing, both scores and descriptive information are recorded.

When a decision is to be made, one can apply some formal rule to the various facts or can combine them impressionistically. For example, a teacher may assign a course grade by strictly averaging the tests, or may form an overall impression that this student is "doing B work even if he did slump at the end" and that one is "not really as good as his tests suggest." The psychometric tester tends to prefer the impersonal procedure, while the impressionist thinks an informal method is more flexible and realistic.

The psychometric tester's insistence on numerical scores influences his choice of tests. Some testers bombard the subject with one test after another, seeming to have almost a mystical faith that the numbers will reveal how to solve the subject's problems. In his concentration on measurable variables the tester may ignore equally pertinent aspects of the individual for which no scorable instruments have been developed. In child guidance it is easy to obtain measures of ability, and fairly adequate instruments exist for obtaining an "emotional adjustment" score. These gross scores, however, tell only a small part of the story, and the psychologist should certainly go on to investigate the child's image of his mother, his father, and his teacher, and what activities in his life give him the greatest satisfaction, even if none of these questions can be answered by a number on a scale or taken into a statistical formula.

This analytical procedure, which can be called neither psychometric nor impressionistic, is being increasingly discussed under the label "the experimental analysis of behavior." Emphasis is placed on determining exactly what situations cause the subject difficulty: what words he misspells, where he goes off the track in solving rate-time-distance problems, what companions and play settings trigger aggressive responses. While this determination can be made impressionistically, it is more common now to advocate an objective tabulation of responses, in full detail. The spirit, then, is more psychometric, but the findings are not compressed into a few scores. The analysis of the case is likely to extend over a considerable period, and so be integrated with remedial efforts; it therefore does not conform to the pattern of "a test."

Emphasis on critical validation.   Finally, we come to the question of critical validation. Psychometric testers are taught to distrust judgments based on tests and observations. Ideally, a psychometric tester accompanies every numerical score with a warning regarding the error of measurement, and every prediction with an index that shows how likely it is to come true. The impressionist is less likely to carry out formal validation studies, often being satisfied to compare impressions based on one procedure with impressions gained from another. Validation of qualitative interpretations and "portraits" is much more difficult than validation of scores and requires a greater readiness for self-criticism on the part of the psychologist.

The most critical issue, indeed, between psychometric and impressionistic testing is that of confidence in the psychologist. Those who develop and advocate rigorous psychometric procedures regard the tester as an erratic instrument whose unregulated interpretations obscure the truth. Those who prefer less structured procedures regard the observer as a sensitive and even indispensable instrument. The impressionist does not deny the danger of bias and random error in judgment. He, however, fears that narrowing the focus to what can be represented in a numerical score on a standard procedure throws away most of the psychologically important information. The gains from intuitive observation and interpretation, he believes, more than offset the errors it introduces.

Most testers occupy an intermediate position—intermediate between obsession with scores and unrestrained use of intuition. Formal, strictly objective procedures are combined in some manner with judgment, except in mass classification programs such as military processing.

The impressionistic style places great responsibility on the test interpreter. He must be an artist, sensitive to observe and skillful to convey his impressions. Some psychologists are presumably much better judges of personality than others. The psychometric method seeks procedures that everyone can use equally well. The objective test is a camera pointed in a fixed direction; every competent photographer should get the same picture with it. Thus psychometric testing aims to reduce measurement to a routine technical procedure. To the extent that it succeeds, it reduces the need for an authoritative, "wise" professional psychologist. A similar conflict between the technical and the artistic ideal is found in medicine. Laboratory tests assume more and more of the burden of medical diagnosis, yet doctors have great respect for the legendary genius who diagnoses unerringly the malady overlooked by the tests.

11. *"Psychometric testing trusts the judgment of the test constructor, where it is unwilling to trust the tester as observer." Is this a defensible statement?*
12. *Distinguish between* structured *and* standardized.
13. *In what respects are the following procedures unstructured?*
    a. *In the Ayres handwriting test, pupils are told to write the Gettysburg Address neatly, doing as much as they can in a fixed time.*
    b. *In the Draw-a-Man test of mental development, the child is told to "draw the best man you can."*
    c. *In a recorded pitch-discrimination test, the subject hears two tones and responds "H," "L," or "N," according as the second tone appears higher than, lower than, or no different from the first.*
14. *What are the advantages and disadvantages of the biographical checklist as compared with the essay?*
15. *Is the issue between psychometric and impressionistic testers one that can be settled by suitable factual research?*
16. *Does experimental analysis of behavior make demands on the psychologist's wisdom, or is it a purely technical procedure?*

Classification of Tests

Tests might be classified in many ways. We shall place tests in two broad classes, the first being those that seek to measure the *maximum* performance of the subject. We use these when we wish to know how well the person can perform at his best; they may be referred to as tests of ability. The second category includes those tests that seek to determine his *typical* performance, i.e., what he is likely to do in a given situation or in a broad class of situations. Tests of personality, habits, interests, and character fall in this category, because characterizations like "shy," "interested in art," and "anxious when in disagreement with a superior" describe the individual's typical behavior.

There are ambiguities in this classification system, since typical behavior and ability do not separate neatly. This is clearly the case when we think about "typical behavior in a situation where he is encouraged to do his best." From one point of view a test may measure ability to add numbers rapidly and accurately. From another, it may measure resistance to stress, persistence, and carefulness. The difficulty we find here is a reflection of the theoretical inadequacy of the age-old distinction between intellect and emotion. The classification scheme is a convenience in organizing our discussion, not a basis for theory.

Tests of Ability

The distinguishing feature of a test of ability is that the subject is encouraged to earn the best score he can.

The goal of the tester usually is to bring out the person's best possible per-

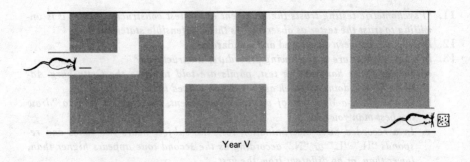

Year V

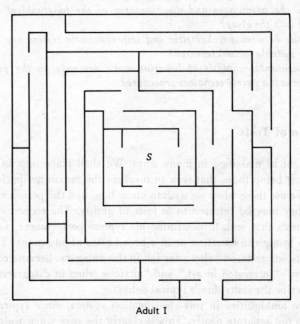

Adult I

Figure 2.2.   Two of the Porteus mazes.
The subject is required to trace the correct path through a maze. A failure is judged whenever his pencil enters a blind alley. He is then given further trials on the same maze. When he gets one maze correct he goes on to a more difficult one, continuing until he fails several trials at a particular level. *Copyright © 1933, The Psychological Corporation. Reproduced by permission.*

formance, and this means that the subject must understand what response is wanted (i.e., what is considered a good performance) and must want to do well. To define the task so that the subject can show his best behavior, the directions need to be clear and explicit, even to explaining what sorts of errors will be penalized. But no test directions tell the subject how to approach the task; style of performance, then, reflects personality (typical behavior). The Porteus maze

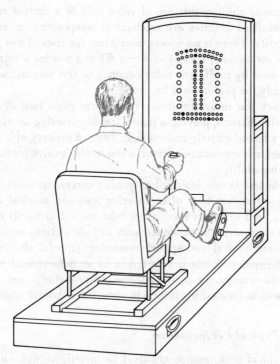

Figure 2.3.   **The Complex Coordination Test.**

(Figure 2.2) is used as an observation technique in which the tester looks for evidence of planning and foresight, as well as being an ability test the numerical score of which represents speed and correctness.

Some ability tests pose familiar tasks: for example, a road test for a driver's license. Others require the person to do something completely unfamiliar. The Complex Coordination Test (Figure 2.3) requires a person who has never flown a plane to operate a "stick" and "rudder bar" just as if he were flying. Flashing lights signal for certain movements. If he can follow the directions and make prompt, coordinated responses he gets a high score. This task reproduces one aspect of the flyer's job; other things being equal, a person who is superior on this test will be a superior pilot.

Tests measuring maximum performance are referred to as mental tests, intelligence tests, etc. We shall not define these terms formally; indeed, most of the terms have no well-established definition. One large group of tests we shall refer to as *measures of general mental ability*. They seek to measure those mental abilities that are valuable in almost any type of thinking. Tests of this sort are often called "intelligence tests," but that name leads to controversy because "intelligence" has so many meanings. General abilities may be contrasted with the more specialized abilities that are of value only in a limited range of tasks. Among the specialized abilities are mechanical comprehension, sense of pitch, and finger dexterity. There is no widely used name for tests of this sort; we shall refer to them as *measures of special abilities*. While a test for a single specialized ability may be used by itself, it is more common to test several such abilities at once so as to study the person's ability profile.

A *proficiency test* measures ability to perform some task significant in its own right: reading French, playing a piano, trouble-shooting an airplane engine. It is ordinarily a test of directly trained skill. Tests of mastery of a school subject are usually called achievement tests. Such a test might involve proficiency, knowledge, or reasoning ability.

An aptitude test is one intended to predict success in some occupation or training course—there are tests of engineering aptitude, musical aptitude, aptitude for algebra, and so on. In form, these tests are not distinctly different from other types. An engineering aptitude test may include sections measuring general mental ability, mechanical and spatial reasoning (special abilities), and proficiency in mathematics. A test is referred to as an achievement test when it is used primarily to examine the person's success in past study, and as an aptitude test when it is used to forecast his success in some future course or assignment.

Tests of Typical Performance

Tests of typical performance are used to investigate not what the person can do but what he does. There is little value in determining how courteous a girl applying for store employment can be when she tries; almost anyone of normal upbringing has the ability to be polite. The test of a suitable employee is whether she maintains that courtesy in her daily work, even when she is not "on her best behavior." Any inspector with proper vision and training should be able to detect defective parts. A test that determines how well he spots defects when trying especially hard would measure vision rather than carefulness. The chief difference between the good and the poor inspector is that the latter permits himself to be distracted and careless in run-of-the-mill duty.

For cheerfulness, honesty, openmindedness, and many other aspects of behavior, a test of ability has almost no practical value. Most people can produce a show of the behavior when it is demanded. But those who act cheerfully, honestly, or impartially when they know they are being tested may not do so in other situations. If we are hiring an executive whose past success guarantees his ability, we also wish to know *how* he usually operates. Does he supervise closely, down to the last detail? Or does he outline a general task and turn his subordinates loose? Is he equally concerned with production, human problems, and finances? Does he prefer long-range planning or quick adaptation? Knowing his pattern is necessary to place him properly in the organization.

In tests of ability a high score is desirable, but in most tests of typical performance no particular response can be singled out as "good." For example, there is nothing good or bad about interest in engineering. One who has this interest can use it, but one who does not finds other worthwhile activities. Likewise, people show wide variation in dominance-submission in social relations. We cannot say that any certain degree of dominance is best, since our world has places for persons of all types.

The person's characteristic behavior is our best clue to his personality. Habits have predictive value in themselves; what a person does once he is likely to do again. Most psychologists would object, however, to assuming that a person's observable habits *are* his personality. New situations continually arise, and a description of his customary behavior does not directly indicate what he will do in a new situation. A youth may have a reputation as a womanhater, but some girl will come along who arouses a quite different response. A clinician who establishes warm relations with most clients will encounter some who arouse only hostile feelings in him. Because we do not wish to regard these exceptional reactions as capricious and unexplainable, we interpret reactions in various situations as reflections of a more basic and consistent "personality structure" or belief system, out of which new behavior develops. The structure has to be inferred from behavior that can be observed at the present time. The psychologist hopes that when he understands the structure he will be able to predict the person's responses even to new situations.

Testing of typical performance is difficult. It has been accomplished, with greater or less success, in a variety of ways. These methods may be divided into behavior observations and self-report devices.

Behavior observations. Behavior observations are attempts to study the subject when he is "acting naturally." Observations are made both in standardized test situations and in unstandardized or "natural" conditions.

The standardized observation requires that each subject be placed in essentially the same situation. Personality may be observed during a mental test, during a group discussion, or while the subject is walking a rail blindfolded. Special tasks are often devised which give an especially good opportunity for observation. These tasks may be referred to as *performance tests of personality.*

The standardized observation permits relatively exact comparison of persons who are not normally seen in similar circumstances. Moreover, it reveals characteristics that could be seen only occasionally in everyday life. Such procedures have been used, for example, to observe typical reactions to frustration. The person commences a task and is prevented in some way from attaining his goal. The way he reacts gives insight into his emotional control. In one famous study, preschool children were given the opportunity to play with ordinary, reasonably interesting toys. Then they were allowed into an adjoining room with extremely attractive toys. After a period of play in this room, they were herded back into the first room, and a wire screen was placed between them and the attractive toys.

The children reacted in many ways: pounding on the fence, regressing to simple play with rocks, trying to pry under the fence, or going off to take a pretended nap. The observers recorded each child's behavior. In general, games after frustration were less mature and less constructive than before.

If an observation is to bring to light typical behavior, the subject must not know what is being observed. The observer may be concealed, or the subject may be led to believe that he is being tested on one behavior while something else is observed. Thus when reaction to frustration is being studied, the subject may be told that his mental ability is being tested. His responses when he is frustrated by difficult questions are usually genuine and little disguised.

Typical behavior may also be observed in samples of the person's ordinary daily activities—"in the field," as it were. Children on the playground reveal a good deal about their habits and personality; so do noncoms leading platoons, and workers in the office. Field observations may use elaborately standardized recording procedures—even videotape—or may, on the contrary, consist merely of an impressionistic judgment. The baseball batting average is a summary of systematically recorded field observations. The industrial supervisor's merit ratings are also based on observation, but the judgments are almost completely unsystematic.

Self-report devices. The subject has had much opportunity to observe himself. If he is willing, he can give a helpful report of his own typical behavior. Questionnaires are used to obtain such reports. The crucial problem in self-report, if it is to be interpreted as a picture of typical behavior, is honesty. If the person tries to give the best possible picture of himself instead of a true description, the test will fail of its purpose. Even when he tries to be truthful we cannot expect him to be detached and impartial. His report about himself is certain to be distorted to some degree.

Most self-report inventories offer a fairly comprehensive picture of personality. Some of them, however, are specialized in their coverage. There are study-habit inventories, interest inventories, social attitude inventories, and so on. Other tests are designated as "adjustment inventories," "character tests," etc.; such a name suggests the way in which the score is to be interpreted but does not identify a distinctive form of instrument.

It is generally agreed that personality questionnaires should not use the word *test* in their titles (American Psychological Association, 1966). If an instrument is marketed under the title "The Jones Dominance-Submission Test," employers, teachers, or others with limited psychological training may think that a person's dominance is being directly measured. If the instrument merely asks the subject questions about himself, he can describe himself in any way he likes. A title such as "The Jones Dominance Questionnaire" or "The Jones Dominance Inventory" is less likely to give an impression of trustworthiness than "The Jones Dominance

Test." It is desirable to use some term such as *questionnaire* whenever the word *test* might be misinterpreted.

17. *Classify each of the following procedures as a test of ability, a self-report test, observation in a standardized situation, or observation in an unstandardized situation:*

a. *An interviewer from the Gallup poll asks a citizen how he will vote in a coming election.*

b. *A television producer wishes to know what program features appeal to different types of listeners. He presents a show to a small audience, who press signal buttons to indicate whether they enjoy or dislike what they are seeing at each moment.*

c. *A test of "vocational aptitude" asks the subject how well he likes such activities as selling, woodworking, and chess.*

d. *A spelling test is given to applicants for a clerical job.*

e. *Inspectors in plain clothes ride buses to determine whether operators are obeying the company rules.*

f. *During an intelligence test, the examiner watches for evidence of self-confidence or its absence.*

g. *In a test of "application of principles in social studies," students are told of a conflict about a proposal to admit Negroes to a community college without giving them entrance examinations. They are asked what the college should do and to give reasons to support the choice.*

h. *An inspector in a stocking factory is supposed to detect all stockings with knitting faults. To check her efficiency, at certain times a number of faulty stockings that have been marked with fluorescent dye are mixed into the batch for inspection. The dye is invisible to the worker, but by turning an ultraviolet lamp onto the stockings after inspection the supervisor can readily locate any faulty stockings the inspector missed.*

18. *Classify each of the following tests, using as many of the descriptive terms discussed in the text as are clearly applicable.*

a. *The Study of Values consists of printed questions, such as*

In your opinion, can a man who works in business all the week best spend Sunday in

a. trying to educate himself by reading serious books

b. trying to win at golf, or racing

c. going to an orchestral concert

d. hearing a really good sermon

The subject answers each question by checking whichever answer he prefers. Answers are scored by a numerical key to determine how important "aesthetic," "religious," and other values are for him.

b. *In a certain "mechanical aptitude" test, the subject marks illustrations of tools and other objects to show which go together (e.g., hammer and anvil).*

c. *A Picture Arrangement Test item presents a set of four pictures which, arranged in the correct order, tell a story in the manner of a cartoon strip (see Figure 7.3). Each picture is on a separate card. The cards are presented* *in a random arrangement and the subject arranges them to make an intelligible story.*

    d. *In a dexterity test the subject mounts washers on rivets and places each rivet in a hole on a board, as rapidly as possible.*

19. *Classify the procedures used by Miss Kimball, the school psychologist described in Chapter 1, according to the terms used in this chapter.*

SUGGESTED READINGS

Baldwin, Alfred L. The role of an "ability" construct in a theory of behavior. In D. C. McClelland & others, *Talent and society.* Princeton, N.J.: Van Nostrand, 1958. Pp. 195–233.

    Baldwin discusses the nature of ability and the theoretical requirements of ability tests. His argument that only voluntary behavior shows ability, as distinguished from habit, amplifies our distinction between maximum performance and typical performance.

Barrett, Richard S. Guide to using psychological tests. *Harvard Business Review,* 1963, *41,* No. 4, 138–146. (Reprinted in Fleishman, 1967.)

    A statement addressed to businessmen, explaining how systematic follow-up studies are used so as to decide whether a test is useful in hiring and job placement. Refers to several criticisms of tests and evaluates their legitimacy. The stance here is, appropriately, psychometric.

Bennett, Chester C. The drugs and I. In James G. Miller & L. S. Uhr (Eds.) *Drugs and behavior.* New York: Wiley, 1960. Pp. 596–609.

    A clinical psychologist describes his experience as a subject in a laboratory where LDS, chlorpromazine, and other drugs are administered and tests are used to evaluate changes in mood and behavior. The testing procedures described include both self-report and performance measures of personality.

Lyman, Howard L. Score interpretation, and Types of test. In *Test scores and what they mean.* Englewood Cliffs, N.J.: Prentice-Hall, 1963. Pp. 1–24.

    A simple introduction pointing out alternatives open to the tester and possible difficulties that make serious study necessary before tests can be used competently.

Melton, Arthur W. (Ed.) Problems and techniques of mass testing with apparatus. In *Apparatus tests.* Washington: Government Printing Office, 1947. Pp. 22–53.

    The aptitude testing program discussed in these reports was the most elaborate one ever conducted. This chapter shows what had to be taken into account in standardizing procedures so that men tested in California could be compared precisely with men tested in Texas.

Porteus, Stanley D. *Porteus Maze Test—fifty years application.* Palo Alto, Calif.: Pacific Books, 1965.

    A biography of a test whose career has spanned the years from 1914 to the present, with lively discussion of its application as a measure of maximum performance and of typical behavior (impulsiveness). The research with the test covers aborigines, drugs, and delinquents, as well as more conventional topics.

Thorndike, Robert L. Educational decisions and human assessment. *Teachers College Record*, 1964, *66*, 103–112. (Reprinted in Flynn & Garber, 1967).

Thorndike expands on the position taken in this chapter, that tests are used for decision making. He offers a strategy to minimize difficulty arising from the limitations of measurement data.

Wohl, Julian. Traditional and contemporary views of psychological testing. *Journal of Projective Techniques*, 1963, *27*, 359–365. (Abridged in Payne & McMorris, 1967.)

Amplifies our psychometric-impressionistic distinction. Excellent in showing the limitations of a narrowly psychometric approach, but unduly optimistic about how easy it is for the tester to "be an expert in personality appraisal (and) dynamic psychology."

Administering Tests

3

Some tests are sufficiently simple for any intelligent adult to give; a few are so subtle that months of special training are required before a tester can get trustworthy data. A group test usually requires less training to administer than an individual test. When the tester has no responsibility save to read out printed directions, any conscientious, nonthreatening person should be successful. Skill is required when it is necessary to question the subject orally, and to use follow-up questions when the first answer is unclear.

The tester should take pains to give every subject a chance to exhibit his ability, and to obtain results comparable to those of other testers. The importance of rigorous adherence to prescribed procedure is especially obvious in the great competitive testing programs for scholarship awards and college admissions. The Scholastic Aptitude Test of the College Entrance Examination Board is given in 1000 American centers and several hundred foreign ones. At 9 A.M. on a particular Saturday in January, the seal is broken on the test package in each center: in Bronxville and Berkeley and Bell Buckle, Tennessee, in Gstaad and Beirut and Kodaikanal. The completed papers pour into the scoring centers and reports go out to the colleges. A boy in Beirut may be in competition with one in Berkeley for admission to the same college, and the selection procedure is unfair unless the two are tested in an identical manner.

To assure fair testing, the tester must become thoroughly familiar with the test. Even a simple test presents stumbling blocks, but they can be avoided if the tester studies the manual in advance.

The tester should maintain an impartial and scientific attitude. Testers are usually keenly interested in the persons they test, and desire to see them do well. As a result, the beginning tester is tempted to give hints to the subject or to coax him toward greater effort. It is the duty of the tester to obtain from each subject the best record he can produce; but he must produce this by his own efforts, without unfair aid. The tester must learn to suppress not only direct hints but also those unconscious acts that serve as cues to the subject.

This is especially a problem when each question is given orally. On a mental test item on which the child is supposed to receive only one trial, his answer may show that he did not comprehend the question. The tester will often be tempted to repeat the question "since the child could certainly have answered correctly if he had understood what was wanted"; this must not be done, since the test directions permit only one trial. Adjustments are sometimes warranted. For example, the result might be discarded (rather than scored as wrong) if an outside disturbance caused the child's failure.

Unintended help can be given by facial expression or words of encouragement. The person taking a test is always concerned to know how well he is doing, and watches the examiner for indications of his success. Suppose he is given the task: "Repeat backward, 2–7–5–1–4." He may begin "4–1–7 . . ."; if the examiner, on hearing the "7," permits his facial expression to change, the subject may take the hint and catch his own mistake. The examiner must maintain a completely unrevealing expression, while at the same time silently assuring the subject of his interest in what he says.

It is important that the subject want to cooperate with the tester. A teacher who knows and likes a child can often secure more spontaneous and representative performance than a stranger called in to administer tests. The tester acquainted with the subject, however, will be less impartial and must be unusually circumspect in following procedures. No rules can be given for the establishment of rapport, but the tester who likes people will develop many techniques. The person who proceeds coldly and "scientifically" to administer the test, without convincing the subject that he regards him as an important human being, will get only limited cooperation. Evidences of poor rapport are inattention during directions, giving up before time is called, restlessness, or finding fault with the test.

Two Specimen Tests

This chapter gives a general introduction to test administration. It cannot, of course, make the reader into a skilled tester; that comes only with practice. To illustrate this and the next three chapters, we digress here to describe the Bennett Mechanical Comprehension Test and the Block Design test in some detail. These tests are important in themselves, but we present them here so that we can refer to them to illustrate general principles of testing. If possible, the reader should take each of these tests himself.

Mechanical Comprehension Test

The Mechanical Comprehension Test (MCT) originated by George K. Bennett is one of the most widely used tests of special ability. The first form appeared in 1940; other forms for various purposes were published commercially, and special forms were developed for vocational selection and classification. The DAT battery for high-school guidance includes a form of the test, and in 1969 two "wide-range" forms were produced to replace some of the original versions of MCT. A list of the current forms and their purposes was given in the catalog excerpt in Chapter 1 (p. 14).

The manual for one version of the test begins with this description of purpose:[1]

The Test of Mechanical Comprehension measures the ability to perceive and understand the relationship of physical forces and mechanical elements in practical situations. This type of aptitude is important for a wide variety of jobs and for engineering and many trade school courses.

. . . .

Mechanical comprehension may be regarded as one aspect of intelligence if intelligence is broadly defined. The person who scores high in this trait tends to learn readily the principles of operation and repair of complex devices. Like other aptitude tests, it is influenced by environmental factors, but not to an extent that introduces important difficulties in interpretation. Formal training in physics appears to increase the score by not more than 4 points. Care has been taken to present items in terms of simple, frequently encountered mechanisms that do not resemble textbook illustrations or require special knowledge.

The test booklet carries instructions to the student and draws his attention to two specimen items (Figure 3.1). The manual carries the following directions to the tester:

Distribute the test booklets and then distribute the answer sheets. Then say:

You have been given a test booklet containing questions, and a separate answer sheet for your answers. Write on only the answer sheet; make *no* marks on the booklet.

If the answer sheets are to be hand scored locally, it is permissible to start with "Directions when only Side 1 is used." If the answer sheets are to be machine scored start with "Directions When Sides 1 and 2 Are Used," and make sure the examinee uses a No. 2 pencil.

The directions go on to tell the examinee how to record his name, the date, and other background information, using a grid like that shown in Figure 4.2. The

[1] Quoted material in this section reproduced by permission of The Psychological Corporation.

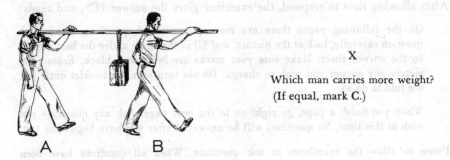

X

Which man carries more weight?
(If equal, mark C.)

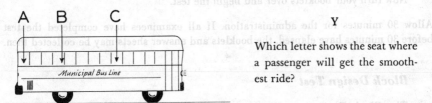

Y

Which letter shows the seat where
a passenger will get the smooth-
est ride?

Figure 3.1.   Mechanical Comprehension Test items.
These are specimen items from forms S and T of the Bennett Mechanical Comprehension
Test, which are being prepared for publication in 1969. *Copyright 1940, 1941, 1942,* ©
*1967, 1968 by The Psychological Corporation, New York, N.Y. All rights reserved. Re-
produced by permission.*

only part of these instructions worth repeating here is these words to the
examinee:

> Be sure to make heavy black marks, filling the entire circle. If you make a mis-
> take, erase very carefully. Don't go outside the circle.

The directions to the tester proceed:

Tell the examinees to find the answer spaces on Side 1 of the answer sheet, and say:

> Now fold back the cover of your booklet and turn it so you can see page 2.
> (Demonstrate.) Look at the second paragraph of directions on page 2 while
> I read them aloud to you.

> Look at Sample X on this page. It shows two men carrying a weighted object
> on a plank, and it asks, "Which man carries more weight?" Because the object
> is closer to man "B" than to man "A", man "B" is shouldering more weight; so
> blacken the circle under "B" on your answer sheet.

> Now look at Sample Y and answer it yourself. Fill in the circle under the
> correct answer on your answer sheet.

After allowing time to respond, the examiner gives the answer (C), and reads:

> On the following pages there are more pictures and questions. Read each question carefully, look at the picture, and fill in the circle under the best answer on the answer sheet. Make sure your marks are heavy and black. Erase completely any answer you wish to change. Do not turn over the booklet until you are told to do so.

> When you finish a page, go right on to the next page. Ask any questions you wish at this time. No questions will be answered after you have begun the test.

Pause to allow the examinees to ask questions. When all questions have been answered, say:

> Now turn your booklets over and begin the test.

Allow 30 minutes for the administration. If all examinees have completed the test before 30 minutes have elapsed, the booklets and answer sheets may be collected then.

Block Design Test

The Block Design test illustrates how tests evolve. S. C. Kohs (1923), a clinical psychologist, invented the procedure. The subject is to construct prescribed designs out of colored one-inch cubes originally sold for children's play. The Kohs test was one among a large number of mental tests invented during the 1920s, when applied psychology first came into prominence. As schools began to hire psychologists to examine children, demand arose for standardized collections of tests. A psychologist acting as editor collected tests by various authors, improved the directions, materials, and scoring procedures, and applied the whole set to a large group of typical pupils to obtain standards of comparison. Several such collections were made. The Block Design task was used in many of these collections, as it measures nonverbal analytic and synthetic reasoning with a wide range of difficulty. Revision and restandardization has continued down to the present day. Each modification alters the number of items or the directions, or introduces new designs. Sometimes the modification is a radical extension; Ohwaki prepared cubes with surfaces of different textures, to test the blind (see Dauterman & Suinn, 1966).

We shall describe Block Design (Figure 3.2) in the WAIS version (manual, 1955, p. 47).

The instructions begin:

Start with Design 1 for all subjects. Take four blocks and say *You see these blocks. They are all alike. On some sides they are all red; on some, all white; and on some, half red and half white.* Turn the blocks to show the different sides. Then say *I am going to put them together to make a design. Watch me.* Arrange the four blocks slowly into the design shown on Card 1, *without* exposing Card 1 to the subject.

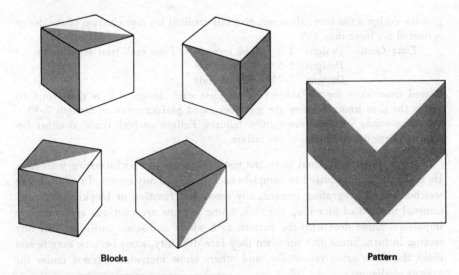

Blocks   **Pattern**

Figure 3.2.   Block Design test materials.
Pattern copyright 1940; © 1955 by The Psychological Corporation, New York, N.Y. Reproduced by permission.

Then, leaving the model intact, give four *other* blocks to the subject and say *Now make one just like this.* If the subject successfully completes the design within the time limit, score 4 points and proceed to Design 2.

If the subject fails to complete the design within the time limit or arranges the blocks incorrectly, pick up his blocks, leaving the examiner's model intact, and say *Watch me again.* Demonstrate a second time using subject's blocks, then mix them up, still leaving the examiner's model intact, and say *Now you try it and be sure to make it just like mine.* Whether subject succeeds or fails on this trial, proceed to Design 2.

Occasionally a subject will try to duplicate the examiner's model exactly, including the sides. When this occurs on Design 1, tell the subject that only the top needs to be duplicated.

A second sample is administered in a similar manner. The test proper begins with Design 3. The directions are:

Designs 3–10. Place the card for Design 3 before the subject and provide him with four blocks. Say *Now make one like this. Tell me when you have finished.* When the subject indicates he has finished or at the end of the time limit, mix up his blocks and present Design 4 with the remark *Now make one like this. Go ahead; let me know when you have finished.* Follow this procedure for all succeeding designs. When Design 7 is reached, take out the five other blocks and say *Now make one like this, using nine blocks. Be sure to tell me when you have finished.* For Design 10 [which has an irregular outline], do not permit the subject to rotate the card to give the design a flat base. However, give full credit if his reproduction of the design is rotated not more than 45°.

Time Limits   Designs   1–2   60 seconds   (Time each trial separately)
                 Designs   3–6   60 seconds
                 Designs   7–10   120 seconds

Record time taken for the subject to complete each design if it is done correctly within the time limit; bonuses are given for rapid performances on Designs 7–10.

Discontinue   After 3 consecutive failures. Failure on both trials of either Design 1 or Design 2 is considered one failure.

As in other individual tests, the tester observes the performance with care. He notes the time required to complete each task, and any errors. In addition, he watches for any revealing remark, any emotional reaction or blocking, and any unusual method of attacking the task. Some persons are cautious and some are impulsive. Some deal with the pattern as a whole and some consider each tiny section in turn. Some give up when they face difficulty, some become erratic and make the same error repeatedly, and others show increased interest under the greater challenge.

1. *If MCT were administered individually, could profitable observations be made?*
2. *Can you think of any questions a subject might ask that the MCT directions do not cover?*
3. *Wechsler's directions specify only that four blocks are to be "mixed up" after each trial. Could this procedure be standardized more exactly? Should it?*
4. *Wechsler prescribes that each sample should be demonstrated only twice. Even if the subject is unable to do the task on the second sample, the tester proceeds to the next design. Is this a wise procedure?*
5. *The manual is not regarded as sufficient to prepare one to give the Wechsler test. The tester learns by observing an experienced tester and discussing procedures with him. What do you think you could learn about giving the Block Design test that the manual did not tell you?*

Procedure for Test Administration

Conditions of Testing

Certain general problems of administration are common to all tests. The first of these is the physical situation where the test is given. If ventilation and lighting are poor, subjects will be handicapped. On speed tests particularly, their scores will be lower than they deserve if they do not have a convenient place to write, including sufficient space to spread out materials. Subjects must be placed so that they can hear directions and see demonstrations clearly. Very large rooms are bad for group testing, unless proctors are stationed to watch subjects closely. The large room has the disadvantage that a person may hesitate to ask a question about unclear directions that he would raise before a smaller audience. This may be solved by having him raise his hand so that a proctor will come to his seat and answer his question.

The state of the person tested affects the results. If the test is given when he is fatigued, when his mind is on other problems, or when he is temporarily upset, results will not be a fair sample of his behavior. Occasionally it is necessary to test a person at an unfavorable time, as when psychological examinations must be given to an accused person during pretrial study of his case. Tests to be used in classification and guidance of college freshmen are frequently given in the midst of a hectic week of orientation, college activities, establishment of new friends and living arrangements, and adjustment to an adult world. Sometimes a freshman who later proves to be normally intelligent does very badly on place-ment tests because of homesickness, distraction, emotional exhaustion, or un-identified causes. While tests given under these conditions do have predictive value for most of the group, some individual scores are misleading. If a test must be given at a psychologically inopportune time, the only correct procedure is to maintain an adequately critical attitude toward results. Conditions can often be improved by spacing tests to avoid cumulative fatigue, providing for adequate rest on the night before tests, and administering the program with a minimum of bustle and confusion.

Military classification tests have often been given to soldiers just after induc-tion when they lack sleep, are recovering from a farewell party, or feel ill from inoculations. In one study men who took a second form of such a test after be-coming stabilized in Army routines raised their scores 11.25 points on the average. This was enough to raise a man from the category of potential noncom to that of potential officer (Duncan, 1947).

Alert subjects are more likely to give their best than subjects who are tired and dispirited. But equally good results can be produced at any hour of the day if the subjects want to do well. Fatigue apparently affects motivation rather than the ability one can summon up. The most thorough inquiry into hour-by-hour variation was conducted by Air Force psychologists (Melton, 1947, pp. 49–51). In one study of 2500 cadets being classified at Buckley Field, Colorado, they found striking differences in psychomotor test performance (finger dexterity, rudder control, discrimination reaction time, etc.). In general, performance was at its peak between 10 A.M. and 3 P.M. In an attempt to confirm and interpret this difference with further tests of nearly 9000 cadets at other places, negligible dif-ferences were found. The inconsistency has not been explained, but it appears that under most operating conditions fluctuations during the day can be avoided. The experience at Buckley Field warns the tester not to close his mind to the possi-bility of error from unexpected sources.

Control of the Group

Group tests are given to reasonably mature and cooperative subjects who expect to do as the tester requests. Group testing, then, is essentially a problem in command. For efficient testing, subjects must follow instructions promptly and all must do the same thing. This attitude is to be maintained without interfering with the opportunity of individuals to ask questions. One person should be in charge, standing in front of the group where he can see all members. He will find helpful the adage "Never give an order unless you expect it to be obeyed." False starts, preliminary attempts to call the group to order while late-comers are finding seats, and ineffectual rapping for attention make it more difficult to secure compliance when work begins. The tester should have full attention when he starts to talk, so that repetition will not be necessary.

Directions should be given simply, clearly, and singly. A complex instruction: "Take your booklet, turn it face down, and then write your name on the answer sheet," will lead to misunderstanding and confusion. It is better to break the instruction into unmistakable simple units: "Take your booklet." (Hold a sample up, and watch the group to be sure everyone has taken his booklet before proceeding.) "Turn it face down." (Demonstrate and wait until everyone has complied.) "Now take your answer sheet." (Exhibit a sample, and wait for compliance.) "Write your name on the blank at the top, last name first." The subjects have a chance to ask questions whenever they are necessary, but the examiner attempts to anticipate all likely questions by full directions.

Formal commands in a firm, audible, but polite tone are effective for controlling a group. A quasimilitary manner may enhance the "inhuman" character of the test situation and give some people the feeling that the examiner is not interested in their welfare. Effective control may be combined with good rapport if the examiner is friendly, avoids an antagonistic, overbearing, or fault-finding attitude, and is informal when formal control is not called for. After establishing control, for example, he may relax his "command manner" and make informal comments about the test and its purpose; this does not interfere with his resuming formal control for the test proper.

Emergencies arise that prevent uniform testing of all persons. Occasionally, for example, a person becomes ill during the test and must leave the room. Usually it will be possible to indicate that the test is invalidated and provide for a makeup on another occasion, perhaps with a different form of the test. The goal of the tester is to obtain useful information. There is no value in adhering rigidly to a testing schedule if that schedule will give false information.

6. *An employment office gives all applicants an intelligence test when their applications are filed. One man takes the test, together with several friends, and the group leave together. Ten minutes later he returns, greatly agitated: "Was I*

supposed to turn over the last page? I thought I had finished when I got to the bottom of page 9, so I looked back over my answers. I had plenty of time, and I'm sure I could have done well on the last page—my friends say the questions there were easy." What should be done in this case, if at the bottom of page 9 the booklet carried the printed statement "Go on to the next page?"

7. *In testing a group of college freshmen to obtain information for use in guidance, the examiner finds that a student newly arrived from Latin America is having great difficulty following directions because of unfamiliarity with English. The student asks many questions, requests repetitions, and seems unable to comprehend what is desired. What should the examiner do?*

8. *In the course of a clinical analysis of a preschool child who is believed to be poorly adjusted, tests are requested. The psychometrist finds the child negativistic. After cooperating reluctantly on two tests the child becomes inattentive and careless on the third. Assuming that the test results are needed as soon as possible, what should the tester do?*

Directions to the Subject

The most important responsibility in test administration is giving directions. The purpose of a standardized test is to obtain a measurement that may be compared with measurements made at other times; *it is imperative that the tester give the directions exactly as provided in the manual.* The tester's task is to follow the printed directions, reading them word for word, adding nothing and changing nothing.

The standard directions usually invite the subject to ask questions after the directions have been read. In answering such questions, the tester must not add to the ideas expressed in the standard directions, since such supplementation gives today's subjects an advantage over those tested at another time. The directions are part of the test situation; in some tests the way the subject follows directions is intended to influence his score.

The most troublesome questions concern matters not discussed in the standard directions. Examples are: "Should we guess if we are not certain?" "How much is taken off for a wrong answer?" "Are there any catch questions?" "If I find a hard question, should I skip it and go on, or should I answer every question as I go?" The published directions to the test were evidently not adequate if they ignored these topics. When the tester refuses to give an answer to the questions about guessing—and he must refuse if the scores are to be compared with norms—some subjects will guess and some will not. Therefore, while the directions are superficially standard, the procedure becomes unstandardized because subjects interpret indefinite instructions, each in his own way. Sometimes the tester will decide to supplement the directions. When he does so, he is in effect creating a new test. The change may get better information. But the norms for the original test cannot be used, and the test really should be given a new name so that no one will be misled.

Attempts to test skill in flying have shown the crucial importance of defining the task clearly for the subject. In making a check test on ability to execute a maneuver, testers found it necessary to tell the pilot exactly how the performance would be scored. When they omitted this, one pilot kept his attention on maintaining altitude perfectly, whereas another of equal ability earned a different score because he concentrated on holding the plane's heading steady. Test directions should be free from ambiguities. When the tester must use a standard test for which directions are imperfect, he faces a difficulty for which there is no ideal solution.

It is becoming increasingly common to administer tests by tape recorder. This assures uniform procedure; the tape can even control the timing of the test, thus freeing the tester from concentration on his stopwatch. Not only the directions, but the test items themselves can be presented on the tape, though in that case the items are usually also put before the examinee in printed form. The relatively poor reader should be helped by the oral presentation, which is an asset when one is primarily interested in testing reasoning or some other skill independent of reading.

9. *The Bennett MCT directions are printed in the student's test booklet, and also read word for word by the examiner. (The only difference is the sentence in which the examiner asks if there are any questions.) Why is it desirable to read the directions aloud instead of allowing the student to read to himself?*

10. *How would you answer the following questions raised by students after hearing the MCT directions?*
   a. *Is this a speed test?*
   b. *If I am not sure of the answer should I mark what I think is best?*

11. *The California Test of Mental Maturity consists of twelve sections, each containing a different type of item. The sections are separately timed, each requiring 3–10 minutes. Is there any reason why a high school seeking data for guidance should not give pupils one or two sections of the test each day until all of it is taken, rather than giving it in one or two sittings as the manual suggests?*

12. *The Bennett directions are vague as regards timing: "Little is gained by allowing more than thirty minutes." The DAT form of the test is definite. "At the end of 30 minutes, say 'Stop!'" What are the advantages and disadvantages of the two procedures?*

Judgments Left to the Examiner

While the directions will be standardized in many respects, it is unwise to standardize the tester's procedures too rigidly. Precisely the same action or remark by the examiner can have a different significance for different subjects, and if so, rigid procedure itself introduces an unstandardized element into the testing. This may be illustrated first with regard to the problem of terminating a test. Directions for most tests place some limit on the time allowed to solve any problem or to work on any subtest (see the Block Design directions, for example). To conform to the directions, the tester need only use his stop watch attentively. When no time limit is stated, it is still necessary to stop the painfully conscientious subject who works long after he has done his best.

Sometimes credit is allowed only when a task is done in (say) two minutes, but the directions do not tell the examiner to stop the subject at that time. The tester must decide whether to let the subject work after he has passed the credit limit or to interrupt him. This is one of the situations where the art of testing comes into play; no rules can prescribe how to terminate an unsuccessful trial.

In an ability test like Block Design, success on one problem has an encouraging effect during the next, but the effect of failure depends on the tester. In the tester's eyes, the subject fails when he does not complete the task within the time limit. If the subject is allowed to continue without interruption, however, he may finish the task and think that he has succeeded. This, of course, tends to help his subsequent performance. But another subject, even with extra time, may be unable to solve the problem. If he apparently is becoming confused and upset, it probably is best to terminate the problem and give him a fresh start. To let him continue might only increase his discouragement. In the absence of definite instructions on procedure, the tester should observe the subject's attitudes carefully and choose whatever course seems likely to have the best effect on his subsequent performance.

Terman and Merrill (1960, pp. 47 ff.), in their advice to examiners giving the Stanford-Binet test, further illustrate desirable variation in tactics:

> Following a standard procedure does not restrict the examiner to a stilted or formal manner. Indeed, the acquisition of testing skill consists initially in learning to work effectively within a specific frame of reference. . . .
>
> The order in which items appear within a given subtest is based upon the relative difficulty of the items, and it is, therefore, advisable not to alter the order of presentation. For example, the level of difficulty of the second and third items of the Ingenuity Test [water-jar problem, see Average Adult level, Table 7.2; see also pp. 640 f.] hinges upon the use that the subject is able to make of the experience he has gained in the solution of the first and simplest problem.
>
> The accepted practice is to limit changes in test order to *practical* requirements of testing. Thus, it is sometimes advisable, in order to secure the child's effort when a certain type of test (such as repeating digits or drawing) is found to arouse resistance, to shift temporarily to a more agreeable task. When the subject is at his ease again, it is usually possible to return to the troublesome task with better success.
>
> To elicit the subject's best efforts . . . [is] the *sine qua non* of good testing, but the means by which these ends are accomplished are so varied as to defy specific formulation. The address which puts one child at ease with a strange adult may belittle or even antagonize another.
>
> Keeping the subject encouraged contributes much to the maintenance of satisfactory rapport. This can be accomplished in many subtle, friendly ways; by an understanding smile, a spontaneous exclamation of approval, an appreciative comment, or just the quiet understanding between equals that carries assurance and apprecia-

tion. Any stereotyped comment following each test becomes perfunctory and serves no purpose other than to punctuate the tests. In general it is effective to praise frequently and generously, but if this is done in too lavish and stilted a fashion it is likely to defeat its own purpose. Expressions of commendation should be varied and should fit naturally into the conversation. The examiner should remember that he is giving approval for effort rather than for success on a particular response.

Under no circumstances should the examiner permit himself to show dissatisfaction with a response, though he may smilingly refuse to accept a flippant answer obviously intended to "test the limits." With younger children, especially, praise should not be limited to tests on which the child has done well. Young children are characteristically uncritical and are often enormously pleased with very inferior responses. In praising poor responses of older subjects, the examiner should remember that the purpose of the commendation is to insure confidence and not to reconcile the subject to an inferior level of response. In the case of a failure that is embarrassingly evident to the subject himself, the examiner may take occasion to point out that he doesn't expect the subject to be able to do all these things, or he may interject, *"That was a good try!"* . . .

Although the examiner should always encourage the child to believe that he can answer correctly if he will only try, he must avoid the practice of dragging out responses by too much urging and cross-questioning. To do so robs the response of significance and discourages spontaneous effort. While the examiner must be on his guard against mistaking exceptional timidity for inability to respond, he must also be able to recognize the silence of incapacity or the genuineness of an *"I don't know"* from the child who knows when he knows not!

The competent examiner must possess in a high degree judgment, intelligence, sensitivity to the reactions of others, and penetration, as well as knowledge of and regard for scientific methods and experience in the use of psychometric techniques. No degree of mechanical perfection of the tests themselves can ever take the place of good judgment and psychological insight of the examiner.

There are cases so abnormal that no procedure laid down by the test constructor can give sensible results. Shapiro (1957) tells of the 7-year-old girl who was uncooperative and at times aggressive toward the tester. The first session was wasted; the child simply would not do the test. The second session started equally unhappily. Finally the psychologist slammed one of the playroom toys against the wall. Said the child, smiling at last, "Do it again." After a bit of routine cooperation—child fetching toy and psychologist smashing it against the wall— they were pals, and in due time, the girl had settled down to take the test, earning a Stanford-Binet score in the normal range. Shapiro tells of another oddity: the woman who could earn a respectable score on a test only when she took it for the second time (though score changes are small for other subjects).

Guessing

At the start of an objective ability test, some subject is likely to ask, "Should I guess when I am not sure?" Sometimes the test directions include an answer to this question, but even where advice to guess or not to guess is given, some ambiguity remains. It is against the rules for the tester to give supplementary advice; he must retreat to such a formula as "Use your own judgment." The discussion that follows is intended to clarify the guessing problem for the tester and test developer but should not influence procedure in giving a standard test.

To simplify, we can speak as if items fall into two categories: those where the subject knows the answer, and those he cannot answer. If the item calls for a choice of alternatives, the subject has a chance of picking the correct response even on the items he does not know. If there are two alternatives, as in a true-false item, he will succeed by chance alone on 50 per cent of his guesses. Some scoring rules assume that any wrong choice represents an unlucky guess. The number of lucky guesses is estimated as a fraction of the number of wrong guesses, and that amount of credit is subtracted. The final score on a true-false test is then "number of items right minus number marked wrong," i.e., total number of items marked correctly less the number thought to have been marked correctly by guessing. If there are n choices per item, the chance probability of a correct guess is $1/n$ and that of an unlucky guess is $(n - 1)/n$. For every $(n - 1)$ incorrect guesses, we expect one correct guess, on the average. Hence the correction formula most often used is "Right minus Wrong/$(n - 1)$." On a 50-item test with three choices per item, a person who gets 36 right and 10 wrong receives a score of 31 (i.e., $36 - 10/2$). In a test with a liberal time allowance and comparatively easy items, subjects usually mark every item. When that happens, the rank order of the scores remains the same whether the score used is "number right" or $R - W/(n - 1)$.

A correction formula is desired because some people guess more freely than others. The scoring formula attempts to wipe out gains due to guessing. Unfortunately, the logic described above does not describe the situation fairly. The basic assumption is incorrect, and the formula does not truly "correct for guessing." You cannot divide items into those the subject knows perfectly and those he does not know at all. There are items he knows fairly well but is not positive of, and others where he has hazy knowledge.

"Guessing" is not a matter of pure chance. Even on the items he knows least about, the guesser's experience and common sense should permit him to choose correctly more often than he would if he selected answers by rolling dice. A truly testwise person can even beat the game when he knows nothing about the test content. There is the story of the visiting American psychologist who earned a good mark on a Japanese multiple-choice achievement test even though he could read none of the language. His strategy was to favor the longest alternative on each item, to avoid using the same response position in close succession, etc. To be sure, a test constructor can balance his test to foil such tricks.

A person who guesses *intelligently* on 10 five-choice items can expect to get perhaps 4 items right, instead of the 2 items expected by chance. Four right answers would give him a formula score of 2½ points. Since a person who does not guess receives a score of zero on the same 10 items, the score is raised by willingness to gamble.

Some subjects mark only the items they are very sure of. Others mark any item they think they understand, and still others mark every item. This difference in tendency to gamble is not eliminated by any change of directions or penalties. As the penalty becomes more severe, guessing diminishes, but the bold still take more chances than the timid. Moreover, the person who takes chances on one test tends to do more guessing on tests in other subjects (Torrance & Ziller, 1957; Slakter, 1969).

Despite correction formulas, the person who gambles on every doubtful item is likely to gain more than he loses. No test constructor is consistently skillful in writing misleading alternatives that the guesser is likely to pick in preference to the right answer. Therefore the person taking a test is usually wise to guess freely. (But remember that the tester is not to give his group an advantage by telling them this trade secret!)

From the point of view of the tester, tendency to guess is an unstandardized aspect of the situation that interferes with accurate measurement. Most European group tests remove the opportunity for blind guessing by presenting items where the subject must construct the answer. American group tests, however, are almost always in multiple-choice form.

The systematic advantage of the guesser is eliminated if the test manual directs everyone to guess, but guessing introduces large chance errors. Chance errors multiply when everyone guesses, and the cumulative influence on accuracy of measurement outweighs the advantage of "do not guess" instructions. It is usual now to inform subjects that wild guessing is to their disadvantage, but to encourage them to respond when they can make an informed judgment as to the most reasonable answer. The following advice given to College Board applicants is much fairer than strict instructions not to guess:

When the test is scored, a percentage of the wrong answers is subtracted from the number of right answers as a correction for haphazard guessing. It is improbable, therefore, that mere guessing will improve your score significantly; it may even lower your score. If, however, you are not sure of the correct answer but have some knowledge of the question and are able to eliminate one or more of the answer choices as wrong, your chance of getting the right answer is improved, and it will be to your advantage to answer such a question.

Probability scoring. A recent ingenious proposal invites the student to report his exact degree of uncertainty and scores him in such a way that the more honest he is, the higher his score tends to be. Several scoring rules are available. One variant asks him to divide 100 points among the alternatives, betting it all on one choice if he feels certain, spreading it evenly if he is without a clue, or placing points in any other way that will express the odds. The scoring rule is to *square* the number of points he bets on wrong answers, and to penalize him by the sum

Table 3.1. Calculation of scores based on the student's stated probabilities

Choice	How the student feels	How he might bet			His score if (a) is correct			His score if (b) is correct			His score if (c) is correct		
		1	2	3	1	2	3	1	2	3	1	2	3
a	0.70	1.00	0.40	0.70				1.00	0.40	0.49	1.00	0.16	0.49
b	.20	–	.30	.20	0.00	0.09	0.04				.00	.09	.04
c	.10	–	.30	.10	.00	.09	.01	.00	.09	.01			
d	.00	–	–	–	.00	.00	.00	.00	.00	.00	.00	.00	.00
Score					1.00	.82	.95	.00	.51	.50	.00	.75	.47

of these squared numbers. The numbers are treated as decimal fractions, not as whole numbers, so that the penalty on an item can range from .00 to 1.00. A credit of 1.00 per item, before penalty, is allowed so as to keep scores above zero. (For details and rationale, see di Finetti, 1967, and Shuford, Massengill, & Albert, 1966.)

How this works is seen in Table 3.1. We consider a four-choice item, and assume that the student is pretty sure a is correct but cannot confidently rule out b and c. Almost certainly, if the test were to be scored conventionally, he would answer a; this response distribution is shown in the table as a bet of all the chips on that answer—pattern 1. In response pattern 2 we have him trying to hedge, putting chips on each of the possible answers. Finally, in 3, he does as instructed, expressing the odds exactly as he sees them. Then the scoring is figured out by squaring the entries under all the wrong answers, and subtracting the total from 1.00. Clearly, the very best thing he can do is to put all the chips on a provided that a is correct; but if it is wrong that pattern is heavily penalized. Pattern 2 permits less variation of scores than 1 or 3, and sometimes gives a better result; but its "expected value" is not so good. If the subject sees the odds as 70–20–10, his expected score—on the average over many such bets—is 0.70 times what he earns if a is right plus 0.20 times the b-correct score plus 0.10 times the c-correct score. For (2): $0.70 (0.82) + 0.20 (0.51) + 0.10 (0.75) = 0.76$. For (3) a similar calculation gives 0.81. A person comes out best in the long run if he "calls them just as he sees them." An irrational caution or love of gambling might cause the subject to depart from this rule, but he will lose by it.

One can admire the ingenuity of this gamesmanship—it is literally an application of the mathematical "theory of games and strategies." But perhaps guessing behavior does not have enough influence on test scores to justify such elaborate machinery. The technique is probably useful as an instructional device, to help the student face and report his uncertainties.

13. *Bennett Form AA items (with very few exceptions) have two alternatives. The test is scored* $R - \frac{1}{2}W$, *for no stated reason. What effect will this formula have as compared to* $R - W$? *Does it favor or penalize the rash guesser?*

14. *Should test directions tell the subject what scoring formula will be used?*

15. *When scores are "corrected for guessing," some person may receive a nega-tive score. What does this mean? Is he less able than a person scoring zero?*

16. *Compute scores for each of the following persons by the usual correction formula:*

Test 1, true-false.	*A has 20 right, 6 wrong, 7 omitted.*
	B has 22 right, 8 wrong, 3 omitted.
Test 2, three-choice.	*C has 15 right, 6 wrong, 4 omitted.*
	D has 18 right, 3 wrong, 4 omitted.
Test 3, five-choice.	*E has 20 right, 6 wrong, 9 omitted.*
	F has 6 right, 6 wrong, 23 omitted.

17. *In a time-limit test of mental ability using multiple-choice items, how rapidly should the subject work, in view of the fact that higher speed leads to more errors?*

18. *Some instructors advocate scoring achievement tests by formulas that penalize guessing very heavily, such as "Number right minus twice number wrong." What effect would this have on validity of measurement?*

19. *In Table 3.1, work out the scores obtained if (d) is correct.*

20. *In a probability-scored test, what should a student do if he is totally uncertain? What score will he get?*

Motivation for Taking a Test

In making a physical measurement—for instance, weighing a truckload of wheat—there is no problem of motivation. Likewise, in weighing a person, when we put him on the scale we get a good measure no matter how he feels about the operation. But in a psychological test the subject places himself on the scale, and unless he cares about the result he cannot be measured.

Incentives that Raise Scores

In ability testing, our problem is like that of the industrial manager who wants a high rate of production. Effort and productivity depend on the reward the person foresees. The most direct reward for good test performance is being hired for a job or being given a desirable assignment. Equally powerful and more universally available as a source of motivation is the desire to maintain self-respect and the respect of others. Effort is stimulated also by sheer interest in the task, by the habit of obeying authority, and by the friendliness of the tester. No single tactic works with all children, as was noted in the quotation from Terman and Merrill above. An attempt was made in one study to get children to persist in a monotonous "game" that consisted of dropping marbles into holes. The investigator found that praise worked with primary-grade children who had older brothers or sisters in their families; their persistence averaged 4 minutes when the experimenter looked on, and 7 minutes when he praised them. But first-born children persisted 4 minutes when the investigator was passive and dropped to 2½ minutes when he praised them (Gilmore & Zigler, 1964).

The test score is not readily altered by simple incentives. There have been many attempts to raise test performance by prizes, pep talks, and monetary payments for increases in score. Such attempts almost invariably fail to improve ability scores appreciably over those earned under the regular conditions of administration. These incentive studies generally offered rewards for compliance with an authority.

When, instead, the tester intensifiies the subject's concern to do well, scores improve. Flanagan (1955), in a study of a large number of aviation cadets, looked for careless and unmotivated performance under various conditions. His evidence was obtained by counting the number of cadets who used stereotyped patterns of marking the answer sheet, such as the sequence A B A B A B, and the number earning chance scores on easy items. Even though the tests affected the cadets' duty assignments, a few cadets gave these completely meaningless responses. On a memory test, which was fairly typical of the entire series of tests, two cadets per thousand showed stereotyped patterns, and five obtained chance scores. High-school students were given a similar test with no particular incentive, merely being told that research data were being collected. Here there were four stereotyped-response papers per thousand, and 21 chance scores. In another school where the students expected that they would receive a full report on the tests together with counseling, there were no stereotyped responses, and only three chance patterns per thousand. Research data collected with tests have uncertain meaning unless the subject is given a personal reason for taking the test. If he is merely asked to cooperate in an experiment, his responses are likely to be casual. He may sabotage the study by trying to miss items, or, according to Rosenthal (1966), he may try to "help" the experimenter by guessing what the hypothesis is and trying to supply data that support it.

Motivation to do a task well or to make a good impression is learned. During his early years, the child develops attitudes toward himself and toward task performance that have a profound influence on his response to tests and to school assignments. The typical middleclass child learns to work hard because he obtains praise, tangible rewards, and special opportunities when he achieves well. The lowerclass child very often learns to take assignments less seriously and to work barely enough to keep out of trouble. His self-respect depends most on his relations with his classmates outside of school, and relatively little on the approval of adult authorities (Eells et al., 1951).

Motives that Reduce Scores

The subject may frankly wish to do poorly on a test (see Pollaczek, 1952). There are times when pupils try to limit their scores on mental tests because a school has a classification plan in which, it is rumored, the better students will be required to do extra work. If, in military classification, men suspect that passing certain tests qualifies one for an unpopular assignment, there is a temptation to fail deliberately. Another instance is the boy who deliberately failed his school subjects so that instead of being promoted he would be kept in the grade where his less intelligent friends were to remain.

When the subject wishes to earn the best score he can, his very desire to do well may interfere with good performance. When one is tense, he overlooks errors that he would readily correct otherwise. In psychomotor tests, tension leads to poor coordination and erratic movements. In a verbal test, the subject who fears criticism of his answers may attempt to escape it by being overcritical of himself. In clinical tests, anxious patients frequently find fault with their own answers or elaborate them to include all possible variations and qualifications. In doing this they may spoil an answer that would have received credit.

Test anxiety. Anxiety over tests is generated at an early age by the attitudes of teachers, parents, and other children. Sarason and his associates developed a special questionaire to measure "test anxiety," using such items as "When the teacher says she is going to give the class a test, do you get a nervous (or funny) feeling?" (Sarason *et al.*, 1958). They found substantial individual differences, which remained fairly stable on a later retest. The median elementary-school child admits to 12 anxiety symptoms on the list of 43 covered by the questionnaire. Anxiety increases gradually through the school years. Test anxiety is common among all kinds of pupils, though it is a bit more common among the dull ones.

The detrimental effects of anxiety may be increased by the very tactics the tester uses to elicit the subject's best efforts. Sarason and his associates (1952) used his questionnaire to identify Yale freshmen with high and low anxiety (HA and LA groups, respectively). They were given five trials on a stylus maze. Half the students received "ego-involving" (EI) instructions which stressed that this was an intelligence test and would be used to assist in interpreting freshman entrance tests. The NEI ("not ego-involved") group, on the contrary, was told that the examiner was standardizing the maze task; and that no one would examine individual standings. Error scores are shown in Figure 3.3. We find that the NEI groups had intermediate scores, there being little difference between the HA–NEI and LA–NEI subgroups. In the low-anxiety group, EI instructions had a small, generally helpful effect. The subjects with high anxiety about tests, however, did much worse when threatened by the emphasis on doing well than they did under emotionally neutral conditions. Urging students to try hard on a learning task also had different effects on different personalities in the study of London, Conant, & Davison (1966). Subjects who are easily hypnotized performed worse after urging (and also worse while under hypnosis) than subjects hard to hypnotize.

How anxious and defensive reactions interfere is shown by G. Wiener

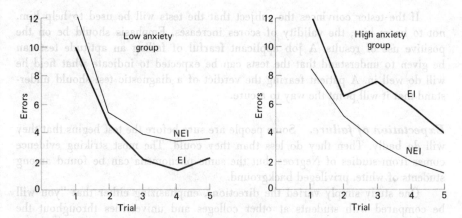

Figure 3.3. Maze performance under ego-involving (EI) and neutral (NEI) instructions.
Sarason, Mandler, & Craighill, 1952. Reproduced by permission.

(1957). "Trustful" and "distrustful" student nurses were selected by a questionnaire. Each nurse took the Wechsler Picture Completion test, which asks what is missing in a picture (e.g., one eyebrow in a sketch of a face). Distrustful subjects were inclined to deny that anything was missing when the answer did not come to them immediately. Likewise, on Similarities ("How are *praise* and *punishment* alike?") the distrustful students were more inclined to deny that the words were alike. Distrustful students averaged 2.7 suspicious comments on the two tests compared to 0.9 for the trustful students. To measure the effect, Wiener compared scores on PC and Similarities with a vocabulary score that presumably is not affected by suspiciousness. He concluded that extreme suspiciousness lowers the IQ by about three or four points. In Wiener's words: "People who say, 'There is nothing missing in that picture!' are responding to internal needs rather than to the testing situation." This is a maladaptive response, and necessarily lowers scores.

Threats are ever present in testing: a delinquent fears that his punishment will depend on the test results; a child fears that a poor intelligence rating will disappoint his parents and diminish their affection; a college girl fears that failure will force her to leave her campus friends and return to the farm; an anxious patient fears that a test will prove him insane. Fears such as these can be listed without end. A striking example is the case of the young reserve officer, extremely eager to serve in time of war, who failed his physical examination twice because the importance of passing made him emotional—and the emotion always brought his blood pressure over the acceptable limit. A series of "reconditioning" treatments eventually made it possible for him to take the test calmly. The disrupting effects of emotion on physiological responses have their intellectual counterparts.

If the tester convinces the subject that the tests will be used to help him, not to harm him, the validity of scores increases. Emphasis should be on the positive use of results. A job applicant fearful of failing an aptitude test can be given to understand that the tests can be expected to indicate what field he will do well in. A patient fearing the verdict of a diagnostic test should understand that it will point the way to a cure.

Expectation of failure.   Some people are sure before the test begins that they will do badly. Then they do less than they could. The most striking evidence comes from studies of Negroes, but the same phenomena can be found among students of white, privileged background.

One study simply varied the directions, emphasizing either that "you will be compared with students at other colleges and universities throughout the United States" or "with other students at this university." The Negroes were undergraduates in a segregated university in a Southern state. The average raw scores (on a digit-symbol, speed-of-substitution task) were approximately as follows:

	"Local comparison"	*"National comparison"*
Easy task	34	33
Hard task	26	22

No such difference between conditions was found for whites (at another college in the same city; Katz, Epps, & Axelson, 1964). The authors do *not* conclude that the "hopeless struggle" condition reduced effort. On the contrary, the Negroes said that they cared more about doing well under the national-norms condition. One theory is that excessive concern gives rise to task-irrelevant thoughts which are distracting.

A companion study crossed two experimental variables. A group could have a white or a Negro tester, and it could be told that the digit-symbol task is "a research instrument for studying eye-hand coordination" or that it is "an intelligence test." No one expects Negroes to be inferior in coordination, and a research study involves little personal threat; under the first set of directions the Negro students score higher with a white tester. Under intelligence-test, personally evaluative conditions, white and black testers get the same results. Blacks tested by a black score a little better than those tested by a white under the research-on-coordination condition. Those tested "on intelligence" by a white do much worse than those given a "coordination" test by a white (Katz, Roberts, & Robinson, 1965).

These studies do not directly yield recommendations for test procedure. When a test is given to reach decisions about individuals, it is improper to state a false purpose or a false plan of interpretation. If one were sure how race, sex, age, and personal style of the tester will affect scores, he would choose the tester likely to elicit the subject's best performance. And the tester will certainly do what he can, within the limits of truth, to raise the subject's expectancy of success. The vagueness of this advice indicates that testing is an art, and always will be.

21. *Mandler and Sarason (1952) comment, "It is questionable whether intelligence test scores adequately describe the underlying abilities of individuals with a high anxiety drive in the testing situation." On the other hand, it can be argued that a person who is not motivated to avoid failure will perform below his best level. Which argument seems correct? How could you test whether anxiety lowers or raises ability scores?*

22. *Hebb and Williams (1946) devised a test to measure the intelligence of rats. The test consisted of a set of mazes to be run, success being scored if a direct path to the foodbox was taken. What problems of motivation would need to be considered in administering this test?*

23. *In an "agility" test used by the British Armed Forces at one time, each man was tested separately while his squad of perhaps twenty others watched. The task called for running back and forth along a cross-shaped pattern, transferring rings from one post to another.*
    a. *What effect on score would be expected from being tested in a group rather than without an audience?*
    b. *What effect would be expected as a result of announcing each man's score at the end of his trial—to be applauded if good?*
    c. *What advantage or disadvantage would a man have who came last in the group?*

24. *On a personality questionnaire, a person reports something discreditable about himself. Can one suggest any reason other than a strong desire to be honest?*

25. *An anthropologist giving psychological tests to Eskimos for purposes of cross-cultural research, tells how the participation of subjects was obtained: ". . . not because they knew me or had any investment in my procedure, but because I had a tenuous identification with another white member of this community. . . . In one such community, the Public Health nurse . . . simply stepped outside her house and waited in ambush, so to speak, for some prospect as the Eskimos walked down the path . . . beside her house. Such subjects were told in a kindly, but peremptory, fashion that he or she was to do whatever I asked." (C. Preston, 1964).*
    a. *Does this method of recruiting have any effect on the interpretation of Preston's Eskimo records on mental tests and personality measures?*
    b. *Is your answer to question a modified by learning that two subjects thought the study was intended to locate persons who should be locked up in a mental hospital?*
    c. *An editor of a journal considered it worthwhile to devote one hundred pages to publication of a detailed account of the test results on 167 subjects. What are the arguments for and against his decision?*

Preparing the Subject for the Test

The motivation most helpful to valid testing is a desire on the part of the subject that the score be valid. This is not the normal competitive set where one desires a high score whether it is true for him or not. It is a scientific set, a desire to find out the truth even if the truth is unpalatable. Ideally, the subject becomes a partner in testing himself.

Too often an autocratic approach is followed, something like "Take this test and I shall decide what is to be done with you." Most testers would disclaim any intention of dictating, yet it is true that tests have most often been used for the private information of the tester, who then bases recommendations on them.

Cooperation between tester and subject is not an impossible goal. Psychotherapy is based on diagnostic testing; decisions of school administrators depend on standard tests; the employment manager must take responsibility for hiring the best-qualified applicants. Responsibility cannot readily be transferred to the person tested, but the subject can be made a part of the tester's team. The tester can take him into confidence as to the purpose of the testing and portray the test as an opportunity to find out about himself, just as the physician often tells the patient what medicine is being given and what good results are to be expected from it. If a fair measurement is to the subject's advantage and he knows it, he will have little motive to provide an untruthful picture. Perhaps the most "autocratic" of the current uses of testing is in industrial hiring—necessarily so, since the goal of testing is profit to the firm. Yet the tests given in the hiring line are to the advantage of the person tested. The very facts regarding turnover that lead the employer to screen applicants are facts that would reassure the worker if he knew them. If he does well on the test, he can have confidence that he will make good on the job. If he does badly, he is unlikely to last on the job. The failure on the tests saves him from wasting time in a dead end; he can begin instead to accumulate experience and seniority in another job for which he is fitted.

The desirability of preparing the subject for the test by appropriate advance information is increasingly recognized. It was formerly the common practice in counseling centers to administer a test battery routinely to every person coming in, and to base the first counseling interview on the test results. Now counseling more often commences with one or two interviews that help the person define his problem. The interview gives him a more realistic understanding of what tests can do, reduces anxiety about the test results, and helps in the choice of tests.

Some of the great nationwide testing programs, like that of the College Entrance Examination Board, orient applicants by means of information booklets. The booklet describes the test, gives advice on efficient work procedures, and displays specimen items. This increases the applicant's confidence and reduces the disadvantage an applicant inexperienced in taking standard tests might otherwise have (Halpern & Sasajima, 1966).

Coaching and test sophistication. Preparation may be carried to extreme lengths. Until recently the British gave a test near the age of 11 to determine what secondary education a child would receive. This decision opened or closed the gate to most professions and to financial and social status. Parents paid private tutors to prepare the child by special after-school lessons; in some districts two-thirds of the candidates received such "black-market" coaching. Coaching for the arithmetic and language tests consisted chiefly of additional drill. Coaching for a test of general mental ability included study of tests used in past years, practice on reasoning problems used in typical mental tests, and instruction on how to solve test problems rapidly. Preparation of this sort guarantees that the coached pupils perform at their best, but perhaps gives them an improper advantage.

Studies of the effects of coaching differ in procedure and results. If the person has no previous experience with objective, speeded tests, coaching may increase his score quite a bit. The results of a British comparison (Alfred Yates *et al.*, 1953; 1954; see also J. W. French & Dear, 1959) show what can be expected among reasonably well-educated pupils today. Gains are measured by repeating the same test after the experimental interval. According to these studies: (1) "Control" groups gain (on the average) about 2–3 points in IQ, merely as a result of taking the first test. (2) "Coached" groups gain about 5–6 points, after having been told about tests and having had numerous representative items explained by the teacher. (3) "Practiced, uncoached" groups gain about 6 points, after taking from four to eight tests without special explanation. (4) "Practiced and coached" groups may gain 8–10 points. The gains from a longer period of coaching are no greater.

All the gains from coaching appear to be small. Half a dozen points added to a score might be enough to push a college applicant over the borderline for a particular college, but coaching will not carry the really poor prospect past the examination hurdle. The conclusion of French and Dear is that "an eager College Board candidate should not spend money on special coaching for the SAT. He would probably gain at least as much by some review of mathematics on his own and by the reading of a few good books."

The most important point to be made about coaching for a test is that if it occurs there is something wrong with the system. In a society in which life at the top is much better than the life of the majority *and* one make-or-break decision can take away a young person's chance for high status, the tests that influence the decision take on an all-too-rational importance. It is the system that is irrational. There are many kinds of talent and these talents emerge over the years, so there is no one right age at which to sort people out. In some developing nations a young man has to complete the academic course to escape a life as hoe-wielder. Parents become abnormally sensitive to news that certain high schools win the most places in the college admission test, that certain lower schools get the most graduates past an earlier test hurdle and into these prestige high schools, and even that certain kindergartens increase the child's chances in life. Coaching for the kindergarten entrance examination follows! Since private tutoring is costly, the overselective system gives an advantage to the children from the upper classes.

Let us distinguish between two types of special preparation. Teaching arithmetic gives the pupil an advantage on the test, but this extra training presumably will also make him a better student. Teaching him how to solve mazes, however, is beneficial only in tests presenting maze items; it is unlikely to improve his later schoolwork. Training on abilities that are a useful part of the curriculum is good for the child and the community.

26. *Do the statements on coaching argue for or against using maze items in an academic selection test?*

27. *What explanation would you give the subject in each of the following cases?*
    a. *College freshmen are to be tested to determine which ones may fail because of reading deficiency.*
    b. *At the end of a course in industrial relations for foremen, an examination on judgment in grievance cases is to be given.*

28. *How could a "cooperative" point of view in testing be adopted:*
    a. *By a school principal who wishes to divide his eighth grade into sections on the basis of scholastic aptitude?*
    b. *By a veteran's counselor who must approve the plan of a handicapped veteran to go to college and prepare for dentistry?*
    c. *By a consulting psychologist who is asked by a social agency to diagnose and report on a potential delinquent?*

29. *What implications do the investigations of coaching have for those who use mental tests to select scholarship winners?*

30. *In Japan a young man's career opportunities depend very much on his ability to capture one of the limited number of openings in a good university. Vacancies are filled on the basis of entrance examinations and school records. Magazines bearing such titles as* Student Days, Examiners' Circle, *and* Period of Diligent Study *have large circulations. These magazines deal with topics of interest to candidates including information about typical test materials (though the actual test questions are of course guarded). Would such magazines increase or decrease the validity of the tests?*

31. *In a competitive mental test to be given all youth applying for higher schools, two policies are possible. One is to devise new types of test items each year, so that knowledge about previous examinations would be of no help. The other alternative is to use the same types of questions every year (for example, number series) but change the items used. Evaluate these alternatives from the*

point of view of the test maker, the student, and the person interpreting the results.

32. *Which of these types of preparation for a scholastic aptitude test make one more likely to do good work in college?*
    a. *Vocabulary-building exercises.*
    b. *Advice about whether to guess when in doubt.*
    c. *Therapeutic counseling to reduce fear of failure and feelings of inadequacy.*
33. *In some college residence halls, students build up files of the examinations they have taken. From the point of view of the professor teaching the course year after year, do these files increase or decrease the validity of measurement?*

Testing Procedure as Standardization of Behavior

The psychometric tester tries to standardize the state of the subject, as well as the test stimuli. His procedures are designed to *eliminate* individual differences —to eliminate, that is, variation in every characteristic save the one that his test is supposed to measure.

To clarify this, consider the physiological measure of basal metabolism rate. If a doctor wants a BMR measure, he requires his patient to fast for 8 hours before the test. This eliminates differences in eating habits that would affect oxygen utilization. For the test itself, it is necessary to reduce the patient's bodily activity to an absolute minimum by putting him into bed; every patient is, in effect, reduced to a standard activity level. The BMR, calculated from the oxygen intake and the carbon dioxide exhaled, is a useful measure of the patient's physiological state. This measure is taken in an artificial "standard condition" that almost never occurs in real life. The person's metabolism rate as he goes about his daily affairs is not much like his BMR, since it is affected by his eating, activity, and other variables.

Psychological tests are similarly designed to extract one variable, purified as much as possible, from the total life activity. The psychologist is concerned if some students fail to understand his directions because this irrelevant difference will affect his results. He is concerned if some students receive coaching, if some are especially anxious about the test, if some interpret the test as a speed test while others think carefulness counts most. All these sources of variation blur his measurement. He tries, in setting the stage for a test, to reduce all his subjects to a "standard state" of motivation, expectation, and interpretation of the task.

One might evaluate personality attributes by observing behavior in everyday affairs. The meaning of this behavior is uncertain, however, since different subjects may be trying to do quite different things. If the situation is more definitely structured so that all subjects have the same goal in mind, differences are more certainly attributable to personality. For this reason, many tests of persistence, reaction to frustration, flexibility, and other traits are disguised as measures of ability. The subject is given a definite task and motivated just as for an ability test. He does not realize that the tester will pay attention chiefly to how he goes about the task.

Testing as a Social Relationship

The tester has been accustomed to think of himself as an unemotional, impartial task-setter. His traditions encourage the idea that he, like the physical scientist or engineer, is "measuring an object" with a technical tool. But the "object" before him is a person, and testing involves a complex psychological relationship. The traditional concern with motivation and rapport recognizes this fact but, as illustrated in the foregoing sections, leads to little more than a recommendation that the tester be pleasant and encouraging, and that he help the subject understand the value of the test. This, we are beginning to suspect, barely touches the real social-psychological complexities of testing.

As Schafer (1954, p. 6) has said,

The clinical testing situation has a complex psychological structure. It is not an impersonal getting-together of two people in order that one, with the help of a little "rapport," may obtain some "objective" test responses from the other. The psychiatric patient is in some acute or chronic life crisis. He cannot but bring many hopes, fears, assumptions, demands and expectations into the test situation. He cannot but respond intensely to certain real as well as fantasied attributes of that situation. Being human and having to make a living—facts often ignored—the tester too brings hopes, fears, assumptions, demands and expectations into the test situation. He too responds personally and often intensely to what goes on—in reality and in fantasy—in that situation, however well he may conceal his personal response from the patient, from himself, and from his colleagues.

The subject coming for an individual test almost invariably is in difficulties. He may have been referred by some authority who demands that he be tested; if so, the tester may be simply another authority to rebel against. Other subjects are self-referred. One might expect cooperation when the subject is asking for help, but he too may come with motives that conflict with the tester's objectives. The very fact that he has had to seek psychological help may disturb the person who wants to be independent. He may have doubts regarding his own adequacy that he attempts to suppress by every available strategy. It is commonplace to discover, behind a college student's self-referral for remedial reading or vocational counseling, a problem of sexual adjustment or emotional conflict with parents. The student, focusing his attention and that of the psychologist on a superficial or nonexistent problem, is using an unconscious sleight-of-hand to conceal the problems he does not want to face. None of us is willing to expose himself completely, or even to learn the whole truth about himself, yet the job of the tester is to penetrate personal secrets. Often the clinical examiner must try to bring to the surface the whole personality—sexual attitudes, feelings of inadequacy, hostilities and wishes the patient is ashamed of, and so on. Even when the tester has a much more limited aim, the patient may believe that his intimate desires and anxieties will be exposed by the tests. The popular literature on psychology and psychiatry being what it is, the subject may expect the psychologist to be pruriently concerned with tabooed areas. Or he may view the tester as a modern magician from whom no truth can be hidden.

These attitudes define a role the tester is expected to play. The tester's self-conceptions define another. When tester and subject meet, therefore, their mutual demands may support each other or may pull in opposite directions. A client who wants to escape responsibility may fall into the hands of a tester who likes to dominate and to pose as infallible. This tester is unlikely to sense that the client's seeming passivity is a guard designed to keep the tester from probing into an unstated problem. The situation is little better if the tester is one who cannot comfortably take responsibility. Pressed by the client to make a definite recommendation, this insecure tester will retreat from responsibility. He will pile test upon test, so that the mass of data will relieve him of the burden of judgment. He will qualify his interpretations and mask them in technical jargon. Finally, he terminates the counseling with "All tests can do is give you a basis for making your own decision." By this he avoids a counseling relation—longer, more intimate, but uncomfortable—in which he could bring the client to understand his passivity and hesitancy.

Schafer points out that the tester chooses his profession because it satisfies his needs. The tester may be one who, feeling inadequate in social relations, can obtain reassurance from seemingly objective instruments. He may prefer the brief and distant contact of objective testing to the demanding personal relations that teachers and therapists have. He may be answering doubts about himself by comparing himself favorably at every turn with those he tests. Or, on the contrary, he may be one who seeks grateful and dependent reactions from subjects.

All these patterns can distort testing procedures and test interpretations. The overly "objective" tester may be unwilling to give the subject the emotional support required to reduce resistance and elicit his best performance. He may be quick to detect difficulties that can be treated unemotionally (limited vocabulary, for example) but overlook emotional needs. The competitive tester may be too ready to identify weaknesses. (Wilson tells us that when he trained intelligent convicts to test new inmates, he had to supervise constantly to prevent their making procedural errors to reduce the subject's score and so magnify their own superiority.) The tester who seeks emotional support from patients may be too lenient, all too willing to overlook weaknesses in the record.

Tester bias. The history of science records numerous instances of self-delusion even by highly trained observers. Many of the errors are self-serving—slanted not to gain material rewards but to confirm the beliefs that seem reasonable and desirable to the observer. Rosenthal (1966) has discussed this matter exhaustively both in terms of historical incidents and in terms of experiments on bias. It is sufficient here to mention just a few of his incidents and findings:

● In studies of telepathy a recorder writes down the subject's attempts to guess the symbol on which a "transmitter" is concentrating at a given moment. Recorders who believe in telepathy make errors in the direction favoring telepathy—7 of those to every 4 against. Disbelievers make one favorable error for every two unfavorable (p. 11).

● Laboratory technicians counting blood cells through a microscope take check readings on the same slide. They agree more closely than the standard procedure (which involves sampling variation) would allow. Evidently discrepant readings are suppressed (p. 5).

● Student experimenters are told (untruthfully) that the rats they are to run have been genetically selected for brightness. These rats learn a maze faster than those run by experimenters told they are running a dull strain (pp. 158 ff.).

● Student testers are led to think that college students normally give a sizable number of responses to an inkblot. They get about 50 per cent more responses than other testers led to expect few responses.

Tests may seem to be objective, but the risks of error are such that Rosenthal urges the replication of an experiment by investigators who *disbelieve* the hypothesis. In practical decision making, even the best standard procedure cannot prevent subtle influences on scores when the tester expects the pretty little girl in the starched dress to do well, or when the tester's social conscience demands that his Negro subjects show up well.

Granting that both tester and subject come to the situation with a full complement of human motives, some of which they are not aware of, what should the tester do about it? At this point, with research on these motives almost entirely lacking, we can make only common-sense suggestions. The first of these is "Know thyself." The more the tester knows of his own personality, of his preferences for different types of subject, and of the biases he brings to test interpretation, the greater the chance that he can meet each situation properly. The second suggestion is Schafer's recommendation that the social situation itself be considered an important way of understanding the subject, and that his strategies, demands, and resistances themselves be taken into account in interpreting scores. His view is well summarized in this paragraph (1954, pp. 72–73):

There are those who would object that this total-situation approach violates the objectivity of test interpretation. Only in the narrow and false sense in which objectivity has been usually conceived is this true. The ideal of objectivity requires that we recognize as much as possible what is going on in the situation we are studying. It requires in particular that we remember the tester and his patient are both human and alive and therefore inevitably interacting in the test situation. True, the further we move away from mechanized interpretation or comparison of formal scores and averages, the more subjective variables we may introduce into the interpretive process.

The personality and personal limitations of the tester may be brought into the thick of the interpretive problem. But while we thereby increase the likelihood of personalized interpretation and variation among testers, we are at the same time in a position to enrich our understanding and our test reports significantly. The more data we use, after all, the greater the richness and specificity of our analyses—and in the long run the more accurate we become.

Schafer's view obviously demands impressionistic interpretation, and is not fully acceptable to psychometric testers. His view need not be accepted, since no evidence is offered that these complex interpretations can indeed be made accurately. Those who reject Schafer's recommendation must find their own solution to the problem of interpersonal dynamics. Even a strictly poker-faced administration of an individual mental test is an hour-long stress situation, every moment of which involves emotional interaction between tester and subject.

The Computer as Tester

Though testing by computer is not yet ready for use, it is no doubt practicable. A computer can operate a typewriter, a set of display lights, a slide projector, and other apparatus. It can plot out diagrams on the face of an electronic tube. Hence it can present almost any item used in ability and personality tests, in the warm tape-recorded voice of a skilled human tester if desired. The subject's response by pushbutton or by a "light pen" that touches a selected spot on the tube-face can be timed and scored automatically. For constructed responses, the subject types his answer; some aspects of the constructed response can be scored by ingenious preprogrammed rules. Test norms and interpretative information are stored, so that the computer can prepare a profile, a verbal description, or any other type of report that does not rest on the impressions of a human observer.

Testing by computer may sound futuristic, but devices almost this automatic were used in military training in the 1940s. Today, training by computer is in operation. In some experimental schools the child comes every day to the computer classroom, takes his place before the computer and display tube, types in his name, and hears through the earphone "Good morning, Terry. Yesterday you learned the words *man* and *pan* and *fan*. Now you see the word *man* and three pictures. Which picture goes with the word?" Terry touches the tube to indicate his selection, is praised (or corrected if wrong), and off he goes through the rest of the review and into the new lesson. From the start, he is hearing something different from what the child in the next seat is hearing, since the computer takes into account its record of previous work completed by each child. Even when two children start together, as soon as one makes errors the sequence for him is modified to provide explanation, additional drill, or a short diagnostic test. A record of Terry's progress is maintained for the teacher, and cumulative data on the errors of all pupils help the program designer to identify and improve troublesome points in the instructional scheme.

The procedure is not limited to single school systems. Long-distance lines can carry enormous amounts of information, so that a central computer can manage faraway classrooms. This opens fascinating possibilities. For example, advanced training in a specialized technical subject can be provided to men in all outposts of a firm (perhaps even to men on all the ships of a Navy) when only a few experts in the central facility are qualified in the subject. It might be thought that the computer is adapted only to literate and emotionally stable subjects. But preschool children respond well to automated displays. The machine also was able to elicit responses from and thus gradually improve back-ward schizophrenics who would only sit and stare mutely in response to a visitor or psychiatrist (Skinner, Solomon, & Lindsley, 1954; Lindsley, 1965). Their machine displayed an exciting picture whenever a button was pushed. The patient had to "work" to get this reward. Once his interest was captured, he was on his way to renewed communication with the world.

The real question is not feasibility, but advantage. It is too early to evaluate computer testing. Some of the possible advantages we list will not work out in practice, and some possibilities we cannot envision will be discovered. Among the features to consider are the following.

● Excellence of standardization. The computer will deliver precisely the stimulus called for by the program, with no unintended variation in timing, tone of voice, or prompting.

● Sequential administration. The test items need not be the same for everyone. As the person succeeds, the computer tests his limits with harder tasks; as he does poorly, the computer offers tasks at a lower level. Greatest time can be given to testing aspects of performance where weakness (or exceptional talent) appears. Something like this is done by the psychologist testing one individual at a time, but a computer method can do it more systematically.

● Precision of timing. While speed is not generally emphasized in current testing, precise timing of individual responses may be valuable, especially in investigating learned skills and in evaluations of brain damage.

● Release of human testers for other duties. Insofar as testing is a routine function, it is a waste to use a well-educated tester.

● Patience. The computer's patience is inexhaustible. If the deteriorated schizophrenic does not make a move for four hours, the display simply waits for him. If the distractible child can only be captured for testing by four preliminary sessions with Disney cartoons, the computer administers them without fidgeting. These long-drawn-out procedures are not even expensive. The computer's costly time is called on only when the subject makes a response; while "waiting," it is dividing its time—a millisecond here a millisecond there—among the thousand subjects who *are* responding.

● Control of bias. Excellence of administration itself precludes most biases;

certainly the computer is not going to take the shiny face and starched dress into account. The computer may also diminish such long-distressing problems as test anxiety and "Hawthorne effect." When—in schools, mental hospitals, and industrial training—it becomes daily or weekly routine to have a session in the automated classroom, no special anxiety attends any one day's questions. Indeed, since errors are handled gently and constructively, most anxiety should disappear. Every training session can serve as a "test." One can insert a special series of questions to test an ability outside the usual run of lessons, in such a way that the pupil does not suspect that a special test is taking place. One can even administer experiments without the pupil's knowing that he is in an experiment, simply by modifying the computer programs for subjects selected at random.

Now it is true that something is lost when all testing or training is impersonal. One major question for research is what, precisely, the human interaction adds, and how it can be capitalized on. The loss may be surprisingly small. Swets and Feurzeig (1965) describe an experimental program for teaching (and testing) the art of medical diagnosis. Here is an excerpt from a conversation via typewriter between student physician and computer, where every response of the computer is regulated by rules that take the student's response into account. The student has been given a report on a patient's symptoms and is to ask for information or to suggest a suitable diagnosis. The student draws his responses from a standardized, but rather long, list. Student remarks appear in capitals below. All other statements are typed out by the computer.

> Begin the physical examination as soon as you are ready.
> PHYSICAL EXAM?
> Fine. What in particular would you like to know?
> CHEST EXAM?
> It is common practice in the medical profession to begin an examination by checking the patient's general appearance.
> GENERAL APPEARANCE?
> Acutely prostrated, lying in bed on his right side. Looks acutely ill, sweaty, apprehensive, but alert. Paroxysmal cough, bringing up a little rusty streaked sputum. Breathing with difficulty.
> EENT EXAM?
> Check all of the vital signs first!
> TEMPERATURE?
> 103.
> BLOOD PRESSURE?
> 150/84.

At a later stage, after laboratory tests have been ordered and reported on, the student attempts a diagnosis:

> PULMONARY INFARCTION.
> There's no question of the need to account for this possibility. . . . But rule it out, won't you, on the basis of the history of shaking chills, high temperature, and somewhat excessive WBC.

ACUTE PYELONEPHRITIS.
Very good. You should think of acute pyelonephritis. It's consistent with many of your
patient's signs and symptoms—but not all. Wouldn't you want some signs of dysuria
to support this diagnosis? And what about the respiratory symptoms in the history and
findings? You'd better reevaluate the evidence.

FRIEDLANDER PNEUMONIA.
A wise thought—but off the mark. You don't have the usual Friedlander pneumonia
gelatinous type sputum nor the Klebsiella organism—do you? Hold off on this diagnosis for awhile.

34. *In what way could sympathy and love for children bias a tester? What parts of
    the testing process would be affected by this bias?*
35. *If social factors and examiner differences affect individual tests more than group
    tests, does this imply that group tests are better measuring instruments?*
36. *Does a formal and impersonal attitude toward all subjects standardize the test-
    ing relationship?*
37. *It is suggested that a correction be made for tester bias. A few points could be
    added to, or subtracted from, the IQs each tester records, the correction being
    determined from a study of tests he has given in the past. Evaluate the sug-
    gestion.*
38. *Can the "superior performance" of rats whose experimenters think they are
    bright be attributed to any causes other than error in recording or error in
    procedure?*
39. *What acts or judgments of the tester—short of gross error—might modify the
    scores subjects earn.*
    a. *in an individually administered vocabulary test?*
    b. *in a group-administered vocabulary test?*
    c. *in an individual story-completion test in which the subject's response is tape-
    recorded and scored, by persons other than the tester, for aggression and hos-
    tility themes.*

SUGGESTED READINGS

Biber, Barbara, & others. Stenographic record of psychological examination. In *Life
and ways of the seven-year-old.* New York: Basic Books, 1952. Pp. 631–639.

> A record of remarks made by examiner and subject before and during a series of
> performance tests of mental ability, including the Porteus maze and several form-
> boards. Note the many places at which the examiner digresses from the test into
> other conversation in order to maintain rapport.

Katz, Irwin. Review of evidence relating to effects of desegregation on the intellectual
performance of Negroes. *American Psychologist,* 1964, *19,* 381–399.

> Katz summarizes findings on Negro performance in examinations and experi-
> ments, in order to identify what incentives, threats, and social conditions affect
> their performance, particularly in mixed-race groups. The results are interpreted

in terms of such concepts as anticipated probability of success, effects of stress, and social compliance. Practical suggestions are made.

Mollenkopf, William G. Time limits and the behavior of test takers. In *Educational and Psychological Measurement*, 1960, 20, 223–230.

Discusses the desirability of defining for the subject whether he is to strive for speed or accuracy, and whether corrections for guessing compensate for the gains some people make by rushing through the test.

Schafer, Roy. Interpersonal dynamics in the test situation. In *Psychoanalytic interpretation in Rorschach testing*. New York: Grune & Stratton, 1954. Pp. 6–73.

In a thought-provoking discussion of the motives with which the tester and subject approach each other, Schafer speculates regarding defenses in the tester's personality (dependence, overintellectualization, sadism, etc.) that may reduce his effectiveness.

Shapiro, M. B. Experimental method in the psychological description of the individual psychiatric patient. *International Journal of Social Psychiatry*, 1957, 3, 89–103. (Reprinted in Savage, 1966.)

Describes discrepancies between the ideal scientific measurement situation and the realities of the clinic, and suggests how the clinician with limited time can operate to provide adequate answers to the most vital questions.

Towbin, Alan P. Psychological testing from end to means. *Journal of Projective Techniques*, 1964, 28, 86–91.

In a statement addressed to clinical testers who deal with patients referred by therapists for testing, Towbin argues against the "Kafkaesque" tradition that makes the tester an efficient, detached observer of the impact of the test instrument on the patient. He favors an interactive style that makes the tester a part of the therapeutic activity.

4

Scoring

Scoring Procedures

Any student who has tried to understand why he received a low score on some essay examination must realize how difficult it is to define a good answer and to assign proper credit for a partially correct response. Starch and Elliott (1912, 1913) provided conclusive evidence on the faults of impressionistic scoring as long ago as 1912. They presented a pupil's English composition to a convention of teachers and asked volunteers to grade it. On a percentage scale, the grades assigned ranged from 50 to 98. This evidence of disagreement could perhaps be dismissed, since judging a composition is influenced by preferences for various styles. To drive home their point, however, Starch and Elliott had a geometry paper graded in the same way. The scores ranged from 28 to 92, presumably because of variation in the credit given to neatness, partial solutions, etc.

No scientific research on behavior can be done nor can sound practical decisions be reached if scoring standards vary erratically. One solution is to develop rules for judgment that all scorers will follow. The other possibility is to use items where the subject is to choose the right answer from among alternatives the test provides; once the initial key is fixed, no judgment is required.

Scoring of Constructed Responses

There are a great variety of tests that use open-ended questions for which the subject must construct his own response. Not only recall tests and essay tests, but Block Design and other complex problem-solving, and most psychomotor tests and job-performance tests fall in this category. Such tests call for judgment in scoring, but methods can be devised that permit considerable objectivity.

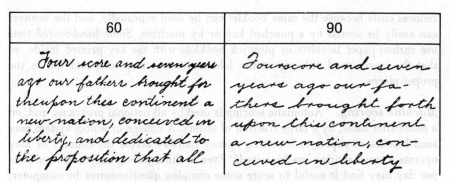

60	90
Four score and seven years ago our fathers brought for theupon this continent a new nation, conceived in liberty, and dedicated to the proposition that all	*Fourscore and seven years ago our fathers brought forth upon this continent a new nation, conceived in liberty*

Figure 4.1.   Part of Ayres' scale for scoring handwriting samples.
Reproduced by permission of the present publisher, The University of Iowa.

Ayres, for example, produced a guide for scoring pupil handwriting (Figure 4.1). The guide displays handwriting specimens representing various levels of quality; to determine the score the teacher locates the sample most similar to the pupil's work. Product-rating scales can be developed for judging quality of sewing, shopwork, etc. Objective methods have not been completely successful for scoring tests in which the subject produces a verbal response, but variation among scorers is reduced by guides that show the approved scoring for representative answers. Noteworthy examples are the scoring manual for the Stanford-Binet test of intelligence (Terman & Merrill, 1960) and that of Atkinson (1958) for scoring the presence of "achievement" themes in interpretations given to pictures.

Special precautions must be taken when constructed-response tests are used to compare effects of experimental treatments. The scorer who believes that one treatment is superior may unconsciously tend to give higher scores to the subjects who had that treatment. To prevent such bias, it is necessary to mix all records together so that the scorer does not know which group any person belongs to. This procedure is called "blind" scoring. Blind scoring might be desirable in everyday use of tests also, to prevent preconceptions about the subject from affecting the score, but the risk is rarely great enough to justify this inconvenient refinement.

1. *The question "Why should people wash their clothing?" is to be used in an oral intelligence test for adults, to test comprehension of common situations. Prepare a set of standards for judging correctness of answers. Make your rules so clear that scorers would be able to agree in scoring new answers.*

Scoring of Choice-Response Items

The scoring guide for a choice-response test consists of a list of the answers to be given credit. Several efficient procedures for obtaining and scoring responses have been devised. Separate answer sheets are used for the majority of tests. This reduces costs because the same booklet can be used repeatedly, and the answers can easily be scored by a punched key or by machine. Some hand-scored tests use carbon-paper booklets or pinprick booklets with the key printed inside, so that the scorer need only rip at the fold and count responses that fall in the proper places.

Machine scoring. Automatic scoring is used by all national programs, and, on a mail-order basis, by a large fraction of testers. A college or school system may send batches of papers to a scoring agency halfway across the country or may operate a small scoring machine itself. Even a clinic testing only a few subjects per day may find it useful to score some complex questionnaires by computer. Machines can handle locally made tests as well as standardized ones.

Machine procedures vary, but their elements are similar. There must be an answer sheet, designed to collect responses in a form the machine can read. The subject indicates his answer to a question by blackening a certain space on the form. The scoring device interprets responses by a position code. The machine reads the answer by means of a light-sensitive photocell or by detecting the electrical conductivity of the pencil mark. Face-sheet information can be recorded in machine-readable form with the aid of an alphabetic grid like that shown in Figure 4.2. Figure 4.2 shows some of the techniques of the Measurement Research Center at Iowa City. Their answer sheets can collect up to 480 responses on a single page. Forms can also be printed with the test questions alongside the answer spaces, though several pages are then required for the usual test. Machine scorable forms for children in the early grades may ask the child to put an X through whichever of several pictures is correct. The mark need not be precisely located.

Each type of equipment requires its own answer sheet, so that decisions about scoring have to be made at the time test materials are purchased. The service that costs least per case for one user will not be the most economical for another user. The first user, indeed, must reexamine the costs every year or so, since changes in volume of work may make it wise for him to shift to another service that follows a different pricing policy.

Machines can score as high as 9000 papers an hour. Both sides of the sheet are read at once and compared with scoring keys held in the computer memory. Scores and part-scores are printed onto the answer sheet or a score roster. Information can be rearranged; a school may get an alphabetic list of students, or a list by classrooms, or a list arranged in order of scores—or all these. A separate report to go to the student may be printed. A statistical summary for the batch of papers is routinely prepared. Norm tables, stored in the computer, translate scores into comparative form. While scoring and reporting can be done very rapidly, service at a scoring center is likely to take a week, because of the work backlog at peak periods and the need for inspection of the work before it is delivered.

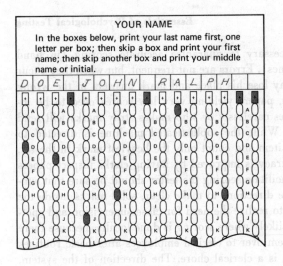

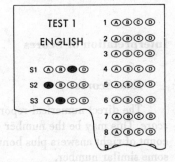

Figure 4.2.   Answer-sheet formats used with the MRC scoring system.
Reproduced by permission of American College Testing Program and Measurement Research Center.

Constant vigilance is necessary to guarantee accurate scoring (in hand scoring as much as with machines). Errors are not frequent, but when they occur they are serious. A student may lose his place and mark answers in the wrong column; to guard against this, papers yielding very low scores need to be inspected. The student who erases carelessly or who makes stray marks will send false signals to the machine. While the sophisticated machine is directed to examine all the choices for an item and count only the heaviest mark in the set, scoring agencies find that accuracy is improved by having clerks inspect papers and make some erasures. To facilitate scoring the tester should be sure that subjects understand and follow the directions to make clear, solid marks inside the printed spaces. It is important to realize the need for close supervision and spot-checking. Trouble is especially likely where scoring is done locally, because there is a temptation to turn the system over to clerical employees after basic routines have been established. Scoring is a clerical chore. The direction of the system, however, must be the responsibility of a well-qualified person who takes seriously the lesson of experience: "If anything can go wrong, it will."

Nearly all booklets of test questions sold commercially are designed to be used many times, all responses being placed on separate sheets. Some purchasers have found that they can print their own answer sheets for less than the publisher's price. Such answer sheets are not suited for machine scoring, which requires a certain crispness of paper and precisely located printing. Moreover, it is short-sighted to save money on answer sheets. The publisher's higher charges cover costs of quality printing, costs of research on further development and revision of the test, costs of new tests in preparation, and a financial return to author and publisher. Far more money for all these purposes comes from sale of answer sheets than from sale of booklets. If answer-sheet income were cut off, either advances in testing would be slowed, or booklet prices would be raised.

2. *What effects upon the character of tests and their use might be expected to follow from the availability of a machine that makes it possible to obtain virtually an unlimited number of scores from a single answer sheet, at negligible cost?*

Interpretation of Scores

Raw Scores

The direct numerical report of a person's test performance is called his *raw score*. This may be the number of questions he answered, the time he required, a count of right answers plus bonuses for fast work and less penalties for errors, or some similar number.

Raw scores can easily be misinterpreted. Willie's report card shows a 75 in arithmetic and a 90 in spelling. His parents can be counted on to praise the latter and disapprove the former. Willie might quite properly protest, "But you should see what the other kids get in arithmetic. Lots of them get 60 and 65." The parents, who know a good grade when they see one, refuse to be sidetracked by such irrelevance. But what do Willie's grades mean? It might appear that he has mastered three-fourths of the course work in arithmetic, and nine-tenths in spelling. But Willie objects to that, too. "I learned all my combinations, but he doesn't ask much about those. The tests are full of word problems, and we only studied them a little." Willie evidently gets 75 per cent of the questions asked, but since the questions may be easy or hard, the percentage itself is meaningless to his parents. We cannot compare Willie with his sister Sue, whose teacher in another grade gives much easier tests so that Sue brings home a proud 88 in arithmetic. It could be, too, that Willie's shining 90 in spelling is misleading, if the spelling tests are restricted to the words assigned for study. We cannot interpret psychological test scores as we do physical measures. Physical measuring scales generally have a true zero and equal units along the scale; this permits us to say, for example, that one boy is twice as tall as another, or has attained 60 per cent of his probable adult height. We cannot make statements like this about psychological measures. Suppose Willie scored 10 per cent in spelling. Would this mean that he knows only one-tenth of the words he should? No, for the teacher probably did not ask about easy words that Willie was sure to know. Even a score of zero on the test would not mean zero ability to spell. The difference between Willie with a score of zero and the model pupil who earns 100 is perhaps a difference in ability to spell only twenty words out of an active vocabulary of several thousand —if those twenty constituted the test. The same argument applies to tests of reasoning ability. A raw score of 80 may appear to represent ability twice as great as a raw score of 40. The test does not include the problems everyone can solve, however; if people were tested on every possible problem calling for reasoning, the true ratio might be 140 to 180, or 1040 to 1080. Even an infant, looking toward the door when he hears his mother's footstep, shows some degree of ability to reason. Absolute zero in any ability is "just no ability at all."

Differences in raw scores do not ordinarily represent "true" distances between individuals. Suppose, on DAT Mechanical Reasoning Form A, Adam gets 53 points, Bill gets 56, and Charles gets 59. The raw-score differences are equal. Is Charles truly as different from Bill as Bill is from Adam? We cannot be sure, since the score difference depends on the items used. Judging from the published norm tables for twelfth-graders, if these same boys took Bennett Form AA the "equal differences" would be replaced by unequal ones: Adam would get 44 points, Bill would get 45, and Charles 48.

The only way one can meaningfully talk about "equal differences" is to bring in some practical criterion that provides a standard of value. Different standards will lead to different numerical scales for the same test. On the DAT the three boys' raw scores are equally spaced. Their probabilities of passing a college engineering course may be 0.70, 0.90, and 0.96, respectively. Their most likely freshman grade averages may be D, C+, and B—. And their respective probabilities of later success in a very demanding engineering firm may be 0.0001, 0.05, and 0.50. "Equal intervals" on one scale are quite unequal on the other.

3. *Decide whether an absolute zero exists for each of the following variables and, where possible, define it:*
   a. *Height.*
   b. *Ability to discriminate between the pitches of tones.*
   c. *Speed of tapping.*
   d. *Gregariousness, seeking the companionship of others.*
   e. *Rifle aiming.*

4. *If several pupils in Willie's class move away and are replaced by newcomers, will his raw score in arithmetic probably change? His rank in his class?*

5. *If a different set of test questions were used in arithmetic, would Willie's raw score change? His rank?*

6. *Alfred, a college freshman, is to receive guidance on his academic plans, and is given four tests of ability. Scores are presented in four different ways. Interpret separately each row of scores.*

	Vocabu-lary	Verbal reasoning	Nonverbal reasoning	Mechanical compre-hension
Raw score	116	32	44	48
Per cent of possible points	77	73	80	71
Points above average	24	10	20	0
Rank among 260 freshmen	104	113	161	136

7. *Is it sensible for a school to fix a numerical standard for assigning course marks on the basis of test averages? (For example: 93–100 = A, 85–92 = B, etc.)*

8. *Some schools "grade on the curve," assigning As to a fixed proportion of the pupils, Bs to another proportion, etc. Is there any logical basis for fixing these percentages?*

9. *Two runners train for the mile. One, between his junior and senior years, reduces his time from 4:16 to 4:04. The other starts with a time of 5:16. What time must he achieve for us to say that he has made as much improvement as the first runner?*

Criterion Reference

Taken by itself, the raw score on a psychological test has little or no significance. To understand it we must bring in additional information, either about the task or about the performance of other persons tested. There are two basic ways of bringing additional facts to bear, which Glaser (1963) has christened *criterion reference* and *norm reference*. A test is said to be *criterion-referenced* when provision is made for translating the test score into a statement about the behavior to be expected of a person with that score. A test is *norm-referenced* when the translated score tells where the person stands in some population of persons who have taken the test. The same test can be used in both ways. An example of a criterion-referenced statement is "James' score indicates that we can expect him to solve 68 per cent of a large set of linear equations having whole-number coefficients less than 10." An example of norm reference is "James performed better in solving linear equations than 80 per cent of a representative sample of ninth graders."

During most of the history of psychological testing, test specialists have emphasized norms, but criterion reference and norm reference are both useful. The former tells what the person is able to do, the latter tells how he compares with others. The former is useful in judging him as an isolated individual, the latter in judging his ability to compete. We can anticipate that in the future there will be considerably more effort by test developers to prepare interpretative guides that indicate expected behavior.

There are two basic types of criterion reference:

• A content-reference scale describes the subject's level of performance on content like that in the test. In a sense, it simply summarizes the behavior the person has just shown. The Ayres scale has this character; an Ayres score of 60 means that a performance resembles the standard samples of 60-level handwriting. Another example: "This vocabulary score implies ability to interpret 80% of words at the difficulty level illustrated by *obvious, overwhelm, persuasive,* and *sentiment.*"

• An expectancy statement predicts behavior in a situation unlike the test. For example: "A student with this vocabulary score who enters training for accountant has a 4-to-1 chance of completing the course." An expectancy statement may refer to future success or to some present performance different from the test. A reading test might be interpreted by means of a list of books the child with a given score can be expected to understand.

Content scales. Interpretation in terms of content requires a scale having clearly defined levels of difficulty. An excellent interpretative statement is "reads material from the news columns of the *New York Times* at the rate of 280 words per minute, when told to be able to summarize it." (To say only, "reads 280 words per minute" would mean little.) Other statements in the reading scale could refer to easier and harder materials or to different rates on the same material.

The most direct way to give meaning to a raw score is to display the actual content of the test, but this is impractical in a summary report. Nor can a long test readily be inspected. Ebel (1962) therefore proposes that scores be interpreted in terms of specimen tasks. From a mathematical reasoning test, for example, he would select ten representative items, and reproduce these on the report sheet together with the statement: "James' raw score is 17. Persons with that raw score can, on the average, solve six of these ten problems." The statement is derived by tabulating the responses of many persons at raw-score level 17. For a reading test, one could display paragraphs ordered from easy to difficult, stating that (e.g.) "a test score of 93 implies ability to comprehend paragraphs up to and including level f."

Content-referenced interpretation is not sensible unless the test content is significant in its own right. We are little interested in knowing what complexity of block design a person can assemble successfully; the Block-Design task is not significant in the world at large. When the test task is significant in itself, we not only find the content interpretation meaningful but can often bring an established standard to bear. The teacher may say, for example, that no one will be allowed to take up the study of shorthand with a typing speed less than 50 words per minute.

One may also translate attitude scores into a direct statement of the person's beliefs. Thus, using a scale developed by Kelley, Ferson, and Holtzman (see Holtzman & Young, 1966), it would be possible to translate one numerical score as implying readiness to endorse statements like these:

Negroes living in White neighborhoods lower the standards of cleanliness.

Separate churches for White and colored people should be maintained, since church membership is a matter of individual choice.

Another score can be interpreted as mildly favorable to integration, implying endorsement of:

The fact that there is no racial segregation in certain European countries indicates that desegregation can be made to work here.

The Army's desegregation policy is an advance toward interracial understanding.

A still more extreme score would be interpreted as implying rejection of the negative statements and endorsement of (for example) "I would not hesitate to join a fraternity or sorority which admitted Negroes."

One might likewise represent readiness to become angry by a scale listing provocations that range from very mild annoyances to violent abuse, indicating the level at which this person is likely to respond angrily. Reference to a content scale is not very informative unless there is an orderly progression of the content the scale refers to. Difficulty of mathematics problems provides a scale on which we can locate the person, and so does the favorableness of an attitude. It might be difficult to describe musical preferences along a lowbrow-to-highbrow scale, however. A single scale-position is inadequate to describe a man who enjoys Bach, Vivaldi, and shout-and-sway jazz, but avoids Lombardo, Stravinsky, and grand opera. Saying that he likes 60 per cent of the selections in a mixed list implies little about what he likes.

Expectancy tables. To arrive at an expectancy table, the test developer or test user administers the test to a large number of persons and subsequently observes their success. The results can be formed into an experience table such as Table 4.1. This table is based on application of a scholastic aptitude test to 920 fresh-

Table 4.1. Expectancy table for first-semester freshman achievement

Score on general ability test		Probability of earning a point-hour ratio of at least				
		1.00	1.50	2.00	2.50	3.00
Raw score	Percentile rank	(D av.)	(Proba-tion)	(C av.)		(B av.)
114–150	90–	100	99	93	80	56
102–113	80–89	100	96	91	60	30
92–101	70–79	100	95	90	60	29
83–91	60–69	99	90	78	41	27
75–82	50–59	98	87	74	25	13
66–74	40–49	97	80	62	25	13
56–65	30–39	96	79	61	17	5
48–55	20–29	95	75	47	13	4
39–47	10–19	95	63	33	7	2
0–39	– 9	87	58	29	3	1

SOURCE: Bingham, 1951, based on data from G. B. Paulsen.

men at Ohio State. A student's counselor directs his attention to the row of the table corresponding to his score; the entries show how likely the student is to attain any particular grade average. This explanation is more definite and more complete than any other system of norms can offer. As Bingham says (1951, p. 552), "The counselor of an entering student who has scored in the lowest decile range (lowest tenth) on this test can now show him these expectancies, and point out, if it seems advisable, that his chances of keeping off probation (Point-Hour Ratio = 1.50) are a little better than even; that he has one chance in a hundred of earning high honors; and that in any event much depends on the persistence and strength of his own determination, a powerful factor not measured by this or any other psychological test."

Expectancy data may also be charted (Figure 4.3). The chart, though less precise than the table, shows trends dramatically. The charts illustrated are based on three different tests; it can be seen that the dexterity test is a much less accurate predictor than the other two. Besides interpreting scores for individuals, the expectancy table gives information on the value of a test (see Chapter 5).

Another use of the expectancy chart or table is to compare two tests. We often wish to ask, for example, whether a poor student's achievement is normal for his mental ability, or lower. It is not correct simply to subtract the ability score from the achievement score, even when both measures are expressed on a common numerical scale. Forming a ratio ("accomplishment quotient") is equally wrong. Such techniques have a built-in bias; they tend to call the person with a high ability score an underachiever, and vice versa (Thorndike, 1963a).

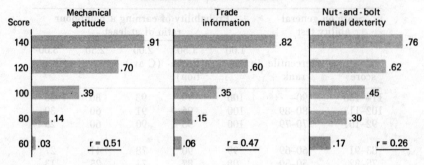

Figure 4.3.   Expectancy charts for aircraft-armorer trainees.
Personnel classification tests, 1946.

The correct procedure is to set up an expectancy chart or table that reports what achievement-test score persons with a certain raw score on the ability test ordinarily reach. In place of the raw score one may sometimes use a mental age; to use an IQ as the baseline, however, is not advisable.

10. *Which of these scales is criterion referenced?*
    a. *A vision test is keyed to report in such terms as "at a 12-inch distance, can read 10-point, or larger, type."*
    b. *A measure of "dental age" is obtained by comparing a child's teeth to a chart showing what teeth are ordinarily present at age 5, at age 6, etc.*
    c. *A sociometric test yields the information that six children out of 30 name Bobby as "a good person to play with."*
11. *"20–20 vision" means being able to see at 20 feet what the average person can see at that distance. "20–100" vision means being able to see at 20 feet what the average person can see at 100 feet. Is this scale criterion-referenced or norm-referenced?*
12. *For each of these decisions, would you prefer a test that is criterion-referenced or one that is norm-referenced?*
    a. *Susana's teacher wants to know the maturity of Susana's interest so that she can select literature for her to read.*
    b. *A girl reports many symptoms of anxiety, and the counselor wishes to decide whether this degree of anxiety is unusual at her age.*
    c. *A school wants to provide intensive exercise for all boys whose physical fitness is poor.*
    d. *Ruby transfers from another school. The counselor wants to know whether her ability in Spanish is good enough for her to enroll in an advanced section.*
    e. *The school wants to report Roger's spelling ability to his parents.*
13. *Is it reasonable to call the Ayres handwriting scale (Figure 4.1) a criterion-referenced measure?*

14. *Expectancy tables prepared for local use are clearly meaningful. Can expectancy tables profitably be included in test manuals, in view of the fact that probability of success on a job depends on local conditions?*
15. *Interpret this information about scores of a prospective aircraft armorer, prior to training: mechanical aptitude, 120; trade information, 140; nut-and-bolt test, 100.*

Percentile Scores

The easiest way to make comparisons is to rank scores from highest to lowest. Reporting that a person stands third out of 40 conveniently states his position relative to others. Ranks depend on the number of persons in the group. If we wish to examine change in standing from one occasion to another we have difficulty because the size of the group changes. To avoid such difficulties, ranks are changed to percentile scores (also called percentile ranks and centile ranks). A *percentile score* is the rank expressed in percentage terms. Various writers use various terms: percentile score, percentile rank, percentile, centile—all have the same meaning.

A person's percentile rank tells what proportion of the group falls below him. Suppose there are 40 persons, 2 superior to A and 37 poorer. Then we arbitrarily divide case A (and all persons tied with him, if any) between the two groups, saying that 2½ cases are above him and 37½ below. Since 37½ is 94 per cent of 40, his percentile score is 94.

By this method of computation, the person exactly in the middle of the group is at the 50th percentile. The 50th percentile is called the *median*. The median can be thought of as the performance of a "typical" person.

A graphic procedure using a smooth curve is often used to compute percentiles. The graphic method disregards irregularities in the distribution of scores in a particular sample and therefore gives a better estimate of what may be expected when further groups are tested. Computing Guide 1 demonstrates this method, using Bennett MCT scores for a ninth-grade class.

Raw scores and percentiles have distinctly different frequency distributions. In Figure 4.4 raw scores for the ninth-grade class have been plotted. The distribution is high at the center and tapers away at each end. To prepare the lower part of Figure 4.4, each raw score was changed to its percentile equivalent (without smoothing) and the number of persons in each interval on the scale from 0 to 100 was tallied. This distribution is nearly rectangular. With larger samples the percentile distribution becomes almost perfectly rectangular. Persons near the middle of the raw-score scale are spread apart; persons at the end are squeezed together. Often, a large percentile difference near the median represents a small difference in performance. Conversely, the difference between the 90th and the 99th percentiles, though it looks small on this scale, may be as great as the difference between a five-minute and a four-minute mile. To take this into account,

1. Begin with the raw scores (these are scores of 75 ninth-grade boys on Bennett Form AA).	37	43	27	44	27	27	26	31	35	42	50
	35	43	36	26	50	47	36	26	32	32	38
	36	21	24	40	39	35	38	36	38	21	17
	26	35	22	18	50	30	38	50	16	45	8
	34	26	34	28	41	27	39	41	30	23	33
	22	31	36	40	54	24	22	8	33	42	41
	41	31	34	36	32	20	22	34	41		

2. Identify the highest score and the lowest score. If there is a wide range, choose a class interval of 1, 2, 5, 10, 20, etc., and divide the range into classes of equal width. Fifteen or more classes are desirable.

Highest score = 54; lowest score = 8; range = 46.

Class interval of 5 will be used. (A smaller interval, such as 2, would be preferable but would be inconvenient in this computing guide.)

3. Tally the number of cases with each score.

4. Write the number of tallies in the Frequency (f) column. Add this column to get **N**, the number of cases.

5. Begin at the bottom of the column and add frequencies one at a time to determine the cumulative frequency, the number of cases below each division point.

6. Divide the cumulative frequencies by **N** to determine cumulative percentages.

Scores	Tallies	Frequency (f)	Cumulative Frequency	Cumulative Per Cent
			75	100
50–54	卌	5	70	93
45–49	//	2	68	90
40–44	卌 卌 //	12	56	75
35–39	卌 卌 卌 //	17	39	52
30–34	卌 卌 ////	14	25	33
25–29	卌 卌	10	← 15	20[b]
20–24	卌 卌	10	5[a]	7
15–19	///	3	2	3
10–14		0	2	3
5– 9	//	2	0	0
		—		
		75		
		N		

[a] 5 cases fall below 19.5; 15 below 24.5; etc.
[b] 20 per cent of the cases fall below 24.5; 20 is the cumulative percentage corresponding to a raw score of 24.5.

record forms separate the 95, 90, and 80 percentile points widely, usually crowd 60, 50, and 40 together, and spread out 20, 10, and 5. For an example, see Figure 4.9.

Averaging two percentile ranks gives a result different from that obtained when the average of the corresponding raw scores is expressed as a percentile rank. Raw scores of 14 and 22 average 18, which has a percentile equivalent of 6. The percentile equivalent of 14 is 4, and that of 22 is 13. If we had made the

7. Plot cumulative percentage against score. (In practice, a large sheet of graph paper would be used.)

8. Draw the smooth curve that best fits the points plotted.

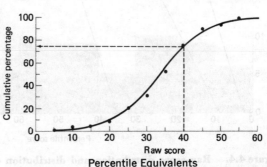

Percentile Equivalents

Raw	%ile	Raw	%ile	Raw	%ile
12	2	24	17	36	60
13	2	25	20	37	64
14	3	26	22	38	67
15	3	27	26	39	71
16	4	28	29	40	74
17	5	29	33	41	77

9. Determine the percentile equivalent of a score by reading from the curve. (The lines on the chart show how one finds that the percentile equivalent of a raw score of 40 is 74).

COMPUTING GUIDE 1. DETERMINING PERCENTILE EQUIVALENTS

mistake of averaging percentiles, our answer would have been 8½ instead of 6. While one rarely makes a serious error by averaging percentiles, percentiles should not be averaged. The median is the proper measure of central tendency for percentiles.

Percentile scores cannot be compared unless the groups on which the conversions are based are similar. Purdue Pegboard norms are based on industrial

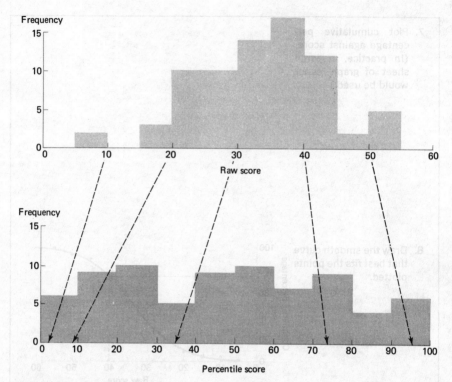

Figure 4.4.   Raw-score distribution and distribution of percentile equivalents for same group.

trainees; Form AA of MCT gives norms for engineering freshmen. A person at the 75th percentile for each test according to these norms does not have equally high standing in each ability. For MCT, separate tables for industrial trainees are available, and we find that a score at the 73rd percentile among freshmen is at the 90th percentile among trainees. Whenever percentiles are used, the norm group involved must be kept in mind.

In the manual for the Bennett test, the user finds a collection of percentile conversion tables permitting him to compare his subject with various reference groups. One such table is reproduced here (Table 4.2). This can be used like the table prepared in Computing Guide 1, although the tables are arranged differently.

A score of 39 falls at the 80th percentile in the norm table, even though it was at the 68th percentile of the small class (Computing Guide 1). The median of the small class (34) is higher than the median of the standardization group; the class is evidently a superior group. This demonstrates the value of carefully collected norms. A person who is just average in mechanical comprehension would not be especially encouraged to choose a mechanical field. The median

Table 4.2. Bennett MCT norms
for boys in grade 9

Percentile	Score
99	54
95	47
90	44
85	41
80	39
75	38
70	36
65	35
60	33
55	32
50	31
45	30
40	29
35	27
30	26
25	23
20	22
15	20
10	17
5	14
1	5
Number of cases	833
Mean	30.8
s.d.	10.4

SOURCE: MCT manual, 1947.

student within this class, however, can be encouraged. He is at the 63rd percentile for the reference population, and it is this larger group with whom he will compete after high school.

16. *Interpret the following record of ability test scores for one person, where all scores are percentile scores based on a random sample of adults: Verbal, 54; Number, 46; Spatial, 87; Reasoning, 40.*

17. *Estimate Alfred's percentile score in each of the four tests he took (question 6 p. 84).*

18. *Why does the table of Bennett norms begin at 1 and stop at 99, instead of ranging from 0 to 100? What percentile score corresponds to a raw score of 60 (perfect)?*

19. *Scores usually change when a test is repeated, because of chance errors of measurement. If each of the following persons changes two points up or down in raw score on MCT, how much would his percentile score change?*

   a. *A person with a percentile score of 55 on the first test.*
   b. *A person at the 95th percentile on the first test.*
20. *The scores below are the times, in seconds, required by a group of persons to perform an easy Block Design problem. Prepare a table of percentile equivalents for this group:*

52	34	41	42	46	45	27	48	35	35	38	29	54	36	33	30
48	39	44	36	36	34	51	40	30	33	37	41	56	32	48	35
37	28	28	45	31	39	31	27	35	36	34	42	38	33	33	31
39	28	36	33	37	36	34	54	34	32	33	38

21. *According to the table prepared in problem 20, how much difference in seconds does a difference of 10 percentile points represent?*

Standard Scores

Mean and standard deviation. The second common way to summarize performance of a group is to use the mean and standard deviation. The *mean* $(\bar{X})$ is the arithmetical average obtained when we add all scores and divide by the number of scores. The *standard deviation* (s.d. or s) is a measure of the spread of scores. The variation of two sets of scores may be different even though the averages are the same. Figure 4.5 shows the smoothed distribution of scores of two classes taking the same test. Even though the groups are similar in mean ability, the distributions are not at all alike. Group B contains far more very superior and inferior cases and therefore has a larger standard deviation.

   The standard deviation is in effect an average of the departures of persons' scores from the group mean. We might measure the spread of scores by finding how far each person is from the mean and averaging (ignoring the direction of deviation). Instead of doing this, we square each deviation, and average the squares. This average is called the *variance* of the distribution. The standard deviation is the square root of the variance. There are more direct procedures for computing the standard deviation that give the same or nearly the same result. The reader should consult a text on statistics for such formulas and the related theory.

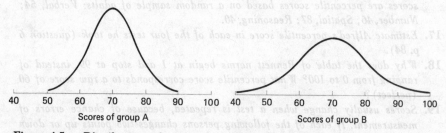

Figure 4.5.   **Distributions of scores of two classes on the same test.**

Conversion scales. It is difficult to compare scores from tests of different lengths unless we convert the raw scores to a common scale. Instead of percentiles, a "standard score" scale based on the mean and standard deviation is often used. Such a scale reports how many standard deviations above or below the mean the person is. For MCT, in the ninth-grade class, the mean is 33.20 and the s.d. is 9.80. A raw score of 43 is one s.d. above the mean, and the standard score is +1. A standard score of −1.5 would be 1.5 s.d. below the mean. The corresponding raw score is 33.20 − (1.5)9.80 or approximately 18.

Computing Guide 2 shows how to convert raw scores to a standard-score scale with a mean of zero and with each s.d. above the mean counted as one unit. This we call a "zero ± one" scale, referring to the numbers assigned the mean and the standard deviation. Testers often use a "50 ± 10" scale that sets the mean at 50 (to avoid negative scores) and sets each s.d. equal to 10 points. As Figure 4.6 shows, changing raw scores into standard scores does not alter the form of the distribution (except for slight changes due to regrouping).

Whereas the Bennett test presents norms in percentile form, Wechsler Block Design norms are in standard-score form (called "scaled scores" by Wechsler). As an example, Table 4.3 displays norms for people aged 20–24. The range of converted scores is from 0 to 19, because Wechsler chose to set the mean equal to a standard score of 10, and to count each s.d. above or below the mean as 3 standard-score points.

1. Begin with the raw scores to be converted.	Assume $x = 33.2$, s.d. $= 9.80$
2. To obtain z scores, express each raw score as a deviation from the mean. Divide by the s.d. $z \text{ score} = \dfrac{\text{raw score} - \text{mean}}{\text{standard deviation}}$	For raw score 50: $z = \dfrac{50 - 33.2}{9.80} = \dfrac{16.8}{9.80} = 1.7$ For raw score 25: $z = \dfrac{25 - 33.2}{9.80} = \dfrac{-8.2}{9.80} = -0.8$
3. To obtain scores on 50 ± 10 scale, multiply each z score by 10 and add to 50: $50 + \dfrac{10 \, (\text{raw score} - \text{mean})}{\text{standard deviation}}$	For raw score 50, $z = 1.7$ $50 + 10 \,(1.7) = 67$ For raw score 25, $z = -0.8$ $50 + 10 \,(-0.8) = 42$

COMPUTING GUIDE 2. CALCULATION OF STANDARD SCORES

Table 4.3. Standard-score equivalents of raw scores for the Block Design test, ages 20–24

Scaled score	0	1	2	3	4	5	6	7	8	9
Raw score	0	1	2	3–8	9–12	13–16	17–20	21–24	25–28	29–31
Scaled score	10	11	12	13	14	15	16	17	18	19
Raw score	32–34	35–37	38–40	41–43	44–45	46–47	—	48	—	—

SOURCE: Wechsler Adult Intelligence Scale Manual, p. 103. *Copyright © 1955 by The Psychological Corporation, New York, N.Y. All rights reserved. Reproduced by permission.*

One can develop standard scores using other values for the mean and s.d. Table 4.4 summarizes several standard-score systems now in use. While there have been logical reasons for many of the variations, only confusion results from so large a variety. In the writer's opinion, test developers should use the system with mean 50 and s.d. 10 unless there are strong reasons for adopting a less-familiar scale. If it is desirable to keep converted scores below 10 so that they

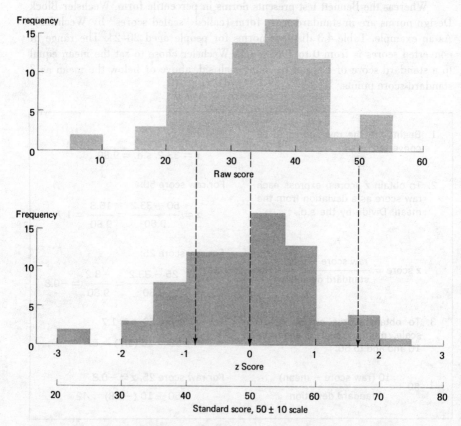

Figure 4.6. Distributions of raw scores and standard scores for the same group.

Table 4.4. Standard-score systems

Mean set equal to	s.d. set equal to	Standard score corresponding to 1 s.d. above mean	Standard score corresponding to 2 s.d. below mean	Name of system, remarks
0	1	1	−2	z scores, prominent in mathematical theory of testing
5	2	7	1	Stanine scores
10	3	13	4	Used for Wechsler subtests
50	10	60	30	Most widely used system
100	15 or 16	115 or 116	70 or 68	Deviation IQ used by many mental tests
100	20	120	60	Used for aptitude tests of U.S. Employment Service

will fit into one column of a standard punchcard for statistical operations, the stanine scale (pronounced *stay-nine*) is recommended. The z conversion is used in statistical and theoretical work, but is not often used by test interpreters. The remaining systems may be expected to die out in time.

The College Board scale is so often encountered that its peculiarities need to be explained. The scale is based on the distribution of college applicants in 1941. In theory today's conversion table assigns the score of 500 to whatever score on this test would have been earned by the average 1941 applicant, this being determined by special test-equating methods. (How closely this theory matches reality is discussed by E. Stewart, 1966.) Since college freshmen today are better prepared than in 1941, the score of 500 is *not* the average of today's distribution. A college that has learned to expect good performance from applicants with a Board score of 600 can make that same interpretation year after year, since the level of ability required to earn that score does not shift with the changing distribution of applicant ability.

22. *The 1960 Stanford-Binet test fixes the mean IQ at 100 and the standard deviation at 16. Express on a 50 ± 10 scale the following IQs: 100, 84, 132, 150.*

23. *In Computing Guide 2 what standard score corresponds to a raw score of 40? 48? 4?*

24. *Draw a figure to show the relation between raw scores and standard scores in Computing Guide 2.*

25. a. *Compute the mean and standard deviation for the Block Design scores given in problem 20, p. 94.*

    b. *How does the mean compare with the median computed previously?*

    c. *What is the approximate percentile rank for a score 2 s.d. above the mean in this distribution?*

Age and grade scales. This is as good a place as any to mention—and condemn—a popular but archaic conversion known as "age equivalents" and "grade equivalents." Whatever score the average 7-year-old earns is converted to an "age-equivalent" score of 7; thus a 5-year-old or a 10-year-old may have a converted score of 7.0. Whatever score the average fifth-grader earns at the start of the school year is converted to 5.0 on the "grade-equivalent" scale; an eighth-grader who makes the same score is said to be performing at the fifth-grade level. Whereas the standard score compares the pupil with a group of which he is a member, these scales compare him with other kinds of groups.

Grade equivalents generate such misleading statements as "The average Mexican-American child entering the seventh grade here is two grades behind the Anglo children in performance." Such a child's converted score of 5.0, however, may not be very far below that of the Anglos in his class. Perhaps a third of the entering seventh-graders of Anglo extraction are also "2 years behind." How much progress is made in one year varies from one school subject to another. According to national norms for the Stanford Achievement Test (Intermediate II, Form W), the middle two-thirds of entering seventh graders range from 5.0 to 10.0 in language usage, i.e., from the fifth-grade to the tenth-grade level. Now the reason is not that the ablest pupils have mastered the ninth-grade curriculum in language; they are not 2 or 3 years ahead in that sense. It occurs because the average pupil, ordinarily coming from a home where elegant language is not prized, is still making a good many commonplace errors when he enters grade 10. The child from a home where good usage is stressed earns a "grade-equivalent" of 10.0 on an intermediate test, but would not do so well on a test dealing with tenth-grade content.

In the writer's opinion, grade conversions should never be used in reporting on a pupil or a class, or in research. Standard scores or percentiles or raw scores serve better. Age conversions are also likely to be misinterpreted. A 6-year-old with mental age 9 cannot pass the tests a 12-year-old with mental age 9 passes; the two simply passed about the same fraction of the test tasks. On the whole, however, age equivalents cause less trouble than grade equivalents, if only because the former are not used for policy decisions in education.

The Normal Distribution

The frequency distribution shown at the top of Figures 4.3 and 4.5 is jagged, but if more cases were added and smaller class intervals were used it would become relatively smooth. The smooth curve as shown in the top portion of Figure 4.7 is the most likely shape of that distribution. This distribution is not perfectly symmetrical, but it tails off on both sides. Most tests yield distributions of this general character. It is sometimes advantageous to convert the score scale so that every test has the same distribution form. The normal probability curve is used for this.

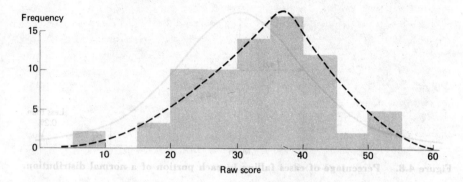

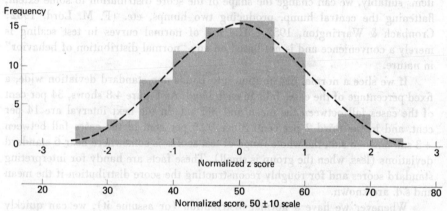

Figure 4.7. Smoothed distribution of raw scores and distribution of normalized scores.

The normal curve (Figure 4.8) is a smooth, symmetric frequency curve having important mathematical properties. The standard deviation is the distance from the mean to the point on the shoulder of the normal curve that separates the convex, hill-like portion from the concave tail. The normal curve is important in the theory of probability and is used in statistical analysis to determine whether a particular experimental result may be a chance occurrence.

Many biological measures such as heights of American men fall into a nearly normal distribution, perhaps because chance combinations of chromosomes determine much of the variation. In psychological tests also, it is very common to obtain approximately normal distributions of scores. Early investigators thought it a natural law that abilities are normally distributed. It is now realized that such a statement is meaningless, since the shape of the distribution depends on the scale of measurement as well as on the subjects' experiences. Distributions of test scores depend on the way the test is constructed. By selecting

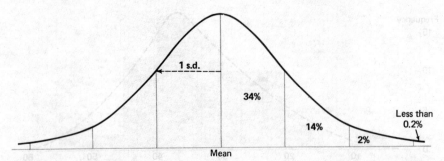

Figure 4.8.   Percentage of cases falling in each portion of a normal distribution.

items suitably, we can change the shape of the score distribution to some extent, flattening the central hump, producing two humps, etc. (F. M. Lord, 1952; Cronbach & Warrington, 1952). The use of normal curves in test scaling is merely a convenience and is not based on any "normal distribution of behavior" in nature.

If we slice a normal distribution into bands one standard deviation wide, a fixed percentage of the cases falls in each band. As Figure 4.8 shows, 34 per cent of the cases fall between the mean and +1 s.d. In the next interval are 14 per cent, and in the third 2 per cent. Since 99.6 per cent of the cases fall between +3 s.d. and −3 s.d., the whole range of test scores is somewhere near 6 standard deviations (less, when the group is small). These facts are handy for interpreting standard scores and for roughly reconstructing the score distribution if the mean and s.d. are known.

Whenever we have a normal distribution (or assume it), we can quickly convert standard scores to percentiles and vice versa. Below the mean are 50 per cent of the cases. Below +1 s.d. are 50 + 34 or 84 per cent of the cases; hence a standard score of 60 (on the 50±10 scale) corresponds to the 84th percentile. Scores are somewhat easier to interpret if all tests are reduced to a scale having a known distribution. For this purpose, some test developers create *normalized standard scores*. These scores are obtained by stretching a distribution to make it nearly normal, and then changing to a standard-score scale.

In our illustrative distribution of ninth-grade MCT scores, 95 is the percentile equivalent of a raw score of 50, and Table 4.5 indicates that the corresponding normalized standard score is 66. This compares with a standard score of 67 (not normalized) obtained in Computing Guide 2. Such small changes, stretching out the scale at the upper end and compressing it at the lower end, produce the distribution shown at the bottom of Figure 4.7. This distribution is more symmetric than the raw-score distribution. If more persons had been included, the smoothed distribution would be essentially normal.

26. *What percentile rank corresponds to a score 2 s.d. above the mean? To a score 1 s.d. below the mean?*

Table 4.5. **Relations between standard scores and percentile scores, when raw scores are normally distributed**

Distance from mean in s.d. units (z score)	Standard score (50 ± 10)	Percentile score	Percent of cases in "tail" of curve	Percentile score	Standard score (50 ± 10)	Distance from mean in s.d. units (z score)
3.0	80	99.9	0.1	0.1	20	−3.0
2.9	79	99.8	0.2	0.2	21	−2.9
2.8	78	99.7	0.3	0.3	22	−2.8
2.7	77	99.6	0.4	0.4	23	−2.7
2.6	76	99.5	0.5	0.5	24	−2.6
2.5	75	99.4	0.6	0.6	25	−2.5
2.4	74	99.2	0.8	0.8	26	−2.4
2.3	73	99	1	1	27	−2.3
2.2	72	99	1	1	28	−2.2
2.1	71	98	2	2	29	−2.1
2.0	70	98	2	2	30	−2.0
1.9	69	97	3	3	31	−1.9
1.8	68	96	4	4	32	−1.8
1.7	67	96	4	4	33	−1.7
1.6	66	95	5	5	34	−1.6
1.5	65	93	7	7	35	−1.5
1.4	64	92	8	8	36	−1.4
1.3	63	90	10	10	37	−1.3
1.2	62	88	12	12	38	−1.2
1.1	61	86	14	14	39	−1.1
1.0	60	84	16	16	40	−1.0
0.9	59	82	18	18	41	−0.9
0.8	58	79	21	21	42	−0.8
0.7	57	76	24	24	43	−0.7
0.6	56	73	27	27	44	−0.6
0.5	55	69	31	31	45	−0.5
0.4	54	66	34	34	46	−0.4
0.3	53	62	38	38	47	−0.3
0.2	52	58	42	42	48	−0.2
0.1	51	54	46	46	49	−0.1
0.0	50	50	50	50	50	0.0

27. *In a normal distribution, what is the relation of the mean and median?*

28. *Assuming that scores are normally distributed on a test where the mean is 60 and s.d. is 8, interpret the following scores: Sara, 64; Harriet, 68; Charles, 87; Bob, 48.*

29. *Using Figure 4.8, interpret each of the following z scores in percentile terms: 3.0, 0, −2.0.*

30. *Translate the following percentile scores into standard scores on a 50±10 scale: 10, 42, 85.*

Comparison of Systems

Since a manual sometimes offers more than one type of conversion table, the user needs some basis for deciding when to use each system of scores. Choice of system is important also when he prepares norms for his own institution.

The percentile score has these advantages; it is readily understood, which makes it especially satisfactory for reporting to persons without statistical training; it is easily computed; it may be interpreted exactly even when the distribution of test scores is nonnormal. The disadvantages of the percentile score are these: it magnifies small differences near the mean that may not be important, and it reduces the apparent size of large and practically important differences in the tails of the distribution. Also, it is often less appropriate for statistical analysis.

The advantages of standard scores are these: differences in standard score are proportional to differences in raw score; use of standard scores in averages and correlations gives the same result as would come from use of the raw scores. The disadvantages are that standard scores cannot be interpreted readily when distributions are skewed, and that untrained persons may misinterpret them. In general, statisticians prefer standard scores while those who interpret tests directly to laymen prefer percentiles. Nonpsychologists can learn to interpret standard-score scales. High-school teachers and parents quite comfortably discuss Pete's Scholastic Aptitude Test score of 650 alongside his IQ of 112 from some other test. The former is a standard score on the 500 ± 100 scale, and the latter a score on the 100 ± 16 scale.

Normalized standard scores have become increasingly popular. These spread out cases in both tails of the distribution and yet can be readily translated into percentiles. The DAT profile form shown in Figure 4.9 illustrates typical current practice. Percentiles are plotted, but the spacing corresponds to normalized standard scores.

31. *A teacher wishes to convert scores on class examinations so that his record book will show at a glance how well a person is doing and can average all tests equally in the final grade. Should he use raw, percentile, or standard scores?*

32. *In a certain college, all freshmen are given a "scholastic aptitude test." The results are to be mimeographed and confidential copies given to all professors. Should the report use raw scores, standard scores, or percentiles?*

Profiles

Derived scores make it possible to compare standing on one test with standing on another. This is illustrated in the Differential Aptitude Tests, a set of eight

Name   Grade   Sex
FINCHLEY ROBERT   11   M

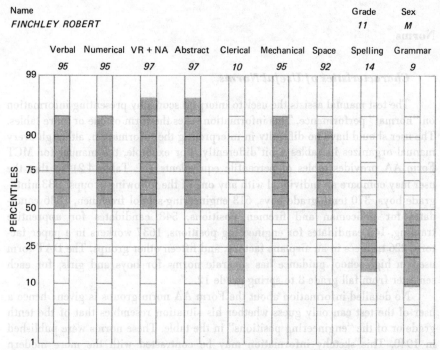

Figure 4.9.   Profile of Robert Finchley on the Differential Aptitude Tests.
Bennett, Seashore, & Wesman, 1951. The current profile form is copyright © 1961, 1963 by The Psychological Corporation, New York, N.Y. All rights reserved. Adapted by permission.

tests, one of which is a form of the Bennett MCT. The tests vary in length and in difficulty, so that from the raw scores alone one cannot identify the person's best performance. After raw scores are changed to percentiles (or normalized standard scores), one can plot a profile showing his comparative standing in all fields. The profile shown in Figure 4.9 compares a high-school junior to the norms for junior boys. Robert is almost equally outstanding in all the reasoning tests, but three scores on tests that do not require reasoning are exceptionally low.

One must be careful in profile interpretations: equal percentiles do not mean equally good performance. If almost everyone can count, and almost no one can carry a tune, the fiftieth percentile on the former means poor performance and the fiftieth percentile on the latter is good (see p. 486).

33. *Rearrange the DAT subtests in random order and sketch a new profile for Robert Finchley. Do you get the same impression regarding the consistency of his performance and the location of his peak abilities? Is any one ordering of subtests better than another, for profiling?*

34. *Why are percentiles spaced nonuniformly in the DAT profile?*

Norms

Characteristics of Useful Norms

The test manual assists the user to interpret scores by presenting information on "normal" performance. This information takes the form of one or more tables. The user should have no difficulty in interpreting the information, although every manual organizes its tables a bit differently. For example, the manual for MCT Form AA provides tables of percentile equivalents (cf. Table 4.2) so that the user may compare an individual with any one of the following groups: 833 ninth-grade boys, 370 tenth-grade boys, 613 engineering-school freshmen, 1836 candidates for policeman and fireman positions, 548 candidates for apprentice training, 145 candidates for engineering positions, 1637 workers in a paper factory, 226 trainees in an airplane factory, and fifteen other groups. The DAT form used in high-school guidance has separate norms for boys and girls, for each semester from fall grade 8 to spring grade 12.

No detailed information about the Form AA norm groups is given; hence a user of the test can only guess whether his situation resembles that of the tenth grade or of the "engineering positions" in the table. These norms were published in 1940. This sketchy information may be contrasted with the more modern description given in the manual for DAT Mechanical Reasoning (1966, p. 3–2).

Schools . . . came from 95 communities in 43 states representing all major geographic areas. In some communities the entire school population in grades eight through twelve was tested; in some, all students in one to four grades were tested; in some larger cities, representative classes (as judged by the local research director) were tested. More than fifty thousand students from 195 schools are included in the norms. These schools are listed. . . .

Almost all of the testing was done during September, October, and November, 1962.

The discussion then goes on to compare the sample with the school population as a whole with respect to geographic distribution and size of school.

Some testers attach too much importance to norms in selecting tests and in interpreting scores. Some are unduly impressed by the number of cases used in compiling the norm tables. We shall see, however, that the size of the standardizing sample alone does not indicate how satisfactory the norms are.

Norms are unimportant when one intends only to identify individual differences within a group or is concerned only with the person's absolute performance. For example, norms are of little use to the employment manager who wishes to hire the ten most promising applicants, or to the manager who knows from actual trial that persons with scores of 72 on test A make satisfactory punch-press operators.

In guidance and clinical work, norms are important. The person's position relative to his group has to be considered. A child who scores at the 20th percentile on a test of readiness for first grade will have difficulties in school, but children in this range can be handled in school. However, if the norms place a child at the 2nd percentile, we do not expect him to fit into the regular program.

Norms play a particularly important part in evaluating educational programs by means of standardized tests. The school officials and the public can be relatively satisfied if the end-of-year performance of the pupils matches the national average, and will be dissatisfied if that is not the case. To be sure, communities differ, and one may therefore try to make an allowance by comparing the achievement-test results with the mental-ability tests given at the start of the year. When that is done, the norms for the ability test also become important in the evaluation. Indeed, what the school really needs is a distribution combining aptitude and achievement data in such a way that the school can compare its achievement mean with the distribution *of school means* for schools that draw from the same aptitude range.

So great is the demand for dependable information of this type that tests sold to schools are often normed in a painstaking way. Lennon (1964) tells us that the typical publisher spends about fifty cents for each case included in the norm group—counting the cost of drawing the sample, soliciting cooperation, testing, and analyzing results; when the norm group for an achievement battery may run to 100,000 cases, it is clear that a serious effort is being made.

Nonetheless, as Lennon goes on to say, these efforts do not produce truly comparable norms for different tests. Because of different technical decisions (about, for example, whether to stratify the sample with respect to intelligence-test scores of pupils) and because of different degrees of control over data collection, the national average in fifth-grade arithmetic reported for one test may be higher than the average performance reported for a similar test. When the State of California directs every school district to give a nationally standardized test and report publicly how well its fifth-graders are doing, and leaves the choice of test to the school district, there is an understandable tendency for teachers to select the test whose national norms set "average performance" at a low figure. The marketplace may thus tend to reward the publisher who has been less careful than others to obtain accurate norms.

Specialized norms. For many test interpretations, local norms are far more important than wide-area norms. A child at the 20th percentile in the typical first grade would be at the 2nd percentile in some other school that enrolls pupils from a select neighborhood. One example of such school-to-school differences is given in Table 4.6.

Table 4.6.   School-to-school differences in Mechanical Reasoning scores
              of ninth-grade boys

City	Name of school	Approximate number of cases	Mean	s.d.
Worcester, Mass.	Commerce	60	28.3	12.7
Worcester, Mass.	Five other schools	190	29.4	11.9
St. Joseph, Mo.	Benton	70	30.3	11.7
St. Joseph, Mo.	Lafayette	70	35.8	10.7
St. Paul, Minn.	Wilson	50	34.0	10.3
Independence, Mo.	Chrisman	175	37.6	12.4

SOURCE: DAT manual, 1947.

The most useful norms permit the tester to compare the subject with his prospective companions and competitors. The manual for the Wechsler intelligence scale gives norms based on adults in general. But a boy who is above the average for his age, compared to people in general, may be below average among college freshmen. If we wish to forecast his success in college, we need Wechsler norms based on college students alone. More than that, we need to know the norms for the particular college he plans to attend.

Sections of the country, occupational groups, and schools vary. Geographical differences are illustrated in Table 4.7. The SSCQT was given for several years to young men who might wish to attend college; those earning scores of 70 and over were generally allowed to postpone their military service until completion of college. The test, designed to be as fair a measure of scholastic aptitude as possible, called for verbal and quantitative reasoning. There are large differences among regions: in the Midwest and East the average registrant did well enough

Table 4.7.   Geographical differences in Selective Service College
              Qualification Test scores

Residence	Percentage of freshmen registrants scoring below				
	50	60	70	75	80
New England	1	4	44	71	92
Middle Atlantic	1	3	40	69	92
East North Central	2	4	45	74	94
West North Central	1	5	44	73	93
South Atlantic	6	11	57	78	94
East South Central	7	15	66	85	97
West South Central	9	16	63	84	95
Mountain	2	4	46	75	94
Pacific	2	5	45	72	93

SOURCE: *Statistical Studies of Selective Service Testing*, 1951–1953. Educational Testing Service, 1955. Adapted by permission.

to be exempt from immediate draft, whereas in the South only 40 per cent of the registrants performed at this level. More detailed data taking size of school into account (Dailey, 1962) show even greater regional differences.

Whenever he can, the test interpreter should prepare norms for the local groups with which he deals. A high-school counselor could profitably use information about the score distribution for all boys in his high school, for boys in the shop curriculum, for boys who later attend the local college, and for workers in certain large local industries. He falls back on published norms because it takes time and effort to accumulate local norms or because, as is often the case, he cannot possibly accumulate local norms. A clinician, for example, has no chance to prepare norms for a random sample of 60-year-old men, yet he needs to compare the men he tests with a community average. No teacher or superintendent from a superior school can take pride if his group merely reaches the national norms; no one from a handicapped school district should be condemned if his group cannot attain the national average. The only fair basis for comparing schools is to judge each school against schools with similar organization, similar curricula, and similar promotion policies. Rarely are published norms based on such meaningful segments as "New England public elementary schools, in cities with population 2000 to 10,000" or "Southern rural elementary schools."

Norms are not "standards." A common mistake is to assume that all pupils in the ninth grade should reach the ninth-grade norm. This is of course a fallacy; 50 per cent of the pupils in the standardizing sample fall below the norm. Furthermore, the test shows only what schools are doing at present. It is highly unlikely that the schools are doing so well that the national average represents what pupils could attain with the best teaching methods. The teacher whose class reaches the average has no cause for complacency. There is much room for the development of better educational methods.

35. *A high-school girl's performance on the Mechanical Reasoning test can appropriately be compared with girls' norms, boys' norms, or the combined norms, depending on the decision to be made. Illustrate.*

36. *How do you explain the geographical differences on the SSCQT? Is it sound national policy to encourage more students from one region to attend college than from another?*

37. *Assuming a normal distribution, what standard score corresponds to a raw score of 40 in each of the schools in Table 4.6?*

38. *In a particular college that admits all high-school graduates who apply, the median score of the freshman class is at the 65th percentile of the published norms for freshmen for the Henmon-Nelson test. What factors might account for this deviation?*

39. *Would local norms or national norms be most useful in interpreting each of the following?*

   a. *A personality test given to indicate whether a prisoner is psychotic.*

   b. *An intelligence test given to an infant considered for adoption.*

    c. *A reading test given to determine if a high-school boy needs individual remedial instruction.*
40. *The Otis-Lennon Mental Ability Test has a form for use in the last half of kindergarten. One type of conversion produces a "deviation IQ," a standard score on a 50 ± 10 scale. There are separate conversion tables for each three-month age bracket from 5-0 to 8-5. A score of 30, for example, is converted to DIQ 100 if a child is 5 years and 10 months old, and to 74 if the child is 8 years old. How do you explain the fact that a perfect score on the test is converted to the IQ "above 150" if the child is 5 or 6 years old, and to IQ 132 if he is 8? Is it reasonable to suppose that IQs of bright children drop in this period?*

What the Manual Should Report

    Except when the primary use of a test is to compare individuals with their own local group, norms should be published at the time of release of the test for operational use. Norms presented in the test manual should refer to defined and clearly described populations. These populations should be the groups to whom users of the test will ordinarily wish to compare the persons tested. The test manual should report whether scores vary for groups differing in age, sex, amount of training, and other equally important variables (American Psychological Association, 1966).

    All these principles have been violated at times in the past. Tests have been published with no norms. Others have offered norms based on inadequate samples, and samples have been poorly described. The historic difficulties in this aspect of test interpretation are pointed out forcibly in these remarks by a test publisher (H. Seashore & Ricks, 1950):

    Legitimate and illegitimate general norms abound in current test manuals. People-in-general norms are legitimate only if they are based upon careful field studies with appropriate controls of regional, socioeconomic, educational, and other factors—and even then only if the sampling is carefully described so that the test user may be fully aware of its inevitable limitations and deficiencies. The millions entering the armed forces during World War II provided the basis of some fairly good norms on young adult men, though mainly on tests not available to the public. The standardization of the Wechsler Intelligence Scale for Children is a recent attempt to secure a representative smaller sample of children aged 5–15 for setting up tables of intelligence quotients which may be considered generalized norms for children. The earlier work of Terman's group to set up good national norms on a small, well-chosen sample is well known. In the standardizing of some educational achievement tests, nationwide samplings of children of each appropriate grade or age and from different types of schools in all parts of the country are sought in an effort to produce norms that are truly general for a given span of grades or ages.

    Unfortunately, many alleged general norms reported in test manuals are not backed even by an honest effort to secure representative samples of people-in-general. Even tens or hundreds of thousands of cases can fall woefully short of defining people-in-general. Inspection of test manuals will show (or would show if information about the norms were given completely) that many such massed norms are merely collections of all the scores that opportunity has permitted the author or publisher to gather easily. Lumping together all the samples secured more by chance than by plan makes for impressively large numbers; but while seeming to simplify interpretation, the norms may dim or actually distort the counseling, employment, or diagnostic significance of a score.

With or without a plan, everyone of course obtains data where and how he can. Since the standardization of a test is always dependent on the cooperation of educators, psychologists and personnel men, the foregoing comments are not a plea for the rejection of available samples but for their correct labeling. If a manual shows "general" norms for a vocabulary test based on a sample two-thirds of which consists of women office workers, one can properly raise his test-wise eyebrows. There is no reason to accept such norms as a good generalization of adult—or even of employed-adult—vocabulary. It is better to set up norms on the occupationally homogeneous two-thirds of the group and frankly call them norms on female office workers. Adding a few more miscellaneous cases does not make the sample a truly general one.

If the manual describes the norm sample adequately, the user can judge the norms by these questions:

• Does the standard group consist of the sort of person with whom my subjects should be compared?

• Is the sample representative of this population?

• Does the sample include enough cases?

• Is the sample appropriately subdivided?

Norms for any group must be a fair representation of that group. A fair sample is assured when the test maker takes a strictly random sample of the population (e.g., of all American college freshmen). Since this is difficult, the test maker usually tries to obtain a mixture of cases from all segments of the population; for college students, he would draw on large and small colleges, private and public, from all sections of the country. If any segment is too heavily represented, the norms will be biased.

In a small sample, accidental inclusion of a few additional good or poor cases will make the norms unrepresentative. In large samples, such variations should cancel out. No fixed number of cases is required for dependable norms. It is better to keep the sample strictly representative, and small, than to accumulate large numbers of cases that may not be representative.

Even when the norm sample is large and representative, it should ordinarily be subdivided if important, clearly identifiable subgroups earn different average scores. On tests like MCT boys do much better than girls. Boys' norms are needed because in a course to which mechanical insight is relevant the competition will consist almost wholly of boys.

Because of the desire to keep norm groups homogenous, Negro children were excluded from the standardization samples of most earlier tests. Some recent standardizations have taken pains to include a suitable fraction of Negroes.

Others have prepared separate Negro norms; e.g., for the Draw-a-Man Test (Kennedy & Lindner, 1964), for the Stanford-Binet (Kennedy, Van de Riet, & White, 1963).

41. *For the usual purposes of testing in schools, should a Negro pupil be evaluated against Negro norms or norms for all kinds of pupils?*

42. *For Form CC, the difficult version of MCT intended for use in engineering schools, separate norms are reported for 148 engineering freshmen at Princeton, and for four groups at Iowa State College: 325 engineering freshmen, 175 agricultural engineering freshmen, 121 sophomores in architectural engineering, and all engineering seniors (108). It is reported that the subgroups of senior engineers were so similar that separate norms were not required. How adequate are these norms? What other tables, if any, would be desirable?*

43. *How would you proceed to get a thoroughly representative sample of adult men in Chicago to use as a standardizing group for a 30-minute mental test? Assume that you have sufficient research funds to pay each man $5.00 for taking the test.*

44. *Consult the manual of some recently published test and discuss its norms.*
   a. *How clear is the description of the selection of cases?*
   b. *How judicious was the selection of cases? Is the correct population truly represented?*

45. *The U.S. Employment Service has a test for statistical typists. It wishes norms for employed statistical typists so as to decide, as persons are tested in the future, how each one compares with persons now in such work. To obtain norms, State employment services in a large number of the States were asked to test employed typists (U.S. Employment Service, 1968b). Consider the following aspects of the sampling plan.*
   a. *Would you take an equal number of cases from each cooperating State, take whatever number each one could conveniently provide, or what?*
   b. *What restrictions would you place on work experience of persons admitted to the sample?*
   c. *Would you prevent the agencies from testing government typists, whom they could locate relatively easily?*

46. *Norms on an individually administered test of mental ability and a group test of achievement for Southeastern Negro pupils were prepared in 1960, so that proper interpretations could be made in child guidance clinics and schools. White testers were used, in the belief that most testers will be whites for some years to come (Kennedy et al., 1963), but Negroes often perform better for black testers. Do you agree with the decision to base norms on white testers?*

47. *Norms vary in different segments of the population. Would a criterion-referenced interpretation show similar variation?*

Norms by Calibration

In the future, test norms may often be constructed statistically by calibrating a new test (or a test needing new norms) against another test that is already well normed. Indeed, one test publisher has gone on record that this is a necessity, to avoid a present lack of comparability among norms for educational tests (Lennon, 1964).

The calibration process is like the procedure the maker of an aneroid barometer uses when he places marks on its dial so that readings agree with an accurate mercury barometer. Rarely has a psychological device had norms good enough to be taken as a standard for other tests. In 1960, however, the so-called Project Talent administered an experimental set of tests of various abilities and personality characteristics to a strictly representative sample of American high-school students, perhaps 5 per cent of the age group in school.

The developer of a new test for high-school ages could use these data as a basis for standardizing. To do so, he would select whichever of the experimental tests measures about the same thing as his test does. For example, a new form of MCT could be calibrated against whatever test or combination of tests measures mechanical comprehension in the experimental battery. Call this the anchor test. The test developer would apply both the anchor test and the new MCT to the same sample. This sample should be reasonably representative of high-school boys (for example, it should not be restricted to boys in a technical high school), but it can be fairly small and need not be exactly representative. Data for girls would be collected on another sample.

The *equipercentile* method is then used to establish what scores on the anchor test and MCT represent the same level of ability. The scores on the second test is taken as equivalent to whatever score on the anchor test falls at the same percentile in the calibration sample. Suppose we have the following information.

Raw score on anchor test	Percentile rank in national sample for grade 9 boys	Percentile rank in boys' calibration sample	Raw score on MCT having same percentile rank in calibration sample
80	98	99	60
60	82	88	52
40	63	70	43

One would conclude that a score of 60 on MCT is equivalent to a score of 80 on the anchor test and we therefore expect it to fall at the 98th percentile of a national sample of ninth-grade boys. The same procedure could be applied to get more specialized norms; e.g., to get norms for boys in technical schools, one could sort out the Talent cases so as to use just the boys from such schools. Once MCT is matched to an anchor, any norms, expectancy tables, or other research on the anchor test can be used to interpret MCT. There are various technical difficulties in this process, however (Angoff, 1962, 1964, 1970). Attractive though the idea of using previously normed anchor tests is, the method has been used only in a limited way. The excellent Talent sample has been put to use only in developing late-adolescent norms for tests the armed services apply to their inductees (Dailey *et al.*, 1962).

Obsolescence of Norms

Test norms become obsolete. On general mental tests, for example, adults score higher on the average than adults did a decade or two ago. These changes may be attributed to an increasing level of education or other social changes.

It is essential that norms be verified when a test is altered. Changes of items or format can make the test easier or harder, and can even alter its meaning. For example, a "structural visualization" test was made by cutting a circular disk into nine pieces of irregular shape, for the subject to reassemble. Originally this test was made of heavy aluminum. After it had been in use for some years, the manufacturer began to use wood instead. The mean time for the wooden test is 182 seconds, whereas the original test has a mean of 140 seconds for the same subjects (J. Wilson & Carpenter, 1948). The published norms were made meaningless by the change; it was a serious error not to revise the manual when the test was modified. Awareness of such difficulties caused the developers of DAT to prepare separate norms for each of three types of answer sheet available for use with the Clerical Speed and Accuracy Test. Differences in marking time required produce such differences in performance as these (medians for tenth-grade boys):

IBM 805 answer sheet	50–51 points
MRC answer sheet	42 points
Digitek answer sheet	47–48 points

Whatever reference group is used for test norms, they are sooner or later rendered irrelevant by social changes. Today's college applicants are not like any reference group that could have been assembled a few years ago: there are more colleges, and more students going to those colleges. Economic and social forces have changed the probability that bright students from working-class homes will apply to college. Recent changes in curriculum and educational procedures have equipped the high-school graduate with different abilities. Similar changes take place in other reference populations, yet it is impractical to revise norms every few years except in program tests like college entrance tests administered on a large scale.

Many experts think that test consumers place too much emphasis on norms. As Angoff (1962) pointed out:

These principles can be stated here: *One*, that the meaning that is invested in a scale at the time of its definition is not lasting; indeed, there is some question whether it is useful. The real meaning in a scale is the meaning given to it by the user over a period of time with experience and familiarity and with normative aids. *Two*, that a scale has a reasonable chance of being [becoming] meaningful to the user if it does not change. . . . There is hardly a person . . . who knows the precise original definition of the length of the foot used in the measurement of height or distance, or which king it was whose foot was originally agreed upon as the standard; on the other hand, there is no one here who does not know how to evaluate lengths and distances in terms of this unit. . . . Its usefulness derives from the fact that it remains the same over time and allows us to familiarize ourselves with it.

Angoff is saying that with experience we build up criterion-referenced interpretations in our heads, and then rely less and less on norm reference.

48. *If you were to bring out a new mechanical comprehension test in 1970 would you be willing to use the 1960 Talent data as a basis for your norms? in 1980? What do you need to know about society to decide such questions?*

49. *When the admissions officer applies an expectancy table to a score on the College Board scale, is he making any assumptions about the stability over time of the population or of the situation?*

SUGGESTED READINGS

Ebel, Robert L. Content standard test scores. *Educational and Psychological Measurement*, 1962, *22*, 15–25. (Reprinted in Mehrens & Ebel, 1967.)

Ebel argues for greater effort by test developers to produce content-referenced interpretations, and illustrates how this can be done for a mathematics test and a vocabulary test.

French, John W. Schools of thought in judging excellence of English themes. In *Proceedings, invitational conference on testing problems, 1961*. Princeton: ETS, 1962. Pp. 19–28. (Reprinted in Anastasi, 1966.)

This study investigates why graders disagree, and what information the constructed response, properly graded, offers that the choice-response test does not. The factor-analytic technique used here is not easy to follow, but the main results can be grasped before the reader learns about factor analysis in our Chapter 10.

Lennon, Roger T. Norms: 1963. In *Proceedings, invitational conference on testing problems, 1963*. Princeton: ETS, 1964. Pp. 13–22. (Reprinted in Anastasi, 1966.)

A publisher's frank evaluation of both the excellence and the inadequacy of present "national norms."

Lyman, Howard B. *Test scores and what they mean*. Englewood Cliffs, N.J.: Prentice-Hall, 1963.

An excellent treatment of virtually all topics in this chapter. The book-length presentation directed to the beginner manages to go deeper into each topic and yet keep discussion clear and simple. The reader will find the chapters on norms, profiles, and "What can we say?" (on score interpretation) the most interesting.

Seashore, Harold G. Methods of expressing test scores. *Test Service Bulletin*, 1955, No. 45. New York: Psychological Corporation. (Reprinted in Jackson & Messick, 1967, and Gronlund, 1968.)

A dozen scales for reporting test scores are compared, including stanines, percentiles, College Board scores, and so on.

Womer, Frank B. Test norms, their use and interpretation. Washington, D.C.: National Association of Secondary School Principals, 1965. Pp. 56.

A simply written account of the procedures used to establish norms for tests used in schools, followed by a discussion of misconceptions that arise in using norms.

Test Validation

Need for Critical Evaluation of Tests

When a teacher investigates the ability of his pupils, he looks for the best mental test available. An industrial psychologist selecting workers for an office wishes to try the best test of mental ability. The clinical psychologist studying a child whose learning is defective needs the mental test that will give the most accurate results. Each user asks, "What is the best test of mental ability?" But the test that best serves one of them is probably not best for the others.

The test purchaser has a confusing problem. He is faced with long tests and short tests, famous tests and unfamiliar tests, old tests and new tests, ordinary tests and novel tests. The catalog of a leading test distributor offers 25 tests of general mental ability and 15 devices for appraising personality. Each was produced by a psychologist who thinks his test is in some way superior to the others on the market. He is frequently correct.

Different tests have different virtues; no one test in any field is "the best" for all purposes. No test maker can put into his test all desirable qualities. A design feature that improves the test in one respect generally sacrifices some other desirable quality. Some tests work well with children but not with adults; some give precise measures but require much time; some give satisfactory total scores but are inferior for detailed diagnosis.

Tests must be selected for the purpose and situation for which they are to be used. In measuring readiness of a child for first grade, what tests are pertinent depends on the instructional plan. Tests that select superior supervisors in one plant are valueless in another. Clinicians choose different tests for patients of different kinds. No list of "recommended tests" can eliminate the necessity for careful choice by the user.

The user has to evaluate developments. New tests are produced, new uses of tests are discovered, and new findings about old tests are brought to light. Of some 1200 tests described in the 1965 *Mental measurements yearbook,* over 900 were new or had been supplemented by significant new information since 1959.

Ability to judge tests is important for many people who will never choose tests themselves. The business executive may turn his selection and promotion problems over to psychological consultants. The psychiatrist or juvenile-court judge may place full responsibility for choice and interpretation of tests on clinical psychologists. Nonetheless, these consumers of test results ought to know how tests are evaluated and must be aware of the common weaknesses of tests. Industrial consultants sometimes recommend testing programs that other psychologists regard as overelaborate or of dubious validity; the executive needs to know something about testing if he is to ask the right questions. There is an understandable tendency for the clinical tester to become overenthusiastic about the procedures in which he is expert, and to make his recommendations too confidently. The judge must be ready to ask pointed questions.

Those who receive reports from psychologists frequently depart from the recommendations made. Such departures are necessary and justified, insofar as they give proper weight to facts not available to the tester. But giving great weight to supplementary impressions and little weight to objectively observed behavior spoils more decisions than it helps. If the user of test information knows how a test is validated, he can decide whether his own impressions are substantial enough to deserve comparable weight.

1. *Improving a test in one way weakens it in another. What advantage, and what disadvantage, comes from each of the following changes?*
   a. *Lengthening a test.*
   b. *Making it interesting to children.*
   c. *Making it more diagnostic of strong and weak points.*
   d. *Giving it as an individual test instead of as a group test.*
2. *This is a letter received by a psychologist from an industrial personnel manager hiring office and factory workers. How would you answer it on the basis of the paragraphs above, knowing that the tests mentioned are representative of their type?*

   ". . . Just now we are planning the use of the following tests: Otis intelligence and Minnesota Multiphasic Personality Inventory, and aptitude tests related to our openings, such as the Bennett test. Does this seem to be a well-balanced testing schedule for industry? Are there tests that you think preferable to these?"

3. *It has been suggested that the American Psychological Association award a Seal of Approval to all well-prepared tests. Discuss the advantages and disadvantages of such a system. Would this plan eliminate the need for critical judgment by users?*

The Test Manual

The manual (often supplemented by a technical handbook) is the principal source of information about the quality of a published test. The manual provides directions for testing, scoring procedures, and research findings.

Manuals are not always as useful as they should be. Some manuals omit facts users need or gloss over unfavorable evidence. Even a generally excellent manual may have inadequate sections.

Prominence and popularity are not necessarily signs of quality in tests. In clinical psychology and counseling particularly, fads in testing flourish. In Schafer's words (1954, p. 6), ". . . a boom town excitement has characterized clinical psychology until very recently. News of a 'good' test, like news of striking oil, has brought a rush of diagnostic drillers from the old wells to the new." Techniques rushed into application far in advance of adequate research include projective tests such as the Rorschach, formulas for detecting brain damage from intelligence tests, and so-called tests of creativity. Many fads in testing fade quickly, but some invalid tests retain "best-seller" status for a generation.

The failure of persons making use of psychological tests to take negative evidence and unfavorable reviews into account has in some instances reached scandalous proportions. To name a name, consider the Bernreuter Personality Inventory, produced in 1931 when research on tests of this kind had barely begun. A recent review (Becker, 1965) echoes complaints that have been widespread for thirty years:

The test is easily faked to give an emotionally stable, somewhat outgoing profile, and while successful and unsuccessful employees of various sorts are occasionally differentiated, the differences are so small as to preclude their usefulness in making decisions about individuals. . . .

The Bernreuter can also be criticized on other grounds besides its failure to do any job well enough to justify its existence. The publishers and author have made no attempt to improve the test throughout the 32 years of its existence. Its cumbersome scoring system remains, its six scores are still retained when two would do [see p. 522], and its current manual contains no information which was not available in 1935, although over 300 studies have been undertaken using the test. The consumer seeking a personality inventory would be well advised to look elsewhere.

These remarks are accompanied by the reminder that the test is still a bestseller and as late as 1953 sold a million copies a year. One has the impression that the test' is sold primarily to firms using it to screen job applicants, and that certain management consulting firms directed by nonpsychologists are responsible for much of its use.

The quality of tests has improved more or less steadily. Publishers as well as the better-trained consumers are now ready to examine critically the quality of test material and technical information regarding test effectiveness. It is now recognized that satisfactory tests require long periods of development. Authors are often advised not to release new tests on which research is inadequate, though tests of similar quality would have been accepted for publication twenty years ago. Test construction has increasingly been taken over by the test publishers, who have added technical staffs for this purpose.

"Program" testing is on the increase. Such a test is developed to fit the needs of a particular large institution or cooperating group of institutions, and used only under its control. Examples are an admissions test for medical schools, a test for awarding college scholarships on a competitive basis, and a battery for applicants seeking Air Force officer training. Such uses often require that questions be kept secret from those to be tested. Many of the tests are patterned on tests that have already been standardized and validated. Program tests should be developed as carefully as tests published for general use. Though technical information about the quality of the tests is not readily available, investigators who need the information can borrow an outdated form for inspection, and can obtain memoranda on research carried out for the institution.

Even the newer tests have marked limitations. These limitations may result only from the fact that no one test can do everything, but they may also be the result of inadequate research and refinement. Some popular tests do not succeed in measuring what they were intended to measure. The author's description of a test understandably advertises its favorable features, and test manuals can seriously mislead the uncritical reader. As recently as the 1950s an aptitude battery for vocational guidance was published with what seemed at first glance to be impressive evidence of validity; but nearly all the "evidence" had been collected on an entirely different set of tests used in military selection. The only connection between the two batteries was a vague resemblance in plan. An even more deplorable violation is described by Rosenbaum (1967). A promotional flyer publicizing a new test was mailed to business executives after an article on the test appeared in a business journal. The flyer "guaranteed" that any applicant scoring A or A— on the test would do well on the job, though evidence had been collected only on very small samples. A number of executives replaced their existing testing programs with the new miracle-claiming test. Two or three years of use showed that the new test did not select particularly good workers and it was dropped.

A good manual is difficult to prepare. The more research there is on the test, the harder the task of summary. The manual must be clear enough that any qualified user can comprehend it—and clear enough that the reader who is not qualified will realize that he is not. Yet the information must be precise enough to satisfy specialists in test research.

The Test Standards

National organizations interested in measurement have prepared standards to aid in writing and using manuals. *Standards for educational and psychological tests* (1966) is a revision of recommendations originally issued in 1954 and 1955. The *Standards* indicate what information the manual should contain. Many of the recommendations are accompanied by examples illustrating good or poor procedure; Figure 5.1 gives an extract to illustrate their form and content. The major subdivisions of the *Standards* are: Dissemination of information (2 pp.), Interpretation (3 pp.), Validity (12 pp.), Reliability (7 pp.), Administration and scoring (2 pp.), Scales and norms (3 pp.).

Test titles frequently mislead: we shall later have forceful things to say, for example, about references to mental "capacity." One finds such absurdities as a 1968 catalog listing of the Iowa Silent Reading Test—New Edition; the adjective was appropriate when the edition appeared in 1942. There has been a perhaps regrettable tendency to attach names of universities to tests: Stanford, Minnesota, Columbia, etc. Such naming may suggest that the test is somehow endorsed by the university, which is never the case. The test is the personal product of one or two scholars on the faculty. By the time the test is revised, the reviser may have no connection with the university named in the title. Thus no author of current forms of the Stanford Achievement Test has been associated with Stanford. In plan, the test is faithful to the original model generated by some Stanford professors in the 1920s; using the familiar name attracts purchasers who were satisfied by older versions. In 1967, when the persons who revised the Stanford test also brought out a wholly new test for a different purpose, they attached to it the label "The Stanford Diagnostic Test in Reading"; such use of the trade name is hard to defend.

A recent copyright is no indication that the test is up-to-date in conception. In some instances a new copyright date covers such a small change as the issuance of an answer sheet to fit a new scoring service; in others, although the test has been reorganized, data collected on the original test are put forward in the new manual. To get norms for a restructured edition of the Stanford-Binet, records collected 20-odd years earlier were rescored according to the new plan. The use of the old data had a justification in this case, because of the cost of collecting a national standardization sample for an individual test. The Stanford-Binet authors had to reanalyze the old, expensively collected data or take a much thinner recent sample.

F. Scales and Norms

F1. Scales used for reporting scores should be so carefully described in the test manual as to increase the likelihood of accurate interpretation and the understanding of both the test interpreter and the subject. ESSENTIAL

F1.1. Standard scores should in general be used in preference to other derived scores. The system of standard scores should be consistent with the purposes for which the test is intended, and should be described in detail in the test manual. The reasons for choosing that scale in preference to other scales should also be made clear in the manual. VERY DESIRABLE

[Comment: The most widely used conventions are as follows: for a two-digit standard score, a mean of 50 and standard deviation of 10; for a one-digit standard score, a mean of 5 and a standard deviation of 2 (as in stanines). The foregoing are proposed as ways of standardizing practice among test developers. It is expected that institutions with established systems will continue to retain them as suited to their purposes. The manual should also specify whether the standard scores are linear transformations of raw scores or normalized.]

F1.2. Whenever it is suggested in the test manual that percentile scores are to be plotted on a profile sheet, the profile sheet should be based on the normal probability scale or some other appropriate nonlinear transformation. **VERY DESIRABLE**

F1.3. If grade norms are provided, tables for converting scores to standard scores or percentile ranks within each grade should also be provided in the test manual. DESIRABLE

[Comment: At the high school level, norms within courses (e.g., second-year Spanish) may be more appropriate than norms within grades.]

F2. If scales are revised, new forms added, or other changes made, the revised test manual should provide tables of equivalence between the new and the old forms. This provision is particularly important in cases where data are recorded on cumulative records. ESSENTIAL

[Comment: New forms of a test should be equated to recently determined standard score scales of other forms in order that the user may be confident that the scores furnished by the new forms are comparable with those of earlier forms.]

F3. Local norms are more important for many uses of tests than are published norms. In such cases the test manual should suggest appropriate emphasis on local norms and describe methods for their calculation. VERY DESIRABLE

F4. Except where the primary use of a test is to compare individuals with their own local group, norms should be published in the test manual at the time of release of the test for operational use. ESSENTIAL.

Figure 5.1.   Extract from the *Test Standards*
Copyright 1966, American Psychological Association and reproduced by permission.

Test Reviews

The trend toward improved test construction and manuals was accelerated by the work of Professor O. K. Buros, who began to release critical reviews of tests in 1934. These critical listings now take the form of *Mental Measurements Yearbooks,* the most recent of which appeared in 1965.

Nearly all tests currently marketed in English-speaking countries, and some program tests, are reviewed in the Buros series. Each test is examined by two or more specialists chosen because of their practical experience and technical knowledge. Reviewers discuss proper uses of the test and draw attention to any questionable claims made in the manual. Test reviews may also be found in journals, particularly *Journal of Counseling Psychology.* Although these reviews help in choosing tests, the purchaser must still judge tests for himself. He will find that reviewers sometimes disagree in judging a test, most often because they approach it from different points of view. Sometimes a reviewer gives much attention to rather petty faults, and the reader must weigh these criticisms against the merits of the test. On the other hand, reviewers occasionally fail to notice faults. Even with a well-balanced review of a particular test, the final decision to use it or not to use it depends on the specific situation, which only the prospective user knows.

We have already discussed some of the qualities that make a test suitable or unsuitable. Chapter 1 drew attention to the necessity of choosing a test the user is competent to give and interpret. Chapters 3 and 4 introduced other considerations, including clarity of directions, immunity to coaching, convenience of scoring, objectivity, and adequacy of norms. All these considerations are important because they affect directly or indirectly the power of the test to improve decisions.

The quality that most affects the value of the test, however, is its validity. Validity is high if a test gives the information the decision maker needs. No matter how satisfactory it is in other respects, a test that measures the wrong thing or that is wrongly interpreted is worthless. We shall devote the remainder of this chapter to the process of test validation and the information it produces.

4. *Compare with the preceding paragraph the following remark. "Validity is the ability of a test to predict something other than itself." (Cattell & Warburton, 1967, p. 32.)*

Types of Validation

A test that helps in making one decision may have no value at all for another. This means that we cannot ask the general question "Is this a valid test?"

The question to ask is "How valid is this test for the decision I wish to make?" or "How valid is the interpretation I propose for the test?"

Decisions are based on a person's expected future performance as predicted from the test score. If these expectations are confirmed, the test was useful; if what happens later is not consistent with the predictions, the test was worthless or harmful. In selection or classification, the psychologist wants to improve decisions. He wants to pick workers who turn out more work, students who learn more, parolees who do not commit crimes. To examine whether predictions are sound, one must make a follow-up study. The psychologist gives the test, makes his predictions, and waits to see what happens. He obtains a record of the outcome (foreman's rating, school grade, or probation officer's report, for example). This record, which we speak of as a criterion, he compares with the prediction. This is a straightforward empirical[1] check on the value of the test— a *criterion-oriented* or *predictive* validation.

Sometimes a test is proposed to substitute for some cumbersome method of collecting information already in use. If the existing method is considered useful for decision making, it is appropriate to ask whether the new test agrees with the present source of information. In this comparison, the existing procedure is accepted as giving the information desired. For example, tests intended for clinical diagnosis are compared with the judgments made by a psychiatrist who interviews each patient, or a test of proficiency in radar maintenance is compared with ratings made by shop supervisors. If there is agreement, the test measures what the other procedure does. If there is little agreement, the test may have value but it is not equivalent to the original procedure.

In studies like these, the two kinds of information are obtained concurrently, i.e., at very nearly the same time. Logically, predictive and concurrent validation are the same, and most writers apply the term *predictive* to both. Where one intends to emphasize that no time elapsed between measures, the study is spoken of as a *concurrent* validation.

The designer of a new test will suggest its validity by comparing it concurrently with an established test. A group test of mental ability is likely to be correlated with the familiar Stanford-Binet individual test. A test that agrees with the Binet test measures "whatever the Binet test measures" and may be relied upon for the same purposes. This procedure is helpful only if the test used as criterion is accepted as meaningful and important. There is little value in knowing that three questionnaires of "neurotic tendency" agree, if none of the tests measures anything save ability to see through the test and give a favorable self-description. Likewise, a psychologist who distrusts psychiatric diagnoses would hesitate to use them as a criterion for a personality test.

When tests are used to evaluate educational or therapeutic programs, a different kind of validation may be needed. The program is trying to produce a certain change in behavior; to evaluate its effectiveness, the tester needs to

---

[1] An *empirical* method involves collection and analysis of data. It is contrasted with purely logical methods of arriving at conclusions.

observe just that type of behavior. When a course is supposed to teach American geography, it is not fair to test its effectiveness by questions limited to the geography of New England. The tester interested in evaluation asks, "Does this test represent the behavior I consider important in its own right?" Instead of comparing scores with other scores as in empirical validation, he compares the test tasks with the content and behavior he wishes to know about. This process is called _content validation._ The content validity of the geography test would have to be studied by checking its items against an outline of the geographic concepts the students are intended to learn and the kinds of problems they are being trained to handle.

Sometimes a test is used to arrive at a description of the individual that will be used for many purposes. Sometimes, also, a test measures outcomes for scientific rather than immediately practical purposes. In these applications, the test results are translated into general psychological terms. Instead of reporting that an experimental treatment "has increased the score on the Jones test," the psychologist wants to make the broader interpretation that "anxiety" has increased. The concept _anxiety_ is part of a psychological theory. The theory describes what persons with strong anxiety tend to do under various conditions. Whenever a tester asks what a score means psychologically or what causes a person to get a certain test score, he is asking what concepts may properly be used to interpret the performance. This type of theoretical concept is called a _construct,_ and the process of validating such an interpretation is called _construct validation._ In order to show that a given construct applies to a test, it is necessary to derive hypotheses about test behavior from theory related to the construct and to verify them experimentally. The theory of "anxiety" accepted by the tester might include such expectations as the following: anxiety increases when subjects are exposed to a threat of electric shock; neurotics are more anxious than nonneurotics; anxiety is lowered by a certain drug; anxious persons set high goals for themselves. Each of these expectations can be tested by an experiment or a statistical study. Construct validation is much more complex than the other types of validation, as our later discussion will show.

Table 5.1 summarizes the types of validation.

With so many different ways to examine validity, each applying to a particular use or interpretation of the test, it is clear that no test developer can carry out all the studies that would be illuminating. The test user cannot expect the manual to provide exhaustive evidence, yet he does not wish to use a test whose validity is dubious. What can he legitimately demand of the test developer? The _Test standards_ indicate that the developer assumes the burden of proof whenever he recommends the test for a certain use. "The manual should report the validity of each type of inference for which the test is recommended." Most tests have a few principal uses for which their validity has been thoroughly studied, and this research answers the questions of the majority of test users. The user who wishes to apply the test in a novel way has to make his own validity studies to justify his interpretation.

Table 5.1. Questions asked in validation research

Question asked	Procedure	Principally applied to	Example
	CRITERION-ORIENTED		
How do measures of some valued performance (criterion) relate to the test scores?	Give test. Collect data on the criterion, ordinarily after the person has spent some time in training, on a job, or in therapy. There may be different treatments for different groups. Examine the correspondence of criterion scores to test scores.	(a) Tests used in selecting employees and students.	(a) Admission test for law students is checked against later marks.
		(b) Tests used in deciding what treatment should be given a patient or student.	(b) To find out what sort of persons respond well to an antidepressant drug, the drug is given to people with different personality test scores.
		(c) A test intended to substitute for a more cumbersome assessment procedure.	(c) Diagnosis of brain damage from Block Design performance is compared with a neurological examination.
	CONTENT		
Do the observations truly sample the universe of tasks or the situations they are claimed to represent?	Examine the test items and the responses called for. Compare with a full description of the universe the test is supposed to represent.	(d) Tests used to evaluate educational programs	(d) Content of a test of shorthand ability is compared with content of office correspondence.
		(e) Observation procedures in research on typical behavior.	(e) A schedule for observing what questions children put to their teachers is checked for representaton of types of lesson, time of day, etc.

Question asked	Procedure	Principally applied to	Example
	CONSTRUCT		
How can scores on the test be explained psychologically? Does the test measure the attribute it is said to measure?	Set up hypotheses regarding the meaning of test scores, stating how high scorers and low scorers are expected to differ, or what influences are expected to alter scores. Test the hypotheses one by one.	(f) Tests interpreted as measuring mental processes or personality traits. Includes tests used to describe the individual in diagnosis or guidance. Includes outcome measures in scientific research and educational evaluation.	(f) A test of art aptitude is studied to determine how largely scores depend on art training, on experience in Western culture, on mental set to be unconventional, etc. A measure of "suggestibility" is studied experimentally to see if scores are influenced by (e.g.) previous relations with the tester.

No matter how complete the test author's research, the person developing a selection or classification program should conduct validation research in his own situation. The psychologist or educator evaluating a training program must check out the content validity of the proficiency tests for that particular program. In this chapter we concentrate on understanding the material presented in test manuals. In Chapter 13 we shall discuss how the tester can conduct his own criterion-oriented validation studies. Construct validation will be illustrated as we study each type of test (particularly in Chapters 8 and 18).

The Bennett manual (Form AA) is fairly typical, though briefer than many recent manuals. It summarizes criterion-oriented studies made in industry and military training. These studies indicate that the test often has considerable predictive value for mechanical trades and engineering. The manual gives no information on the test as a predictor of school and college grades (but the manual for the DAT version, when it appeared several years later, covered this). Correlations of MCT with several intelligence tests and with other mechanical aptitude tests are reported. This feature informs the tester about the possibility of substituting MCT for one of the other tests, and clarifies whether the test is really giving new information. The uses proposed for MCT did not make content validation a central issue.

How well does this information fill the counselor's needs? Counselors need to advise students regarding many questions of vocational specialization, yet correlations are reported only for scattered occupations. It would be impossible to conduct separate validations for all the vocations various counselees will consider. The list would have to cover architecture, aeronautics and hydraulics, metalworking and woodworking, design, construction, maintenance, and so on ad infinitum. Even when a predictive study has been made for a specific occupation, one must recognize that not all jobs within the occupation make the same demands. The counselor therefore will rarely be able to translate an MCT score into a definite prediction of vocational success.

The counselor has to know what the "mechanical comprehension" measured here signifies. How much does it depend on specific training? This can be examined by finding out how much scores increase during a shop course or a physics course. Does it apply solely to mechanical-manipulative occupations, or to all work that requires reasoning about forces and motion? This can be judged from the available prediction studies. Are individual differences stable enough to justify long-range predictions? This calls for a long-term follow-up. Does mechanical comprehension imply skill in handling tools and machines? The answer comes from the comparison of MCT scores with scores on apparatus tests.

The Bennett AA manual does not include all this information. Older tests, in general, were published without comprehensive validation, and even the best manual must leave some questions unanswered. The modern DAT manual, after 57 pages of validity data, concludes with a statement urging the counselor to prepare expectancy tables for courses in his own school and for jobs in his own community. The test constructor is not expected to answer every last question about validity before publishing his test, but he is expected to give the test user a fair impression of the dependability of the interpretations he recommends.

5. *A typing test that has excellent content validity for the original user may have poor content validity for some other user. Illustrate this statement.*
6. *Why would it be valuable to find out "what a test of pharmacy aptitude measures," if we already know that it predicts success in pharmacy school?*

Validation Against a Criterion

The Criterion

An investigator studies predictive validity when his primary interest is in bettering some outcome. The outcome is what we want to improve by our professional decisions: the employee's production on a job, the patient's response to therapy, the counselee's satisfaction. In research on such matters, one collects evidence as to how good the outcome is; this report is called a *criterion*.

Suppose that a wholesale hardware concern wants to hire good salesmen. The outcome that interests the firm is the sales each man will make. For research, we need a numerical index of success. Perhaps "amount sold in 6 months" will serve. This criterion measure would be compared with test scores recorded before the men were hired, to learn how well the proposed test predicts. If the test is unrelated to the criterion, it is invalid for selecting salesmen for this firm. A single predictive study does little to clarify the psychological meaning of a test, but it does indicate the test's usefulness for one practical situation.

The hardest part of predictive validation is to obtain suitable criterion data. If the 6-month record does not really represent "selling success," the test has not been given a fair trial. Look at the weaknesses of the criterion suggested above. In the first place, it represents only the wholesale hardware business, so that at best we can judge the test for this one use; additional predictive studies will be required if the test is considered for hiring men to sell insurance or machine-tools. Although "amount sold" appears to be a fair basis for judging success, some men were assigned more desirable territory than others, so that sales do not reflect ability alone. Suppose we control this by comparing each man's sales with normal sales in his territory. We still have not considered the possible effect on business of variable factors, such as poor crops in one region. Another problem is that sales alone may not be what we desire from a salesman. A high-pressure salesman may build up sales on a first trip but, by overselling, create problems that will eventually harm the firm's business.

A common type of criterion is the rating or grade. Aptitude tests are validated against marks earned in school. Industrial predictors are validated against ratings by supervisors. These ratings are not entirely satisfactory as criteria. The judge may not know the facts about the person. Often a rating reflects the personal relation between man and supervisor rather than the quality of the man's work. When a test fails to predict a rating, it is hard to say whether this is the fault of the test or of the rating.

7. *Criticize each of the following criteria:*
   a. *Ratings of student teachers by their supervisors, as an index of teaching ability.*
   b. *Number of accidents a driver has per year, as an index of driver safety.*
   c. *Number of accidents a driver has per thousand miles, as an index of driver safety.*

8. *A test for preschool children is validated in three ways: (1) Intelligence is defined as ability to learn responses with which one has had no previous experience. The test items are examined and found to fit this definition. (2) Scores on the test, given at age 3, are found to be related to reading skill and vocabulary knowledge at the end of the first grade. (3) Scores on the test, given at age 3,*

Table 5.2.   Data on ten hardware salesmen

| Salesman | Test score | | | Criterion measure | Criterion rank C | Test rank | | |
	1	2	3			1	2	3
A	30	45	34	$25,000	6	4	7	7
B	34	64	35	38,000	2	2	3	5½
C	32	32	35	30,000	4	3	9	5½
D	47	52	31	40,000	1	1	5	9
E	20	74	36	7,000	10	9	1	4
F	24	50	40	10,000	9	7	6	1
G	27	53	37	22,000	7	5	4	3
H	25	36	30	35,000	3	6	8	10
I	22	71	32	28,000	5	8	2	8
J	16	28	39	12,000	8	10	10	2

are found to be related to scores on the Stanford-Binet test given at age 16.

a. *What possible uses of the test are warranted, on the basis of each of these studies?*

b. *Would it be possible for a test to show high validity by method (2) and to lack validity according to the other two procedures?*

9. *A study-habits inventory asks such questions as "Do you daydream when you should be studying?"*

a. *What criterion would you use to determine empirically whether the inventory really measures study habits?*

b. *What criterion would you use to determine whether the inventory predicts success in college?*

c. *Which validation study would be most useful?*

10. *Criticize the procedure indicated in the following report of a study of success of students who graduated from a teachers' college:*

> *"The correlation between all thirty of the predictor variables and the school superintendents' ratings was only 0.17, but that between the variables and marks earned during four years of college was 0.79. Since college marks were predictable on the basis of the thirty variables and the superintendents' ratings were not, the marks were substituted for the ratings as a criterion of success."*

Correlation Coefficients

A correlation coefficient is a statistical summary of the relation between two variables. It is the most common way of reporting the answer to such questions as the following: Does this test predict performance on the job? Do these two tests measure the same thing? Do the ranks of these people today agree with their ranks a year ago?

To illustrate, consider ten hardware salesmen who were given three tests when hired. After 6 months, when the criterion records are in, we have the information in the left portion of Table 5.2. The problem is to judge which test

Example

1. Begin with the pairs of scores to be studied.

Man A (30, 25,000)

2. Rank men from 1 to **N** (number of men) in each set of scores. (Note that the lowest man must have rank **N**, unless he ties with someone.)

Man A has ranks 4, 6
N = 10

3. Subtract the rank in the right-hand column from the one in the left-hand column. This gives the difference **D**. (As a check, make sure that this column adds to zero.)

Man A: 4–6 = −2

4. Square each difference to get **D²**

Man A: $(-2)^2 = (-2)(-2) = 4$

5. Sum this column to get ΣD^2

6. Apply the formula:

$$r = 1 - \frac{6(\Sigma D^2)}{N(N^2 - 1)}$$

$$r = 1 - \frac{6(36)}{10(100 - 1)}$$

$$= 1 - \frac{216}{990}$$

$$= 1 - .218$$

$$r = 0.782$$

Man	Scores Test	Scores Criterion (C)	Ranks Test	Ranks Criterion	Rank Difference (D)	Squared Difference (D²)
A	30	$25,000	4	6	−2	4
B	34	38,000	2	2	0	0
C	32	30,000	3	4	−1	1
D	47	40,000	1	1	0	0
E	20	7,000	9	10	−1	1
F	24	10,000	7	9	−2	4
G	27	22,000	5	7	−2	4
H	25	35,000	6	3	3	9
I	22	28,000	8	5	3	9
J	16	12,000	10	8	2	4
					$\Sigma D = 0$	$\Sigma D^2 = 36$

COMPUTING GUIDE 3. RANK-DIFFERENCE CORRELATION

is the best predictor. This is hard to judge by scanning the raw scores, since each test has a different range.

One way to simplify the data is to change them to ranks, as in the right portion of Table 5.2. (On test 3, two men tie. Since four men do better than these two, we consider these two as occupying the fifth and sixth positions and assign each one the rank 5½.) Now we see that E, poorest on the criterion, has very low rank on test 1, high on 2, average on 3. Man F, also poor as a salesman, is below the median on 1 and 2, but at the top in 3. Before reading ahead, study Table 5.2 to estimate how valid each test is for selecting hardware salesmen.

Rank correlation.   To obtain an index of agreement, we compute a correlation. A procedure useful in small studies is the rank-difference correlation. Computing Guide 3 shows the steps in determining r_{1C}, the correlation relating test 1 to the criterion C.

When the computations for all three tests are performed, we have these correlations between test and criterion:

$$r_{1C} = 0.782$$
$$r_{2C} = -0.090$$
$$r_{3C} = -0.754$$

A positive coefficient shows that high standing on the test goes with high standing on the criterion. A negative coefficient shows that high standing on the test goes with *low* standing on the criterion.

A zero coefficient means that one cannot predict the criterion from the test. A correlation of 1.00 or –1.00 shows perfect relationship; when this occurs, the criterion score (or rank) is predicted exactly. Test 1 identified the best salesman and the second-best accurately, but the third-best salesman ranked sixth on the test, which lowered the correlation. The larger the correlation, whether positive or negative, the more accurate the prediction. On test 3, a low score picks out a superior salesman. From these data we conclude that either test 1 or test 3 is a good predictor for this firm.

Product-moment correlation.   We have introduced the rank-difference correlation because it is easy to explain and compute, but it is not often used in professional work with test scores. Most prominent is the product-moment correlation, obtained directly from the scores themselves.

Pairs of scores can be plotted in a "scatter diagram." Figure 5.2 does this for some of the data of Table 5.2. We set up a chart with the first variable (test score) along the horizontal axis and the second variable (sales) along the vertical axis. Man A is plotted above 30 on the horizontal axis (test 1), and opposite $25,000 on the vertical axis (criterion). He can be seen that criterion scores correspond to test scores: as score 1 arises, C tends to rise.

Figure 5.3 shows scatter diagrams corresponding to various sizes of coefficient. There are two slanting lines in each diagram. One shows the expected

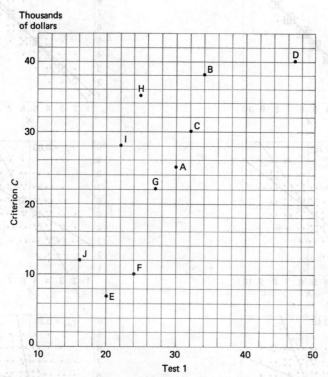

Figure 5.2. **Scatter diagram for test 1 and criterion C.**

average value of Y, for each value of X; the other (dashed line) shows the average X for each Y. These are *regression lines*. It is evident that a scatter diagram contains the same information as an expectancy table (p. 87). The line showing the average Y for each X is steep when the correlation is high, indicating a marked relation of outcome to test score. Observations fall near the regression line when the correlation is high. (For more realistic scatter diagrams, see pp. 224 and 422.)

When $r = 1.00$, one variable is predicted perfectly from the others. Everyone with a given X has the same Y score. With $r = 0.60$, prediction is only approximate. People who stand at 8 on X average near 7 on Y, but they spread from 3 to 9. An employer wishing not to lose any applicant whose Y score is 8 or better would have to hire everyone with an X score of 4 or better.

When the correlation is less than 1.00, one measure is influenced by some factor not affecting the other measure. Random errors of measurement lower correlation. So do causal factors not involved equally in both variables. For example, intelligence and school marks correlate only moderately because many

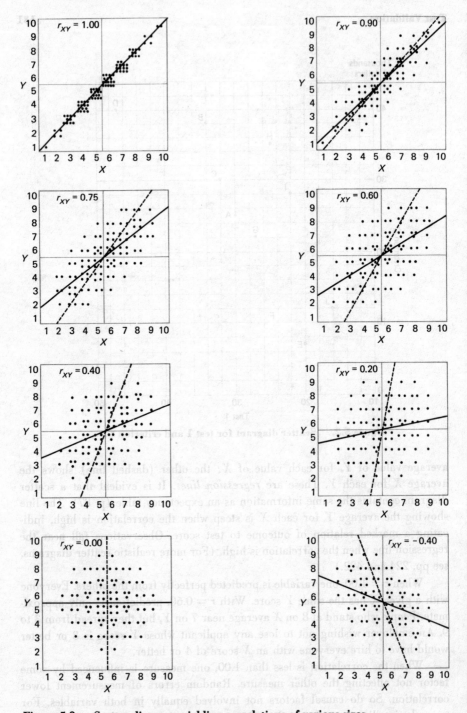

Figure 5.3.   Scatter diagrams yielding correlations of various sizes.

factors besides mental ability influence the marks: pupil effort, teacher bias, previous school learning, health, and so on.

It is incorrect to interpret a high correlation as showing that one variable "causes" the other. There are at least three possible explanations for a high correlation between variables A and B. A may cause or influence the size of B, B may cause A, or both A and B may be influenced by some common factor or factors. The correlation between vocabulary and reading may be taken as an example. Does good vocabulary cause one to be a good reader? Possibly. Or does ability to read well cause one to acquire a good vocabulary? An equally likely explanation. But to some extent both scores result from high intelligence, a home in which books and serious conversation abound, and superior teaching in the elementary schools. A theoretical understanding of the processes involved, or data from controlled experiments, permit us to draw conclusions about causes that underlie a correlation. Without such information, the only safe conclusion is that correlated measures are influenced by a common factor.

Results vary when we compute a statistic on different samples. Even if subjects are drawn at random from a single population, the correlation coefficients between two variables will differ from sample to sample. The larger the sample the more dependable the correlation, if the sample is random. Correlations may fluctuate a great deal from sample to sample. If the two scores correlate 0.30 in a large population, in ten random samples of 100 cases each the product-moment correlations could vary thus: 0.17, 0.47, 0.34, 0.31, 0.24, 0.39, 0.20, 0.25, 0.28, 0.45. If samples, instead of being random, come from different firms or communities, the fluctuation will be even greater.

Computing Guide 4 is provided primarily to add to the reader's understanding. There are many more efficient computing procedures, the choice depending on the calculating equipment available. The most common procedure employs a procedure a bit different from that of our computing guide, using raw scores rather than deviation scores; it arrives at the same result. In the computing guide it is evident that persons above the mean on one variable and below the mean on the other lower the correlation. A person who has a large positive deviation on both variables (or a large negative deviation on both) makes the coefficient higher.

11. *How large a correlation would you anticipate between the following pairs of variables?*
    a. *Age and annual income of men aged 20 to 50.*
    b. *Age in January, 1930, and age in March, 1950.*
    c. *Scores on two intelligence tests, given the same week.*
    d. *Annual income and number of children, among married urban men.*
    e. *Maximum and minimum temperature in Wichita, day by day for a year.*
12. *Compute rank correlations 2C and 3C.*
13. *How much would the rank correlation in Computing Guide 3 change if person J had been replaced by a person with score 21 and criterion $26,000?*

	Example
1. Begin with the pairs of scores to be studied.	Man A (30, 25,000)
2. Compute the mean for each column.	$M_X = 27.7$, $M_C = 24,700$
3. Form deviation scores x (test) and c (criterion) by subtracting the mean from each score.	Man A: $(x = 30 - 27.7 = 2.3;$ $c = 25,000 - 24,700 = 300)$
4. Compute x^2 and c^2.	Man A: $2.3^2 = 5.29$; $300^2 = 90000$
5. Multiply x by c to form xc.	Man A: $(2.3 \times 300 = 690)$
6. Sum the x^2, c^2, xc, x, and c columns. Use Σ to denote "sum of."	
7. Enter the sums in the following formula:	

$$r_{xc} = \frac{N\Sigma xc - \Sigma x \Sigma c}{\sqrt{(N\Sigma x^2 - (\Sigma x)^2)(N\Sigma c^2 - (\Sigma c)^2)}} \qquad \frac{10(685400)}{\sqrt{10(686.10)}\ \sqrt{10(1254100000)}}$$

$$= \frac{6854000}{82.8 \times 112000} = 0.740$$

Note: In practical calculation steps 2 and 3 would usually be omitted and calculations would be made from raw scores.

	Scores		Deviation scores			Squares and products	
							c^2	xc
Man	Test(X)	Criterion (C)	Test (x)	Criterion (c)	x^2	($\times$0000)	($\times$00)
A	30	$25,000	2.3	300	5.29	9	6.9
B	34	38,000	6.3	13,300	39.69	17689	837.9
C	32	30,000	4.3	5,300	18.49	2809	227.9
D	47	40,000	19.3	15,300	372.49	23409	2952.9
E	20	7,000	−7.7	−17,700	59.29	31329	1362.9
F	24	10,000	−3.7	−14,700	13.69	21609	543.9
G	27	22,000	−0.7	−2,700	.49	729	18.9
H	25	35,000	−2.7	10,300	7.29	10609	−278.1
I	22	28,000	−5.7	3,300	32.49	1089	−188.1
J	16	12,000	−11.7	−12,700	136.89	16129	1368.9
Sum			0	0	686.10	125410	6854.0

COMPUTING GUIDE 4.   PRODUCT-MOMENT CORRELATION

14. *Obtain a combined score by subtracting score 3 from score 1 for each man. Correlate ranks on this with the criterion. Would it improve prediction to use both tests?*

15. *Transform the information in Figure 4.3 (p. 88) for the mechanical aptitude test into a scatter diagram. (The criterion has only two values, average-or-above, and below-average.)*

16. *Prepare scatter diagrams relating tests 2 and 3 to the criterion.*

17. *What is the expectation of earning above average on Y, if a person has a score of 8 on X? Determine this for each value of* r *in Figure 5.3.*

18. *What possible causal relations might underlie each of the following correlations?*
    a. *Between amount of education and annual income of adults (assume that* r *is positive).*
    b. *Between average intelligence of children and size of family (assume that* r *is negative).*
    c. *Between Sunday-school attendance and honesty of behavior (assume that* r *is positive).*

19. *Beginning with the information in Figure 5.3, prepare an "expectancy table" similar to Table 4.1, corresponding to each of the following values of* r: *1.00, .90, .40, .20.*

Typical Validity Coefficients

Correlations between test and criterion are called validity coefficients. Table 5.3 lists fairly typical coefficients of predictive and concurrent validity, taken, in each case, from the test manual. Some test-criterion combinations exhibit much greater validity than others. The variation in results for the Short Employment Tests should be particularly noted in Table 5.3.

It is unusual for a validity coefficient to rise above 0.60, though that is far from perfect prediction. Although we would like higher coefficients, any positive correlation indicates that predictions from the test will be more accurate than guesses. Whether a validity coefficient is high enough to warrant prediction from the test depends on such practical considerations as the urgency of improved prediction, the cost of testing, and the cost and validity of the selection methods already in use. To the question "What is a good validity coefficient?" the only sensible answer is, "The best you can get." If a criterion can be predicted only with validity 0.20, the test may still make an appreciable practical contribution. Naturally, a greater contribution is required to justify an expensive, inconvenient procedure than an inexpensive one.

In interpreting a correlation, the range of the group studied must be considered. The correlation is smaller in a select group than in a group containing a wide range of ability. High-school achievement would predict college marks with a validity much above .60 if all high-school graduates, including those with poor records, went on to college. The validity of the Iowa Tests for advising pupils whether to plan on going to college is higher than the instrument's validity for selecting among the high-school graduates who apply for college admission, because the latter group is already restricted. One demonstration of this point is found in Figure 5.4, which tabulates validity coefficients for 94 law schools. The

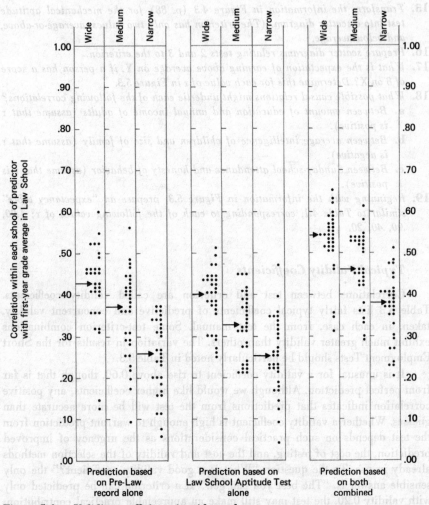

Figure 5.4. Validity coefficients in wide- and narrow-range groups.
Coefficients for 94 law schools are classified according to the spread of talent in the entering class. Arrow indicates median correlation. Wide-range classes have a large s.d. on LSAT (74.4 to 97), and narrow-range classes a small s.d. *Unpublished data supplied by W. B. Schrader. For a report on a less complete study, see Schrader, 1968.*

schools were divided into three groups, according to the variation of the entering class on the aptitude test. A narrow-range group is one that can select severely, filling its class with an excellent quality of applicant, or one that tends to draw applicants from only a narrow range of ability. It is evident that, with either the aptitude test or the previous grade record as a predictor, the validity coefficients are considerably higher in the wide-range group. Note also the very wide variation of validity coefficients; in some schools the test has validity above 0.40, and in some schools the validity is near zero. (For further discussion of the effects of range on validity, see pp. 431 f.)

Time considerations. In evaluating relations between a test and a criterion, the time separating the two measurements must be taken into account. As a general rule, the greater the time-lapse, the less the correlation; but some predictions hold up over long periods.

A short-term study indicates an upper limit to the long-term predictive value of the test in similar samples. Sometimes an employer or counselor uses a test to make long-range predictions even though there have been no long-term studies. An employer who finds that certain tests sort out his present workers in the same order that the criterion does is likely to consider it a sound basis for selecting further employees. If, however, the best present employees have changed during their years on the job, a long-term prediction on new workers might be invalid. A "concurrent" correlation, between two measures at about the same time, is not secure evidence that the test predicts into the future.

Concurrent studies were appropriate when Strong produced his questionnaire to identify vocational interests; he would have had to wait twenty years to find out if the test really predicted what work each college student would like in middle adulthood. Strong published his inventory in 1928, offering as evidence of validity the fact that the scores distinguished middle-aged men of different occupations from each other. For instance, the Physician scores of doctors averaged much higher than those of nondoctors. But the purpose of the test is not to find out whether a middle-aged man is a doctor; it is to find out if a young man will, as he grows older, be satisfied with that career. If the direction of a man's interest at 40 is the same as at 20, then the concurrent validation on older men does show that the test is relevant to vocational choice at 20. Until long-term follow-up studies were made, users of the Strong test had to assume stability of interests. After publication of the test, Strong continued to accumulate evidence by following men for 20 years or more and by 1954 was able to verify that the test indeed makes fairly valid predictions over a long period.

A concurrent study may be carried out by administering the test to persons whose criterion performance can be observed immediately. An aptitude test designed for entering medical students may be applied to men who are graduating from medical school and compared with their grades. If the test fails to identify those with superior grades, it will probably be discarded without investing several years in a follow-up study of entering students. A test intended to identify potential neurotics is checked first by determining whether it distinguishes present neurotic cases from some nonneurotic group such as medical patients coming to the same clinic. A predictive study comes later.

One need not be unduly suspicious of concurrent data; under many circumstances concurrent and predictive correlations agree well enough. A number

Table 5.3. Illustrative validity coefficients

Test	Sample	Criterion	Type of validity	Coefficient
California Short-Form Test of Mental Maturity	100 children referred to a guidance department	Wechsler individual test	Concurrent	0.77 for total score
Iowa Tests of Educational Development	634 students in six Iowa colleges tested in grade 9	Grade point averages as college freshmen	Predictive	0.58
Short Employment Tests:	51 operators of proof machines in a large bank	Supervisor's merit ratings of job performance	Concurrent	
Verbal				0.15
Number				0.25
Clerical				0.37
Short Employment Tests:	80 skilled operators of bookkeeping machines in a bank	Records of production on ten days	Not stated	
Verbal				0.10
Number				0.26
Clerical				0.34
Short Employment Tests:	262 students in a one-year secretarial training course	Satisfactory completion of course vs. noncompletion or noncertification	Predictive	
Verbal				0.15
Number				0.48
Clerical				0.47
Short Employment Tests:	52 stenographers and clerks in an industrial concern	Ratings of job performance	Predictive	
Verbal				0.45
Number				0.08
Clerical				0.31
Thorndike Dimensions of Temperament	147 graduate students in education	Self-ratings on same dimensions	Concurrent	0.43–0.73 for ten scores
Thorndike Dimensions of Temperament	Students in a residential unit; five groups of about 60 each	Ratings of subject by acquaintances	Concurrent	0.24–0.49 for ten scores

of correlations with achievement measures are reported in the 1966 manual for the SRA High School Placement Test. The "concurrent" measures were four months apart, with the criterion collected first; the "predictive" measure was collected nine months before the criterion. While there are differences between paired values for the same high-school class, the concurrent correlation is the smaller of the two about half the time. A similar report in the employment setting comes from the U. S. Employment Service. In some 70 studies of diverse occupations, validities for subtests of GATB (described in Chapter 11) averaged 0.20 against concurrent job-proficiency criteria and 0.22 against similar criteria collected some (unstated) time after testing. Such agreement can be expected when (a) one sample is not more restricted than the other; (b) the abilities under test are sufficiently developed for ranks to be fairly stable; and (c) the elapsed time for the prediction is not extreme, or there has been no radical intervention following the predictive testing.

While we have spoken of concurrent studies as giving an "upper limit" estimate, there are times when the concurrent study gives too low a value. When the concurrent-criterion group has survived training and a period of service on the job, dropouts and discharges have removed many poor men from the sample. The test is not given credit for its ability to identify such men in advance. Sometimes the concurrent-criterion group covers a wide range of age and education, and higher ratings tend to be given to men with more seniority. But these men, out of school for a long time, will not do so well on the test and the test looks bad. When the test is applied to current applicants who are much the same in age, validity might be fine.

Example of validity information. Let us now examine some of the data given in the DAT manual, for that version of MCT. The data offered include correlations with subsequent course grades, a 4-year follow-up of school achievement, and a follow-up of post-high-school careers. Only a brief extract can be considered here.

Table 5.4 gives some of the coefficients relating mechanical comprehension to course grades in science and shop. It is obvious that one cannot speak of "the validity" of a test for a certain field, save as a shorthand expression for a general trend. The variation of coefficients is great. Many explanations can be offered: sampling fluctuations, differences in course content, differences in reliability of grading, differences in level of ability, etc. Figure 5.5 demonstrates even more clearly the similar radical fluctuations among validities against industrial criteria for repairmen in industry.

Data from many different studies have been summarized here. Samples were sometimes small, but most of the variation probably comes from differences in job requirements or in the nature of the group tested. Whenever many coefficients are obtained for the same test against the same type of criterion, variation such as this is found. Only when work or instructional conditions are highly standardized is a second validity coefficient likely to duplicate a first. When training follows a uniform plan, when the level of ability is held constant by selection, and when the criterion is based on objectively measured performance, validity coefficients are as stable as the size of the sample allows. It is because of situation differences that the tester must validate the test in his own school or factory, or must fall back on a psychological rather than a purely statistical interpretation.

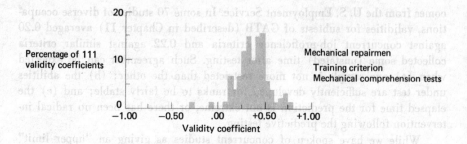

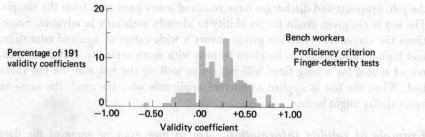

Figure 5.5.   Tabulation of validity coefficients from different studies of the same occupation.
Ghiselli, 1966, p. 29.

While the publisher is expected to include representative validity studies in the manual, much further evidence accumulates after the test is distributed. Only a thorough search of professional journals can locate all this information. Among the journals in which criterion-oriented validations are reported are *Educational*

Table 5.4.   Validity of the Mechanical Reasoning Test as a predictor of course grades for boys

Course	Grade	Location	Time between test and marks	Number of cases	Validity coefficient
Industrial arts	9	Mt. Vernon, N.Y.	1 year	67	0.39
	9	Worcester, Mass.	4 months	89	0.20
	9	Worcester, Mass.	1 year	79	0.05
Woodworking	10	Independence, Mo.	3 months	42	0.30
General science	9	Mt. Vernon, N.Y.	1 year	84	0.19
	9	Columbia, Mo.	8 months	88	0.50
Physics	11	Schenectady, N.Y.	3½ years	42	0.47
	—	White Plains, N.Y.	1–2 years	41	0.41
	12	Edgerton, Wisc.	½ year	27	−0.32

SOURCE: DAT manual, 1966, p. 5–13, pp. A–5 ff.

and Psychological Measurement, Journal of Applied Psychology, and *Personnel Psychology.*

20. *How long a time should elapse between test and criterion measurement when*
    a. *the U.S. Employment Service wishes to test men to determine which ones have had enough experience to be referred to contractors who have vacancies for electricians?*
    b. *a pencil-paper test is proposed for identifying students entering junior high school who have emotional difficulties and should be singled out for counseling?*
21. *How can you account for the difference in size between the two sets of validity coefficients for Thorndike Dimensions of Temperament (Table 5.3)?*
22. *Which of the following describes concurrent validation, and which describes predictive validation? In which instances would some other time interval between measurement and collection of criterion data be more informative?*
    a. *The Short Employment Tests are found to correlate 0.91 with the General Clerical Test, which has been used for some time as a predictor of job success.*
    b. *A manual for the Henmon-Nelson Test of Mental Ability reports correlations with high-school course marks assigned one month later.*
    c. *A correlation is calculated to determine how well a certain test distinguishes patients diagnosed as schizophrenic from those diagnosed as brain-damaged.*
    d. *School records of delinquents and nondelinquents in high school are searched to learn what scores collected in the elementary grades correlate with present delinquent status.*
23. *A test of ability to understand spoken words is validated by administering it to first-graders at the end of the year, and correlating it with their reading ability at that time. The coefficient is fairly high. Would you expect a similarly high predictive-validity coefficient*
    a. *if the test is used at the start of the first grade to predict end-of-year reading?*
    b. *if the test is used at the end of the first grade to predict response of poor readers to a special remedial reading program?*
    c. *if the test is used with 4-year-olds, to predict later success in grade 1 reading?*
24. *Would the attitude of present employees, taking a test in a concurrent-validation experiment, be the same as the attitude of applicants taking the test?*
25. *Some MCT coefficients are as high as 0.50. With this validity, what is the likelihood that a person who is above average on the test will be above average on the criterion? (Use Figure 5.2)*
26. *How do you account for the fact that the validity of the MCT as a predictor in physics is not higher than 0.50?*
27. *What facts might the principal of the school in Worcester obtain to determine why MCT predicted shop grades poorly, as compared to results in some other schools? Should these facts be included in the test manual?*
28. *Account for the variation in validity coefficients for industrial repairmen found by Ghiselli.*
29. *The 1967 manual for the Adaptability Test, intended for industrial selection, reports validation studies by reporting that 77 per cent of clerical employees in*

the raw-score range 25–33 had been previously rated A by their superiors, 64 per cent in the range 22–24, 55 per cent in the range 19–21, and so on. Evaluate this unorthodox form of report on validity.

Construct Validation

Construct validation is an analysis of the meaining of test scores in terms of psychological concepts or "constructs" (Cronbach & Meehl, 1955). Every test is to some degree impure, and very rarely does it measure exactly what its name implies. Yet the test cannot be interpreted until we know what factors determine scores. As one experienced clinician has said (Kent, 1937, pp. 422–423),

When a child of reading age is referred to the clinic because of his failure to learn to read, it is of the first importance to ascertain whether his mental capacity is or is not within normal limits. A composite test which contains reading matter . . . discriminates against the subject whose inability to read is due to any cause other than mental retardation. A test which calls for oral response discriminates very seriously against the child who by reason of speech defect or impediment is unable to make himself understood. It is little more than a farce to use a timed test or a test containing timed items for a psychotic subject whose mental processes are pathologically slowed up. What we measure by the test may be significant, but it is something quite other than what the test is intended to measure.

Such items as this writer criticizes would probably correlate with criteria of school success, and would probably be judged to have "content validity" as a sample of significant adaptive performances. The difficulty is that the test cannot be interpreted as a measure of a coherent psychological quality.

Sometimes the tester starts with a test that he wishes to understand better. Sometimes he starts with a concept for which he wishes a measuring instrument. The interpretation of a test is built up very gradually, and probably is never complete. As knowledge develops, we arrive at a more complete listing of the influences that affect the test score, and at some estimate of the strength of each influence. At present, the interpretation of even the best-established psychological tests falls far short of the ideal—this, because theories of ability and personality are incomplete and hazy.

Whereas predictive validity is examined in a single experiment, construct validity is established through a long-continued interplay between observation, reasoning, and imagination. First, perhaps, imagination suggests that construct A accounts for the test performance. The investigator reasons, "If that is so, then people with a high score should have characteristic X." An experiment is performed, and if this expectation is confirmed, the interpretation is supported. But as various deductions are tested, some of them prove to be inaccurate. The proposed interpretation must be altered either by invoking a different concept, by introducing an additional concept, or by altering the theory of the concept itself. The process of construct validation is the same as that by which scientific theories are developed (Cronbach, 1970).

The user of the test wants to know how the test can be interpreted, and how confidently. The manual should indicate what interpretation the author advises, and should summarize the available evidence from all types of studies relevant to this interpretation. If the user wishes to make some other interpretation, he must examine all the evidence on the test in the light of his own theory.

There are three parts to construct validation:

Suggest what constructs might account for test performance. This is an act of imagination based on observation or logical study of the test.

Derive testable hypotheses from the theory surrounding the construct. This is a purely logical operation.

Carry out an empirical study to test one hypothesis after another.

The actual sequence of operations need not be so neatly ordered. Often one accumulates experience with a test before offering an interpretation. Sometimes the test is used for a long time before any theory is developed around it. This was true, indeed, for MCT.

What do we mean when we talk of explaining performance on MCT? Essentially, we mean being able to state what influences affect the score and what influences do not. Once it was thought that there were three "intelligences"—verbal, mechanical, and social. To validate the interpretation that the MCT measures "mechanical intelligence," we would have to know what this quality is. If it is said that mechanical intelligence is an inborn ability to perform all tasks involving apparatus, we can begin research. We find that the MCT correlates 0.68 with a pencil-and-paper test of reasoning with forms, but only 0.08 to 0.39 with various dexterity tests. We are inclined, therefore, to interpret it as a measure of nonverbal problem solving rather than of manipulative performance. When we find that boys do much better than girls, we become suspicious of the view that the aptitude is inborn. Perhaps it represents experience with mechanics, or even knowledge acquired in school. Research on that point shows that scores increase only a little after a course in physics. Hence scores may depend on experience, but not on training in theory.

It is necessary not merely to identify an influence but to find out how strong it is. The writer once suspected that much of the MCT score depends on knowledge of a few specific principles (e.g., gears, levers), each of which is involved in several items. But when separate scores were obtained on each type of item, these scores correlated highly. Since a person high on gear problems was high on other items, it was unnecessary to introduce the concept of subtypes of mechanical comprehension. Such specific knowledge could account for only a tiny part of the differences among persons.

It is already evident that no single type of research is used in construct validation. The following incomplete tabulation of procedures indicates the diversity of methods and shows how each is relevant to MCT.

• Inspection of items. This is sufficient to rule out some explanations; thus it is easily seen that neither arithmetic nor verbal reasoning affects scores.

It is also seen that the machines illustrated are those common in Western culture, not in primitive Africa; this reminds us to consider cultural background in interpreting the test outside industrial nations.

• Administration of test to individuals who "think aloud." This may show that quite irrelevant features of the test (e.g., an obscure drawing) affect the score. It may show that some people succeed by an intuitive perception of answers that others reach by painstaking logic. This would suggest that a good score means different things for different persons.

• Correlation with practical criteria. Learning what jobs MCT predicts clarifies what types of mechanical work it relates to.

• Correlation with other tests (and factor analysis). If MCT correlates highly with a general mental test, it need not be interpreted in terms of a special mechanical aptitude. As a matter of fact, MCT performance does depend to a substantial degree on general mental ability and spatial reasoning.

• Internal correlations. The study of items based on different mechanical principles, described above, is of this type.

• Studies of group differences. The comparison of boys and girls is an example.

• Studies of the effect of treatment on scores. Training in physics proved not to affect MCT greatly.

• Stability of scores on retest. If scores are unstable, one could not interpret mechanical comprehension as a lasting, vocationally significant aptitude. An obtained correlation of 0.69 between ninth- and twelfth-grade scores for boys promises a reasonable degree of stability, but also shows that rank in this aptitude is far from fixed.

To defend the proposition that a test measures a certain variable defined by a theory, one looks basically for two things. The first is *convergence* of indicators. There need to be two or more different kinds of data that are regarded as suitable evidence that a person is high or low on the variable. If these indicators agree, despite their surface dissimilarity, we place greater faith in the proposed theoretical interpretation. The fact that the maze test correlates with a verbal reasoning test tends to support the view that both of them are measuring some general intellectual ability. The second kind of evidence is *divergence* of indicators that are supposed to represent different constructs. If a test is said to measure "ability to reason with numbers," it should not rank pupils in the order a test of sheer computation gives, because the computation test cannot reasonably be interpreted as a reasoning test. The test interpretation would also be challenged if the correlation with a test of verbal reasoning is very high, because this would suggest that general reasoning ability accounts for the ranking, so that specialized ability to reason with numbers is an unnecessary concept. These and other aspects of construct validation will become clearer as we examine validation studies on particular tests.

30. *Kohs (1923, pp. 168 ff.) wished to argue that the Block Design test measured "intelligence," defined as "ability to analyze and synthesize." He then offered the following types of evidence (plus others) for his claim. How does each of these bear on construct validity? (The Stanford-Binet test was at that time recognized as the best available measure of intelligence but was thought possibly to depend too heavily on verbal ability and school training.)*

  a. *Logical analysis of the "mental processes" required by the items.*
  b. *Increase in average score with each year of age.*
  c. *Correlations as follows:*

Binet score with age	*0.80*
BD score with age	*0.66*
BD score with Binet score	*0.81*

  d. *Correlations:*

Binet score with teachers' estimates of intelligence	*0.47*
BD score with teachers' estimates of intelligence	*0.23*

  e. *Correlations:*

Binet score with vocabulary	*0.91*
BD score with vocabulary	*0.77*

  f. *Correlations between successive trials:*
    on Binet 0.91; on BD, 0.84.

31. *Which of the variables in Kohs' study are acceptable as criteria of pure intelligence?*

Content Validation

Tests are often thought of as samples from a universe of observations that would be of interest. A reading test presents paragraphs of the kind the college student will need to comprehend. Observations of teaching skill sample a range of lessons and observers. A questionnaire on cultural interests touches on a limited number of cultural opportunities, out of a much larger number of possibly relevant items. Judging the adequacy of the content of the test is the process called content validation. Adequacy of content is especially important for tests that measure outcomes of education or training.

Adequacy of content is attained by defining the universe appropriately and representing the universe fairly in the test. The definition ought to cover (1) the kinds of tasks, stimuli, or situations over which the universe ranges; (2) the kinds of response the observer or scorer ought to count; and (3) the injunction to the subject. Change in any one of these changes the nature of the task. It is impossible to defend any one universe definition as correct. For some purposes one would want to confine reading selections to text material, and for other purposes one would want the universe to range over fiction, newspapers, and instruction manuals. But if the definition is made clear the prospective user can decide whether the test aims at the universe he is interested in.

Sampling is best guaranteed by systematically mapping out subdivisions

Table 5.5.   Correlations of tests having similar form
              and tests having similar content

	Correlation	Correlation corrected for unreliability
Tests similar in form, different in content:		
Verbal tests: mechanical vs. electrical	0.63	0.79
Pictorial tests: mechanical vs. electrical	0.64	0.86
Tests similar in content, different in form:		
Mechanical: verbal vs. pictorial	0.61	0.71
Electrical: verbal vs. pictorial	0.51	0.74
Tests different in both form and content:		
Mechanical verbal vs. electrical pictorial	0.49	0.63
Electrical verbal vs. mechanical pictorial	0.45	0.59
Internal-consistency reliability coefficients:		
Mechanical verbal	0.89	
Mechanical pictorial	0.82	
Electrical verbal	0.71	
Electrical pictorial	0.67	

SOURCE: Conrad, 1944.

of the universe and collecting the desired number of items for each subdivision. This prevents such faults as an overemphasis on passages from economics texts, or selection of passages that are too simple to be representative. Test manuals for achievement tests often describe the process by which a suitable distribution of content was achieved.

The form of the task is as important as the content. A measure of knowledge is not valid, for instance, if the person who knows a fact misses an item about it because of verbal difficulties. The Navy Mechanical Knowledge Test contained four types of items: mechanical facts, tested verbally; mechanical facts, tested pictorially; electrical facts, tested verbally; and electrical facts, tested pictorially. Similar content produced lower correlations than similar form (Table 5.5). In other words, the form of the items largely determined the score. Another study provides even stronger evidence that the verbal element in tests may be undesirable. Training of Navy gunners had been validly evaluated by scores made in operating the guns. As an economical substitute, verbal and pictorial tests were developed. Identical information was tested in the two forms, the same question being asked in words alone or by means of pictures supplemented by words. Questions dealt with parts of the gun, duties of the crew, appearance of tracers when the gun was properly aimed, etc. The pictorial test had a correlation of 0.90 with instructors' marks based on gun operation, whereas the validity of the verbal test was only 0.62. The verbal test was in large measure a reading test; it correlated 0.59 with a Navy reading test, while the picture test correlated only 0.26 with reading (Training Aids Section, 1945).

Speed is relevant and important in tests of typing attainment or reading facility, or in tests of arithmetic for cashiers. Speed is irrelevant when we wish to know how large a pupil's vocabulary is, how much science he knows, or how accurately he can reason. Speeding can usually be justified in proficiency tests only if the test is intended to predict success in a task where speed is helpful.

Perhaps the most general maxim to ensure content validity is this: *no irrelevant difficulty*. Reading is irrelevant to proficiency in gunnery. Reading of long sentences is irrelevant to the task of messenger boy, but reading everyday phrases is not (see Figure 9.3). Wherever a task can be simplified without making it a false example of the universe, it should be simplified.

Some test constructors try to make items harder by offering treacherous alternatives or by requiring fine discriminations, because they believe that a good test "spreads out people." But where content validity is the aim, discrimination among persons is not. If every applicant for the job of messenger has enough reading ability to cope with the tasks of that job, it is improper to discriminate on the basis of a hard reading test, and so to benefit the better-educated applicant.

The correlation of the item with the whole test is sometimes examined, and low-correlating items dropped. Thus Bennett, in making the new forms S and T of MCT, tried 180 items (some new, some taken from older forms with or without revision). When these were given to a suitable population of boys in the later years of high school, item scores were correlated with the total score on the items taken. No student took more than a third of the items. Only 136 items had correlations greater than 0.20, and the final forms were chosen from these items to get the desired degree of interform similarity and difficulty. Items on electricity rarely survived this screening because of their difficulty; evidently understanding of electrical phenomena is something boys do not pick up through everyday experience. Items "on extraterrestrial events" did not correlate with the pool as a whole and they too were discarded. Persons who understand the effects of low gravity may or may not be particularly knowledgeable about the forces one deals with in daily life.

Dropping items with low correlations may *reduce* content validity. The chief value of the statistical analysis is to point out ambiguities. A badly written item that confuses good students has no place in the test. The test constructor who examines an item with an unsatisfactory correlation may see a flaw that explains the errors of good students: a double negative, a supposedly true statement that the critical reader can find an exception to, a too-plausible alternative answer, etc. If such a flaw is found, the item should be rewritten. Dropping a particular item probably will not spoil the content validity of the test. The danger is that many of the poorly constructed items will fall in the same content area. When they are dropped the test loses its representativeness.

The low correlation may indicate that the item differs psychologically from the bulk of the test. A proficiency test usually samples mixed content. Dropping unusual items "purifies" the test, but the instrument then no longer represents the intended universe. A person might master the verbal portions of chemistry and still be badly confused on the quantitative parts of the course (such as balancing equations). To drop the quantitative sections just because they correlate less with the total than do verbal items makes the test a false sample of the content. On the other hand, if a question correlates poorly with the total because it requires knowledge of a certain chemical compound that few pupils have read about, the item ought to be replaced. The special content it brings in is an irrelevant difficulty.

Many popular testing techniques allow response styles to affect scores. A *response style* is a habit or a momentary set causing the subject to earn a different score from the one he would earn if the same items were presented in a different form. In true-false tests particularly, some people have the habit of saying "true" when in doubt, while others are characteristically suspicious and respond "false" when uncertain. If the tester has included a large proportion of true statements in his test, the acquiescent student will earn a fairly good score even if his knowledge is limited. Other response styles include tendency to gamble, working for speed rather than accuracy, and use of a particular style in essay tests.

We have spoken of defining a universe and sampling from it. This is a pleasing and logical ideal, but test construction rarely reduces to such simple terms. Most often the test constructor has some general idea of the task or situation he wishes to observe the subject in, but he cannot give a neat definition. An investigator wants to measure sociability of preschool children: Can he catalog the situations in which sociable behavior arises? Can another investigator list all the human relations problems a foreman should be able to deal with? Can a third truly define the universe of situations in which scientific reasoning is to be shown by a science student? Obviously not.

Examining content validity therefore requires judging whether each item—and the distribution of items as a whole—covers what the tester wants to measure. This judgment rests on the test user more than on the test author. The pattern set by the test author will rarely correspond perfectly to what the tester intended to measure. How close a correspondence should be demanded is a highly subjective judgment, unless there happens to have been a correlational study showing whether one performance can substitute for something a bit different.

32. *A tester wants to measure attitude toward blacks, so as to compare schools having different programs of student activities. What is the universe from which he will draw test items?*

33. *Skill in the use of library reference materials is to be measured at the end of a college freshman course. Define a universe of tasks from which the test might be drawn.*

34. *The Morse code consists of a short alphabet of characters. The receiver must respond to units made up of several characters in rapid succession; the most difficult part of the task may be to separate one letter from the next.*
   a. *Describe an appropriate test for a person learning to receive ordinary nonsecret communication in English.*
   b. *Describe an appropriate test for a person learning to receive secret (encoded) messages of the form* GFVG JHBI YGTA FBSJ. . . .
35. *In a written test for drivers, how could the tester decide how many questions to devote to speed laws, how many to safety rules, how many to interpretation of signals, etc.? Would the decision reached have any effect on a learner's chance of success? Would it have any effect on the way he studies for the test?*
36. *A test is carefully balanced to cover the kinds of knowledge and skill in high-school physics that the college physics course expects students to have. A teacher finds that his emphasis is distributed quite differently. Is the test a proper basis for grading students? For decisions about college admission? For judging the adequacy of the high-school course?*

SUGGESTED READINGS

Cronbach, Lee J. Test validation. In R. L. Thorndike (Ed.), *Educational measurement.* Washington: American Council on Education, 1970. (In press)
   A thorough discussion of problems of validation with emphasis on educational tests. The sections on validation of descriptive interpretations will be especially useful in connection with the present chapter.

French, John W. Validation of new item types against four-year academic criteria. *Journal of Educational Psychology,* 1958, *49,* 67–76.
   This predictive study compares different types of tests for college applicants in terms of their power to predict grades and successful completion of college work. The study is unusual because of the large number of measures used, the large sample in each college, and the repetition of the experiment in many colleges. Note particularly the degree to which results differ for different criteria and different colleges.

Glaser, Robert, & Klaus, David. Proficiency measurement: assessing human performance. In R. M. Gagné (Ed.), *Psychological principles in system development.* New York: Holt, Rinehart and Winston, 1962. Pp. 419–474.
   This paper, written from the perspective of training research rather than the classroom, indicates factors making for content validity, and suggests superior methods of constructing and using proficiency tests.

Peak, Helen. Problems of objective observation. In L. Festinger & D. Katz (Eds.), *Research methods in the behavioral sciences.* New York: Holt, Rinehart and Winston, 1953. Pp. 243–299.
   This chapter, directed toward the social scientist choosing a measurement procedure for a research project, discusses the qualities that make a procedure satisfactory. Peak outlines many methods used in establishing construct validity.

Validity. *Standards for educational and psychological tests and manuals.* Washington: American Psychological Association, 1966. Pp. 12–24. (Reprinted in Jackson & Messick, 1967; abridged in Gronlund, 1968; and Barnette, 1968.)

This section of the recommendations introduces the four types of validity, lists information about validity to be included in test manuals, and gives specific examples of good and bad practice. It is suggested that the reader compare the manual of some recent test with these recommendations.

Other Characteristics
Desired in Tests

An Interpretation of "Error of Measurement"

In a 3-minute work sample Mary types 162 words, or 54 words per minute; how well does this figure represent Mary's skill? Suppose the teacher requires typing at 50 w.p.m. before a student is allowed to study shorthand. Is Mary above this level? Or would she be likely to average below 50 if we measured more thoroughly? Mary produced 65 w.p.m. last week. Does today's score of 54 show that she has declined in skill, perhaps having changed her technique for the worse? Or is the change no more than a commonplace "error of measurement"?

No single observation is entirely representative of the person. The obtained score indicates only roughly the level of the person's ability or typical behavior. To know how trustworthy it is, we examine the consistency among measurements. Consistency can be checked by applying the same test repeatedly or by using similar tests.

Test scores vary from one measurement to another. Attention and effort change from moment to moment. Over longer periods, score changes come from physical growth, learning, changes in health, and personality change. If we employ different test items for each measurement, another type of variation is introduced. The person who is lucky on one trial, finding items that are easy for him, will encounter unfamiliar items on some other trial and earn a lower score. To these factors must be added the unaccountable "chance" effects. Chance effects enter even when we use the same procedure twice in rapid succession; the two scores differ to some extent because of guessing and instantaneous lapses of attention.

The decision that a student has completed a course or that a patient is ready for termination of therapy must not be seriously influenced by chance errors, temporary variations in performance, or the tester's choice of questions. An erroneous favorable decision may be irreversible and may harm the person or the community. Even when reversible, an erroneous unfavorable decision is unjust, disrupts the person's morale, and perhaps retards his development. Research, too, requires dependable measurement. An experiment is not very informative if an observed difference could be accounted for by chance variation. The less accurate the measuring instrument, the harder it is to find a significant difference between groups. Large error variance is likely to mask a scientifically important outcome. Taking a better measure improves the sensitivity of an experiment in the same way that increasing the number of subjects does.

To be sure, accuracy is less important than relevance. A highly accurate test does us no good if what it measures is irrelevant to the intended decision or conclusion. But if two tests are equally relevant, the more accurate test will yield more valuable reports.

"Error of measurement" is a familiar concept, but an ambiguous one. The test score is subject to many unwanted influences. Test theory shows how to estimate the effect of unwanted influences and permits judgments about the relation between the actual score and the score that could be obtained by thorough measurement. Here we examine only a part of that theory. (Extensive presentations of current theory in these matters are to be found in Lord & Novick, 1968; Stanley, 1970; and Cronbach et al., 1970.)

Sources of Variance

A particular observation is only one of many observations that might have been made. Mary was tested from 10:10 to 10:13 on May 5 by Mr. Brown; she was asked to type a passage from a news report on the United Nations; her paper was scored by Alice Gates, Mr. Brown's student helper. No one was especially interested in how well Mary could type at 10:10; a measure at any other hour of the day would have been equally relevant. Nor did anyone wish to measure her rate on this news report; any similarly difficult, unfamiliar selection would serve. We could accept a different tester and a different scorer. There are at least five distinguishable influences on Mary's score: tester, day, time within the day, passage typed, and scorer.

Other testers, days, passages, etc., might have been employed for Mary's test. Mary's score depends on which conditions are chosen. On some days Mary feels livelier. Some passages are easier for her than others, because some words are easier for her to spell and some sentences easier for her to carry in mind. Probably tester and scorer effects are small, but they should not go unconsidered. If Alice Gates is careless in penalizing for spelling errors, the scores she gives will be higher than those of a more careful scorer. Each of these variations in experimental conditions is a *source of variance*, because if Mary were retested her score would change.

As a second example, consider how variations in conditions of observation affect the rating a preschool child receives on friendliness. An obsever is to rate each child after observing him for 5 minutes in each of three situations: in the sandbox, on playground equipment, and at the juice break. The most evident sources of variation are:

● Observer. Some give more generous ratings. Some may be especially generous in rating cute redheads, some in rating children belonging to racial minorities. Observers have different concepts of "friendly" behavior. Consequently, their reports on the same event are likely to differ.

● Situation. This sample of three situations by no means exhausts the events of the preschool day. Perhaps a certain child would be less friendly to his peers if observed in a competitive game, or in a setting in which there is an adult to play up to.

● Occasion. Even in a defined situation such as the juice break, behavior varies from day to day. Weather, companions, objects present, etc., change; the child's mood varies; and behavior changes accordingly. The problem of analyzing "error of measurement" becomes that of estimating how greatly scores are affected by each such change.

1. *If a typing test has standard directions, how could a change of tester change Mary's score?*
2. *Could the typewriter used for the test affect Mary's score? Can you think of further sources of variance affecting the typing test?*
3. *What are possible sources of variance in MCT scores of a job applicant?*
4. *What sources of variation might produce variation among several Block Design tests given to a person?*

The Universe Score as the Desired Information

"What is Mary's true typing ability?" This must be interpreted as, "What would Mary's score be if a large number of measurements were collected and averaged?" The particular test score Mary earned is just one out of a *universe* of possible observations, any of which the investigator would be willing to base his conclusion or decision on. If one of these scores is as acceptable as the next, then the mean, called the *universe score* and symbolized here by M_p (mean for person p) would be the most appropriate statement of Mary's performance in the type of situation the test represents.

The universe is a collection of possible measures "of the same kind," but the limits of the collection are determined by the investigator's purpose. If he needs to know Mary's typing ability *on May 5* (for example, so that he can plot a learning curve that includes one point for that day), the universe would include observations on that day and only that day. He probably does want to generalize over passages, testers, and scorers—that is to say, he would like to know Mary's ability on May 5 without reference to any particular passage, tester, or scorer. In deciding whether to admit Mary to the study of shorthand the teacher is not concerned with typing ability on May 5; he needs an estimate of typing performance valid for several weeks or months. The teacher is now concerned with a universe of passages, testers, scorers, *and days*. In either of these examples, the investigator would be best satisfied if he could learn Mary's universe score. Since that is not possible, her observed score has to substitute. Insofar as the two disagree, there is "error of measurement."

The person will ordinarily have a different universe score for each universe. Mary's universe score covering tests on May 5 will not agree perfectly with her universe score for the whole month of May. Her universe score for many testings on the UN news report will not exactly equal her average over diverse selections. Some testers call the average over a large number of comparable observations a "true score"; e.g., "Mary's true typing rate on 3-minute tests." Instead, we speak of "universe score" to emphasize that what score is desired depends on the universe being considered. For any measure there are many "true scores," each corresponding to a different universe.

When we use a single observation as if it represented the universe, we are generalizing. We generalize over scorers, over selections typed, perhaps over days. If the observed scores from a procedure agree closely with the universe score, we can say that the observation is "accurate," or "reliable," or "generalizable." And since the observations then also agree with each other, we say that they are "consistent" and "have little error variance." To have so many alternative terms is confusing, but not seriously so. The term most often used in the literature is "reliability." The author prefers "generalizability" because that term immediately implies "generalization to what?" To generalize over scorers is not the same thing as generalizing over passages. There is a different degree of generalizability for each universe. But "generalizability" is an awkward, mouth-filling word. We shall therefore use one of the simpler equivalents when a precise expression is not required.

Testers have long recognized that there are many ways to define "error." The formal theory that separates sources of variance, and distinguishes one universe score from another, has taken shape only fairly recently. Nearly all writing about error of measurement and nearly all statistical reports in test manuals still rely on the older, simpler theory. While we present the current version of the concepts here, we shall refer also to the older concepts to help the reader understand published reports.

The older methods of analysis do not separate the sources of variation. They deal with a single source of variance, or leave two or more sources entangled. In the next several sections we shall confine attention to such relatively simple methods of analysis; we then examine how they may be extended.

5. *A teacher's rapport with pupils is judged by asking pupils to respond to a number of questions such as "Does your teacher give fair marks?" The most evident sources of variation are the questions (since other similar questions could be asked), the pupils, and the occasion. For what type of decision or investigation would one define the universe to include*
   a. *all possible pupils and questions, with observations limited to this particular semester?*
   b. *all similar questions, but only these particular pupils at this particular time?*
6. *A questionnaire covering feelings about the self and emotions is given to all patients coming to a clinic for a general medical checkup, to determine which ones should probably have a psychiatric interview. What universe of observations does the questionnaire score represent?*
7. *As a criterion in a selection study a life-insurance company determines how much business each salesman brings in during a certain 6-month period. What universe does this criterion represent?*
8. *In a certain university, doctoral students in psychology must show proficiency in a foreign language by making a correct summary of the ideas in a short selection written in the chosen language. The selection is taken from a professional journal or book in the student's special field. To what universe is generalization intended? Is the universe the same for all students?*

The Standard Error of Measurement

Suppose, for the moment, that we are interested in Mary's level of typing ability on May 5 only, but wish to generalize over all suitable passages and all times during that day. (This discussion ignores any effect the tester and scorer have.) If it were worth our trouble, we could carry out dozens of 3-minute tests using different passages. If we allow a warmup period before starting the first test, and suitable rest periods, all these measures would be reasonable samples from the universe. This information could be charted in a distribution of scores (Figure 6.1). Whereas the distributions in Chapter 3 represented scores of many persons, here we have a distribution of many scores for one single person. *The mean of the distribution is a good estimate of Mary's universe score.* Any one observed score is a sample from the distribution, and provides a relatively inexact estimate.

If the observed score is 54 and the universe score is 49, the discrepancy is 5 points. If we take the observed score as an estimate of Mary's universe score, the "error of measurement" is 5 points. An *error of measurement* is a difference between a person's universe score and his score on one observation.

The tester does not know the person's universe score, so he cannot determine the error in any particular observed score. But he can estimate how large such errors tend to be. By using methods presented below, he estimates the standard deviation of the distribution for a single person. This standard deviation of observed scores is called the *standard error of measurement* for that

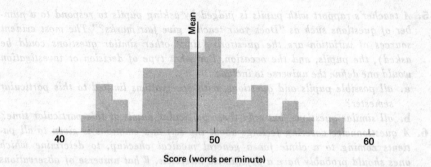

Figure 6.1.   Distribution of scores for Mary on many typing tests.

person. It may be symbolized by s.e.m. (The standard deviation of the person's observed scores is the same as the standard deviation of the errors of measurement. Do you see why?)

Communication engineers speak of "signal" and "noise" in discussing the accuracy of transmissions; this provides a useful analogy for us. The signal (universe score) is the information we would like to have—and could obtain if there were perfect reception. But instead we get a signal distorted by interference or noise. The "snow" on the television screen, the static in the radio, the departure from the universe score that results from testing a pupil at a particularly good or bad moment—these all constitute "noise." The greater the noise, the less we can be sure of the underlying signal.

Coefficients of Reliability or Generalizability

If scores spread over a 100-point scale, an error of 5 points has little effect on a person's standing. If the range is only 10 points, a 5-point error has an enormous effect. Testers therefore compare the size of errors with the total range of scores. Figure 6.2 compares the spread of MCT scores for ninth-grade boys with the variation arising from the standard error of 3.7. It is evident that a boy's standing changes considerably from one observation to another.

The statistic commonly used for summarizing such a comparison is a ratio of two variances which we call a *coefficient of generalizability* or, in the older terminology, a "reliability coefficient." The information desired about individual differences is contained in the universe scores, the signal. The information obtained is a composite of signal and noise. This leads us to the ratio

$$\frac{\text{Signal}}{\text{Signal-plus-noise}} = \frac{\text{Variance of universe scores}}{\text{Variance of observed scores}}$$

The symbol $r_{xx'}$ (or something similar) generally denotes this ratio. The ratio tells what fraction of the information reported about individual differences comes from "true" differences in universe score.

If we have made two independent observations X and X' on many persons,

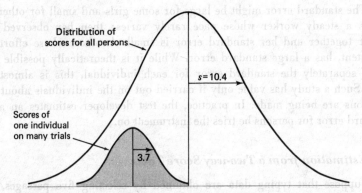

Figure 6.2. **Distribution of scores for one boy on the Mechanical Comprehension Test.**
These are compared with the range of individual differences for all boys of his age.

the correlation $r_{XX'}$ estimates this variance ratio. However a coefficient is obtained, it can be interpreted as the expected correlation between two observations that belong to the universe. It is also true that the variance ratio equals the *squared* correlation of the observed score with the universe score. (For proof, see Lord & Novick, 1968.)

9. *For a certain test that measures the threshold of pitch discrimination the standard error of measurement (over trials) is 3 cycles. Comment on the statement that "this test locates the person's threshold within 3 cycles."*

Estimation Procedures

A single observed score tells nothing about the error of measurement. To investigate the magnitude of errors, we must have two or more observations per person. The study of error is an essential part of instrument development. The test developer collects the required information, perhaps uses it to improve the instrument, and reports it in his test manual so that a tester can decide whether the finished test is accurate enough for his purposes. The person who applies a published test rarely makes his own investigation of generalizability (unless the application is part of a research study). He must, however, interpret the studies others have published.

Estimation from Observations on One Pupil

If we had several tests for Mary on May 5 (say, a dozen or more), this would give a distribution of observed scores as in Figure 6.1. Their standard deviation would estimate the standard error for Mary.

The standard error might be large for some girls and small for others. One girl is a steady worker whose pace rarely varies; then her observed scores cluster together and her standard error is small. Another, whose effort is inconsistent, has a large standard error. While it is theoretically possible to calculate separately the standard error for each individual, this is almost never done. Such a study has value only if carried out on the individuals about whom decisions are being made. In practice, the test developer estimates an average standard error for persons he tries the instrument on.

Estimation from a Two-way Score Table

Suppose that typing data are obtained by selecting five passages, A, B, . . . E, and administering them to all members of a typing class, with rest periods between. Then the scores of the pupils form a two-way table as shown at the top of Table 6.1. We could calculate the standard error for each individual and then take the mean or median. Or we might average the squares of the standard deviations (variances) and take the square root. The procedures described below are convenient indirect methods of doing just this.

A common statistical technique known as two-way analysis of variance can be applied to this table, and from this "components of variance" can be estimated. Since our emphasis is on interpretation, we shall not discuss the mathematical rationale for this analysis or the computational procedures. Table 6.1 shows enough steps of the calculation to connect this discussion with that in a statistics text, but it is not complete enough to serve as a computing guide. (Nearly every statistics text shows how to compute the mean squares for a two-way table; a few books take the further step of breaking the mean squares into the components of variance; e.g., McNemar, 1969, pp. 351, 454–458 ff., Hays, 1963, pp. 422–423, 438.)

Components of variance. The observed score is made up of components. Let X_{pi} be the observed score for person p under condition i. (In this example the "conditions" are passages A, B, C, etc.) Let M_p be the universe score for p (i.e., the average of X_{pi} over all conditions in the universe). Let M_i be the mean score for condition i, the average of scores on selection i for all persons in the population. And let M be the mean score for all observations, i.e., the average over all persons and all conditions. Then the observed score is the sum of several separate components or "effects":

$$X_{pi} = M + (M_p - M) + (M_i - M) + (\text{residual})$$

The first term, M, is a general average of typing speed, a baseline against which other effects are judged. The "person effect" $M_p - M$ describes the superiority or inferiority of p to the average person. If p types more rapidly than the average person does, $M_p - M$ will be positive. The "condition effect" $M_i - M$ indicates

Table 6.1. **Analysis of hypothetical data for five observations of typing rate**

Pupil (p)	Observed scores X_{pi}				
	A	B	C	D	E
Mary A.	54	57	51	50	51
Sue A.	52	55	56	53	52
Joan C.	50	46	49	52	50
Betty D.	52	51	52	43	54
Nora F.	53	53	43	47	50
. . . .					
. . . .					
. . . .					
Average	52.2	53.0	51.4	51.2	51.7

Number of persons $n_p = 25$

Number of conditions $n_i = 5$

From analysis of variance:

MSp : Mean square for rows (persons) $= 50$

MSi : Mean square for columns (conditions) $= 10$

MSr : Mean square for residual $= 3$

Estimated variance of person effects (universe scores):

$$\frac{1}{n_i}(MSp - MSr) = \frac{1}{5}(50-1) = 9.80 \quad \boxed{\text{Component for persons}}$$

Estimated variance of condition effects:

$$\frac{1}{n_p}(MSi - MSr) = \frac{1}{25}(10-3) = 0.28 \quad \boxed{\text{Component for conditions}}$$

Estimated residual variance:

$$MSr = 3.00 \quad \boxed{\text{Residual component}}$$

Estimate of $s^2{}_X = 9.8 + 3.0 = 12.8 \quad \boxed{\text{Observed-score variance}}$

Estimate of $r_{XX'}:s^2{}_{M_p}/s^2{}_X = 9.8/12.8 = 0.77 \quad \boxed{\text{Coefficient}}$

whether condition i tends to produce high or low scores. If all passages are equally difficult and the time of administration makes no systematic difference, then $M_i - M$ will be zero for every condition.

The "residual" includes any influence that makes a particular observed score higher or lower than we would predict from our knowledge of the corresponding M_p and M_i. The influences that enter the residual are worth illustrating in some detail, because the residual usually contains the largest errors. The residual term includes such effects as these:

- Passage C is easier for Sue than for most pupils, because she happens to be familiar with its subject matter.
- While Joan was working on selection B her effort slackened and she fell below her usual pace.
- As Nora is a poor reader, her score drops when a selection uses long sentences. All pupils score a bit lower on such selections, but Nora is handicapped a great deal.
- Momentary inattention caused Betty to make three transposition errors on Selection D, though she makes no more than one error on the usual selection.

In Table 6.1 the variance component for persons is estimated to be 9.80. This is the estimated universe-score variance. The square root of this, 3.1 w.p.m., is the standard deviation of the distribution of accurate typing rates for pupils like these. The component for condition effects is extremely small (0.28), and the corresponding s.d. for M_i is 0.5 words per minute. Evidently the average rate of typing differs only slightly from selection to selection and from one hour to another. The residual component is also small here, but in many studies it is large.

The error variance equals the sum of the components for conditions and residual, since both of these contribute to variation among a person's scores. Here, they add to 3.28, and s.e.m. = 1.8.[1]

Coefficient alpha.   The variance ratio is $s^2_{M_p}/s^2_X$. The numerator (signal) is the variance component for persons. A variance s^2_X for observed scores could be calculated directly for any column of observed scores in Table 6.1, but it is preferable to estimate the variance of the typical column by adding the components for persons and residual. This estimates s^2_X to be 12.8. The variance ratio or coefficient 9.80/12.8 is 0.77. This coefficient tells how well scores obtained by testing under just one condition—here, administering a single passage—represent universe scores.

The estimate of $r_{XX'}$ in Table 6.1 is often called an "alpha" coefficient, and we may use the special symbol α_1 to indicate that two-way analysis of variance

---

[1] We have defined the error of measurement to include the condition effect. Another kind of "standard error" disregards the condition effect, even when it is not zero. This standard error, which we denote by s_E, appropriately indicates the error in measuring individual differences, provided that all persons are observed under the same condition. When conditions have equal means (e.g., when tests are equivalent), the two standard errors are the same.

or an equivalent procedure has been used. (This is also referred to as an "intraclass correlation".) The subscript applied to α indicates that the coefficient refers to the accuracy of just one observation. There is a coefficient α_k for scores obtained by combining k observations, estimated by methods presented below.

Short-cut internal-consistency formulas. If we were concerned with the accuracy of a composite score based on five typing tests, we might compare it with a composite from five other selections. It is equally reasonable, however, to look at the consistency within the composite, since if its parts agree they would probably agree with the five parts of the next composite. One useful formula is:

$$\alpha_k = \frac{k}{k-1}\left(1 - \frac{\text{Sum } s^2_{X_i}}{s^2_{X_t}}\right)$$

where $s^2_{X_i}$ is the variance of part-scores X_i for each part in turn and $s^2_{X_t}$ is the variance of the sum of k part scores. In Table 6.1, for example, we could calculate a variance $s^2_{X_i}$ for each column, and get a total score for each row, X_t, whose variance we could also calculate.

A shortcut is available if the parts are items scored zero and one. Then if P_i is the proportion passing item i and $Q_i = 1 - P_i$, then $s^2_{X_i} = P_i Q_i$.

$$\alpha_k = \frac{k}{k-1}\left(1 - \frac{\text{Sum } PQ}{s^2_{X_t}}\right)$$

This formula is referred to as KR 20 (after the originators, Kuder and Richardson).

The procedure takes another twist when the investigator divides his test into just two parts, usually by scoring the odd and even items separately. The odd scores and even scores are entered in

$$\alpha_2 = 2\left(1 - \frac{s^2_{\text{odd}} + s^2_{\text{even}}}{s^2_{\text{total}}}\right)$$

This is a "split-half" coefficient. The formula is really just the first α_k formula, with $k = 2$. Since the k observations are half-tests, the formula estimates the accuracy of a single whole test. Another procedure is to correlate odd and even scores and correct the result by the procedure of Table 6.3 (p. 171) or the Spearman-Brown formula:

$$r_{11} = \frac{2r_{\frac{1}{2}\frac{1}{2}}}{1 + r_{\frac{1}{2}\frac{1}{2}}}$$

The result is nearly identical to α_2.

Correlation between observations. Test developers often arrive at a coefficient simply by calculating the correlation between two columns of scores, say,

from two administrations of a test. The result ordinarily differs negligibly from
the result obtained from the α_1 formula. The procedure is declining in prominence because it gives less information than the complete breakdown of components and because it does not apply directly when there are more than two
observations.

10. *To investigate accuracy of scoring, three observers are asked to watch through
a one-way window while a mental test is given, to keep a record, and calculate
an IQ. In this way, three IQs are obtained for each of 20 children. What information is represented in each of the following?*
    a. *the variance component for persons*
    b. *the variance component for observers*
    c. *the residual component*
11. *Calculate an α coefficient from these facts:*
$$s^2_{odd} = 20 \qquad\qquad s^2_{even} = 22 \qquad\qquad s^2_{x_t} = 60$$
12. *Calculate an α coefficient for a 10-item test, knowing that $s^2_{x_t}$ is 90 and the
respective items have variances: 3, 1, 5, 2, 2, 4, 3, 3, 1, 4.*

More Complex Procedures

The best way to study errors is to represent several sources of variation
systematically in the experimental design, and to estimate the effect of each. These
procedures take many different forms, and we can give only a sketchy impression
of them here. (For a fuller account, see Cronbach *et al.*, 1970). These complex
methods have not so far been used in preparing test manuals, but they are appearing with increasing frequency in the research literature.

The investigator decides what sources of variation to evaluate. To take a
simple example, suppose he wants to find out how typing scores are affected by
two sources of variance: passage typed, and occasion. Then he should administer
at least two selections, each on at least two occasions. To minimize the effect of
recall, he probably will divide each passage into two parts, and administer one
part on each day. Suppose that he selects two passages, cuts each in half, and
gives halves of two passages on each of two days. Then he has four scores for
each person. The analysis estimates the amount of error arising from the
sampling of passages, that arising from occasions, and a residual representing
momentary effects. This explains the variation among scores, and helps him
design a measuring procedure to reduce the major sources of error. More would
be learned if the study were made still more complex—e.g., by having each test
scored by two or more scorers.

Since such studies can become hopelessly complex, one expects a test
developer to study only the sources most likely to interfere with accuracy. An
exhaustive investigation is impossible.

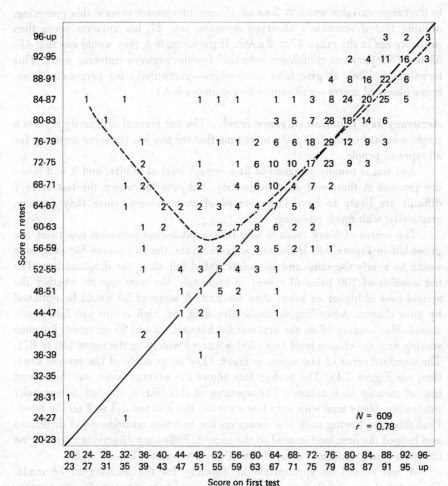

Figure 6.3. Test and retest scores on pitch discrimination.
Ford et al., 1944.

Interpreting Findings on Reliability

Meaning of the Standard Error

Once we have calculated a standard error, we can infer how far observed scores will depart from the universe score. To do this, testers assume that errors of measurement are normally distributed. Then, in accord with Figure 4.7, two-thirds of a very large series of observations that might be made on a person will fall within a range of two s.e.m. (universe score ± 1 s.e.m.) and 95 per cent fall in the range universe score ± 2 s.e.m. (Some interpreters reverse this reasoning, arguing that if someone's observed score is, say, 47, his universe score then probably lies in the range 47 ± 2 s.e.m. If the s.e.m. is 3, they would say that 41–53 is a "95 per cent confidence interval" for the person's universe score. This technique is likely to give false conclusions—particularly for persons with extreme observed scores—and cannot be recommended.)

Accuracy as a function of score level.   The test manual ordinarily reports a single standard error. It is risky to assume that the test has the same accuracy for all types of people.

Any test is usually designed to fit a certain level of ability, and it will measure persons at that level most accurately. Subjects for whom the test is very difficult are likely to have large errors of measurement, since they perform erratically, with much guessing.

The scores of Navy recruits who took a pitch-discrimination test twice are presented in Figure 6.3. If the test were accurate, the two scores for each man would be nearly the same and all points would fall along the diagonal line. The test consists of 100 pairs of tones; in each pair, the man reports whether the second tone is higher or lower than the first. A score of 50 would be obtained by pure chance. According to the scatter diagram, high scores are fairly consistent. Men scoring 85 on the first test fell between 72 and 95 on retest. But men scoring near the chance level (e.g., 55) scattered widely on the retest (40 to 87). The standard error of low scores is great. (For an example of the reverse situation, see Figure 7.4). The broken line shows the average score, on the second test, of men in each column. The upcurve of this line at the left is especially interesting. Many men with very low scores in the first test did well on the retest. Probably men having such low scores on the first test misunderstood directions and judged the first tone instead of the second. Following directions correctly on the retest would shift their scores from 70 items wrong to 70 items right.

A test should be appropriate in difficulty for the decision to be made. Figure 6.4 shows distributions of scores on several tests given to the same group. The very easy test A may be quite satisfactory for measuring differences at the lower end of the group. Test A is unsatisfactory for measuring most of the group, since variation of only a few points causes a subject to drop from the top of the group to the average. Furthermore, it does not distinguish between the persons tying at 100 though the subjects probably are not equally able. The failure of this test to detect differences among superior persons is referred to as a "ceiling effect." Test B is difficult. The top scores are spread out, but differences at the low end of the scale are too small to distinguish individuals dependably. Test C spreads out cases at both ends of the scale. Tests yielding roughly normal distributions are preferred when it is necessary to distinguish all along the scale. If our decision requires us only to distinguish the best men, test B is efficient. If we need only to eliminate the poorest men, we could use A.

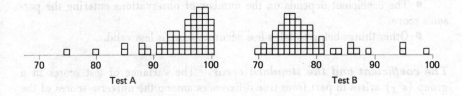

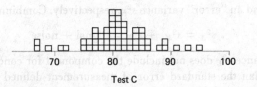

Figure 6.4.   Distributions of scores for several tests given to the same group.

13. *Which distribution in Figure 6.4 would be most desirable in each of the following cases?*
    a. *A psychologist wishes to measure liberalness of attitudes, to study its relation to voting habits.*
    b. *A college wishes to pick out freshmen needing special training in reading.*
    c. *A test for college guidance measures interest in medicine.*
    d. *An employer wishes to select the best statistician from a group of applicants.*
14. *The California Test of Personality, Elementary, contains several subtests, one of which is Feeling of Belonging. A low score on this questionnaire is said to indicate maladjustment. According to the test manual, the percentile rank corresponding to each possible score is as follows:*

Score	1	2	3	4	5	6	7	8	9	10	11	12
Percentile rank	1	1	1	1	1	5	10	15	25	40	65	90

   a. *How would a boy's standing in the group change if his score changed two points?*
   b. *What is the shape of the raw-score distribution? What does this distribution imply regarding the usefulness of the test?*

Meaning of the Coefficient[2]

Several general principles apply to the interpretation of the reliability coefficient:

● The coefficient tells what proportion of the observed-score variance is non-error variance ("signal," or wanted information).

● The coefficient depends on the spread of scores in the group studied.

[2] The argument of this section is simplified by neglecting (a) the distinction between values calculated from actual data and the theoretical values for the population of persons, and (b) the possible lack of equivalence among measures from the same universe. Carefully constructed forms of the same test are likely to have equal

● The coefficient depends on the number of observations entering the person's score.

● Other things being equal, a less accurate score is less valid.

The coefficient and the standard error. The variance of test scores in a group ($s^2{}_X$) arises in part from true differences among the universe scores of the persons tested. It arises in part from accidents of sampling one observation from the universe rather than another. These two sources generate the universe-score variance $s^2{}_{Mp}$ and an "error" variance $s^2{}_E$, respectively. Combining them,

$$s^2{}_X = s^2{}_{Mp} + s^2{}_E = \text{Signal} + \text{noise}$$

This error variance $s^2{}_E$ does not include the component for conditions. Therefore s_E is smaller than the standard error of measurement defined above unless the measures in the universe have equal means (see footnote, p. 160).

The division of variance into two parts can be illustrated for the MCT. For one sample of ninth-graders $s_X = 10.4$ and $s_E = 3.7$. The variances are

for observed scores	$s^2{}_X$	$= 108.2$
for errors	$s^2{}_E$	$= 13.7$
for universe scores	$s^2{}_{Mp}$	$= 94.5$ (by subtraction)

The standard deviation of universe scores, then, is $\sqrt{94.5}$ or 9.7.

The corresponding coefficient is estimated as follows:

$$\frac{\text{Variance of universe scores}}{\text{Variance of observed scores}} = \frac{s^2{}_{Mp}}{s^2{}_X} = \frac{94.5}{108.2} = 0.87 = r_{XX'}$$

When a manual reports only the coefficient, we can calculate the corresponding $s^2{}_E$ by means of the formula

$$s^2{}_E = s^2{}_X - s^2{}_{Mp} = s^2{}_X (1 - r_{XX'})$$

The coefficient tells what proportion of the test variance is due to "true" individual differences. In MCT 87 per cent of the variance comes from universe scores and 13 per cent from "error" corresponding to accidents of one particular testing (Figure 6.5).

The coefficient and the range of ability. Errors of measurement are most troublesome when we need to compare persons who differ only moderately. When we are hiring one person out of a group of applicants, the final decision often hinges on a difference of a few points between the best and next-best man. In

---

means, standard deviations, and equal intercorrelations. This is not so likely to be true for work samples, observations, or ratings from different acquaintances. The mathematical statements in this section are only approximately valid for actual data.

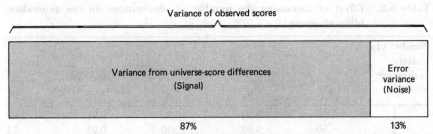

Figure 6.5. Composition of observed-score variance for MCT in grade 9.

such a case slight errors of measurement often lead us to hire the less-qualified man.

Since $s^2{}_X = s^2{}_{M_p} + s^2{}_E$, it is easily seen that when $s^2{}_{M_p}$ changes, the ratio $s^2{}_{M_p}/s^2{}_X$ changes correspondingly. We calculated a coefficient of 0.87 for MCT when s_{M_p} was 9.7. If we apply the test to a group where s_{M_p} is 5, the ratio drops to 0.64 ($= 25/[25 + 14]$). If we mix junior-high school students from various grades we might find s_{M_p} as large as 12, in which case r rises to $144/[144 + 14]$, or 0.92.

A test accurate enough to discriminate within a wide-range group may be unsatisfactory in a selected group. A rather crude mental test can be used to identify which of the pupils entering school are to be suspected of serious handicaps; but to divide the possibly handicapped group, so as to determine who is finally placed in a special class, requires a much more accurate test.

15. *For a college-entrance test the test manual reports a reliability coefficient of 0.95 for a college applicant population where s_X is 20. What, then is $s^2{}_X$? $s^2{}_M$? $s^2{}_E$? What will each of these, and the variance ratio, be in a group of freshmen actually admitted to a certain college, if s_X in that group is 10?*

16. *A reading test is to be used in grades 4 through 6. The manual should report a coefficient calculated for each grade level separately. Why?*

17. *An ability test is to be used to select employees. Should the reliability coefficient be determined on satisfactory employees or on applicants? Why?*

18. *Illustrate kinds of measurement for which s.e.m. and s_E are unlikely to be the same (i.e., for which means of observations are probably not equal).*

Effects of Changing the Number of Observations

A long test is generally better than a short test because, with every question added, the sample of performance becomes more adequate. A single addition problem is a very poor sample of ability, since the number combination presented may be particularly hard or easy. By asking more questions of the same general sort, we get a better estimate of ability to add.

Table 6.2.   Effect of increasing the number of observations on the generalizability of scores

Number of tests averaged[a] (k)	s^2_E	$s^2_{M_p}$	s^2_X	Coefficient (variance ratio)	s_E
1	1.00	9.80	10.80	0.91	1.00
2	.50	9.80	10.30	0.95	.71
3	.33	9.80	10.13	0.97	.58
5	.20	9.80	10.00	0.98	.45
10	.10	9.80	9.90	0.99	.32
100	.01	9.80	9.81	0.999	.10

[a] If tests were summed, instead of averaged, the entries in the variance columns would be multipled by k^2.

Long tests are less influenced by chance. If a test has only 5 multiple-choice items, a few people might get all items correct just by guessing. In a 50-item test, one would have to be extraordinarily lucky to get a high score by guessing. Variations due to guessing tend to cancel out. Three 15-minute observations of a child's social behavior provide a poor sample of his typical behavior; thirty observations, however, surely would give a dependable record.

Consider what happens as we make more and more observations. When k uncorrelated scores are averaged the variance of the average drops to one-kth the variance of a single measure. Error scores may be considered uncorrelated, and this law applies to them. Consequently, as k changes we get the effect shown in the second column of Table 6.2. The universe-score variance is constant. Hence as k increases the coefficient approaches 1.00. The more observations we average, the more closely the result agrees with the universe score (Table 6.2).

The signal-noise ratio.   The changes in the coefficient are described by the Spearman-Brown formula, named for the British psychologists who introduced it. (See p. 161 for the version of that formula used when $k = 2$.) Instead of calculating by that type of formula we may use a handy table. We change $r_{XX'}$ to a "signal-to-noise" ratio (S/N). Table 6.3 gives for each value of r a corresponding signal-noise ratio (obtained by calculating $r \div 1 - r$). The signal is unchanged no matter how many observations we average. The noise (averaged) declines in proportion to k. Hence *the signal-noise ratio changes in proportion to k.* This gives us the very simple procedure illustrated in Table 6.3 for estimating r for various values of k.

The example shows how to proceed when r for a short test is known and r for a test k times as long is desired. The table can be applied also to estimate r for a reduced number of observations. If we go from three observations to only one, $k_2/k_1 = \frac{1}{3}$. Since the initial S/N ratio was 1.500, the final one is 0.500. The corresponding r is 0.33.

There is another way of using the table. Suppose the measure now has a coefficient of 0.75 and we would like to increase r to 0.90. How much observation is required? The table indicates that S/N(0.75) is 3 and S/N(0.90) is 9. Then $k_1:k_2 = 3:9 = 1:3$; so we would have to triple the number of observations.

These procedures are often used in deciding how the accuracy of a test would be changed if the number of items were altered, assuming that changing the length does not change the nature of the test. Unless one is careful, added items or added periods of observation may not cover the same behavior or ability as the original test and the formula is misleading. Short tests are preferred, other things being equal. Too long a testing period bores the subject and makes him uncooperative. When morale is high, however, one can give very long batteries successfully. Shortening a test to a few items will destroy its value, but not much is gained by lengthening a test beyond 100 items per score except in a competitive examination in which a few points make a great difference. The Bennett MCT has sixty items and requires about 30 minutes for adolescent subjects. This is a usual length for a test yielding a single score.

One must examine the accuracy of every score he intends to interpret. Some testers, knowing that a test as a whole has a large coefficient, place faith in its part scores also, but a part score based on a few items is of limited value. A test manual should give the standard error and the reliability coefficient for every part score whose interpretation is recommended.

Several sources of variance contribute to the error of measurement. When we make additional observations we sample some of these conditions more thoroughly. Consider two procedures for obtaining a more accurate typing score. We might decide to administer three passages, all on the same day. Or we might decide to administer three passages, each on a different day. Both observations are "three times as long" as the original one-passage test. But they are not equally good bases for estimating the universe score over passages and days. The first one samples passages three times but samples days only once. Day-to-day variation is sampled no better than in the original study. Three-passages-on-three-days samples each source of error three times. It therefore gives a better basis for the intended generalization.

Testers used to think that any method of increasing the number of observations by a certain multiple has the same effect. This is untrue. Without going into all the complications of the problem, we can state when the signal/noise calculations and the Spearman-Brown formula apply. In obtaining the original coefficient, certain components varied from observation to observation. The analysis given above tells what to expect if we sample all those components and only those components more thoroughly. (For example, suppose the original study applied all five passages on the same day. Only the passage was systematically varied. Applying the S/N table does not tell us what we gain by testing on more days, or

Table 6.3. **Conversion of reliability coefficient to signal-noise ratio**

Coefficient	S/N	Coefficient	S/N	Coefficient	S/N	Coefficient	S/N
.01	.0102	.26	.3514	.51	1.041	.76	3.167
.02	.0204	.27	.3699	.52	1.083	.77	3.348
.03	.0309	.28	.3889	.53	1.128	.78	3.545
.04	.0417	.29	.4085	.54	1.174	.79	3.762
.05	.0526	.30	.4286	.55	1.222	.80	4.000
.06	.0638	.31	.4493	.56	1.273	.81	4.263
.07	.0753	.32	.4706	.57	1.326	.82	4.556
.08	.0870	.33	.4925	.58	1.381	.83	4.882
.09	.0989	.34	.5152	.59	1.439	.84	5.250
.10	.1111	.35	.5385	.60	1.500	.85	5.667
.11	.1236	.36	.5625	.61	1.564	.86	6.143
.12	.1364	.37	.5873	.62	1.632	.87	6.692
.13	.1494	.38	.6129	.63	1.703	.88	7.333
.14	.1628	.39	.6393	.64	1.778	.89	8.091
.15	.1765	.40	.6667	.65	1.857	.900	9.00
.16	.1905	.41	.6949	.66	1.941	.905	9.53
.17	.2048	.42	.7241	.67	2.030	.910	10.11
.18	.2195	.43	.7544	.68	2.125	.915	10.76
.19	.2346	.44	.7857	.69	2.226	.920	11.50
.20	.2500	.45	.8182	.70	2.333	.925	12.33
.21	.2658	.46	.8519	.71	2.448	.930	13.29
.22	.2821	.47	.8868	.72	2.571	.935	14.38
.23	.2987	.48	.9231	.73	2.704	.940	15.67
.24	.3158	.49	.9608	.74	2.846	.945	17.18
.25	.3333	.50	1.00	.75	3.000	.950	19.00
						.955	21.22
						.960	24.00
						.965	27.57
						.970	32.33
						.975	39.00
						.980	49.00
						.985	65.67
						.990	99.00
						.995	199.00

SOURCE: Cronbach & Gleser, 1964.

Conversion of reliability coefficient to signal-noise ratio (*Continued*)

Use of the signal-noise ratio

Procedure. To infer the coefficient for k_2 observations when the coefficient for k_1 is known:

1. Enter the table with the coefficient r for k_1 observations and read the corresponding S/N.
2. Multiply this by k_2/k_1. This gives the S/N ratio for k_2 observations.
3. Enter the S/N column with this value and read the corresponding coefficient for k_2 observations.

Example. For the average of 3 observations, the coefficient is known to be 0.60. What will the coefficient be if 6 observations are combined? $k_2/k_1 = 6/3$ or 2. Opposite the coefficient 0.60 we read S/N = 1.500. This is multiplied by 2 to get the new S/N = 3.000. In the S/N column we locate 3.000 and read opposite it the coefficient 0.75.

---

by scoring each paper twice. It does tell us what we gain by using k passages on a single day rather than one.) To plan an efficient study sampling each of several components requires a more complex calculation (see Cronbach *et al.*, 1970).

Effect on the validity coefficient. An inaccurate test cannot be a good predictor. The error portion of the test score will not correlate with any criterion; consequently, the greater the error variance the lower the validity coefficient. There are simple relations between validity (r_{XC}, if C stands for the criterion) and reliability ($r_{XX'}$).

• r^2_{XC} must be less than $r_{XX'}$. This comparison of a squared correlation with an unsquared one looks odd. The explanation is that $r_{XX'}$ equals $r^2_{XM_p}$. So r^2_{XC} is less than $r^2_{XM_p}$—i.e., X cannot correlate higher with an outside variable C than it does with its own universe mean M_p. To give an example: For MCT, $r_{XX'}$ is 0.87 in the group we have been discussing. Then—disregarding sampling errors in a small study—it cannot possibly predict shop grades with r^2_{XC} above 0.87; hence the validity coefficient r_{XC} cannot exceed 0.93 ($\sqrt{0.87} = 0.93$). While r_{XC} *might* exceed $r_{XX'}$, this almost never happens.

• As many observations of X are combined, the ratio $r^2_{XC}/r^2_{XM_p}$ (which equals $r^2_{XC}/r_{XX'}$) remains constant. This is represented in Figure 6.4. The upper curve exhibits the change in reliability as more measures are taken; it follows the Spearman-Brown formula. The lower curve shows the *squared* validity coefficient, assuming that the universe score for X correlates 0.60 with the criterion C. Once the measure X has attained a reliability of 0.80 or so, further lengthening improves validity only very slowly (Figure 6.6).

While it clearly improves prediction to take extra observations, practical

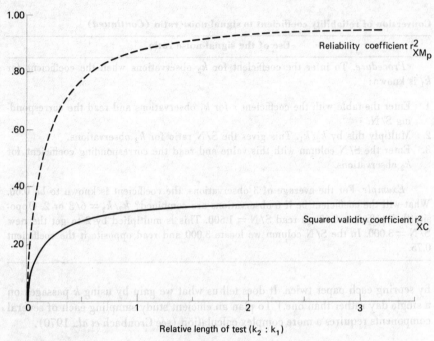

Relative length of test ($k_2 : k_1$)

Figure 6.6.   Effects of changing the number of observations.

conditions set limits on the time and effort one can invest. Moreover, it often is better to invest one's time in measuring several variables, each relevant to the intended decision, than to measure one variable thoroughly and collect no data on the others.

Generalizability studies contribute to test validation by showing the importance of various influences and so explaining the test. We have mentioned observations on pre-school children. Friendliness can be observed by two or more observers, in several kinds of situation with two or more occasions of observation in each situation, etc. The investigator learns about "friendliness." Is it stable, or highly variable from day to day? Is it general, or does it depend on the situation? Does friendliness depend so much on who one's companion is that the concept of general friendliness and unfriendliness is inappropriate? Interpretations such as this go far beyond the mere estimation of accuracy.

Efficiency gained through branching procedures. The traditional test gave the same questions to all subjects. The mathematical theory of error distributions suggests that efficiency can be gained by "branched" testing in which the test is divided into two or more stages. Every subject takes the same first-stage test, and those who succeed move on to a relatively difficult second-stage while those who do poorly receive easier questions at the second stage. This branching process can be continued any number of times; statistical adjustments permit adjustment of scores so that ultimately all subjects are described on the same scale of ability. In theory, this permits one to shorten testing time without sacrificing accuracy (Cronbach & Gleser, 1965). One does not require a computer to carry out branched testing of this type. He may use some kind of self-scoring answer sheet so that the student calculates his own score for the first page of the test. (One procedure uses a plastic sheet on which the answer spaces are covered by an opaque paint. The student scrapes off the paint to indicate his response; below the paint is printed a number to indicate whether he gets credit or not.) A table at the foot of the page instructs those with scores above 10 to turn to page 22 of the test booklet, and similarly sends students of lesser ability to appropriate second-stage tests. One report indicates that such a branched test obtains information whose accuracy is comparable to that of a conventional test three times as long (Linn, Rock, & Cleary, 1969).

19. *The coefficient for a single MCT score is 0.87. With the S/N table, determine the cofficient for a composite based on two forms of the test.*

20. *A spelling test of 30 words has a reliability coefficient of 0.80. What reliability would be expected if 90 words were used?*

21. *In World Series baseball, some pinch hitters reach batting averages as high as 0.750, whereas the best regular players rarely exceed 0.400 for seven games. How can this be explained?*

22. *A test has validity 0.25 for some criterion and a reliability coefficient of 0.60. If the test were made very long, what value would the reliability coefficient approach? the validity coefficient?*

Alternative Experimental Procedures and Their Implications

The investigator carrying out a generalizability study makes two or more observations per person and examines how well they agree. Certain conditions vary from one observation to the next; their influence enters the "error" variance. Some other condition is held constant from one observation to the next; the analysis treats its effect on the standing of individuals as part of universe-score variance. This is incorrect, unless the universe definition calls for holding that condition constant. An experiment that holds too much constant over-estimates the universe-score variance, overestimates the coefficient, and under-estimates the standard error of measurement.

The reader of a study must ask the pointed question: Are there significant sources of error that this estimate of error fails to take into account? When the answer is "Yes," he will not know how much to allow for that further source of error, but he will at least proceed with extra caution. If scores are obtained by having two judges score every test paper, the agreement of the scores evaluates only one source of error: that coming from the observer. The coefficient tells how well from one scoring we can generalize to the score a universe of judges would assign to that same performance. It tells, not how well we have sampled the person's behavior, but how well we have sampled judgments.

Variation classified by stimulus conditions and occasion. Two sources of variation, stimuli and occasions, loom particularly large in planning measurement procedures, and their effects are most often examined in test manuals.

Data are always collected in a specific situation even though the investigator is interested in a general quality. The general characteristics of the individual will affect his response to all situations or problems drawn from the same class; they will tend to make his performances consistent. His specific reactions to each problem also affect his score, and since these specific reactions depend on the stimuli presented, they are a source of inconsistency. In MCT, for example, the investigator wants to measure the general quality of ability to comprehend virtually any mechanical situation. But the score on any one form depends to some extent on the particular items chosen. Table 6.4 distinguishes between general and specific influences on the score.

It also distinguishes between temporary and lasting characteristics. One wants to know the person's standing capability in mechanical comprehension, but when we test him on a certain day there are temporary influences that raise or lower his score, as we see in sections III and IV of the table.

Comparisons that hold occasion constant. The test developer often reports a study of the consistency of two or more scores collected on the same occasion. He may administer two forms of a test, with an appropriate rest period between. This is an alternate-form study. Or he may divide a single test into two or more equivalent parts, and get a score for each section. This is an internal-consistency study.

The alternate-form or internal-consistency procedure tells how well the test score agrees with similar scores obtained at the same time. Suppose Forms S and T of MCT are administered in close succession. In this study the several kinds of variance are allocated as follows:

Counted in universe-score variance	*Counted as error*
Lasting–general	Lasting–specific
Temporary–general	Temporary–specific, and chance

Any lasting-general attribute (e.g., ability to interpret mechanical diagrams) affects both tests in the same way. It enters into any form of the test and hence into the universe score. Temporary-general attributes (e.g., a severe headache) cause the observed scores to depart from the universe score (defined over forms and days). But they make the two scores consistent, and so the procedure fails to

Table 6.4. Sources of test-score variance classified

I. Lasting and general characteristics of the individual
  1. General skills (e.g., reading)
  2. General ability to comprehend instructions, testwiseness, techniques of taking tests
  3. Ability to solve problems of the general type presented in this test
  4. Attitudes, emotional reactions, or habits generally operating in situations like the test situation (e.g., self-confidence)

II. Lasting and specific characteristics of the individual
  1. Knowledge and skills required by particular problems in the test
  2. Attitudes, emotional reactions, or habits related to particular test stimuli (e.g., fear of high places brought to mind by an inquiry about such fears on a personality test)

III. Temporary and general characteristics of the individual (systematically affecting performance on various tests at a particular time)
  1. Health, fatigue, and emotional strain
  2. Motivation, rapport with examiner
  3. Effects of heat, light, ventilation, etc.
  4. Level of practice on skills required by tests of this type
  5. Present attitudes, emotional reactions, or strength of habits (insofar as these are departures from the person's average or lasting characteristics—e.g., political attitudes during an election campaign)

IV. Temporary and specific characteristics of the individual
  1. Changes in fatigue or motivation developed by this particular test (e.g., discouragement resulting from failure on a particular item)
  2. Fluctuations in attention, coordination, or standards of judgment
  3. Fluctuations in memory for particular facts
  4. Level of practice on skills or knowledge required by this particular test (e.g., effects of special coaching)
  5. Temporary emotional states, strength of habits, etc., related to particular test stimuli (e.g., a question calls to mind a recent bad dream)
  6. Luck in the selection of answers by "guessing"

SOURCE: After R. L. Thorndike, 1949, p. 73.

count their effect as error. This makes the universe-score variance and the coefficient too high, if for the tester's purpose the temporary effects are noise rather than signal.

The forms employ different items. Therefore, a lasting-specific attribute such as knowledge about the airplane rudder increases one score but not the other. A lasting-specific attribute counts as error. This is appropriate, since we desire to measure mechanical comprehension in general, not comprehension of a few particular machines. Temporary-specific influences, such as distraction, also enter the error term, as they should.

There is no important reason to distinguish internal-consistency coefficients from form-to-form, same-day coefficients. It is proposed to generalize over a universe of forms. The part-scores are treated as if they were short parallel forms. The parts ought to be just as similar as two test-forms would be.

The part scores must be experimentally independent, so that errors on one part are not linked to errors on another. Independence is violated when a highly speeded test is scored by halves in odd-even fashion, because the person who gets stuck on an odd-numbered item will not reach the end of the test and will thereby get a lower score on *both* the odd and even parts. There is a lack of independence also if understanding one problem helps the person solve the next. Wherever such linkages are possible, a proper internal-consistency study must divide the test into physically separate parts and administer them separately. In particular, the parts of a speed test must be given separately, each with its own prorated time limit, if valid conclusions about the consistency of the parts are to be reached.

Nonindependence gives spuriously high coefficients. One demonstration of this employed the speeded PMA tests, for which some investigators had been reporting ordinary split-half coefficients. Anastasi and Drake (1954) gave the half-tests with separate time-limits in order to get a proper estimate, and compared this result with a coefficient from the improper single-administration method. The results for four tests were as follows:

	Single administration	Separate halves
Verbal	0.94	0.90
Reasoning	0.92	0.87
Number	0.92	0.83
Space	0.90	0.75

Whether parts of a test need to be highly similar depends on how similar we expect tests in the universe to be. Sometimes we are thinking about a universe of randomly parallel tests. When we speak of typing skill, for example, we refer to an average rate over a broad class of passages (e.g., business letters, newspaper selections, etc.). We would be willing to use any selection drawn at random from the broadly defined universe. Hence our study would compare randomly similar passages, parallel only in the sense that they belong to the universe. To get two scores by splitting the United Nations passage, and timing each half separately, would be a poor procedure because the stimuli are too similar. Ability to spell *Secretariat* would raise the score on both parts—but would not be generally significant. In the usual test in which successive items range over different topics, one can consider the items and half-tests to be randomly similar. Using items on odd and even halves to get part scores is proper if each test in the universe consists of randomly assembled items. This is a reasonable assumption for MCT or a vocabulary test.

The random-content assumption is not suitable when the tests in the universe follow a definite plan. It may be agreed that all forms of a mathematics test for college entrance should have a certain number of algebra items, a certain number of geometry items, etc. The various tests constructed to fit this plan are "stratified parallel." If the investigator sees the test as belonging to a universe of stratified-parallel tests, the parts formed for an internal-consistency study should be stratified. The easiest procedure is to divide each subgroup of items down the middle so that algebra (for instance) is as prominent in one half-test as in the other. The analysis of variance and alpha procedures can be modified to estimate the coefficient for a universe of stratified-parallel tests (Rajaratnam, Cronbach, & Gleser, 1965).

Comparisons over a time interval (stability). A second prominent type of investigation compares measures separated by a time interval (retest, or delayed alternate-forms procedure). One may look on the separate occasions as more or less interchangeable samples from a period of time or he may look on the data as reflecting systematic trends over time.

If one is trying to estimate the aggressiveness of a child when he enters preschool, as a baserate for an experiment, day-to-day variation is considered to be random error. One checks the magnitude of this error by observing on two or more days a week or so apart. The usual statistical analysis indicates how well the score X derived from observations on one, two, or k days agrees with a score M_p that might be obtained from an exhaustive sampling of behavior in this period. One applies similar reasoning to MCT correlations for testings separated by a week or a month. In studies like this, one does not have to be greatly concerned with the precise length of interval, or with whether the same test form or two different forms are used. But the two testings should be far enough apart to minimize memory effects. With a design in which several occasions are sampled and the same items or situations are presented repeatedly, the allocation of variance is:

Counted in universe-score variance	Counted as error
Lasting–general	Temporary–general
Lasting–specific	Temporary–specific, and chance

If a different test form or situation is encountered on each occasion, lasting-specific variance is treated as error.

Any trait may change systematically with time. The best procedure for studying this would be to obtain form-to-form coefficients for different time intervals, but ordinarily one has data for only one or two intervals. A set of stability data for the Stanford-Binet Scale is presented in Figure 7.4 (p. 224). This gives a retest correlation over about a week of 0.91. As the time interval increases the correlation declines. Over a 4-year interval the retest correlation is

Table 6.5. Specimen evidence on generalizability of Mechanical Reasoning Test

Procedure and interpretation	Sample	r	Mean	s.d.	s_E
Split-half	202 boys, grade 8	0.87	42.7	9.6	3.4
(generalizability over	212 boys, grade 9	0.85	45.5	8.6	3.3
sets of items)	913 boys, average within				
	grades, 9–12	0.87	47.4	8.8	3.1
	199 girls, grade 8	0.72	35.9	7.6	4.1
	221 girls, grade 9	0.79	37.2	8.1	3.7
	930 girls, average within				
	grades, 9–12	0.79	38.2	7.9	3.6
Form-to-form,	112 boys, grade 8	0.70	39.4	8.5	4.7
tests 1–2 months apart	121 boys, grade 9	0.82	44.8	9.1	3.9
(generalizability over	108 girls, grade 8	0.68	32.2	6.9	3.9
forms and occasions)	113 girls, grade 9	0.59	37.9	7.3	4.7
Form-to-form, tests	140 boys, grades 9, then 12	0.69			
three years apart	183 girls, grades 9, then 12	0.60			
(generalizability over					
forms and occasions)					

SOURCE: DAT manual, 1966, pp. 4–1 ff., 6–1 ff.

only 0.74 and over 11 years it is only 0.68. An important fraction of the test variance at age 7 reports individual differences that can be measured accurately at the present moment but that will change with time.

The tester must interpret information on stability in the light of his purposes. If he intends to make long-range predictions or to measure a trait that is supposed to be constant, he wants stability over long periods. There are other uses of tests for which long-time stability is of little importance. The breakdown in Table 6.4 is somewhat arbitrary. An effect that lasts for a month (e.g., a child's disturbance due to a parent's absence) is temporary from the point of view of a year-to-year study, and "lasting" from a week-to-week viewpoint.

Table 6.5 gives a sample of the information a modern manual provides for a version of MCT. There are a number of interesting comparisons to be made. The month-to-month, form-to-form correlations are lower than those from split-half analysis. The latter procedure is commonly used by test developers. It is less expensive and it gives a higher coefficient. But surely the coefficient over forms given a month apart is a better indication of the error that concerns the counselor or employment officer who uses such a test. (In Table 6.5 there is astonishingly little drop from the 1-month coefficient to the 3-year coefficient. But the 3-year coefficient is of little worth when no s.d. is given; the sample may be atypical.)

26. *A teacher gives a standardized test of knowledge of scientific facts to his class in chemistry. Several students make scores lower than he had expected.*
   a. *He asks, "Could it be that I gave a form of the test that included many questions these particular pupils happened not to know? Would their scores have changed much if they had been asked other questions of the same type?" What type of study answers this question?*
   b. *He asks, "Could the performance of these students be due to the fact that they were having an 'off' day? Does a pupil's score on tests of this type vary much from day to day?" What type of study is most helpful in answering this question?*
27. *Which types of variance in Table 6.4 are to be regarded as "error" when a questionnaire regarding emotional problems is used for this purpose:*
   a. *To select high-school pupils with whom the counselor should have an early conference.*
   b. *To identify recruits likely to break down in service.*
   c. *To identify the area within which a pupil has conflicts, as a preliminary to a counseling interview.*
28. *Interpret these facts about a test measuring "liberality" of political attitudes.*

Coefficient from two forms taken at same sitting	*0.90*
Coefficient from two forms, one year apart	*0.60*
Coefficient from test, and retest with same form one year later	*0.65*

29. *In speaking about hearing tests for children a writer says: "Physical and psychological changes from day to day may make tests at two sittings less valid than a complete test at one sitting. We find that we get worse results on cloudy days than on sunny days."*
   In what sense is the word valid used? Can you defend the contrary statement that scores at two sittings would be more valid than a complete test at one sitting?

The Bandwidth-Fidelity Dilemma

Multiscore tests—i.e., tests that present a profile of two, five, or even twenty scores for interpretation—are hard to evaluate. The statistical treatment of profiles is more complex than the treatment of single scores. Even when there is agreement on the statistics, qualified investigators differ sharply in the value they assign to such tests. The problem is partly technical and partly a matter of value judgment. One has a certain time at his disposal for testing. Should he use that time to get a good measure of one dimension or to make several separate measurements? If he chooses the latter course, each separate score will be based on a relatively small sample of behavior and will be less accurate than the one-dimensional measure. Heterogeneous data (from varied situations) can be lumped into a single score. For example, information on diverse questions posed during an employment interview can be recorded simply as an interviewer's summary rating on merit. If one prefers, the interviewer can rate the man on half-a-dozen qualities, or can even mark a checklist of numerous specific characteristics. The same holds true for a test. Ability in arithmetic computation can be reported as a single score, or the report can give a complete list of whichever addition combinations the subject is weak on.

Compressing behavior into one or two scores loses detailed information. But attempting to capture rich detail by using many scores, each from a small sample of behavior, gets poor information. A high-school counselor would obviously prefer 10-minute tests of five abilities to a 50-minute test that samples mechanical reasoning exhaustively and tells nothing about verbal, numerical, abstract reasoning, and clerical abilities. He risks getting flimsy data if he goes so far as to substitute ten 3-minute tests for the 30-minute MCT—but it is hard to define a perfect balance between breadth of coverage and precision.

This is the bandwidth-fidelity dilemma. We encounter it in debates about the proper number of aptitudes to take into account in selection and guidance, in debates about the wisdom of preparing a 10-subtest profile for the Wechsler Scale of Intelligence, and even in an argument about whether it is justifiable to separate "mental ability" from "achievement." The argument is equally vigorous in the personality domain. Some investigators doubt that one can extract any more from a questionnaire than the conclusion that the subject reports good or poor adjustment; others prepare elaborate descriptive profiles.

The terms "bandwidth" and "fidelity" come from Shannon's "information theory" (1949), developed for the study of electronic communication systems. Home music systems have made "high fidelity" familiar to everyone. The complementary concept of bandwidth refers to the amount or complexity of information one tries to communicate in a given space or time. The fidelity of disk recording depends upon the width of the groove; if grooves are crowded together to put more music on a record, fidelity suffers. Similarly with a tape: the greater the tape speed, the greater the fidelity—but the less the information on the reel. With other things held constant, any shift in the direction of greater fidelity reduces bandwidth; bandwidth is purchased at the price of fidelity. Any communication system must compromise between bandwidth and fidelity. The record industry settled on the 33-rpm "long-play" record; the FCC allows the FM station a bandwidth of 22 kilocycles.

When many decisions are to be made, each requiring a different sort of information, the best solution is to allow a large amount of time for gathering information. In clinical diagnosis of children with behavior problems, hundreds of tests and observations might shed light on different aspects of development. An employer hiring an executive can likewise raise a very large number of questions. But time is inevitably limited. While no general rule can be given as to the best division of limited testing time, it is clear that the greatest amount of time should be given to the most important questions. When several questions are of about equal importance, it is more profitable to use a brief test giving a rough answer to each one than to use a precise test answering only one or two questions (Cronbach & Gleser, 1965).

Yet the scores traditionally used are the ones whose value is best demonstrated, and any proposal to add scores has to be challenged. There is the rub. The psychology of individual differences can only advance by becoming more complicated, by introducing additional variables (which are usually subvariables within the older main variables). Hence everyone who introduces a new kind of score is increasing bandwidth. But new proposals are hypotheses that await validation. So many of the proposals eventually prove unsound that the skeptics who are deeply suspicious of *any* proposal to make the profile more complicated are correct most of the time. The tension between the innovators and conservatives is entirely constructive. Which voice one should heed in choosing tests for his own decisions depends very much on the decision. It is the purpose to be served and the way tests will be interpreted that determines whether limited bandwidth or low fidelity is more acceptable.

The position taken in this book is that of hoping for benefits from each innovative proposal, since that is the only way progress in testing can come, while insisting that each proposal to increase bandwidth prove its merit. In particular, this means looking for evidence that each score added to the profile (and each difference between scores in the profile) is reasonably generalizable—and then going on to ask for evidence that such refined information relates to nontest variables.

The classical psychometric ideal is the instrument with high fidelity and low bandwidth (Cronbach & Gleser, 1965). A college aptitude test tries to answer just one question with great accuracy. It concentrates its content in a narrow range, using homogeneous items to increase reliability. Its parts are highly correlated, hence part scores give little information for choosing between majors or diagnosing weaknesses.

At the opposite extreme, the interview and the projective technique have almost unlimited bandwidth. In some studies with personality tests, scores are assigned on more than forty variables, all on the basis of about an hour's testing. An individualized description may bring in even more variables.

There are tests with intermediate bandwidths, and a particular technique may be used as a narrowband method by some testers and as a wideband method by others. Validity studies substantiate Shannon's principle: increases in complexity of information are obtained only by sacrificing fidelity. The Wechsler Verbal IQ is highly valid for many predictions. Patterns of subtest scores are of some but quite limited value. Interpretations of responses to single items are distinctly untrustworthy. One or two main scores summarize dependable information in the usual test; if one makes supplementary breakdowns he should be fully aware of their doubtful accuracy.

This does not do away with all problems. It does not settle debates about homogeneity in test construction. It does not answer psychologists (notably Guilford and R. B. Cattell) who consider broad composites that combine distantly related tasks positively misleading; they prefer to risk reporting subscores of doubtful validity and reliability. Users are rarely sophisticated enough to place just the right weight on that flimsy information. All too often, a complex report overwhelms the user. Teachers, psychiatrists, and persons counseled find it hard to separate solid conclusions from loosely verified speculations.

The issues are philosophical as well as practical. Is it better to take some risk, making use of information that may not be sound? Or is it better to shun all such information, and stop with scores that present an incomplete and featureless picture?

Other Considerations in Test Selection

As Chapter 5 said, the fundamental basis for choosing a test is validity—whether we can interpret the test soundly, and whether the information obtained serves our purpose. Information on reliability is supplementary. It sometimes warns us that validity will be limited just because of error of measurement, and it sometimes helps us to plan a more accurate data-gathering procedure. Additional considerations enter into the selection of a measuring procedure. At some point, for example, the gains in accuracy from increasing the number of observations further will be insufficient to justify the cost and inconvenience. We may examine briefly these supplementary considerations, starting with one that is not at all technical.

Appeal to the Layman

When a patient loses faith in the medicine his doctor prescribes, it loses much of its power to improve his health. He may skip doses, and in the end he may decide doctors cannot help him and let treatment lapse altogether. For similar reasons, in selecting a test one must consider how worthwhile it will appear to the subject who takes it and to oth *r* laymen who will see the results.

If an applicant for a job is given an employment test that he considers silly or unrelated to the job, he is likely to be resentful. This will make it difficult to obtain valid scores. If he is not hired, he may excuse his failure by criticizing the test; what he says to his friends damages public relations and makes it harder to obtain job applicants. Even the successful man may feel that he was hired in spite of the test, and begin work antagonistic toward management. Some satisfactory workers have had little schooling and are distrustful of tests that probe their weaknesses; catch questions and questions that seem childish are especially likely to arouse criticism.

If a test is interesting and "sensible," taking it is likely to be a pleasant experience. This not only tends to make the scores valid but also helps to establish good relations between the personnel worker and the subject. An Italian bus company contracted with psychological laboratories in two cities to give tests to applicants for jobs as drivers. After a few months, it was found that most of the applicants were traveling to Rome—going as much as 100 miles farther than necessary—because the Rome center had elaborate testing apparatus while the second center used simple equipment to measure the same aptitudes. The applicants thought the elaborate tests fairer and more dependable. British experience with War Office selection boards is a second case in point. The selection board observed candidates during several days of field testing, apparatus tests, discussions, etc. Before this system was established, men from the ranks rarely applied for commissions because they thought the tests previously used gave an advantage to applicants from good homes and good schools. They regarded the selection board as a fairer system through which a man can show his true ability. This attitude was of great assistance in recruitment of officers.

The story would be incomplete without the most dramatic example of all. In 1967 "New Left" students at a Japanese university called a strike, armed themselves with clubs and barricaded the main building—all this to protest a proposal to install a multiple-choice examination as part of the admissions procedure! As a result the university was closed for months, until officials agreed not to adopt the new tests. It is not easy to be sure that the students really cared about the tests; perhaps they merely used the issue as a focus for rebellion. Nor is it certain that the testing proposal would have been rejected if the ground had been better prepared. As it is, the highly competitive admission to Japanese universities continues on the old system. Every university administers its own essay examination, and the student takes the examinations for several universities. Then all university work stops for six weeks while the faculty grades the essays and decides whom to admit. Such a system was functional in days when few students went to the few universities then in existence. It is staggeringly inefficient today and would be on the way out—if failure to "appeal to the layman" had not blocked all progress. Now that the examinations have become a political battleground, a rational system may be long in coming.

A large audience passes judgment on the psychologist's tests. The British military selection program had to satisfy a Labor cabinet insistent that poor boys have a fair chance to become officers, the parents of the boys tested, and the old-line officers who trained the accepted men. A psychologist who installs a highly valid industrial selection program will find it in the ashcan a year later unless he convinces both management and the union that the test is fair. Users of test results have strong prejudices. If a group of social workers is accustomed to mental test A, the psychologist who substitutes mental test B in his case reports will encounter difficulty. Even if test B is more accurate than A, the social worker may disregard results from B because the test does not have his confidence. So important is user acceptability that the psychologist working with teachers, industrial personnel men, or physicians must often use a test that would be his second or third choice on the basis of technical qualities alone.

A test that seems relevant to the layman is said to have "face validity." Adopting a test just because it appears reasonable is bad practice; many a "good-looking" test has failed as a predictor. Civil service examiners, for example, prepared two tests to measure ability in aphabetic filing. One gave five names per item—John Meeder, James Medway, Thomas Madow, Catherine Meagan, Eleanor Meehan—and asked which name would be *third* in alphabetical order. The other test required the subject to place a name in the proper place in a series; for example:

Robert Carstens   A_____

Richard Carreton

B_____

Roland Casstar

C_____

Jack Corson

D_____

Edward Cranston

Though the makers were confident that the tests called on the same skill, and though both tests had reliabilities above 0.80, they correlated 0.01 (Mosier, 1947).

Such evidence as this (reinforced by the whole history of phrenology, graphology, and tests of witchcraft!) is strong warning against adopting a test solely because it is plausible. If one must choose between a test with "face validity" and no technically verified validity and one with technical validity and no appeal to the layman, he had better choose the latter. The job of the tester is, after all, to get information that improves decisions. The tester should seek and usually can find a test with both face validity and technical validity.

30. *A testing-training procedure for executives asks the man to work through an "in-basket" of communications of various sorts (memos, letters, policy directives, etc.) and mark each piece for suitable action (call a meeting, file, etc.). To make the task more realistic, one organization puts new postage stamps on the letters that supposedly came through the mail, cancelling them itself. The cost is perhaps 20¢ per executive. Does this refinement seem to be justified?*

Ease of Application

In most fields, one can choose between tests to be administered by untrained persons and tests to be given only by an expert. The test that is simpler to apply will have more complete directions and simple objective scoring, and requires no observation or judgment by the tester. The more complex test offers more comprehensive findings, but only in the hands of a well-qualified tester. Attention should also be paid to the adequacy of supplementary materials that assist the user in drawing conclusions from test results. This is especially important when a psychologist is choosing a test whose results many other persons will consult.

A test manual may present all the important information about the test and yet fail to communicate to the reader. Lennon found, indeed, that large numbers of schoolteachers fail to grasp even simple factual statements in an achievement test manual (Lennon, 1954). The person in charge of a testing program must educate all those who will give or interpret tests; he cannot rely on the manual to convey the insights they need.

Equivalent or Comparable Forms

Equivalent forms are tests measuring the same thing at the same level of difficulty, so that equal raw scores have the same meaning on each form. They are especially valuable when each person is tested twice—at the beginning and end of an experiment, or to check on an undependable first score. The use of new questions rules out the effect of memory.

Two tests are said to be *comparable* when their raw scores can be converted to the same derived-score scale. Some school achievement tests are organized in a series at different levels of difficulty so that the pupil may be tested each year. Although the tests are not equivalent, a scale is provided so that performances on the easier test and the harder test can be compared to evaluate the pupil's progress. Another type of comparability is seen in the DAT profile chart, which permits comparison of mechanical comprehension with other abilities by showing the rank of each score in the same norm group. Though useful, such comparisons introduce problems that will require attention later (Chapter 11).

31. *Published aptitude and achievement tests usually have equivalent forms. Only a few personality questionnaires do. For what uses would such forms be advantageous?*

Cost

The cost of the usual test is only a few cents, but when one is testing a large number of persons, a difference in cost may be worth some attention. Fortunately there is little relation between the cost of tests and their quality, so that even a limited budget permits the use of well-constructed tests. Cost is greatly reduced when it is possible to use an answer sheet and a reusable question booklet. The reusable MCT booklet costs about 22 cents per copy (in packages of 25). The answer sheets cost an additional 5 cents. In determining the cost of a test, one must consider not only the cost of the materials but also the cost of scoring.

A more inclusive cost figure is suggested by the charge Science Research Associates makes for full service on one of its batteries that provides several subtest scores for each pupil. Sixty cents per pupil covers rental of booklets, answer sheets, scoring, reporting of names and scores, and a basic statistical summary.

32. If a clinical tester is examining a criminal to establish whether he is mentally responsible, he may have to present his results in court and stand cross-examination on them (I. Frank, 1956). In what ways might his choice of tests differ from those he would use in examining a similar case at the request of a hospital psychiatrist?

33. A certain examination for French secondary-school admission was deliberately made very difficult to obtain a skewed distribution, since only a small number of places was to be filled. When the children told of the questions at home, parents organized protest meetings that ultimately brought the problem to the attention of the Minister of Education, who decided to give a second test to those who had failed. Do you agree with this decision?

34. What changes might automation on a large scale be expected to make in
   a. the time at which tests are given in educational institutions
   b. the way test findings are used in educational institutions
   c. the way test-development agencies operate and are financed

35. Answer a and b above, considering mental hospitals rather than educational institutions.

Evaluating a Test

We have now introduced nearly every concept that is used in judging the adequacy of a test. Subsequent chapters will describe the various types of tests and apply these concepts. In that application, the concepts will be explained more completely. Even though the reader needs to study those chapters before he attempts to draw conclusions about particular tests, we can here summarize the concepts and present a form useful in evaluating any test.

The development of a testing program requires, first of all, a clear purpose. As we pointed out earlier, one must search for a test that fits the decision to be made, not just for "a good test of reading" or "a good personality test." It is unrealistic for the student of testing to evaluate a test in the abstract, yet he cannot consider all possible applications simultaneously. For this reason, it is suggested that any test manual be approached with a definite measurement problem in mind. Our form carries a space for entering this purpose, which might be specific (selecting girls for training as punch-card clerks) or rather general (obtaining information to be filed for subsequent use in counseling high-school pupils as problems arise).

Ordinarily the tester's situation restricts the type of test that may be considered. It determines the choice between group and individual tests, the age or ability range, and the level of interpretative skill to be used. Thus a test to be given for later reference in high-school counseling will be a group test (since individual testing of a whole school is not practicable), will have to cover the whole range of a normal population, and will have to be suitable for interpretation by counselors and probably by all teachers and administrators. With such crude specifications in mind, one turns to publishers' catalogs, the Buros *Year-*

Table 6.6.   A form for evaluating tests

1. Title
2. Author
3. Publisher
4. Forms and groups to which applicable
5. Practical features
6. General type

7. Date of publication
8. Cost, booklet; answer sheet
9. Scoring services available and cost
10. Time required

11. Purpose for which evaluated
12. Description of test, items, scoring
13. Author's purpose and basis for selecting items

14. Adequacy of directions; training required to administer
15. Mental functions or traits represented in each score
16. Comments regarding design of test
17. Validation against criteria: number and type of cases, criterion measure, time interval, result
18. Other empirical evidence indicating what the test measures
19. Comments regarding validity for particular purposes

20. Generalizability (procedure, cases, result)
21. Long-term stability (procedure, time interval, cases, result)
22. Norms (type of scale, selection of sample)
23. Comments regarding adequacy of above for particular purpose

24. Comments of reviewers
25. General evaluation
26. References

books, texts on measurement or applied psychology, etc., and makes a list of tests to consider. The form presented in Table 6.6 is a convenient record of facts and opinions regarding tests examined in detail.

The top section (entries 1–10) includes simple descriptive facts that can often be obtained from the catalog. They are for the most part self-explanatory. It is suggested that you enter (6) one or two words to describe the general type, so that completed analysis forms may be filed by categories. In the specimen form filled out for the Bennett MCT (Table 6.7), we have inserted simply the word aptitude. The summary for MCT that appears here is not a full appraisal. We shall discuss evidence on mechanical comprehension further in Chapter 11.

Table 6.7.   Evaluation form for MCT

1. *Title.* Mechanical Comprehension Test
2. *Author.* George K. Bennett (with co-authors in some forms)
3. *Publisher.* Psych. Corp.
4. *Forms and groups to which applicable.*
    AA: high-school boys, job applicants
    BB: experienced workers, advanced students
    CC: engineering students, high-level job applicants
    W-1: high-school girls, female job applicants
    S, T: wide-range forms for high-school students, job trainees and applicants,
         experienced technicians
    Other versions in DAT battery (high school); also versions in French and
    Spanish.
5. *Practical features.*
6. *General type.* Aptitude
7. *Date of publication.* Basic versions published in 1940s. New forms S and T pub-
    lished in 1970.
8.[a] *Cost, booklet,* 22¢; answer sheet, 5¢
9. *Scoring services available and cost.* Adaptable to any machine scoring system.
10. *Time required.* 30 min.
11. *Purpose for which evaluated.* Vocational guidance of high-school students.
12. *Description of test, items, scoring.* Pictures of simple apparatus. Questions in
    3-choice form (5-choice in CC) as to what will happen to an object when force
    is applied, which of two structures is most stable, etc. Objective scoring (number
    right in recent forms). Only one overall score obtained.
13. *Author's purpose and basis for selecting items.* Intended to measure an ability
    required in many jobs and training courses. Past experience is allowed to affect
    scores, but the items require understanding rather than rote knowledge. Items
    were put through various stages of criticism and tryout; items retained were
    those discriminating high scorers (on the total test or a pooled Mech. Comp.
    score) from low scorers.
14. *Adequacy of directions; training required to administer.* Directions are unusually
    clear and simple. Classroom teacher can handle. Some answer sheets for older
    forms involve awkward matching of arrows to line up with booklet.
15. *Mental functions or traits, represented in each score.* General experience with
    machines common in Western world, understanding of simple principles of
    motion, energy. Formal physics helpful to some extent. Solutions can be intuitive
    or deductive; more rigorous deduction required in CC. Unspeeded. No claim is
    made that the test measures an innate aptitude.
16. *Comments regarding design of test.* Highly efficient. Use of correction formula
    in scoring unnecessary but harmless.
17.[a] *Validation against criteria.* Manual gives reference to numerous military and
    industrial studies in which MCT was correlated with grades in technical training
    or job ratings. Coefficients range from 0.30 to 0.60. Manual is often not clear as
    to time separating test and criterion. A separate compilation of studies by

Ghiselli (1966, pp. 122–123), confirms these validities, with slightly poorer results against job proficiency criteria.

Evidently generally useful, though the test usually must be supplemented by verbal measures. Information is lacking on usefulness of the test for prediction in high-school courses, or on long-range predictions from high-school testing. Such data are available for DAT version. Form CC has validities 0.28 to 0.50 for college freshmen, with performance in technical courses as criteria. Note that range is restricted, compared to h.s. group.

18.[a] *Other empirical evidence indicating what the test measures.* Study of 1471 applicants for fireman-policeman jobs shows that high-school physics raises scores about ½ s.d. on AA. (This information is needed—and not now available—for CC, where the effect of physics or math might be greater.)

Form AA correlates about 0.50 with general mental tests in wide-range groups; BB and CC correlate 0.20–0.30 among applicants to engineering school. Considerable overlap with spatial tests (0.50 with Minn. Paper Form Board in wide-range group, 0.66 with College Board spatial test among engineering-school applicants). Correlation of 0.30 with tool dexterity test. Factor-analytic studies[b] show a mechanical-experience factor prominent in the test. But loadings of general mental ability and spatial or visualization ability are so high that perhaps the concept of a separate *mechanical* reasoning ability is unnecessary.

19. *Comments regarding validity for particular purposes.* Test has predictive value for jobs or courses involving nonroutine machine operation. Overlaps general and spatial tests, so that its contribution would depend on the situation.

20.[a] *Generalizability.* Split-half method, coefficient = 0.84 (Form AA, 500 ninth-grade boys). Similar coefficients for other forms, lower in groups of restricted range. Interform correlation about 0.80 for BB *vs.* CC. Preliminary evidence for S and T indicates higher reliability for those forms.

21. *Long-term stability.*[c]

22.[a] *Norms.* Each manual offers several columns of percentile norms for various groups in schools and industry. In the older manuals, selection of groups is poorly described (e.g., "833 ninth-grade boys," "417 applicants for unskilled jobs"). For CC, tables are given separately for two specific engineering schools.

23. *Comments regarding adequacy of above for particular purpose.* Reliability of 0.80 is low for guidance. A second test should be given if a few points' difference in score would alter a decision. Difference between MCT and other aptitude scores will often arise from errors of measurement alone.

The norms have limited usefulness; the counselor ought to obtain norms for his school, for special courses in the school, and if possible for the local job market. Stability is insufficient to permit confident use of the test for long-range predictions earlier than twelfth grade.

24.[a] *Comments of reviewers*

"The manuals of directions are models of conciseness and honesty. . . . There is little doubt that the test measures comprehension of many mechanical principles, but its value for prediction has been questioned on the ground that several items involve principles or facts which one is unlikely to encounter in

Evaluation form for MCT (Continued)

---

everyday mechanical experience, outside of a physics course" (Charles M. Harsh, in Buros, 1949, p. 720).

"The *Test of Mechanical Comprehension* . . . should prove to be a useful tool especially to those persons engaged in educational and vocational guidance. It should also find increasing usage in the technical school and the industrial employment office. It is an attractive test; the items are intrinsically interesting; all the forms appear to have been well constructed; and they are easy to give. The range of usefulness of the test will undoubtedly increase as more validity data are made available" (George A. Satter, in Buros, 1949, p. 723). (Note: Much evidence on validity has appeared since the date of this comment.)

25. This is an exceptionally popular test, various versions having been prepared and widely used; there are many studies showing the relevance of the test to performance in mechanical work. The concreteness of the test makes it appealing. Being unlike tests commonly encountered in school, it dramatizes the concept of special abilities for the counselee.

The new forms S and T could be helpful in bringing the ninth grader to examine his aptitudes, but the DAT battery which includes a version of MCT is preferable for this purpose because it gives comparable data on other aptitudes. This battery is also useful later in high school, when more definite vocational and educational plans are being made. Even where a mechanical comprehension test is wanted by itself, MCT Form S perhaps has no advantage over the DAT version of the test, though further research may show one or the other to have somewhat better reliability or validity.

MCT is a measure of understanding acquired through general exposure to tools and machines; it does not depend on training or technical experience. There is some question as to whether MCT information adds much of value if general and spatial abilities have been measured. MCT indicates whether the person has the concepts useful in profiting from training; it does not guarantee proficiency without training, and it has nothing to do with manual aspects of performance.

---

[a] Refers to older forms. Comparable information on Forms S and T not available at this time.

[b] The meaning of information of this sort will be considered in Chapters 10 and 11.

[c] See Table 6.5. Stability will be discussed in Chapter 11.

The date of publication (7) is not highly significant. Some older tests are excellent. Indeed, as Anastasi remarks (1967), ". . . the effectiveness of a test is likely to increase markedly as more and more data accumulate from long term longitudinal studies and other research conducted with the test." An old test should ordinarily be scrutinized with special care, however, since some items may be obsolete, the norms may no longer be pertinent, and the manual is likely to be incomplete. Moreover, the interpretation that seemed appropriate when the test was published may be inconsistent with more recent findings.

The date of the manual is one of the places in which publishers sometimes introduce misleading information. It is possible to copyright the test manual every year so that it looks up-to-date, even though no real revision has been made. Such embellishments will not confuse the reader unless he gives undue weight to superficial values. Some half-truths can be spotted by any alert reader, while others are identifiable only by an expert. If the reader finds that the manual or test advertising is untrustworthy in one respect, he must of course view all the remaining information with suspicion. The scientific and ethical quality of the manual, however, does not always match the quality of the test. A few excellent tests have manuals that contain misleading or confusing statements.

The next·step is to form an impression of the test by examining the items, the scoring principles, and the aims the author had in mind in preparing the test. It is this impression that largely determines the appeal of the test to the subject and to other laymen. Under (12) in the form, one can describe the items superficially and should also list the titles of subtests to be separately scored. Attention should be given to the objectivity of scoring.

The author's stated intentions (13) help one to understand the nature of the test, though it perhaps can also serve some quite different purpose. The manual will usually indicate whether the author was interested in selection, guidance, clinical use, or classroom evaluation, and will often tell what aptitudes or traits he had in mind in preparing items. The source of items is particularly important if the test is to be interpreted on the basis of its content.

Many test manuals report statistical studies used in selecting items. These reports are rarely significant to the test purchaser. The item-selection procedure is best judged by its fruits, namely, the evidence on validity and generalizability. If content validity is of primary interest, statistical analysis is less informative than an examination of the content itself. Sometimes an old-fashioned manual reports a correlation of an item score with a total score as an "item-validity coefficient." This information is not a validity coefficient and should be ignored.

Directions (14) can be examined with regard to their clarity and the extent to which they standardize the test.

An armchair analysis of the test items should be made (15) to judge what abilities, experiences, work habits, or personality traits influence the score. Such an analysis is required for each of the subscores to be interpreted. One cannot hope to identify all the contributing variables, but the attempt brings to mind questions to be used in interpreting validity studies. The report should state what the score seems to indicate, whether this is what the author intended or not. It should also list irrelevant variables likely to distort scores. It is usually desirable for the reviewer to take the test or to administer it to a suitable subject.

Empirical evidence of validity (17–18) may be of various sorts. Spaces are provided for validation against criteria and for other studies bearing on construct validity. While some users examine only the evidence presented in the test manual, one can evaluate the test better if he considers data published elsewhere.

For some tests, the volume of research is so great that it can only be summarized or sampled. Under heading *18* any study might be listed that helps to establish what the score measures. One might list, for a mechanical aptitude test, evidence of its overlap with general intelligence, of its degree of speeding, or of the extent to which physics students earn better scores than those who have not studied physics. Factor analyses are often relevant to this question. Here particularly it is necessary to select the most significant information from that available.

The final evaluation of validity (*19*) is the most important single entry in the form. Does the test give the information needed to make the intended decision? What degree of confidence can be placed in it? What level of psychological training is required to interpret the test as proposed? To reach such an integrated conclusion, it is necessary to weigh positive and negative evidence, to decide which of several contradictory findings is most trustworthy, and to judge the body of evidence as a whole. It is especially important to note what necessary evidence on validity is lacking.

Entries *20–21* consider error of measurement. This information is usually presented in the manual and needs only to be summarized. Subscores as well as totals should be discussed. Norms (*22*) must be examined critically for representativeness, and for relevance to the user's own situation.

It is of course important to examine whatever critical reviews of a test are available, and the record form includes a space (*24*) for quotations that summarize the reviewer's evaluation. The general evaluation (*25*) is a final summary of the advantages and limitations of the test for the particular purpose, considering both its technical and its practical features. It is appropriate to compare the test with others having the same general function. One can also point to supplementary information that should be taken into account along with the test. Special ways of applying the test, over and above its use as a measuring instrument, should be noted. These would include making supplementary observations during the test, examining responses to obtain clues for diagnosis, using test responses as a point of departure in a counseling interview, etc.

An analysis of this sort for every test under consideration (whether the analysis is put in writing or not) provides a basis for a total testing program. A program is more than a list of good tests. A program will be designed so as to minimize wasteful overlap and timed so as to get each piece of information when it will be most helpful. Testing cannot be planned by itself. In industry or the armed forces it must be dovetailed with recruiting, training, and assignment. In the clinic, testing must be considered as part of the whole therapeutic effort. The final program states what tests will be given and when, and how the results will be used in assigning the person or in helping him to understand himself.

36. *Examine the manual for Forms S and T of MCT (which should have been published by the time this book appears) and decide whether it alters the evaluation given in Table 6.7.*

37. *Reviews of Forms S and T should appear in 1970 and 1971, and validity studies should appear in journals starting in 1972. How would you proceed to locate this information?*

SUGGESTED READINGS

Anastasi, Anne. Reliability. In *Psychological testing* (3d ed.) New York: Macmillan, 1968. Pp. 71–98.

A textbook chapter covering the theory of measurement error in a traditional vein. Our treatment gives greater prominence to the analysis of variance and the related formulas, whereas Anastasi stresses correlations between observations.

Bauernfeind, R. H. The concept of test reliability. In *Building a School Testing Program* (2d ed.) Boston: Houghton Mifflin, 1969. Pp. 98–117.

A presentation of essential concepts directed to the classroom teacher who is constructing tests or selecting standardized achievement tests on the basis of information in the manual.

Dobbin, John E., and others. [Critical reviews and appreciations of the *Test Standards*.] *Educational and Psychological Measurement*, 1966, *26*, 751–811.

Eight persons, whose background ranges over all types of testing and responsibilities from publishing to the firing-line use of tests, comment on the *Standards*. Note to what extent these various writers agree, and which aspects of the *Standards* draw critical fire. In particular, do the reviewers agree in identifying the same weaknesses and limitations of the *Standards?*

Wesman, Alexander G. Reliability and confidence. *Test Service Bulletin,* 1952, No. 44. New York: Psychological Corporation. (Reprinted in Remmers *et al.,* 1957; Flynn & Garber, 1967; and Gronlund, 1968.)

A simple presentation of the major difficulties in the interpretation of reliability coefficients reported in test manuals.

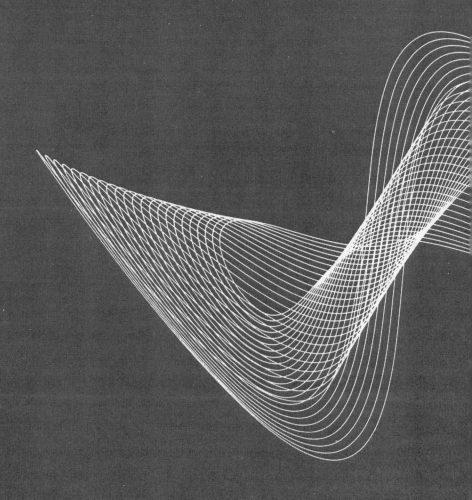

part II

Tests
of Ability

7

General Ability: Appraisal Methods

The Emergence of Mental Testing

Tests Before Binet

The outstanding success of scientific measurement of individual differences has been that of the general mental test. Despite occasional overenthusiasm and misconceptions, and the fact that the established tests are rendered obsolescent by recent conceptual advances, the general mental test stands today as the most important technical contribution psychology has made to the practical guidance of human affairs. Among mental tests, none has been more influential than that fathered by Alfred Binet. A history of mental testing is in large part a history of Binet's scale and its descendants.

The first systematic experimentation on individual differences in behavior arose from the discovery that astronomers differ in reaction time. In 1796, an assistant named Kinnebrook at Greenwich Observatory was engaged in recording, with great precision, the instant when certain stars crossed the field of the telescope. When Kinnebrook consistently reported observations eight-tenths of a second later than those of his superior, the Astronomer Royal, he was thought incompetent in his work and was discharged. Twenty years later, it was realized that even competent observers respond to stimuli at different speeds and that the variations are more or less normally distributed. Hence astronomers cannot consider one report strictly correct and all others wrong. Differences like these gradually came to be recognized as significant facts about the human system for processing information, rather than as annoying errors of observers.

Physiologists, biologists, and anthropologists were stimulated by the scientific climate of the 19th century to measure a great variety of human characteristics. Notable among these workers was Francis Galton, whose interest in individuality developed from his cousin Charles Darwin's newly published theory that differences among species derive from variation within species. During the latter half of the 19th century, Galton invented ways of measuring physical characteristics, keenness of the senses, and mental imagery. These methods, though not developed fully by Galton, served as models for later tests. In addition, Galton (1869) demonstrated that outstanding intellectual achievement occurred unusually often in certain families. Genius, evidently, was not an accident or a gift of capricious gods, but a lawful phenomenon to be investigated scientifically.

At this time, psychology was only beginning to emerge as an objective science. It was suggested that mental processes—or at least their products—could be observed under standard conditions. Scientific observations, supplementing or even replacing introspection and philosophical speculation, could describe exactly the relation between the mental and physical worlds. This was the aim with which Wundt opened the first psychological laboratory in Leipzig in 1879, and he and his colleagues did triumphantly establish quantitative psychological laws comparable in form to those of physics. Believing that psychological research should analyze behavior into its simplest elements, he designed techniques to measure very limited functions. Wundt, trying to identify general laws governing all minds, was not concerned with individual differences. His laboratory procedures and particularly his interest in quantitative research, however, had a strong influence on early tests. In the United States, as early as 1890, J. McKeen Cattell was using a mixture of procedures from Wundt's and Galton's laboratories to measure sensory acuity, strength of grip, sensitivity to pain from pressure on the forehead and memory for dictated consonants. Cattell came to the study of individual differences out of sheer curiosity, but he quickly became excited about the practical value of identifying superior individuals for responsible jobs. This line of effort unfortunately collapsed when the new tests measuring simple elements of behavior proved to have no relation to significant practical affairs. The crucial study was Wissler's, on test scores of Columbia University students (1901). He correlated their marks with each of the Cattell tests, finding such negligible correlations as the following: reaction time, -0.02; canceling a's rapidly on a printed page, -0.09; naming colors, 0.08; auditory memory (recall of digits), 0.16. We now recognize that low correlations were certain to result no matter what mental functions were tested, because Wissler's brief tests were quite inadequate samples of behavior, and his group was so highly selected that differences within it were hard to detect. The disappointment that followed the Wissler study, however, delayed attempts to base an applied psychology on the findings of the laboratory.

Wundt tested narrow, elementary reactions that could be precisely defined, using stimuli that could be accurately controlled. The tests had validity in the same way that a chemist's measure of the freezing point of a substance has validity; the result describes a clearly defined characteristic and is readily interpreted at a superficial level, no matter how much remains to be learned about the underlying process.

Tests of this sort have an obvious content validity, and continued investigation in the laboratory spins a web of theory between these measures and theoretical constructs. Their validity for predicting behavior outside the laboratory, however, has usually been negligible (except as a defect in color vision or another sensory quality is a handicap in some practical task).

For practical prediction, tests constructed on quite another principle have been more successful. When a complex performance is to be predicted, a sample of that very performance will often prove to be a good predictor. To minimize effects of specific training and to obtain a test of wide applicability, the test will sample, not the criterion task exactly, but the general type of intellectual or motor performance required by the criterion task. The Bennett MCT is of this nature.

This kind of practical testing came into psychology from medicine. Clinicians dealing with mental defectives and pathological cases needed diagnostic tests. Psychiatrists looked for tasks that would distinguish normal from abnormal subjects, and distinguish among various types of mental disorders. Kraepelin and other 19th-century psychiatrists observed reasoning, and steadiness of effort in continuous work. Their tasks had some resemblance to requirements of life outside the laboratory. Though few tasks of this period survive in present-day diagnosis, clinical tests are still chiefly concerned with complex processes. Alfred Binet, to whom we turn in a moment, was a physician by training and he chose tests that could distinguish between clinical groups, no matter how obscure or complex the "psychological meaning" of the tests.

The Binet tests had practical value for the physician, the educator, the social worker, and, in modified form, for the employer. The practical general mental tests of today are much closer to worksamples of life performance than to the narrow psychophysical measures of Wundt. In predicting school performance and adjustment to work, and in assessing the severity of mental disorder, the practical tester has found complex tasks far more relevant than tasks that isolate elementary reactions. The practical tests in general use today are much like those of the 1920s. Current tests differ from those of the earlier generation just as 1970 automobiles differ from those of 1920: more efficient, more elegant, but operating on the same principles as before.

Investigators continue to study the more elementary processes, and occasionally one is found to have practical significance. For instance, information on the brain functioning of a mental patient is obtained by having him report whether he sees a steady or flickering light when the stimulus light actually goes on and off many times per second (see p. 623). We are far from a theory that can explain complex behavior in terms of elementary reactions. "Stimulus-response psychology"—from Wundt to Skinner—has on the whole had little influence on the study of individual differences. The great influence has come from the functional orientation that emphasizes the purposive, deliberately adaptive nature of behavior.

Binet Defines Intelligence

About 1890, Alfred Binet became interested in studying judgment, attention, and reasoning. Being interested in complex mental processes, he tried a greater variety of tests than his predecessors. In studies published between 1893 and 1911 he tried to find out just how "bright" and "dull" children differ. Having little preconception regarding this difference, he tried all sorts of measures: recall of digits, suggestibility, size of cranium, moral judgment, tactile discrimination, mental addition, graphology—even palmistry. He found, as did others, that sensory judgment and other simple functions had little relation to general mental functioning, and he gradually identified the essence of intelligence as "the *tendency to take and maintain a definite direction;* the *capacity to make adaptations* for the purpose of attaining a desired end; and the *power of auto-criticism*" (translation by Terman, 1916, p. 45; italics added).

The stage was set, then, for the call in 1904 to produce the first practical mental test. Paris school officials had become concerned about their many nonlearners and had decided to remove the least capable children to schools in which they could be taught a simplified curriculum. The officials could not trust teachers to pick out the cases of genuine mental deficiency. There was a risk of segregating the able child who was making no effort and the troublemaker the teacher wished to be rid of. The officials wanted to identify the dull from good families whom teachers might hesitate to rate low, and the dull with pleasant personalities who might be favored by the teacher. Therefore they asked Binet to produce a method for distinguishing the genuinely dull. Binet's scale was published in collaboration with Simon in 1905, with revisions in 1908 and 1911.

The person making the first mental test is in the position of the hunter going into the woods to find an animal no one has ever seen. Everyone is sure the beast exists, for he has been raiding the poultry coops, but no one can describe him. Since the forest contains many animals, the hunter is going to find a variety of tracks. The only way he can decide which tracks to follow is by means of a preconception, however vague, about the nature of his quarry. If he seeks a large flat-footed creature he is more likely to bring back that sort of carcass. If he goes in convinced that the damage was done by a pack of small rodents, his bag will probably consist of whatever unlucky rodents show their heads.

Binet was in just this position. He knew there must be something like intelligence, since its everyday effects could be seen, but he could not describe precisely what he wished to measure. Some workers, then and now, have objected to this circular and tentative approach whereby mental ability is described only after the test has been made.

But to define a psychological quality a priori—before a period of investigation—is to leap into the dark. The faculty psychologists prior to Binet had defined mind as a bundle of separate faculties such as reasoning, memory, attention, and sensory discrimination. Tests were designed for the separate dimensions but no one of the abilities so measured seemed to have any relation to performance in everyday affairs. Terman (1916, p. 151) explained this as follows.

The assumption that it is easier to measure a part, or one aspect, of intelligence than all of it, is fallacious in that the parts are not separate parts and can not be separated by any refinement of experiment. They are interwoven and intertwined. . . . Memory, for example, cannot be tested separately from attention, or sense discrimination separately from the associative processes. After vainly trying to disentangle the various intellective functions Binet decided to test their combined functional capacity without any pretense of measuring the exact contribution of each to the total product.

Modern diagnostic tests do obtain useful information about distinct (though still complex) aspects of ability. In Binet's time, however, it was a great contribution to set aside the idea of separate functions in favor of the concept of a pervasive, general intelligence. Having started with the idea that some children were bright and some dull, he found quickly that those who were best in judgment were also superior in attention, vocabulary, etc. In other words, the tests were correlated. This implies that all these performances tend to develop together. If various intellectual tasks usually rank people in the same order, it is convenient to think of a general mental ability that enters all the tasks. But that ability is not a single process. Like blood pressure, it is a surface indication of the way in which all parts of the organism are working together.

Binet refined his idea of intelligence by trial and error. If color matching does not correlate with other estimates of mental ability, it must not be influenced by the common factor. If knowing certain information does correlate with the tests of reasoning, both must measure the same thing to some extent. Out of a study of his best test items, Binet came to his famous description quoted above.

We shall use the term *general ability* in a loose, comprehensive sense to refer to any of the tests influenced by the Binet "hodgepodge" tradition. Later, we shall encounter more refined concepts of general ability that emphasize analytic processes distinct from trained achievements. The shift in meaning will be clear in context.

At the turn of the century there was a great demand, especially in America, for objective methods of investigation. Although Thorndike was using experimental tests on animals, American psychological research had been dominated by introspection, anecdotes, and questionnaires, all of which were as fallible as the person reporting. Educational and social research had likewise been little more than the collection of opinions. Binet's method, impartial and independent of the preconceptions of the tester, was welcomed enthusiastically as a research technique and as a means of studying subnormal children.

In 1910, Lewis M. Terman began experimentation with the Binet tests, and in 1916 he produced the Stanford Revision which extended Binet's scale to normal and superior children. The Stanford-Binet (SB) had immediate popularity; instruments like it were prepared in all parts of the world. Other tests also appeared at this time, but the outstanding popularity of the Stanford test made its conception of mental ability the standard. The acceptance of the Stanford test was due to the care with which it had been prepared, its success in testing complex mental activities, the easily understood IQ it provided, and the practical results it quickly produced. The instrument has been central to psychological research and practice for many decades. Indeed, from 1920 to 1940 the main function of the clinical psychologist was to "give Binets" in schools and other institutions. Some clinicians did a great deal more than calculate IQs, but only in the 1940s did working with the individual truly begin to take precedence over classifying the subject and putting a report on file. Psychologists who regarded the recording of a score as the end of their responsibility usually held the view that a person's rate of mental development, and the level he will ultimately reach, are essentially fixed.

1. *What do the following definitions of "intelligence" include that Binet's definition does not, and vice versa?*
   a. *"The ability to do abstract thinking" (Terman).*
   b. *"The power of good responses from the point of view of truth or fact" (E. L. Thorndike).*
   c. *"The property of so recombining our behavior patterns as to act better in novel situations" (Wells).*
2. *Would the same sort of test items be called for by each of these definitions?*
3. *Is previous learning included in intelligence by these definitions? By Binet's?*

Interest in Selecting the Talented

Throughout the latter part of the 19th century, ideas about social institutions were strongly influenced by the Darwinian conception that the environment automatically selects the fittest organisms for survival. Galton, Spencer, and others in England saw education as preparation for responsibility, and expected the fittest persons to go furthest. A sound system would be one in which the persons having the greatest capacity were given greatest encouragement and greatest responsibility. This concept of an efficient, democratic society as one where "the cream would rise" was also prominent in American thought (Persons, 1950).

If some persons were naturally more "fit" intellectually than others, and more likely to benefit from education, this seemed to imply that ability is unidimensional, and that persons can be ranked from fittest in intellectual capacity to least fit. The influential British psychologist Charles Spearman spoke of a central (general) ability which he called g. Whereas Binet had been willing to consider personality and emotion as contributing to intellectual functioning, Spearman sought to isolate the purely intellectual element, i.e., to observe "mind" in its strictest sense. While some useful reasoning tasks were devised by Spearman and his students, their more fundamental influence was on the aims of testing and on test interpretation. In particular, their work encouraged (1) a sharp separation of intellectual powers from acquired understandings and from emotion and temperament; (2) ranking persons along a single dimension; and (3) interpreting the score as a measure of pure intellectual capacity. Only gradually have psychologists broken away from this thinking.

Binet's tests were originally designed as part of a clinical examination. American investigators appreciated this intensive study of the test performance, but they placed far more emphasis on the numerical score. Terman put forth as his definition of intelligence "the power of good responses from the point of view of truth or fact", which pointed toward a numerical assessment of superiority or inferiority and away from Binet's description of processes. In the spirit of Terman's definition, if a child had learned to read and count at an early age, this was simply evidence that the child was indeed intellectually superior. American testers of this period made no effort to rule out items that depended directly on instruction, though they did intend that all subjects should have had a fair opportunity to learn the words, concepts, and skills the test called for.

Some preliminary attempts at group testing had been made by the time the United States entered World War I, and it was suggested that these procedures could be used to screen the thousands of men being inducted into the army. The probable misfits could be rejected, and the remainder could be sorted into groups that would receive training for high, low, or intermediate responsibilities. Leading psychologists quickly assembled a test the final version of which became famous as Army Alpha. Alpha tested simple reasoning, ability to follow directions, arithmetic, and information. It was easily administered and interpreted, and the fact that soldiers holding greater responsibility earned high scores was considered to be striking evidence of its validity. Data such as those shown in Figure 7.1 were widely discussed in the press. Since success apparently could be predicted by group tests, schools and industry were quick to adopt them. Alpha itself appeared in a civilian revision, and comparable tests by Otis and others were widely applied in selecting employees and in assigning schoolchildren to fast and slow sections. The American Council on Education, representing the country's colleges and universities, commissioned L. L. Thurstone to prepare annual editions of a test that could be used in admission and guidance of freshmen. The ACE Psychological Examination was administered to nearly all college freshmen until about 1950, when other tests took its place.

Army Alpha and many of the tests that followed it made little attempt to measure abilities independent of prior education. (An arithmetic subtest, for example, is surely not a measure of native intellectual powers alone.) Nonetheless, these tests were generally regarded as measures of capacity for intellectual

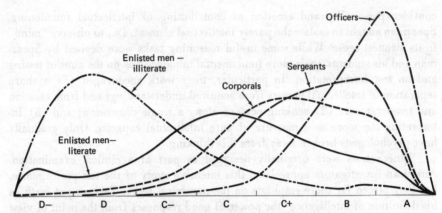

Figure 7.1.   Alpha scores of Army personnel of various ranks.
Yoakum & Yerkes, 1920.

development. While a number of psychologists warned that the tests measure only the person's development to date, and that the inference about underlying capacity is hazardous, the general impression among test users during the 1920s and for some time thereafter was that the tests did indeed select those "fittest to survive" and most meriting encouragement. The data in Figure 7.1, which tend to support this view, were widely reproduced in textbooks for psychologists and teachers. Other data from the same source (Figure 7.2) suggest that the group tests of the period were reflecting past educational opportunity rather than naked potential for taking responsibility. But in a climate of opinion where most people believed that talent is inborn and should be detected as early as pos-

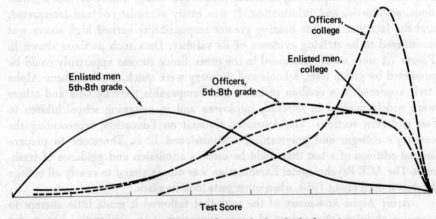

Figure 7.2.   Alpha scores of officers and men, by level of education.
The divisions of the score scale do not correspond perfectly to the letter grades of Figure 7.1.
Data from Yerkes, 1921, pp. 766–767.

sible, the message of Figure 7.2 was unwelcome. Data classified in this way were much less widely reproduced than Figure 7.1. Psychologists making clinical interpretations of course tried to allow for any subject's educational disadvantages, but only recently has the broader public become sensitive to the importance of experience in developing abilities.

Much misuse or misinterpretation of mental tests arises simply from the labels "intelligence" and "capacity," as they suggest that inborn potentiality is being measured. Performance on the tests is influenced by many things not included in this concept of "intelligence." Each test calls for knowledge, skills, and attitudes developed in Western culture, and better developed in some Western environments than in others. A mental test gives only indirect evidence on "potentialities," as we can observe potentiality only when it has flowered in performance. We cannot assume that all children in the same culture or all those who have attended the same school have had equal opportunities to develop the abilities we test. Even children raised together in the same home receive different stimulation and different degrees of encouragement. One way to emphasize that the test is a sample of one type of intellectual performance is to call it a "test of general scholastic ability"—implying that it measures an ability that presently exists (not a "potential") and that is helpful in most schoolwork. A similarly unambiguous label in a test for adults would be "test of verbal and numerical reasoning abilities."

As we proceed, it will be clear that there is no one thing that general-ability tests measure. Some of the tests in this category put substantial emphasis on school achievements such as arithmetic, whereas others employ tasks that can be performed without any use of verbal concepts. "Intelligence" and "general mental ability" are thoroughly ambiguous terms. The difficulties are to be removed not by announcing a definition but by a close examination of the tests and the research on them. In the course of this and the three following chapters, both the variation and the central consistency among concepts of general ability will become reasonably clear.

Alongside tests intended to report general ability, there sprang up a great number of measures of more specialized abilities. In 1919, for example, Seashore produced his so-called Measures of Musical Talent which tested abilities to discriminate pitch, timbre, rhythm, and the like. While these abilities are clearly necessary in musical performance, the name of the test is unsatisfactory, since it hints that these abilities are inborn and that a person who scores high on the test can be made into a brilliant performer. It is now known that these discriminations are trainable, so that a child who scores low does not have to be rejected from musical education; and it is certain that distinguished musicianship requires abilities far subtler than those Seashore tested. MCT is an example of tests prominent in employee selection; it overlaps to some extent with a test of general ability, but requires additional understandings that some bright people lack.

The emergence of such varied tests convinced psychologists, by the 1940s, that ranking of persons along only a single dimension gives an insufficient report on aptitudes; different jobs require different aptitudes, and bright persons are better along some lines than others. During World War II attention was given to assigning men to the type of training in which they could do well rather than to merely sorting them as excellent, fair, or poor. Tests used by the Air Force to choose a bombardier differed from those to select a pilot, for example. Spearman's view that intellect can be reduced to one key element has been replaced by far more complex conceptions. Despite this, a composite measure of intellectual performances is almost always used in practical testing today, with scores describing specialized abilities serving as supplementary data.

4. *Suppose an agricultural experiment station were to test the yield of various varieties of corn. For hybrid G, specimens yield, on the average, 47 pounds per plant.*
    a. *Does it mean anything to say that hybrid G seeds have a "potential" of 47 pounds? What is required for the "potential" to be realized?*
    b. *Might seeds of hybrid F, measured at an average of 42 pounds, have a greater "potential"?*

Wechsler's Scales for Clinical Appraisal

The group test was designed to yield a numerical measure, not to describe *how* the individual functions. Each version of the Binet scale was likewise intended to produce a single score, though the psychologist also noted significant descriptive information he observed. From the earliest days of individual testing, there were other tests designed especially to facilitate clinical description. Thus Porteus developed a series of mazes in which the child is to trace the correct path (Figure 2.2). The child's score reflects general adaptive ability, but the observer also obtains information on his ability to take advantage of his mistakes, his manner of reacting to frustration, etc. The maze is particularly suitable because the process by which the child solves the problem is clearly observable.

David Wechsler developed his scale out of experience as a clinical psychologist at Bellevue Hospital operated by the city of New York, where adult social derelicts of many sorts had to be tested. These people might be mentally defective, psychotic, or illiterate. The person's intellect was important to consider in decisions about his disposition, and the psychological examiner was expected to make some judgment about the nature of the disorder or handicap underlying any low score. Wechsler prepared the 1939 Wechsler-Bellevue Scale to provide for such clinical evaluations. Having been designed for children, some of the Stanford-Binet tasks seemed childish to adult subjects. Proper norms for adults were lacking. Furthermore, the SB tasks were predominantly verbal, and provided too limited a range of diagnostic clues for Wechsler's purpose. While

Wechsler's conception of mental ability was similar to Binet's, he felt it necessary to look beyond the composite performance to separate scores on different tasks. He therefore prepared ten or more subtests for each age level, each subtest containing one type of task: mazes, recall of information, memory for digits, etc. The original Wechsler-Bellevue has now been replaced by better-constructed and better-standardized forms that reach down to preschool ages. As with the Binet, there have been adaptations and translations throughout the world.

Wechsler's test became available just at the moment when clinical psychology was emerging as a full-fledged profession. During World War II military hospitals had to deal with great numbers of patients showing emotional disturbance or brain damage; there was particular concern for diagnosis, as quite different recommendations would be made for different types of disturbance. Wechsler believed that the profile of his subtest scores was a diagnostic indicator, that is, that brain-injured patients were especially low on certain subtests, schizophrenics on others, etc. His test became the standard instrument in military clinical testing and when clinical psychologists went to work in veteran's hospitals, public mental hospitals, and child-guidance clinics after the war, the test retained its prominence. With the appearance of the children's scale in 1949, the Wechsler scales came to dominate testing practice.

Strange ironies attend the history of test development. Binet set out to identify mental defectives, yet the most famous piece of research with his scale was Terman's follow-up of superior children. Wechsler tried to prepare a new type of mental test for adults, in the belief that adults and children differ in their interests and approach to work. Yet today his technique is popular as a children's test. Wechsler's secondary hope in developing the test was that patterns of subtest scores would provide a ready means of clinical diagnosis. Pattern analysis proved to have little validity and is no longer depended upon.

The simple interpretation of test profiles that Wechsler originally suggested has been replaced by other types of thinking. No rule can transform a Wechsler profile into a psychiatric diagnosis, and such an interpretation would in any event be inappropriate for normal children and adults. But it is highly suggestive to observe that a subject hesitates on an easy item when it follows a previous failure, or that he adequately repeats a string of digits but becomes confused when asked to repeat a somewhat simpler string backward. These observations, combined with the tester's clinical experience and theoretical knowledge, suggest a picture of the individual much richer than the IQ alone provides.

Wechsler emphasized that performance is a complex product of biological development and experience. Like Binet, he wished to consider the individual whole, and was quite unwilling to separate intellectual from emotional processes. Emotional forces may heighten attention, persistence, and adaptability or they may impair ability to mobilize intellectual resources. Since anxiety, self-confidence, desire to impress the tester, and so on are clearly learned reactions, Wechsler scores have never been thought of as measuring potential independent of experience.

Description of the Wechsler and Binet Scales

Wechsler Test Materials and Procedure

The Wechsler series in use today consists of three tests: WPPSI for children from age 4 to 6½ (introduced in 1967), WISC for ages 7 to 16 (1949), and WAIS for older subjects (1955). The three scales have the same general pattern, with five or six subtests producing a Verbal score (hereafter denoted V) and five more generating a Performance (P) score, both together giving the Full Scale score. The subtests at different age levels are similar but not identical (Table 7.1). In addition to the subtests regularly used in a scale, there are alternate tests. Thus, in WISC, Digit Span constitutes a sixth Verbal subtest that may be employed if one of the regular tests is somehow spoiled during administration or the tester particularly desires to observe Digit Span performance.

Table 7.1.   Subtests of the Wechsler scales for various ages

Preschool-Primary (WPPSI)	Children (WISC)	Adults (WAIS)
VERBAL		
Information	Information	Information
Comprehension	Comprehension	Comprehension
Arithmetic	Arithmetic	Arithmetic
Similarities	Similarities	Similarities
Vocabulary	Vocabulary	Vocabulary
(Sentences)	(Digit Span)	Digit Span
PERFORMANCE		
Block Design	Block Design	Block Design
Picture Completion	Picture Completion	Picture Completion
	Picture Arrangement	Picture Arrangement
	Object Assembly	Object Assembly
Animal House		Digit Symbol
Mazes	(Mazes)	
	Coding	
Geometric Design		

Parentheses indicate tests used as alternates or supplements.

Verbal tests. The following items, not taken from actual Wechsler forms,[1] indicate the character of each subtest at various levels of difficulty:

Information
How many wings does a bird have?
Who wrote "Huckleberry Finn"?
Comprehension
Why do automobiles have tires?
Why do married people who want a divorce have to go to court?
Arithmetic
Jane had 2 candies and her mommy gave her 1 more.
How many did she have altogether?
How many hours will it take to drive 240 miles at the rate of 30 miles an hour?
Similarities
Puppies grow up to be dogs and kittens to be _____.
In what way are water pipes and streets alike?
Vocabulary
What is a prince?
What does *formulate* mean?
Digit Span
Examiner says a string of numbers at rate of one per second; when he finishes, subject recites the group. Other strings are given which the subject is required to recite backward. Easiest items present 3 digits forward, 2 backward; most difficult items, 9 forward or 8 backward.
Sentences
Child is to say back to examiner a sentence such as

Jerry has two dogs and a new blue scooter.

These subtests were selected to fall within general mental ability, and yet to silhouette different processes. Some depend directly on education, though not on specialized studies. Others require analysis and judgment.

Performance tests. Among the performance subtests, we have already (Chapter 3) examined Block Design. Figure 7.3 illustrates some other performance subtests.

[1] Publishers are reluctant to authorize reproduction of actual test items because a professional textbook may fall into the hands of people who will take the test in question or whose children will take it. This might give an unfair advantage. There is some risk of misrepresenting the test when the specimen items have not gone through the full tryout and editing process. In this book, we sometimes employ actual items, sometimes items prepared by the publisher that were dropped from the final form, and sometimes items that are roughly parallel in structure to actual items. While the items in this section are parallels to items from the three Wechsler scales, we cannot be sure without tryout that the parallel to a WPPSI item, for example, will fall at the preschool level of difficulty; for this reason, items are not identified with levels.

Picture Arrangement

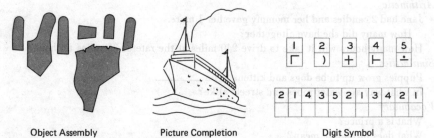

Object Assembly   Picture Completion   Digit Symbol

Figure 7.3.   Items from Wechsler Performance subtests.
Copyright © 1955 by The Psychological Corporation, New York, N.Y. All rights reserved.
Reproduced by permission.

These tests illustrate Wechsler's concern for variety. Block Design, for example, requires analysis of a complex whole, breaking a pattern into elements. Object Assembly gives the parts and requires the person to discover how they go together. Bonuses for rapid performance are allowed.

Digit Symbol requires the person to fill in the proper code symbol under each number, doing as much as he can in a short time. (Our illustration shows only five symbols; the actual test uses ten.) The code remains in front of the subject as he works. He can continually refer to the code, or he may carry it in his head. The test might appear to be a work sample of learning ability, but the motor abilities required to copy figures rapidly have a large influence on the score (Murstein & Leipold, 1961).

In Picture Arrangement, a story is told in three or more cartoon panels; they are presented in random order, to be arranged correctly. Here the subject must identify a complex whole from disorganized parts. (This test was not used in the preschool scale because the task could not be explained adequately to young children.)

Performance tasks are especially helpful in studying problem children, psychiatric patients, the mentally retarded, and persons with limited education. They make minimal demands on verbal facility, they permit significant observations of the process of performance, and they appeal to subjects who resist school-like tasks. V and P rank subjects differently, and hence do not measure exactly the same characteristics.

The Wechsler is comparatively simple to administer, requiring about one hour. Subtests are administered one after the other, in any order that seems likely to maintain interest. In some subtests all items are presented; in others, the examiner shifts to the next subtest when the subject has clearly gone as far as he can. In some of the verbal tests, the examiner must make rather sensitive judgments as to the correctness of an answer since it may be necessary to request the subject to elaborate his meaning. Answers that seem wrong may be judged correct after the subject explains himself. When the subject is responsive and friendly the examiner is tempted to interact more freely, to give more praise, and to give more opportunity to clarify answers (Masling, 1959). Scorers often disagree about borderline answers (Walker, Hunt, & Schwartz, 1965); supplementary scoring aids (e.g., Massey, 1964) are helpful.

5. *Which of the Wechsler subtests described have the following characteristics?*
   a. *The score is affected by educational background.*
   b. *The test demands experiences common to the persons in the urban American culture.*
   c. *The test requires problem solving or reorganization of knowledge rather than mere recall.*
   d. *The test measures very simple mental processes such as Cattell and Wissler investigated.*
6. *Have a friend make up a Digit Span test by preparing two strings of digits of each length from five digits to twelve. Then have him give the test to you, reading off each string at a steady rate, without emphasis. Judging from your experience, what processes are required to do well on the test? What might account for a poor performance, in a high-school student who performs at an average level on other Wechsler subtests?*

Stanford-Binet Materials and Procedure

While the Wechsler scales are more often used today than the Stanford-Binet (SB), the latter is equally sound and some testers continue to prefer it. Moreover, such a large fraction of the research literature is based on the Stanford-Binet that an understanding of the test will continue to be necessary.

Binet thought of intelligence as a steadily growing power, and so proposed a scale or ladder of tasks. His measurement finds out how far up the ladder the child can go before the tasks become too difficult. For any level on the ladder Binet selected tasks that average children at that age are just mastering. The tasks for young children involve relatively simple discrimination and recall, whereas those for middle childhood require intellectual manipulations (Table 7.2). The entire scale includes many more levels than the table shows, with six subtests at each level. Each subtest has several items, of which we show only one or two.

Verbal Absurdities (Form L-M, Year IX)[2] is a rather typical task.

[2] Items copyright 1916 by Lewis M. Terman, 1937 by Lewis M. Terman and Maud A. Merrill, © 1960 by Houghton Mifflin Company. This and other items from the Stanford-Binet reproduced by permission of the publisher.

Procedure: Read each statement and, after each one, ask, "What is foolish about that?". . . If it is not clear that the subject sees the absurdity E must say, "Why is that foolish?"

(a) Bill Jones's feet are so big that he has to pull his trousers on over his head.

(b) A man went one day to the post office and asked if there was a letter waiting for him. "What is your name?" asked the postmaster. "Why," said the man, "you will find my name on the envelope."

(c) The fireman hurried to the burning house, got his fire hose ready, and after smoking a cigar, put out the fire.

(d) In an old graveyard in Spain they have discovered a small skull which they believe to be that of Christopher Columbus when he was about ten years old.

(e) One day we saw several icebergs that had been entirely melted by the warmth of the Gulf Stream.

Scoring is objectified by a scoring guide that illustrates acceptable and unacceptable answers. In an absurdities item, the subject is expected to recognize clearly the central absurdity, and not to bring in irrelevant matters.

The SB has somewhat different content at different ages, as is indicated by Sattler's armchair classification summarized in Table 7.3. Some of Sattler's distinctions are subtle, and other interpreters of the test would no doubt modify his categories. The correlations in Table 7.2, and the predominance of language and verbal reasoning items in the counts of Table 7.3, indicate that the total score on the SB is heavily weighted with verbal abilities. Only at the preschool levels can many as half the items reasonably be classed as nonverbal—in the sense that only simple words and sentences are to be understood or given in responses.

The 1916 SB had only one form. Two forms were provided in 1937, but testers tended to concentrate on Form L. In 1960 the test was reissued with just a single form (called L-M).

The examiner attempts to start the child on easy tasks, ordinarily those located a year below his actual age—lower, if he is suspected to be below average. The child moves upward, level by level, until at some level he fails all the subtests. Levels are spaced 6 months apart from ages 2 to 5, one year apart from age 5, and even more widely above age 14. A 9-year-old would begin with tests at year VIII and, if he passed those, would continue until he reached his limit of ability. Some 9-year-olds would be unable to go beyond the 11-year level, whereas others would still be passing a few tests at the 14-year level. One hour, more or less, is required for testing.

Since the child encounters considerable frustration in a succession of failures, Hutt (1947) proposed to alternate easy and hard items. He found that well-adjusted children earned the same IQs on his "adaptive" procedure as on the usual test, but badly adjusted children averaged 4.5 IQ points higher. However, any departure from standard administrative practice changes the meaning of scores. Hutt's nonstandard method will yield higher IQs on the average than the procedure by which the test was standardized. This argument has been used

Table 7.2. Representative tasks from the Stanford-Binet

Year	Task	Correlation with whole test	Nature of Stimulus	Nature of Response
II-6	Points to toy object "we drink out of"	0.55	Verbal	Motor
	Shows doll's hair	0.63	Verbal	Motor
	Names *chair, key*	0.70	Object	Verbal
	Repeats "4–7"	0.63	Verbal	Verbal, memory
IV	Names *gun, umbrella*	0.79	Picture	Verbal
	Recalls name of object (dog) when covered by box	0.53	Object	Verbal, memory
	"Brother is a boy; sister is a. . . ."	0.56	Verbal	Verbal
	Matches circles, squares	0.75	Picture	Motor
	"Why do we have houses?"	0.70	Verbal	Verbal
VI	Defines *orange, envelope*	0.67	Verbal	Verbal
	Gives examiner 9 blocks	0.77	Verbal	Motor
	Maze	0.69	Object	Motor
	"An inch is short; a mile is. . . ."	0.67	Verbal	Verbal
IX	Examiner notches folded paper; child draws how it will look unfolded	0.62	Object	Drawing
	Verbal absurdities	0.83	Verbal	Verbal
	Reproduces design from memory	0.60	Picture	Drawing, memory
	Repeats "8–5–2–6" backward	0.52	Verbal	Verbal, memory
	Computes change from a purchase	0.62	Verbal	Calculation
XII	Defines *skill, juggler*	0.79	Verbal	Verbal
	Finds absurdity in picture	0.51	Picture	Verbal
	Defines *constant, courage*	0.85	Verbal	Verbal
	Completes "The streams are dry . . . there has been little rain."	0.72	Verbal	Verbal
Average Adult	Defines *regard, disproportionate*	0.86	Verbal	Verbal
	Explains how to measure 2 pints of water with a 5-pint and a 3-pint can	0.70	Verbal	Verbal
	Explains a proverb	0.73	Verbal	Verbal
	Compares *laziness* and *idleness*	0.80	Verbal	Verbal

Source: Adapted from Terman & Merrill, 1960, pp. 69 ff.

to account for some gains in IQ that might otherwise be attributed to intellectual growth during preschool.

When tests are given in the usual manner, the investigator often finds gains

Table 7.3. Percentage of Stanford-Binet L-M subtests judged as falling into seven content categories

					Percentage of subtests classified as			
Age level	Number of tests	Lan-guage	Reasoning	Memory	Conceptual	Social intelli-gence	Numerical reasoning	Visual-motor
2-5	42	26	21	10	5	17	0	21
6-10	31	19	10	19	16	16	10	10
11-14	23	30	26	17	9	9	9	0
AA-SAIII	26	31	15	12	27	0	15	0
Tests representative of category		Naming objects; rhymes	Orientation; verbal absurdities	Memory for sentences; for digits	Similarities; proverbs	Comprehension; picture absurdities	Making change; ingenuity	Form board; copying a square

SOURCE: Adapted from Sattler, 1965.

of 10 IQ points between the start of the preschool program and the test the following spring. But when the pretest is given by an adaptive procedure like Hutt's, to reduce frustration, the average pretest score is higher than under standard administration, and no fall-to-spring gain appears (Zigler & Butterfield, 1968). Apparently the child coming to school for the first time is lacking in emotional and attentional readiness, and so his full ability is not displayed under the standard test procedure. Standard testing works satisfactorily after several months of school, when he has become accustomed to solving problems on adult demand.

A somewhat similar comment about test procedure is made by Eysenck (1957), who compares the usual test to the "massed practice" conditions of the psychological laboratory. When a person is required to work at a test for a long, uninterrupted period, his effort and accuracy fall off. Eysenck suggests that this decrement may be greater for some types of personality than for others. No one has provided evidence, however, that a "spaced" test—with sections given on different days—elicits higher scores or has greater validity.

7. *In a Wechsler subtest (except for Vocabulary), every subject starts at the beginning of the subtest. In the SB, one does not administer the easiest items to older subjects. What differences in the designs of the tests justify this difference in procedure? Why should one not start the SB with the easiest items and work upwards?*

8. *Judge the following answers to the problem "Bill Jones's feet are so big . . ." (from Pintner et al., 1944, p. 60) as right or wrong:*

   a. *You can't put them on because his legs are joined together.*

   b. *You can't put your trousers over your head because your legs are in them.*

   c. *He's supposed to put the trousers over his feet.*

   d. *A man couldn't put his pants over his head.*

9. *There are Digit Span items mixed into the SB, two or three digit items being followed by items of other kinds before the next digit item is reached. Children seem to recall longer strings of digits in this format then they do in the Wechsler format (Hutton, 1964). What explanation can you offer? Does this fact suggest anything about the comparative validity of the two formats?*

10. *A statement such as the following is often made: "The same set of items, administered at two different ages, is very likely to measure different mental processes in the older group." What could be meant by that statement? Illustrate.*

The Intelligence Quotient and Other Scores

The IQ as a Standard Score

Most tests of general scholastic ability provide tables for converting raw scores into "intelligence quotients." These converted scores are nothing more than standard scores, but instead of the customary mean of 50 and standard deviation of 10, the IQ conversion fixes the mean at 100 and the standard deviation at 15 or 16. A person whose raw score is 2 s.d. above the mean for his age is assigned an IQ of 130. The IQ scale is anachronistic; scores of this form have no advantage over standard scores expressed on the 50±10 scale. The only justification for the 100±15 scale is that intelligence quotients have been used in the psychological literature for many decades, so that a body of lore has grown up about what can be expected of a child with IQ 60 or IQ 120.

To understand how the IQ came into psychological tradition, and why it is fading from the scene, we go back to 1916. Binet had arranged his test as a ladder, and suggested describing each child in terms of the level he reached on the ladder. This level came to be called the child's *mental age*. This, however, describes the child's present status, and those who saw the test as a measure of potential wanted to describe the child's rate of development. Dividing the mental age by the chronological age was suggested, and when Terman scored the Stanford-Binet this way he set the pattern for other mental tests, and for reports on test results in the literature.

The IQ of this period was a "ratio IQ," formed by expressing the child's age in months, dividing it into the mental age in months, and moving the decimal two places to the right. A child of chronological age (C) 7 and mental age (MA) 7 would thus have an IQ of 100. A child of CA 10 and MA 12 years 6 months would have an IQ of 125. The ratio IQs were distributed more or less normally, with standard deviations in the neighborhood of 15 or 16. About 46 per cent of the population had SB IQs in the range 90–109, about 4 per cent above 130, and about 3 per cent below 70 (See Table 7.5. These figures are taken from the 1937 standardization of the Stanford-Binet [Terman & Merrill, 1960], the last large-scale standardization of an individual test giving ratio IQs).

Teachers and other nonpsychologists have become accustomed to receiving reports in the form of IQs; this impels test developers to provide for an IQ conversion. When the Differential Aptitude Test battery appeared in 1947, it offered a profile of eight aptitudes each scored on the 50±10 scale; interpretation was to be based on the profile. While the test was widely accepted, demands from schools for something like an IQ compelled the test authors to offer a supplementary scale that converts the sum of the verbal and numerical scores into an IQ-like measure. Before this extra score was offered, teachers often requested that an "IQ test" be administered in addition to the DAT.

When testers came to realize that the ratio IQ was unsatisfactory, for reasons to be indicated below, and yet had to provide some measure like it to appease their clients, they turned to the standard-score form of IQ, known as a "deviation IQ." The standard-score conversion is such that the distribution of deviation IQs is similar to that traditionally found for ratio IQs. Some testmakers (including Wechsler) have defined the deviation IQ to have a standard deviation of 15, some 16 (as in the 1960 SB), and occasionally one has used an out-of-line value such as 20. The recent *Test Standards* suggest that any test reporting deviation

IQs should design the conversion so that in an unselected population of a given age the mean and standard deviation will be 100 and 16, respectively.

Differences in the choice of s.d. and, indeed, the difference between ratio and deviation IQs are less critical than differences in the practices of test standardizers. If a test is standardized on schoolchildren, the average score is not truly representative of all children of the indicated age and should not be set equal to an IQ of 100. But it is not clear just how to correct the standardization for the absence of out-of-school subjects. The effect of variations in standardization is shown in research on the Pictorial Test of Intelligence (manual, 1964, p. 21; Houghton Mifflin). This test was standardized on a small but apparently representative sample of children (about 150 at each age), using a 100 ± 16 scale. When a separate group of 32 first-graders took this test (PTI) along with SB and WISC, the results were:

	Mean	s.d.
PTI	114	8
SB	114	18
WISC	102	10

This group of children was not randomly selected, so we need not be surprised that the data do not show mean 100 and s.d. 16. But this leaves us puzzling over the low mean for WISC and the high s.d. for SB. Such inconsistencies are often found when different tests are compared. Other studies (see Littell, 1960 and Estes, 1965) have found WISC and WAIS means lower than SB means when both are given to the same cases in the normal and superior ranges. With defectives, WISC IQs average higher than SB IQs (Fisher, Kilman, & Shotwell, 1961). Evidently one test or the other was standardized on an unrepresentative sample, but we have little basis for judging which is at fault.

The principal conclusion is that an IQ in isolation can be given only a very rough interpretation. One cannot conclude that an IQ of 130 on one test represents the same degree of superiority as an IQ of 130 on another. The tester who becomes familiar with a particular test in a particular population builds up his own reference system, so that each level of the IQ scale comes to have meaning for him—but this could be accomplished with any other type of score.

Faults of the ratio IQ. The ratio IQ arose out of the idea that a child's rate of mental development reflects his potentiality. It was thought that a 4-year-old who has mental age 5 is developing 25 per cent faster than the average, and will continue to develop at this faster rate until adulthood. This implied that for any given child the plot of MA in successive years forms an ascending straight line (except for errors of measurement). Any linear trend obviously breaks down in adulthood. Mental test scores of adults are very little higher than those of adolescents. Since the average score at age 40 is about the same as at 15, it makes no sense to refer to someone as having reached "mental age 40." It was for this reason that Wechsler, setting out to build a scale for adults, introduced the deviation IQ. A 40-year-old with IQ 125 does not match the average 50-year-old; the deviation IQ reports only his standing among others of his own age.

In childhood also, the expected linearity of development failed to occur. When enough data had accumulated to trace the growth of individuals the lines proved to be not at all straight (see page 231).

This brings us to the chief limitation of deviation IQs: the 100 ± 15 scale differs from that of other tests and no ready comparison—e.g., of general ability with mechanical comprehension—is possible.

The quotient form of score is not suitable for many tests introduced for the purpose of vocational guidance. Some of these abilities (e.g., pitch discrimination) showed little correspondence to age; they reach their full development during childhood. Such scores could not sensibly be reported in terms of "age level reached." Moreover, it may be inappropriate to compare the subject with the average person of his age. Conclusions about a high-school student in a college-preparatory program, for example, rest far more on how he compares with similar students than with unselected adolescents. For guidance, the usual practice is to put all test scores on the same standard-score or percentile scale. For a young child one would use a reference population of the pupil's own age, and possibly of the same sex and education status. By midadolescence, educational status is a better basis for norms than age.

Educational selection and the IQ distribution.   While comparing a person with the population is of some value, practical decisions require us to estimate how he will fit into a more selected group. Even when the child enters school, his companions are not representative of the population, for some subnormal children are institutionalized or cared for in the home. Community and neighborhood differences restrict the range. Through the grades there is slow but continuous elimination, especially where children are permitted to leave school to work. The superior child is less likely to leave school, and the end result is a gradual rise in the average. A study made in the 1940s of dropouts in five school systems permits us to construct Table 7.4. While the statistics would differ today, the general pattern is no doubt similar. (Some recent evidence is offered by Stice & Ekstrom, 1964.) The very dull tend to drop out as early as the law allows. Those below IQ 85 tend to fall a year or two behind others of the same age, and to drop out of high school. The IQ range in high school is unrepresentative of the adolescent population, and college groups are even more selected (Table 7.5). On a group test for school ages the mean IQ of 100 represents the average of pupils in school.

Since the range of abilities varies from school to school and from class to class, most decisions must be based on local norms. Wolfle's report (1954, p. 147) on college students provides an important warning against overgeneralizing in

Table 7.4. Educational records of 2500 seventh-graders

| | Intelligence Quotient | | | | |
	Below 85	85–94	95–104	105–114	115+
All cases in Grade 7	400	575	650	575	400
Dropouts in Grades 7 and 8	93	30	14	5	2
Remainder entering Grade 9	307	545	636	570	398
Dropouts in Grades 9 and 10	241	171	143	78	29
Remainder entering Grade 11	66	374	493	492	369
Dropouts in Grades 11 and 12	52	65	81	55	25
Remainder continuing to graduation	14	309	412	437	344

SOURCE: Dillon, 1949.

interpreting an IQ. He studied 41 representative colleges, using a score scale roughly comparable to an IQ. In the most selective of the 41 colleges, the middle 50 per cent of the entering freshmen fell between 126 and 137; in the lowest, the middle range was from 99 to 117. A student who would succeed readily in one college would be far below his competitors in another.

A student choosing among colleges needs to know what competition he will face in each college. Counselors can now obtain such information from reference books (College Entrance Examination Board, 1967; American College Testing Program, 1967–68) which tabulate for each college the scores of applicants, of

Table 7.5. Percentage distribution of IQs

IQ	Standardizing sample ($N = 2904$)	High-school graduates ($N = 21,597$)	College entrants ($N = 1093$)
140 and above	1.3 ⎫	9.7	31.7
130–139	3.1 ⎬ 12.6		
120–129	8.2 ⎭		
110–119	18.1	22.8	46.1
100–109	23.5	29.9	18.1
90–99	23.0	23.2	4.0
80–89	14.5 ⎫		
70–79	5.6 ⎬ 22.7	14.3	.1
Below 70	2.6 ⎭		

Note: The standardizing sample data are for ratio IQs on the 1937 Stanford-Binet (Terman & Merrill, 1960). High-school data are for group tests as recorded in school files (Semans et al., 1956). College data are for Wechsler-Bellevue and WAIS administered to freshmen at San Jose State College (Plant, 1958).

persons accepted for admission, and of freshmen actually enrolled. They some-times report the grade expectation at each score level, and other information rele-vant to the high-school student's decision. For some States there are handbooks that provide norms and expectancy tables for every college in the State.

11. *If for age 15 the standard deviation of mental ages is 2 years and 10 months, find the deviation IQ corresponding to an MA of 16.*

12. *It was once the practice to define a "feebleminded" child as one having a ratio IQ below 70, the SB ordinarily being used for measurement at that time. What facts given above cast doubt on the wisdom of such a definition?*

13. *The use of a 100 ± 16 standard-score scale for general mental tests makes the comparison with other ability measures difficult. Other ability tests could be reported on the 100 ± 16 rather than the 50 ± 10 standard-score scale. Are there any arguments against agreeing to use the 100 ± 16 scale for all standard-score conversions?*

14. *A high-school senior is considering three colleges. His aptitude tests suggest that he will be at the 80th percentile among freshmen at college A, the 50th at B, and the 20th at C. C is a "prestige" school, and A is thought to have an un-distinguished faculty. Which should he choose?*

Mental Age

The mental age score indicates the age at which the average child does as well as this subject has done. John, who is 5, earns a mental age of 8 if he does as well as the average 8-year-old. Scoring of SB would be simple if the child passed all tests to a certain level and failed all tests after that level. Because the failures enter gradually, the mental age is determined by adding credits (usually two months per test) for each test passed. The total credit in months is converted into a mental age in years and months (usually written thus: 5–8 for 5 years, 8 months). For tests not built on the ladder principle, point scoring is used, and the average score earned by 8-year-olds defines what a child must do to be credited with "MA 8."

The mental age serves essentially the same purposes as a raw score. As with any total score, one can reach the same MA in different ways. Two children with the same score have received the same number of credits, but they are not neces-sarily similar in pattern of development. A bright young child will reach a mental age of 8 by passing a different set of tests than a subnormal adolescent who also has MA 8 (Magaret & Thompson, 1950). Among those having the same MA, the brighter children tend to go furthest on tasks that require analysis and judgment, whereas the duller children earn much of their credit on tasks for which schooling or experience gives a marked advantage (e.g., information items).

The MA is an estimate of present performance and of promise in the imme-diate future. Superior children who are younger than the other pupils in a class tend to equal the performance of average children; they do worse than superior children of the normal age. In making decisions within a group of varied age (e.g., in sectioning of classes) the mental age or the raw score gives more relevant information than the IQ. In research also, if it is desired to equate groups, to separate groups unequal in present ability, or to correlate some other variable with mental ability, *the mental age should be used rather than the IQ*. In equating, it is preferable to consider both the MA and CA.

The possible difference in results is illustrated in a report where both MA and IQ were correlated with raw score on the Illinois Test of Psycholinguistic Abilities (McCarthy & Kirk, 1961). Each sample had an age range of six months. Correlations were as follows:

Age group	2½	3	3½	4	5	6	7
Correlation for MA	0.33	0.49	0.55	0.71	0.61	0.56	0.70
Correlation for IQ	0.14	0.39	0.55	0.67	0.60	0.54	0.69

Use of IQ rather than MA is particularly misleading at early ages and in groups with a wide age range.

The IQ, percentile, or standard score is more pertinent than the mental age or raw score when a long-range comparison involving more than one age group is attempted—for example, when one wants a rough estimate of how a present 6th grader will rank among 18-year-olds. Standard scores or percentiles are also preferred for "sideways" comparison of measures of different types at the same age.

Wechsler started with an interest in testing adults, for whom the concept of mental age is inappropriate. When he brought out the children's scale, he was forced to produce a sort of mental-age conversion. He buried the conversion in appendices to his manuals and discouraged its use, and in this he may well have been wise. But the failure to compute and use a total raw score is a serious omission in research with the Wechsler and in practical work in which comparisons are made among children varying in age.

Wechsler Scaled Scores

We have already described the Wechsler V, P, and Full Scale IQs as standard scores with mean 100 and s.d. 15. Subtest scores are also converted to a standard score, though not to an IQ. Different subtests have different numbers of items, and the number of credits per item varies; consequently, subtest raw scores are hard to compare. Wechsler provides a table for each age level, translating the subtest raw score into a scaled score. The scaled score has a mean of 10 and an s.d. of 3 in the age group. For WAIS, scaling is based only on ages 20–34. The ten or eleven scaled scores constitute the individual's profile.

15. *Three children have the following scores:*

	CA	*MA*	*IQ*
Mack	7–6	10	130
Ray	10	10	100
Ted	10	13	130

Which boys are most similar? Can one say that any two of them are truly alike in mental ability?

16. *Why is the choice between MA and IQ scores less critical in grade 9 than at school entrance?*

17. *An investigator wants to know if rate of learning is correlated with mental-test performance. He measures learning rate by finding out how long a child requires to master a certain task. Should this be correlated with MA or with IQ?*

Precision of Scores

The two chief questions about precision in measurement of general ability are the adequacy of sampling of the person's present behavior and the consistency of scores from one period of the person's life to another. The latter question, traditionally referred to as the question of "constancy of the IQ," bears more on the interpretation of the score than on the thoroughness of the measurement, and therefore will be treated later.

As Chapter 6 emphasized, one can generalize from an observed score to alternative universe scores. A multifacet study is required to disentangle the many sources of error. Such designs have not yet been applied to individual mental tests, and we are forced to piece together various simpler studies to draw conclusions about the precision of Wechsler and SB scores. We shall give a representative estimate for each type of score, ignoring the variation from study to study.

Table 7.6. How well WISC and SB estimate the person's universe score

Score	Standard error of measurement	Coefficient[a]
WISC (age 9 and up)		
Full Scale IQ	5.0	0.89
Verbal IQ	6.0	0.85
Performance IQ	7.5	0.75
V-minus-P	9.2	0.52
Subtest score	1.5	0.75
Stanford-Binet		
IQ	5.0	0.91

[a] Of generalizability, over tasks and occasions, within an age group.

What universe is a score such as the SB IQ thought to represent? There are four obvious possibilities:

(1) Many measures on the same day, using parallel forms of each task. For example, if the test includes Verbal Absurdities, every form would have its own Verbal Absurdities items.

(2) Many measures on the same day, using forms each of which has its own tasks. For example, one form would include Verbal Absurdities, one would include Vocabulary, one Verbal Analogies, etc. Each test as a whole would represent the same broad domain of tasks as the others.

(3) Like (1), save that the measures are taken on different days in the same period. Day-to-day fluctuations are now counted as a source of error.

(4) Like (2), save that measures are taken on different days in the same period.

Testers usually make the kind of interpretation implied by universe (4). That is, they see the Wechsler or SB score as representative of the person's status during a period; they don't care particularly about his ability on the day he happens to be tested. And they look on the test tasks as representative of a broader domain of intellectual tasks.

The Stanford-Binet authors correlate Form L with Form M given on another day. They thus count day-to-day and task-to-task variation as sources of error (since L and M have few tasks in common). Hence the data in Figure 7.4 (see also Table 7.5) tell us how well an SB IQ estimates the universe score for universe (4).

Wechsler reports split-half studies, which bear on universe (1) and thus do not recognize some important sources of error. Task-to-task variation can be evaluated on the basis of intercorrelations he reports and day-to-day variation can be inferred from retest studies or from studies in which both WISC and WAIS have been given the same persons. Putting all this information together gives the rough estimates in Table 7.6 for V, P, and Full Scale IQs for age 9 and above. WISC at age 7 seems to measure less accurately than at older ages. The few estimates available on WPPSI are not far from those in Table 7.6. For a subtest score one is interested in generalizing over measures on different days with different items of the same fixed sort. The subtest estimate in Table 7.6 is of this type. (It should be recognized that the standard error for subtests is on a 10 ± 3 scale while that for IQ is on a 100 ± 15 scale.) Subtests are not equally accurate; Object Assembly and Digit Span are poor, Block Design and Vocabulary are good.

A standard error of 5 points for an IQ implies that the observed IQ may be as much as 15 points from the person's universe score. Most errors will be 5 points or less, and for practical purposes the tester would probably report a calculated IQ of 90 by saying "the IQ is estimated to fall in the range 85–95." But the universe score falls outside those limits for at least a third of the persons

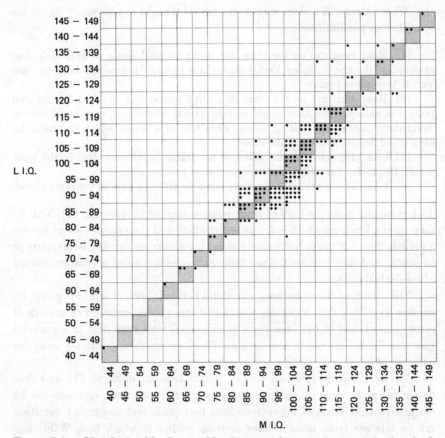

Figure 7.4.   IQs obtained by 7-year-olds when tested on two forms of the Stanford-Binet.
Terman & Merrill, 1960, p. 11.

tested. For a P IQ, the interval has to be a good deal wider—e.g., 82–98. Subtest scores are inaccurate, and to emphasize this it is highly desirable for the profile to display each subtest score as a band rather than as a point. A scaled score of 8 would be plotted as a band between 6 and 10. Note particularly that the Verbal-Performance difference is less accurate than either IQ alone. Wechsler wisely recommends that no attempt be made to interpret a V-P difference smaller than 15 points. The departure of a subtest score from the average of all V or P subtests should not be interpreted even tentatively unless it is 3 points or more.

The tester must become familiar with the peculiarities of the test he uses. Standard errors of SB IQs, for example, are much greater for bright children than for those far below normal (Figure 7.4). On the Wechsler, there are practice effects that give an advantage of perhaps 5 IQ points on a retest within a few months.

Writers desiring to lighten the burden of routine clinical testing suggest using short scales (e.g., Vocabulary and Block Design alone) in place of the full Wechsler. The justification put forward is that the IQ estimated from two or three subtest scores correlates around 0.90 with Full Scale IQ (for references, see Mumpower, 1964). This is fallacious evidence because the two measurements are not independent; the short form is included within the long form and consequently the correlation is *raised* by errors of measurement. It therefore cannot be interpreted like an ordinary correlation of 0.90. The correlation of the BD–Vocabulary combination with an independently determined total score is about 0.75. The short form sacrifices a good deal of precision and misses descriptive information the full scale offers. A short form may properly be used in research in which conclusions are reached by comparing groups of subjects. In case work a short form can be used for a hasty initial survey, but is not a proper basis for a serious decision.

It has been suggested that the Wechsler can be used to check results from the SB, though we have already seen that the IQ conversions are not truly comparable. The scales are not completely equivalent in content; correlations tabulated by Littell (1960) are in the neighborhood of 0.80 for SB with V, 0.65 with P, and 0.80 with Full Scale. Since the reliability coefficients are around 0.90, somewhat different abilities influence the scores.

18. *Fargo et al. (1967) administered the two forms of the Peabody Picture Vocabulary Test to children, once as an individual test and once as a group test by means of a TV screen in the classroom. The order of forms and methods of presentation were counterbalanced in different subgroups of subjects. It was found that the mean score was almost exactly the same, regardless of mode of presentation. Why is this finding insufficient to justify the conclusion that group administration is a satisfactory substitute for individual administration? What other relevant facts should have been reported?*

19. *Using Figure 7.4, determine what percentage of the children have Form M IQs five points greater than Form L, and how many five points less, when the L IQ is in each of these ranges: 40–84; 85–114; 115–149. (Since the data are coarsely grouped, count all cases in the diagonal squares and half the cases in any square next to the diagonal as falling within five points of each other.)*

20. *If a scorer allows credit for a response that most experienced scorers of the test would allow no credit for, or vice versa, a scoring error has been made. Under what circumstances could such errors raise the form-to-form correlation for the test?*

SUGGESTED READINGS

Brown, Elinor W. Observing behavior during the intelligence test. In E. Lerner & L. B. Murphy (Eds.), Methods for the study of personality in young children. *Monographs, Society for Research in Child Development*, 1941, *6*, No. 4, 268–283.

Responses of two 4-year-olds to the Stanford-Binet are presented to show that performance depends on personality and response to the examiner, as well as on intellect. Informative for those who have not seen a demonstration of individual mental testing.

Richards, T. W. Mental test performance as a reflection of the child's current life situation: a methodological study. *Child Development*, 1951, *22*, 221–233. (Reprinted in Hartley & Hartley, 1958.)

A child's Binet performance from age 3 to age 10 fluctuated from IQ 115 to IQ 140. Richards traces observation records, parent attitudes, and personality tests to show that test changes correspond to changes in the pressures and satisfactions in the child's life.

Terman, Lewis M. The discovery and encouragement of exceptional talent. *American Psychologist*, 1954, *9*, 221–230. (Reprinted in various books of readings.)

This lecture surveys some of the principal American work with mental tests, including Terman's follow-up of exceptional children. Terman reviews the childhood differences between those who succeeded in later life and those whose careers were mediocre, emphasizing the cultural factors that bring talent to fruition.

Witkin, H. A., and others. Cognitive patterning in mildly retarded boys. *Child Development*, 1966, *37*, 301–316.

This paper criticizes the Wechsler, emphasizing a distinction between fluid and crystallized abilities that will become increasingly prominent in the next three chapters of this book. Witkin finds the conventional IQ unfair, arguing that it labels many children retarded though they have good thought processes.

Young, Michael. *The rise of the meritocracy, 1870–2033.* London: Thames and Hudson, 1958. Penguin edition, 1961.

A Labor Party adviser presents a mock history of the rise and fall of the testing movement. Particularly under attack is the philosophy that some people ("more talented") are better than others and should be screened off for special encouragement and responsibility.

General Ability: Research and Theory

Consistency and Change in Test Scores

Test Intercorrelations

This chapter surveys most sorts of evidence collected over the past fifty years that provide a background for interpreting tests of general mental ability and for developing a theoretical conception of intellectual performance. Chapters 9 and 10 will extend the discussion. We begin with correlations among the parts of the Wechsler.

An ambivalence runs through all interpretations of mental-test correlations. There is a need to emphasize, on the one hand, the consistency among tests that is usually found, which is a justification for the whole testing enterprise. It is encouraging to find correlations in the neighborhood of 0.80 between Wechsler and Binet IQs, for they claim to fulfill similar functions. On the other hand, it is necessary to scrutinize the gap between such a correlation and the still higher correlation level that would convince us that the tests are reporting exactly the same information except for errors of measurement. Virtually every correlation between two ability measures implies both a similarity and a difference, and both have to be attended to. Statistical uncertainty is also to be kept in mind. Correlations vary from sample to sample, and no numerical value applies everywhere.

Table 8.1 summarizes intercorrelations for Wechsler subtests. Only a summary can be given, since for each age there are 45 or more pairs of subtests and an equal number of correlations. The data here are representative except that we ignore the poorer subtests.

Discussion may begin with the fact that V and P correlate in the neighbor-

227

Table 8.1. Summary of intercorrelations for Wechsler subtests

| | | Median of intercorrelations | | |
Subtests	Age	with V subtests	with P subtests	Median reliability
Information, Comprehension,	4–6	0.51	0.36	0.82
Arithmetic, Similarities,	10–14	0.61	0.36	0.80
Vocabulary	25–34	0.59	0.52	0.85
Block Design, Picture	4–6	0.47	0.50	0.83
Completion, Mazes	10–14	0.35	0.38	0.78
	25–34	0.52	0.57	0.83

Data are from manual for Wechsler Scales and from Wechsler (1958). Reliabilities are split-half coefficients (generalization over items). Neither the reliabilities nor intercorrelations are lowered to reflect day-to-day fluctuations. Among adults PA rather than Maze correlations were counted.

hood of 0.60 (WPPSI and WISC). Since their reliability coefficients are much higher than this, the two abilities are distinct in childhood. If the V-P separation had much explanatory power, V subtests ought to correlate high with other V subtests and relatively low with P subtests; for P, just the opposite. The table confirms that V-with-V correlations are rather high, considering the brevity of each subtest. But P subtests correlate with V subtests almost as strongly as with each other. Hence "performance abilities" does not mark off a coherent set of tests and is not a distinct concept. The Wechsler P score is determined by the general ability common to both V and P tests and by a number of more specific abilities. The low reliability (0.52) for the V-P difference reinforces this conclusion. To get a really adequate measure of the domain of "performance abilities" one would need to apply 10 or 15 different tasks (though one might use relatively few items of each type). We shall later consider the concept of a "fluid-analytic" ability that might serve better than Wechsler's concept of an ability running through all performance tasks.

1. *Is a high or a low correlation between subtests desirable in a general mental test?*

Changes with Age

When one wishes to study the growth of mental ability, and its possible eventual decline with aging, the appropriate data come from a *longitudinal* study in which the same persons are tested repeatedly, over long time spans. But investigators are unwilling to wait a whole generation for data to ripen, and therefore fall back on a *cross-sectional* design, of testing a different sample of subjects at each age level. A cross-sectional study permits comparison of means and standard deviations but yields no age-to-age correlations. There is an intermediate technique of using several samples, and following each one for a few years. For example, one might test samples of age 3, 6, and 9, and retest annually for three further years. This is an *overlapping longitudinal* design.

Level of performance (growth). The advantage of the longitudinal design is that the comparisons are for a fixed group of subjects. In drawing samples of different ages for a cross-sectional comparison, there is always a risk that the older group will be more select than the younger one (or—not so likely—less select). The overlapping design guards against this; a comparison of the original 6-year-old distribution with that for original-3-year-olds-turned-6 warns the investigator if the groups are not comparable.

When a long age span is under consideration, differences between older and younger samples may represent changes in society. Most of the data that have been compiled on trends in score during adulthood were obtained cross-sectionally, by comparing distributions for (say) 20-, 40-, and 60-year-olds all tested during the same year. Such studies consistently report a decline in average score during adulthood. In the 1955 standardization of WAIS, for example, 60-year-olds and 20-year-olds did about equally well on V, but 30-year-olds were superior to both. On P, the peak was at age 25, and the drop after that age was steep. The groups belông to different eras. The 60-year-olds were educated when relatively few Americans finished high school, and when the schools were very likely less effective than they are today. By 1990-odd, when Wechsler's 20-year-old sample reaches 60, they ought to outperform the 60-year-old standardization group of the 1950s. This prediction is supported by the finding, for example, that men drafted in World War II did considerably better on Army Alpha than recruits in World War I (Tuddenham, 1948). Implication: norms for mental tests must be redetermined periodically.

There are now several sets of data from longitudinal studies, some of them following the same individuals for 20 or more years (Bayley, 1955; Bradway & Thompson, 1962; Owens, 1966; Berkowitz & Green, 1963; Jarvik, Kallman, & Falex, 1962.) Figure 8.1 is based on an especially systematic study that contrasts cross-sectional findings with those from the more informative overlapping longitudinal design. The authors selected 25 men and 25 women in each of the intervals from 25 to 70 years of age, tested them, and then retested 5 years later. The samples were cross-sectional, but the 5-year spans were longitudinal and could be linked up to give a corrected picture of growth. The left panel of Figure 8.1 gives the cross-sectional report; in the past such curves were thought to indicate that mental decline sets in quite early in life. What the left panel does show is the comparative disadvantage of today's older persons, presumably due to their less complete education. The right panel shows that on three of the four tests there was a rise in score during each 5-year period of middle adulthood. Growth apparently levels off in the 50s and turns down, but not very sharply. The standard

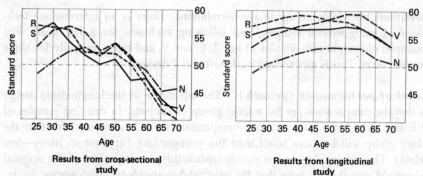

Figure 8.1.   Trends in average ability scores with age.
Data from Schaie & Strother, 1968.

scores used by the authors are based on their own population, but it would not be seriously wrong to think of 50 as corresponding to an IQ of 100, 55 to an IQ of 108, etc., among subjects at the youngest ages. Since Wechsler determines IQs against a cross-sectional norm group, his norms collected 10 or more years ago will clearly be inappropriate for middle-aged persons in the 1970s and later.

It is not surprising that verbal ability should rise, since the adult has continual opportunities to use and build his vocabulary. The early decline of the reasoning score is puzzling, and hard to confirm or contradict on the basis of other studies. The tests used are the Primary Mental Abilities battery, and its reasoning test is of a highly abstract sort that may simply bore older persons. One kind of item is Letter Series (mnoqrsuvw___) and another asks one to select the "different" group in a set such as RFRG MHMI XBBY PLPM.

The data from all the studies taken together make it evident that mental ability maintains itself in adulthood, at least to the point of senile disorders. Appreciable declines seem to occur after age 60 in speed tests but not in others. The rapid early development might be indicative of biological maturation, which is rapid during early years and slower later. It is equally plausible that the rise reflects educational effort and opportunity, which are great in early years and slight in adulthood. (Horn & Cattell, 1967, however, offer some cross-sectional evidence that "crystallized" abilities directly acquired through education may improve during adulthood.)

Standing within age group (stability). Studies of IQ stability have three types of implications. First, they tell how much confidence we can have in making long-range predictions for the individual and in using the test score in educational and vocational planning. Second, they bear on the theoretical question as to whether rate of intellectual development is fixed and perhaps largely determined by heredity. Third—as the evidence is that rate of development is far from constant—they enable us to look for factors associated with increases and declines in intellectual standing (compared to one's age group), and so perhaps to learn how to foster intellectual development.

Three case records illustrate a few of the many patterns of intellectual development that can occur (Figure 8.2). Scores from individual tests (SB from 4 to 16) are expressed on a 0 ± 1 standard-score scale, with the average of the cases in Bayley's longitudinal sample defining the zero line. We observe that test scores rise and fall erratically in early childhood; this is borne out in the correlations of Table 8.2. For the Wechsler, there are similar data, consistent with those for SB (Gehman & Matyas, 1956; Bayley, 1957):

Age at first test, 7 years; interval, 4 years; correlation, 0.77

Age at first test, 16 years; interval, 3 years; correlation, 0.96.

When the SB was given twice, at ages 6–7 and 9–10, to Negro children in a small Southern community, the correlations were 0.77 for girls and 0.62 for boys (Baughman & Dahlstrom, 1968, p. 112). While these values are lower than the corresponding Bayley figure for whites, the difference seems to be accounted for by the smaller range of the Baughman-Dahlstrom sample.

Tests for young children have not been very satisfactory, for reasons to be examined in detail later. By age 4, when language functions are well established in most children, some are exhibiting superiority that will last, and some are showing deficient vocabulary and comprehension that will be a handicap if not overcome. The mental test at age 4 correlates 0.70 with a mental test at 16, and equally high with intellectual motivation at that age (Kagan & Freeman, 1963). This justifies our taking preschool IQs seriously. But they are far from fixed: the three cases in Figure 8.2, nearly equal at age 4, pull apart over the years. Some children very high or low at 4 drift to the middle of the range. Bayley now em-

Table 8.2. Correlation of mental test with test at a later age

Approximate age at first test	Name of first test	Years elapsed between first and second test			
		1	3	6	12
3 months	California First-Year	0.10(CFY)	0.05(CP)	–0.13	0.02
1 year	California First-Year	0.47(CP)	0.23	0.13	0.00
2 years	California Preschool	0.74(CP)	0.55	0.50	0.42
3 years	California Preschool	0.64	—	0.55	0.33
4 years	Stanford-Binet	—	0.71	0.73	0.70
6 years	Stanford-Binet	0.86	0.84	0.81	0.77(W)
7 years	Stanford-Binet	0.88	0.87	0.73	0.80(W)
9 years	Stanford-Binet	0.88	0.82	0.87	—
11 years	Stanford-Binet	0.93	0.93	0.92	—

SOURCE: Bayley, 1949. Some entries have been estimated from closely related data in Bayley's report. Initials indicate second test; W stands for Wechsler-Bellevue, forerunner of WAIS. Where no initial is given, the Stanford-Binet is the second test.

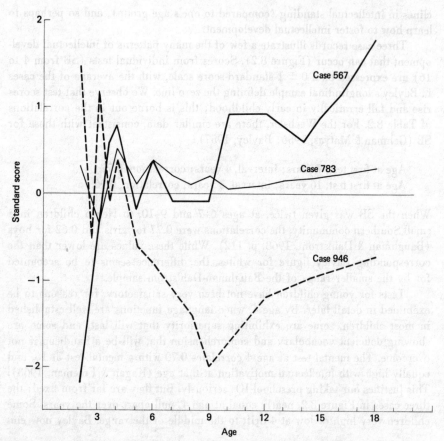

Figure 8.2.   Records made by three children on successive mental tests.
Honzik et al., 1948.

phasizes the stability rather than the change of her cases: "By four years of age the children's levels of intellectual function are fairly well set, and except for a few individual cases their IQs remain relatively stable . . . at least through the next 17 years" (Bayley & Schaefer, 1964, p. 22).

Case histories of IQ change suggest causes, and also warn that simple causal hypotheses are likely to be false. Case 783 has very nearly a constant standing, just slightly above the group mean. Yet he had a poor health history, an insecure and underprivileged home background, poor grades, and emotional symptoms such as stammering and enuresis. "There never was a time in his history when he was not confronted with extreme frustrations." Case 946 had IQs as low as 87 and as high as 142. Her parents were immigrants, and unhappily married; their conflict led to a divorce when the girl was 7. At 9, with her mother remarried, the girl was insecure at home and excessively modest. The later recovery perhaps reflects better adjustment to her family. The third case (567) shows consistent improvement. This girl's early years were marked by grave illnesses in the family, and the girl herself was sickly and shy. After age 10, her social life expanded and she developed rewarding interests in music and sports. This blossoming is paralleled in the test scores. The frequency of large changes is suggested by a follow-up study of a group of problem children, retested after 5–9 years (R. Brown, 1933). Three per cent changed as much as 30 IQ points, and 13 per cent changed 20 points or more. For further data on IQ stability, see pp. 286 ff.

Comparisons of children and adults who gain in IQ, or decline in IQ, are hard to summarize. In the first place, the personal characteristics are often recorded at the end of the change period, and may reflect changes that accompanied the growth, rather than its antecedents. Second, the characteristics associated with rapid growth differ with age and sex. Nonetheless, one arrives at a strong impression that among children with the same IQ at the start of a period, gains are likely to be shown by those who vigorously and independently engage in exploring their world. Gainers are described as comparatively aggressive, nonconforming, willing to work for a reward, and, of course, as having intellectual interests. The warmth and authority pattern of the home contribute complexly to development (Owens, 1966; Bayley & Schaefer, 1964; Sontag, Baker, & Nelson, 1958).

In general, changes in intellectual standing seem to be associated with radical changes in the child's opportunity for learning or his emotional readiness to profit from them. These factors work together, as is illustrated in the following case.

Danny adapted poorly to kindergarten and therefore was singled out to take the SB; his MA of 4–2 supported a decision to keep him out of school for the year. Lowell (1941) reports a record covering the next seven years, including these test data:

2–2–34	Age 5–0	MA 4–2	IQ 82
5–9–35	Age 6–4	MA 6–2	IQ 98
6–8–37	Age 8–5	MA 9–4	IQ 111
12–3–40	Age 11–11	MA 15–9	IQ 132

After one year, Danny's Binet score seemed normal. He was placed in the first grade in September 1935 in spite of poor social adjustment. The teachers complained that Danny seemed to live in a world of his own, was poor in motor coordination, and had a worried look on his face most of the time. The mother was called in, and only then was light thrown on his peculiarities.

The mother explained that while Danny was still a baby his father had developed encephalitis. In order for the mother to work, they lived in the grandparents' home, where Danny could be cared for. Danny's high-strung, nervous old grandfather was much annoyed by the child's noise and at times expostulated so violently that Danny became petrified with fear. The grandfather's chief aim was to keep things quiet and peaceful at any cost. When Danny was excluded from kindergarten the mother took him from the grandparents' home.

The next few years were a period of educational and emotional growth for the starved child. He amazed his teachers with his achievement. He became an inveterate reader and could solve arithmetic problems far beyond his grade level. He was under a doctor's care much of the time and was also treated by a psychiatrist because of his marked fears. He made friends with boys in spite of physical inferiority.

2. *The text states that differences between older and younger subjects represent "social changes," but the only change discussed is improved education. What other social changes might cause the test scores of 50-year-olds to be higher (or lower) in 1980 than for similar 50-year-olds in 1950?*

3. *Changes in the education of adults clearly justify a demand for revised norms. Are there similar reasons for regarding the Binet norms based on children tested in the 1930s as obsolete today?*

4. *It is suggested that one reason for poorer scores of older subjects in many cross-sectional studies is that they have less motivation for taking tests. Does this seem reasonable? If there is such an effect, how does it modify the interpretation of Figure 8.1?*

5. *Cattell (1963, p. 19) contrasts test of "fluid" ability that emphasize nonverbal reasoning with tests that put more emphasis on learned achievements including verbal ability (see p. 282, below). He believes that the population average on tests of the former sort has not increased during the past generation, whereas all investigators have found later adults doing better on verbal ability tests. Suppose that this hypothesis is confirmed by further studies; what explanations can you offer for failure of the two types of test to show corresponding increases?*

6. *Danny gained 2 full years in mental age during the 15 months between his first and second tests, at a time when he was not yet in school. What possible explanations for the rapid improvement in score can be suggested?*

7. *Is it reasonable to suppose that emotionally disturbed children have less stable mental-test standings than adjusted children?*

8. *Brown reports the frequency of large IQ changes over a period of two years or so. How do these frequencies compare with the shifts that would arise from error of measurement alone?*

9. *It is found that adult men who graduated from a certain representative State University 30 years ago earn scores today that have a distribution similar to the scores of today's freshmen on the same mental test. These men tested today (on another test) average considerably better than they did when they were given that test as freshmen. The two comparisons are based on different but similar tests. How can the two findings be reconciled?*

Practical Correlates

The ultimate justification for using individual mental tests is that they indicate what can be expected in practically important situations. The Cattell-Wissler tests dropped from sight just because they were unable to predict academic performance. While the SB and Wechsler have been accepted as relevant to practical decisions, we can display little direct evidence of this relevance. Originally, the practical relevance was supported by the consistency between test scores and clinical impressions formed by observers, e.g., in homes for retarded children. With the passage of time, case histories of children who had been given Binet tests piled up and tended to reinforce psychologists' view that the test has practical relevance. Terman and his associates (see Oden, 1968) followed a sample of children with high SB scores. Here are a few of the facts about their careers: 90 per cent entered college and 70 per cent graduated. At an average age of 40, the 800 men had published 67 books, more than 1400 scientific and professional articles, and more than 200 short stories and plays. They had more than 150 patents to their credit. As Terman's last report said (1954): "nearly all the statistics of this group are from 10 to 30 times as large as would be expected for 800 men representative of the general population." The evidence of better-than-average academic, professional, marital, and financial success, and of adult mental health, argues that the mental test is practically significant, though Terman's high-scoring children very likely had physical and environmental advantages besides. We should note also the discrepancies between SB performance and later attainment. Some of Terman's bright boys—not very many—failed in college, or served a prison term, or had unhappy marriages and careers.

An interesting demonstration of the significance of intellectual superiority in childhood is Catherine Cox Miles' attempt to estimate, from recorded biographical facts, the IQs various famous and creative persons would have had in early life. A child who, according to report, achieved something at age 5 that most children achieve at age 8 would be estimated as having an IQ of at least 160. "Voltaire wrote verses from his cradle; Coleridge at 3 could read a chapter from the Bible. Mozart composed a minuet at 5; Goethe, at 8, produced literary work of adult superiority" (Cox, 1926, p. 217). The minimum IQs that could account for the recorded facts about these men were estimated as: Voltaire, 180; Coleridge, 175; Mozart, 160; Goethe, 190.

At the other end of the scale is a follow-up on three groups tested as children: "very low" (SB IQs under 70), educated in classes for the retarded; "low" (IQs 75–85); and an "average" group. At age 50 information was obtained on each group, and a limited number of subjects were retested. Table 8.3 shows that adult success is related to childhood classification, but both the rise in the IQ and the large number of the low group who supported themselves in semiskilled labor and such posts as foreman imply that childhood retardates often perform in the normal range as adults.

Studies of the predictive validity of individual tests on representative samples are scarce, because the tests are ordinarily applied only to cases referred for special study.

Table 8.3.   Adult achievement of persons classified by childhood IQ

	Very low (IQ below 70)	Low (IQ 75–85)	Average
Institutionalized or totally dependent	11%	3%	0%
Entirely self-supporting	65%	93%	96%
In unskilled labor	44%	29%	—[a]
Mean or median, childhood IQ	60	81	107
Mean, adult IQ	82	89	107

[a] Not reported.
SOURCE: Baller, Charles, & Miller, 1967.

Table 8.4 gives correlations of Wechsler scores with grade average or rank in graduating class. The criterion includes work completed before the test as well as after; a strictly predictive study would give slightly lower r's. For the same persons, group tests gave results like those for V. V predicts as well as Full Scale; P adds nothing to prediction of marks. A college comparison shows SB and WAIS to be equally related to marks (Gianell & Freeburne, 1963). For

Table 8.4.   Correlations of school marks with Wechsler scores

	High school	College
Information	0.54	0.48
Comprehension	0.55	0.33
Arithmetic	0.45	0.19
Similarities	0.50	0.39
Digit Span	0.37	0.04
Vocabulary	0.65	0.46
Digit Symbol	0.34	0.15
Picture Completion	0.33	0.20
Block Design	0.29	0.19
Picture Arrangement	0.22	0.07
Object Assembly	0.17	0.12
Verbal	0.63	0.47
Performance	0.43	0.24
Full Scale	0.62	0.44

SOURCE: Conry & Plant, 1965; see also Olsen and Jordheim, 1964.

ninth-graders, SB correlations with achievement tests a year later are (Bond, 1940):

With reading comprehension	0.73
With reading speed	0.43
With English usage	0.59
With history	0.59
With biology	0.54
With geometry	0.48

A third-grade SB correlates 0.74 with an achievement measure three years later (Churchill & Smith, 1966); a kindergarten WISC correlates 0.57 with a reading test in grade 5 (Ames & Walker, 1964). The size of such correlations will vary with the time interval, the nature of the instruction, the criterion, and the range of the sample. The general conclusion is that the mental test predicts with fair— but only fair—accuracy.

Occasionally, outside of school, a performance test predicts better than a verbal test. For a sample of borderline defectives, adjustment in the community of correlated 0.77 with Porteus maze score, 0.57 with SB. Mental defectives who succeeded in holding down jobs outside an institution were those with Wechsler P greater than V (Appell, Williams, & Fishell, 1962). In a school for the retarded, SB predicted a rating of response to classroom education better than Porteus (0.81 vs. 0.59); but for a rating on response to occupational training the correlations were 0.66 and 0.75. Southern Negro adolescents were tested, and rated on adequacy of everyday behavior. The Porteus score cleanly discriminated the cases judged to be behaviorally retarded from the nonretarded, assigning IQs 24–84 to the former and 102–132 to the latter. Wechsler V IQs were low, and similar in the two groups: Wechsler P IQs were 38–75 in the retarded, 50–83 in the nonretarded (Cooper *et al.*, 1967).

10. *If Bond had measured achievement at the same time he gave the SB, those scores would also have predicted end-of-year achievement. Why, then, should a school ever wish to use a mental test to predict achievement?*

11. *The correlation of SB IQs with grades of medical-school seniors was found to be only 0.15 in one study. The average IQ of these men was 131 (Mitchell, 1943). Explain why the correlation was so small.*

12. *Garrett (1965, p. 62) discusses a boy with IQ 148 (MA 9–6 at CA 6–5):* "... *a very bright youngster. He should be ready for high school by age twelve or earlier. He should now be in fourth grade if he is ready for it socially." A school psychologist (Finley, 1965, p. 916) attacks this an an obsolete view. The "learning patterns" of a 9½-year-old, she says, differ greatly from those of a boy like this, and acceleration such as Garrett recommends is rarely advised today.*

What facts presented in this chapter support either the Garrett position or that of Finley? What other facts would be relevant in deciding what policy on acceleration a school system should adopt?

Processes Considered in Test Interpretation

The meaning of "intelligence" or "general mental ability" has evolved gradually. Binet invested ten years of research before he arrived at his characterization of mental ability (p. 200), and research with his and other tests has been modifying our conception down to the present day. We shall introduce here some of the main streams of interpretative research and extend the discussion in the next two chapters.

Proposals To Subdivide the IQ

We have just been discussing differences between practical correlates of V and P. This traditional distinction has some basis in reality, yet we saw earlier that correlations among P subtests are too small to support the conception of a unified "performance" ability. As we proceed we shall examine concepts that are beginning to supplant the V-P interpretation.

The verbal-performance distinction.   When a person does much better on performance tests than on verbal tests, we suspect a language handicap. One who learned English late in life, who has had a very limited education, or who suffers from deafness will perform badly on tests of word knowledge and verbal reasoning. Such persons have difficulty in understanding the verbal test and may also have poorly developed ability to reason verbally. Verbal handicaps reduce a performance score only slightly. Many children and adults regarded as defective if classified only by their verbal comprehension are able to perform nonverbal tasks at an average level. We may assume that a person who has developed normal performance ability would do equally well in verbal tasks if he had had normal experience. When we can identify restrictive factors in his past history, this interpretation can scarcely be challenged.

Poor verbal ability is easily understood in the case of the child from a bilingual home (Table 8.5), the child who has had difficulty in learning to read, and the adult who dropped out of school at an early age. For many others who show P greater than V no cause can be identified. The psychologist is unable to say whether such differences are due to unidentified background factors, to accidents of learning history, or to some physiological deficit that interferes with verbal learning.

When P is well below V, the explanation may be emotional. A painstaking, overcautious approach will lower the P score; undue caution is interpreted as

Table 8.5. Mean IQ of monolingual and bilingual preschool children on the Binet test and a performance test

Test	Mean IQ for monolinguals ($N = 106$)	Mean IQ for bilinguals ($N = 106$)	Difference[a]
Stanford-Binet	98.7	90.9	7.8
Atkins Object-Fitting	89.0	97.5	−8.5

[a] Significance tests show that neither difference can reasonably be attributed to chance.

SOURCE: Darcy, 1946.

having emotional origins. Performance tests generally demand a longer period of sustained attention than the shorter items of individual verbal tests, and more often require deliberate analysis (see below). They therefore provide a greater opportunity for confusion or frustration to disrupt performance. Porteus (1950) discusses studies in a reformatory, where maladjusted delinquents were compared with law-abiding, well-behaved inmates. The adjusted and maladjusted groups had similar Binet IQs, but on the Porteus maze the maladjusted group dropped about 10 points below the others.

When P is lower than V, one also considers the possibility that V is artificially elevated. Some students and adults make a great effort to learn new words. The tester sometimes observes in such a subject a love of big words and an effort to give impressively complicated answers to simple questions. The person with one-sided verbal development often does better on recall questions (Information, Vocabulary) than on items demanding thought (Comprehension, Similarities).

Analytic and crystallized abilities distinguished. A test is a sample of performance in a social situation in which an intellectual demand is made. Even the simplest test task requires coordination of many processes. Digit Span may on the surface appear to assess only short-term memory, but the subject must cooperate and make an effort, have adequate hearing and ability to focus attention, be familiar with the names of numerals, and be able to say a string of numbers he has in mind. Any emotional obsession will generate "noise" that impedes his attention and recall. The person may possess some special techniques (e.g., rhythmic grouping) that improve his score.

Binet's characterization views the response as a complex process involving direction of attention, rearrangement of concepts and images, and regulation through self-criticism; Wechsler added an emphasis on the emotional component. Shyness with strange adults, lack of confidence, and dislike for "schoolish" tasks all affect scores. A self-critical person may say "I don't know" because he is dissatisfied with the best answer he can formulate; a person less sensitive to niceties may give an answer that is passable. Fear may cause a child to "freeze up" so that he cannot find a new mode of attack on a problem when his first one is blocked.

Binet considered tests requiring "judgment" to be closest to the heart of intelligence, though he saw a mixture of other abilities and techniques as being relevant. Spearman gave a similarly central place to the ability to notice and extract relationships. The Matrices test (p. 269) illustrates in a rather pure form what Spearman had in mind. As practical testing developed, information and vocabulary were seen to have *predictive* value greater than that of tests that place more emphasis on relational thinking and judgment (see Table 8.4).

Today there is increased discussion of these two types of tests as representing opposite ends of a continuum. At one end are tests calling for "analytic" or "fluid" ability; at the other, tests of trained or "crystallized" ability.

The extensive research by Herman Witkin and his associates (1954, 1962) has shed considerable light on the distinction. He has concentrated on some unusual ability tests, one of which should be described here. The Embedded Figures Test (EFT), based on the work of the Gestalt psychologists and particularly Kurt Gottschaldt (1926), presents a structured but unfamiliar geometric pattern and asks the subject to find it in a larger complex field (Figure 8.3). Versions of EFT were published in 1969 by Consulting Psychologists Press.

Correlation studies suggest that EFT has little or nothing in common with Wechsler Vocabulary and Comprehension, but is a good measure of whatever Block Design, Object Assembly, Mazes, and Picture Completion have in common (D. Goodenough & Karp, 1961; Witkin *et al.*, 1962, p. 70, and Witkin *et al.*, 1966). These tests, and EFT, all require that the subject analyze a complex whole, paying attention to relevant information and disregarding the irrelevant. They are said, then, to measure fluid or analytic abilities.

A group of "educable mentally retarded" boys (ages 11–21) was tested on WISC (Witkin *et al.*, 1966). Their V and P means were 69 and 73. A rescoring separated verbal comprehension (Inf. + Comp. + Voc.) from "analytic" abilities (BD + PC + OA); those means were 61 and 77—a striking separation. Interpreting this, Witkin protests that both society and the mental tester are using verbal competence to "route children through life," neglecting analytic ability. Parents are likely to sense that something is wrong with the child who is laggard in verbal skills, and the school is likely to refer such a child for mental tests while overlooking children who are normal verbally and weak analytically. The low-verbal, normal-analytic child will be classed simply as having a low IQ unless the tester is sensitive to patterning in the performance. The low-analytic, normal-verbal child may even be regarded favorably by his teachers because he is more docile.

Witkin and others (1962) employed an extensive battery of tests and interviews with children of various ages in order to study the total functioning of children high and low in analytic ability. An earlier report (1954) deals with

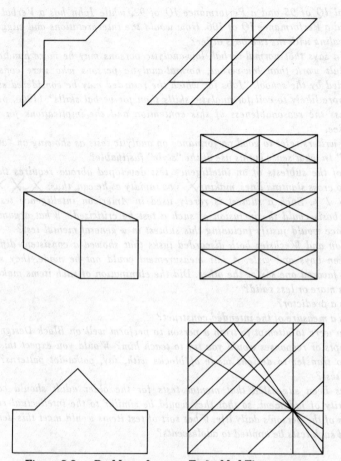

Figure 8.3.   Problems from an Embedded Figures test.

adults. Witkin has used several theoretical terms more or less interchangeably to describe high-analytic persons: field independent, highly differentiated, less prone to interference. The reader may wish to look ahead to p. 628 for our discussion of these results.

13. *Comment on this statement: "A person's true level of mental ability is shown by whichever IQ, verbal or performance, is higher."*

14. *Suppose one is faced with Binet's original problem of deciding whether a pupil failing in school could profit from the regular curriculum. If the pupil is bilingual, would the SB or a performance test serve better?*

15. *Bill and John, two 15-year-olds, are referred to the school psychologist because both are failing in 9th-grade work, their courses being social studies, English, general science, and art appreciation. Both have IQs of 93, but Bill has a*

Verbal IQ of 95 and a Performance IQ of 92, while John has a Verbal IQ of 87 and a Performance IQ of 106. How would the interpretations and suggestions for dealing with the two boys differ?

16. *Witkin says that normal-verbal, low-analytic persons may be more handicapped in adult work than low-verbal, normal-analytic persons who were considered retarded by the school. "Jobs for which the retarded may be considered suitable are more likely to call for analytic skills than for verbal skills" (1966, p. 313). Discuss the reasonableness of this contention and the implications for school practice.*

17. *Some writers refer to good performance on analytic tests as showing an "analytic style." In what sense is this use of the "style" justifiable?*

18. *One of the subtests of an intelligence test developed abroad requires the subject to cross slanting lines, making ✕'s as rapidly as he can, thus: ✕ ✕ ✕ ✕ ✕ / / / /. Such a subtest is rarely used in American intelligence tests. On what basis could the inclusion of such a test be criticized? What argument or evidence would justify including this subtest in a general mental test?*

19. *Terman and Wechsler both discarded tasks that showed a consistent difference between boys and girls. A fair measurement could not be made, they said, if items favored one sex or the other. Did the elimination of such items make their scales more or less valid?*
    a. *as a predictor?*
    b. *as a measure of the intended construct?*

20. *If you were to attempt to train a person to perform well on Block Design, what concepts or responses would you try to teach him? Would you expect this training to transfer to designs made of blocks with, say, polka-dot patterns? To a maze test?*

21. *It has been suggested that mental tests for the older adult should call for maturity of judgment, so that they would be similar to the intellectual requirements of the person's daily life. What sort of test items would meet this demand? Could such tests be applied to adolescents?*

Piaget's Account of Intellectual Development

An insistence that "intellect" consists of activity, of the manipulation of relationships and images is found also in the famous research of Jean Piaget at Geneva. Piaget emphasizes analysis, but he assigns a major role in it to overlearned concepts and classification systems.

The intellectually mature 7-year-old is not misled by the gross impression an object offers. He checks the logical consistency of what he sees against what he knows, with the aid of mental structures and operations. Even at age 3 a task requires active adjustments; to foresee what hole in a formboard a triangle will fit—when the triangle points up and the hole points down—requires a mental transformation.

Piaget has offered an elaborate account of ways in which the older child thinks differently from the younger. The infant must learn to make perceptual comparisons and to abstract from his sense impressions ideas or "schemata." His first schemata are merely identifications of objects; for instance, the recognition of his mother as the same person no matter how her dress, posture, and other superficial appearances change. He gradually builds one schema upon another, thereby acquiring tools of thought. Once he realizes that "an object" exists, he can think of it as continuing to exist even when hidden; this stage is necessary before he can be expected to find a hidden object. He later develops ideas of shape, size, identity, order, etc. For example, the preschool child may be able to compare the sizes of two blocks, and yet not to arrange a whole series of blocks in order. A schema or idea such as "order" may first appear in a concrete form; i.e., the child can compare two bead chains only when they are laid out side by side. Then he learns to hold the abstract order in mind so that he can compare, for example, a straight chain with one twisted in a "figure eight." When the idea of order is completely abstracted, he can solve logical problems such as "Town A is north of B, and C is south of B; what can you say about A and C?"

This type of research is beginning to formulate a theory of intellect. Solving any problem, it is argued, calls for the use of certain codes and information-processing devices. The person does not perceive his world as a physical event. Rather, he creates a representation in his mind, assembling that representation with the aid of whatever schemata he knows. This abstract model, being simpler than the world and less variable than perceptual impressions, lends itself to formal, accurate reasoning.

Much of Piaget's research has centered on concepts of conservation of volume, shape, etc.; e.g., that true shape does not change when something is viewed from a new angle, or volume when some liquid is poured into a new container. The observations in effect take an inventory of the intellectual structures the child has at his disposal. Such a listing of specific processes and concepts might seem to contradict the idea of any general adaptive or analytic ability. The position of the Geneva researchers, however, is that the overall mental-test score is a suitable tool of applied psychology, while the detailed inventory is needed to construct a theory of how ability accrues (Inhelder & Matalon, 1960, p. 136).

The inventory of intellectual structures, as seen by the Genevans, is a complex act of inference, not a simple tabulation of successful and unsuccessful performances. Inhelder (1968, p. 282) indeed goes so far as to say:

Our experiments have nothing in common with tests, but tend to be an exchange of views, a relatively unstructured conversation about experiments of elementary physics which arouse the child's curiosity. In most tests the child, once given the instructions, finds himself in front of problems to be solved. In our method the examiner is in some way part of the experiment. . . . The subject's contact with the the facts of the experiment must be accompanied by interindividual exchange. The elaboration of the rational notions necessitates a discussion which, at this level of development, cannot be entirely interiorized. . . . The examiner must adapt himself to each case in order to stimulate the child, follow the lines of his thought, and at the same time, direct it toward crucial points.

This is a distinctly nonbehaviorist way of examining intellectual performance; the concern is with internal mental operations (see also p. 346). That this kind of mental diagnosis is filled with hazards is made clear not only in Inhelder's volume on clinical methods but in Smedslund's (1969) methodological analysis. Smedslund's recommendation is to introduce crosschecks, testing for a particular mental structure by many methods. The problem, as he sees it, is not to describe what the subject does but to learn "the meaning of what the subject does."

A conventional behavioral test measuring the child's possession of an ability in the Piaget inventory usually correlates with tested mental age. This is true for a conservation-of-volume test using two balls of clay (Goodnow & Bethon, 1966). After a child has agreed that they are equal, one is flattened into a pancake. On the table are two identical containers of water, and the child is asked which will have the higher water level after the ball is put into the first and the pancake into the second. The child is said to conserve volume if he predicts that the two levels will be the same. The test was applied to older and younger, brighter and duller children (as classified by the CTMM group test), with the results in Table 8.6. Success matches MA rather than CA, and there is a hint here as in other studies that on Piaget tasks bright young children do better than duller children of the same MA. Although tests based on Piaget's concepts relate to MA, some of them may be distinct enough to have supplementary value in educational diagnosis (Freyberg, 1966). No general statement can be made, as "Piaget-like" tests created by different investigators vary even more widely among themselves than conventional mental tests do.

According to O'Bryan and MacArthur (1969), the Piagetian tasks fall into several groups. They separate three kinds of ability; a 9-year-old who is advanced in one of the three may or may not be advanced in the others. The first, "reversibility A," has to do with flexibility in regrouping objects. The second, "reversibility B," is found in tasks requiring conservation of spatial patterns. Finally, there is a separate ability identified with conservation of volume and area. This third ability correlates moderately with mental age. The second ability is rather strongly related to fluid ability. And reversibility A is correlated rather little with these tests, and correlates substantially with the Torrance measures of divergent thinking that we will encounter in Chapter 12 (p. 395).

Conceptual maturity is most evident when the child's abstract reasoning overrides misleading appearances. Young children misjudge the equality of different shapes made from the ball of clay; they tend, for example, to see the pancake as larger than the ball. A more subtle test than the one above may be required to determine whether a child has truly mastered a concept. Smedslund (1961) asked 5-year-olds and 8-year-olds to judge the comparative weight of two lumps of clay, originally identical, after one had been flattened. The 5-year-olds said

Table 8.6. Mastery of the concept "conservation of volume" as a function of mental age

	Group					
	1	2	3	4	5	6
Mental age	8–7	8–8	11–3	12–1	12–1	15–11
Chronological age	11	8	8	11	11	11
Status	Dull	Av.	Sup.	Av.	Av.	Sup.
Percentage passing volume test	28	44	65	62	56	75
Overall percentage passing on Piaget tasks (median of seven measures)	28	44	60	65	62	91

SOURCE: Goodnow & Bethon, 1966.

that the two were unequal. Then Smedslund trained the children by a reinforcement procedure in which the balance was used to verify their judgments on trial after trial. After training, these children did indeed give the "equal" response. But Smedslund tested the limits of their learning with "extinction" or "contradiction" trials. He secretly pinched off some of the clay, or added an extra bit, so that the judgment of "equal" was contradicted by the balance. The young children accepted their errors with a sort of "you can't win 'em all" reaction; they had not truly been forming a mental representation of constancy of weight. Eight-year-olds, in a similar test, responded as the concept of weight dictated: "Something is wrong with the scales" or "Some got lost"—and scrambled down from their chairs to look on the floor for the missing clay. The training, then, served not to erase but to expose more clearly the superiority of the older children. Vigotsky (1962) has made the provocative suggestion that conventional mental-test procedures, even when using tasks requiring analysis, do not measure these resources in the best way. The usual test is a measure of immediate adaptation, whereas one is allowed a much greater opportunity to become familiar with everyday problems. Vigotsky believed that the first few trials of a task like Block Design may reflect mostly past learning and accidental choice of a suitable strategy. He suggested that the child be given a period of coaching on the task. Once all children are provided with an efficient strategy for Block Design and an adequate opportunity to become familiar with it, one would proceed to find out how difficult a design each child could manage, using designs not seen during the familiarization exercises. Rankings after coaching would probably differ from those obtained on the usual 5-minute test. Whereas testers have hitherto regarded special training as illegitimate, Vigotsky suggested that coaching will increase validity—assuming, of course, that all children get the same help. Vigotsky's idea is given some support by a study applying special tests to children of very low IQ. Performance after coaching was clearly a better measure of ability than a test given without coaching (Schuchman, 1960).

The Role of Task Familiarity

In one sense, all mental ability is achieved—through observing, comparing, making attempts to attain goals, and reflecting on experience. But some tests are directly related to training received in school or out. Some SB and Wechsler tasks are taken from school lessons, e.g., reading a paragraph, and arithmetic. Vocabulary, Information, naming the parts of the body, and tying a shoelace require simply a demonstration of responses the person has surely been taught.

Since it is agreed that a mental test measures acquired abilities, it might appear that all the abilities—including analytic ones—can be produced by direct training. This is a dream that goes back to Binet, who suggested that psychologists might invent programs of "mental orthopedics" to accelerate mental growth. The specific responses required by any set of test items can indeed be taught. So can a rule that applies to a large class of tasks, for example, a technique of arithmetic. For any schema or analytic skill, it is conceivable that effective training can be devised. Smedslund's experiment warns that the training must be subtle, and so must the methods used to appraise it.

But we are not interested in training for the test tasks alone. The aim of intervention is to develop ability to cope with a wide range of intellectual tasks. A successful method of training on the Block Design task, if widely applied, would redefine school achievement to include that task. Such training would contribute to intellectual development, properly speaking, only if it radiated out into better maze performance, better picture-completion performance, and better performance on other unpracticed tasks. So far, we have no clearly valid methods of developing analytic abilities faster than they emerge in a normally rich environment (see also p. 306).

22. *Which items in Table 7.2 depend on previous school learning?*
23. *Which items would offer a child from an upperclass home an advantage over a child from a slum home?*

Influence of the Culture

There have been many attempts to compare the mental abilities of nations and racial groups by means of performance tests or translated verbal tests. Differences in group averages are often found, but they are small. The groups overlap greatly. This is evidence in itself that no one racial group has a monopoly on talent. While group comparisons have no practical importance, they might be of scientific interest if the tests were a fair basis for comparison.

A test shows how well persons tested have developed *along those lines*, not how they rank on all tasks. And since some cultures provide opportunity to acquire the needed background and others do not, the comparison gives no basis for conclusions about innate differences. Sometimes an author suggests that a certain test, usually a performance test, is "culture free" or "culture fair"—that is, that standings do not depend on the socializing experiences the person has had. But experience affects all behavior. Surely there is no task that all children have had an equal opportunity to prepare for.

In a primitive tribe living on the edge of the desert, scores on most performance tests were quite a bit below the European average for the same age. On a test that called for assembly of colored mosaics (similar to Block Design) these children averaged slightly above the European norms (Fahmy, 1954). Color plays a large part in the ceremonies of this culture and in the children's games. This evidently helps their test performance by giving them experience in examining patterns or by developing their interest in such tasks.

Direct training probably influences only a few performance measures, but learned attitudes and motivations affect all tests. Children of the educated classes in Western nations are taught from early years to take intellectual matters seriously. The child is rewarded for answering adults' seemingly pointless questions. He shares puzzles and word games with his playmates. These experiences cause him to take artificial problems seriously and teach self-criticalness and competitiveness.

The Zuñi Indians, however, teach cooperation rather than competition. Zuñi children have races. But a child who wins several races is scolded for having made others lose face. He is taught to win some races to show he is capable, and then to hold back and give others an opportunity to win. White teachers sent Zuñi children to the blackboard for arithmetic drills, with instructions to do a problem and turn their backs to the board when finished. Instead, the pupils faced the board until the slowest had finished, then all turned. This was to them simple courtesy; in their eyes, the teacher had asked them to show off. Obviously, a group speed test gives misleading results among the Zuñi. An individual test fares no better. The first subject may fail some items deliberately, because he fears the next child will be unable to answer. Intelligence tests are adequate only for comparing persons with similar experience. Anglo-Americans would perhaps do badly on a test developed by a Zuñi psychologist, using questions that differentiate between good and poor members of Zuñi culture.

Racial comparisons have frequently been misinterpreted because certain liberals want to prove that there are no innate differences in ability and certain conservatives want to prove that nonwhite groups will not profit from improved opportunity. Balanced accounts of the many studies and of their possible interpretations are given in L. E. Tyler, 1965, pp. 299–323, and Anastasi, 1958, pp. 542–575. The issue of racial differences has recently been reopened by Jensen (1969), who takes the position that Negroes are, by heredity, lower in fluid ability than whites. The argument is extremely complex, and critics have pointed to numerous weaknesses in Jensen's case (Kagan et al., 1969).

Even the simplest percepts and concepts are defined by the environment and by cultural demands. By middle childhood, an American sees the world as mapped out in straight lines. A map for him is a picture of spatial relations. But straight lines are nearly absent in some primitive communities, and a map may be only a temporal picture of the sequence of landmarks one passes in following a familiar route (Dart & Pradhan, 1967). For children in such a culture, the "simple" squares and triangles of Block Design are as hard to fix in mind as jigsaw-puzzle shapes are for us.

Even among Western nations acculturation varies. Children in urban Israeli and American schools were judged to have equal ability, as they were equal in repeating back the main ideas of a story and in learning digit-symbol pairs. But a surprise retest given without warning 48 hours later showed that the American children had forgotten half the digit-symbol pairs while the Israelis had forgotten only a quarter. For meaningful learning (story test) there was no difference on the retest. Evidently the Americans are conditioned to dismiss meaningless associations from their minds while the Israelis are set to retain anything presented in school (Harari & McDavid, 1966). We must accept Liverant's (1960) conclusion that to decide "what is or is not intelligent behavior involves a cultural value judgment" and that a person's variation in efficiency from task to task must be explained by examining his expectations and the rewards available.

24. *In what ways, if any, might cultural differences affect performance on each of the following tests?*
    a. *Formboards (fitting blocks into variously shaped holes)*
    b. *Wechsler Picture Arrangement*
    c. *Porteus mazes*
25. *One could modify the Picture Arrangement test to fit other cultures by redrawing the pictures to represent scenes in each type of community. Would such adapted tests provide a suitable basis for crosscultural comparisons?*
26. *Assume that Picture Arrangement is adapted as described in the preceding question. Then would Picture Arrangement or Block Design be more nearly "culture fair?"*

Diagnosis of Styles and Disorders

"Diagnosis" can mean many things. It may describe the individual in terms of his observed style (e.g., caution), it may suggest inferences about his motivations and reactions to tasks and persons, or it may attempt to locate him in a category of psychiatric disorder. The mental test provides some basis for all three types of interpretation, though one would hesitate to take this one sample of behavior as definitive. Three types of information may be taken into account: observations of style of work, the content of answers, and the pattern of subtest scores.

A sample of the information an examination yields is indicated by the following record, Mark, 8 years old, had a Binet MA of 8–8. On some performance tests, however, he reached an MA of 9–6 (Biber *et al.*, 1952).

The most striking feature of Mark's examination was his extreme lack of confidence and his desire to do what was expected of him. This was manifested by his constant reference to the examiner. . . . to see whether the expression on the examiner's face indicated approval.

In the Healy Completion [fitting small blocks into square holes to complete a picture] the examiner noticed that once when she gave him a friendly smile he was content to leave an inferior solution, as if he were guided much more by his wish to please than by his own good intelligence. Although she busied herself with papers and tried to pay as little attention as is compatible with a test situation, it was impossible to prevent this. The directions in the Healy Completion to look the work over carefully and see if there are any changes to make seemed to imply criticism to Mark, and he removed a block which was correctly placed and substituted a blank. His first responses were all good. In this test, he placed the first three accurately; then, apparently, he began feeling anxious or uncertain, and the last three he placed were blanks. It seemed that he was using the blanks as a way of avoiding committing himself to a mistake, and that he felt that he would rather do nothing than to get the wrong result. This test was the most plainly motivated by his desire for approval, although there were indications of it throughout the other tests as well.

In the Pintner-Paterson series, he seemed to be less conscious of the examiner, probably because he felt more sure of himself in these tests. When he was uncertain, as in the Ship and Triangle Tests [formboards], he would look up shyly as he worked. Several times he commented, "That's easy."

The first part of the [Porteus] maze series he enjoyed, working quickly, accurately, and with ease. After his first failure in Year VIII, he seemed much more uncertain and slow. After practically every one he said, "I'm not going to do any more of these." With constant encouragement, he went on and completed Years X, XI, and XII, although he had four trials on Year XII. Toward the end of the series, there was little evidence of real effort on his part, but rather he seemed to be going through the motions because the examiner urged him on.

Probably no test results on Mark are completely accurate because other factors besides ability are so definitely involved in his behavior. Difficulty . . . simply discouraged him and left him tense and uneasy. He was responsive to praise, but always with a questioning expression, as if he were trying to ferret out what one really thought of him.

Response content sometimes reveals disturbances of thinking or emotional processes. Feifel (1949) reported that mental patients and normals respond to vocabulary items in different ways. Asked what an envelope is, normals said "a container," "a receptacle for paper," "something to put a letter in," etc. Typical patient responses were "a piece of paper you fold," "you write letters," "it's sticky on top so you can paste it down," and "to mail." Strauss (1941) asked mentally defective delinquents, "What ought you to do before undertaking something very important?" (1916SB, Year X). Their answers included: "Don't touch anything that doesn't belong to you," or "Run away from a guy who is going to take it. Go tell him nothing of the people that owns them." Defining *pity*, one of them answered, "Don't take pity on somebody, shoot them and kill them." Glasser and Zimmerman (1967) list similar clues found in WISC responses.

Wechsler found some association between patterns of subtest scores and particular types of mental disorder, and has recommended the test for classifying patients. Many clinicians develop formulas for combining subtest scores into indices supposedly characteristic of brain-damaged patients, schizophrenics, etc. An illustration of these clinical hypotheses is Schafer's statements about the Wechsler-Bellevue in psychopathic character disorder (1948, p. 54):

> The characteristic pattern is a superiority of the Performance level over the Verbal, low scores on Comprehension and Similarities and high scores on the tests of visual-motor coordination and speed [Object Assembly, BD, Digit Symbol]. Often the Digit Span score does not drop, reflecting the characteristic blandness. Frequently Picture Arrangement is conspicuously high. This is especially true for shrewd "schemers." If Picture Completion is high, over-alertness or watchfulness is probably characteristic. . . .
> Qualitatively the chief feature is usually blazing recklessness in guessing at answers. . . . "George Bernard Shaw wrote Faust," "Magellan discovered the North Pole," "Chattel means a place to live (chateau)," "Ballast is a dance (ballet)," "Proselyte means prostitute," and so forth. . . . The over-all pattern will indicate that this is a bland, unreflective, action-oriented person whose judgment is poor, whose conceptual development is weak, but whose grasp of social situations may yet be quick and accurate.

Some proposals for diagnostic interpretation have been little more than plausible guesses or generalizations from small, unrepresentative samples. Even the suggestions based on sound research have limited practical value, because group means can differ significantly even when distributions overlap greatly (Rabin, 1965). There is theoretical justification for expecting brain damage to impede one type of performance more than another, or for expecting psychopaths to suffer where pretentious, incautious responses are penalized. The effect of personality is masked, however, by the effects of ability, experience, attitudes in taking the test, and random errors. Studies agree that on the average schizophrenics have Verbal IQs higher than Performance IQs. But when we look at Rapaport's data (1945, Appendix II), we find that only 31 out of his 72 schizophrenics have Verbal IQs five points or more above the Performance IQ. Even among the highway patrolmen used as a comparison ("normal") group, a third showed this "sign of schizophrenia."

Basing diagnosis on multiple signs reduces errors of classification, but not enough. Wechsler and Jaros (1965) provide some evidence for a WISC scoring formula to separate schizophrenics from normals. The rule would call 2 per cent of the normals schizophrenic, while correctly identifying 40 per cent of those judged to be schizophrenic by a complete clinical study. The formula rests chiefly on the fact that schizophrenic children have irregular profiles. Previous research (Patterson, 1953, pp. 41–76; Guertin *et al.*, 1966, pp. 402–403) has been unable to confirm the diagnostic significance of this type of scatter, and the Wechsler-Jaros formula may not stand up under further study.

It will be noted that Schafer did not propose to identify psychopaths by a numerical formula. He examined the *nature* of the errors and successes to arrive at a qualitative picture of the personality. The Wechsler scale is in some ways superior to other tests or interview procedures as an aid in forming such impressions, because the questions are the same for all subjects, are varied, and elicit revealing responses. If the clinician wishes to describe the subject, he should consider the Wechsler subtests individually and qualitatively (with due awareness that he may be interpreting random variation). The clinician must not regard an impression formed in this manner as a diagnosis. The impression is useful, but it is not a scientific conclusion. The Wechsler yields a general measure of mental ability and sometimes a significant V-P or crystallized-vs.-analytic difference, and beyond that can offer hints leading to further study of the individual.

27. *Harper (1950), comparing 245 schizophrenics with 237 normals, established reliable differences and offered a formula for combining standard scores on subtests:* $0.28\ Inf - 0.15\ Comp + 0.17\ DSp - 0.19\ Pic\ Com + 0.25\ BD - 0.35\ DSym$ *(+ other small terms). A "cutting score" halfway between the mean for normals and the mean for schizophrenics was used. In a new sample, 68 per cent of schizophrenics fell beyond the cutting score. The formula is thus shown to be truly discriminating. In view of the large number of misclassifications, what value does the formula have in practice?*

28. *According to Harper's formula, schizophrenic profiles tend to have a high point on Block Design and a low point on Digit Symbol.*
   a. *Can you explain this?*
   b. *Could you give an equally convincing explanation if the opposite had been found?*

29. *What advantage would there be in using an "intelligence" test to diagnose abnormal personalities, over using a "personality" test having similar validity for that purpose?*

30. *Schafer calls BD and OA "tests of visual-motor coordination and speed" and Witkin calls them "analytic." Can these labels be reconciled, or can one be defended as sounder than the other?*

31. *What description of the patient's thought processes is suggested by each of these responses to "Why should we keep away from bad company?" (Schafer, 1948).*
   a. *Your friends will talk about you; if we want to live in a good environment we must choose good company.* (IQ = 107)
   b. *I don't know if that necessarily holds true. To prevent picking up their bad habits, I guess.* (IQ = 123)
   c. *It's a trend toward living the same kind of a life, get bad yourself.* (IQ = 127)

32. *Match the responses in the preceding question to these answers to "Why do we have laws?" given by the same three patients.*
   a. *Govern the behavior of people. [E queries.] There has to be some maintenance of order by which government policies are carried out as well as personal behavior of individuals.*
   b. *To have a law-abiding group of people; otherwise they would corrupt the city.*
   c. *To make good citizens out of us; to keep the unruly under control.*

33. *Does the Wechsler-Jaros study indicate how many errors a clinician will make if he classifies the children it tests on the basis of the proposed formula?*

34. *Do the theories discussed above leave room for the possibility that improving the diet of disadvantaged children could benefit intellectual development? (For hypotheses of this sort, see Scrimshaw, 1968.)*

35. *Valett has published a Binet "profile form" on which the tester can circle each item passed. Items have been classified into six categories: general comprehension, visual-motor ability, arithmetic reasoning, etc. Valett proposes that the level reached in each category be plotted to form a profile for clinical analysis of weaknesses and that it be used to give a report to parents that does not stress the IQ. What facts about the construction of the SB make this proposal unsound?*

Summary Evaluation and List of Individual Tests

For school-age children and adults, the Wechsler is the dominant individual test. Those who prefer the SB are comfortable with its administrative pattern, like its varied tasks, and have so much experience with the test that they gain more from it than the average tester does. Most of the evaluative comments that apply to the Wechsler also apply to the SB.

The Wechsler has many virtues. It spreads over a variety of significant tasks and provides comparable scores from age 4 upward. It is easy to administer though not foolproof. The majority of today's clinical testers have been using one or another form of the Wechsler throughout their professional lives. This background helps at every turn; knowing when to probe into a response, when to call off a test because the subject is insufficiently attentive, what expectations to associate with a score, and what weight to put on deviant subtest performances.

The Wechsler's virtues are those of an aid to clinical observation rather than of a scientific measuring instrument. It is primitive in conception, embodying tasks that clinicians found useful in the early days of testing. Since these tasks were originally devised, psychological theory has advanced on many fronts; this theory did not enter into the design of the Wechsler and enters only indirectly into the profile organization and the interpretation. Measurement theory also has made advances by means of which a more efficient test could surely be engineered. It should be possible to obtain equally precise scores and equally rich observations in two-thirds the testing time. It should be possible to design a new structure for such a test with the aid of the "hierarchical" concepts of ability that we shall reach in Chapter 10. Unfortunately, specialists in quantitative measurement have given most of their attention to group tests, neglecting the improvement of individual measurement.

The most serious questions about the Wechsler relate to the organization and interpretation of the profile. The design encourages testers to draw conclusions from zigs and zags in the profile that represent nothing but error of measurement or that lack well-validated meaning. The distinction between V and P is of uncertain value, and P is not well measured. Very likely the test series that someday replaces Wechsler's will retain several of his tasks, but it can be expected to introduce new tasks tied to well-defined theoretical constructs.

While no other test rivals the Wechsler and Binet for general individual appraisal at ages 7 and above, practical tests for special purposes exist. Here we draw attention to a selection of special tests. We list tests for ages below 7, though these remain to be discussed later. The list is confined to current tests; detailed information on others can be found in the older Buros yearbooks and in Anastasi's text (1968). The reader should consult test reviews (see p. 121) for a more complete critique of the tests listed here. We do not list tests for which there is no commercial edition. The *Annual Review of Psychology* is the best single guide to studies on such tests. Each listing gives the test title, the author(s), the publisher, ages or grades for which suited, and remarks about the test's nature, purpose, and quality.

• Bayley Mental and Motor Scales of Infant Development; Nancy Bayley; *Psych. Corp.* Ages 1 month to 30 months. Two instruments, one appraising the child's attention and adaptive behavior, the other appraising coordinations. An accurate, well-investigated, practical instrument (see pp. 260 f.).

• Goodenough-Harris Drawing Test (formerly called Draw-a-Man); Dale B. Harris, based on an earlier test by Florence Goodenough; *Harcourt.* (See Harris, 1963.) Preschool to 15 years. The child is asked to draw the best man he can, and the best woman. Scoring takes into account the basic structure of the drawing (e.g., are the arms attached properly to the trunk? see Figure 8.4) and details of features, clothing, etc. Simple to administer; scoring rules carefully prepared. The test is used by clinicians as a supplement for WISC or SB; it is not a substitute.

Though the test can be applied in all cultures it is not free of cultural influence. Among Hopi Indians, boys' IQs averaged 117 while girls' averaged 100, the difference increasing with age. Not coincidentally, the male Hopi produces the ceremonial art of the tribe (Dennis, 1942; see also Dennis, 1966).

• Illinois Test of Psycholinguistic Abilities; S. A. Kirk and others; *Illinois.* Ages 2½ to 9. Intended to diagnose language abilities, isolating functions suggested by a theoretical model. In its present form the test seems to give clinically useful information on children who have extremely irregular profiles, but the validity studies (McCarthy & Olson, 1964) do not clearly support the underlying theory. Among the major alterations needed to allow secure interpretation is the

Credit

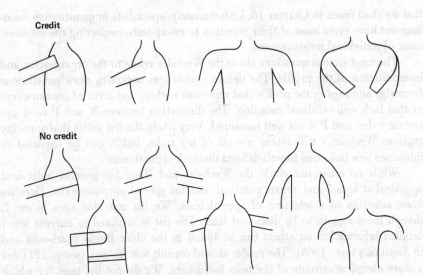

No credit

Figure 8.4.   Illustration of precise scoring rules for an individual mental test.
This is one of 71 items the scorer of the Goodenough-Harris Drawing Test must consider. For a full-face drawing, credit is allowed if "shoulders are continuous with neck and arms, and 'square,' not drooping. If arm is held from the body, the armpit must be shown." There are similar verbal standards for the side view. *D. Harris, 1963, p. 255.*

inclusion of *two* distinct short tasks for each ability (for a reason explained on p. 297).

● Peabody Picture Vocabulary Test; Lloyd M. Dunn; *American Guidance Service.* Ages 2½ to 18. A word is spoken and the child points to the appropriate picture. Useful in a clinical examination of the retarded or handicapped, as it reflects vocabulary development independent of ability to express ideas. Not sufficiently broad or thorough to be used in place of SB or WISC (Rice & Brown, 1967).

● Porteus Mazes; S. D. Porteus; *Psych. Corp.* Ages 3 to adult. The subject works through a series of paper mazes of graded difficulty (see Figure 2.2, p. 36), and is stopped whenever he enters a blind alley. He is given two trials on each maze. A premium is thus placed on planning, foresight, and inhibition of impulsive response (Porteus, 1965). Combines a measure of directed attention with a measure of emotional control, and as such is useful in studies of delinquents and in prediction of adjustment (see pp. 239, 639).

● Stanford-Binet Scale; L. M. Terman and Maud A. Merrill; *Houghton.* Ages 2½ to adult (see pp. 211 ff.).

● Wechsler Intelligence Scales; David Wechsler; *Psych. Corp.* 4 years to adult (see pp. 206 ff.).

36. It was said earlier that the SB and Wechsler do not measure entirely the same things. What appear to be the main differences in psychological meaning of the two scores?
37. For research, if not for clinical testing, it would be advantageous to administer Wechsler subtests to groups. Which of the subtests could be translated into a group form (possibly administered by sound tapes and slides, or even videotape) without seriously changing the meaning of scores? For which of these subtests would group administration sacrifice important opportunities for observation?
38. Statistical and psychometric research has concentrated on group tests rather than individual tests. What reasons can you suggest?

Intellectual Development in Early Childhood

The mental ability of the young child has received increased attention since 1960, thanks to both scientific and political concerns. During the 1940s and 1950s child psychologists had given greatest attention to emotional development, a center of interest both in progressive education and in Freudian thought. Abilities were neglected, partly because the research of the 1930s had stressed "maturation" as a sufficient explanation of the emergence of speech, locomotion, and other abilities. In the 1950s reforms were initiated in science and mathematics teaching (and later in other subjects); the new instruction stressed modes of reasoning and concept formation in those fields, rather than skills and facts alone. New types of lessons were proposed for the elementary and even the primary grades. When psychologists were asked to supply guidance for this attempt to sharpen the schoolchild's analytic powers, the most obviously relevant investigations were those of Piaget.

In a particularly influential volume, Intelligence and experience, J. McV. Hunt (1961) condemned the lingering belief that "intelligence" is predetermined and used Piaget's data to convince social workers, teachers, and other users of psychology that the child learns to be intelligent through actively investigating his environment. In the 1950s and 1960s experimental psychologists were giving increased attention to symbolic and mediating processes, thus bringing learning theory to bear on intellectual development. Though one school of thought continued to explain behavior in terms of passive conditioning, as regulated by stimuli and reinforcements from outside, theory increasingly dwelt on the active processes by which even the young child organizes and uses his experience.

Simultaneously with this renewed insistence by psychologists that intelligence is to a large degree an accomplishment rather than something that unfolds by itself, the disadvantages suffered by the lowerclass child, and particularly the Negro, came to the full attention of political leaders. As these children generally were inferior in readiness for schooling, offering equal education would not by itself enable them to take an equal place in society. It was shown that the lowerclass home environment was likely to inhibit intellectual development rather than to stimulate it (Strodtbeck, 1965; Hess & Shipman, 1965). The early years are formative years, and accumulated handicaps are difficult or impossible to overcome. The very fact that mental test score at age 4 correlates 0.70 with score in late adolescence (Table 8.2) has suggested that stimulation and training must start early to be of much benefit.

With the aim of enabling disadvantaged children to profit from regular schooling, Federal legislation initiated special preschool programs of various sorts. Some of the programs operate for only a few weeks prior to first-grade entrance, some for a year or more. A few experimental programs start with young infants. The legislation carries an unusual provision requiring annual measurement of the effects of the programs with objective tests. The character, rationale, and chances for success of several such programs are considered by Hess and Bear (1968).

Both the new curricula in the primary grades and the educational programs for the disadvantaged can be described as attempts to raise the child's intelligence. Certainly they wish to improve his ability to focus attention and analyze a situation, to organize experience and generalize, to form new concepts, and to substitute logical consistency for impulse. The new mathematics curricula are intended as much to increase the child's aptitude for learning further mathematics as they are to teach him how to work particular problems. The preschool programs are intended to increase the child's readiness to perform efficiently as a learner in the primary grades. Because the improvement of mental ability is seen as a goal, the SB and other mental tests have frequently been used to measure the educational effectiveness of preschool programs in the 1960s.

The mental tests for preschool years developed prior to 1960 were not very satisfactory. They could objectively locate subnormal and superior performance, but they did not give the descriptive breakdown of intellectual functioning required for formal evaluation of preschool programs or for research. The inadequacy of preschool tests reflected a lack of demand for such tests from practitioners, since measurement and diagnosis went on mostly in schools and clinics serving older children. It also reflected the difficulty of studying young children. An investigator of early childhood must exercise far more patience in obtaining access to representative children, in conducting psychological examinations, and in following up his subjects over a period of years than the investigator who finds his subjects conveniently assembled for him in schools.

There has been a great deal of recent test development to serve the new demands. Some of the tests represent the culmination of a long period of research and some are spur-of-the-moment constructions. Some are given focus by a theoretical formulation and some, like WPPSI, aim for a broad sample of the child's functioning. While we shall describe some of the new tests, it is too early to reach conclusions about their merits and potential contributions.

39. *What arguments can be offered to support the view that mental tests, soundly interpreted, contribute to equal opportunity for children from disadvantaged sectors of society?*

40. *Mischel (1968, p. 141) notes that Binet and Simon said that they were trying to measure intelligence "as it is at the present moment." He goes on to say that they were "not [concerned] with other predictions or postdictions." Is there any point in measuring ability if no prediction is to be made?*

Testing in Infancy

Limitations of tests for infants.   One may judge the content of a mental test in three ways: (1) He may make a task analysis—that is, he may examine the stimuli and the responses required, asking whether they can reasonably be considered a sample of behavior regulated by intellect. (2) He may ask about prediction, accepting a mental test at a later age as a criterion, and ask whether the tasks in hand forecast later standings. (3) He may examine the tasks in the light of a conception of the development of mental ability, and ask whether the acts and processes required are stages on the path toward mature intellectual functioning. The first and second viewpoints dominated thinking about mental tests until recently, and in the light of those questions infant tests have been inadequate. The third viewpoint is subtly different, in ways that will become clearer as our discussion proceeds.

A task analysis leads one to say that observations on infants do not sample and probably cannot sample mental ability. Psychologists from Binet onward have emphasized problem solving. But one cannot set a task for the infant, since he neither understands commands nor has been trained to do what he is asked. To study the first year of life is to study the infant's spontaneous behavior and his conditioned reactions and habits. In the second year, limited tasks can be set for him.

We may regard the child's behavior as purposive when he reaches for a ring, but even if he succeeds we credit him with visual-motor coordination rather than with intellectual analysis. He analyzes to some extent in order to imitate the examiner and place one block atop another, but this is scarcely problem-solving. The opinion that prevailed before 1960 is that expressed by Boynton (see Monroe, 1941, p. 629): "When the Linfert-Hierholzer Scale attempts to measure intelligence in terms of the child's ability to follow visually a ball or to use a spoon in eating, or when Charlotte Bühler looks for intelligence in a child's smile or in the fact that he seeks a lost toy, it is apparent that the procedure involves matters which neither the layman nor the psychologist would regard as integral aspects of intelligence at a later age."

From a predictive point of view infant tests fare even less well. The performance of the infant is unstable from day to day because his mood and attention vary. His rate of development is not steady; the one who is ahead of schedule at 6 months may be far back in the pack at 8 months. In Figure 8.2 we saw that the plot of an individual's standings zigzags erratically until age 3. A test at 12 months correlates only 0.47 with one at 24 months, and a negligible 0.13 with a test at year 7 (Table 8.2). There is one questionable finding that needs to be considered before we write off hope of prediction from infant tests. When a subset of items having to do with vocal expression at ages 6 to 12 months was extracted from the Bayley data, they did predict verbal IQs at school age and in adulthood. But this was true only for girls, and the small sample size gives us no grounds for confidence in the finding (Cameron, Livson, & Bayley, 1967).

A response that is just being formed is present on some days and absent on others. Moreover, the age at which a response emerges may be as much a reflection of special stimulation or lack of stimulation as of the child's ability to develop the response. Twins, for instance, are slower to speak, very likely because their attention is going into nonverbal interaction when other children are practicing sounds to themselves.

One can accept the view that the timing of development in infancy is not much correlated with later attainments, and yet believe that developing mental ability is worthy of observation. Mapping the infant's performance sheds light on the nature of development, permits one to test the effect of extra stimulation, and may—when sufficient theory has been established—suggest special treatment for particular kinds of children.

Piaget has argued that sensorimotor advances in infancy are steps on the path toward forming concepts. One of the early concepts of the child, he says, is that of "the permanent object." The child who crawls after a ball that has rolled behind a screen is showing that he knows the object is there. The evidence is even clearer when he goes to the ball after it has been screened from sight, wrapped in a cloth, moved across the table, and put behind a second screen (Inhelder & Matalon, 1960, p. 427). The child masters the idea of equality by pairing off objects ("one cookie for you and one for Mary and one for me"), first by physically laying the items alongside each other, later by glancing back and forth the needed number of times to check the pairing, and ultimately by holding in mind and comparing numbers. Abstract concepts and symbols grow out of and gradually replace sensorimotor controls, hence they are not an entirely different type of accomplishment.

If this position is accepted, when the infant displays a sense of "the permanent object" at about the normal age we have a sign that he has achieved one step along the path to reasoning. We need not argue that the child who attains this concept first is the brightest. We might be concerned, but not yet alarmed, if a child is considerably behind the norm in attaining the concept. Only as we amass extensive observations of children who display a certain lag in development will we know what action to recommend, if any. As of now, we have one well-established conclusion: skills develop poorly in a bleak environment in which there is nothing to arouse attention and encourage exploration. One of these skills or habits, that of directing continued attention to an object, was recognized as a central part of intelligent behavior in Binet's first studies; Piaget has now made manipulative exploration (e.g., the infant's turning an object in his hand) seem equally important.

Stott and Ball (1965) questioned experienced psychologists about tests for young children. Among tests for infants, the ones most often used were the Gesell Schedule and that of Psyche Cattell. The Cattell Scale (1940) is organized much like the Stanford-Binet, though with observational items. The Gesell Schedule (Gesell & Amatruda, 1947) samples both intellectual and motor activities. It is a cross-section of things babies normally can do. The clinicians replying to Stott and Ball were particularly critical of the emphasis on physical and motor development in these scales, and of the lack of correlation between infant scores and later mental-test scores. While the critics thus echoed the old task-analysis and predictive viewpoints, they regarded both scales as helpful in picturing the infant's development.

The technique of factor analysis (Chapter 10) groups items that are particularly correlated, i.e., that tend to rank persons in the same order. These groupings indicate what the test covers, and indicate ways of dividing the test to get subscores. Stott and Ball analyzed several sets of infant tests; we shall reduce their complex report to a simple summary of findings for the Cattell scale. The items have large intercorrelations. Items most representative of the scale as a whole at the 6-month level are

> Regards cube,
> Follows ring in a circular motion with eyes,
> Regards spoon.

All involve active, directed attention. There is a subset of items involving undirected hand activity. By 12 months individual differences in score depend mostly on directed use of hands. Purposive movements seem quite relevant to the study of intellectual development, even though they have only short-run predictive power (Cavanaugh et al., 1957). The data suggest that one could get separate scores for reaching movements, persistent examination of objects, etc., by making several observations of each type. The Cattell Scale is as suitable as any of the older tests for infants, but a revision is needed to take advantage of current theory, to improve reliability, and to obtain proper norms.

It perhaps seems inconsistent to say that certain performances are steps toward abstract thinking and yet do not predict later mental status. It is true that the infant who earns a superior score at 12 months has made a rapid start, because of a favorable constitution or favorable living conditions. This does not mean that he will advance rapidly in the next year. Behavior sometimes requires a period of consolidation; this gives "late starters" a chance to overtake this superior child. Perhaps, too, the living conditions that favor early development are not the best for second-year progress. Warm encouragement (for example) sometimes promotes development and sometimes stifles it by making life too easy. We should not be surprised to find the pace of development uneven.

The Bayley Scale. Nancy Bayley, whose work we have referred to several times, has assembled a Scale of Mental Development (*Psych. Corp.*). There are companion schedules for appraising motor development, for interviewing the mother, and for observing the infant's social behavior. Although the instrument as a whole is new, most of the items were introduced in Bayley's studies of the 1930s and a few come from Cattell and Gesell. Therefore a whole generation of research enriches the interpretation. The scale is applied between ages 1 and 30 months; a child's scores are interpreted by comparison with the mean and standard deviation for babies of his age. The Bayley scale is much better standardized than any other instrument for infants and the split-half reliability is as high as that of the Wechsler or SB (Bayley, 1965; Werner & Bayley, 1966). Because babies are particularly prone to "off-days," the examiner must more often reject a testing as invalid than is the case at older ages.

The Bayley Scale is more varied in content than earlier tests, judging by the Stott-Ball factor analysis (1965). The following items represent the range of content at 6 months (each item being accompanied here by Bayley's suggestion as to the function measured) :

Sustained inspection of ring (alertness of an exploratory type)
Turn to observe moving spoon (goal-directed attention)
Vocalizes displeasure (extrovertive responses, not goal centered)
Smiles at image in mirror (social response)

At 12 months, the emphasis is on communication and concepts, including imitation and obedience to simple commands. While a substantial number of the items require controlled movement, Bayley's items demand deliberate and complex behavior, and hence the task analysis suggests that it is truly a "mental test" for the 1-year-old. Earlier than that, it is more a sample of attentiveness and responsiveness. Bayley does not think of the scores as predictors of later status, save for the mentally defective. The Bayley Scales will no doubt become a standard procedure for appraising development in the first months of life. The Bayley Scale, like Wechsler's, is the product of an experienced tester who knows what responses yield suggestive information. It is not derived explicitly from a theory. The experimental studies of young children now in progress in various laboratories seem likely to analyze response processes more intensively.

Some of this work is producing a more tightly structured concept of infant development and its measurement. While Bayley has worked in the tradition of Binet, seeking a cross-sectional, hodgepodge measure of development, perhaps one can show that one competence or response pattern grows out of another. If so, one could begin to map out how far the child has progressed along each sequence. Kohen-Raz (1967) has applied the Guttman scaling technique to organize the Bayley items into five such sequences. (These correspond only imperfectly to Bayley's four categories.) They are: an eye-hand scale, a manipulation scale, an object-relation scale, an imitation-and-comprehension scale, and a vocalization-and-social-contact scale. It may seem strange to pair dissimilar functions, but the grouping is determined by the sequence of development. Thus in the imitation and comprehension scale, one part of the sequence is this set of items (numbers, in months, refer to the latest standardization):

(9.4) Puts cube in cup on command
(9.7) Stirs with spoon in imitation
(10.4) Attempts to imitate scribble
(11.2) Holds crayon adaptively
(14.0) Spontaneous scribble
(15.3) Shows shoes or other clothing or own toy
(17.8) Follows directions with doll

These are assembled in a sequence because a child rarely shows one of the later responses prior to those listed earlier. The connection is sometimes a strictly logical one; scribbling has to follow crayon-holding. But the data provide evidence that imitative behavior is a forerunner and perhaps provides necessary preparation for command-following. The order is not just an order of "difficulty." The items "Imitates words" and "Says two words" (12–15 months) fall in another scale, because some children reach those responses earlier or later than they pass the tasks where directions must be obeyed.

A similar idea, testing developmental sequences suggested by Piaget's observations, enters scales by Uzgiris and Hunt (unpublished). The tasks and observations resemble those of Bayley, and the scale groupings have much in common with those of Kohen-Raz: visual pursuit and permanence of objects, development of means for achieving desired environmental events, development of schemata in relation to objects, development of causality, construction of the object in space, and development of imitation. The new scales will correlate with Bayley scores. A sequence of the Guttman sort has to have predictive value over at least modest time intervals, since the infant can reach the 2-year-old level on schedule only if he passes through the earlier parts of the sequence at a normal time.

While the demonstration of strands of development in infancy is a step forward, the strands can surely not be considered separate. There are cross-connections. A child's progress along one chain is partially dependent on his progress along other lines. He may move ahead at an unusual rate along one line, but there will be some forward step he cannot take until supporting skills that form part of other chains have been achieved.

A further kind of investigation illustrating the possibilities of intensive analysis comes from studies of attention and recognition. Kagan and others (1966) displayed sculptured faces to the infant and recorded the duration of his fixation, smiling, vocalization, and heart rate. There were four faces: a normal one, a scrambled one with features out of place, one with eyes smoothed out, and one totally featureless. All faces elicited the same length of fixation, but the child's smiling differed with the stimulus. Four-month-olds changed heart rate most when shown the normal face, and 8-month-olds when shown the scrambled face. It is suggested that the heart rate changes when the infant is puzzling about an *almost* interpretable stimulus; the change, then, indicates what visual patterns the infant has stored up. This is, literally, an attempt to read the child's mind. Such a study argues that only a simultaneous study of several aspects of response is an adequate indication of complex internal processes.

41. *On the Bayley Scale, retests after one week showed high consistency for most items including Lifts cup by handle, Looks for fallen spoon, and Imitates words. Low consistency was found for such items as Holds cup to drink from (in response to examiner's example), Cooperates with examiner in games, and Vocalizes displeasure. How do the two sets of items appear to differ? Can you explain the variability of the second set?*

Preschool Testing

Problems and dissatisfactions. The Stott-Ball study dealt with tests for preschool children as well as infants. The clinical testers who responded to the questionnaire used the Stanford-Binet much more often than other instruments and were generally favorable to it. (WPPSI was not yet available.) The most significant complaints had to do with a certain cumbersomeness of administration, and with its limitations as a diagnostic test because there are few items of any one type.

Tests at the preschool level may be criticized from the task analysis, predictive validity, and "precursor" viewpoints. Some Stanford-Binet tasks clearly require adaption to novel demands, but a good many cover what the child has been taught—e.g. pointing out a doll's eyes, shoes, etc. The heavy emphasis on such learning is hard to defend.

There have been several predictive studies that compare IQs in later years with performance on single tasks at preschool ages. SB subtests often prove to be spectacularly successful predictors. WAIS V IQs in adulthood are predicted with r's over 0.80 by obeying simple commands, identifying how common objects are used, and picture vocabulary at age 2½ to 3. Picture vocabulary, memory for sentences, and other tasks (usually having a verbal component) predict the P IQ with r 0.70 and over. Verbal knowledge is what predicts; nonverbal tests rarely predict well. While the best subtests predict well, the overall IQ at age 3 (on SB) correlated only 0.60 with adult V and 0.54 with adult P. The prediction is evidently impaired by inclusion in the preschool test of numerous items that require little adaptation and little use of concepts (Bradway & Thompson, 1962; Bayley, undated).

A test is a much stranger experience for the young child than for one who has had months or years of school experience. The pressures on the child who is carried off from home for a test are sympathetically described by Moriarty (1961, pp. 14 ff.):

> At the beginning of our contact, he faced the relatively new experience of some form of separation from the mother. . . . it is possible that separation was sometimes interpreted as a form of rejection or displacement in the mother's affections. Separation from the mother at the examining room door in some cases . . . occurred only because of the small child's inability to override adult pressures for separation. . . .
>
> It seems inevitable that a trip with new people to a new place, particularly to the shy, retiring children, must have been somewhat confusing . . . [and] left no room to predict what might be about to happen. Only a few of the children cried. On the whole, they were more likely to come along quietly with their uneasiness reflected in facial solemnity and bodily stiffness. . . . Some children seemed to be open and free in five or ten minutes. Others were not entirely comfortable even after two or three sessions of an hour each. . . .
>
> He was often asked to defer his wishes to continue playing with the blocks or beads or to control his spontaneous enthusiasm to go on to less interesting objects or tasks which he was required to handle in specific ways, sometimes repeating or working rapidly when the reason was not immediately obvious. . . . Such concentrated attention was unusual . . . confining and in some cases irritating . . . at times boring and fatiguing. . . . [To many children, however, the tests were] stimulating and pleasant.

Refusals on single items or sections of a test are fairly common at ages up to 6. Rust (1931) found that a child often passes an item he has refused if it is presented again on another day. If credit were allowed for such passes-after-refusal, one-quarter of the 3-year-olds tested would raise their IQs by 15 points or more.

The insecure child's performance in a strange task with a strange examiner may be far below his potential. McHugh (1943) gave the SB to pupils entering kindergarten and then retested them after two months. Their mental-age scores increased nearly six months during this period and their IQs by 6 points, on the average. Tasks requiring oral response showed twice as much change as tasks calling for manipulation (see also Zigler & Butterfield, 1968). Particularly dramatic is the report of a new testing procedure in a school for ghetto children in New York City (Palmer, unpublished). IQs below 70 were recorded rather commonly when ordinary procedures were used. Testers were instructed to delay the testing of each new case until the child was fully at ease. This meant that the child would visit the examiner daily, perhaps for as many as seven days, each time spending half an hour in games or other casual interaction. When the examiner judged that the child was emotionally prepared, the test was given. Among children given this emotional conditioning for the test, IQs of 70 and below were not found.

These observations cause us to question the validity of plans used to evaluate effects of preschool training. A common evaluation plan compares scores after a year or so of instruction with the scores children earned when they entered, or with the scores of a control group given no training. The stresses Moriarty describes are a part of school activities, and hence familiar to the child who has been in school; this alone might improve post-test scores.

The Moriarty study provides one fact that strongly supports the use of the test as a basis for observation even when the validity of the score itself is doubtful. Ratings were made of adjustment and resourcefulness during the test; these did not correlate highly with the test score, but they correlated 0.50 to 0.70 with an overall rating of "coping capacity" based on a thorough study of each child.

Recent preschool tests.   The child's success in schoolwork is usually a criterion that tests are supposed to predict. But a measure of his success in learning can also be used as a predictor. The Kindergarten Evaluation of Learning Potential (KELP) asks the teacher to instruct the child—as a part of the day-to-day curriculum—in such tasks as block design, printing his name, and interpreting safety signs (J. A. R. Wilson & Robeck, 1964). The teacher is to make note of his progress. Such a record of success in learning is said to predict first-grade success. It correlates as high as 0.73 with the Stanford-Binet (in one sample of children from good homes). This high correlation suggests that the SB is a good measure of learning ability. Possibly a measure like KELP is a better predictor of learning for disadvantaged children than SB is, but no clear evidence is at hand. Correlations of 0.63 to 0.81 between KELP and first-grade ratings were found for children ranging down into the lower classes (but there was one teacher for whose class the coefficient was only 0.28.—Robeck & Wilson, 1964). There is no present basis to argue that KELP is a better measure than the conventional test.

Instead of attempting to "measure" the child, a novel instrument by Boehm takes an inventory of the concepts the child can use, in accord with the suggestion of the Geneva investigators referred to earlier. Boehm identified a large number of operating concepts such as "above," "larger than," "same color," etc., that the child has to use in primary-grade schoolwork. She then devised one item to measure whether the child does or does not have command of the concept. The items, as seen in Figure 8.5, call for a multiple-choice response to a dictated question. This introduces a good deal of random error into the inventory. It is a simple matter to generate parallel versions of all the items, and it would probably be a good idea to work the material into a series of exercises with about five items per concept, to reduce the chance of accepting a lucky guess as evidence of mastery. There are dozens of significant concepts, so the test would be spread over

Mark the boy who is **nearest** the school.

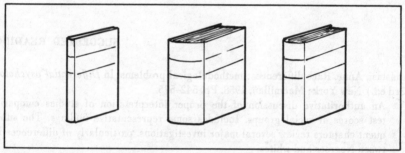

Look at the books. Mark the book that is **thickest**.

Figure 8.5.   A preschool inventory of basic concepts.
Items from a version of the Boehm Test of Basic Concepts. (Items here two-thirds
actual size.) *Copyright © 1967 by The Psychological Corporation, New York, N.Y.
All rights reserved. Reproduced by permission.*

several days if that suggestion were followed. The purpose of the survey, of
course, is to identify topics the child, or the group as a whole, needs to learn.
The instrument has also been used for evaluation of preschool instruction; it
is scheduled for publication. An instrument rather similar to Boehm's is being
prepared for 1970 publication by California Test Bureau. This, the Tests of
Basic Experience by Margaret Moss, is organized around school subjects such
as social studies and science.

Several authors have compiled checklists of development which range over
mental, motor, and social development. The data may come from the observations
of the preschool teacher, interviews with the mother, or from a direct "test." Such
a checklist is likely to be useful in sensitizing the teacher to the differences within

a class, and may also play a part in evaluating preschool programs. The devices are not regarded as measures of mental ability.

42. *Would statistical information (reliability, norms, etc.) be useful for a test like Boehm's?*
43. *At preschool ages, a writer says, "testing is a highly interpersonal process—a feature that increases both the difficulties and the opportunities presented by the test situation." Explain. Is this more true at age 5 than at age 10?*
44. *In testing children without school experience, what procedures might reduce the pressures Moriarty describes?*
45. *One of the three explanations offered for change in performance during early preschool experience is that the child may become more ready to interact with adults and attend to tasks. Has his mental ability, as defined by Binet, improved? Was the first test valid or invalid?*
46. *If giving credit for passes-after-refusals often raises IQs, would you recommend that a tester using the SB allow such credits?*

SUGGESTED READINGS

Anastasi, Anne. Race differences: methodological problems. In *Differential psychology* (3rd ed.) New York: Macmillan, 1958. Pp. 542–575.

An authoritative discussion of the proper interpretation of studies comparing test scores of racial groups. Includes some representative findings. The subsequent chapters review several major investigations, particularly of differences between Negroes and whites.

Inhelder, Barbel, and Matalon, Benjamin. The study of problem solving and thinking. In P. H. Mussen (Ed.), *Handbook of research methods in child development.* New York: Wiley, 1960. Pp. 421–455.

Two of Piaget's collaborators describe methods used in research in his laboratory and elsewhere. Emphasis is placed on "taking an inventory" of the operations and concepts used from infancy to adolescence, rather than on a numerical score "which may be perfectly justified in applied psychology . . . , but is of little value in a study of the thought mechanisms involved."

Moriarty, Alice. The concept of coping. In *Coping patterns of preschool children in response to intelligence test demands. Genetic Psychology Monographs,* 1961, *64.* Pp. 13–26.

Describes and interprets reactions of preschool children to the test situation and illustrates how the test discloses adjustment devices used by the child.

Stott, Leland H., and Ball, Rachel S. Intelligence: a changing concept. In *Infant and preschool mental tests: Review and evaluation. Monographs of the Society for Research on Child Development,* 1965, *30,* No. 3. Pp. 4–45.

Surveys controversies of the past century regarding intelligence as a fixed capacity and as a product of developmental experience. Summarizes views of leading figures from Galton to Guilford and Piaget.

Zeaman, David, and House, Betty J. The relation of IQ and learning. In R. M. Gagné (Ed.), *Learning and individual differences.* Columbus, Ohio: Merrill, 1967. Pp. 192–212.

A summary of studies connecting mental-test measures with laboratory measures of learning, particularly in the retarded.

General Ability:
Group Tests and Their Use

Individual tests permit an appraisal of the qualities of the person's performance that is perhaps more important than the quantitative score. The group test is used primarily for obtaining numerical scores: its impersonal administration and multiple-choice form provide no basis for qualitative interpretation. A group test is not simply a less expensive and perhaps cruder version of the individual test. Group tests have their own content, often selected to predict school or work performance rather than for psychological meaningfulness. The technical quality of a group test may .be superior to that of the usual individual test, if only because research on a truly large scale is practical during the development of a group test.

Time limits play only a minor part in individual tests, although bonus credit may be allowed for rapid solution of, for example, a Block Design problem. The group test is almost always timed, and in older tests each subtest had its own short time limit. Modern practice is to set liberal time limits, which simplifies test administration and makes quality of performance the critical matter.

In interpreting a group test one assumes that the subject understands the nature and purpose of testing, and wants to do his best. When this is not the case, scores are invalid. The examiner giving an individual test is likely to be aware of invalid performance because he can sense the subject's tension or his failure to understand directions. Group testing permits no similar attention to individuals. It is the only practical solution, however, to the problem of screening large numbers of job applicants, recruits, or students. Its aim is to improve the average quality of decisions in an institutional setting. When thorough understanding of an individual is required, the flexibility and intimacy of the individual test usually make it much more satisfactory. School psychologists use group tests to locate pupils who should be studied individually.

Representative Instruments

Most of the early group tests used the hodgepodge principle of the Binet scale. Mixing problems cut down the influence of any one specialized ability such as arithmetic, and the score depended mostly on the abilities relevant to all problems. As the makers of the famous Army Alpha put it, the aim was to find tasks all related to the criterion (e.g., success in the Army) and having little relation to each other. The mixed test with items in haphazard order or with many short subtests, yielding just one score, was the most common type of group test until the 1940s. The majority of items were verbal. Nonverbal tests were also produced; indeed, at the very outset of group testing the nonverbal Army Beta was developed for illiterate soldiers who could not take Alpha. In the years since 1940 general-ability tests have usually been organized to offer two main scores, one verbal and the other nonverbal or (at advanced levels) quantitative.

Sometimes a test is confined to a single type of item. Charles Spearman was the leading spirit in a British attempt to find items that measure mental ability and nothing else. He sought pure measures that would correlate with intellectual performances of all types but would not depend on specialized achievements such as vocabulary and arithmetic. According to Spearman's research the best measures of the "general ability (g)" were abstract-reasoning problems. He described g as facility in "apprehension of one's own experience, the eduction of relations, and the eduction of correlates"—i.e., in making observations and extracting principles. Spearman's g is close in conception to Piaget's views regarding the adolescent's formal use of logical systems (though not to the concepts Piaget applies to younger children). This g reappears today in the concept of fluid or analytic ability. The meaning of Spearman's abstract phrases is nicely illustrated in the matrix test, to which we now turn. We shall use g and "analytic ability" as synonyms, continuing to refer to general-purpose tests as measures of general mental ability.

A Homogeneous Test: Matrices

The "figure-analogy" task ranks alongside vocabulary items as a most popular technique for measuring mental ability. The matrix version of the task was invented by L. S. Penrose and J. C. Raven in England and published as Raven's Progressive Matrices Test in 1938 (Figure 9.1). Raven, following Spearman's theory, desired to measure the ability to perceive relationships. The subject is directed to select the design that completes the pattern. Figures are altered from left to right according to one principle, from top to bottom according to another. The subject must identify these principles and apply them.

The matrix device is highly flexible. The possible range of difficulty is

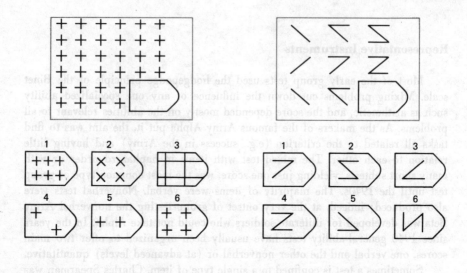

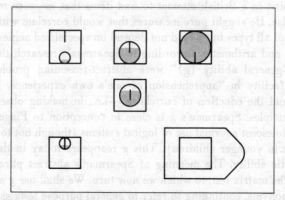

Figure 9.1.   Matrix items at three levels of difficulty.
The first and second items are like those in the Progressive Matrices, being of the usual
difficulty. The third item is a very difficult matrix in free-response form, designed for testing
college graduates.

enormous, as can be seen in the examples given. The test may be administered
individually or in groups, and may be speeded or given with a liberal time
allowance. For the less mature subject, the item can be a formboard; he chooses
a block and fits it into the blank space. The directions are simple, verbal understanding playing little part. Indeed, the verbal element can be eliminated by using
pantomime.

No one matrix test is used widely; psychologists in all parts of the world
have developed tests of their own. These unstandardized versions can be used
for hiring employees or selecting students for special courses, with little fear

that the items will become known in advance. The disadvantage of this variety is the lack of comprehensive data on any one form. Even the several versions of the matrix test prepared by Raven are poorly standardized. The directions offer certain options regarding the use of practice items and time limits, and thus one user's results may not be comparable to another's.

The matrix test correlates substantially with individual tests. The results depend on the form of the matrix test and the sample of persons; E. Barrett's (1956) correlation of 0.75 with WISC seems to be representative. Though the matrix test requires no words, it relates no more closely to Performance IQ than Verbal IQ; both correlations are around 0.70. Further information comes from the Goodnow-Bethon (1966) study of Piaget-type tasks. The balls-of-clay problem (which tests an overlearned concept) correlates with WISC but not with matrix scores. On the other hand, a task requiring formal, systematic thought (the child is to form all possible pairs from discs of four colors) is strongly related to matrix performance. The matrix test requires the child to analyze, extract concepts, and integrate them. The concepts required are familiar to almost everyone; the difficulty comes in trying to manage them all at once. The matrix is less dependent on education than most tests, though scores are depressed in cultures offering little education. Just because the matrix does not reflect school learning, it is customary to use a vocabulary test along with it.

A matrix test was the principal test for military classification in Great Britain during World War II. This test was chosen to make sure that normally intelligent recruits were not rejected because of poor education. Secondary education was completed by relatively few British youth at that time. The fact that the matrix is a narrow sample of abilities limited its military usefulness. Tests combining analytical, verbal, and numerical abilities more accurately predicted performance in training. Specialized spatial-mechanical tests such as the Bennett MCT generally made a better contribution to prediction of success in mechanical jobs. The matrix test was most helpful in predicting performance in visual signalling and radar operating (Vernon & Parry, 1949, pp. 235, 244). Experience such as this has led the practical tester to give more attention to the specialized abilities than formerly. A pure measure of g is usually not so good a predictor as a composite of g with verbal, spatial, or the other abilities required by the course or job to which the person is assigned. One reason SB and Wechsler V are successful predictors is that they call for the more specialized abilities in about the same combination that schooling itself does.

The abstract nonverbal measure has one special function in school testing. It calls attention to pupils who have good ability to direct attention, process information, and regulate thought, but who are below standard in reading and verbal development. A test that mixes verbal and nonverbal components together gives a discouraging report on some children who could do much better work if given suitable help. The nonverbal test is also useful in employee selection where educational beckground of applicants varies widely. Among African tribesmen being trained to operate heavy mining machinery, the matrix test predicted performance ratings with validity 0.51. This coefficient was based on performance after two practice tests; in line with Vigotsky's suggestion (p. 245), such a measure proved to be more valid than measurement before practice (Ombredane et al., 1956).

A Two-Score Test: Lorge-Thorndike

Representive of the tests used by schools and in educational research is the series originally prepared by R. L. Thorndike and the late Irving Lorge. The series has changed somewhat in successive editions. At present the measure for grades 3–13 has eight subtests, five verbal (V) and three nonverbal (NV). One item from each subtest appears in Figure 8.2, each item here being at about fifth-grade difficulty. The measure for primary grades (called the Cognitive Abilities Test) has four subtests: Vocabulary, Picture Classification, Relational Concepts, and Quantitative Concepts. In this test, the examiner reads each item, allowing about 15 seconds for the child to respond by circling or crossing out a picture. The item types in Figure 8.2 have been used repeatedly in group tests. Arithmetic reasoning and some vocabulary measure such as synonyms almost always appear in tests for grades 3–8. Classification, analogies, and number-series tests are close to Spearman's concept of g and to the matrix test.

Each section of the Lorge-Thorndike is administered with a time limit (e.g., nine minutes for Number Series). The authors say that the items progress so steeply in difficulty that only occasionally does a child have insufficient time to attempt all the problems he is capable of solving. This was verified in tryouts in which children were given extra time, but could not improve their scores appreciably. The total working time is 62 minutes, plus time for giving out materials and presenting directions.

The LT has an unusual "multilevel" feature which makes for economy of time and materials. Synonyms, for example, has 60 items ascending in difficulty. Fifth-graders may be told to take the "Level C" items, which means that they begin with item 11 ("unsuccessful," as in Figure 9.2) and continue to item 35 ("conviction"). An 11th-grade group, told to take the "Level G" items, starts at item 31 ("exclamation") and goes to 55 ("usurer"). This has several virtues. The pupil, taking items suitable for his grade, does not spend time on items he is sure to pass. Nor does he bang his head against impossibly difficult ones where in the end he is likely to guess and so introduce random error. The several levels are reported on a common scale. If a particular fifth grader does very badly (or very well) he can be given a lower (higher) level of the alternate form. The score so obtained compares him with the rest of the class and yet measures him at his own level. Furthermore, the school can test throughout the range of grades from 3 upward while purchasing only a single test booklet.

FIGURE CLASSIFICATION

NUMBER SERIES

6   7   7   9   9   9   12   12 →   12   13   14   15   16

4q   5p   6o   7n →   6n   7m   7n   8m   8n

FIGURE ANALOGIES

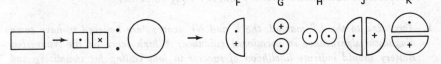

SENTENCE COMPLETION

Not every cloud gives _____.

   weather   shade   sky   climate   rain

VERBAL CLASSIFICATION

walnut   almond   filbert

   lime   broccoli   bean   pea   pecan

ARITHMETIC REASONING

Mrs. Sterne bought a 5¾ lb. chicken at 52¢ a pound. How much did the chicken cost her?

   $263.75 $27.68 $2.99 $.57¾   none of these

VOCABULARY

unsuccessful   awkward   stupid   failure   slow   dirty

usurer   lawyer   sovereign   teacher   interest   moneylender

Figure 9.2.   Items from the Lorge-Thorndike Intelligence Tests.
Copyright 1954 by Irving Lorge and Robert L. Thorndike; copyright © 1964 by Houghton Mifflin Company. Reproduced by permission.

Verbal and nonverbal deviation IQs are based on a carefully planned national sample. Percentile norms for pupils in each grade are also offered.

MacArthur & Elley (1963) found a correlation of 0.63 between the Raven

Matrices and LT NV, and other evidence indicating that the two are about equally good measures of g. Correlations with Wechsler IQs are of about the following size:

> Wechsler V with LT V,   0.8 ; with NV, 0.8
> Wechsler P with LT V,   0.6 ; with NV, 0.7
> Full Scale   with LT V,   0.8 ; with NV, 0.8

The following facts give some impression of the accuracy of the LT (and of other group tests of similar length):

Correlation of two forms on different days: V, 0.85–0.94 ; NV, 0.81–0.92
Correlation of V with NV : 0.66−0.75
Standard error of IQ: V, 4–5 points; NV, 5–6 points[1]
Interpretable difference between V and NV IQs; 15 points

1. *According to the LT manual, the V and NV scores "are believed to have some diagnostic significance in vocational guidance. A high score on the Nonverbal Battery should indicate likelihood of success in jobs calling for visualizing and for thinking in concrete terms. A high score on the Verbal Battery will indicate probable success in jobs in which language and ideas expressed in words play a part" (Manual for Administration, Multi-Level Edition, 1964, p. 40).*
   a. *What evidence would be required to justify this suggestion? From what particular jobs might the evidence be obtained?*
   b. *How does this interpretation compare with suggested interpretations of Wechsler V and P?*
   c. *Would an NV IQ of 130 lead to the same vocational expectation when accompanied by a V IQ of 110 as when accompanied by a V IQ of 90?*
2. *An out-of-date LT manual suggested the following interpretation. Why was it unsound? (Hint: Will the combined error of two tests be larger or smaller than the error on one test?)*
   "The average standard error of a LT Verbal IQ is [about 4] IQ points. Suppose that a teacher had Verbal IQs for Form A, on a class of 30 pupils. If they were all to take Form B of the tests, she could expect about 20 of the second set of IQs to be within [4] IQ points of the first. . . ." (Examiner's Manual, 1957, p. 10, slightly edited.)

Two College Admission Tests

The principal aptitude tests applied to college freshmen are the SAT and ACT. SAT, the Scholastic Aptitude Test of the College Entrance Examination Board, is required of all applicants to colleges participating in the College Board program. This includes most of the traditional private colleges and universities, particularly in the Eastern United States. Competition for places in some of these colleges is keen, and in admission decisions considerable reliance may be placed on the aptitude score, along with achievement tests and school records. The

---

[1] Counting day-to-day and form-to-form variation as error.

American College Testing Program, which uses the ACT test, primarily serves public college and university systems.

SAT gives two scores. A Verbal score is based largely on paragraph comprehension. Passages from the types of reading material used in college assignments are given, together with questions requiring fairly deep understanding of what is presented. An effort is made to avoid passages the understanding of which depends on knowledge acquired in high-school courses. A Mathematical score requires mathematical reasoning, drawing conclusions from tables, etc. Most of the items can be solved by arithmetic or simple algebra, plus ingenuity; but the person who has taken advanced mathematics will be able to make use of his specialized techniques. The test is essentially a job sample, since much of college work consists of reading for meaning, and in some programs mathematical reasoning is essential.

ACT is even more explicitly a measure of what has been learned in school. The test is a sample of skills and knowledge required in college. The content emphasizes things that almost every high-school student has studied: reasoning about basic mathematics, correcting a paragraph to improve clarity and grammar, reading and evaluating reports in science, reading and reasoning in social science. Some items require specific concepts and techniques as well as general skills.

Both tests use standard-score scales. SAT has its own 500-point scale described earlier (p. 97). On the ACT scale the average high-school senior earns about 16, and about 90 per cent of college-bound seniors fall in the range 12–28 (possible range 1–36). Whereas the SAT scale has an s.d. of 100, the ACT s.d. is about 5; the ACT authors believe that a finely divided scale encourages test users to give too much attention to small, unreliable differences. Each test is long: working time is 180 minutes. A long test is considered necessary because the test is used for important decisions and must discriminate within a population known to be superior. The main scores have form-to-form coefficients over 0.90.

A number of statistical services are offered for colleges that use ACT. Scoring is centralized, and the computer prepares for the college a score distribution for its own prospective applicants, to serve as local norms. Moreover, a college can later report grades of students to the central office and get back a report on the local validity of ACT scores as predictors. This analysis is much more thorough than most colleges could make for themselves.

The LT manual reports correlations with both of these tests, for samples of modest size:

	LT V	*LT NV*
SAT		
V	0.8	0.4
M	0.6	0.7
ACT Composite	0.8	0.4

Table 9.1. Distribution of cases, at three levels of ACT composite score, on SAT V + M

Standing on SAT	Standing on ACT		
	Lower quarter $N = 1128$	Middle $N = 2258$	Upper quarter $N = 1128$
Upper quarter	14 (1.2%)	287 (12.7%)	820 (72.7%)
Middle	404 (35.8%)	1555 (68.9%)	303 (26.9%)
Lower quarter	711 (63.0%)	416 (18.4%)	5 (0.4%)
	(100.0%)	(100.0%)	(100.0%)

SOURCE: American College Testing Program Technical Report, 1965, p. 40.

Allowing for day-to-day variation, SAT-V and ACT measure about what LT-V does. ACT and SAT do not invariably agree. Scores for both tests in three colleges provide the data for Table 9.1. Substantial agreement is evident here, and also in tabulations for the separate verbal and quantitative scores. The many discrepancies arise from content emphasis, from fluctuations caused by an occasional student's "off day," and from minor errors of measurement that pull a student from the middle group across the border into the top or bottom quarter (and vice versa).

3. *Arranging to give tests for a national testing program is troublesome to high schools, especially since each program of tests has to be given three or four times a year to accommodate those who cannot come on a single fixed date. It is suggested that all colleges agree to accept either ACT or SAT so that only one test is taken by any college applicant. What arguments for and against this proposal can be advanced? What is your conclusion?*
4. *What conclusions can be drawn from Table 9.1?*

A List of Group Tests

Chapter 8 listed individual tests in current use. Here we briefly describe group tests; the list is far from complete, as there are dozens of such tests. The list concentrates on those most actively used today, along with some little-known tests of unusual interest. The reader should not select a test for use without consulting the manual and more complete test reviews.

● American College Testing Program (ACT); anon.;[2] *ACTP*.
A test of achievement in school subjects, used for college admission purposes; there are separate English, mathematics, social studies, and natural science scores, as well as a composite. Administered on certain dates each year as a "program" test (see p. 275).

---

[2] An entry of "anon." indicates that the test was prepared by the staff of some organization. The responsibility for test design is shared so widely that listing the many cooperating authors would not be informative.

● California Test of Mental Maturity (CTMM); E. T. Sullivan, W. W. Clark, E. W. Tiegs; *CTB*.
Levels from kindergarten to adult. Has unusual variety of items, good format, and a continuous series of levels. The full test requires over one and one-half hours at school ages. Separate Language and Nonlanguage IQs are offered, but there is little evidence to indicate the practical significance of differences between the two IQs. Subscores for memory, logical reasoning, etc., attempt to provide a profile of abilities, but these subscores have dubious validity and should be given little attention. CTMM IQs run higher than those for other tests, due to some fault in norming. A "Short-Form 70" is scheduled for 1970 publication. This is similar to the older long form, save for not attempting to measure kindergartners. Possibly careful construction will make this a satisfactory instrument, but the older Short Form suffered from limited reliability.

● Cooperative School and College Ability Tests (SCAT); anon.; *ETS*.
Levels for grades 4 to 12. The original SCAT, still in use, was a test rather like the SAT, requiring about 2 hours to get dependable Verbal and Quantitative scores. Because a test of this length was not popular with schools, a 1-hour test called SCAT Series II was constructed. The Verbal score is derived from vocabulary items prepared in an analogies form that requires close analysis. The Mathematics score is a mixture of items requiring simple reasoning with familiar concepts and items requiring some command of algebra and other course content. Validity for predicting grades probably suffered little from the shortening of the test.

● Culture Fair Intelligence Tests; R. B. Cattell and A.K.S. Cattell; *EITS*.
Levels for age 4 to college. A short nonverbal test designed to measure fluid ability. The test is independent of language skill, but tests abilities that some cultures are more likely to develop than others. (Scale 1, for use up to mental age 8, has additional verbal subtests.) The test is less precise than most and is not adequately normed. For complex reasons, there are two IQ conversions, one to a 100 ± 16 scale and one to a 100 ± 24 scale; the latter should not be used. Reports of IQs on this test should be checked to make sure which scale they came from. The test has no advantage over the nonverbal sections of tests such as the Lorge-Thorndike.

● Fundamental Achievement Series; George K. Bennett and Jerome E. Doppelt; *Psych. Corp.*
Adolescent and adult. A new kind of test for employment use developed in response to the charge that tests emphasizing school learning are unfair to many potentially competent workers. Items require the type of reading and arithmetic essential in even unskilled jobs such as messenger work and taxi driving (Figure 9.3). Directions and nonreading items are presented by sound tape. Well suited to persons with education below 8th-grade level, but has a limited range in abler groups. The norms are sketchy, but probably local norms for applicant or trainee populations are more important than published norms.

6.

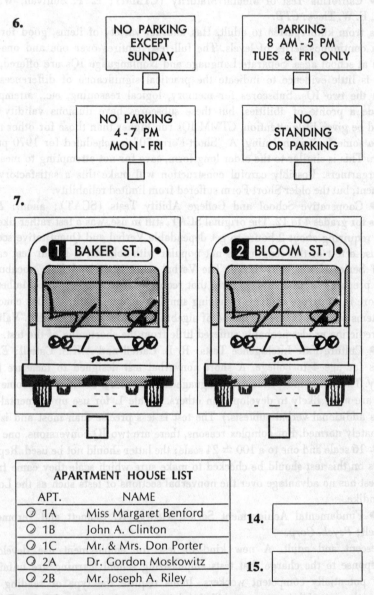

| NO PARKING EXCEPT SUNDAY □ | PARKING 8 AM - 5 PM TUES & FRI ONLY □ |
| NO PARKING 4 - 7 PM MON - FRI □ | NO STANDING OR PARKING □ |

7.

① ● BAKER ST. ●   **② ● BLOOM ST. ●**

□   □

14. ▢

APARTMENT HOUSE LIST

APT.	NAME
⊘ 1A	Miss Margaret Benford
⊘ 1B	John A. Clinton
⊘ 1C	Mr. & Mrs. Don Porter
⊘ 2A	Dr. Gordon Moskowitz
⊘ 2B	Mr. Joseph A. Riley

15. ▢

Figure 9.3. An "achievement" test to measure the probable success of ill-educated employees.

Items are taken from the Fundamental Achievement Series (see p. 277). The instruction telling which box to mark, or what information to write in the blank space, is presented by tape. *Copyright © 1968 by The Psychological Corporation, New York, N.Y. All rights reserved. Reproduced by permission.*

There is insufficient experience to indicate what decisions such a test is valid for.

● Henmon-Nelson Tests of Mental Ability; M. J. Nelson and others; *Houghton.*
Grades 3–6, 6–9, 9–12, college. Uses "spiral omnibus" pattern in which item types are mixed together, with a steady rise in difficulty. Includes information items, proverb interpretation, figure analogies, etc. Efficiently scored 30–40-minute test that predicts marks. No subdivision at lower levels. College test offers V and Q scores, but value of Q score is questionable. Speeded; score depends heavily on reading skill.

● Kuhlmann-Anderson Measure of Academic Potential; F. Kuhlmann and Rose G. Anderson; *Personnel Press.*
Eight overlapping booklets for kindergarten to grade 12. Separate V and Q scores for grade 7 and above, but the V–Q difference is rarely reliable. A confidence-band technique (see p. 370) reduces risk of misinterpretation of the difference. Tests for early grades give a single score, based on varied, mostly nonverbal tasks. Perhaps the best of the omnibus tests that emphasizes analytic ability. (Research results in this book are usually not from the most recent form.)

● Lavoie-Laurendeau Group Test of General Intelligence; G. Lavoie and Monique Laurendeau; *Institute for Psychological Research, Montreal.*
A French-language group test derived from Wechsler tasks; subtests include Vocabulary, Comprehension, Picture Arrangement, etc. Gives V, NV, and Full Scale IQs. The test is standardized on French-speaking pupils in Montreal.

● Lorge-Thorndike Intelligence Tests; I. Lorge, R. L. Thorndike, Elizabeth Hagen; *Houghton.*
Kindergarten through high school. See pp. 272 ff.

● Miller Analogies Test; W. S. Miller; *Psych. Corp.*
Superior adults. 100 very difficult verbal-analogy items. Administered only at licensed centers; severe restrictions protect the security of items, since the test is used by graduate schools to test applicants. Sizable validity coefficients for predicting success in graduate study are reported, despite the narrow range of ability within which the test must discriminate. Also widely used for this purpose is the Graduate Record Examination, a difficult version of SAT.

● Otis-Lennon Mental Ability Test; Arthur S. Otis and Roger T. Lennon; *Harcourt.*
Levels for kindergarten to grade 12. A recent revision of the pioneering tests Otis developed around 1915, which have appeared in many versions. The lowest level presents a row of pictures; the teacher reads a sentence containing a somewhat uncommon word or a concept, and the child circles the corresponding picture (e.g., "the picture of the thing that was not made by any person"). At higher levels, items are a mixture of various simple types of reasoning and vocabulary. The tests are in omnibus form, all items contributing to a single score. Norms are well prepared. Scores obtained in kindergarten and early first grade should be viewed with caution; the primary tests are less reliable than

the advanced levels, and children often change considerably during their early
schooling. Data on stability are not available.

● Progressive Matrices; J. C. Raven; *Psych. Corp.*, distributor.
Ages 5½ to adult. Efficient, properly standardized forms are badly needed. See
pp. 269 ff.

● Scholastic Aptitude Test (SAT) ; anon.; *CEEB.*
Administered to applicants for admission to affiliated colleges; not sold for general use. See pp. 274 ff.

● Tests of Educational Ability; Thelma G. Thurstone; SRA.
Grades 4–6, 6–9, 9–12. Subtests measure vocabulary, reasoning (using figure
classification or letter series), and arithmetic. An adequate test for predicting
marks. Subscores, each derived from one type of item, are of little value. There
is another version, STEA, with forms for kindergarten to grade 12. The reliability of these short forms is inadequate.

● Wesman Personnel Classification Test; A. G. Wesman; *Psych. Corp.*
Adults. A well-constructed power test intended for use in employee selection.
Manual describes local validation studies carried out by industrial users.

5. *In an adult counseling center, adults with varying educational backgrounds and
vocational goals must be given advisement. Prepare what you consider to be a
minimum list of general ability tests (group and individual) needed to cope with
all nonpsychiatric cases.*

6. *Prepare a minimum list of general ability tests needed by a school psychologist
who is expected to diagnose any pupil, age 6 to 16, whose behavior or school
work is considered to be unsatisfactory.*

7. *Would a group or an individual test be preferable*
   a. *in screening applicants for teaching positions in a large city?*
   b. *in testing juvenile delinquents prior to decisions about probation?*
   c. *in research on trends in the intelligence of immigrants?*
   d. *in selecting secretarial employees for a university?*

8. *In a subtest of CTMM (Elementary) pupils listen to a story about "The Pack
Train." In the story, a man goes to a mining camp by pack train, passing a glacier
and being threatened by a grizzly bear. After hearing the story, pupils go on to
take other sections of the test. After an elapsed time of 25 minutes, the pupils
are asked questions about the story. What characteristics and abilities would help
a pupil to earn a high score?*

9. *The manual for the Otis-Lennon Mental Ability Test goes to some length to convey that the test does not measure "native endowment," and that ability level is not
fixed. The items are considered to measure verbal and numerical abilities requisite
for success in schoolwork. As it goes on to discuss score interpretation, the manual
uses the following phrases, among others, to refer to the person's test performance:
"general abstract reasoning ability," "potential for learning," "brightness,"
"mentally gifted" (high scores). How satisfactory are these terms for communi-
cating to the teacher? Which term or terms would you prefer to use?*

The Spectrum of Ability Tests

Group tests, like individual tests, have a wide range of contents, serving different aims. At one extreme is the Matrix test, so pure a measure of abstract reasoning that for practical use it has to be supplemented by measures of knowledge and skill; at the other extreme the ACT instrument draws its items almost directly from school lessons.

We can examine this range, and the possible functions of tests of each type, with the aid of the spectrum of Figure 9.4. This spectrum, while suitable for present purposes, will be made considerably more complicated in the next chapter. At the lower end of the spectrum are tasks that sample directly the content of schoolwork, making minimal demands for adaptation or transfer. They are trained abilities. The answers often depend on conventions (e.g., spelling) or on conclusions the person could not reach for himself. At the other end are analytic tasks in which knowledge and particular concepts play little part. In EFT and matrices the person has to extract, not recall, an answer.

Perhaps it is most helpful to think of the scale in terms of transfer of learning. When a person learns to make response R to stimulus S, a later test that presents the identical stimulus S demands recall. But if the stimulus is modified or embedded in a new context, the subject must transfer his knowledge. If the new stimulus and the old are much alike, little transfer is required. If the new stimulus is unfamiliar, so that the subject must analyze and be ingenious, he has to transform what he learned. Even a task quite remote from past lessons calls on learned habits and mental structures. The logical regulation of thought required by the matrix task is the product of learning even though the person has never before seen this task. But the skills and aptitudes employed are not the product of direct training.

At the lower extreme of the scale are tests of information and familiar skills. Such tasks require no reasoning; a brilliant but uninformed person would be unable to answer. Tests for student selection and guidance sometimes contain items requiring routine application of rules, rapid computation, and other abilities that have been directly trained in school.

Some tests measure "general educational development"—i.e., competence in skills and intellectual processes that are useful in handling almost any subject matter. Paragraph reading and table reading are examples of tasks at this level. Each stimulus is new to the subject, so transfer is required, but there is little demand for ingenuity. Also at this level are quantitative reasoning items that can be solved by translating a paragraph into numerical or graphic form and applying elementary mathematical principles.

Level B moves further from things directly taught. The tasks demand reorganization of knowledge. In making a verbal test of the C or D type one would

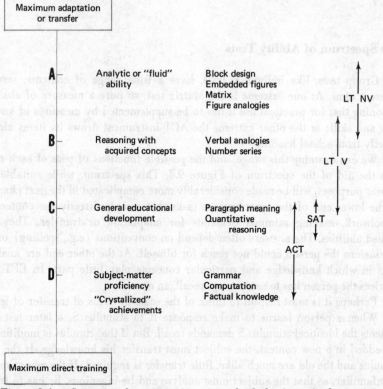

Figure 9.4. Spectrum for comparing tests of scholastic aptitude or general ability.

construct difficult items using rare words. The person who can retrieve the pertinent knowledge from his head has an advantage. A verbal problem at the B level uses words familiar to the subjects, but in novel combinations, as in LT subtests 2, 4, and 5.

The A tasks require analysis and reasoning; advanced knowledge is rarely helpful. While verbal concepts often help the subject to respond, he need not know the examiner's language. A-level tasks correspond closely to *g*.

Tests tend to correlate higher with their neighbors in the spectrum than with tests farther away. Thus LT NV (Level A-B) correlated only 0.4 with ACT (Level C-D). Many writers have made a distinction like our spectrum, though each uses different language (Guttman, 1965a, 1965b; Schlesinger & Guttman, 1969; Horn & Cattell, 1966; Humphreys, 1967). The spectrum is oversimplified; for example, it does not make the useful distinction between verbal and mathematical abilities. At a later point we shall expand this scheme into a complex "hierarchical structure." While that cannot be clearly discussed until additional basic concepts have been presented, the reader will find it profitable to look ahead now to that section (pp. 331 ff.).

The typical group mental test for adolescents and adults is predominantly verbal, making demands on both reading and vocabulary. A poor reader's score is sure to be limited no matter how well he thinks. While verbal items predict success in schooling, a test that requires well-developed vocabulary, reading speed, or comprehension of difficult sentences cannot be interpreted as evidence of deficiency in thought processes. A group "nonverbal" measure and an individual "performance" score are not alternate versions of the same test. Verbal concepts are helpful in working out a Figure Classification problem, whereas they are not especially important in Block Design and Digit Symbol. Persons with strong conceptual development are likely to have an advantage in analytic tasks even if stimulus and response are nonverbal. A deaf person is likely to be handicapped even on so-called nonlanguage tests. He is likely to be equally handicapped in everyday reasoning, just because he is at a disadvantage in acquiring concepts.

10. *Insofar as possible, locate the Wechsler subtests on the continuum.*
11. *It would be possible to design lessons to train persons to solve matrix problems. If such training were regularly offered, would this change the nature of the spectrum or simply move the matrix test toward Level D?*
12. *What sort of directions and associations would have to be stored in order to enable a computer to solve problems of each of the following types? How does this relate to the classification of items on the continuum? (Assume that the computer can "read" words and drawings, call on a memory, and "hear" commands.)*
    a. *Digits Backward*
    b. *Verbal Opposites*
    c. *Verbal Analogies*
    d. *Mazes*
    e. *Figure Classification*
13. *In Figure 9.4, illustrations of Level A are all figural. Is there any justification for regarding figural tests as more purely "analytic" than others in our culture? In all conceivable cultures?*
14. *Are the terms "analytic task" and "reasoning task" synonymous?*

Overlap of General-Ability Tests and Achievement Tests

Some experts contend that we are only fooling ourselves when we call some tests "achievement" tests and others "aptitude" tests, because the two really measure the same thing. Whether this criticism is warranted depends on the content of the aptitude test; it applies most forcefully to tests toward the D end of the spectrum. It also depends on the educational experience of a group. Persons who have been educated together will tend to rank the same way on both types of test; there will be less consistency between tests in a sample of persons who have had different types and amounts of education. The effort is made to limit the "achievement" demands of aptitude tests to matters encountered in every school. Group tests overlap with achievement to a greater degree than individual tests because they depend on reading and arithmetic. Attitudes toward schooling may also influence scores; the child discouraged about his schoolwork may see the aptitude test as more of the same frustrating stuff.

LT V correlates highly with achievement batteries given within the same 24-month period; the manual reports correlations as high as 0.88. The correlation for NV is consistently 0.10–0.15 lower than that for V. We can use statistics like this to interpret the criticism that mental tests are indistinguishable from achievement tests. The variation on the ability test can be divided into two portions: the "reliable" proportion that could perhaps be predicted and explained, and the "error." The size of each fraction is given by the coefficient of generalizability (over forms and days). Then the "reliable" part is divided: one part, equal to the squared correlation with another measure, indicates the overlap; the remainder is the independent portion, distinct from what the second measure covers. For one set of LT data we get the breakdown in Figure 9.5; other samples give the same general impression. We estimate here that 76 per cent of V duplicates information in the achievement test, and 15 per cent is new information. Among children with the same achievement, coming from the same educational background, *almost half of the individual differences in verbal IQ are due only to random errors of measurement.* A similar conclusion would hold for other group tests with considerable verbal loading. For most children continuing in the same school a verbal aptitude test leads to the same prediction that a direct measure of past achievement would.

The NV score overlaps much less. Among children with the same achievement, about three-fourths of the differences in nonverbal IQ are due to some accurately measured ability independent of achievement.

Tests that correlate substantially, as do verbal IQ and achievement measures, may still differ sufficiently in content to bring out important group differences, for example in the study of developmental trends or evaluation of treatments. A cross-sectional study by Baughman and Dahlstrom (1968), for example, finds that white boys and white girls in a certain community have about the same average, at each age from 7 to 14, on the Stanford-Binet and on the total score for the Primary Mental Abilities group test. They tie also on the Stanford Achievement Test up to age 12; then the boys, on the average, drop noticeably behind the girls. This has to be interpreted as some sort of adolescent rejection of school.

15. *"It is doubtful whether overall predictions of achievement in elementary school are particularly useful except where extreme deviates are being considered." Do you agree with the statement? Can the fourth-grade teacher use information about the pupil's MA, if it is within 1 year of the group average?*

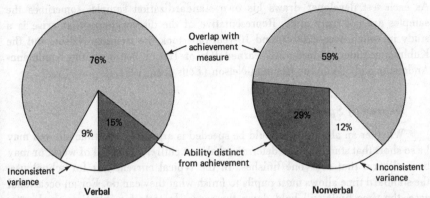

Figure 9.5. Overlap of Lorge-Thorndike scores with a concurrent measure of achievement.

16. *A committee of testing specialists made the following recommendations (among others) to state school officials regarding desirable testing programs* (Identification and Guidance of Able Students, 1958). *Classify the recommended tests on the spectrum and indicate what published tests seem to meet these specifications.*

   a. *For selecting college scholarship winners, if there is a statewide competition, the final examination should measure use and comprehension of the English language, quantitative reasoning, and ability to handle problems of comprehension in basic fields of knowledge including the sciences.*

   b. *In grades 6 or 7 there should be a scholastic aptitude test as little dependent on academic skills as possible—i.e., a reasoning test based on material not directly taught in school. In addition the test should probably yield a score based on verbal and quantitative material.*

   c. *In grade 10 or 11 there should be a test oriented primarily toward predicting college success. Its contents should probably be in the region where aptitude and achievement merge.*

17. *What reasons can you give for or against the above recommendations insofar as they concern type of test and placement?*

18. *Among college entrants, boys tend to surpass girls on tests of mathematical abilities and girls surpass boys in literary interpretation. How would you take these facts into account in planning a test to be used in a statewide public competition for scholarships?*

Problems of Design and Validity

Comparability of Scores

Just as there are doubts as to the comparability of Wechsler and SB IQs, so IQs from group tests may not be comparable from age to age and test to test.

As each test developer draws his own standardization sample, sometimes the samples are not truly alike. Representative of the discrepancies that arise is a study in which over 2200 9- and 10-year-olds took the Henmon-Nelson and the Kuhlmann-Anderson tests: 137 earned IQs of 120 or better on the Kuhlmann-Anderson, and 524 on the Henmon-Nelson (Eells *et al.*, 1951.)

Degree of Speeding

Whether an ability test should be speeded is arguable. The time allowed may be so short that standings are determined almost entirely by speed of work, or may be so liberal that everyone finishes. In the typical current test for school use, the standard time allows most pupils to finish what they can do. For an occasional case, the time limit will hold down the score. In tests for selecting employees, time limits tend to be short, and speed affects standings.

We cannot tell whether speeding of a test makes for better or worse prediction until we know whether the criterion task calls for speeded performance, and what type of speed it calls for. When the criterion task does not demand the type of speed involved in the test, speeding the test introduces an irrelevant variable. For academic prediction the level of task difficulty a person can cope with independent of speed is more relevant than his speed. Hence with a long testing time, an unspeeded test is a more valid predictor than a speed test covering the same material. If only a short time is available for testing, however, a speeded test will be more reliable than an unspeeded test. As a result, the *short* speeded test has greater predictive validity than the still shorter test that everyone is sure to finish (F. Lord, 1953).

Speed and level of performance may be regarded as independent aspects of ability (Nummenmaa, 1960). While practical tests have increasingly emphasized power, a few psychologists believe that speed of producing and checking hypotheses is an important aspect of problem-solving ability, and one that should be measured. Possibly there would be an advantage in measuring speed and power separately, but studies to support the validity of the proposal are lacking.

Stability

As test scores are unstable when behavior patterns are being acquired, we would expect a pencil-and-paper test score to be unstable in the earliest school years. For one first-grade test the correlation between two forms given at about the same time was 0.91—but the retest correlation over a 4-month interval was only 0.76. Likewise, early predictions of criteria are likely to be poor; for example, 0.50 for prediction of an achievement test in grade 3 from Lorge-Thorndike in grade 1.

Once children are accustomed to school and have stabilized their work habits, group tests for successive ages give fairly stable rankings. IQs obtained

2 years apart are likely to correlate in the range 0.65–0.80, so long as the two forms have similar content (Bradshaw, 1964; LT technical manual, 1965; Finley, Thompson, & Cognata, 1966). There are long-range correlations of 0.75 and higher between tests in adolescence and retests 20–40 years later (e.g., Haan, 1963, p. 11; Owens, 1966). Despite this stability, the tester should not rely on an old mental test for a critical decision. Some young people change their rankings considerably in a 3-year period.

The tester must also be cautious when some subjects have had little experience with conventional group tests. "Test sophistication" enables a person to do much better on later tests than on his first try. In England, where objective tests are not much used, Watts (1958) found year-to-year gains attributable to practice not only on initial testing but on the second, third, and even the seventh test.

Just what will happen to a student with a given IQ is difficult to predict. He may do well in school and college and enter a profession, or he may drop out of school and remain in an unskilled job.

Figure 9.6 is a follow-up study of students who graduated from high school in Flint, Michigan, in 1943. Ten years later the investigator obtained information about the subsequent careers of 97 boys. The boys are divided according to Kuhlmann-Anderson IQ in grade 9. For each group, the figure charts high-school grades, college history, and occupation ten years after graduation. The data deserve detailed study; they indicate the uncertain predictive value of high-school test scores, while at the same time showing that such scores have a definite relation to future success. We shall mention only a few of the relations that can be traced in the figure. There is appreciable correspondence between IQ and grades; practically no one in the lowest IQ level earned superior marks. Boys in the lowest group were more likely than others to be in unskilled jobs. Only a very few, with good grades, entered college. About one-third of the group with IQ 90–104 entered college, and half of them were graduated. The occupational status of high and middle IQ groups *who went to college* is the same. Among those who did not go to college, occupational level corresponds somewhat to IQ. The most striking finding is that, regardless of IQ or high-school average, every student who finished college was in an upper-level occupation 10 years after completing high school. The predictive significance of a 9th-grade IQ would differ somewhat in other times and other places; it would be desirable for any high-school counselor to perform his own follow-up study in order to establish expectancies for his school.

The fact that boys with IQs below 100 can succeed in college is hard to explain in any general way, but the individual cases often are quite understandable. Alex, though he had an IQ of 93 in grade 9, eventually became a lawyer. The IQ was not inaccurate: he had 93 on a retest some months later, and 113 on the Stanford-Binet. Alex had lived in a boarding home during his early school years following the death of his mother, and suffered from a sense of inadequacy that led him into aggressive, offensive behavior. A counselor felt that Alex had ability even though his tests and grades were poor. Under the counselor's encouragement he improved his marks to the B level and transferred to a college-

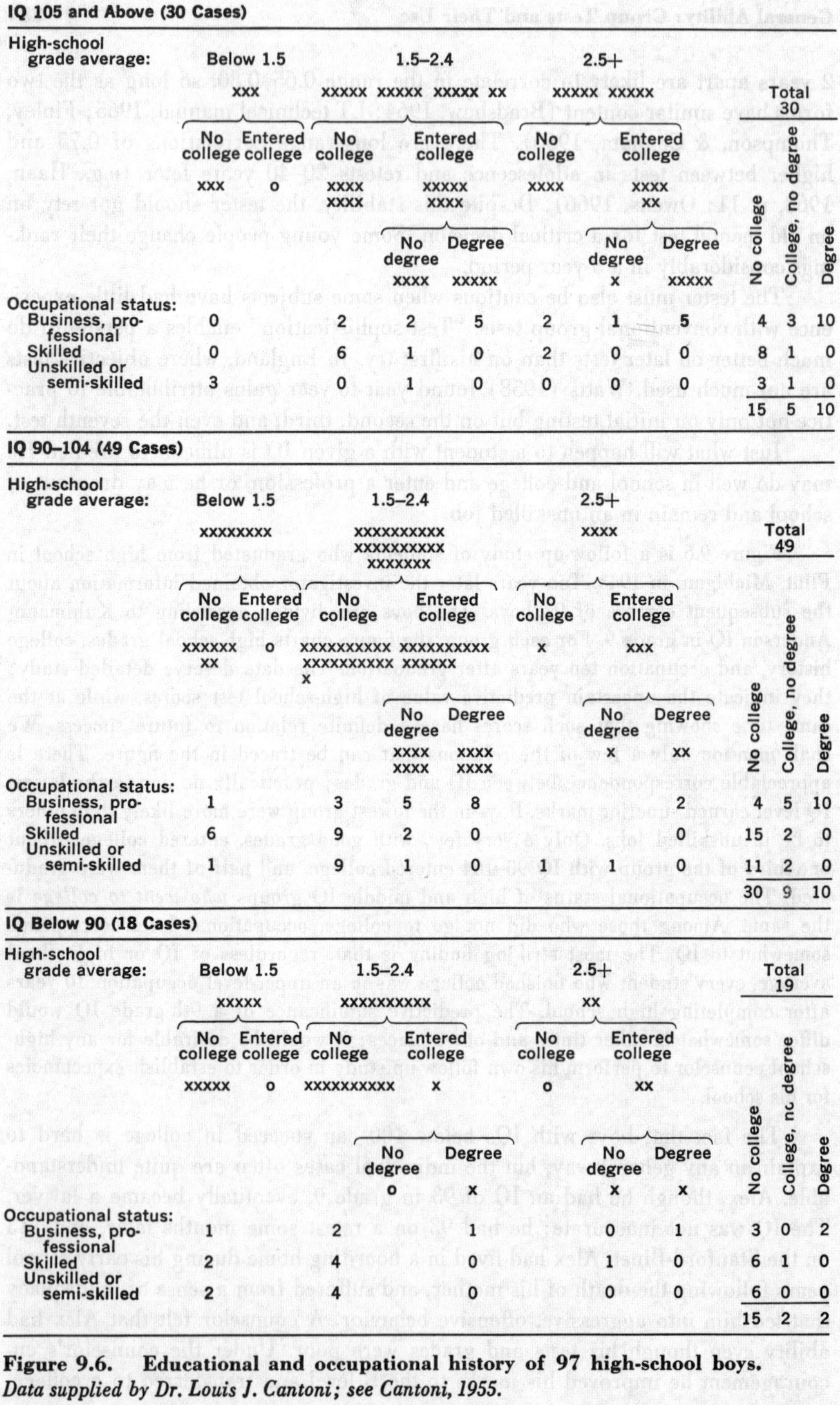

IQ 105 and Above (30 Cases)

High-school grade average:

```
                 Below 1.5          1.5–2.4                    2.5+                      Total 30
                   xxx        xxxxx xxxxx xxxxx xx        xxxxx xxxxx

               No coll | Entered     No coll | Entered          No coll | Entered
                 xxx   |    o        xxxxx   | xxxxx xxxx         xxxx  | xxxxx x
                          xxx          xxx   |
                                            No deg | Degree          No deg | Degree
                                             xxxx  | xxxxx              x   | xxxxx
```

Occupational status	Below 1.5: No college	Below 1.5: Entered college	1.5–2.4: No college	1.5–2.4: No degree	1.5–2.4: Degree	2.5+: No college	2.5+: No degree	2.5+: Degree	No college	College, no degree	Degree
Business, professional	0		2	2	5	2	1	5	4	3	10
Skilled	0		6	1	0	2	0	0	8	1	0
Unskilled or semi-skilled	3		0	1	0	0	0	0	3	1	0
Total									**15**	**5**	**10**

IQ 90–104 (49 Cases)

High-school grade average:

```
                 Below 1.5                 1.5–2.4                     2.5+                Total 49
                xxxxxxxx          xxxxxxxxxx xxxxxxxxxx xxxxxxx         xxxx

               No coll | Entered     No coll | Entered          No coll | Entered
               xxxxxx  |   o        xxxxxxxxxx xxxxxxxxxx | xxxxxxxxxx xxxxxx    x   | xxx
                  xx                          x        x
                                            No deg | Degree          No deg | Degree
                                             xxxx  | xxxx               x   | xx
                                             xxxx  | xxxx
```

Occupational status	Below 1.5: No college	Below 1.5: Entered college	1.5–2.4: No college	1.5–2.4: No degree	1.5–2.4: Degree	2.5+: No college	2.5+: No degree	2.5+: Degree	No college	College, no degree	Degree
Business, professional	1		3	5	8	0	0	2	4	5	10
Skilled	6		9	2	0	0	0	0	15	2	0
Unskilled or semi-skilled	1		9	1	0	1	1	0	11	2	0
Total									**30**	**9**	**10**

IQ Below 90 (18 Cases)

High-school grade average:

```
                 Below 1.5          1.5–2.4              2.5+              Total 19
                  xxxxx          xxxxxxxxxx               xx

               No coll | Entered     No coll | Entered          No coll | Entered
                xxxxx  |   o        xxxxxxxxxx |  x              o     |  xx

                                            No deg | Degree          No deg | Degree
                                              o    |  x                x   | x
```

Occupational status	Below 1.5: No college	Below 1.5: Entered college	1.5–2.4: No college	1.5–2.4: No degree	1.5–2.4: Degree	2.5+: No college	2.5+: No degree	2.5+: Degree	No college	College, no degree	Degree
Business, professional	1		2	0	1	0	0	1	3	0	2
Skilled	2		4	0	0	0	1	0	6	1	0
Unskilled or semi-skilled	2		4	0	0	0	0	0	6	0	0
Total									**15**	**2**	**2**

Figure 9.6. Educational and occupational history of 97 high-school boys. *Data supplied by Dr. Louis J. Cantoni; see Cantoni, 1955.*

preparatory curriculum. His personal adjustment also improved. After war service Alex entered college and completed his law course successfully (Cantoni, 1954).

The rather large number of "late bloomers" like Alex warns against making a definite and final separation of students into "academic" and "nonacademic" programs at or before the start of high-school. To be sure, it is hard to teach complex ideas to dull pupils, and their presence in the mathematics or French class will impede the instruction of the ablest. Many potentially able students, however, will not be recognized as such in the ninth grade. Any grouping plan must make provision for the student whose ability begins to show itself midway through high school. He must be able to shift his program and fulfill college requirements without too much loss of time; otherwise, much of his talent will be wasted.

Predictive Validity

Academic prediction. If one is comparing students who have been in the same class, the high correlation between aptitude and achievement tests means that it makes little difference which we use. When one compares persons coming from *different* educational backgrounds, the general ability test is more suitable. In comparing pupils at the beginning of a school year, the mental test gives much the same opportunity to pupils coming from various schools, whereas an achievement battery might not.

In decisions regarding the admission of college students, high-school grades or class ranks usually predict better than mental tests, but it is hard to compare grades from different schools, especially small ones. A combination of high-school grades with a group mental test commonly predicts college grade averages with validity 0.60–0.70 in colleges that are not especially selective. The coefficient for the test alone is usually around 0.50; long tests with educational loadings may predict with validity 0.60 by themselves (Munday, 1967). Such tests predict better than measures of fluid abilities, since those who have done well in past schoolwork are most likely to meet the demands of colleges. It is tests at Levels C and D of the spectrum, then, that are most strictly tests of "scholastic aptitude" —i.e., probability of success in further conventional schooling. Fluid abilities do not predict so well, a matter discussed further below (p. 295). There is, for example, the report of Meyers, Attwell, & Orpet (1968) that a Raven test during kindergarten predicted achievement test score in the fifth grade with $r = 0.39$. The test also predicted *language* IQ in grade 5 with $r = 0.35$.

Holland and others argue with some justice that a college that selects students on the basis of probable academic performance rejects students with fair academic promise who are outstanding along other lines. Nonacademic achievement can be judged by a questionnaire on musical, scientific, literary, and leadership activities (e.g., Have you ever won an award in a science fair?). These records of accomplishment correlate negligibly with grade record or with test scores (Holland & Richards, 1965, 1967; see also p. 477), but they do correlate with subsequent accomplishment.

Vocational prediction. The relation of mental ability to occupational level has been recognized since the first use of Army Alpha. Every comparison shows higher mental test scores among men in more prestigeful, more demanding occupations. For example, World War II soldiers who had been lawyers in civil life had a median on the General Classification Test of 62 (on a scale where the median for all men was 53); the median for general clerks was 58, and that for plumbers was 51. The lowest medians (around 45) were for farm workers, miners, and laborers. While differences such as these are significant, the overlap of groups is equally noteworthy. The plumbers (disregarding the extreme 10 per cent at each end of the distribution) ranged from 36 to 61. Some were far below the median for laborers, and some did as well on the test as the average lawyer.

While it was once thought that the differences implied a necessary relation between mental test score and occupational performance, it is now recognized that additional schooling explains most of these results. The mere fact that the sons of the well-to-do have a good chance to stay in school and also to get a good position contributes to the correlation. We know that the person who does badly on mental tests is likely to do badly in school. One can scarcely say that poor ability causes poor learning, or that poor learning causes poor ability—there is a spiral relationship. The person who gets off to a poor start fails to learn and then is ill-prepared for the next demand. Those with poor school records tend to leave school earlier. Completing college gives a license to enter the path toward executive-professional work regardless of whether the school training contributes directly to competence. The dropout who gets on-the-job training can perform in some occupations just as well as the person who has survived several additional years of schooling.

Direct studies of the predictive validity of mental tests for occupational selection frequently give encouraging results, though the results depend on the occupation and on the criterion. On the whole, tests have excellent validity for predicting grades at the end of training. A version of the Army General Classification test had correlations above 0.60 with grades in occupations as diverse as air conditioning and printing (AGCT manual, 1960). A compilation of virtually all studies in the literature showed an average validity of 0.42 against end-of-training criteria even though many of the correlations had been reduced by the weeding of the least able men from the sample. Correlations with measures of job performance averaged only 0.23 (Ghiselli, 1966, p. 121).

One especially interesting result comes from a follow-up of workers in the home office of an insurance company. Nearly 700 workers hired between 1937 and 1949 were tested on a short general mental test at that time. New workers enter in the lower job categories and are promoted as their performance shows merit. The correlation between responsibility held in 1954 and score at time of hiring was 0.60. Fifty-four per cent of those in "decision-making jobs" had had scores of 120 and over; only 5 per cent with scores 0–99 and 19 per cent in the 100–119 range held these high-ranking jobs (Knauft, 1955). The insurance company found a high correlation because the level-of-responsibility criterion spanned many jobs. Within one job (e.g., office manager), the correlation of the test with a later merit rating would surely be lower.

The coefficients for any job title range from very high to negligible, depending upon the range of ability in the group tested and the demands of the specific job. According to Ghiselli, average validities for group mental tests *against job proficiency* fall in the following ranges:

> Low (0.25 and below) Service occupations, machining workers,
>   packers and wrappers, repairmen, record
>   clerks, assemblers
> High (above 0.25) Managerial and professional, computa-
>   tional work, some sales jobs

Somewhat similar results are reported by the USES. Correlations for general mental ability are above 0.40 for success of accountants, electronics foremen, mechanical inspectors, and bindery workers, for example. In contrast, correlations are below 0.15 for electronic-toothbrush assemblers, venetian-blind assemblers, stocking inspectors, and meat-packing workers (GATB manual, 1967).

To ask about the relevance of general ability to prediction is to ask too limited a question. There are many abilities, and the employer or the person seeking a vocation cannot base the decision on just one. This is clear in Figure 9.7, which describes three female applicants for an office job in terms of test scores. Obviously, the choice among them cannot be made until the employer states his requirements precisely. We shall have much more to say on vocational aptitudes—of which general ability is only one—in the next three chapters.

19. *Characterize the occupations for which general ability is a good predictor.*

20. *Describe an office job for which applicant A (Figure 9.7) would be an excellent prospect. Do the same for C.*

21. *If literary achievement in high school (e.g., publications) correlates only 0.10– 0.20 with a test on English usage and with high-school grades (Holland & Richards, 1965), does this imply that scholastic aptitude is unimportant for excellence in writing?*

Ability to learn. Not represented directly in the spectrum of ability tests is ability to learn. This has been a principal concern of ability testers, and yet it is one of the most obscure aspects of individual differences. Binet, charged to find out which children could profit from schooling, intended to measure ability to

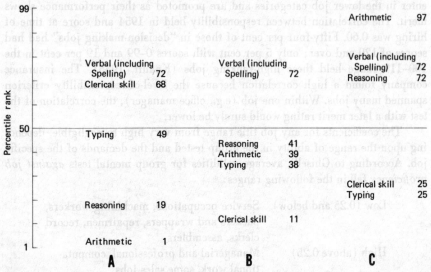

Figure 9.7.   Test-score portraits of three female job applicants.
Guion, 1965, p. 10.

learn, and mental testers following him very often described the intelligence test as a measure of learning ability. This belief has been sharply challenged, notably in papers by Woodrow (1946) and J. Anderson (1939). Anderson contended that children with high mental ages do not gain more from year to year than duller children—they finish higher, but they also started higher. Woodrow found negligible correlations between mental tests and gains in laboratory learning. Such conclusions are open to question on technical grounds, but they posed a challenge worth taking seriously. Ability to learn rapidly is an important intellectual power; it should be measured if possible. Anderson and Woodrow considered the mental test a summary only of past learning. Crystallized ability helps where new knowledge builds on old. But what helps one to master lessons so novel that everyone starts even?

Only recently have there been substantial studies of the relation between conventional tests and rate of learning. The work of Stevenson & Odom (1965) is illustrative. They gave CTMM to fourth- and sixth-graders, and also put them through a number of learning tasks. One type required the child to learn, from trials-with-correction, a series of arbitrary responses. For example, sets of three drawings were presented repeatedly, one set at a time, in scrambled order; in each set, one drawing was designated as the desired response. On the first appearance of the set the child could only guess, but on later appearances the successful learner would recall the right answer. Two tasks of this sort called for rote discrimination learning; a third called for concept attainment. The learning scores intercorrelated 0.40 or better. (For our purposes, we give a single correlation; the authors gave data for separate grade and sex groups.) Correlations of learning scores with MA were essentially zero. The learning measures are not very reliable, but even so, if the mental test were appreciably related to learning, the correlations for MA should be 0.25 or better. There was a fourth learning task, uncorrelated with the three tasks just described. This was a paired-associates task requiring the child to recall which word had been paired, a few trials earlier, with a certain nonsense syllable. *This* learning score correlated about 0.45 with MA. (The correlations with Language and Nonlanguage MAs were nearly identical.) This is puzzling. MA correlates with one learning task as highly as the reliability of the learning-score permits, but does not correlate with three other measures of learning. The rest of the studies on this problem give equally variable results (see Gulliksen, 1968, and G. Olson *et al.*, 1968).

We conclude that "learning rate" or "ability to learn" is not a satisfactory construct. Learning *of what?* And *from what instruction?* There are many kinds of learning task, and often a person who is excellent in one is poor in another. Brighter children seem to have an advantage in a task in which one can use mediation. For example, they do better at paired-associates learning where one can make up a meaningful sentence to connect the stimulus and response words. Older and brighter children are more likely to have acquired this technique. Jensen and Rohwer (1965) indicate that one can teach this trick to children of school age, and when this is done the learning of the test-dull child very nearly matches that of the test-bright child. Additional evidence comes from studies by Flavell and his associates (see Moely *et al.*, 1969); many children who score poorly on a test can do very much better when they are given enough experience and guidance to proceed efficiently. It is becoming increasingly clear that what we measure when we expose a child to a task for the first time is quite different from what we measure when he has learned how to play the game. Too many studies of individual differences have employed very short tests or very short learning periods. To obtain information relevant to school situations, we need to test how well the child can do after he has spent several periods on a certain kind of task, and has been given the sort of coaching a teacher can provide. There is a suspicion afoot that education calls for analytic ability just because the materials are capable of being put into meaningful relationships *and* the instructor has either failed to so display the relationships or has given an explanation that is hard to follow. Then one has to use his brains!

Despite the perplexities that arise when we try to explain low correlations of mental tests with learning, two general statements account for a great many findings. First, it is true that in instruction that presents connected materials— whether by a programmed text, a live teacher, or some more exotic method—the pupils high in mental age learn more than those low in mental age. Hence MA does represent one kind of ability to learn. When, however, the material is rote in nature, and no meaning can be supplied by the learner (as in many laboratory

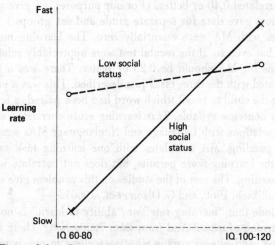

Figure 9.8.   Learning rate related to IQ in advantaged and disadvantaged children.
This finding is controversial, in the light of the most recent evidence (Rohwer, in press). *Jensen, 1968b, 1968c, p. 34. Based on studies by Rapier and others.*

tasks), good general ability gives little or no advantage. There is some reason to think that rote memory is a separate ability. Good performance on a truly rote task may occur as often among those we call "dull" as among the bright.

Studies by Jensen and his students have produced evidence that complicates the matter further. When paired-associate and other learning tasks that do not depend on school background are administered to children from typical middle-class homes, there is a healthy correlation of learning rate with IQ. But when data are collected for poor children, whether of Old American stock or some minority, there is virtually no relation (Figure 9.8). Thus the disadvantaged child has considerably greater learning ability than the conventional mental test with its heavy cultural loading gives him credit for.

Possibly a learning sample would make a good test to predict a pupil's response to certain kinds of instruction. In a sense, Wechsler's Digit Span tries this, but without much profit, since Digit Span has low correlations with other parts of the Wechsler, with school marks, and with other learning measures. The KELP measure mentioned in the last chapter uses a learning sample, but perhaps it adds nothing to the Binet score. One little-known learning test suggests a line of departure. The Semantic Test (Figure 9.9) is designed to require conceptual learning, and yet to be usable with illiterates. The intention of the author, P. J. Rulon, was to identify educable illiterates among Army draftees. The meaning of certain symbols is taught by pantomime. The subject starts with two-choice "decoding" problems and works up to the harder items pictured. In Figure 9.9 the upper panel shows that the first symbol stands for "cow," etc. The first phrase

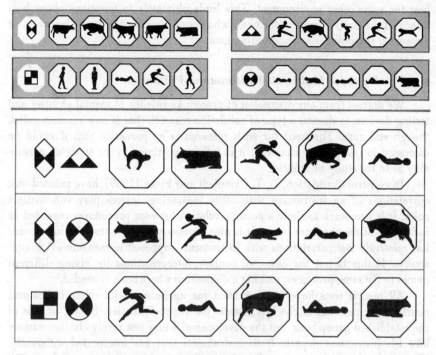

Figure 9.9.   Items of the Semantic Test of Intelligence.
Rulon & Schweiker, 1953. Reproduced by permission of the estate of Dr. Phillip J. Rulon.

is "cow jumping," and the fourth picture should be circled. Correlations show that this worksample of learning is more a measure of ability to profit from training, and less a measure of attainment, than other mental tests (Rulon & Schweiker, 1953). Learning of artificial languages has been used successfully also to test aptitude for instruction in foreign languages (Carroll, 1965).

There is no adequate basis today for judging how many types of learning ability there may be, or for judging whether a test like Rulon's is truly distinct from the *g* of Matrices and other such tests. Tests of fluid ability and learning abilities draw attention to individuals for whom past schooling has not been fully effective. Some modified educational treatment should help them, but we can make no general statement about what treatment is likely to be effective.

Recent shifts in conceptualization are forcing a fresh look at many questions for which the answers laid down by past research are inadequate. We need to ask separately, for example, about the long-term predictive implications of different types of abilities, rather than merely to talk about the stability of the IQ. Moreover, we need to trace how those predictive effects work out in different types of learning environment. An ability or style (e.g., curiosity and independence) that promotes learning and development in one environment is very likely not the best for some other environment. This leads ultimately to questions about how to adjust the environment to the child who shows superiority in rote learning, or nonverbal reasoning, or concept attainment.

The Need for Multitrait-Multimethod Validation

We digress from our discussion of present knowledge of mental abilities and testing devices, to discuss a type of validation research that is now recommended, though still rare. The need for such research is so pervasive that it could be discussed in many other chapters; it is fully as pertinent to the study of personality as to the study of abilities.

In construct validation, D. T. Campbell and Fiske (1959) have pointed out, correlations of an instrument with other measuring devices play two distinct roles. It is necessary to show a *positive* relation between procedures regarded as indicators of the *same* construct. It is also necessary to show that the instrument has *relatively low* correlations with instruments supposed to measure *other* constructs. If this is not the case, we confuse interpretations by giving different names to the same processes, making a distinction where none is needed.[3]

All mental tests have been checked for agreement with other indicators; nearly every new test is checked against the Binet, Wechsler, Raven, or one of the established group tests. But the developer of a new test rarely clarifies exactly how his instrument departs from instruments that are interpreted differently. That is why the confusion regarding the overlap of achievement tests and general-ability tests developed. Studies of indicators of distinct constructs, including the factor-analytic studies to be examined in the next chapter, have begun to make the useful distinction between fluid-analytic tests and crystallized, education-loaded abilities.

The Campbell-Fiske recommendation regarding intertest correlations does not go far enough. In any study designed to test a construct interpretation or to explore the significance of a trait, it is important (a) to measure the trait or ability construct by at least two substantially different procedures (multimethod) and (b) to measure subjects on one or more additional traits that offer alternative explanations of the phenomenon to be used as a dependent variable (multitrait). To illustrate most simply, consider further the studies reported above showing that the Porteus maze score correlates with a number of indicators of adjustment in the workaday world better than Binet or Wechsler does. This satisfies the second requirement by making it clear that not just any mental test would have these correlations. The first requirement is not satisfied: only the Porteus, among the various possible measures of fluid ability, was used. Hence we cannot say whether the adjustment of the high-Porteus group is explained by general ana-

---

[3] In the Campbell-Fiske language, one shows "convergent" and "discriminant" validity by these two types of correlational evidence, respectively. To reduce the number of "kinds of validity" to be kept in mind, we shall not employ those terms.

lytic ability, or by carelessness and impulsiveness, or by some specific quality to be found in maze tests and not in other types of tests. The investigator who advances the "analytic ability" explanation ought, as a minimum, to employ a *second* analytic test such as the matrix or EFT as a predictor, along with such contrasting nonanalytic tests as (say) Comprehension, a space-relations test, and a test of impulsiveness. If the several analytic tests show equally high correlations with the indicators of later adjustment, and the other three types of tests show rather low correlations, his conclusion is well-supported. But if the supporting high correlations from the tests advanced as measures of the construct, or the supporting low correlations from all the others, do not appear in the data, he has to alter his theory.

Studies like this have a multitrait-multimethod design. By measuring two or more distinct traits, we can rule out prominent counterinterpretations. By using two distinct methods to measure the key trait, we demonstrate the appropriateness of a broad construct; here, agreement of indicators would justify a conclusion about analytic ability rather than about "maze ability" or, even narrower, "ability on mazes given and scored according to Porteus directions."

A distressing example of the absence of such a design is the Witkin work on EFT. He wants to interpret the test as a measure of a style of life, a general intellectual approach, which he has sometimes labelled "field independence" and sometimes "analytic ability or analytic approach." He has brilliantly demonstrated that high scorers on EFT are different, in most of their behavior, from low scorers. We shall review those findings in Chapter 18. Witkin has wisely measured this trait or style by radically diverse methods, including the pencil-paper EFT and other tests involving postural discriminations. He shows consistencies among scores on these tests and also shows that the scores have consistent relations to his criteria of life style and personality. Unfortunately, nearly all his research contrasts high scorers on this one dimension with low scorers. Since we know that his tests are substantially correlated with g, we are not at all certain that "field-dependence" is anything more than a measure of general adaptive ability. Worse, since general mental tests are correlated with educational histories, we cannot be sure that Witkin's criteria would not have correlated with measures of crystallized ability. To show that the results are not explainable by all mental development including nonanalytic school learning, Witkin should have carried *at least one measure* of "ability supposedly distinct from field independence" through all his research. His theory would be supported if he found that each effect he attributes to field dependence is unrelated to the supposedly irrelevant ability.

This issue is pervasive in mental testing. An investigator too often stops after showing that his novel ability measure has the correlations he anticipated for it. He does not show that his measure has any criterion relations *in addition to* or stronger than those found for past cultural advantage and educational success, as measured by MA. It is this more than anything else that leaves us today without knowledge as to what educational treatments will work for the child with good fluid ability and poor crystallized ability; no one has found out what treatments the former predicts *better than the latter.*

The identical problem arises in the personality area. No one knows whether the correlation of a questionnaire score on, for example, "anxiety" with some effect is due to the particular trait of anxiety or simply to a general tendency to give an unfavorable self-report. Only rarely does a study of anxiety include a measure of general self-esteem as a check measure. Only if anxiety gives a strong relation and self-esteem a weak one can we defend the narrow interpretation and reject the broader one.

Tests and Cultural Differences

The Issue of Fair Employment Practice

A challenge to the use of mental tests in employment has arisen as a part of the current concern for rights of minorities. When legislation required employers to open jobs to all qualified persons, without regard to race, sex, and other irrelevant variables, it was noted that mental tests were a barrier keeping members of some minorities, particularly Negroes, out of jobs. Sometimes the poor test scores proved only that these Negroes, poorly schooled, were ill-qualified for the job in question. But it was suspected than an employer who did not want to employ Negroes could use the test as a barrier even though the test had nothing to do with job qualifications. One famous case charging that an applicant's rights had been violated by requiring a general ability test went all the way to the Illinois Supreme Court. Even when there is no intention to discriminate, selection on the basis of tests may reduce the chance that a qualified Negro or Puerto Rican will be hired.

The issues here are easily confused. No law can reasonably compel an employer to take a poorly qualified worker in preference to one who will perform well on the job. Employment on merit is not an unfair practice (Ash, 1966). It is likewise meaningless to argue that the mental test, properly administered and scored, is "unfair." The tasks are objective and the low scores of uneducated persons, including those from minorities, demonstrate a true deficiency in abilities. (To be sure, the testing atmosphere must be such that the applicant feels encouraged to do his best; see pp. 60 ff.)

The real issue is relevance. If the tested abilities are not truly required on the job or could be developed by a practicable training program, then the test tells nothing about the man's prospective merit as an employee. The man's poor performance in school is ancient history. Its aftereffects lower his scores on certain kinds of tests. Whether these aftereffects lower his job performance is an open question, to be established by validity studies in each particular employment situation. Several studies comparing validities of tests on whites and blacks in similar employment situations were compiled by Kirkpatrick *et al.* (1968). The results are highly inconsistent from one study to another; the samples are small, and the statistical analysis concentrates on correlations rather than on the regression equations that would be more suitable. Nonetheless, the evidence does indicate that for some companies and positions tests have different validity in different ethnic or socio-economic groups. Sometimes the discrepancy gives an advantage to the majority applicant and sometimes to the minority applicant. The burden of validation rests on the employer who proposes to use any test (Wallace, Kissinger, & Reynolds, 1966; McLain, 1967). He must show either that the test is a content-valid sample of work to be done on the job and that defective skill could not be remedied by economically feasible training, or that the proposed selection rule will indeed pick men who are superior performers on the job, within the minority group as well as the majority. He should consider the possibility that a different type of test is needed to select the best employees among applicants with limited educational background. One example is the "fundamental achievement" test (p. 278). Another special approach is to provide "orientation" to familiarize the applicant with test-taking skills, before the regular test is given.

The problem is complicated by the fact that a mental test irrelevant to *job* performance may predict success in training. To be sure, one wants to select men who will survive training. But if the training presents difficulties not inherent in the job, this barrier may be unfair. When a job is nonverbal, it is hard to defend a training program that relies heavily on reading, and that judges success by written tests. Very likely a redesign of the training to reduce the demand on school-learned and abstract abilities would be a good investment for the firm. Public relations would be improved by opening the job to a larger fraction of the community. The firm would have a larger pool of workers available, within which it could select on truly job-relevant abilities. And very likely the new training program would prove to produce better workers (Maslow, 1969).

This is a suitable place to draw the reader's attention to data on public attitudes toward mental tests, even though they are not concerned solely with employment. Using opinion-polling methods, investigators asked whether representative American adults favor use of "intelligence, IQ, or aptitude" tests for various types of decisions; the results are shown in Figure 9.10. The reader will have to evaluate the findings in the light of his own views. They can be seen as a sharp challenge to most present practices, or as evidence for the need to educate the public regarding the relevance of tests. Many persons evidently see the mental test as measuring not what a man is but "what he might be." And the public does not see much merit in undeveloped potentiality.

22. *Do you favor using a mental test to decide what persons should be eligible for jury duty? Would any other sort of test serve better?*

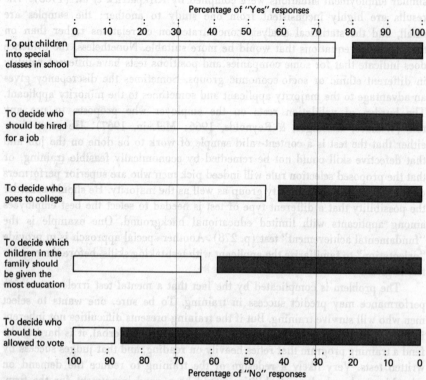

Figure 9.10. **Proportion of Americans endorsing various uses of intelligence tests.**
Brim, Neulinger, & Glass, 1965, p. 130.

23. *It is suggested that some job applicants from disadvantaged groups earn poor scores because of unfamiliarity with tests, and that therefore an applicant who falls below the acceptable standard should be allowed further opportunities to pass the test. What precautions are required to make sure that information from such additional tests is a valid basis for decisions?*

24. *One proposal to minimize discrimination is to set a different cutting score for the minority group. If management is satisfied to hire the upper 50 per cent of white applicants, it is suggested that the cutting score for minority-group applicants be set at the median of the minority-group. Evaluate this proposal (which Doppelt & Bennett, 1967, discuss).*

25. *As in the insurance company mentioned, entry jobs are used to identify persons who can be promoted to higher levels of responsibility. A person who scores low on a general ability test may be fully qualified for the entry job, and yet be unlikely to qualify for promotion. Is it fair for the company to give preference to high-scoring persons in filling vacancies in the entry job?*

26. *Tests are more objective than interviews and letters of recommendation. Therefore, say Doppelt & Bennett (1967), testing job applicants "is a friendly rather*

than a hostile act to those who come to the job market from backgrounds of limited opportunity." How can testing be seen as "friendly" when it is known that the average score in such a disadvantaged group is well below the average of all applicants?

27. *Among the studies of Kirkpatrick et al., the largest number of differences between whites and blacks appeared in a study of nursing students in Washington, D.C. The data given below are for a representative predictor and criterion. The Academic score is similar to SAT. Ignoring the fact that the sample was small, discuss whether the data indicate that there is unfair bias in using the Academic score as a basis for admission decisions. In particular: Who, if anyone, is favored and who is unfairly hindered by screening on this test?*

	Academic score		Obstetric nursing exam		Predictor-criterion r
	Mean	s.d.	Mean	s.d.	
Whites	301	9	574	103	0.60
Blacks	293	7	548	103	−0.04

Testing in Developing Nations

Closely related difficulties arise in attempts to test students and workers in newly independent, economically developing countries. New industries, and the replacement of Europeans by native workers, create high-level positions for which natives must be selected and trained. Education is limited, and schools are uneven in quality. Tests and testing procedures that work well in Western cultures fail with these school children and adults; in fact, American test items may work badly even in European cultures (Ortar, 1963). When a pictorial test is used, translating a picture into the abstract concept it supposedly portrays may be troublesome, so that "nonverbal" tests are not always more suitable than verbal tests.

Schwartz (1963) found that minor elements of test-taking procedure cause great difficulty for the African subject. Even the simplest test presents an overwhelming number of strange requirements. The African finds it just as difficult to figure out where to put his answer on an elaborate answer sheet as to decide on the answer itself. Simplified procedures help him to show his ability. Schwartz and other workers suggest such devices as these: putting all items on a single page or, if the test is long, passing out just one sheet at a time; using the same format for every test; providing extensive practice exercises; demonstrating what is wanted by film or pantomime; and using very simple language for directions. It is desirable also to encourage the most effective test-taking by, for example, pacing a speed test.

Test items should be comprehensible in the light of subject's cultural background. A mechanical comprehension test ought to be based on objects common in village life, not on objects known only to persons already participating in the industrialized fragment of the culture. There is the further difficulty that drawings are unfamiliar; such Western conventions as perspective and shading communicate nothing. This seems not to impair understanding of the matrix diagrams, but it renders pictorial tests invalid. When pictures must be used, as in testing mechanical comprehension, one should try pictures and revise them, and should train subjects to interpret the specific pictures in the test.

The key in all these suggestions is to remove *irrelevant* difficulties—not to make the test easy for everyone, but to make sure that any difficulties arise from the weaknesses the test is intended to detect.

28. *Which of the suggestions for testing in Africa would be likely to improve the validity of tests for American job applicants who have attended school briefly and irregularly?*

Testing the Disadvantaged Child in School

Mental tests used in schools have, like employment tests, been challenged by persons concerned with the problems of minorities. Objections from Negro parents became strong enough in New York City that the school board ordered an end to group mental testing in the early grades (Loretan, 1965; Gilbert, 1966). It can be argued that the mental test is a democratic device that helps the able child receive due recognition, no matter what his race. As John Gardner has said (1961, p. 48), "The tests couldn't see whether the youngster was in rags or in tweeds, and they couldn't hear the accents of the slum." The critics, however, stressed just the opposite effect. The majority of pupils from ghetto homes tested much below the norm. When they also did badly in schoolwork, a teacher was likely to say "they are working up to their ability level" and accept the result, making no effort toward remedial procedures.[4] When pupils are sorted into fast and slow sections, the majority of the Negro children have been placed in the slow groups and given an undemanding program rather than a stimulating

---

[4] A side remark may be made regarding a much-publicized study which seems at first glance to support with hard data the claim that merely giving mental tests has a prejudicial effect. After a mental test was given, for certain children picked at random the teachers were told that a spurt in intellectual development could be expected during the year. According to the published report (Rosenthal & Jacobsen, 1968) and numerous press accounts, the IQs of these children rose during the year by startling amounts. Rosenthal himself has pointed out the danger that investigators will tend to obtain data that support their preconceptions; this study is a case in point. The data that he dramatizes are selected, focusing on one of several studies and on one out of three tests within the selected study. A close examination of the study with the aid of a proper statistical analysis convinces me that the data as a whole show no significant effect (see Snow & Elashoff, 1969). There are some large gains for a few young children who scored at a chance level on the first test, which was too hard for kindergartners. Their gains, computed from an erratic base, are meaningless.

one designed to overcome handicaps. It is significant, in view of Witkin's remarks referred to above (p. 240), that black children score below whites, on the average, in Vocabulary but not in Block Design (Jensen, 1968a). But a Negro handicap in nonverbal tests is found in another study (see below).

The opposition to tests rests in part on the belief that the test is designed for the white middleclass child, and does not give the slum child a fair chance. The middleclass child is encouraged to develop verbal abilities and to reason critically; such training is much less common in lowerclass homes. This does not show the tests to be unfair; abstract and critical reasoning is indispensable for full participation in a complex and technical civilization. But it justifies our thinking of the low-scoring slum children as culturally handicapped rather than as inferior from birth. To interpret IQs as inherited and fixed *is* unfair. (Genetic faults produce some IQs below 50. Special diets may help subjects in whom the genetic defect is metabolic.)

The problem of the slum child is partly motivational. As Havighurst points out (Eells *et al.*, 1951, p. 21):

> With the exception of a minority who urgently desire mobility for their children, lower-class parents tend to place little value on high achievement in school or on school attendance beyond minimum age.

> When the middle-class child comes to a test, he has been taught to do his very best on it. Life stretches ahead of him as a long series of tests, and he must always work himself to the very limit on them. To the average lower-class child, on the other hand, a test is just another place to be punished, to have one's weaknesses shown up, to be reminded that one is at the tail end of the procession. Hence this child soon learns to accept the inevitable and to get it over with as quickly as possible. Observation of the performance of lower-class children on speed tests leads one to suspect that such children often work very rapidly through a test, making responses more or less at random. Apparently they are convinced in advance that they cannot do well on the test, and they find that by getting through the test rapidly they can shorten the period of discomfort which it produces.

As with the experimental handicap, the motivational handicap does not mean that the test is wrong. The test is validly reporting an ineffectiveness that will block adaptation in school and life unless the motivation is radically altered.

There is considerable interest in the effect of environmental handicaps and opportunities on the status of racial minorities. It has been suggested, for example, that inferior schooling causes the Negro child to lag further and further behind the white child. The best available data come from a national survey on *Equality of educational opportunity* (Coleman *et al.*, 1966). A serious attempt was made to draw a truly representative sample of pupils in each grade; analysis was made within geographical regions, and city children were separated from rural children. As one part of the study a nonverbal test somewhat like the Lorge-Thorndike and the verbal portion of SCAT were administered, using forms appropriate to the grade.

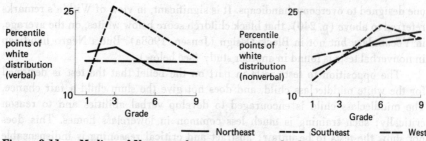

Figure 9.11.   Median of Negro performance expressed relative to percentile points of the white distribution for the same region and school grade.
Nonverbal data for the 3rd grade were not in usable form. *Based on data reported by Coleman et al., 1966, pp. 221–243.*

The selected results (see Figure 9.11) give a general impression of the findings and also will illustrate some of the difficulties of drawing conclusions from survey data. We have chosen three out of five regions, and ignored non-metropolitan data; results there would differ only in detail from those shown. (Our charts look a bit different from the charts given by Coleman on his pages 254 ff.; in part this is because we use a different statistical procedure and in part because there are discrepancies among his charts.) We have located the Negro median roughly against the white percentile scale for the region; reading off exact percentiles is not warranted. On both tests the Negro median is low compared with that for whites in their region, though of course the Negro range extends well above the white median. The disadvantage maintains itself with little modification throughout the grades. The Negroes appear to overcome some of their initial nonverbal (test-taking?) disadvantage, and perhaps to fall behind a bit in verbal performance. The authors suggest that the "hump" in the third grade data (verbal) is due to a ceiling effect; the test was too easy to allow for the ablest third graders to pull ahead. Another possibility is that early schooling does overcome some of the handicaps children bring with them from impoverished homes.

We invite the reader to draw his own implications. He should take into his thinking the following points. The analysis does not recognize socioeconomic status in any way. The study deals only with children who remain in school; dropout rates tend to be greater among the poor. The study compares children in the same grade, not children of the same age; those who do badly in school tend to lag behind a year or two, if they do not drop out. Middleclass children have conspicuously better educational opportunities than poor, black children, and home-school cooperation is better on the whole. Finally, one can speculate as to whether the educational handicap implied by a given standing is the same in all grades—that is, what does it mean educationally to be at the 25th percentile in a third grade, and in a ninth grade?

The lowerclass child has a true disadvantage in intellectual development because of lack of stimulation at home, sometimes aggravated by poor schooling later. The next question is, do tests exaggerate that disadvantage? In an effort to get items that discriminate, some testers introduce irrelevant difficulties, for instance making up items that depend more on experience than reasoning. Says A. Davis (1951):

> The type of problem in present tests, which is clearly biased, may be illustrated by the following:
>
> A symphony is to a composer as a book is to what?
>
>   paper   sculptor   author   musician   man
>
> On this problem 81 per cent of the higher socio-economic groups marked the correct response, but only 51 per cent of the lower socio-economic group did so. In an experiment designed by Professor Ernest Haggard we made a problem similar to that just read, but we used words and situations common to all social groups of children. This problem was read to the pupils:
>
> A baker goes with bread, like a carpenter goes with what?
>
>   a saw   a house   a spoon   a nail   a man
>
> On this culturally fair problem, 50 per cent of each socio-economic group gave the correct answer.

This difficulty has not been entirely eliminated from more recent tests. LT Verbal Analogies, for example, contains a few concepts that are clearly class-biased such as "linen handkerchief," "gladiolus," and "mansion." Probably a more basic source of trouble for the lowerclass child is the use of many concepts that only the child who reads widely will learn.

Davis suggested that some types of tests might be fairer than others, but the evidence denies this. Performance tests show about as much disadvantage for the lowerclass child as verbal tests, and all subtests of group tests show about the same differences (Havighurst & Janke, 1944, 1945; Eells et al., 1951). Davis and Eells designed a test (Figure 9.12) intended to interest lowerclass children and test their reasoning on familiar matters. The test appeared to have little educational loading—but the lowerclass child does no better on it than on the usual test (Charters, 1963).

There is one additional line of argument about "bias" in tests. A test would surely be considered biased if, among those who perform equally well in school, those from one racial group had high test scores and those from the other had low scores. Such a test untruthfully predicts greater success for the former group. It gives them an improper advantage in the teacher's eyes and in any selection procedure. The statistical question is this: If we predict grades from an ability test, using the expectancy table for whites as the basis for prediction, will grades for Negroes fall along the same trend line or will they be higher than predicted from the test? The College Entrance Examination Board made studies of this type in three integrated colleges. In two Eastern colleges, there was neither overprediction nor underprediction for the Negroes. In a college in the Southwest there was a slight but reliable tendency for the test interpretation to predict

"Each boy is trying to take three packages home. Which boy is starting to load the packages the best way so he can take all three home?"

(No. 3 is scored as right)

Figure 9.12.   **Specimen items from the Davis-Eells Games.**
Questions below the figure are read aloud to the group by the tester. *Copyright 1953, Harcourt, Brace & World, Inc. Reproduced by permission.*

a *higher* score for the Negro than he actually would earn (Cleary & Hilton, 1968).

This evidence seems to dispel the notion that there is serious bias in the usual test. The test is giving realistic information on the presence of a handicap. To condemn the test seems, as Doppelt and Bennett remark, like the ancient practice of killing the messenger who brought bad news to the emperor.

The critical problem is not one of modifying tests but of inventing educational procedures suitable for children who are prepared neither intellectually nor motivationally for the traditional school. It is in this spirit that the Educational Testing Service has prepared for the New York City schools a set of procedures that is at the same time instructional and diagnostic. "Let's Look at Children" consists of exercises to develop discriminative abilities, perseverance, conceptual reasoning, and other elements missing from the child's intellectual performance. Some tasks are borrowed from reading-readiness instruction, some from Piaget's laboratory procedures, some from mental tests. The teacher is encouraged to help the child with the lessons, noting where he has difficulty and where he does well—but never falling back into the role of emotionally neutral tester. The KELP materials discussed earlier are used similarly (p. 264). The entire approach is highly reminiscent of Soviet thinking. The Russians, opposed on doctrinal grounds to the concept of innate differences, and on political grounds to a system in which children from "better" families have an advantage, have always opposed Western-style testing. They rely heavily on the teacher's classroom observations to guide instruction, and on tests of subject-matter attainment for academic selection (Anan'ev *et al.*, 1961). Recent Soviet research on mental development has much in common with that of Piaget and his followers (Galperin, 1968).

It is too early to judge whether any of the current instructional procedures will actually increase readiness for subsequent schooling, and whether the observations will give information helpful in planning for the child. A summary of present knowledge in these matters is offered by Hess and Bear, 1968. Psychologists are confident that *some* instructional procedure can be devised that will be suited to the disadvantaged child. It is possible that different procedures will suit different children. If so, testing procedures that emphasize diagnosis rather than a single prediction will be needed to choose the method for each child.

29. *Middleclass children taking a multiple-choice test tend to select the most plausible of the incorrect choices, when they make an error. Lowerclass children scatter their errors over all the wrong choices, plausible or not. What does this suggest about the validity of the test?*

SUGGESTED READINGS

Anastasi, Anne. Psychology, psychologists, and psychological testing. *American Psychologist*, 1967, 22, 297–306.

    Anastasi reviews recent criticisms of ability testing and adds criticisms of her own. She then goes on to state what uses of conventional tests are justified and what developments in psychological theory would make tests more useful.

Deutsch, Martin, and others. Guidelines for testing minority group children. *Journal of Social Issues* (Supplement), 1964, 22, 129–145. (Abridged in Payne & McMorris, 1967).

    A committee advises those who use tests regarding the errors, technical and philosophical, that are likely to be made when a given score is assigned its usual meaning though earned by a child from a minority home. Various special studies and special interpretation procedures are proposed.

Doppelt, Jerome E., and Bennett, George K. Testing job applicants from disadvantaged groups. *Test Service Bulletin*, 1967, No. 57. 5 pp.

    A review of the ways in which tests are said to be biased against job applicants from minority cultures, and a critical analysis of proposals to eliminate biases.

Hebb, D. O. The growth and decline of intelligence. In *The organization of behavior*. New York: Wiley, 1949. Pp. 274–303.

    Clinical studies after brain surgery and studies of animals are described that indicate that innate potential can be distinguished from comprehension developed in a particular culture. Hebb's theory emphasizes the importance of appropriate early experience to develop ability.

Turnbull, W. W. Review of Academic Promise Tests. In O. K. Buros (Ed.), *Sixth Mental Measurements Yearbook*. Highland Park, N.J.: Gryphon Press, 1965. Pp. 766–767.

    A generally favorable but incisive review of a test battery that offers four subscores. Attention focuses on the issue of whether the inclusion of a figure-classification subscore improves the battery. (The present writer concurs with

Turnbull that it does not.) The detailed criticisms shows how one may criticize a certain general-ability test for school use even though most of the prominent tests have about equal reliability and predictive validity.

White, Sheldon H. Some educated guesses about cognitive development in the pre-school years. In R. D. Hess and R. M. Bear (Eds.) *Early education: current theory, research, and action.* Chicago: Aldine, 1968. Pp. 203–214.

Up-to-the-minute thinking about attempts to improve the intellectual per-formance of children. This is a summary comment on a conference in which many experimenters and preschool educators presented their approaches; White reviews the main themes and conflicts of view. He comments particularly on whether developing intellectual performance means the same thing as "raising the IQ."

18

Factor Analysis: The Sorting of Abilities

Nearly all the tests considered to this point grew out of Binet's original discovery that complex tasks measure general adaptive ability better than simple tests of reaction and discrimination do. To supplement the omnibus test, separate measures of verbal, mechanical, numerical aptitudes, etc., were designed, and many of them proved valuable in guidance and personnel classification. We might merely describe these tests and summarize data on their validities, but such a catalog would be endless. It will be better to emphasize the modern techniques of classifying abilities that guide the development and interpretation of such tests.

Factor analysis is a systematic method for examining the meaning of a test by studying its correlation with other variables. The investigator administers a large collection of tests to the same persons. The analysis tries to determine how many distinct abilities are being measured reliably and which ones enter each test, to detect additional "trace" abilities that could be measured reliably if the tests were modified, and to reduce the confusion that results when the same ability is given different names in different tests. Factor analysis, by studying what traits go together, clarifies measures of interests, attitudes, and personality as well as measures of ability. The purpose of this chapter is to clarify what factor analysts are doing and to review competing suggestions about the grouping of abilities.

The technique of factor analysis is laborious, though the basic idea is as simple as correlation itself. There are various techniques, each of which produces a somewhat different picture of the same data. Since factor analysis studies a set of tests as a whole, the conclusions drawn about a test vary according to what other tests are analyzed along with it. Despite these complications, a number of conclusions have emerged from factor analysis. The variation among studies is confusing, just as it confuses the beginning student of geography to find different maps picturing Greenland in different ways. These differences are of little concern to the nonspecialist; the important thing is that all maps agree that there is such a large island in the North Atlantic.

Theory of Factor Analysis

Interpreting Sets of Correlations

Looking at a collection of scores such as the Wechsler subtests, the psychologist must ask: Just how many different abilities are present? The word *ability* in such a question refers to performances, all of which correlate highly with one another, and which as a group are distinct from (have low correlations with) performances that do not belong to the group.

To take a specific example, Wechsler Vocabulary items call for recall of word meanings, and Wechsler Similarities items call for verbal comparison of concepts. Are these measures of the same ability? Or do some people consistently do well on one and not on the other? For a group of adolescents we have these data:

Form-to-form correlation of Vocabulary on same day = 0.90
Form-to-form correlation of Similarities on same day = 0.80
Correlation of Vocabulary and Similarities   = 0.52

The two tests evidently overlap. About 52 per cent of either test can be regarded as representing a shared ability or "common factor." Twenty per cent of the Similarities variance is due to form-to-form variation. This leaves 28 per cent

Table 10.1. Intercorrelations of three tests for Navy recruits

	A	B	C
A		.81	.69
B			.69
C			

To simplify tables, each correlation is presented only once. The correlation of A with B (or B with A) is .81. Entries could be made symmetrically below the diagonal if desired.
SOURCE: Conrad, 1946.

that must be due to some distinct ability that is not tested by Vocabulary. Likewise, 38 per cent of Vocabulary is due to an ability not involved in Similarities. There is a common factor of verbal facility or reasoning, but each test also involves something extra. Hence the two tests do involve distinct abilities.

Factor analysis works along these general lines, starting from correlations. Binet applied such reasoning when he decided that his tests, all having a substantial relation to each other, must reflect a pervasive general intelligence. Wissler, whose tests had very small intercorrelations, concluded correctly that his tests had very little in common and therefore represented different abilities.

The factor concept can be illustrated by means of a series of correlation tables. We start with Table 10.1, the correlations of three Navy classification tests with each other. These data suggest two conclusions:

Because the correlations are generally positive, the tests must have something in common.

Tests A and B have more in common than either has in common with test C.

The reasonableness of such a result is clear when we find that A is the General Classification test, B the Reading test, and C the Arithmetic Reasoning test. Probably the common element in all three tests is a composite of general reasoning ability and past learning. Two verbal tests may well have more in common than either has in common with a mathematical test.

In Table 10.2 the pattern reflects the presence of two distinct abilities. One ability is common to the Vocabulary and Arithmetic tests. Some other ability is common to the Turning test (placing pegs in holes) and the Assembly test (assembling a rivet and washer). The former is presumably a verbal-educational ability and the latter a psychomotor ability. A formal factor analysis goes beyond inspection and calculates the strength of each influence (by methods much more defensible than our rough estimates for Vocabulary and Similarities above).

1. *Table 10.3 presents correlations between six tests of the Navy classification battery. Does there appear to be a single common factor among all these tests? If so, what might be its psychological nature?*

2. *Which pairs of tests in Table 10.3 seem to have the greatest overlap?*

Table 10.2. **Intercorrelations of four measures for adult workers**

	Arithmetic Reasoning	Turning	Assembly
Vocabulary	.66	.06	.14
Arithmetic Reasoning		.03	.16
Turning			.38
Assembly			

SOURCE: GATB manual, 1967, III, p. 27.

Table 10.3.   Intercorrelations of six Navy classification tests

	Reading	Arithmetic Reasoning	Mechanical Aptitude	Electrical Knowledge	Mechanical Knowledge
General Classification	.81	.69	.60	.53	.49
Reading		.69	.56	.51	.46
Arithmetic Reasoning			.61	.47	.41
Mechanical Aptitude				.53	.55
Electrical Knowledge					.78
Mechanical Knowledge					

SOURCE: Conrad, 1946.

Three Types of Factors

A correlation table reports how much a particular test has in common with each other test in turn. If there are 50 tests, it takes 49 comparisons to describe the findings on one test. A factor analyst introduces composite variables or "factors" that can be readily interpreted, and describes the test by its relations to these few key variables. The process is like that of locating someone's home. Jones lives next to Smith and Adams, half a block from Brown and White, three blocks from James, Thomas, and Shultz. This description (which resembles a row in the correlation table) is useless if the person seeking Jones does not know where these others live, and inconvenient when he does know. So we introduce a reference system. We locate Jones as north of Main Street and west of State. Or we say he lives on this side of the highway, beyond the railroad tracks, halfway to the golf course. We can place any home in these reference systems. Both descriptions are correct, but they differ in completeness and communication value.

Three types of factors are distinguished: general, group, and specific. A *specific factor* is present in one test but not in any of the others under study. A *group factor* is present in more than one test. A *general factor* is found in all the tests. If all correlations among a set of tests are positive, one can find a general factor. If there are any zero or negative correlations, a general factor does not appear (Figure 10.1). How a factor is classified depends on what tests enter the analysis. If we analyze only numerical tests, numerical ability shows as a general factor. Put a few numerical tests into a mixed collection and the analysis reveals the same ability as a group factor. Use just one numerical test in the battery, and the numerical ability will be specific.

A factor is an explanatory variable. The factor analysis tells which characteristics help a person to do well on each test. The analysis produces a *factor loading* which can be thought of as a correlation between the test score and the factor score. The square of the loading tells what proportion of the test variance

Correlations within sets of three variables:

1	2	3		4	5	6		7	8	9		10	11	12
1	.0	.0		4		.7	.7		7		.5	.0		10		.6	.6
2		.0		5			.7		8			.0		11			.4

Corresponding factor patterns
(general factor heavily shaded; group factor lightly shaded)

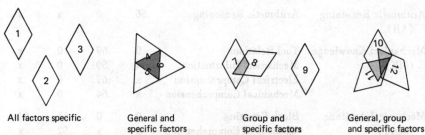

| All factors specific | General and specific factors | Group and specific factors | General, group and specific factors |

Figure 10.1.   Illustrative factorial relations among tests.

can be explained by the factor. Thus one can say that 52 per cent of the variance in Similarities is accounted for by, say, a "verbal comprehension" factor. (The label put on the factor is always a matter for debate.)

Factors in a Navy classification battery. Let us examine the loadings for the Navy tests the correlations for which were presented in Table 10.3. These tests had various part scores. Peterson was asked to determine how many different abilities were being measured, so that testers could report to classification officers all the scores giving different information without reporting the same ability under different names.

Though all the tests have something in common, Peterson chose not to report a general factor. Instead, he looked for group factors, and arrived at the factor loadings in Table 10.4. To interpret the factors, inspect the tests in which each appears. Factor I appears to be verbal ability developed through education; it covers what Guttman has called "verbal achievement" tests. This variable is often given the label *v:ed*. Factor II reflects mechanical knowledge, and factor III involves reasoning about numbers or spatial relations or both. (Interpretation is never clear when only a small number of tests are analyzed.)

The 12 tests produced only three sizable common factors. Each test contains a specific ability but the only specific loadings large enough to take seriously are those for Block Counting and Surface Development. Hence almost all the information in the twelve scores can be reported in five scores—three for group factors and two for the large specifics.

Looking only at the large factors would imply that GCT, Reading, and AR duplicate one another, and that since each test is reliable the Navy could drop

Table 10.4. Factor analysis of Navy classification test scores

| Test | Subdivision | Factor Loading[a] | | | |
		I	II	III	Specific
Reading	Reading	.70	0	0	x
General Classification	Opposites	.76	0	0	x
(GCT)	Analogies	.73	0	0	x
	Series Completion	.68	0	x	x
Arithmetic Reasoning	Arithmetic Reasoning	.56	0	x	x
(AR)					
Mechanical Knowledge	Tool Relations	0	.69	0	x
(MK)	Mechanical Information	x	.59	0	x
	Electrical Comprehension	x	.67	0	x
	Mechanical Comprehension	x	.64	0	x
Mechanical Aptitude	Block Counting	0	0	.61	.64
(MAT)	Mechanical Comprehension	0	x	.52	x
	Surface Development	x	x	x	.65

[a] x indicates factor loading between 0.20 and 0.50; 0 represents negligible loading, below 0.20. In this analysis there are small correlations between factors which the discussion in the text ignores.

SOURCE: D. A. Peterson, 1943.

two of them. Many factor analysts would have made precisely this recommendation. But Peterson did not, and he was correct. Specific factors and minor group factors may be important to validity. Table 10.5 shows how the three tests predicted grades at a training center. In courses that involve arithmetic, AR predicted better than GCT or Reading. It would have been a mistake to drop the AR test; evidently it does contain a small but useful specific.[1] It would be a mistake to merge AR with other measures of factor I, since the classification officer then could not give it extra weight in choosing men for certain schools. While factor analysis suggests profitable groupings, final decisions on test design depend on validity data.

3. *The Wechsler test can be scored to emphasize information about a general factor, about group factors, or about specific factors present in various subtests. Demonstrate the truth of this statement.*

4. *Confidence may be manifested in a variety of situations: making a speech to a woman's club, taking one's car apart to repair it, piloting a jet plane, or going to a show instead of cramming for a test. Give three alternative explanations of the nature of confidence: one in which it is considered as a general factor, one*

[1] Possibly sampling error or some other defect of the Peterson analysis caused its loading to be unduly small. As with any empirical result, factor analyses need to be confirmed by successive studies.

Table 10.5.   Validity of tests loaded on the $v:ed$ factor for predicting service-school grades

Training course	Arithmetic Reasoning	GCT	Reading
Basic engineering	.38	.31	.30
Electrician's mate	.57	.55	.42
Fire control	.34	.25	.34
Quartermaster	.53	.37	.36
Cooks and bakers	.33	.54	.40
Storekeeper	.43	.16	.26

SOURCE: Frederiksen & Satter, 1953.

in which it is divided into group factors, and one in which it is considered as a number of highly specific factors. Which theory do you think is most adequate?

5. Confidence is to be considered in selecting astronauts. How would a psychologist test confidence for this purpose if he believes it to be a broad general trait? How would he proceed if he considers confidence to be specific to a particular situation?

6. What correlation pattern in a set of three variables would be required to produce a general factor without group or specific factors?

The Machinery of Factor Analysis (Optional Section)

For readers who wish to gain some idea of how an investigator carries out a factor analysis, we shall now discuss the computations in as simple a form as possible. Computing Guide 5 applies one type of factor analysis to a small set of tests. Twenty or more tests ordinarily go into a factor analysis, and the work is done by a high-speed computer. The investigator feeds test scores into the computer; out come factor loadings.

It is a mistake to trust the computer blindly, as dozens of decisions are made that affect results. The investigator can give an order to the computer regarding each decision, and so control the process. When he gives no order, the computer does whatever the computer programmer wrote in as routine procedure; this will not give the clearest result for every investigation. There is no one "right" way to do a factor analysis any more than there is a "right" way to photograph Waikiki Beach. The uninspired photographer will snap the same old view past the Royal Hawaiian toward Diamond Head. The thoughtless factor analyst will let the computer turn out an equally standard factor structure. But in either case, a look from a different angle is likely to be more interesting and more informative.

We employ here the "square root" method, which is simple and illustrates clearly the judgments required. Some investigators want factor analysis to be a strictly "objective" procedure, in which the psychological ideas of the inves-

COMPUTING GUIDE 5.   EXTRACTING FACTORS FROM A TABLE OF CORRELATIONS.

This computing guide demonstrates the elements of a factor analysis. The method used is the "square root" method which is easiest to compute. We have not mentioned all possible short-cuts and computational checks. Computer methods of factor analysis are able to use some techniques not shown here.

A. Construction of Table R.
1. The procedure requires several tables, and paper ruled in tabular form is helpful.
2. On one sheet lay out a table with seven rows and seven columns, leaving extra space at left, right, and bottom. Down the left side list the names of the tests in abbreviated form.
3. Fill in the correlations between pairs of tests. We shall refer to any cell by a pair of numbers like this: (2,1). This means the first cell of column 2. In general, the yth cell of the xth column is (x,y).
   Example: Test 1 is Figure Classification; Test 2 is Number Series. We have found out (from the 1962 test manual) that their correlation is 0.507. This is placed in cells (2,1) and (1,2).
4. Fill in the diagonal cells (1,1), (2,2), etc. In this example we shall use split-half reliability coefficients, also from the test manual.
   Example: The manual reports a coefficient of 0.711 for Test 1, so this value is entered in (1,1).

B. Extension of Table R.
1. Define pivot variables. The pivot variable is a single test or a combination of tests that can be used to construct a frame of reference. In this example we have decided to define these two pivot variables:
   I. Sum of tests 4, 5, and 7 (all verbal)
   II. Sum of tests 1, 2, and 3 (all nonverbal)
2. Provide an extra column and row in table R for pivot variable I—this will be column 8 or row 8. Fill in this column by adding the entries for columns 4, 5, and 7 in each row.
   Example: To fill (8,1), add (4,1), (5,1), and (7,1).
   $$0.317 + 0.482 + 0.367 = 1.166$$
3. Assign column 9 and row 9 to pivot variable II. Fill each cell of column 9 by adding the entries for columns 1, 2, and 3.
4. Place in (1,8) the same value as in (8,1). Reproduce each other value of column 8 in row 8. Do the same for column and row 9.
5. Fill (8,8) by adding (4,8), (5,8), and (7,8).
   Fill (9,8) by adding (1,8), (2,8), and (3,8).
   Fill (8,9) with the value from (9,8).
   Fill (9,9) by adding (1,9), (2,9), and (3,9).

C. Extraction of first factor.
1. Set up a new table F with two columns, headed I and II, and with 9 rows. The procedure we use will place a first reference factor to coincide with I. The second factor will coincide with the information in II after I is eliminated (partialled out).

COMPUTING GUIDE 5. (Continued)

2. Find the square root of the value in cell (8,8) of R. (This is the diagonal entry in the column corresponding to I.)
3. Divide each cell of column 8 by this square root and place the result in the corresponding cell of column I of table F. We shall refer to this yth cell of column I as [I,y].
Example: (8,1) = 1.166. The square root of (8,8) is 2.529.
1.166 ÷ 2.529 is 0.461. This is [I, 1].
4. Set up a new table just like R in form, with 9 rows and 9 columns. Label this G_1. Fill in cell (x,y) of G_1 by multiplying [I,x] by [I,y].
Example: [I,1] multiplied by [I,1] = 0.461 × 0.461 = 0.213. This goes in (1,1) of G_1. To fill (2,1), multiply 0.383 by 0.461 = 0.177.
(Hint: Every cell to the lower left of the diagonal is equal to the corresponding value above and to the right of the diagonal. Therefore one can compute the values above the diagonal and simply copy them in the correct place below the diagonal.)
5. Set up a table R_1 in the same form as R. Fill cell (x, y) by subtracting the (x, y) value in G_1 from the (x,y) value in R.
Example: For cell (2,1), 0.507 − 0.177 = 0.330.
Table R_1 shows how much correlation there is between two tests after we eliminate that part of the correlation that can be assigned to variable I.

D. Extraction of second factor.
The procedure is exactly like that followed in C, with these small substitutions.
2. Find the square root of (9,9).
3. Place quotients in column II of F.
4, 5. Label the new tables G_2 and R_2. Enter products of [II,x] with [II,y] in G_2.

E. Completion of factor table.
1. The numbers in rows 1–8 of F are the factor loadings that are the main result of a factor analysis. Additional useful numbers are added to the table. First, square each number from [I,1] to [I,8] and add; put this sum below the I column. Do the same for the II column.
2. Add the squares of [I,1] and [II,1]; put this beside column II in a new column. Do the same for rows 2–8.
3. Enter in the "remainder" column the diagonal entries (1,1) to (8,8) of R_2.
4. Subtract the entry in (1,1) of the original R from 1.00 and enter the difference in the "error" column. Do the same for each row.
5. The three values in any row—sum of squares, remainder, and error—should add to 1.00.

F. Plot of factor loadings.
1. Diagram the factor loadings as shown in the illustration.

COMPUTING GUIDE 5. (Continued)

Table R   (The printed numbers are supplied at the start of the analysis)

		1	2	3	4	5	6	7	I	II
Fig. Class.	1	.711	.507	.547	.317	.482	.431	.367	1.166	1.765
Numb. Series	2	.507	.843	.548	.296	.383	.368	.290	.969	1.898
Fig. Anal.	3	.547	.548	.873	.354	.430	.521	.387	1.171	1.968
Sent. Comp.	4	.317	.296	.354	.770	.593	.470	.702	2.065	.967
Verb. Class	5	.482	.383	.430	.593	.864	.494	.675	2.132	1.295
Arith. Reas.	6	.431	.368	.521	.470	.494	.821	.604	1.568	1.320
Vocabulary	7	.367	.290	.387	.702	.675	.604	.824	2.201	1.044
Pivot I		1.166	.969	1.171	2.065	2.132	1.568	2.201	6.398	3.306
Pivot II		1.765	1.898	1.968	.967	1.295	1.320	1.044	3.306	5.631

$$\sqrt{6.398} = 2.529$$

SOURCE: Correlations reproduced from Technical Manual for the Lorge-Thorn-dike Intelligence Tests (original Separate Level Edition), 1962.

Table G_1

	1	2	3	4	5	6	7	I	II
1	.213	.177	.213	.376	.389	.286	.401	1.166	.602
2	.177	.147	.177	.313	.323	.237	.333	.969	.501
3	.213	.177	.214	.378	.390	.287	.403	1.171	.605
4	.376	.313	.378	.666	.688	.506	.710	2.064	1.067
5	.389	.323	.390	.688	.711	.523	.733	2.132	1.102
6	.286	.237	.287	.506	.523	.384	.539	1.568	.810
7	.401	.333	.403	.710	.733	.539	.757	2.200	1.137
I	1.166	.969	1.171	2.064	2.132	1.568	2.200	6.396	3.305
II	.602	.501	.605	1.067	1.102	.810	1.137	3.305	1.708

Table R_1

	1	2	3	4	5	6	7	I[a]	II
1	.498	.330	.334	−.059	.093	.145	−.034	0	1.163
2	.330	.696	.371	−.017	.060	.131	−.043	0	1.397
3	.334	.371	.659	−.024	.040	.234	−.016	0	1.363
4	−.059	−.017	−.024	.104	−.095	−.036	−.008	0	−.100
5	.093	.060	.040	−.095	.153	−.029	−.058	0	.193
6	.145	.131	.234	−.036	−.029	.437	.065	0	.510
7	−.034	−.043	−.016	−.008	−.058	.065	.067	0	−.093
I	0	0	0	0	0	0	0	0	0
II	1.163	1.397	1.363	−.100	.193	.510	−.093	0	3.923

$$\sqrt{3.923} = 1.981$$

[a] Sometimes the actual subtraction gives a very small number which is the result of rounding error. The true value of zero has been used instead.

Table G_2

	1	2	3	4	5	6	7	I	II
1	.344	.414	.404	−.029	.057	.151	−.028	0	1.163
2	.414	.497	.485	−.035	.068	.181	−.033	0	1.397
3	.404	.485	.473	−.034	.067	.177	−.032	0	1.363
4	−.029	−.035	−.034	.002	−.005	.013	−.002	0	−.099
5	.057	.068	.067	−.005	.009	.024	−.005	0	.192
6	.151	.181	.177	.013	.024	.066	−.012	0	.509
7	−.028	−.033	−.032	−.002	−.005	−.012	.002	0	−.093
I	0	0	0	0	0	0	0	0	0
II	1.163	1.397	1.363	−.099	.192	.509	−.093	0	3.924

COMPUTING GUIDE 5. (Continued)

Table R$_2$

	1	2	3	4	5	6	7	I	II
1	.154	−.084	−.070	−.030	.036	−.006	−.006	0	0
2	−.084	.199	−.114	.018	−.008	−.050	−.010	0	0
3	−.070	−.114	.186	.010	−.027	.057	.016	0	0
4	−.030	.018	.010	.102	−.090	−.049	−.006	0	0
5	.036	−.008	−.027	−.090	.144	−.053	−.063	0	0
6	−.006	−.050	.057	−.049	−.053	.371	.077	0	0
7	−.006	−.010	.016	−.006	−.063	.077	.065	0	0
I	0	0	0	0	0	0	0	0	0
II	0	0	0	0	0	0	0	0	0

Table of factor loadings F

	I	II	Sum of sq.	Re- mainder	Error
1	.461	.587	.557	.154	.289
2	.383	.705	.644	.199	.157
3	.463	.688	.687	.186	.127
4	.816	−.050	.668	.102	.230
5	.843	.097	.720	.144	.136
6	.620	.257	.450	.371	.179
7	.870	−.047	.759	.065	.176
I	2.529	0	—	—	—
II	1.307	1.981	—	—	—
Sum sq. 1–7	3.091	1.394	4.485	1.221	1.294
%	44	20	64	17.5	18.5

Plot (axes I and II): II 1.0; NS 2; • 3 FA; 1 FC; .5; •6 AR; 5 VCI; I; .5; 4 SC; 7 V; 1.0

tigator have no influence on the results. I do not agree. Judgment is indispensable, and it is better to have the choices made by the psychologist than by the computer technician.

The square-root method is mathematically crude, and not the best for all or even most purposes. The reader who proposes to conduct factor analyses will need to study such books as those of Horst (1965) and Harman (1967), and may need to examine special procedures described in *Psychometrika* and the Cattell (1966) handbook. The procedure most often used today is "principal axes with normalized varimax rotation," described in the texts cited. Among advanced procedures, a procedure of particular merit is the one called "Procrustes." For a particular problem it may be best to use some other exotic variety: "three-mode analysis" (Tucker, 1965); "alpha factor analysis" (Kaiser & Caffrey, 1963); or "interbattery analysis" (Tucker, 1958)—to name only three. Our presentation gives the merest hint of the possibilities and complexities of the factor-analytic art.

Analysis of Lorge-Thorndike Data

Computing Guide 5 carries out one possible analysis of correlations for Lorge-Thorndike subtests. The procedure is long, but it consists of a few steps of elementary calculation, each repeated many times.

We start by examining the results in Table F and the plot. Tests 4, 5, and 7 have heavy loadings on the first factor, hypothesized to be verbal ability. The large loadings confirm that it is reasonable to describe the three tests in terms of a common "verbal" ability. We find also that each of the other tests has a loading on I—that is, that they all are explained in part by "verbal ability." Tests 1, 2, and 3, however, are not verbal! We explain the loading either by assuming that some general ability present in verbal tests also enters nonverbal tests, or by pointing out that verbal concepts help in solving nonverbal problems.

Factor II was defined as a composite of whatever information in tests 1, 2, and 3 (nonverbal) is not accounted for by verbal ability. The loadings confirm that this grouping is sensible. The correlations for these three tests in Table G_1 tell us how much of each original correlation is accounted for by verbal ability. The correlations in R_1 (0.33 to 0.37) tell how much correlation is left after the first factor is removed. G_2 tells how much of each correlation is attributable to factor II, and R_2 tells what the tests still have in common after II is also removed.

The numbers at the bottom of columns I and II of F report how potent each factor is, i.e., what fraction of the information in the *set* of tests the factor accounts for. At first glance it appears that the verbal element in LT scores is much stronger than the nonverbal. But factor I also contains all information common to verbal and nonverbal tests; it is not purely verbal.

Error variance arises from the choice of a particular set of items and from moment-to-moment fluctuations in performance. It has no theoretical interest. The "remainder" column of Table F tells what meaningful information is left to be explained by abilities other than I and II. These fractions are all very small except for test 6, Arithmetic. This large remainder shows that AR measures something other than the broad V and NV factors. Does any other test also measure this? To answer, look at R_2. All intercorrelations in column 6 are small. If any test besides AR measured the arithmetic or number factor to an appreciable degree, there would be a corresponding correlation in column 6. It is hard to give a general rule as to when a correlation is large enough to take seriously; the answer depends on the problem and the number of subjects. But it is usually safe to ignore correlations and remainders less than about 0.13. We conclude that AR has a specific factor, in addition to its V and NV components. The present AR test by itself does not give a strong enough measure of the third factor to warrant a separately interpreted score.

Because the squares of factor loadings, plus error and remainder, add to 100

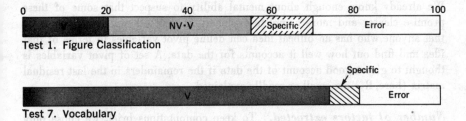

Test 1. Figure Classification

Test 7. Vocabulary

Figure 10.2. Sources contributing to variance of two LT subtests.

per cent, one can prepare a bar diagram (Figure 10.2) to illustrate the makeup of each test. (A pie diagram may also be made; see p. 324).

Decisions Required

We made a number of decisions in the illustrative analysis. The choices have to do with overall method, diagonal entries in R, pivot variables, number of factors, and rotation. We shall discuss the decisions within the square-root method and leave until last the question of overall method.

Choice of diagonal entries. The diagonal cells in R have to be filled, and there are essentially three alternatives: to enter 1.00, or a coefficient of generalizability, or a "communality." Ordinarily the latter is preferred; unfortunately, *how* and *why* one calculates a communality estimate cannot be explained briefly. Using a communality separates off specific factors more completely than other methods do.

Choice of pivot variables. In the square-root method one can place the axes anywhere he chooses. Where an axis is put expresses the hypothesis that a certain test or combination of tests has explanatory value, i.e., that the analysis will make sense. Any set of data can be organized in various ways, and judgment is involved in choosing good hypotheses. Among the many choices open in the LT analysis were these:

Let I be the total of all seven tests (approximately, "general mental ability"). Let II be the difference between the average of 1, 2, 3, and the average of 4, 5, 6, 7 (a verbal-nonverbal difference score).

Let I be test 7 alone (vocabulary). Let II be test 6 (arithmetic). Then see if the tests show any common factors after these achievement variables are removed.

Let I be a "classification" factor (1 + 5); let II be an "arithmetic" factor (6).

We already know enough about mental ability to suspect that some of these promise clearer and more complete explanations than others. But the point is that anyone who has an offbeat idea can define pivot variables in terms of that idea and find out how well it accounts for the data. A set of pivot variables is thought to give a good account of the data if the remainders in the last residual matrix (here, R_2) are small or readily explained.

Number of factors extracted. To keep computations brief, we chose only two pivot variables. Examining the remainders suggested a third variable, defined by test 6. If this were removed, the new residual R_3 would still not be purely an array of zeroes. An investigator determined to squeeze the last drop from the data could invent another dimension to use as a fourth pivot. There is no firm rule for deciding when to stop. But when the investigator extracts small factors, meaningless sampling fluctuations affect his conclusions.

Rotation. The investigator can make a chart of the loadings, taking two factors at a time. Looking at the plots—hard to do when there are more than three factors—he may decide that placing the axes differently will "make better psychological sense." Figure 10.3 shows rotations of the original plot. To make the rotated plot, new axes were laid down on the original plot, the figure was turned around to bring these axes to the horizontal or vertical, and the old axes were erased. Panel (b) shows a rotation that gets rid of negative loadings; this makes better sense than the original plot, because it is hard to explain how an ability test can be negatively related to an ability factor. Panel (c) emphasizes the nonverbal factor; we could have gotten the same result by making $1 + 2 + 3$ the *first* pivot variable. Panel (d) locates one axis so as to represent an overall, general ability. The second axis, at right angles, is a V-NV difference. From each graph one can read loadings that describe the test in terms of new factors I', II', etc. The pictures are equally correct; the choice is to be made on psychological, not mathematical, grounds.

Often a rotation to get a "simple structure" is chosen. In an ideal simple structure, on each factor there are some tests with large loadings and many tests with zero loadings. The table of loadings has many near-zero entries. Investigators who seek such a structure want to explain each test as a composite of just a few independent abilities; they do not want to use "general ability" as a construct. While this mathematical solution clarifies a confused table of original factor loadings, following it with graphic rotation will often produce a more sensible picture.

Choice of overall method. Each method of extracting factors selects part of the information in the tests for interpretation and throws the rest into the remainder column. The centroid method is a square-root method that puts the first factor "right down the middle" of the set of tests. The second and later factors contrast one subset of tests with the others. The result from rotation

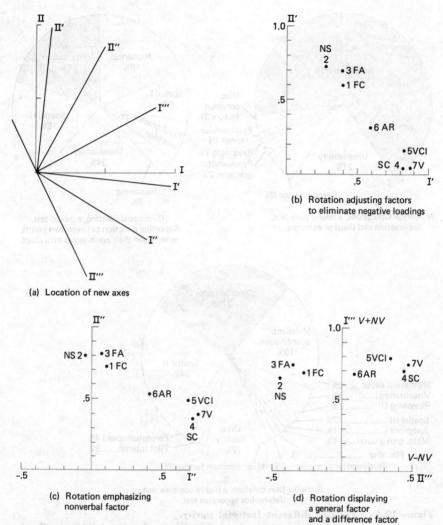

(a) Location of new axes

(b) Rotation adjusting factors to eliminate negative loadings

(c) Rotation emphasizing nonverbal factor

(d) Rotation displaying a general factor and a difference factor

Figure 10.3.   Four rotations of the Lorge-Thorndike loadings.

(d) of Figure 10.3 is much like what the centroid analysis would report, before it is rotated. The principal-axis method does about the same thing as the centroid analysis, but is mathematically more elegant.

On the whole, the decisions about number of factors and rotation have a greater effect on conclusions than the others.

Factors in Three Air Force Tests

To this point, our simple examples have involved few tests and few factors. The usual factor analysis involves twenty or more tests, because a factor is hard

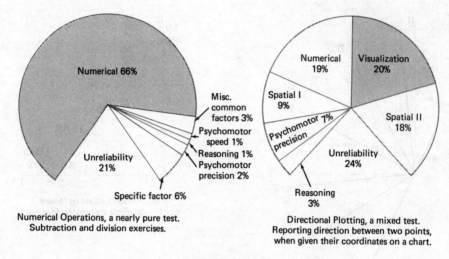

Numerical 66%

Misc. common factors 3%

Psychomotor speed 1%

Unreliability 21%

Reasoning 1%
Psychomotor precision 2%

Specific factor 6%

Numerical Operations, a nearly pure test.
Subtraction and division exercises.

Numerical 19%   Visualization 20%

Spatial I 9%

Psychomotor precision 7%

Spatial II 18%

Unreliability 24%

Reasoning 3%

Directional Plotting, a mixed test.
Reporting direction between two points,
when given their coordinates on a chart.

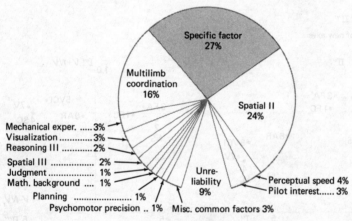

Specific factor 27%

Multilimb coordination 16%

Spatial II 24%

Mechanical exper. 3%
Visualization 3%
Reasoning III 2%
Spatial III 2%
Judgment 1%
Math. background 1%
Planning 1%
Psychomotor precision .. 1%   Misc. common factors 3%

Unre-liability 9%

Perceptual speed 4%
Pilot interest...... 3%

Complex Coordination, a highly complex test.
Job-replica apparatus test.

Figure 10.4.   Tests of different factorial purity.
Factor loadings were determined by analysis of a complete battery of AAF classification
tests. The most prominent factor in each test is shaded. *Guilford, 1947, pp. 828–831.*

to interpret unless it is found in several tests. Figure 10.4 illustrates results from
such a large factor analysis.

The tests were among those used by the Air Force in classifying men for
training as pilots, navigators, etc. The test battery was extensive, including
both pencil-paper and apparatus tests, and thus many diverse factors could be
distinguished.

The three tests are quite different in structure. Numerical Operations can be interpreted in terms of just one large factor, having to do with achievement in arithmetic. Directional Plotting is influenced by four or five simple abilities. In Complex Coordination the subject handles a stick and rudder in response to light signals. A dozen factors contribute at least slightly to the performance, and the largest loading of all comes from a specific factor shared with no other test in the battery (see also Figure 2.3 and pp. 389 ff.).

7. *In the light of the factor analysis, does including the Arithmetic Reasoning test improve the validity of the LT Verbal IQ? What is the justification for including it in the test?*

8. *Read loadings for the Figure Classification test from one of the panels of Figure 10.3 and prepare a bar diagram like that in Figure 10.2. Would use of a different rotation lead to the same diagram? Why?*

9. *Table 10.6 presents a second factor analysis of the Lorge-Thorndike, using a later form of the test having an extra subtest, and, of course, a new set of data. To what extent are the results consistent with or inconsistent with the results from the computing guide?*

10. *Factor analyze the data in Table R of the computing guide, using pivot variables of your own choice.*

The Prominent Systems of Factors

Systems of Parallel Factors

Thurstone's "primary" abilities. Factor analysis was invented by Charles Spearman as a part of his research on *g* (p. 202). When American researchers

Table 10.6.   A second factor analysis of Lorge-Thorndike scores

| | Factor loadings | | | Sum of | | |
Subtest	I	II	III	squares	Remainder	Error
1. Figure Classification	0.75	0.05	0.02	0.54	0.17	0.29
2. Number Series	.78	−0.02	.28	.66	.18	.16
3. Figure Analogies	.85	−0.07	.14	.75	.12	.13
4. Sentence Completion	.66	.43	−0.03	.63	.14	.23
5. Verbal Classification	.73	.38	.04	.67	.19	.14
6. Arithmetic Reasoning	.48	.29	.43	.50	.32	.18
7. Vocabulary	.78	.39	−0.03	.75	.07	.18
8. Verbal Analogies	.78	.08	.03	.62	.20	.18

SOURCE: Technical Manual for the Lorge-Thorndike Multi-Level Edition, 1966. Since no reliabilities for subtests are reported, values from the previous edition are used here, and for the newly added Verbal Analogies test the median of reliabilities for other Verbal subtests is used. The loadings here are derived from unrotated loadings in the manual.

became interested in pursuing not the elusive central ability but the large number of distinct abilities that might be relevant in occupational selection and guidance, the method had to be modified. The methods most widely adopted were those of L. L. Thurstone—particularly his recommendation of "simple structure" rotation, which breaks up any general factor.

The investigations by Thurstone and his students provided a widely accepted classification of abilities. Several alternatives to this classification are being advanced at present, but most of them are elaborations of Thurstone's ideas. Basically, Thurstone thought of test performance as arising from what we may call parallel common factors. That is to say, he looked for a number of distinct abilities, equally simple, each required in many different tasks. He hoped to explain any complex performance by adding several elementary factors. Thurstone acknowledged that parallel factors might correlate with each other, that is, that each elementary task might involve a broad general factor. Thurstone wanted irreducible factors and therefore matched his factors to simple tests wherever he could. A test whose items seemed, on inspection, to require mastery of several mental processes together would not satisfy him as a measure of a pure factor. This aim is in marked contrast to that of Terman and Binet (p. 200).

Thurstone (1938) suggested that the factors he had isolated from a battery of 56 tasks were "primary mental abilities." By this name he intended to suggest that these abilities combine to produce success in any complex intellectual performance, just as green, red, and blue spotlights can be mingled to produce any other hue, or white. Thurstone's primaries have been compared to the chemist's list of elements, but this is not a sound comparison. There is only one answer to the question: What elements make up table salt? In factor analysis there are many answers, equally sound but not equally satisfactory.

The seven factors most prominent in Thurstone's studies were:

V, verbal. Found in Wechsler Vocabulary, Similarities, Information; LT Synonyms and Completion.

N, number. Measured by simple computation tests. *N* and other factors are combined in arithmetic reasoning tests.

S, spatial. Reasoning about visual forms and how they will look if moved about, reassembled, and otherwise transformed. One spatial test is SB paper cutting, in which the child must indicate how a sheet of paper, folded into quarters and notched, will look when unfolded. Block Design involves *S* along with reasoning.

M, memory. Found in tests requiring rote learning, e.g., Digit Span.

R, reasoning. Found in tasks requiring logical inferences, for example, Number Series and Binet water-jar problems.

W, word-fluency. It requires ability to think of words rapidly, as in giving as many four-letter words as possible, all beginning with *C*. It is not strongly represented in any Binet or Wechsler task. The distinction between *V* and *W* is shown in two synonym tests tried by Thurstone. A test requiring the subject to select the best synonyms for rather uncommon words was saturated with V but not W; a test in which the subject rapidly supplies three synonyms for an easy word measured W, not V.

P, perceptual speed. Comparing pictures and symbols rapidly and accurately. This is not prominent in any of the tests studied so far. It enters several "clerical tests" e.g., Figure 11.1, p. 354.

Occasionally, the list of primaries was extended, e.g., by the separate listing of *Deduction* and *Induction*.

Thurstone and his wife published batteries known as the Tests of Primary Mental Abilities or PMA Tests, for various ages (see p. 376).

Air Force findings. The initial Thurstone list was expanded as new sets of data were examined. Air Force studies in the 1940s radically increased the number of factors, as Figure 10.4 indicates. There, in place of Thurstone's S, we find reference to *Spatial I*, *Spatial II*, *Spatial III*, and *Visualization*. Similarly, in place of R the Air Force psychologists distinguished between *Reasoning I, Reasoning II, Reasoning III, Judgment, Integration I, Integration II, Integration III*, and *Planning*. The Air Force investigators listed, in all, some two dozen factors, not counting those concerned with fluency or psychomotor performance.

Often what had appeared originally as a single factor broke into three or more parallel factors in the same domain. Any ability can be subdivided. Instead of "spatial" ability we can measure ability to reason about rotation of two-dimensional shapes in a plane, rotation of three-dimensional shapes in space, and visualization of the three-dimensional figure that can be formed by folding a flat pattern. Any of these can be a group factor, since several tests of each ability can be devised. Even though the factors are all spatial, their correlations with each other may be small. And a complex test (e.g., Complex Coordination in Figure 10.4) may involve one of the subfactors and not the others.

This finding contradicts the notion that there are just a few primary abilities. It tends to erase the distinction between "common" and "specific" factors, since it will usually be possible to invent additional tests covering the specific ability, which then becomes a "group" factor. When the Air Force work made it evident that the list of possible factors was inexhaustible, the concept of parallel factors became unsatisfactory. A description of a task in terms of a dozen factors (as in Figure 10.4) is disorderly and of little theoretical value. One would like an orderly structure in which some factors have a more prominent or more central position, and others are placed in a satellite position.

The French Kit of Reference Tests

The work of the Thurstone school has provided a list of factors (no longer called "primary") and a set of tests for each; these constitute a resource for research. A factor that has been studied in many investigations takes on special value as a reference point for new test development and new theoretical efforts. It is highly desirable, for example, to include in a new factor analysis tests for which there are well-accepted interpretations; this makes much clearer the meaning of new tests and new factors. Any proposed test ought to be checked against old tests to make sure it indeed measures something new. Before a new hypothesis is taken seriously, one ought to make sure that hypotheses involving older, simpler variables, will not suffice. For example, it has been suggested that the Embedded Figures Test, in which the subject is given an irregular shape and must detect it in a large and confused diagram, measures a personality characteristic related to flexibility. But that interpretation is not needed if the EFT score can be accounted for by spatial ability. To check this, one compares it with a test of each spatial factor, and it is much better to use well-tried spatial tests than to make up new ones haphazardly.

The French Kit of Reference Tests (*ETS*) serves such purposes as these. J. W. French (1951) searched the literature based on Thurstone procedures and collated the findings. He then looked for "pure" measures of each important factor, i.e., for tests loaded on that factor and not on other factors in the list.

His original list was revised in 1963 with the advice of other leading investigators, so that the kit now includes tests for all the generally accepted factors. A number of the factors advanced for consideration by only Guilford and his colleagues were added. Table 10.7 lists the contents of the French Kit, giving greatest space to the factors that overlap traditional tests of mental ability. Perceptual factors lead to interesting research, but have played only a minor part in practical testing. Fluency factors will be discussed in the next chapter, and the special Guilford factors can best be discussed as part of his system. The tests listed as illustrations come from the French Kit unless a test discussed elsewhere in this book provides a clear example.

The Kit offers two to four measures for each of the 24 factors; a person wanting a factor score would combine at least two of the tests. Since many factors are usually to be measured in any study, each test is brief and the factor scores are not highly reliable. The tests are sold for research use only and are not to be used for the diagnosis of individuals. Low reliability, of course, lowers correlations with other variables, but in a study with a large sample the relative sizes of correlations can still be interpreted.

From the point of view of French and his advisers, the area represented by the Wechsler, Binet, and Lorge-Thorndike tests breaks up into 7 to 10 factors, though some of them receive little weight in the tests.

Where earlier testers saw reasoning as a general adaptive ability, the French list contains at least three reasoning factors. Just as reasoning is separated from the number-achievement factor *N*, achievement loadings have been stripped from the reasoning tests wherever possible. Figure Classification, representing factor *I*, induction, requires detection of a rule (see Figure 9.2). Syllogistic reasoning (*Rs*) is illustrated by this true-false "nonsense syllogism."

Some apples are coffee cups. Some coffee cups fly kites. Therefore some apples fly kites.

The best informed person has no advantage here, unless he happens to have studied formal logic. The tests for I and Rs might be regarded as measures of

Table 10.7. Factors represented in French Kit of Reference Tests

Domain	French desig- nation	Closely related Guilford catego- ries	French description	Factor tests
Reasoning	I	Several	Induction	Letter Sets, Figure Classification
	Rs	EMR	Syllogistic reasoning	Nonsense Syllogisms, Logical Reasoning
	R	CMS	General reasoning	Necessary Arithmetic Operations
Verbal	V	CMU	Verbal compre- hension	Vocabulary
Number	N	NSI, MSI	Number facility	Addition, Division
Space	S	CFS	Spatial orien- tation	Card Rotations, Cube Comparisons
	Vs	CFT	Visualization	DAT Space Relations (p. 354), Paper Folding
	Mk		Mechanical knowledge	Mechanical Information
Memory	Ma	MSR	Associative (rote) memory	Object-Number Pairs
	Ms	MSU, MSS	Memory span	Digit Span

Additional groups of factors:

Perceptual. Cf (NET) Flexibility of closure; Cs (CFU) Speed of closure; P (ESU, EFU) Perceptual speed; Ss (CFI) Spatial scanning; Le (- - -) Length estimation.

Fluency. Fa (DMR) Associational fluency; Fe (DMS) Expressional fluency; Fi (DMU) Ideational fluency; Fw (DSU) Word fluency; O (DMT) Originality.

Other Guilford factors. Re (NMT) Semantic redefinition; Sep (EMI) Sensitivity to problem; Xa (DFT) Figural adaptive flexibility; Xs (DMC) Semantic spontaneous flexibility.

fluid, analytic ability; it is not certain whether the finer distinction is worth making. Factor R is tested by a task (Necessary Arithmetic Operations) in which numerical skills are unimportant. The subject is to indicate how he would solve a problem, without performing any calculation. For example:

A store marked down the price of a TV set from $200 to $175. What was the per cent reduction? To solve this one would
a. multiply and divide
b. subtract and divide
c. divide and add

All the French measures of R involve arithmetical reasoning, so that "general reasoning" appears to be a poor name for the factor.

Precise description of traditional tests in terms of these factors is impossible, because there has been no comprehensive analysis of them in a battery along with reference tests. The Lorge-Thorndike obviously combines R, I, V, and N in the Verbal IQ; the Nonverbal IQ looks like a nearly pure measure of I. The Binet and Wechsler reach out farther, giving modest weight to S or Vs, Ms, and, very likely, some factors not in French's list. There is also an emotional loading in individual mental-test performance, a matter most unfortunately ignored in all factor analyses of intellectual tasks.

The reader may be interested in Jones' (1954) factor analysis of the SB, and Paul Davis' (1956) analysis of the Wechsler-Bellevue (reported in some detail in Cronbach, 1960, p. 266). In the language of the French system, the traditional IQ is a composite chiefly dependent on V, I, and R abilities. The large question, of course, is how much might be gained by subdividing test scores along these lines, and that question will reenter our discussion in the next chapter.

11. *One student says, "It seems to me the factor analysts are like astronomers trying to discover planets. The astronomer finds a new planet by detecting the pull it exerts on already known bodies. Then he makes more careful studies to check his conclusion and locate the planet exactly. The factor analyst locates one test against already established abilities." How satisfactory is this comparison?*

12. *Another student suggests that factors are comparable to constellations of stars, which the astronomer uses to label portions of the sky (e.g., "The nebula is in Orion"). How apt is this comparison?*

13. *What factor or factors in the French kit seems to correspond to factor I of Table 10.6?*

14. *In Western culture language skills and arithmetic both are taught to all children in school. Does this tend to make the correlation higher or lower than it would be in a culture where schooling is only verbal?*

15. *Return to Peterson's analysis of Navy tests (Table 10.4). How do his factors relate to those of French? Does French's listing suggest why AR performed differently in validation studies than Peterson's first factor?*

16. *What has happened to the traditional distinction between verbal and nonverbal tests in the French listing?*

17. *Insofar as you can judge from the information presented, which French factors represent fluid ability and which represent crystallized abilities?*

18. *WISC now places little emphasis on French factors Ma, Mk, and S. Would the test be improved by inserting subtests involving these factors, in place of some present ones?*

19. *Baughman and Dahlstrom (1968) tested children near the start of kindergarten and again near the end of the school year. They tested a control group in the same months. The average changes were as follows (asterisks indicating significant differences):*

In Stanford-Binet IQ

> **White kindergartners, 7.0; nonkindergartners,   2.0*
> *Negro kindergartners, 1.1; nonkindergartners, −0.2*

In PMA battery total raw score

> **White kindergartners, 21.8; nonkindergartners, 17.6*
> **Negro kindergartners, 23.5; nonkindergartners, 11.5*

a. *What hypotheses can you offer as to why SB and PMA gave different results for the Negro sample?*

b. *How satisfactory is this evidence as an evaluation of the worth of the kindergarten program? (There were about 80 children in each of the four groups, when data from three successive years were combined.)*

The Hierarchical View

The most promising way to view factors is a hierarchical structure in which there are broad factors, each of which accounts for performance in a wide range of tasks, and below these, more specific task abilities to account precisely for the varied tasks in the domain. While there are no mechanical procedures for extracting a hierarchical structure from a correlation matrix, a combination of conventional factor analysis and substantive reasoning can produce a structure that provides a reasonable working hypothesis. The most mature proposal for a hierarchical structure (Vernon, 1965) is still sketchy, and our Figure 10.5 is a combination of ideas from many sources, more an hypothesis than a tested theory. It will serve to illustrate hierarchical thinking.

The hierarchy is the current version of the original Spearman conception of *g* (pp. 202, 269). Today no one contends that the "general" ability enters into every intellectual performance. Some tasks that undeniably measure intellectual performance correlate zero with conventional tasks (Guilford, 1964b). A measure of mental speed (e.g., naming colors rapidly) will not correlate with reasoning tests in middle childhood and adulthood; this is more a crystallized skill than a thought process (see p. 239). While the domain to which analytic ability is relevant may be somewhat narrower than Spearman or Binet once thought, it is still wide. Burt (1958, p. 5) speaks for those who see *g* as the heart of the matter.

In nearly every factorial study of cognitive ability, the general factor commonly accounts for quite 50% of the variance (rather more in the case of the young child, rather less with older age groups) while each of the minor factors accounts for only 10% or less.

By "minor factor" Burt refers (for example) to whatever is left in arithmetic or verbal reasoning tasks after g has been partialled out.

The general ability is seen as a capacity to focus on the relevant part of a complex situation and recognize useful relations. While Matrices, EFT, and Block Design fit the concept, they may not be pure measures; some forms of these tests probably give weight to spatial ability. One can also measure fluid ability with nonpictorial tasks; letter series ($d\ q\ r\ m\ d\ q\ r$ __ __), verbal analogies with familiar words, and syllogistic reasoning (after age 12 or so) seem to qualify.

Cattell has suggested that alongside this hierarchy it may be possible to erect additional hierarchies topped by fluid abilities other than g. He suggests that mental speed may be broadly significant, and also considers a possible fluency domain.

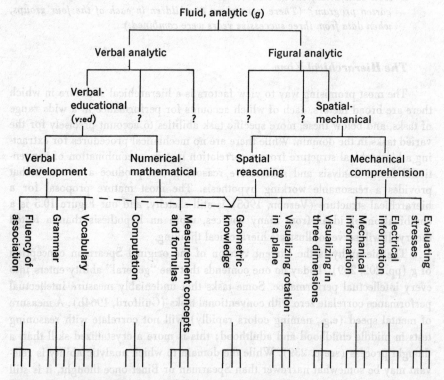

Figure 10.5.   A possible hierarchial structure of abilities.

The spectrum of Figure 9.3 is a simplified version of the hierarchy. Where we were content there to lump the crystallized abilities at the low end of the chart, here we recognize that they are diverse. There are students who develop both verbal and mathematical skills, but there are many who achieve in one direction and not the other. The subdivision in the hierarchy recognizes the relatively weak correlations among narrowly defined abilities (Guttman, 1965 a, b).

Just below the general factor we have separated verbal from figural analytic reasoning; this corresponds to the verbal-nonverbal distinction of the Lorge-Thorndike. The difference probably reflects broad encoding schemes to be mastered—for example, among words the concept of opposites, and among figures the concepts of proportion and rotation. Not every nonverbal task would be called figural-analytic; figural analysis is a positive set of procedures for dealing with graphic structures.

The first two levels are sufficient to illustrate hierarchy. The tests in the two categories of the lower level correlate; this is explained by a common factor which appears at the higher level. Figural reasoning tasks are thought to involve the *g* factor and a group factor of spatial or figural reasoning. This broad spatial factor is in turn subdivided, at lower levels in the chart, into group factors each covering more specialized tasks. Tests tend to have their highest correlations with tests immediately above or below them, and somewhat lower correlations with tests two or more levels away; their correlations with tests at the same level are not necessarily high.

Going on to the third level of Figure 10.5, we encounter a broad factor the British often label *v:ed*. This verbal-educational complex refers to ability to handle tasks like those encountered in school. It enters many kinds of achievement test and jobs requiring paper work, and such tests as Wechsler Comprehension. The mechanical-spatial complex refers to a broad type of comprehension relevant to practical nonverbal tasks. We have labeled only two factors at the third level, but others can be suggested: e.g., a verbal skill in social communication present in some persons who do badly in school tasks, or an ability-to-memorize factor in the figural or verbal domain. Vernon enters a psychomotor ability in this scheme, but we have left it out because such abilities have slight relation to intellect (see Chapter 12).

The fourth level is somewhat like Thurstone's proposals, though Thurstone tended to emphasize simple tests which fit still lower in the hierarchy. Paragraph comprehension and oral interpretation of pictures are examples of tasks in the broad "verbal development" category. At the fifth level one breaks this down. One can continue further, shredding out subcategories such as science vocabulary and art vocabulary (Coffman, 1966); then down, say, to nutrition, and even to subtopics within nutrition. The work of Gagné (1966) shows how such microstructures can be useful in the study of instruction. They can also be useful in diagnosis (e.g., of speech difficulty). Sometimes research concentrates on a very narrow ability, as in Piaget's studies of the concept of volume. But factors below the five levels of our chart are too numerous to be of much use in guidance or in practical decisions about groups (e.g., in personnel classification).

There are many obvious omissions from Figure 10.5, partly because space is limited and partly because too little is known about many abilities to place them reasonably. One might extend the diagram in a musical direction, for example, since there are surely broad and narrow factors of musical comprehension (as distinct from performance, sensory discrimination, and enjoyment). One could insert a dozen subdivisions of verbal development (e.g., spelling, second-language mastery, rhyming). Some of our suggestions are speculative; in Chapter 11 we shall question whether a distinction is warranted between the broad mechanical comprehension and broad spatial factors, and in Chapter 12 we shall question whether a fluency or divergent-thinking ability can be separated in the verbal domain. In one instance we have represented a low level ability as dependent on more than one broad factor. Mastery of geometric principles may well depend on verbal, mathematical, and spatial competence. Many other such crossings might be suggested, particularly when we recognize that what abilities affect success on a task depends on the person's stage of development. For example, figural-perceptual abilities have much to do with ranking of pupils in early reading lessons, even though the correlation of perception tests with reading is negligible later.

To locate a test task in any structure is a bit false, since a particular problem can be solved in different ways. An analytic EFT task may have a strong component of geometric knowledge, for example, if the hidden figures can be given names from the geometry book. Suitable training can provide a crystallized ability to cope with almost any task. No factor analytic scheme should be taken too seriously. A hierarchical mapping of abilities is rather like the schemes used in geographical description. Formally we locate counties within states within continents, but the phenomena that interest us rarely follow the boundary lines. We find ourselves talking about the Mississippi River Basin, the New York market area, and the reception range of Radio Luxembourg. Though we forget the boundaries as we get down to particular problems, the map still helps us to keep our bearings.

The test designer can measure a broad domain by sampling varied tasks, each of which might fit into a lower-level category. Thus the SAT describes verbal-educational ability. Yet its specific items might be subclassified in such rubrics as reading comprehension in history, table reading, time-and-distance problems, etc. These narrower categories refer to group or specific factors among SAT items. But since verbal-educational performances tend to be highly correlated, these minor factors have little influence in final SAT standings. Instead of thinking of the higher-level performance as simply the sum of all the specifics, one can think of the broad categories as representing broad abilities and attitudes that are lost sight of at the lower level. Thus the bright child's consistent attitude of checking responses before committing himself may be easier for us to keep in mind if we recognize it as a component of g than if we say that it is a component of each performance at the lowest level of the chart—though this statement would also be true.

20. *Suggest subcategories that might be useful in a detailed analysis of*
    a. *Computation*
    b. *Visualizing in three dimensions*
21. *What sort of argument or evidence is required to justify placing "measurement concepts and formulas" under the numerical-mathematical heading rather than under "verbal development"?*
22. *Suggest how each of the first ten factors of the French list (Table 10.7) could be fitted into the hierarchy (adding additional branches if necessary, or even suggesting a second hierarchy if the test appears not to involve g).*
23. *Defend the following statement: At every level of the hierarchy there is a cell in which the Embedded Figures Test fits. Can this be said of any verbal or figural task?*

The Guilford Search Model

A current proposal, fully as ambitious as the original claims of Spearman and Thurstone, is Guilford's three-way classification of tasks. Guilford was one of the leaders in the Air Force application of factor analysis, and he pushes the search for factors to its limits. He noted that the original Thurstone factors are not of the same kind; some, such as *Memory*, refer to mental processes or functions, whereas others refer to the content or symbols with which the subject operates. It is natural to wonder whether Thurstone could not have formed factors for verbal memory, number memory, and spatial memory. This suggests at least a two-way classification. Guilford proposes a three-way classification (Figure 10.6), with every test placed according to the "content" it presents and the operation and "product" it requires. Each cell of the system is labeled with three letters, in the order operation-content-product. *CFR*, for example, is *Cognition of Figural Relations.*

Types of content. Let us look first at "cognition of relations" tests.[2] In such a test the subject is to perceive or interpret a relation implicit in the item. Guilford classifies content as *F*, figural; *S*, symbolic; *M*, semantic; or *B*, behavioral. Hence there are four types of cognition of relations: *CFR*, *CSR*, *CMR*, and *CBR* (Figure 10.7).

The figural *CFR* tasks display abstract drawings. The symbolic *CSR* tasks display relations based on the order of letters. The meanings of the words are irrelevant. There are also symbolic tasks that use numbers in a similarly arbitrary

[2] The tests in the Guilford system are being issued by Sheridan Psychological Services.

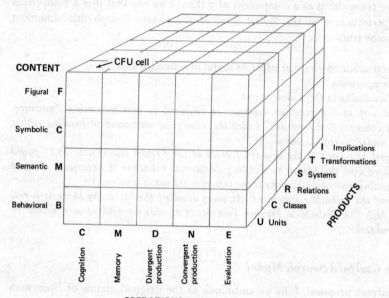

CONTENT

Figural F

Symbolic C

Semantic M

Behavioral B

I Implications
T Transformations
S Systems
R Relations
C Classes
U Units

PRODUCTS

C   M   D   N   E

Cognition

Memory

Divergent production

Convergent production

Evaluation

OPERATIONS

Figure 10.6.   Guilford's model of intellect.

way. In semantic *CMR* items, word meanings carry the relation to be detected. The words employed are commonplace; this is a test of ability to sense relations, not of vocabulary. Finally, behavioral *CBR* tasks display pictures of faces, gestures, postures, etc.

Types of operation.   To examine the list of operations, let us concentrate on Symbolic and Semantic content; the former uses letters and numbers in arbitrary ways whereas the latter focuses on meaning. The five proposed operations are Cognition (C), Memory (M), Divergent production (D), Convergent production (N), and Evaluation (E). In the two sorts of production, the response must be formed by the subject. In Cognition the relation is implicit in the item content and need only be recognized; in Memory it must be recognized and retained. The Evaluation items present alternative answers and require critical comparison.

A Cognition item (Figure 10.7) requires the subject to detect a relation and apply it. A Memory task presents a page of material to be studied, and then a test page where the person must recall and apply relations. For example, an *MSR* (Symbolic) task presents several letter series such as AA AAA AA AAA AA AAA for study. Then the test page gives other series and the subject must mark the ones whose pattern appeared on the study page. For example, he should mark HH HHH HH HHH HH HHH as one of the patterns studied.

FIGURAL

CFR

Figure matrix

Figure analogies

DAT Abstract Reasoning

SYMBOLIC

CSR

These words are ordered; by what rule?

RATED CRATE MORNING
DEARTH SEPARATE

Which answer fills the blank?

ON-NO
TOP-POT
PART-_____

(A) ART   (B) PAT   (C) RAPT
(D) TAR   (E) TRAP

SEMANTIC

CMR

Verbal analogies

Change the order, if necessary:
TREE LOG WOOD PAPER ASH
FLOUR DOUGH BREAD CRUMBS TOAST

BEHAVIORAL

CBR

What is the person marked by the arrow saying to the other?

(a)   "I'm glad you're feeling a little better."
(b)   "You make the funniest faces."
(c)   "Didn't I tell you she'd say 'No'?"

Figure 10.7.   Tests requiring "cognition of relations."
(*After Guilford, 1967*). For uniformity, we have taken some liberties with typographical arrangement. Answers. *CSR:* Position of r; e. *CMR:* No change in first, but in second put TOAST before CRUMBS. *CBR,* c.

The distinction between divergent and convergent thinking is Guilford's most provocative contribution. Convergent tasks have just one acceptable solution per problem. A divergent task is one in which many right answers can reasonably be given, and the subject is to give as many as he can. The Thurstone word-fluency tests measure a type of divergent-symbolic thinking. A Guilford task in the *DSR* (symbolic) category asks subjects to produce the total 7 by combining 1, 2, 3, 4, and 5 in various ways, using each number no more than once per response. Possible answers include $3 + 4$ and $5 + 4 - 2$. A divergent-semantic task *DMR* is to complete the simile

His smile is as wide as a(n) _____ [3]

in as many ways as time permits. For the *NSR* (convergent-symbolic) cell there is a test emphasizing letter arrangement. The rule for the first two pairs must be applied to complete the third pair; e.g.,

    CALM CALL   SELF SELL   HELP _____

For *NMR* Guilford uses another form of verbal analogy:

    (a) BLACK: (b) _____ : : STRONG: _____ , where (a) and
    (b) are opposites.

Each Evaluation item requires careful examination of suggested answers. An *ESR* (symbolic) task presents the pair GRAND–RAN and asks which of the following pairs has most nearly the same relation:

                    COUNTRY–COT
                    RESPITE–SIT
                    LOVING–LOG

The second is considered correct because the letter rearrangement is most nearly like that in GRAND–RAN. An *EMR* (semantic) item is the subtle analogy:

        BIRD:SONG   A. FISH:WATER
                        B. MAN:LETTER
                        C. PIANIST:PIANO
                        D. HORSE:RANCH

Types of product. To fully explain the "product" breakdown would carry us into profitless detail. To be very brief: in the series "cognition of semantic products," we have:

    CMU (units)—Synonyms (Figure 9.2)
    CMC (classes)—Verbal Classification (Figure 9.2)
    CMR (relations)—Verbal Analogies (Figure 9.2; Figure 10.7)
    CMS (systems)—Necessary Arithmetic Operations (p. 330)
    CMT (transformations)—Similarities (p. 209)
    CMI (implications)—Effects

Only the Effects test is new to us. In it, the subject is given a suppositious fact and is asked to list consequences that might follow; e.g., "What is likely to result,

---

[3] This item and others in this section from *The nature of intelligence* by J. P. Guilford. Copyright © 1967 by McGraw-Hill, Inc. Used with permission of McGraw-Hill Book Company and Professor Guilford.

twenty years hence, if it is true that there have been more girls than boys born in the past five years?" Four or more answers are called for. Effects is in part a measure of the divergent ability *DMI*.

The 120 Guilford cells represent fine subdivisions of the ability domain, possibly corresponding to the fourth or fifth level in the Vernon hierarchy.

Value of the system. Guilford's striking proposal, labeled by him "the structure of intellect," attracts much attention. The system is still growing and changing. Just as the original concept of abstract reasoning split into figural, symbolic, and semantic elements, so even the cells in his system are now beginning to divide, *CSU*, for example, becoming *CSU-Verbal* and *CSU-Auditory*. There are empty cells where no tests can yet be accepted as satisfactory, either because the intended tests of the factor fell elsewhere in a factor analysis or because no tests of the factor have yet been designed. Moreover, interpretations for particular tests in the system change as evidence accumulates. Because of these changes, the system can be evaluated only tentatively.

Guilford and his aides have done a prodigious amount of work; very likely they have tested more hypotheses, and used more hours of subject time, than any program of pure research since the start of psychology. The system has functioned well as a suggestive, hypothesis-generating device. Guilford's assumption is that tests can be invented to fit every one of the 120 definitions implied by his diagram. Whereas previous testers made up tests haphazardly, Guilford has tried to invent tasks with particular characteristics; for example, Necessary Arithmetic Operations with its deliberate suppression of calculation, and the various Symbolic tests with their deliberate suppression of meaning. His group has shown much ingenuity in producing such tests. Some of the tests they have devised will have lasting significance.

When Guilford (1967) says that 82 factors of the 120 have been "discovered" or "demonstrated," he provokes disagreement. We note, for example, his statement (1967, p. 60) that by 1956 almost 40 intellectual factors had been demonstrated. But as late as 1963 French and his experts listed only 24 factors, and some of these had been "found" only by Guilford. Clearly, Guilford acknowledges a factor as worthy of attention long before other experts are ready to do so.

Guilford's factor analyses are designed to fit the data to his hypotheses; they do not tell whether his complicated scheme is necessary. Eventually each cell of his scheme must be judged in the light of the detailed data, which already fill two books (Guilford, 1967; 1969). Another book, in preparation, tentatively titled *The analysis of intelligence*, promises to be even more important. Here, we can do no more than illustrate the type of review required.

We focus first on a limited matter. The Guilford scheme denies the conclusion we have previously offered, that Matrix and EFT both measure the same fluid ability. For Guilford, the Figure Matrix task falls in cell *CFR* and Embedded Figures in *NFT*. In the study of O'Sullivan, Guilford, and deMille (1965), we look at correlations for two tests of each type. They report a correlation of 0.32 between their two *CFR* tests (one of which is Matrix), a correlation of 0.27 for the two *NFT* tests (one of which is EFT), and crosscorrelations between the two pairs of 0.24, 0.25, 0.35, and 0.55; the median, 0.30, is at the same level as the within-cell correlations. The two groups of tests are apparently indistinguishable; our earlier conclusion is supported.

As a more complex study, consider evidence regarding *CSU, CSC, CMU*, and *CMC*. These categories are represented, respectively, by anagrams, number classification ("What do 35, 110, and 75 have in common?"), vocabulary, and verbal classification. We have combined correlations from several original reports from Guilford's laboratory (Dunham, Guilford, & Hoepfner, 1966; Hoepfner & Guilford, 1965; Hoepfner, Guilford, & Merrifield, 1964; Nihara *et al.*, 1964; O'Sullivan, Guilford, & deMille, 1965; and Tenopyr, Guilford, & Hoepfner, 1966). In these studies we located the tests Guilford currently recommends as measures of, for example, *CSU* and tabulated their correlations with each other, and with the recommended tests for each other cell. The numbers in Figure 10.8 are approximate medians, weighting each study equally. (Data for two comparisons on *CMC* were lacking.)

To justify introducing a factor, it is necessary to show that the correlations of the tests for that factor cannot be explained by other factors. In particular, tests for that factor should correlate higher with each other than they do with tests in other cells. (This statement has to be modified if tests do not have similar generalizability over forms and occasions.) The results in Figure 10.8 are somewhat consistent with Guilford's structure. The correlations within the boxes (relations between tests Guilford groups together) are higher than those linking tests in different cells. A rough factor analysis suggests that, on the average, the variance of any test in this set breaks down about as follows:

Factor common to all four cells	40%
Group factor identified with the cell	13–25%
Specific factor for the task	20%
Form-to-form variation ("error")	15–27%

The *cell* factors are the ones corresponding to the Guilford hypotheses. For the four cells of Figure 10.8, they are present but weak. To measure one of these abilities with any precision, it would be necessary to combine many tests representing the cell. Such a score would be strongly influenced by the factor common to the four cells (probably *v:ed*) as well as by the cell factor. Table 10.8 considers tests applying different operations to Symbolic Classes. The boldface within-cell correlations ought to be higher than the between-cell correlations. This holds true

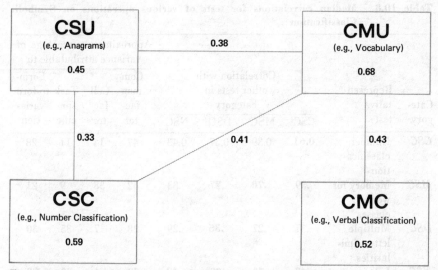

Figure 10.8. Median intercorrelations for certain cognitive tests.

here for *CSC* and *MSC*, but not for *DSC* and *NSC*. After we extract a factor common to the four cells we find that only *MSC* has a sizable cell factor.

Guilford's distinctions, then, reflect very subtle differences between tasks. The fine subdivision appears to add very little to our ability to explain or predict. It will almost certainly be impractical to measure individual standings on the separate Guilford factors, since the cell factors are overshadowed by broad factors such as we found running through Figure 10.8 and Table 10.8. We estimate, for example, that 4 hours of testing would be required to determine, with reliability 0.70, whether a person ranks higher in *DSC* than *NSC*. Guilford's is a fine-grain analysis, and fine-grain analyses are not necessarily useful. The photoengraving process of the newspaper breaks a photograph down into minute gray and black dots; when we look close enough to see that detail, we lose all sense of what the picture is about. The conservative psychologist criticizes Guilford for extracting tiny factors that reflect only unimportant detail; McNemar (1964, p. 872) punfully calls the 120-cell structure of intellect "scatterbrained."

But occasionally a subtle distinction is of practical importance. Differences between isotopes of the same chemical element, for example, can be disregarded for *almost* all practical purposes. The fine distinction between uranium-235 and uranium-238, however, proved to be so important that enormous effort to separate the two was justified. Maybe some Guilford abilities will be worth distinguishing.

The Guilford list is probably best seen as a set of elements that have to be reassembled into a more-or-less hierarchical structure. One approach might be to group tests along the rows or slices or the Guilford diagram, forming a *Cognition of Figures* factor, for instance, running across all products. The present evidence

Table 10.8.   Median correlations for tests of various operations on Symbolic Classification

| Category | Representative test | Correlation with other tests in category | | | | Approximate percentage of variance attributable to | | | |
		CSC	MSC	DSC	NSC	Common factor	Cell factor	Task specific	Form-to-form variation
CSC	Number classification	**0.61**	0.39	0.37	0.43	47	14	11	28
MSC	Memory for word classes	.39	**.70**	.27	.33	32	38	9	21
DSC	Multiple letter similarities	.37	.27	**.35**	.29	28	7	35	30
NSC	Letter grouping	.43	.33	.29	**.42**	38	4	30	28

Boldface type indicates correlation for tests within same category.
SOURCE: Dunham, Guilford, & Hoepfner, 1966.

does not suggest that such groupings will often be coherent. The problem of the "structure" of intellect remains unsolved.

The burden of proof is always on the person who advocates recognition of a new factor. He ought to show

● that the new factor accounts for an appreciable amount of variance that other factors cannot account for, and

● that the newly proposed factor has some interesting correlates with non-test behavior.

A thorough critical review of the Guilford data will in due time indicate which cells (*MSC* appears to be one) have strong enough cell factors to satisfy the first demand, and which regroupings of cells can account for enough variance to be useful. Beyond that, a whole generation of validation studies will be required to show which factors have predictive and explanatory value. In this remark, we do no more than echo Guilford's earlier comment on his own system (1957, p. 20):

If the apparent complexity implied is appalling, what seems to be needed is the courage to face reality. If the next steps do not seem to be clear, then the cure is more knowledge—knowledge concerning the whole list of intellectual factors, their relations to complex mental functioning, and their relations to everyday behavior.

Whatever list of factors one uses to group tests, he should realize that he is not dealing with universals. Tests that separate into two clusters at one age may all cluster together as one factor at an earlier age. Abilities that separate in one culture may develop together as a single factor in another. Factors do not reflect biological nature directly. To be sure, some sensory abilities such as color vision have biochemical and genetic causes. Possibly there are inherited neural processes that make some persons faster in visual perception than others. But task performances generally depend on the use a person has learned to make of his neural structures, and this depends on his experiences. Crosscultural comparisons suggest strongly that it is experience, not heredity, that determines whether verbal and spatial abilities keep pace with each other or split off as separate factors. R. C. Gardner (1960), factoring abilities involved in using a second language in French-English Montreal, found that abilities taught in school grouped together, and that abilities used outside school in interacting with speakers of the second language formed a separate factor. Vernon (1969) has recently studied factor structures in various cultures.

The "social intelligence" hypothesis. We now consider separately the limited evidence on Guilford's interesting proposal to measure a category of "social intelligence." E. L. Thorndike made such a suggestion in the early days of testing, but the idea did not survive because all the tests devised in that era correlated highly with academic ability and seemed not to measure anything independent. Guilford not only expects to separate behavioral from academic abilities, but hypothesizes that there are 30 distinct abilities in the Behavioral domain. His one major study in the domain (O'Sullivan, Guilford, & deMille, 1965) used 23 newly designed tests presenting faces, cartoons, verbal expressions of mood, etc., to be judged in various ways. He concludes that the data show the six factors hypothesized for these tests.

By a procedure similar to that employed previously we get the median correlations in Table 10.9. We have grouped *CFR* and *NFT*, having found that the two are not distinct. For CBR we use four tests, one of which is Social Relations, shown in Figure 10.7; for *CBT* we use three tests. The results for *CBR* are consistent with Guilford's hypothesis; correlations among *CBR* tests run higher than those between *CBR* tests and tests in other cells. This is not true for *CBT*. As a way of sharpening the picture, we apply a technique (not encountered elsewhere in this book) that estimates what correlation we might get by combining a very large number of tests for any factor (Cronbach *et al.*, 1970, Chapter 6). According to these estimates, *CBT* has so much in common with conventional tests that the hypothesized *CBT* ability is unworthy of further consideration. *CBR* has a substantial degree of independence and is evidently worthy of further study; it might prove to be of great significance, practically and theoretically.

We make no effort to evaluate the four other behavioral factors in this study. Further studies, looking into the 24 cells so far unexplored and using improved tests of promising categories, are needed. Considerable work will be required to refine tests for this domain:

● Efficiency needs to be increased. The present behavioral tests require twice

Table 10.9. Correlations for two types of Behavioral tests

Category	Content	Character	Correlation with other tests in category				Estimated correlation of universe score with that for category			
			CBR	CBT	CMR	CFR,NFT	CBR	CBT	CMR	CFR,NFT
CBR	**Behavioral**	**Interpreting pictured social interaction**	**0.29**	**0.18**	**0.20**	**0.13**		**0.62**	**0.54**	**0.44**
CBT	Behavioral	Changing one's conception of a social event	.18	.29	.35	.27	.62		.95	.92
CMR	Semantic	v:ed	.20	.35	.47	.31	.54	.95		.83
CFR,NFT	Figural	Fluid, nonverbal	.13	.27	.31	.30	.44	.92	.83	

Note: Boldface type indicates correlations for tests in same category.

SOURCE: O'Sullivan, Guilford, & deMille, 1965.

as long to achieve a given level of accuracy as conventional tests do; but then, conventional tests have been improved through decades of experience.

• Since task-specific variance is large, it will be necessary to devise several tests for each factor.

• We need clearer evidence as to the number of behavioral factors worthy of attention.

After a decade of work along these lines, the instruments will be ready so that a start can be made toward tracing theoretical meanings and relationships to practical affairs. The behavioral hypothesis may be extinguished by better data, but the findings on *CBR* tests hint that Guilford may have opened a new chapter in the study of abilities.

24. *Show that the critical reasoning of this section is an application of the multitrait-multimethod design.*

25. *What practically important criteria could be used to validate the usefulness of tests in the behavioral domain?*

An Approach to Deeper Theoretical Analysis

The factor-analytic approach is a differential approach, and as such is not easy to integrate with psychology as a whole. Suppose, for example, we ask what changes occur during practice trials on a maze task. We could score many aspects of the performance. Score intercorrelations will tell us about differences between leaders and laggards. But a change common to all subjects will show up in the means and not in the correlations. Useful as factor analysis is in reducing sets of correlations so that their information can be digested, it is not by itself an adequate basis for theory because it neglects noncorrelational findings.

Philosophers have been trying for centuries to work out usable theories to explain thought and problem-solving. Experimental psychology has produced further theories in its century of work. Some of the theories are extremely broad, and consequently vague in their discussion of behavior in a specific situation. Guilford (1967, pp. 312–331) traces a certain rough correspondence between general theories of problem solving and such "operations" as his system concerns itself with. But "insight," "incubation," "flexibility," etc., are not so much theoretical terms as they are labels for events psychologists do not understand.

Theoretical progress probably will require a microscopic analysis of thought and behavior (Bouchard, 1968). The research of Piaget examines such intellectual achievements as the abstraction of the concept of weight; a concept-by-concept description is far more elaborate than a discussion of, for example, "verbal development."

An emerging line of research using the computer as a model requires a similar concentration on detail. Let us introduce this topic, and then try to show

how computer models may be combined with Piaget's theory to suggest a way of interpreting intellectual development. Any such attempt is highly speculative, as we are far from having a true theory of development at present.

Most of the work computers do is conducted according to efficient programs. Efficient, that is, for a computer. The way a computer goes at a task is often not the way a human should or would proceed. Consider alphabetization. A card-sorting machine follows an automatic process. It starts with cards in which each letter of the family name is punched in order in, say, spaces 1–20, and the given name in spaces 21–40.[4] The cards are run through a sorter 40 times, starting with column 40 and working back to column 1. Each pass sorts the cards into 26 piles, depending on the letter punched in each column. After the pass, the cards are picked up in order, those in the A pigeonhole on top, B next, etc. This series of operations will put any number of cards in order.

The human sorter goes at alphabetizing quite differently. Probably he first splits the alphabet into three to five segments (e.g., $A–E$) and sorts on the first letter of the last name. Then he re-sorts the $A–E$ pack into five packs by initial letter. Perhaps he next sorts the A's on all 26 second letters in one pass. Then he takes each pack such as the Ac's and inspects the whole name on each card; he slips the second card ahead or behind the first card, then the third into the proper position, and so on until all the Ac's are in order. His procedure will change with the number of cards to be handled, whereas the efficient scheme for automated sorting is the same whatever the number of cards.

One might, now, study how John Jones alphabetizes and try to describe his process precisely and literally. This would require us to pay very close attention to what he does and the decision rules he uses (rules that he perhaps is not aware of). *Computer simulation* is the process of writing a set of orders such that a computer can carry out an automatic sort in exactly the way the human would, even making mistakes (e.g.. ignoring the difference between Mc- and Mac-) that the human does. The first rule might be "If the pack is more than two inches thick and less than four, sort into five piles, $A–E$, $F–K$, $L–O$, $P–S$, and $T–Z$; if more than four inches thick, start with two piles, $A–K$, $L–Z$." If Jones' behavior is inconsistent, then, the observer can discover rules for choice of procedure or, if he cannot do that, can represent the inconsistency by a probability ("use $F–K$ as a category 80 per cent of the time and $F–L$ 20 per cent"). The success of the simulation is tested by giving Jones, and the computer, several decks of cards to sort and recording the order of the cards after each stage of the process. The simulation is fully successful if judges cannot tell, from the record, which sortings were by Jones and which were done by computer.

The difficulties faced in attempts to simulate are obvious. There are dozens of branching-points where a person chooses his next step. The basis for choice is hard to detect. And since each individual has his own rules, one would need one

---

[4] We simplify by ignoring the coding device that punches numerals rather than letters.

theory to describe Jones, another for Smith, etc.; only by a great creative feat of synthesis will an investigator reach a sound and definite general statement about "how people alphabetize." Now the alphabetization problem is a simple one to simulate, compared with the analysis of problem solving. The behavior is easy to observe, and the cues usable in branching are fairly evident. One can regard decks of the same length as parallel tasks to which Jones almost certainly applies the identical program. With problem solving, however, much of the behavior is unobservable, stored information plays a great part, and there is little reason to think that the program that simulates Jones' solution of one problem will work for another of the same general type. Yet, just because it forces the investigator to pay close attention to what the subject does and to speculate about details of the internal process that cannot be observed, simulation advances the psychology of problem solving. Such research is reviewed by E. Hunt (1968).

A "Simulation" Model for Bead-Chain Performance

We shall restrict ourselves to the bead-chain task which appears in the Binet tests and was studied by Piaget in simple and complex forms. Let us assume that both the child and the computer understand the directions. They are to string beads in the order displayed in a model. Assume that the computer has equipment that performs the following functions: scanning the bin of loose beads, picking up a bead, placing it on the chain, and comparing one chain with another. We do not require that the machinery resemble the human's. Our remarks rely on Piaget's observations and discussion, but the simulation is too sketchy to represent Piaget's views or to constitute a true simulation. Our aim is only to illustrate this approach to theory.

Piaget and Inhelder (1956) varied the bead-chain task, introducing new sources of difficulty in order to see where the subject's performance breaks down. For example, one puts more beads in the model. Adding cards in the alphabetization task makes it harder for the human and requires a shift of process, but does not trouble the machine; adding beads troubles the young child and not the mature adult. Here is something to be explained by developing a different program to represent the young child's procedure. Adding more colors, or placing the model far from the chain to be built, or twisting the model into a complex form loads the system. Which complications cause failure, and what does that suggest?

Piaget finds that young children proceed erratically and impressionistically, and make frequent errors. It is not easy to simulate an impressionistic, haphazard process, so we move on to about age 5 when thought is "preoperational." The child is not yet able to regulate his performance adequately with abstract concepts of order and color names; instead, he picks a bead, mounts it on his chain, and then moves his chain closer to the model to check the correspondence of colors. He does this because he cannot use a mental representation such as "red-blue-blue." Relying on direct sensorimotor comparison, he can correctly

SUCCESSIVE STEPS IN PREOPERATIONAL THOUGHT (ABOUT AGES 4–5)

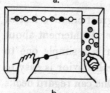

a.

Solves by adding one bead at a time, putting copy alongside model to check, regulating by touch or short eye movements.

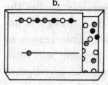

b.

Rod is fixed by tester in offset position. Child solves by adding one bead at a time, regulating by back-and-forth eye movements.

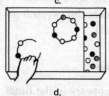

c.

Child solves by breaking circle into parts. Tends to lose his place and reverse direction. Has no concept of "between."

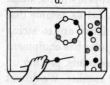

d.

Response is mediated by image of the circle "opened out," transforming the task to one resembling b.

SUCCESSIVE STEPS IN OPERATIONAL THOUGHT (ABOUT AGES 6–7)

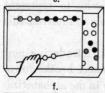

e.

Child is told to make chain in reverse order. He must extract the order, neglecting appearance. The performance is regulated by verbal mediators such as "next to" and "between."

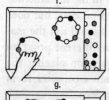

f.

Child is told to make chain in reverse order, from a given starting point.

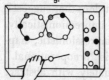

g.

Starting point is given. Child mediates response by naming colors in order while working on each section.

Figure 10.9. The concept of order grows in power.

Problems arranged in the order in which the child masters them, according to Piaget and Inhelder (1956). The child is to construct, on the rod he holds, a chain exactly like the model. The various shadings indicate different colors. *This figure appeared in Cronbach, 1964, and is reproduced by permission of Harcourt, Brace & World, Inc.*

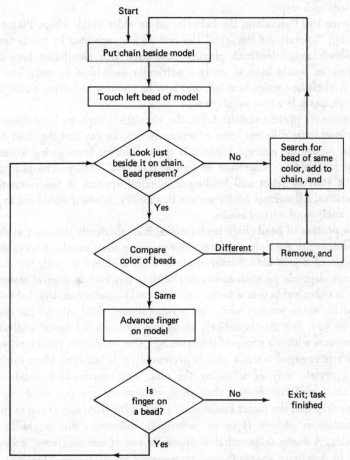

Figure 10.10.   Model of successive actions taken when young
child applies preoperational thought to bead-chain problem.

reproduce a long chain under condition *a* of Figure 10.9 (though he may eventually lose his place). When the wire on which he is to mount beads is anchored
he cannot make a direct comparison and he is very likely to lose his place and make
errors. He tries to get sensorimotor control by pointing with his finger; but this
control breaks down when we keep the model and chain at some distance from
each other.

Figure 10.10 sketches a process that might account for the successes and failures of a child in this period. It is a series of steps, all of one form: try, check, and
correct if necessary. To keep matters simple we have not attempted here to specify
how he chooses a bead from the box, but a full simulation would have to include

that. This process will determine the frequency of wrong selections to be detected by the feedback steps.

Figure 10.11 simulates the behavior of an older child, whom Piaget speaks of as using "operational thought." His actions are regulated by labels carried in mind, sensorimotor feedback playing little part. Our simulation here is a bit indefinite; we would have to study a particular individual to learn how long a string of labels he carries in mind, and how he chooses a starting point, etc., before the program is a true simulation.

Even in its present sketchy form, the simulation explains bead-chain behavior at a level quite different from a factor analysis. To say that the child does not yet know or use the concept *between* is quite different from giving a numerical value of his *v:ed* or "cognition of figural relations" ability. The procedure of picking a starting point and holding it in mind appears in the simulation for older persons. All normal adults possess this ability, hence it would not appear in a factor analysis of normal adults.

The process of bead-chain performance is qualitatively different at different ages. Adolescents are doing different things, using their minds in ways different from those of 6-year-olds. Factor analysis tends to leave us with the statement that a task depends on such-and-such abilities; but such a general statement is false. It is conceivable that a factor analysis could discover that verbal processes are used by older persons while the preoperational child attacks the task in a nonverbal way. But this is unlikely to happen because the factor analyst looks for differences within a group of the same age. One cannot, in any event, say that an ability is engaged when a task is presented; it is engaged when the subject adopts a certain way of attacking the task. This argument is reinforced by J. W. French's (1965) finding that when subjects are grouped according to the processes they use, the factor loadings of a test differ from one group to the next.

Simulations suggest types of individual differences that might be worth recognizing. A dozen skills or habits appear in one of our diagrams; it should be possible to develop a simple diagnostic measure for each one. Then one should know exactly where a child is weak, and which variations of the bead-chain task will cause him to make errors. One could teach some techniques, such as the use of a fixed starting point. More general habits such as carefulness are probably hard to teach. Some of the abilities and habits employed in these programs are fairly general—for example, the older person's tendency to frame in words what he needs next. Successful performance may more often depend on typical behavior—on the habit of using some techniques—than on ability in the usual sense. No doubt the young child *can* name a string of colors and hold a string of four words in mind long before he uses those abilities in making a bead chain.

Task analysis of this sort makes it plain that the common scheme of describing the individual by means of a few scores is a practical strategem rather than a true theoretical analysis (Tuddenham, 1962, pp. 514–521). It suggests that

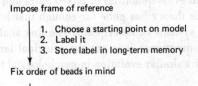

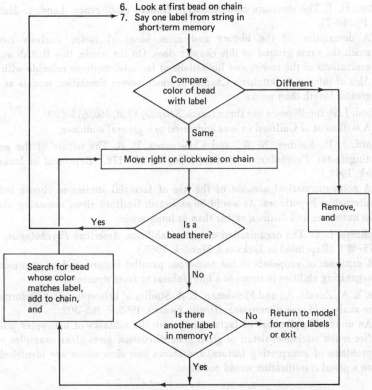

Figure 10.11. Incomplete model of successive actions taken when older child applies operational thought to bead-chain problem.

even Guilford is working with categories too gross to describe the elements of ability. But it does not imply that psychology will be compelled always to deal in terms of tiny bits of behavior, single concepts, and separate types of problems in isolation. The microtheory to which intensive observation and simulation leads should ultimately make for better interpretation of gross behavior. The petroleum chemist thinks about atoms and forces within a particular molecular structure, and he also thinks about gross quantities of mixed gases and gummy residues in a fractionating tower. His theory has gone far enough that he can work back and forth between the two systems of description. The fine analysis copes with difficulties and unresolved questions; it is not the principal language of day-to-day thinking. One hopes for a similar evolution in psychological theory.

SUGGESTED READINGS

Butcher, H. J. The structure of abilities. In *Human intelligence*. London: Methuen, 1968. Pp. 40–71.

A description of the history and main ideas of factor analysis covering much the same ground as this chapter does. On the whole, this British author's evaluations of the merits and limitations of factorial methods coincide with ours. Also of interest is Butcher's Chapter 5, which covers simulation models at much greater length than we do.

Guilford, J. P. Intelligence has three facets. *Science*, 1968, *160*, 615–620.

A statement of Guilford's views addressed to a general audience.

Guilford, J. P., Kettner, N. W., and Christensen, P. R. The nature of the general reasoning factor. *Psychological Review*, 1956, *63*, 169–172. (Reprinted in Jackson & Messick, 1967.)

A nonmathematical account of the use of factorial studies to choose between alternative hypotheses. As would be expected, Guilford views reasoning abilities as numerous and distinct, rather than as integrated.

Humphreys, L. G. The organization of human abilities. *American Psychologist*, 1962, *17*, 475–483. (Reprinted in Jackson & Messick, 1967.)

A criticism of proposals to list numerous parallel factors, and an argument for organizing abilities in terms of a hierarchical or facet structure.

Locke, E. A., Zavala, A., and Fleishman, E. A. Studies of helicopter pilot performance: II. The analysis of task dimensions. *Human Factors*, 1965, 7, 285–302.

An unusual application of factor analysis to the subtasks of helicopter piloting. Not much statistical detail is given. The discussion gives clear examples of the problems of interpreting factors, and shows how dimensions are identified that an a priori classification would not show.

11

Ability Profiles in Guidance

Persons with the same general mental ability have different patterns of strength and weakness. A multiscore test that describes this pattern ought to be useful in selecting a career, a course of study, or a method of individualized instruction. Of the many "differential" instruments developed for this use, we shall examine the Differential Aptitude Tests (DAT) and the General Aptitude Test Battery (GATB), and review evidence on their validity.

Representative Batteries

The Differential Aptitude Tests

The DAT battery is intended primarily for high-school counseling. The eight tests measure aptitudes previous research had suggested as relevant to academic and vocational choices. Among the tests are a modification of MCT, a clerical aptitude test, a spelling test, and a verbal reasoning test. This partial list makes it clear that DAT is quite different from the PMA battery. No attempt is made to isolate simple, pure abilities. Instead the tests measure complex abilities that have a fairly direct relation to job families and curricula. Achievement subtests are included because of their predictive value. A composite verbal-plus-number score is used for essentially the same purposes as a Verbal IQ.

The tests require 6 to 30 minutes of working time. With the addition of time for directions a total of nearly 4 hours is required for the battery. Except for Clerical, the tests are essentially unspeeded. Items from the tests are presented in Figure 11.1 (for Mechanical Reasoning, see p. 47).

VERBAL REASONING

...... is to night as breakfast is to ......

A. supper – – – – corner
B. gentle – – – – morning
C. door – – – – corner
D. flow – – – – enjoy
E. supper – – – – morning

NUMERICAL ABILITY

1. Add	Answer
393	A 7908
4658	B 8608
3790	C 8898
67	D 8908
	E none of these

ABSTRACT REASONING. Which figure is next in the series?

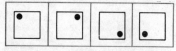

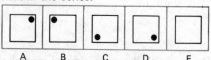

SPACE RELATIONS. Which one of the figures can be made from the pattern?

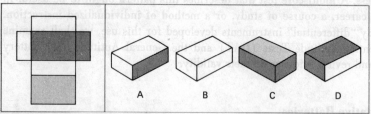

CLERICAL SPEED AND ACCURACY. Underline at right the symbol that is also underlined at left.

AB	AC	AD	AE	AF		AC	AE	AF	AB	AD
a̱A̱	aB	BA	Ba	Bb		BA	Ba	Bb	aA	aB
A7	7A	B7	7̱Ḇ	A̱Ḇ		7B	B7	AB	7A	A7

SPELLING. Which words are incorrectly spelled?

afirmed
omission
neighborhood

GRAMMAR. Which part of the sentence is incorrect in grammar, punctuation, or spelling? Mark E if there is no error.

Ain't we / going to / the office / next week?

A B C D

They were / nearly starved / before they landed / somewheres in Florida.

A B C D

Fig. 11.1.   Items from subtests of the Differential Aptitude Battery.
Items copyright 1947, © 1961, 1962 by The Psychological Corporation, New York, N.Y. All rights reserved. Reproduced by permission.

Table 11.1.   Correlations for DAT administered on two occasions

Form M	Form A							
	VR	Sp	Gr	NA	AR	SR	MR	CSA
Verbal	0.78	0.58	0.70	0.62	0.50	0.53	0.45	0.28
Spelling	0.55	0.83	0.65	0.54	0.35	0.40	0.23	0.27
Grammar	0.59	0.59	0.74	0.58	0.45	0.46	0.34	0.28
Numerical	0.57	0.55	0.56	0.79	0.50	0.44	0.30	0.35
Abstract	0.62	0.36	0.56	0.60	0.69	0.64	0.54	0.35
Spatial	0.52	0.28	0.44	0.41	0.54	0.83	0.57	0.24
Mechanical	0.52	0.16	0.36	0.39	0.44	0.55	0.68	0.20
Clerical	0.14	0.28	0.20	0.36	0.31	0.22	0.02	0.48

Data for two groups pooled. Tests were given to ninth-grade boys, 1 month apart in one school, 7 months apart in another. The correlation of 0.48 between the two clerical tests is lower than other studies report. These data, supplied by The Psychological Corporation, are reported for the samples separately in the 1966 manual, p. 4-4.

The initial publication of this integrated battery in 1947 marked an important forward step. Previously, the counselor desiring tests of this nature had had to make up his own collection, using tests standardized and validated on different samples. Comparison of scores from one test to another was therefore inexact at best. Percentile conversions for all DAT scores have been calculated on the same samples, to give profile shapes as much meaning as possible. The tests are similar in difficulty, hence all can be applied satisfactorily to the same subjects. Correlations for the tests are presented in Table 11.1. The tests involve a general factor, but the correlations between tests are much lower than the reliabilities. This assures us that additional factors are present. (See also p. 368.)

1. *The manual suggests that one may give the DAT in two, three, or six sessions, adjusting the length of session appropriately. Which arrangement would you advocate?*
2. *Prepare a composition diagram like Figure 9.5 to show the breakdown into common and independent elements of these pairs of tests.*
   a. *Verbal-Abstract*
   b. *Numerical-Clerical*
3. *If an adolescent being counseled has been tested with the Wechsler, which of the Differential Aptitude Tests would add the most useful supplementary information?*
4. *In what high-school subjects would you expect Space Relations to predict success better than Abstract Reasoning?*

The General Aptitude Test Battery

In marked contrast to DAT in form and function is GATB. This battery was developed and published by the Federal government and is applied throughout the country to adults seeking work. The construction of the battery was strongly influenced by Thurstone's factor-analytic studies and by three decades of research on job performance. Several of the tests are descended from the pioneer Minnesota series of vocational aptitude tests, which date back to the 1920s. Versions of the tests are in use in many foreign countries.

GATB is given only in or by arrangement with State employment services. The tests are often given in high schools and junior colleges under a cooperative plan that makes the results available to both the school counselor and the employment service. The employment service is primarily concerned with guiding the person into suitable work. There are thousands of jobs in the modern industrial world, each having its own aptitude requirements. When an employer asks for referrals of potential employees, he wants applicants who are likely to succeed. Thus the Labor department, working with State agencies, studies the psychological characteristics of jobs and accumulates information on the meaning of test scores. The variety of occupations studied is endless: accountant, aircraft mechanic, appliance-cord assembler, artificial breeding technician, asparagus sorter, and so on. Prediction for such jobs takes us far beyond the academic and reasoning abilities that have received attention so far in this book.

The diversity of occupations rules out the possibility of a separate aptitude test for each job. At one time, the USES had started to build different tests for each job family, but when the total number of tests passed 100, it became clear that such a collection could not be used for guidance, even if each separate test were valid for one job family. Guidance requires a limited number of diversified tests that can be given to everyone and that can be linked in various combinations to predict in different situations. With this end in view, current forms of GATB use eight pencil-paper and four apparatus tests to measure nine factors:

G – General (a composite of tests titled Vocabulary, Three-Dimensional Space, and Arithmetic Reasoning)
V – Verbal (Vocabulary)
N – Numerical (Computation, Arithmetic Reasoning)
S – Spatial (Three-Dimensional Space)
P – Form Perception (Tool Matching, Form Matching)
Q – Clerical Perception (Name Comparison)
K – Motor Coordination (Mark Making)
F – Finger Dexterity (Assemble, Disassemble)
M – Manual Dexterity (Place, Turn)

We can skip over Vocabulary, Arithmetic Reasoning, and Computation without further description. The Space test is much like that of DAT. Name Comparison, similar to DAT Clerical, requires quick comparison of two lists of names of business firms, identical except for errors of style and spelling.

Tool Matching calls for rapid visual comparison of pictures of tools, alike save for differences in shading. The only reason for showing tools rather than

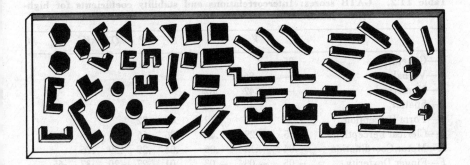

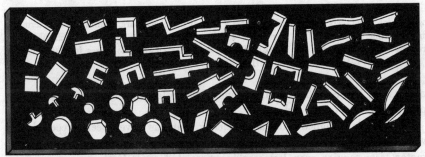

Figure 11.2. Minnesota Spatial Relations Formboard.
Courtesy American Guidance Service, Inc.

abstract forms is to increase the subject's interest. Form Matching is a pencil-paper adaption of a formboard with dozens of irregular holes. In the formboard, pieces of corresponding shape are supplied and the subject is to fit each piece into the correct hole (see Figure 11.2). In the GATB version the shapes are printed in two different arrangements and the subject must match them up. The test appears much like Figure 11.2, but larger. Changing from a formboard to a printed test eliminated dexterity from the score, making it more interpretable as well as easier to administer.

Mark Making, a coordination test, is likewise designed to meet the needs of a program that tests a million people each year. The subject is asked only to make marks like these (*II*) in each square, filling as many squares as he can in sixty seconds.

For the Place and Turn tests, there are 48 pegs inserted into a board. A second board with holes is provided, and the subject transfers the pegs from one board to another as fast as possible, working two-handed. In the Turn test (one-handed), he inverts each peg while transferring it.

The tests named Assemble and Disassemble call for coordination of finer movements. A board contains 50 holes. Using both hands, the person fits a rivet

Table 11.2.   GATB scores: Intercorrelations and stability coefficients for high-school seniors

	G	V	N	S	P	Q	K	F	M
G—General	.85								
V—Verbal	—	.86							
N—Numerical	—	.42	.82						
S—Spatial	—	.40	.34	.81					
P—Form Perception	.43	.34	.42	.48	.72				
Q—Clerical Perception	.35	.29	.42	.26	.66	.74			
K—Motor Coordination	−.04	.13	.06	−.03	.29	.29	.76		
F—Finger Dexterity	−.05	−.03	−.03	.01	.27	.20	.37	.65	
M—Manual Dexterity	−.06	.06	.01	−.03	.23	.16	.49	.46	.73

Intercorrelations are for a sample of 100 boys and girls. We do not report correlations with G for three tests that themselves form a part of the G measure. Stability was determined by retesting 600 boys after 3 months; similar coefficients for girls are much like those reported above, save that the retest coefficient for motor coordination rises from 0.76 to 0.86.
SOURCE: GATB manual, 1967, III, p. 31, 197.

and washer into each hole. In Disassemble, he replaces the rivets in their bin and puts the washers onto a rod.

GATB is designed with an efficiency that has never been exceeded. The working times for pencil-paper tests are close to 6 minutes each. The psycho-motor tests require even less working time, but several minutes are used for demonstration and practice. The entire battery can be given in about 2½ hours. The simple procedures allow trustworthy administration by relatively untrained testers, to subjects who have limited education or poor command of English. The psychomotor tests are so designed that each subject leaves all the materials as he found them, ready for the next subject. No doubt much has been sacrificed for efficient administration. The marked speeding of nearly all the GATB sub-tests may reduce their validity for many purposes. One cannot expect to measure with the precision of DAT, which uses subtests five times as long.

With its access to workers in all areas of the country, all types of industry and agriculture, and most occupational levels, USES was able to obtain a highly representative normative sample. Four thousand cases were drawn from the records on hand to form a group in which occupational, sex, and age groups were properly represented in proportion to census data. Scores on the factors are expressed as 100 ± 20 standard-scores.

Correlational data for GATB appear in Table 11.2. We note the usual com-mon factor running through the pencil-paper tests, and another factor linking the psychomotor tests. The intercorrelations are low enough to give some promise of meaningful separation of aptitudes.

GATB, designed for persons with a sixth-grade education, may not serve school dropouts and others with educational handicaps. The Labor department

Table 11.3. Correlations of DAT with GATB

	G	V	N	S	P	Q	K	F	M
	General	Verbal	Number	Spatial	Form Perc.	Cler. Perc.	Motor Coord.	Finger Dext.	Manual Dext.
Verbal	.78	.72	.54	.54	.21	.41	.29	.20	−.03
Spelling	.66	.66	.57	.21	.03	.51	.32	.08	.10
Grammar	.74	.75	.56	.36	.05	.33	.33	.17	.12
Numerical	.66	.52	.62	.32	.01	.22	.27	.13	.05
Abstract	.68	.48	.45	.56	.14	.26	.21	.17	.00
Space	.59	.49	.24	.72	.21	.22	.19	.35	.11
Mechanical	.62	.56	.25	.68	.13	.09	.24	.39	.08
Clerical	.25	.18	.33	.07	.46	.53	.61	.27	.46

The "GATB Scores" heading spans the nine right-hand columns, and "DAT Scores" labels the row headers at left.

The sample consists of high-school senior boys in one school ($N = 78$); results for girls and for other samples are similar. Correlations larger than 0.50 are in boldface type.
SOURCE: GATB manual, 1967, III, p. 183.

aims to remedy this by developing a pretest to screen out those for whom GATB is likely to be invalid, by providing test-familiarization exercises, and by developing substitute measures that do not require reading (Dvorak, Droege, & Seiler, 1965). In its preliminary form (USES, 1968a), the "nonreading edition of GATB" has the following contents:

G—Matrices, Picture-Word Matching, Oral Vocabulary, Three-Dimensional Space
V—Picture-Word Matching, Oral Vocabulary
N—Coin Matching, Matrices, Oral Vocabulary, and Coin Series
S—Three-Dimensional Space
P—Form Matching, Tool Matching

The regular tests for Q, K, F, and M are used with nonreading subjects. There are a few puzzling matters here. For example, Oral Vocabulary is included in the N score, because its correlation of 0.50 with the original N measure indicates that it helps to improve the agreement between the original N and the "nonreading" N. At present there are no data on the occupational validity of the new form.

Relation of DAT to GATB. The intercorrelations in Table 11.3 shed light on both DAT and GATB. In most samples any DAT score has its highest correlation with the corresponding GATB factor, except that VR and NA often have higher correlations with GATB G than with GATB V and N. The general factor has substantial influence in every DAT score except Clerical; the latter correlates moderately with GATB perceptual-speed tests. (The correlation of 0.61 with K in this table is unusual; other samples give values 0.18 to 0.54.)

GATB factors *P, K, F,* and *M* are not duplicated in DAT. Mechanical Reasoning of DAT has no exact counterpart in GATB, although it overlaps *G* and *S* substantially. Spelling and Grammar overlap GATB *V* quite a bit, but not as much as DAT VR does.

5. *How do you account for the overlap of P and Q, which seems to involve neither reasoning nor dexterity, with the remainder of the battery?*
6. *Are local norms or national norms most relevant in occupational guidance?*
7. *For what types of guidance does the content of GATB seem more useful than that of DAT? For what types is it less useful?*
8. *What do the correlations of DAT-Clerical with GATB tell about its meaning?*
9. *Make composition diagrams to show the overlap and unique content of these pairs of tests:*
   a. *DAT NA and GATB N*
   b. *DAT MR and GATB S*

Validity of Specialized Tests

Spatial Ability

We cannot examine separately the psychological and practical significance of every factor mentioned in Chapter 10, or even of all the scores in the test batteries under discusion. We have selected spatial reasoning and mechanical comprehension for close attention. After reviewing evidence on these factors we shall return to a general discussion of the batteries. Psychomotor abilities will be considered further in the next chapter.

Spatial ability is present in many nonverbal tests of general ability. Many measures of "analytic" ability (e.g., EFT and BD) are spatial in part, but the spatial loading is ordinarily looked on as an impurity in that context. During childhood, boys surpass girls on spatially loaded tests (Sherman, 1967), and this is usually attributed to the activities boys are encouraged to engage in.

Early investigators of vocational aptitudes identified a number of jobs that seem to require reasoning about forms, and spatial tests have since played a part in nearly all research on vocational aptitude. The DAT manual (p. 1-9) speaks of Space Relations in this way:

> The *Space Relations* test is a measure of ability to deal with concrete materials through visualization. There are many vocations in which one is required to imagine how a specified object would look if made from a given pattern, or how a specified object would appear if rotated in a given way. This ability to manipulate *things* mentally, to create a structure in one's mind from a plan, is what the test is designed to evaluate. It is an ability needed in such fields as drafting, dress designing, architecture, art, die-making, and decorating, or wherever there is need to visualize objects in three dimensions.

Table 11.4.   Some validity coefficients for DAT scores against course grades nine
months later

Course	Grade	Location	Number of cases	SR	VR + NA	AR
Geometry	10	Buchanan, Mich.	34	.47	**.54**	**.73**
	10	Wakefield, R.I.	74	**.40**	**.54**	**.48**
	10	Clairton, Pa.	56	.20	**.47**	.22
Solid Geometry	11	Clairton, Pa.	27	.31	**.70**	.00
	12	Clairton, Pa.	37	.38	**.49**	.22
Industrial Arts	10	Edgerton, Wisc.	41	.19	**.45**	**.41**
	10	Tulsa, Okla.	53	**.50**	**.49**	**.47**
Shop	8	Wakefield, R.I.	74	**.53**	**.52**	**.52**
English	10	Buchanan, Mich.	31	.07	.36	.36
	10	Wakefield, R.I.	114	.29	**.55**	.33

Correlations 0.40 and above in boldface.
All data are for boys.
Source: DAT manual, 1966.

Undoubtedly spatial ability is developed through experience (Piaget &
Inhelder, 1956). It does not seem to be increased by the usual geometry course,
but Brinkmann (1966) was able to produce very large gains on DAT Space Relations by giving 3 weeks of direct training on spatial visualization. He did not
go on to study two further important questions: Are these trained students now
better able to perform in practical tasks involving spatial abilities? Does DAT
Space correlate as well with criterion performances in the trained group as it does
in a group not specially trained?

Validity in educational prediction. One might expect spatial ability to be
relevant to certain high-school courses, e.g., geometry and mechanical drawing.
Validity coefficients for several schools are available in DAT manuals; a few
are reported in Table 11.4. For comparison, coefficients are also given for VR +
NA and Abstract Reasoning. The coefficients reported are based on boys, but
results for girls are similar.

Looking first at the correlations for geometry, we see that results vary from
sample to sample, sometimes mysteriously. Insofar as we can judge from these
coefficients, the contribution of SR to prediction of geometry is accounted for by
its general-factor content. Some further evidence is given in Figure 11.5 (p. 372).
Though geometry undeniably requires reasoning about forms, tested spatial ability accounts for little of the variation in geometry marks. The remaining coefficients in Table 11.4 tell the same story: variation from class to class, generally
small positive correlations of SR with the criterion, equally good correlations for
nonspatial tests. For similar data on GATB, see Ingersoll and Peters, 1966. The

tester dare not trust his judgment as to what a test will predict. Spatial ability per se has little power to predict success in nontechnical high-school courses, though it may be quite relevant in a technical course (see below).

In our present concern for specialized abilities we should not fail to note that a differential battery taken more or less as a whole is a good *general* predictor, as good as the tests studied in Chapter 9. Composite scores on GATB predict high-school marks with *r*'s of 0.50 or better, and the longer DAT sometimes does even better.

Possibly the relevance of specialized abilities (i.e., of profile shape) depends on the method by which a course is taught. Hills (1957) studied college mathematics grades, using measures of the space (S) and visualization (Vs) factors as predictors. Spatial Orientation (a measure of S) shows pictures over a boat's prow, as seen from the cockpit. The pictures are paired, and the task of the subject is to locate in the second picture the "aiming point" toward which the prow was pointed in the first scene. The second, measuring Vs, requires the subject to identify how a clock will appear when tilted and rotated. The sequence of movements is described verbally. Hills found consistent correlations of S with criteria in several mathematics courses for engineers, coefficients being as high as 0.55. In courses at the same level for physics and mathematics students, however, S had negligible validities. The relevance of the factor depended on how each course was taught. Validities for Vs were much smaller than for S in the engineering sections, and consistently larger in sections for physics students. S predicted better than general reasoning tests. Further studies of this sort are needed.

Occupational validity. The chief value of spatial tests is in vocational prediction. A study of watch repairing, for example, indicates a marked correspondence between spatial ability and performance, the validity coefficient in one study being 0.69 (DAT manual, 1966, p. 5–58). Validities depend on the precise nature of occupational duties, however; GATB data show that validities of S are negligible for watchmakers in such assignments as balance-wheel assembly and movement assembly, 0.38 in the finishing and casing departments, and 0.50 for men doing specialized work on certain subassemblies. No doubt validities vary even for different groups having the same job title, but the general impression that S is relevant is supported.

A tremendous volume of information on vocational correlates of spatial ability is provided by research on GATB. Table 11.5 gives some of the results, along with data on General, Form Perception, and Manual Dexterity scores. The data were gathered on persons working in or training for the occupation. These were a select group, as is shown by the fact that the mean scores depart from 100 and the s.d.'s are below 20. Seemingly only persons quite superior in space ability are likely to get into engineering and dentistry courses. Drill-press operators, at the other end of the scale, are drawn from the below-average

Table 11.5. Validities of GATB-S against occupational criteria

Occupation	Number of cases	Criterion	Spatial aptitude Mean	s.d.	r	Comparable correlations for G	P	M
Dentist	96	Lecture grades	137	14	0.29	0.24	−0.02	−0.18
	89	Laboratory grades	133	17	.34	.13	.33	.14
Engineer	150	Grade average	134	15	.11	.42	.11	.01
Draftsman	40	Ratings	122	12	.33	.42	.06	.24
Machinist	71	Ratings	114	18	.37	.29	.27	.08
Tabulating-machine operator	203	Ratings	106	18	.20	.34	.10	.10
Bomb-fuse parts assembler	90	Ratings	98	15	.12	.21	.33	.31
Mounter (radio tubes)	100	Production records	101	14	−0.02	.03	−0.02	.54
Upholsterer	49	Ratings	97	17	.43	.24	.25	.32
Poultry laborer	72	Ratings	95	16	.03	.24	.09	.56
Dry-cell assembler	94	Ratings	94	16	.11	.11	.27	.50
Drill-press operator	31	Production records	88	18	.05	.32	.22	.47

Values in boldface are significant $(p > .05)$.
SOURCE: GATB Manual, 1967, III. Some data from 1958 manual. See also USES, 1967b.

workers who remain after those with better aptitude are siphoned into other jobs. Where the s.d. is low, validity would be higher for a less restricted group.

Both general and spatial ability contribute to success as draftsman or tabulating-machine operator; dentists and machinists need form perception besides. Although S and P are both figural, S is important in dentistry lecture courses while P is not. For bomb-fuse assemblers, the quick perception tested by P is much more important than the reasoning tested in S. The radio-tube mounter is likewise engaged in assembly of small parts, but his success depends on dexterity, not on S or P.

Few of the correlations in Table 11.5 are large. Spatial ability alone does not account for success in any of these jobs. Taking all the aptitudes into account simultaneously, however, improves employment decisions. In Chapter 13 we shall explain procedures used to combine aptitudes into a selection formula.

10. *Why are the validities of the GATB tests different for the two dentistry criteria?*
11. *How can one explain the negligible importance of spatial ability in predicting success in geometry courses?*
12. *Osborne and Gregor (1966) find that Surface Development scores of MZ (one-egg) twins correlate 0.91, while for a small sample of DZ (two-egg) twins*

the correlation is 0.20. High correlations for MZ twins are expected when a trait is largely determined by heredity. How can the Osborne-Gregor finding be reconciled with Brinkmann's finding that spatial ability is trainable?

Mechanical Comprehension

The Bennett MCT provided the model for the Mechanical Reasoning test of the DAT battery. Although mechanical reasoning tests predict success in many occupations, there is considerable uncertainty as to whether they measure an independent ability. It will be noted that GATB did not include a mechanical test. Performance on such tests is accounted for to a substantial degree by general, verbal, and spatial abilities, as we saw in Table 11.3. Factor analysis usually shows an additional factor that accounts for a fraction of the variance in the mechanical reasoning or knowledge tests. This factor is interpreted as reflecting information acquired through experience with machines, not as a special type of reasoning.

Adaptations of the Bennett tests have frequently been able to predict success in civilian and military technical specialties (Super & Crites, 1962, pp. 250–254). In the British Army a form of the Bennett test had a validity of 0.59 for selecting truck drivers; no other test was nearly so good (Vernon & Parry, 1949, p. 230). Ghiselli (1966), averaging a very large number of published validity coefficients, reported the mechanical principles test to be a good predictor of training or proficiency criteria for machinists, tool makers, operators of complex machines, bench workers, and the like. Spatial ability is also a good predictor for most of these occupations, though not always so good as mechanical comprehension. In predicting success in learning to fly, the two most significant factors out of 26 factors considered, were *S* and *Mechanical Experience* (followed closely by *Integration, Vs, Psychomotor Coordination,* and *Pilot Interests*; Guilford, 1947, p. 843). The Mechanical Principles test had a validity of about 0.35 in this study. USES has developed tests of job-specific mechanical information, e.g., for a man who claims to be an experienced carpenter, "What do you mean by a 'shore'?" (answer: upright brace). Many men who claim experience in a trade fail on the questions. Such a screening test, used in an employment center, eliminates those who might otherwise be shipped across the country to a plant where skilled men are needed. These so-called "trade tests" have also been used in military classification to check whether men are qualified in the trades where they claim civilian experience. Such tests, because of their reliability, are sometimes more dependable for assigning men than records made in training courses (Vernon & Parry, 1949, p. 244).

13. a. *The Purdue Assembly test is designed to include mechanisms using each important mechanical device: gears, levers, rack-and-pinion, etc. Does such a test assume that mechanical aptitude or comprehension is a single general ability, or that it is a group of specific abilities?*

b. *If the latter theory is true, what implications does it have for selecting students for training in watch repairing?*

14. *Boys surpass girls on the Bennett test. How may this finding be explained?*

15. *One author reported validity coefficients around 0.50 for his mechanical aptitude test. The criteria used are teacher's ranking of engineering drawing trainees (women), experience in mechanical activities, and scores on the Air Force Mechanical Information Test. What other validity studies are needed to support his recommendation that those scoring low on the test should not be hired for mechanical work or should be placed only in routine mechanical jobs?*

Interpretation of Profiles in Individual Decisions

Differential ability tests are used for institutional decisions and for individual decisions (Cronbach & Gleser, 1965). An institutional decision is one in which a factory, a school, a military organization, or the like selects and assigns individuals in order to obtain the best total result—i.e., the greatest possible attainment of institutional goals. This use of the tests rests primarily on efficient statistical combination of scores rather than on psychological interpretation. An individual decision is one that seeks to promote the welfare of one person considered by himself. Such decisions (career guidance, for example) make far less use of statistical rules and far more of psychological interpretation. We shall concern ourselves here with the use of profile information in individual decisions, and turn to institutional decisions in Chapter 13.

In the early days of testing it was hoped that a test profile would permit a definite, final choice of vocation at the time the tests are given. If this were the case, the counselor and client together could reach a decision, and the client could rely on the counselor's interpretation of the tests. Today it is recognized that the client himself must fully understand the test results, for two reasons.

One reason is that vocational choice is not a single throw of the dice; rather, it is a long-term process of development. As a person goes through school and into his first jobs, he has many occasions to narrow his field of concentration or even to transfer to a new one. In high-school courses and introductory college courses he develops new aptitude and interests. Workers change position or change responsibilities within the same establishment. The engineer in a technical firm, for example, may become a manager, a salesman, a creative designer, or an expert on specifications. Wise choice requires self-understanding; no prescription filled out by a tenth-grade or freshman-year counselor can give recommendations to cover these later opportunities for choice.

Secondly, the client is more likely to accept recommendations that he understands. The counselor may be convinced that a freshman should get out of engineering and into advertising. Even though advertising is consistent with the student's talents and interests, he may resist or ignore the recommendation. If he has been visualizing himself as an engineer for years, such a change of program requires him to alter his entire self-concept and may seem like an admission of defeat. To accept the new goal he has to understand the facts the counselor considers significant. The counselor must decide what meaning may justifiably be extracted from scores and must at the same time consider how this information is to be communicated so that the client can use it.

Limitations on Interpretation

A battery of aptitude measures has definite predictive value, as we have seen. At the same time, the scores have distinct limitations.

Profile shape as a function of the norm group. It is necessary to use test norms in order to plot a profile, and the choice of norms influences the profile shape.

The USES profile is ordinarily plotted against norms for adult workers. The profile (Figure 11.3) of a student engineer plotted in the usual manner (upper profile) draws attention to his superior G, V, and S abilities, and places him near the average in dexterity. If instead we base standard scores on data from engineering students, his profile takes on a strikingly different appearance (lower profile). His greatest strength, relative to other engineers, is V. In S, he is just above average; he is average in G, and behind the group in dexterity.

It is important to compare the person with the group he will complete against rather than with "people-in-general."

Uncertainty in prediction. Even when a test is long and accurate, a retest would alter the recommendations for a certain number of persons. Variations in score do not necessarily cause much concern when tests are used for *institutional* decisions. Though a test is seriously wrong in 10 per cent of the cases, the decision maker reaches correct conclusions more often than he could without the data. If an unintelligent man slips by an Army screening test, he can be detected later and discharged at no enormous cost. In individual decisions, however, we cannot be content with a moderate rate of error. A person's entire life is altered if a test score, lower than he would obtain on other testings, leads him to decide not to continue his education, for example.

Suppose it is known that 70 people out of 100 having IQ 110 fail in a certain profession. The counselor cannot make a clear prediction for Walter, IQ 110. Perhaps Walter would do better if tested again. Perhaps other qualities unknown to us make Walter one of the 30 who would succeed, rather than of the 70 who fail. *Almost never is a psychological test so valid that a prediction about a single case is certainly true.*

The counselor who is conscious of unreliability takes precautions. He checks each test result against the case history for consistency. If in doubt, he confirms significant test findings by a second test. He looks for special causes such as lan-

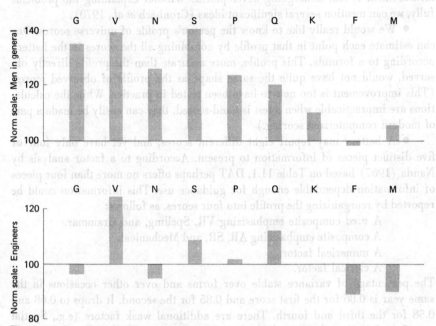

Figure 11.3. Two GATB profiles for the same student engineer.

guage handicaps that might invalidate the test. Most important, he thinks of test performance as placing the subject in a region of the scale, rather than as pegging him firmly at a percentile point. Tests rarely misfire in stating that a student is "somewhat, but not extremely, below average in scholastic aptitude." The statement "Walter is at the 32nd percentile of college freshmen" is almost certainly untrue, in the sense that further data would not precisely confirm it.

Clients and professional workers may trust test data too much. Even when the tester's report is carefully qualified, the person receiving the report is likely to remember only portions of it. A parent, learning that his child's IQ is 87, may forget the tester's cautions about what the test does not measure, the possibility of growth or decline in IQ, and the approximate nature of predictions from it. Instead, the figure itself may stick vividly in mind and be used as a basis for significant decisions for years to come.

Accuracy of profile information. We have made many references to the standard error of scores considered singly. The discrepancies between observed scores in a battery and the corresponding universe scores are likely to be relatively large, because the single tests are rather short. Furthermore, we are interested in differences within the profile, and observed difference scores do not correspond very well to the differences in universe scores. The theory of profile measurement is still undergoing development. Without explaining the problems fully, we can mention several significant ideas (Cronbach *et al.*, 1970).

● We would really like to know the person's profile of universe scores. One can estimate each point in that profile by combining all the scores in the battery according to a formula. This profile, more accurate than the profile directly observed, would not have quite the same shape as the profile of observed scores. (This improvement is too new to have been tested in practice. While the calculations are impracticable when a test is hand-scored, they can easily be made a part of modern computerized scoring.)

● A battery may report eight different scores, and yet have only four or five distinct pieces of information to present. According to a factor analysis by Nanda (1967) based on Table 11.1, DAT perhaps offers no more than four pieces of information dependable enough for guidance use. This information could be reported by reorganizing the profile into four scores, as follows:

A *v:ed* composite emphasizing VR, Spelling, and Grammar.

A composite emphasizing AR, SR, and Mechanical.

A numerical factor.

A clerical factor.

The percentage of variance stable over forms and over other occasions in the same year is 0.86 for the first score and 0.85 for the second. It drops to 0.68 and 0.58 for the third and fourth. There are additional weak factors (e.g., Spatial specific), but according to these data none of them is measured accurately enough to be a basis for guidance. (This one analysis is not a sufficient basis for finally revising the DAT scoring pattern.)

A score too weakly measured to be suitable for guidance may, however, profitably be weighted into a formula for an institutional decision, as was the case with Arithmetic in the Navy battery (p. 314). Even in guidance, there is a positive value in displaying many scores to dramatize for the student the range of vocations open to him. There is nothing wrong with overlap among scores in a profile so long as the interpreter knows not to give attention to the small differences that arise by chance.

● Differences between scores are measured with much less precision than the scores themselves. DAT-VR and NA are reliable, for example, but they overlap, and much of the reliability of each score is due to the overlapping part. When that is subtracted, the remaining score variance contains a high proportion of error (Thorndike & Hagen, 1969, p. 196).

Small differences are generally chance effects. When a difference becomes twice as large as its standard error, there is only one chance in twenty that the person is equally good on both tests. We can have substantial confidence that a retest would confirm such a difference. Table 11.6 indicates how large a difference must be to allow this degree of confidence. For VR and NA scores, the reliability (form-to-form, with a time interval) is near 0.80. The table tells us that a difference between these scores must be at least 12.5 points (on a scale

Table 11.6.   Interpretability of difference scores

Reliability coefficient (average for two scores)	Difference required for interpretation	Proportion of subjects showing interpretable difference, if test intercorrelation is			
		0.00	0.25	0.50	0.75
0.95	6.3	66	61	53	38
0.90	8.8	54	47	38	22
0.80	12.5	37	31	21	8
0.70	15.3	28	21	13	3

In this table, an interpretable difference is defined as one that would occur only one time in twenty, in testing persons for whom the two abilities are actually equal. A standard-score scale with s.d. 10 is assumed.

where s.d. = 10) to be significant. A difference smaller than the required level should be regarded only as a suggestion that must be confirmed by other data. If two tests are highly correlated, few difference scores are large enough for interpretation, and the profile is not very useful for differential measurement. The correlation of VR and NA scores collected at the same time is about 0.60, hence about one-fifth of the pupils have interpretable differences between VR and NA.

Test developers are giving increasing thought to ways of reporting scores so that their unreliability will be kept in mind. One device is the report form for an educational achievement test shown in Figure 11.4. Here the pupil's score is shown, not as a point on the scale, but as a range ("confidence band") within which his ability probably falls. The student can see from the profile that

Figure 11.4.   Portion of the Student Bulletin for reporting scores on the Sequential Tests of Educational Progress.
Given his scores in the form of a "percentile band," the student shades in corresponding portion of the scale. For this case, the shaded areas for Mathematics and Social Studies overlap; the student is told that "it is impossible to say with certainty that the difference is not due to chance." The Social Studies band is higher than the Science band, without overlap; the student is told that he is "really better" in Social Studies than in Science. *Form copyright © 1965 by Educational Testing Service. All rights reserved. Reproduced by permission.*

the difference between social studies and mathematics is not reliable. Current procedures for defining the band are open to serious technical criticism, however.

Stability of aptitude patterns.   Vocational guidance involves an attempt to predict success far into the future. This prediction cannot be made unless the aptitude pattern is stable over several years. Measures of general ability have substantial stability after about the age of 9, when the initial adjustment to schooling is completed. But how early does the pattern of specialized aptitudes emerge?

When DAT is given in grade 9 and again in grade 12, correlations for boys are around 0.80 or better for Verbal and Spelling; near 0.70 for Grammar, Numerical, and Mechanical; and near 0.60 for Space, Abstract, and Clerical (Manual, 1966, p. 6–8). Much of this stability no doubt owes to the general factor. The real question is the stability of differences within the profile, rather than that of the scores taken singly. Table 11.7 summarizes a study of GATB stability in a very large sample. Evidently, the abilities GATB covers develop markedly during high school, so that long-range recommendations are not warranted in grade 9. By grade 11, the scores are showing reasonably good stability, though the profile no doubt changes further during advanced training and work experience. Combining the correlations in Table 11.2 with the stability coefficients for grades 11–12, and applying Table 11.6, we find that for any two of the scores *V*, *N*, *S*, and *P* about 25 per cent of eleventh graders have interpretable differences; likewise, for any pair among *K*, *F*, and *M*. For an intellectual-motor comparison such as *V* with *K*, the percentage of interpretable differences rises to 35. The profile of almost every pupil will contain several interpretable differences, so we can be well satisfied with the stability of the GATB profile by grade 11. (But the *P-Q* difference is not at all stable; evidently these should not be separately interpreted.) Scores of DAT are more stable than those of GATB but the scores have higher intercorrelations; the yield of interpretable differences is about the same as GATBs.

16. *Which pair of DAT measures appears to have the least reliable difference?*
17. *Examine the DAT profile in Figure 4.9. Which score differences appear to be reliable enough to interpret?*
18. *In a test used for guidance, why is it better to examine generalizability by giving two forms several months apart than by testing twice within the same week?*
19. *What might be a sound educational recommendation*
    a. *for a high-school student who is strong in analytic ability and somewhat below average on verbal and numerical tests?*
    b. *for a 10-year-old with marked ability in instrumental music (performance and some composing), fairly good analytic ability, a poor record in school, and below average verbal scores?*

Table 11.7.   Stability of GATB scores

| | Measures having coefficients in each range, when grade 12 scores are compared with scores earned | |
	3 years earlier	1 year earlier
0.80–0.85		G, V, N
0.70–0.79	G, V, N, S, K	S, Q, K, M
0.60–0.69	P, Q, M	P, F
0.50–0.59	F	

SOURCE: Droege, 1967.

Differential Prediction

There can be little long-range differential prediction before grade 11. In grades 7–10, aptitude tests suggest strong points; the pupil will be encouraged to enroll in courses in which these assets will be developed. Low points in the profile need not be taken seriously at such an early age except when, as in numerical and spelling tests, remedial instruction can raise the score. By midadolescence the aptitude pattern is reasonably stable, but even at this age irreversible decisions should be avoided. Later courses and job experience may alter the profile and will certainly add to the student's knowledge about his capabilities and interests.

When a multiscore battery is used for guidance, the intention is to make differential predictions—that is, statements about *which* fields the student is likely to do best in. A proposed interpretation of a score pattern must hold up in many different situations, since the counselor who advises a young man that he will do well in science cannot know exactly what courses and instructional procedures he will face. This makes a much more stringent demand on the test than occurs in selection and classification, where an institution can work out a prediction formula for its own situation (see p. 434), and can accept a prediction of modest validity.

The best evidence on the present usefulness of factorially designed tests for academic prediction comes from J. W. French's studies (1963, 1964) of the prediction of high-school and college marks. We shall discuss a portion of the results in a study of nearly 2000 students drawn from many high schools. They were given tests from the French Kit and some others. The report covers seven scores that were relatively good predictors. Figure 11.5 estimates the correlation a *perfectly accurate* measure of each factor would have with mark in each school subject. A proper combination of the tests predicts each mark fairly well; we would scarcely expect better prediction, considering that many things other than aptitude affect any single mark. The second thing to note is that there are three

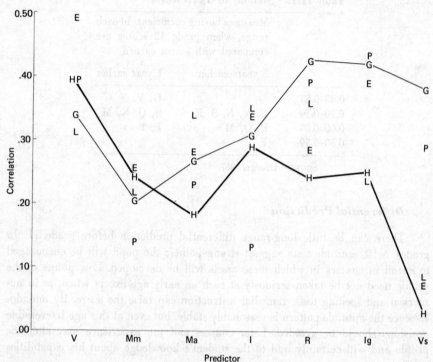

Figure 11.5.   Correlation between high-school marks and differential tests.
Each correlation is corrected for unreliability in the predictor. Courses are E, English;
H, history; P, physics; G, geometry; L, foreign language. Tests are: V, vocabulary; Mm, recall of words in sentences; Ma, recall of number strings; I, letter grouping; R, arithmetic
word problems; Ig, Integration (following directions); Vs, paper folding. *J. W. French, 1964.*

distinct patterns in the correlations; English and History have nearly the same
pattern of correlations; Geometry and Physics have a different pattern. So to
some extent success in different courses does depend on different aptitudes. In
this large study, even quite small differences between correlations are statistically
significant, and the patterns seem to make psychological sense.

With regard to differential prediction, however, the results are discouraging.
The short ability tests in French's study, combined with interest scores, predicted
grades in either English or Geometry with a validity of about 0.50. But even
this elaborate set of scores could predict the *difference* between the two grades
with a validity of only 0.33. Not only is that prediction too weak to be a basis for
guidance, but most of the differential validity came from interest scores rather
than abilities.

The only differential prediction of course marks that is reasonably dependable at present comes from the special relation of quantitative reasoning to math-

ematics and some sciences, economics, etc. (McNemar's tally (1964) of 4096 validity coefficients for DAT finds one other consistent differential pattern, a spelling-to-shorthand connection.)

The failure of differential prediction of marks is probably not due to weaknesses in the predictors so much as to the fact that examining and marking methods in all academic instruction depend on about the same complex of abilities. Reading, verbal understanding, motivation, and work habits put the same students ahead in most courses. If the criterion in geometry or science were broken down in terms of subskills, each measured independently and objectively, perhaps different combinations of V, R, N, Vs, etc., would predict each subskill. Studies by Hills (p. 362) and R. Gardner and Lambert (1965) support such an hypothesis.

Differential prediction of this kind would not tell the student's chances for success, but it might help him and his teacher know where his weaknesses within the course will appear. Once he and his teacher know this, they ought to make special changes in the teaching method to spoil the prediction!

Special ability tests may have some use for short-term prediction and diagnosis in even the present elementary-school program. This is suggested by one isolated study (Reed, 1958) in which the PMA spatial score (visual discrimination) correlated 0.41 with achievement in primary reading whereas verbal ability correlated only 0.27. But in subsequent grades, V correlated 0.52 and S only 0.18, a finding that reflects the shift in instructional emphasis from perception to comprehension. For most elementary pupils, gudiance is best based on broad measures of verbal and nonverbal ability rather than on elaborate profiles whose implications for instructions are unknown.

Differential tests may be of considerable use in *vocational* guidance even though they do not tell which courses the person will find easiest. Vocational predictions will be discussed further in Chapter 13.

Explaining the Score Profile

In counseling, scores must be explained in commonsense terms that help the client to understand his own profile and to understand what tasks the various aptitudes are relevant to.

The DAT and GATB profiles are well designed for such interpretations. Labels such as Numerical Reasoning and Spelling do not sound like mysterious inborn aptitudes; they are clearly measures of a certain type of performance.

Wolfle (1960, pp. 543–544), while acknowledging that global, all-round criteria are easiest to come by and easiest to predict by equally global tests, nonetheless argues for more differential measurement in the search for talent.

The price we pay for using general measures is that we reduce the apparent size of the pool of talent on which we can draw. . . . In [one] study, selection of the top 10% of the children in general intellectual ability, the top 10% in leader-ship, and the top 2% in drawing ability included 16% of the total population (there being 6% overlap). The authors estimate that, had they also included the top 10% each in music, dramatic ability, creative writing, and mechanical ability, they would have brought into their talent development program 25% of the total child popula-tion (DeHaan & Havighurst, 1957).

Clearly the use of special aptitude tests and the use of individual grades and scores rather than averages identifies a larger number of talented young persons and lays the basis for a larger and more diversified talent pool.

This argument, echoed by Holland (see p. 289), is sound enough, but it is mean-ingful only when radically different instructional programs are available to help children of these various kinds.

The safest way to interpret scores is in terms of the items that constitute the test; i.e., "This score shows that you do well on problems like this." Any more elaborate interpretation leads quickly to misunderstanding. Mechanical reasoning is misinterpreted as "mechanical aptitude" though the test does not cover dexterity. The clerical test is misinterpreted as a predictor of success in stenography and typing whereas it actually covers rapid checking of details, im-portant chiefly in routine office jobs. The student may connect spatial ability to art, geometry, and shop courses even though the validity coefficients discour-age such an interpretation.

Some degree of vagueness is absolutely essential. The student should be made to feel that he can improve many of his aptitudes. He should regard the test findings as hints to be checked in other experience. Nothing in our experi-ence with testing justifies making firm individual decisions on the basis of differential abilities.

The case of Sarah Carrell provides an illustration of many of the comments we have made (Bennett, Seashore, & Wesman, 1951).

Early in her junior year, Sarah talked over her test scores with the counselor. Her school work had been satisfactory. She then appealed for help in persuading her mother that it was worth while to finish high school. The mother wished her to go to work since her father had been forced to retire on just a small pension. The mother felt Sarah was over-age (illness in childhood had retarded her one year), and that she would not do well in secretarial training because her school grades were not above average. Moreover, none of Sarah's older sisters had graduated from high school and the mother considered high school of little value for a girl.

Sarah's DAT profile showed that she fell in the middle range of high-school juniors. Her Spelling and Grammar scores were her lowest, at the 25th percentile. Her peaks were Numerical (75th percentile) and Abstract (70). All other scores were at the median. In grade 9, a reading test had placed her at the 58th percen-tile, and the Otis group mental test in grade 8 at the 47th percentile. All these scores agreed with DAT in indicating that Sarah had enough ability to finish school.

The test record was useful in showing Sarah's mother that the girl was superior in numerical and abstract performances. The counselor pointed out that Sarah could expect to do well in calculating and bookkeeping, which she could study if she stayed in school. (NA, AR, and Grammar are the best predictors of bookkeeping marks.) "The mother," says the counselor, "then admitted that her secret desire had been for Sarah to work in an insurance office where her brother-in-law could secure her a job. She conceded that if Sarah was that good, she ought to have a chance to finish school."

Sarah was deficient in language usage, and the counselor should have pointed to its importance in office work. If this deficiency were repaired, Sarah could qualify for almost any office job at a modest level of responsibility.

The DAT scores of Robert Finchley (Figure 4.9) contradict his scores on other tests. His Otis score was at the 55th percentile, his reading speed at the 24th, and his comprehension at the 50th. But on the DAT, he had these percentile scores (Bennett *et al.*, 1951):

VR	NA	AR	SR	MR	CSA	Grammar	Spelling
95	95	97	92	95	10	14	9

His parents were college graduates, and his sister had a good school record. Robert's record had declined steadily during all his school years, and in high school he was doing little of his assigned work. DAT had been given routinely in grade 10, but no effort was made to discuss it with Robert, or even with his teachers, until a year later.

The story of the test scores is clear: outstanding overall ability, with a severe deficiency in clerical speed and in language usage. From the case history it appears that Robert's teachers had begun to regard him as a mediocre student who could not be expected to do well, and that he had come to share their opinion. Robert himself was openly delighted with the test report and put forth more effort as he regained confidence. He became interested in obtaining information on schools of engineering. The record suggests a need for remedial reading, but this could perhaps better be added to Robert's schedule after he gets his current work in hand.

20. *Would GATB have given valuable information to supplement Sarah's DAT scores?*

21. *Why did the Otis test fail to reveal Robert's superiority?*

22. *Is engineering the most suitable goal for Robert?*

23. *Interpret the profile of Ellsworth Newcomb. He has been preparing for engineering, but is making C's in mathematics. His tested interests are in verbal and personal-contact activities. He has done some selling, with success. His DAT percentile scores in grade 12 are:*

Verbal	Numerical	Abstract	Space	Mechanical	Clerical	Spelling	Grammar
86	48	44	40	36	13	73	93

A List of Guidance Batteries

In addition to DAT and GATB, there are a number of multiscore batteries on the market. It is relatively rare that one of these batteries is the subject of independent research, and the user therefore has to be guided primarily by the information in the publisher's manual. The best source of information and comment on older batteries is a report by Super (1958), together with reviews published by Buros. Among the current batteries, the typical school user might want particularly to examine the following (in addition to DAT and GATB):

• Academic Promise Tests; George K. Bennett, Harold Seashore, and A. G. Wesman; *Psych. Corp.*
Grades 7–8. An attempt to provide a measure somewhat like DAT, but with fewer scores, for a younger age group. Stability is a problem; APT scores sometimes seem not to correspond with later DAT scores having the same name.

• Flanagan Aptitude Classification Tests; John C. Flanagan; *SRA.*
High-school seniors. A 7-hour battery with 21 tests, some of them relatively uncommon: tapping, speed of scale reading, etc. Validity information for the scores singly or in proposed occupational composites has not been developed.

• Tests of Primary Mental Abilities; Thelma G. Thurstone; *SRA.*
Five levels covering the range K-12. A battery partly derived from L. L. Thurstone's original list of factors. The scores are not independent. Some scores are unstable, and profile interpretation is not warranted in the early grades. Even for the upper grades, there is little validity research to support profile interpretation.

Helping Counselees Use Test Information

Client-Centered Counseling

In earlier days of psychological service, the counselor was often viewed as an expert passing judgment, like an engineer inspecting a bridge or a physician prescribing for a disease. The modern view is that the counselor does not decide or direct, but rather helps the client think for himself. In directive counseling, the "expert" tells the client what to do. "Client-centered" counseling leads the client to make his own decisions, on the grounds that the important goal is the growth of the client toward maturity and adjustment. A person who has learned to rely on his own judgment has been helped more that one who must seek advice in each new crisis.

Expert advice often fails because factual questions are entangled in emotional attitudes. The true problem is often not the surface problem voiced to the counselor. Suppose Stan Howard, employed on a finishing machine, comes to inquire why he was not promoted to foreman. The directive personnel manager might give the facts, based on tests and ratings, that "prove" Howard would make a poor foreman. He may even give a pep talk on how well Howard produces, about the chance of raising his pay as a workman, and about the undesirability of seeking a job in which he would fail. Howard is likely to nod his head and leave, but he may be far from convinced he should not be a foreman. He may quit and go to another company where he'll "have a chance." Howard may have failed to state or even to recognize that he is anxious to be a foreman because his brother-in-law is a foreman and he wishes equal status. Similar "irrelevant," "nonobjective" factors lurk within the case of the student who studies inadequately, the mother who overrates her child's ability, and the girl who can't learn mathematics. The client phrases his problem to protect the tender spots of his ego. The counselor who relieves a surface problem may be helping the client to avoid facing his real conflicts.

The nondirective methods suggested by Rogers help the client express his feelings. The counselor reflects the client's feeling by rephrasing what the client has said: "You think you'd rather be a foreman than a machine operator"; "It's discouraging when a man who came after you did is promoted over you"; "You feel that the management doesn't trust you." Acknowledging the feelings, instead of trying to prove them false, promotes ultimate adjustment. The client, freed from need to justify or apologize for his attitudes, gains insight into himself.

The client is made responsible. He asks the questions, limits the area discussed, makes the judgments, and decides when to terminate the counseling. If the counselor proposes a test, or suggests that poor arithmetic may be a source of difficulty, or lays down alternative solutions, he is taking responsibility. He risks pushing the client faster than he is ready to move.

The client-centered movement turned away from tests because such instruments do not center on the feelings of the client. Although Rogers himself had once done some test development, by 1946 he was ready to attack the use of tests and other procedures designed to put the counselor in command of the situation:

The counseling process is furthered if the counselor drops all effort to evaluate and diagnose and concentrates solely on creating the psychological setting in which the client feels he is deeply understood and free to be himself. It is unimportant that the counselor know about the client. It is highly important that the client be able to learn himself. (Not to learn *about* himself, but to learn and accept his own self.) In making use of these principles the counselor examines his own attitudes and techniques and endeavors to refine his procedures so as to eliminate all which are not in accord with the basic principles. Thus questions are eliminated from the interview because they invariably direct the conversation, advice is eliminated because it assumes the counselor to be the responsible person, diagnosis and evaluation are put aside because it has been learned that even when they are not voiced they tend to distort the counselor's responses in subtle ways and to break down his full acceptance of client attitudes.

Rogers has modified his position somewhat; he does not see it as appropriate for the counselor to direct the client, but he does emphasize today how important it is that the counselor understand the client—especially, understand his feelings (Rogers, 1964, p. 116). Tests can go only a short distance toward obtaining this type of information, and some doctrinaire Rogerians reject testing altogether (Grummon, 1966). Grummon accepts the Bordin-Bixler approach described below (a bit grudgingly, as their style tends to introduce testing in most cases). But he flatly rejects attempts to "diagnose" the client to define his problem or to understand his abilities and interests:

> Diagnosis or appraisal, being in the external frame of reference, serves no function since, regardless of the findings, the client-centered counselor concentrates his attention only on the client's *internal frame of reference*. Diagnosis is thus a waste of time. Moreover, diagnosis may interfere with counseling for the following reasons: (1) by treating the client as an object, diagnosis tends to violate the conditions seen as necessary for counseling; (2) diagnosis tends to place the locus of responsibility for doing something about the problem on the counselor rather than the client; (3) the gathering of diagnostic information . . . can sometimes dominate the interview; and (4) the counselor may become so committed to a diagnostic formulation that he fails to appreciate and understand significant new attitudes which emerge in later interviews. (Grummon, 1966, p. 83–84).

We shall again encounter an unhappiness with traditional concepts of diagnosis when we consider recent writings on therapy for mental patients (p. 546), but those writings do not regard tests as positively harmful, as Grummon does. They ask how test information can play a constructive role in guiding what the therapist does; and in the counseling field, the parallel question is how to introduce testing so that it helps both the counselor's understanding and the client's move forward.

Tests can be used within a nondirective spirit, to help the client find out about himself. The student who comes with the statement "I'm worried because it takes me so long to learn an assignment" is not immediately seated before a battery of tests. Instead, counseling may go through to completion with no use of tests. Perhaps, in the course of examining his difficulties, he says, "I've often worried about whether I'm as bright as the students I compete with. I thought you people had some tests that would tell about that." Then the counselor supplies him with the means of measuring himself, since he has apparently reached the maturity required to face his question honestly. When tests are delayed, problems come to light that would otherwise never have been voiced. A student may request an intelligence test. Given the test, told that his score is normal, and dismissed, he has been reassured but not necessarily helped. Taking the test may have reduced his tension temporarily but left untouched the basic conflict that set him to wondering about his intelligence. Perhaps he is worrying about changing his major; perhaps he is concerned because his grades in college are lower than in high school. The problem may be as remote from that stated as a worry because his wife's family considers his pronunciation peculiar. Delaying tests permits the client to dig into what really concerns him.

Decisions made by the counselor apparently have less effect on most clients than those they make themselves. Bixler and Bixler (1946) have developed ways to increase the client's involvement in test interpretation and his self-examination. The counselor, they say, avoids giving opinions. The counselor is always tempted to comment on the goodness or badness of scores to build confidence or emphasize the seriousness of symptoms. Such evaluation comes between the client and the score and makes it harder for him to accept the score as a reality. The Bixlers suggest prediction in the form of an expectancy statement instead. A second suggestion is that the counselor should be frank. Low scores must be faced honestly if the client is to gain in self-knowledge. A test score inconsistent with the person's previous impression of himself forces him to take a new look at his plans. Students characteristically overestimate their ability and interest in the vocational field they have chosen. Test results that challenge these distortions can be beneficial, but they generate emotional conflict that the tester must turn counselor to dispel.

What is less obvious is that favorable test results pose problems for the subject. Bordin (1951) tells of the college student who earned a high score on a "scientific aptitude" test because the test included achievement items and he had taken considerable science in high school. Although the student "had made a definite choice of business administration, he was thrown into a state of indecision by this test result, partly because his father was a successful engineer. Later counseling proved that his original choice was well founded and that his indecision would have been short lived if the tests had been properly interpreted to him by someone who could also have helped him to relate these results to his percept of himself as different from his father."

This does not argue against giving information to the subject. Testing is an opportunity for him to find out about himself, and it is better to create a correct self-image than to leave him with false impressions. But the counselor must decide what information the person is able to assimilate. One advantage of tests of educational development in college counseling, as distinguished from tests that appear to measure intelligence, is that the subject usually finds it easier to accept unfavorable evidence about his achievement than evidence of "low intelligence."

The client must always feel free to reject any interpretation. He must be able to say that, though his score is low, he expects to succeed. He must be able to reject his own interest-test score by insisting that he really likes engineering despite a low interest in computation. It is only when he learns that he need not argue with the counselor that he becomes free to examine himself nondefensively. The counselor should help the client recognize his emotional reactions to the test scores. Emotional reactions block rational thinking; the client can use the scores wisely only after he has come to an understanding of his emotions.

These points are illustrated in the following dialogue from a case record (Bixler & Bixler, 1946):

Counselor. Sixty out of one hundred students with scores like yours succeed in engineering. About eighty out of one hundred succeed in the social sciences. . . . The difference is due to the fact that study shows the college aptitude test to be important in social sciences, along with high school work, instead of mathematics.

Student. But I want to go into engineering. I think I'd be happier there. Isn't that important too?

C. You are disappointed with the way the test came out, but you wonder if your liking engineering better isn't pretty important?

S. Yes, but the tests say I would do better in sociology or something like that. (Disgusted)

C. That disappoints you, because it's the sort of thing you don't like.

S. Yes. I took an interest test, didn't I? What about it?

C. You wonder if it doesn't agree with the way you feel. The test shows that most people with your interests enjoy engineering and are not likely to enjoy social sciences—

S. (Interrupts) But the chances are against me in engineering, aren't they?

C. It seems pretty hopeless to be interested in engineering under these conditions, and yet you're not quite sure.

S. No, that's right. I wonder if I might not do better in the thing I like—Maybe my chances are best in engineering anyway. I've been told how tough college is, and I've been afraid of it. The tests are encouraging. There isn't much difference after all—Being scared makes me overdo the difference.

Fact-Centered Counseling

Although emphasis has been placed on nondirective counseling above, it should not be assumed that prescriptive methods are obsolete. They are widely used under many circumstances. Some counselors prefer them. Administrative requirements force a counselor to take responsibility for decisions. When a person is referred for counseling, instead of coming in voluntarily, the counselor cannot stick to client-centered methods.

Those using tests prescriptively emphasize the importance of "objective facts" as a basis for rational decision, in contrast to Rogers' emphasis on the emotional meaning of the facts. The prescriptive counselor tends to think of the client as leaning on someone for direction, and considers tests an especially sound basis for giving the direction sought; in other cases, the problem of counseling is to convince the client that his plans should be changed, and tests are regarded as a forceful type of evidence. The counselor who wishes to bring his client to face the facts takes a stand similar to John Dewey's (paraphrased here from a passage dealing with children, 1938, pp. 84–85).

The suggestion upon which clients act must in any case come from somewhere. It is impossible to understand why a suggestion from one who has a larger experience and wider horizon should not be at least as valid as a suggestion arising from some more or less accidental source. It is possible of course to abuse the office, and to force the activity of the young into channels which express the counselor's purpose rather than that of the client. But the way to avoid this is not for the counselor to withdraw entirely. . . . The counselor's suggestion is not a mold for a cast-iron result but is a starting point to be developed into a plan through contributions from the experience of all engaged in the counseling process.

Prescriptive counselors generally obtain a variety of information, make an interpretation, and bring the client to act on this information. While they respect the right of the client to choose between alternatives of merit and do not force even a wise course of action upon him, their emphasis is on keeping the client from making errors.

The counselor, whatever his technique, wishes the client to have a basis for optimism. The nondirective counselor would prefer that this come through insight, whereas the directive counselor tends to give a pep talk. In either case, however, the client should leave the counseling with a positive plan for action, rather than merely with the knowledge that his former plan was inadequate. Similarly, he must have a feeling that he has some strong qualities, rather than a total feeling of failure because tests have brought to light only weaknesses. In every test performance, there are some praiseworthy aspects. The counselor who wishes to give support will call attention to such features as accuracy, originality, or persistence, in addition to giving the client facts about his score. A counselor working with a normal late adolescent or adult gives him the facts on which recommendations (if any) are based. The counselor who refuses to give scores even in general form sets up a fear in the client that he was not told because his scores were too poor.

The most helpful single principle in all testing is that test scores are data on which to base further study. They must be coordinated with background facts, and they must be verified by constant comparison with other available data. This is the reason that continued counseling by an adviser over a year is more effective than "one shot" counseling in which an answer is given to each new problem by a different adviser. The test score helps the counselor by warning him to look in the record for further symptoms of a particular problem. The score, and study of items within the tests, suggest topics to probe by interview methods. While sometimes it is necessary to act on a problem immediately, it is sound practice to defer a final decision as long as possible, meanwhile seeking confirmation of tentative diagnoses.

24. *Guidance tests are given routinely to college freshmen at the start of the term. It is proposed that the scores be handed back in a group session at which the meanings of the tests, and general principles of test interpretation, are explained. What are the merits and limitations of the procedure? (See Ohlsen, 1963.)*

25. *At what age is it appropriate for counselors or school psychologists to give a child or adolescent information about his abilities?*

26. *Reread the counselor's remarks (p. 380) carefully. Did he at any time suggest what he thought was right, or what he approved? Did he disapprove of any idea of the client?*

27. *In the dialogue quoted, would it be helpful or harmful for the counselor to make these remarks?*

    a. *It's probably better for you to work in an area you like than to follow these tests strictly.*

    b. *Most people develop an interest in areas where they do well; you probably would learn to like social science if you tried it.*

    c. *If you stay in engineering, you should plan to take a course in remedial mathematics.*

    d. *It seems to you that it's wisest to work in the field where your chances are best.*

28. *Which is more likely to be threatening, a report on a general scholastic aptitude test or a report on a battery like DAT?*

29. *Discuss the advisability of delaying final decision in each of these situations. What supplementary information should be sought to confirm the tentative conclusions?*

    a. *A college student who is failing in engineering at midterm seeks a more suitable vocational goal. Aptitude and interest tests suggest journalism.*

    b. *An engaged couple, after a quarrel, seeks the help of a marital counselor. A personality test intended to predict marital adjustment (validity 0.50) shows that their score as a pair is low, in the range in which there is an even chance of divorce.*

    c. *Students applying to enter a graduate school for social work are tested routinely. A girl shows severe neurotic signs on both a questionnaire and a subtle, moderately dependable personality test.*

SUGGESTED READINGS

Bennett, George K., and others. *Counseling from profiles.* New York: The Psychological Corporation, 1951.

    This booklet presents the DAT and a philosophy of counseling, then discusses 30 cases exhibiting a variety of realistic problems in which aptitude profiles are useful.

Bordin, Edward S. Test selection and interpretation, and Illustrations and problems. In *Psychological counseling,* 2nd ed. New York: Appleton-Century-Crofts, 1968. Pp. 295–365.

    Bordin amplifies his view that tests imposed on the client without adequate preparation may delay improvement. He shows by extracts from interviews how skilled counselors deal with such problems as the client who expects tests to make decisions for him and the client who has been forced into counseling.

Lister, James L., and McKenzie, D. H. A framework for the improvement of test interpretation in counseling. *Personnel and Guidance Journal*, 1965, 45, 61–65. (Reprinted in Gronlund, 1968.)

> Counselees frequently ask questions that sound like requests for test-score information, but which, if probed, turn out to be questions about probable outcomes of decisions they face. The authors discuss how the counselor can avoid unjustified projections of test scores into action.

McNemar, Quinn. Lost: Our intelligence? Why? *American Psychologist*, 1964, 9, 871–882. (Reprinted in Chase & Ludlow, 1966, and in Byrne & Hamilton, 1966.)

> A measurement specialist identified with the Stanford-Binet enjoys himself in making a review of evidence offered for replacing the one-score mental test with differential batteries, and for the measurement of creativity by divergent tests (our Chapter 12). The criticism is frankly one-sided and conservative. A rejoinder by Guilford is available (Guilford, 1966).

Thorndike, R. L. The prediction of vocational success. *Vocational Guidance Quarterly*, 1963, 11, 179–187. (Reprinted in Flynn & Garber, 1967.)

> Tests given to young men proved to have little relation to the testees' later success in various jobs. Thorndike presents alternative rationalizations of this finding and discusses the credibility of each one, thus demonstrating how to reason about predictive data.

Other Special Abilities

The preceding chapter discussed the tests most often used in guidance. The present chapter describes additional tests of special abilities including those for psychomotor and creative aptitudes.

Psychomotor Abilities

The only psychomotor performances considered to this point are the simple speed and dexterity measures of GATB. Tests that use more elaborate apparatus and measure more complex abilities have been tried, and many have shown predictive value. Since the tests are costly to construct, maintain, and administer, their use is largely confined to industrial and military classification. Military agencies have provided both the support and the opportunities for most of the research on psychomotor abilities, since they can arrange for uniform testing of large numbers of men and for excellent criterion data. Present knowledge about motor skills, as a practical concern and as a problem in theoretical psychology, is brought together in a symposium edited by Bilodeau (1966).

A Factorial Classification

We may use Fleishman's (1966) list of 11 factors, extracted from dozens of studies, as a basis for organizing our discussion.

Speed: *Speed of Arm Movement, Wrist or Finger Speed* (tapping), *Reaction Time*

384

Simple control: *Steadiness, Aiming*
Coordination: *Finger Dexterity, Manual Dexterity, Control Precision, Multi-
limb Coordination*
Judgment: *Response Orientation, Rate Control*

The three speed factors are readily understandable. *Arm-Hand Steadiness*
and *Aiming* involve simple muscular controls. The first (Figure 12.1) requires
simple positioning free from tremor. Steadiness, rather than strength or speed, is
the key element. The second is found in tests in which dots are to be pencilled
within very small circles; precision and speed are required.

More complicated adaptations enter the other factors. Dexterity factors
appear in tasks requiring a series of responses. *Finger Dexterity* appears in small
movements: picking up nuts and twisting them onto bolts, or using tweezers, etc.
Manual Dexterity refers to movement of larger objects, as in packing spools into
a box. *Control Precision* also involves large movements, but calls for a finer degree of control. This factor appears in Rotary Pursuit and Pursuit Confusion
(Figure 12.1). *Multilimb Coordination* (called *Psychomotor Coordination* in
many early reports) enters tasks in which arms and/or legs must be used simul-

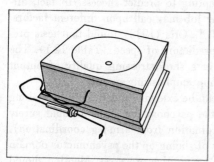

Rotary Pursuit

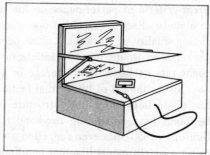

Pursuit Confusion

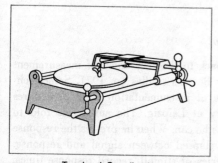

Two-hand Coordination

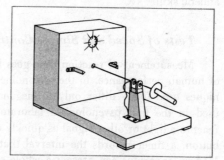

Arm-hand Steadiness

Figure 12.1.   Tests of motor control and coordination.
After Fleishman, 1954, 1956.

taneously, as in operating stick and rudder controls of an airplane. It appears in Complex Coordination (Figure 2.2), Rudder Control, and Two-Hand Coordination (Figure 12.1). The *Response Orientation* factor is observed in tasks that require rapid judgments of the direction of movement required (e.g., choice reaction time, where one throws whichever switch a light signal calls for). Finally, *Rate Control* appears in tests in which the person must judge changes in speed of a target and alter his movements accordingly (e.g., Rotary Pursuit).

For a factor representing complexly controlled movement, there is unlikely to be a "pure" test, since the complicated task is likely to involve intellectual as well as motor factors. Moreover, several motor factors may be involved. Figure 10.4 showed that the Complex Coordination task had loadings not only on *Multilimb Coordination* but on several spatial and perceptual factors and a large specific factor.

Tests of different factors often have very low correlations. A test like GATB *M*—placing 2-inch discs into holes—measures *Manual Dexterity;* the Rudder Control test is primarily a measure of *Multilimb Coordination*. The two correlate only 0.02. There is no general psychomotor ability that makes some persons superior at all manual or athletic tasks. It is, therefore, important to select the right factors for measurement when attempting to predict success. In fact, different criteria of performance on the same job may call upon different factors. In a study of sewing-machine operators, J. L. Otis (1938) found that tests predicting quality of work were often poor predictors of speed (Table 12.1). The worker who would be most satisfactory in a shop stressing quality of output might rate no better than average in a shop emphasizing quality.

Just as the list of intellectual factors can be extended indefinitely by making fine distinctions, so a finer structure in the psychomotor domain could surely be found (e.g., separating two-hand coordination from arm-leg coordination). Guilford (1958) has even suggested a way of slicing up the psychomotor domain to get a search model like that he offers for cognitive processes. Mention should also be made of Fleishman's analysis (1964) of factors in physical fitness or athletic skill.

Tests of Speed and Simple Control

Measurement of reaction time goes back to the very dawn of measurement of human performance, in the astronomer Bessel's studies (p. 197). Some techniques used today differ only in elegance of instrumentation from procedures used in the first psychological laboratory at Leipzig. The subject is told to react to a light or other signal as quickly as he can. When he presses the response button, a timer records the interval that elapsed between signal and response. Modern apparatus can present a whole series of stimuli, record response times, and cumulate the score—all automatically. The signal apparatus is programmed to present signals at irregular intervals. Such automation is valuable for tests

Table 12.1. Prediction of quality and quantity of work of sewing-machine operators

Test	Factor, if known	Correlation with quality criterion ($N = 52$)	Correlation with speed criterion ($N = 52$)
Minnesota Clerical, Names	*Perceptual Speed*	.36	.08
Minnesota Clerical, Numbers	*Perceptual Speed*	.26	.22
Poppelreuter Tracing (time score)		−.31	.45
Poppelreuter Weaving		.27	.21
Paper folding		.30	−.10
Minnesota Spatial Relations (time)	*Spatial*	.24	.28
Minnesota Paper Form Board	*Spatial*	.32	.17
O'Connor Tweezer Dexterity	*Finger Dexterity*	.07	.46
O'Connor Finger Dexterity	*Finger Dexterity*	.20	.27
Minnesota Rate of Manipulation	*Manual Dexterity*	.08	.31
Otis Self-Administering	*v:ed*	.17	.11
Tests with correlations in boldface, combined		.57	.64

SOURCE: J. L. Otis, 1938.

involving varied stimulus patterns because it speeds up testing and precisely standardizes testing procedure.

Although it has often been thought that simple reaction time is relevant to automobile driving and to many jobs, consistent evidence to support this view is lacking. Simple reaction is a different matter entirely from reaction with judgment. Most practical performances depend more on discriminative reaction than on simple reaction. Discriminative reaction time (in which a different button must be pushed for each pattern of light signals) correlates only about 0.30 with simple reaction time (Melton, 1947, p. 102). A discriminative test involves *Response Orientation* or some other judgmental ability.

Arm steadiness is tested by requiring the subject to hold a stylus outstretched in a small aperture without touching its sides. The stylus and base plate are connected electrically, and each contact is registered on a counter. Several studies have found very high correlations between steadiness tests and rifle marksmanship (Humphreys *et al.*, 1936). The tests do not predict pilot or bombardier success. Speed of movement enters GATB scores *K*, *F*, and *M*. In Table 11.5 we noted that factor *M*, involving speed and manual dexterity, correlated 0.30–0.55 with success in many jobs, having a notably high correlation with success of persons mounting wires in radio tubes. Factor *K* has equally large correlations with such jobs as typing, telephone operating, packing, and outboard motor assembling. In general, motor speed is important in overlearned routine tasks.

1. *Which type of psychomotor ability is likely to predict success in each of the tasks listed below?*
   a. *A jigsaw operator is to move a board, about 8 inches square, so that a curved pattern is cut out.*
   b. *A rifleman must hold his sights steadily on a target while resting on an elbow in a prone position.*
   c. *A pistol marksman must hold his sights steadily on a target while standing.*
   d. *An engraver must follow a pattern with great precision, using a small power tool.*
2. *Which factor involves complex movement of small-muscle groups, with little emphasis on speed?*
3. *Which factors do you think are involved in each of these tasks?*
   a. *Riding a bicycle.*
   b. *Typewriting.*
   c. *Cutting dress materials, following a pattern.*
4. *These items are included in the MacQuarrie Test of Mechanical Ability. All are given with short time limits. Which factors does each seem to measure?*
   a. *Dotting; ³⁄₁₆-inch circles, irregularly spaced. Place one dot in each circle.*
   b. *Tracing; a series of 1-inch vertical lines, each with a ¹⁄₁₆-inch opening somewhere along its length. Trace a path through the openings.*
   c. *Tapping; ³⁄₈-inch circles regularly spaced. Put three dots in each circle.*
5. *The Purdue Pegboard requires the subject to place small pegs into holes, first with his right hand, then with his left hand. Loadings for the right-hand and left-hand scores, respectively, on various factors were as follows: reaction time, 0.25, 0.02; arm-hand steadiness, 0.14, 0.06; rate of arm movement, 0.22, 0.13; finger dexterity, 0.46, 0.58. What explanation can you give for the differences observed between right- and left-hand scores?*
6. *The correlation of visual and auditory reaction time is only 0.56. For either test, generalizability over trials is about 0.85. How can the gap between these figures be explained?*

Complex Performance

One principle often followed in designing tests of complex psychomotor ability is that of the *job replica*. If we are selecting workers to perform a particular job, we might observe a worksample, i.e., we might observe the people briefly on the job itself and record their output. If the job requires training after selection or uses expensive equipment, however, the true worksample may be impractical. In such a case, the tester tries to design an apparatus that reproduces much of the original task, without requiring skills that have to be trained.

An excellent example of the job replica is the Complex Coordination test (Figure 2.3). One cannot observe a would-be pilot in an airplane, but the Complex Coordination test gives him a stick and rudder bar that he is to move much as the pilot does. Movements are dictated by signal lights. When a light appears at the top of the left center column, the man pulls the stick so that the right center light will move upward to match it. A sideways movement of the stick controls the light in the top row, and the rudder controls the light running across the bottom row.

This test had a validity of about 0.40 for predicting pilot success and was given the highest weight among all tests used in the World War II selection battery. A factor analysis demonstrated the reason for this high validity: the Complex Coordination test duplicates better than any other test the common-factor composition of the student pilot's task. Table 12.2 (cf. Figure 10.4) gives loadings of the test and of the criterion (graduation from pilot training vs. elimination). The products of the loadings, in the farthest right column, show how much each factor adds to the total validity. The total of these products agrees almost exactly with the observed validity of 0.39. (There are slight variations in validity and factor loadings from one table to another because each is based on a different sample.)

There are three important things to observe in this table. First, the *Multi-limb Coordination* factor made a welcome contribution to validity, a contribution no pencil-paper test could provide. But, second, a large part of the validity of this Complex Coordination test came from factors that could be measured much more cheaply by pencil-paper tests, particularly tests from the spatial-mechanical domain. Third, the specific factor found in this test and not in other coordination tests made no contribution to validity. There was then no special value in a job replica; tests that did not "look like an airplane" could measure the abilities that mattered. To be sure, the fact that the test was a replica may account for its representing the factors in so nearly the right proportions, but ordinarily such weighting can be achieved more easily and more correctly by combining factor scores statistically.

Negative evidence such as this casts doubt on job replicas, however great their face validity. Designing a good replica may be an expensive engineering project; one will not undertake this project unless he is dissatisfied with the predictive efficiency of tests measuring common factors.

A number of job replicas have shown good validity, presumably because their specific content makes a valid contribution. The Metal Filing Worksample, which isolates one element of the dentist's job and measures it directly, correlated

Table 12.2.   Factor loadings of the Complex Coordination Test and
the pilot-success criterion

Factor	Loadings of Complex Coordination Test	Graduation-elimination criterion	Product of loadings (contribution to validity)
Cognitive factors			
Spatial	.49	.34	.167
Mechanical Experience	.20	.26	.052
Visualization	.17	.25	.042
Perceptual Speed	.17	.15	.026
Numerical	.09	.01	.001
Verbal	−.01	−.02	.000
Reasoning	.02	−.02	−.000
Psychomotor factors			
Multilimb Coordination	.34	.22	.075
Complex Coordination (specific)	.37	.00	.000
Interest in piloting	.17	.28	.048
			.405

SOURCE: Melton, 1947, p. 995. The specific factor loading is estimated indirectly.

0.53 with grades in dentistry courses (Bellows, 1940). A trimming test, in which a girl cuts between a pair of narrowing lines with scissors, correlated 0.69 with ratings of trainees in power-sewing-machine operation (Treat, 1929). A hand-tool dexterity test, requiring operations on nuts and bolts with wrench and screwdriver, correlated 0.46 with performance of machinists (Bennett & Fear, 1943). It is not a coincidence that these studies are all very old; job replicas are no longer fashionable.

There is no need to describe the dozens of apparatus tests that have been used. The only one that has appeared frequently in the literature is Rotary Pursuit, its prominence being attributable to its usefulness in laboratory studies of learning. As seen in Figure 12.1, there is a metal disk, perhaps an inch across, set in a plastic turntable. The subject uses a stylus with a hinged handle to follow the disc, his total contact time being recorded electrically. Many variations are possible. In the Pursuit Confusion test, the speed of the target changes, and the subject has to guide his tracking by watching in a mirror rather than by viewing the target directly. The Two-Hand Coordination test involves slower but more complex movement. One handle controls left-right motion of the follower arm, while the other controls front-to-back motion. Both must be moved at the same time, at different speeds, to stay on the target.

7. *The factor loadings for Complex Coordination, squared, give the percentage composition of the test variance. How do the values from Table 12.2 compare with those in Figure 10.4, p. 324?*

General Problems of Psychomotor Testing

Apparatus Differences

Test apparatus is supposed to be standardized, especially when results at one time and place set standards to be used in future selection or guidance. Pieces of apparatus made in the same shop from the same blueprints are rarely identical in performance. Moreover, each apparatus changes over time as electrical contacts become dirty, rubber parts become less elastic, and so on. For example, in the relatively simple Arm-Hand Steadiness Test, a score that is average on one machine would be near the 30th percentile on another (Melton, 1947).

Pencil-Paper Measures of Motor Performance

Apparatus tests are almost never practical in guidance testing, though GATB has succeeded in simplifying its tests enough to permit their use on a large scale. In industrial and military selection also, elaborate apparatus tests may be impractical. Initial cost is not the difficulty: the apparatus used to test tens of thousands of men in the Air Force during World War II cost only some $250,000. The big cost was in time of the tester, who could supervise no more than 6 subjects. Nonetheless, the tests may improve prediction enough to justify their cost—e.g., when a washout in pilot training cost tens of thousands of dollars. With current advances in automation, the quality of machines should arise and the cost of test administration should drop.

Pencil-paper tests are much less costly, and testers would prefer to use them if they measure the same abilities as the apparatus tests. But apparatus tests and pencil-paper tests of motor ability seem to represent different factors, perhaps because the pencil-paper test resents a static display. *Aiming* and *Wrist-Finger Speed* are the factors most clearly entering pencil-paper tests. GATB *K*, which measures *Wrist-Finger Speed*, is the only pencil-paper motor test for which we have considerable validity information. Printed tests should not be used to measure more complex dexterity and coordination (Fleishman & Ellison, 1962).

Trial-to-Trial Consistency

As in the case of performance tests of general ability, inconsistency from trial to trial has been a source of difficulty in psychomotor tests. It will be recalled that, in GATB, *F* and *M* are the least consistent scores. Retest correlations for

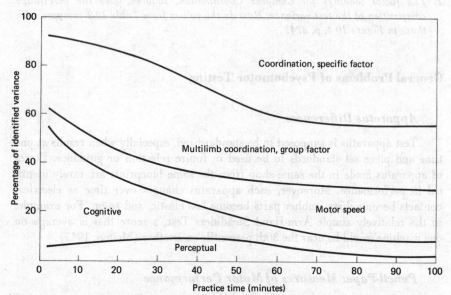

Figure 12.2. Composition of Complex Coordination Test as a function of practice. *Data from Fleishman & Hempel, 1954.* Curves show proportion of variance accounted for by each factor after removing error variance and unidentified minor factors from consideration. Curves have been smoothed, and factors have been combined as follows: *Cognitive* includes *Spatial, Visualization,* and *Mechanical Experience; Motor Speed* includes *Rate of Movement* and *Psychomotor Speed.*

apparatus tests as usually given are in the neighborhood of 0.70. This may be satisfactory when the test is to be combined with several others in a prediction formula.

One might reasonably suppose that extending the test period would give a better sample and so boost accuracy of measurement just as it does for a reasoning test. The accuracy of psychomotor tests does not increase with length in that way, however, because successive periods of performance are not "equivalent." A Rotary Pursuit score for 10 trials has an internal-consistency coefficient of 0.97. The correlation of the first 10 trials with a second 10 trials is only 0.84. While the score from the longer series is less influenced by chance, the long and short series do not measure the same thing. Learning and fatigue make later trials psychologically different from early trials.

On a complicated testing device one cannot show his full skill until he has became familiar with the reaction required. Fleishman and Hempel (1954; Fleishman, 1957) gave 64 2-minute trials on the Complex Coordination test (8 minutes is the usual testing time). The scores, together with reference tests, were factored. Figure 12.2 shows that the factor content of the test varies with the amount of practice. Different men score high at different stages of practice. In the early stages, cognitive factors such as S and Vs are most important, along with *Multilimb Coordination*. The cognitive factors account for little variance when subjects are familiar with the task. *Multilimb Coordination*, a factor common to this test and to other motor tests administered, increases in importance during the first 40 minutes of practice but then drops back. Two factors grow steadily in prominence; *Rate of Movement* and a specific factor that we shall discuss further in a moment. Evidently the early trials measure adaptation to a new task, and intellectual factors play a large part in the variance. At the end, sheer speed has become a prominent source of individual differences.

The substantial specific factor found in Complex Coordination and not in other apparatus tests becomes the largest source of individual differences after the first hour of practice. This factor reflects individual differences generated during the test, probably because the person hits on some unique coordination or work method (Stevens, 1951, pp. 1341–1362). If a man with good general aptitude happens to fall into a bad habit, his final score may be far below his potential. Specific bad habits are highly persistent from trial to trial and even from month to month, as any athlete knows. They are not just a sign of ineptness; the professional coach makes a career of recognizing such faults and eliminating them from the performance of talented athletes. Not all specific responses are harmful; sometimes one stumbles into a fortunate pattern or rhythm that gives him a higher score than his aptitude would have predicted. A habit specific to one test is unlikely to have predictive value. There is no reason to think that a man who falls into a certain bad sequence of actions on this test will form a similar habit when learning to fly a plane. In learning that task, other specific habits will develop. Indeed, we cannot assume that a specific habit represents anything more than an historical accident. If we could wipe the slate clean and let the man practice the task again, he might develop entirely different specific habits and earn a different final score.

Stability data on GATB were presented in Table 11.7. The coefficients for psychomotor tests are lower than for other abilities, but if the motor abilities had been measured precisely at each age, the scores evidently would have shown stability like that of the specialized intellectual abilities.

Validity

Despite popular legends about boys who are "good with their hands," there is no general psychomotor ability. Psychomotor tests must be chosen for each particular job. They can be trusted as predictors only after an empirical tryout. There have been many disappointing studies in which tests that "ought to have" predicted occupational criteria failed to do so (Stevens, 1951, pp. 1341–1362).

We have already discussed the uncertain promise of job replicas. One reason for wishing to avoid the job-replica principle in test design is that it leads to an endless process of inventing and revising tests to cover additional jobs or to take changes in job requirements into account. Vocational guidance could not possibly be based on such tests, since hundreds of tests would have to be given to cover the occupational spectrum. Fleishman believes that a short battery can measure the chief psychomotor factors, and that combining scores from this battery can predict the psychomotor component of any job. At present, no one can say how well the factor scores will predict jobs, and one cannot guarantee that the list of psychomotor abilities will remain short. The factors account for about half of the variance in current tests; the factor scores may capture the valid part of the test information.

While psychomotor abilities are often of value in predicting occupational performance, they tend to be less relevant than intellectual abilities. USES found relatively few occupations in which motor factors were substantially better predictors than the nonmotor factors. The exceptional occupations fall into two broad categories: bench work or assembling (cheese wrapper, telephone diaphragm assembler, paper-pattern folder) and manipulative machine operating (machine clothes presser, bag sealer). Motor tests have excellent validity for these routine jobs (which are also the ones that lend themselves best to automation). As soon as a job becomes less repetitive, perceptual and intellectual factors become dominant.

8. *What function might psychomotor tests play in making school physical education programs more profitable?*

9. *Experimenters wish to study the effect of vitamin lack on motor performance. They plan to test a group, then alter the diet, and test again after some time. Would it be desirable to offer training on the tests before the first measurement?*

10. *Would extending a psychomotor test so that it measures fatigue or endurance raise or lower its validity in job prediction?*

The Search for Creativity

From Galton's *Hereditary Genius* (1869)—at the very beginning of scientific research on aptitude—to the present time, investigators have hoped to uncover the secret of creative talent. And repeatedly they have been disappointed. To be sure, tests of general ability identify persons who are mastering the symbolic tools of the culture and will go on to complete advanced training and enter the professions. As Terman's *Genetic Studies of Genius* and its sequels showed (Oden, 1968), boys with high IQs are likely to enter scientific fields and to produce research and patentable inventions. The traditional tests seem to be much more related, however, to predicting academic success than to predicting which college graduates will be intellectually daring. Many psychologists have claimed success in measuring "creative ability," but the use of this term is as questionable in most instances as was the use of the term "genius" by Galton and Terman. (A line of research on creativity that measures aspects of personality—typical behavior—is not under discussion here. See Barron, 1964.)

Before a test can be accepted as measuring a distinct creative ability, (1) it must be independent to some degree from conventional tests of general ability, and (2) it must be shown that high scorers are especially likely to produce original works of some kind that are excellent for their age and training. Many proposed tests fail to satisfy criterion (1); even if they have rather low direct correlations with general mental tests, this is explained by their low reliability (Thorndike, 1963c; Wallach & Kogan, 1965, pp. 2 ff.). Most of the tests have been announced to the world prior to any solid validity studies.

Tests of Divergent Thinking

Introspective accounts of artists, mathematicians, and other creators have suggested that creativity requires intellectual fluency, or adeptness in recombining observations and ideas. The most thoughtful psychologists have not asserted that associative fluidity is the whole of creativity. Rather, they have argued that this must be integrated with the purposiveness and critical thinking that Binet's definition emphasized, and with a store of knowledge (which is as useful in original thinking as in other thinking). See Guilford's particularly good statement (1965) on this point. The creative person, then, has good ability in the conventional sense, plus something extra. Perhaps, some writers suggest, the creative person will not be found in the highest ranges of IQ and school success, because dutiful learning of school lessons may not be compatible with a free-ranging intellect. Perhaps, to put the suggestion differently, there is good correspondence between rank in conventional tests and rank in creativity, up to IQ 120; but among pupils above that level rank on conventional tests may not agree with rank in creativity (H. Butcher, 1968, p. 103).

Most of the tests suggested as measures of the creative ingredient missing from conventional tests are "divergent." There is no one correct answer and often the subject is asked to give many answers to the same problem, thereby demonstrating his flexibility. The tests may ask one to call up from his mental depths images relevant to a novel situation, or perhaps to generate creative literary or artistic products.

The Torrance tests. The greatest amount of research has accumulated around a set of tests designed by Torrance and now published for research use (*Personnel Press*). The Verbal section contains subtests such as these:

• Ask-and-guess. An intriguing picture is shown. The subject is to guess what might have led to the scene pictured, and what might happen next. A long list of answers is wanted.

• **Product Improvement.** A picture of a stuffed animal toy is shown. The subject is to suggest changes, each of which would make the toy more fun to play with.

• **Unusual Uses.** This test, which originated with Guilford, asks the child to list as many uses as he can think of for some commonplace object, such as empty tin cans. (Space is provided for fifty different answers!)

The Figural test asks the subject to produce drawings, sometimes to tell a story, sometimes to display an object. In each subtest, initial starting points are given. One test, for example, consists of a page of circles. The directions are to make as many different pictures as possible, with the circle a key part of each picture. The tasks are obviously enjoyable, and can be expected to hold the interest of the subject.

The Torrance tests can be administered to groups above grade 4, and individually as low as kindergarten; each half takes 45 minutes of working time. Tasks are separately timed, so that the speed with which one can generate ideas is important.

Scoring tests of this sort is difficult. Torrance developed an elaborate scoring guide, giving both rules and examples. Classroom teachers are able to agree rather well with Torrance's judgment of specimen papers, but only after attentive study of the manual.

For each task, there are three types of score:[1] fluency (total acceptable responses); flexibility (How many of the categories listed in the manual does the subject use?); and originality (count of responses that are not in a standard list of frequent responses and that "require intellectual energy . . . away from the obvious and commonplace"). Within the verbal or figural section the three scores correlate so high that we probably can consider them measures of the same thing.

Form-to-form and retest correlations suggest that, while the scores are not so stable as those for conventional tests of equal length, they are dependable enough for research purposes. Verbal and Figural scores correlate about as highly as V and NV IQs, after we take the greater reliability of the latter into account.

Those who propose to use tests of divergent thinking emphasize that they measure something different from the conventional tests of mental ability. This is partly true, but there is appreciable overlap. Yamamoto (1965b) concludes that the best estimate of the correlation for representative elementary-school pupils is 0.50, after correcting for errors of measurement. This implies that about three-fourths of the variance in divergent-thinking performance is caused by something different from g or $v:ed$. In adolescent samples (Bowers, 1966; Thorndike, 1963c) the overlap is sometimes much greater. This discrepancy is puzzling, and will have to be clarified by further studies.

---

[1] An "elaboration" score, recently added, has not been the subject of much research.

Torrance has not collected systematic norms, which is understandable in view of the scoring labor the test requires. From his reports on classes within the same school, it appears that Figural scores do not increase at all with age, and that Verbal scores change very little after grade 6. No doubt older persons are more inhibited in drawing than younger ones, and the individual administration of the verbal test to younger children may give them some advantage. Possibly, too, scorers inadvertently are more severe in scoring work of older persons. We reported earlier (Figure 8.1) that adults do better on conventionally scored tests as they grow older, at least through age 40 or 50. The same study, however, finds that a word-fluency score drops off very sharply after age 20 (Schaie & Strother, 1968). This anomaly appears very difficult to explain.

The validation available for tests of this sort is unsatisfactory. The correlates of divergent abilities need to be studied for groups in which conventional general ability is held constant. For example, we need to compare high- and low-divergent fourth-graders who have MA 12, and separately to compare high- and low-divergent fourth-graders with MA 9. Divergent production is of little value and may even interfere with intellectual work if it is not accompanied by good convergent thinking; there is no merit in a fluent outpouring of unrealistic, uncritical ideas. Second, we need a report on the strength of the relation in each such study; an investigator all too often stops with the statement that a relation "is significant." The practical significance of the tests is indicated only by a correlation for a representative sample, or a regression line. Third, we need studies involving significant real-life creativity as a criterion. The Torrance test is the best researched of the divergent measures, and yet few studies on it satisfy even one of these desiderata.

The studies now reported include such findings as these. In elementary grades, the drawings of the best divergent thinker are likely to be more original than those of a low-divergent of the same IQ (a 46-case study by Torrance; details unpublished.) But how strong was the relation? And were the drawings good, or only novel? In grade 5, a Torrance score correlates 0.50 with evaluation of imaginative stories with respect to originality, insight, etc. (Yamamoto, 1963, 40 cases). But when Wodtke (1964) repeated the study *and held IQ constant,* the correlation was only 0.24. Six teachers high on the Torrance test were compared with six at the other extreme. In their classrooms the high-divergent teachers asked questions requiring pupils to think rather than factual-recall questions (Torrance & Hansen, 1965). But this compares extreme groups; how strong is the relation for representative teachers? High scoring pupils tend to be more active, more ambitious, and less conforming; they describe themselves as adventurous and humorous. Teachers tend to rate them as more original and more flexible. All this makes the tests seem interesting, but it does not carry us to the point where we can evaluate their practical usefulness.

A classroom criterion was collected by Moss and Duenk (J. Moss, 1966; Moss and Duenk, 1967), who had industrial-arts teachers record incidents in which eighth-grade boys showed creative problem solving during a 9-week pe-

Table 12.3.   Correlations of Torrance scores with observed
creative acts in Industrial Arts classes

	Group I $N = 24$	Group II $N = 32$
Torrance Total	.51	.10
Torrance Verbal	.63	−.10
Torrance Nonverbal	.27	.26
Lorge-Thorndike Verbal	.50	.34
Lorge-Thorndike Nonverbal	.55	.32

SOURCE: Moss, 1966.

riod. This criterion correlated about 0.70 with creativity ratings given by class-mates. The correlations in Table 12.3 are impressive in Group I, especially since IQ correlated little with Torrance scores. In Group II, however, no effect is found, even though the technique of observation was identical. Puzzles like this need to be cleared up before tests of divergent thinking are used widely.

We may mention here a relatively solid study of correlations between tests and ratings of the creativity of scientists in industry. F. Jones (1964) applied a number of conventional tests, plus several of Guilford's divergent measures. Scores on verbal and mathematical reasoning correlated 0.3 with the criterion, and so did a Guilford "ideational fluency" test and a score of the "consequences" or "effects" sort. The convergent and divergent scores combined give a rather good prediction, despite the sample's being select. While two of the divergent measures had practical value, five others had negligible validity.

The Remote Associates Test.   More impressive validation is reported for a test employing a different approach. The Remote Associates Test of Mednick & Mednick (*Houghton*) measures fluency in producing familiar but hard-to-retrieve associations, screening them, and moving on to new associations until a satisfactory one is found. They give three words, e.g.,

blue   cottage   rat

and ask the subject to think of a word that, in everyday usage, is associated with each of these. His thoughts must run off in a number of directions before he discovers the word the authors had in mind; when he does hit on it, its correct-ness is obvious. The task is perhaps not "creative," since one is searching for an old response rather than making up something new. But it is not dissimilar to the search for a simile, or a rhyme, or a mechanical construction to fill a need.

The overlap of RAT with tests of $v{:}ed$ is considerable. Judging from re-ported correlations in highly select groups, it might be as high as 0.70 in repre-sentative samples. But perhaps RAT also involves a fluid ability that does not appear in a measure of g.

Table 12.4.   Studies comparing the Remote Associates Test with criteria of creativity

Sample	Criterion	Mental test used and relation to RAT	Relation of criterion to RAT	Relation of criterion to Mental test
20 university architecture students	Instructor rating: creativity in design	Concept Mastery Test	$r = 0.70$	"Very low relation"
43 graduate students in psychology	Instructor rating: creativity in research	Miller Analogies Test; $r = 0.41$	$r = 0.55$	$r = -0.08$
42 scientists in chemical firm	Level of job to which assigned		$Q = 0.84$	
82 scientists	Were research contract proposals from these men given funds?		75 per cent of funded proposals were from men above RAT median	
37 scientists	As above		Men high on RAT wrote 69% of all proposals and 81% of successful ones	
29 scientists	Patents		Men above median on RAT accounted for 93% of the patents	
214 scientists	Papers, patents, rated scientific productivity		Essentially zero	

Source: RAT manual, 1967.

The manual lists nine studies comparing the test with criteria that seem to reflect practically significant creativeness. The studies summarized in Table 12.4 are representative. Since predicting in a preselected group is inevitably difficult, these substantial correlations justify serious attention to the test. The Concept Mastery and Miller tests are simply measures of high-level vocabulary; their correlations do not provide evidence as to whether RAT accomplishes something that conventional *reasoning* tests cannot.

11. *In discussing creativity Guilford (1964a) says: "Our way of using factor analysis has one great advantage in that we do not have to worry about the criterion prob-*

lem. Factor analysis provides its own criteria." How far can factor analysis go in demonstrating that a test truly measures creativity?

12. *Comment on the following hypothesis (Gallagher, 1964, p. 372). Suggest a plan for collecting evidence on it.*

   "The I.Q. test was validated on school performance during an era when successful school performance often depended on sheer memory work. No wonder vocabulary played so important a role in most I.Q. tests! When the cognitive skills of inventiveness and problem-solving are stressed in schools, new or modified aptitude or ability tests may be needed to predict the successful student. The definition of giftedness or retardation itself is likely to undergo some change."

13. *When an Unusual Uses test asks the Negro lowerclass child to suggest uses for a newspaper, he tends to get a high score because he thinks of things like soaking up spilled grease or putting on the floor when you take a bath. Relate this to the earlier discussion of cultural bias in conventional mental tests. Is Unusual Uses biased in favor of the poor child? Or is his higher score validly so?*

Artistic Abilities

In painting, architecture, and other graphic arts, special talents must certainly play a large part in success. To identify such talents prior to training has proved exceedingly difficult, but several tests of artistic ability have been tried.

Worksamples.   One way of identifying those who will do well in art training is to obtain a sample of the person's creative drawing. This may reflect training to date just as much as talent, but it is a fair basis for comparing persons who have similar training. Merely asking the subject to draw or paint a picture, or to submit a piece of completed work, however, does not make for a standardized comparison. To standardize the task by requiring everyone to draw from the same model, on the other hand, leaves little room for creativeness.

The Horn Art Aptitude test attempts to solve this problem by a job replica calling for high-level creativeness under very slight constraints. In the "imagery" section of the test the subject is given several cards, each bearing a pattern of lines. Around these lines he is to sketch a picture. The pictures are judged by art instructors as to imagination and technical drawing quality. By using careful scoring directions, competent judges can attain a correlation of 0.86 between independent scorings. The other chief section of the test calls for arrangement of rectangles and other simple figures into balanced compositions. The test is intended for use with applicants to art school, most of whom have had previous training. The scores at the beginning of the year correlated 0.66 with grades in a special art course for high-school seniors (C. Horn & Smith, 1945).

Gilbert and Ewing also favor the job-replica principle. Their unpublished Illinois Art Ability Test (based on an item devised by Knauber) asks the subject to draw certain objects (e.g., a table) in perspective. The drawing is scored not only for the technical quality of the perspective but for the extent to which the subject has elaborated or beautified the object. A table that shows attractive lines and proportions receives a higher score than a graceless one. The test requires artistic skill, but it also reflects creative effort and hence attempts in part to measure typical behavior or style. Scoring rules have been developed that permit clerks to score the papers objectively. Two scorings of the same papers correlate 0.94.

A validation study on students of architecture shows several interesting facts (Table 12.5). The test predicts art courses moderately well but gives a poor prediction in engineering drawing. The latter is predicted very well by MCT and a spatial test. The average in other courses, including English and mathematics, is best predicted by high-school marks, a scholastic aptitude test, and a mathematics achievement test. This points to a fact of great importance in vocational counseling. Even though a student possesses special aptitudes in high degree, he cannot use them in a profession unless his academic ability is good enough to carry him through general college courses. Specialized abilities play little part in determining the architect's average freshman grades, where the drawing courses are outweighed by nonspecialized courses. MCT and Art Ability correlate only 0.12 with the grade average.

Analytic Tests. The job replica gives valuable information about students who have had some art training, but it neither clarifies the nature of artistic talent nor gives a basis for comparing untrained persons. For these purposes, it is necessary to test components of artistic ability prior to training. These components have not been adequately identified, and the tests now available are based only on some investigator's hunch as to what makes an artist.

Table 12.5. Correlations of tests with success in freshman architecture courses

Test	General engineering drawing	Freehand drawing	Grade average, other courses combined
Illinois Art Ability Test	0.26	0.42	0.27
Object Aperture Test (spatial)	0.57	0.30	0.27
Coöperative Mathematics Test	0.40	0.27	0.45
ACE (general ability)	0.40	0.25	0.45
Bennett MCT	0.60	0.10	0.09
Rank in high-school class			0.49

Note: The criterion for the drawing courses is a composite of grades and ratings by instructors. The number of cases varies from 27 to 69.

SOURCE: These are unpublished data from a study by W. M. Gilbert *et al.*

Figure 12.3.   Item from the Meier Test of Art Judgment.
The arrangement of the woman's burden has been changed. Which arrangement is better?
Item copyright 1940 by the Bureau of Educational Research, State University of Iowa. Reproduced by permission.

Over a period of more than 30 years, Norman Meier studied characteristics of artists and tried to isolate the elements in artistic ability. He projected a three-part test; the first part, the Art Judgment Test, has been widely used. To create an item such as that in Figure 12.3, a work of art judged to be good was altered in composition, shading, or some other quality so as to damage its aesthetic appeal. The subject is shown the original and altered versions and asked to select the more pleasing one. The second part, Aesthetic Perception, was released in 1963, shortly before Meier's death. It employs the same principle, but the items are more subtle and more demanding. Works of art shown range from North Coast basketry to Picasso-like drawings and sumi-e. There are four versions of each, varying in several respects. The subject has to rank the four in order of merit. Meier's third proposed test, Creative Imagination, never reached the point of release. While there is some evidence that Meier was measuring significant abilities, the evidence is too fragmentary to warrant a statement about the validity of his approach.

Artistic judgment is distinct from ability to perform artistically. Rose Anderson (1951) warns against reliance on the test of judgment as a predictor in the fine arts. Persons who have poor Meier scores are not uncommonly judged to be highly promising by their art teachers. She says that her counseling experience

has led to considerable caution in encouraging clients toward fine-art specialization. On the other hand, the combined results of several tests provide a more adequate basis for appraising potentialities for such applied fields as advertising art, format, interior decoration, costume design, and crafts. The appropriate combination of supporting aptitudes includes superior artistic judgment . . . superior facility for spatial visualization and fine eye-hand coordination, manual dexterity, evidence of drawing ability reflected in the Lewerenz Originality of Line Drawing Test, in the Horn Art Aptitude Test, or in work samples.

Research on artistic abilities is still in a most primitive stage. No systematic research has been done using modern tests and adequate criteria. Most of the tests have been left as they were when first designed as much as thirty years ago, without follow-up research or revision. The nature of artistic aptitude remains an unsolved—and neglected—problem.

14. *What criterion would the Meier test be expected to predict better than the Horn test, and vice versa?*
15. *What aspects of art aptitude do not appear to be measured by any of the tests described?*
16. *Assuming that the validities reported in Table 12.5 are confirmed by further studies, what advice would a counselor give an applicant to the school of architecture who scores at the 80th percentile in the Art Ability Test, MCT, and Object Aperture Test but at the 30th percentile in mathematics and general ability?*

Special Aptitude Tests for Courses and Professions

In the 1920s and 1930s attempts were made to develop aptitude tests for particular school subjects or curricula such as algebra, foreign language, engineering, or law. The test was usually prepared on the basis of a superficial analysis of the course of study. Test problems were based on the type of content to be encountered in the course (e.g., a foreign-language test might require substituting nonsense symbols for words in a sentence; a legal aptitude test would ordinarily present hypothetical problems in legal reasoning).

The introduction of content specially relevant to the course of study did not raise validity appreciably above that which could be obtained with a good measure of verbal abilities or relevant past achievement. Usually a broad-purpose test with one or two scores can make as good a prediction as the special aptitude test. Occasionally a thorough psychological study of some type of training makes it possible to identify pertinent abilities the usual test does not cover.

The best example is the Modern Language Aptitude Test by Carroll and Sapon (*Psych. Corp.*). This test grew out of the attempt to provide intensive training in a variety of foreign languages for officers and diplomats going overseas. The analysis had to concern itself with what makes languages in general easy or hard to learn, among intelligent and highly educated men. Carroll's job analysis, which led him to try numerous tests, eventually arrived at five tasks.

● Number learning. The subject is taught new, artificial names for the numbers 1, 2, 3, 4, 10, . . . , 40, 100, . . . , 400. Then he is to write the numerals corresponding to numbers dictated in the new language. The test, recorded on tape, presumably measures memory and some form of auditory alertness.

● Phonetic script. The subject has to learn to associate certain sounds with printed syllables. The test appears to require an auditory memory helpful in mimicking foreign speech sounds.

● Spelling cues. The subject has to decode rapidly words spelled in an irregular, semiphonetic fashion (e.g., *fnetk fshn*). This depends in part on vocabulary and in part on ability to associate sounds with symbols.

● Words in sentences. The task is to find the word in the second sentence that performs the same syntactic function as the underlined word in the first sentence. For example:

I had little hope of *becoming* rich.

<u>Turning</u> right at the <u>intersection</u> gives you your best chance of <u>avoiding</u> the
    A   B   C
<u>homecoming</u> <u>traffic</u>.
    D   E

● Paired associates, a memory task. The subject studies pairs such as *glang-finger* (2 minutes for 24 pairs), and then is tested.

The whole test requires a bit over an hour; there is also a shorter form, not quite so valid. Since the subtests have reliabilities as high as 0.90, it is striking that their intercorrelations are frequently as low as 0.40–0.50. They evidently do measure rather distinct abilities. The validity coefficients relating test scores to success are consistently high: median of 0.53 in ninth-grade courses, 0.52 for adult intensive courses. The test predicts equally well, no matter what the language. Very likely results would not be the same in courses of a grammar-translation type as in audiolingual courses.

A key question is how much the MLAT overlaps conventional mental tests, and what it adds to prediction from grade records and general tests. The one explicit report on that point comes from a high-school sample in which MLAT predicted with validity of 0.71, but three different general mental tests had validities of only 0.34–0.52. There can be little doubt that Carroll has isolated some important specialized job elements.

Many aptitude tests have been developed in recent years for use in graduate and professional schools. The tests are for the most part measures of general ability or academic achievement, such as might be used for general counseling. They are adjusted in difficulty to the level of students tested, and place extra emphasis on the abilities of obvious interest to the profession in question. This special emphasis may make the test a slightly better predictor than a general-purpose test. Basically, however, such a test is to be regarded as a measure of crystallized abilities and educational development which supplements the undergraduate grade record.

SUGGESTED READINGS

Calandra, Alexander. Angels on a pin. *Saturday Review,* December 31, 1968, *51,* 60.
A divergent fable on the theme of divergent thinking.

Fleishman, Edwin A. The description and prediction of perceptual-motor skill learning. In R. Glaser (Ed.), *Training research and education.* Pittsburgh: University of Pittsburgh Press, 1962. Pp. 137–176. (Also in paperback edition, Wiley, 1964.)
After reviewing the motor factors and their measures, Fleishman reports how progress in learning is related to various aptitudes. He then discusses the research on motor learning in practical skills, and the implications of aptitude studies for training.

Guilford, J. P. Intellectual factors in productive thinking. In M. J. Aschner and C. E. Bish (Eds.), *Productive thinking in education.* Washington: National Education Association, 1965. Pp. 5–20.
Professor Guilford argues that all problem solving is creative, and that divergent thinking is only a part of the process. He relates the ability to sense problems, to generate ideas, and to evaluate one's progress to the elements in his speculative system for classifying tests.

Yamamoto, Kaoru. "Creativity"—A blind man's report on the elephant. *Journal of Counseling Psychology,* 1965, *12,* 428–434.
A good-humored perspective on the philosophical conflicts that have prevented agreement about the nature of creativity and tests for it. Excellent bibliography.

13

Personnel Selection and Classification

When we wish to predict success in task X, it would be convenient if we could look in a test catalog, find a test labeled "Test of Aptitude for Task X," and begin using that test for selection. Unfortunately, the procedure required to establish a selection program is much more complicated. One difficulty is that names are misleading. Tests with similar names measure different things, and sometimes the test intended to predict task X predicts less well than a test made for quite another purpose. To cover the aptitudes that a job demands usually requires more than one test. And, on the other hand, a test of an ability required in a job is irrelevant to prediction if all applicants possess that ability to the required degree, or can learn it quickly on the job. However well a test has been developed and however thoroughly its author has validated it, no one can be sure it will predict in a situation until it is tried out there.

The employment manager or educational admissions officer can accept no test at face value, nor can he accept a test solely on the basis of research conducted elsewhere. Sooner or later, nearly every person using tests for selection or classification must carry out his own validation studies to determine whether his prediction methods are working. While the practicing tester may limit his studies to relatively simple follow-up, it is important to know the full procedure for validation research, since this establishes the basic logic of any study of prediction.

In Chapter 2 we distinguished among types of decisions: selection, classification, evaluation of treatments, and verification of scientific hypotheses. While some prediction is involved in using tests for any of these purposes, the empirical, criterion-oriented validation procedures to be examined in this chapter are most directly relevant to selection and classification. We shall devote the greater part of our discussion to selection, using employee selection for nearly all examples.

The statements are equally relevant, however, to institutional decisions in military, educational, and clinical settings.

Procedures in Prediction Research

To select employees one chooses a number of tests for tryout, determines their predictive effectiveness experimentally, and devises a plan for using test scores in making decisions. The procedure may be crude trial and error: the experimenter assembles a "shotgun" battery of all kinds of tests in the hope that one or more of them will prove effective. Use of this method is declining as we understand better why some tests are valid and others are not. Psychologists developing test batteries today devote considerable thought to the characteristics of the job and the criteria, as well as to the search for promising tests.

The stages in prediction research are these:

• Job analysis, to form hypotheses as to what characteristics make for success or failure.

• Choice of possibly useful tests to measure these characteristics.

• Administration of tests to an experimental group of workers.

• Collection of criterion data that show how these workers succeeded on the job.

• Analysis of the relation between test score and success on the job, and installation of the most effective selection plan.

• Periodic validity studies to check on the continuing soundness of the plan.

Job Analysis

Job analysis sets up hypotheses stating which abilities and habits contribute to or limit success in the job. No machinelike procedure of checking off one by one all possible job elements has ever been found successful. Instead, the psychologist studies the task with whatever insight and psychological knowledge he can muster. Job analysis is an art.

The analyst must first of all be well grounded in psychology. Understanding of motivation, motor habits, and the organization of abilities are required, as well as knowledge of the multitude of tests now available. Motion analysis will suggest what dexterities or coordinations are important. Analysis of the stimuli to which the worker responds may suggest the relevance of perceptual or sensory abilities. One approach is to compare good and poor employees now on the job, observing their performance and products, or comparing them on tests. Study of workers in training is helpful, as their difficulties in learning may identify aptitudes needed. Published research on job success draws attention to tests worth trying and sometimes suggests that certain tests can be eliminated without further trial. While the analyst takes off from the experience of others, unless he brings in new hypotheses he is unlikely to find a better method of predicting.

The job needs to be clearly and rather narrowly defined. One does not analyze the job of salesman: one studies "detail man for a drug firm who calls on physicians" or "salesman in a furniture store selling to a lower-middleclass clientele." Research engineers differ from development engineers, stenographers from clerk typists (Dunnette & Kirchner, 1958). This specificity points to a great difficulty in selection research. Findings in one firm may apply only approximately in another or not at all, because the duties that go with a job title may be entirely different in the two firms.

The specificity of job demands puts a limit on vocational counseling. The person's aptitudes and achievement record tell us something about his chances of survival in training (e.g., in engineering school). But whether he does well or badly on an engineering job will depend on the requirements of that job. The personnel department uses tests fitted to the requirements of the firm, but the counselor cannot guess what firms the man will consider. Even if he did, long-range advice has limited value. Job duties are not eternally fixed, as shown by the radical changes automation has brought to "engineer" and "clerk" alike. It is just this that causes us to stress understanding of oneself and of the world of work as the aim in counseling. The person who survives engineering training has opened the path to many jobs, some right for him and some not.

Let us return to the job analyst. His report about the job must be specific. He should not state that successful workers have "mechanical ability"; he should instead define the ability as "knowledge of and ability to apply principles of gears," or "speed in routine two-handed manipulation, not involving much finger dexterity or adaptation." Such clear definitions open the way to a search for the most appropriate test. The analysis should range over the entire field of abilities, habits, personality characteristics and interests, previous experience, knowledge, physique, and so on.

Impressionistic job analysis places heavy reliance on the opinions of a few observers. A systematic procedure for using more informants and perhaps breaking away from folklore is the "critical-incident" technique (Flanagan, 1954). The analyst asks some person well acquainted with the job to think of an individual who has done excellently on the job, and then to recall one particular incident that showed this person's superiority. The informant then recalls a poor performer, perhaps one who had to be discharged, and the incident that led to the final verdict of unsuitability. These incidents are concrete, and only one stage removed from field observation of good and poor performance, as can be seen in these two examples (H. Preston, 1948):

> This officer was instructed to land his P-80 on runway 15. He pedaled on the right runway but lined up to land on runway 9. He was told to go around and line up and land on runway 15 again. This time he overshot and had tc go around. He was getting dangerously low on fuel so I personally talked him around the pattern, putting

him on his down-wind leg, and instructed him when to turn on base. I asked him if he had runway 15 spotted and he said "Roger." After acknowledging, he flew right by runway 15 and almost "spun-in" trying to turn in on runway 9. Being low on fuel, I told him to go ahead and land. He came in hot and ran off the end of the runway.

In meeting and acting as a pilot for general officers this lieutenant has brought favorable comment upon himself through the accomplishment of the mission. One specific case when when, through no fault of his own, an aircraft was allowed to depart without a retired Major General on board. Immediately upon being confronted by the general—a rather crusty old bird—he, without calling on me or any other superior, arranged for his departure to the original destination in time to overtake his original aircraft.

Incidents, when classified, suggest variables to be measured for predictive purposes and to be included in the criterion.

The critical-incident method collects richly suggestive data, avoiding vague generalities such as "This job requires good judgment." It is not, however, a truly objective method. If the folklore of the business says that truck drivers must have stamina but not necessarily much intelligence, the informant is likely to bring to mind incidents consistent with the stamina theory, and to forget the cases in which drivers made themselves valuable by recognizing mixups in their orders. The person who classifies incidents likewise can introduce stereotypes, but this disadvantage is present in any judgment of job requirements. A systematic study by Andersson and Nilsson (1964) is highly favorable to the critical-incident procedure.

Whereas that method starts afresh with each new job to be analyzed, a general system that may be applicable to one new job after another has been developed by E. J. McCormick (Thornton & McCormick, 1964; McCormick et al., 1967). The Worker Activity Profile is a job-description scale with 162 entries, two of which are as follows:

Interpretation of Information. In various jobs, the worker receives information from charts, graphs, meters, tables, etc., and his task is to "read" and interpret this information, in order to decide upon an appropriate course of action. The difficulty of the task in such cases would vary depending upon such factors as the amount, complexity and completeness of the information presented. Check the activity below which is most nearly like those of the incumbent in terms of the difficulty of interpreting data.

5 _____ reads corporate financial reports as a step in analyzing their financial soundness

4 _____ reads and interprets weather charts in order to make weather forecasts

3 _____ checks farm production records in order to compile summary statistics

2 _____ reads temperature gauges to insure that temperature is within safe limits

1 _____ reads gas meters and records readings on a standard form

0 _____ does no interpretation of data

Depth Discrimination. (Judgment of the distance of an object, or the distance relationship between objects.)

2 _____ makes difficult, precise judgments of distance or depth (e.g., hunter, photographer)

1 _____ makes fairly easy, gross judgments of distance or depth (e.g., taxi driver, nursery man planting trees)

0 _____ seldom or never judges distance

An informant is asked to consider what a particular man, whose work he knows well, is required to do. As in the critical-incident method, he reports on one man, not on a stereotype or composite. He is to check the most difficult or highest level performance required of the man on each scale. The many items of the Activity Profile have been sorted by factor analysis to facilitate summary after reports on many men in a job category have been collected. The extensive and successful application of the method in the Air Force is described by Morsh (1964).

1. *On the two scales of the Worker Activity Profile shown, rate the following occupations.*
   a. *Surveyor*
   b. *Farm owner or manager*
   c. *Newspaper reporter*
2. *What investigations might be carried out to decide on the comparative advantages of the critical-incident and Worker Activity Profile techniques?*
3. *Prepare a list of the abilities composing aptitude for one of the following jobs: making pie dough, operating a calculator of a particular type, driving a taxi, or schoolteaching of some one type.*
4. *For many jobs requiring long training, e.g., physiotherapy, it is undesirable to take girls into training who will probably marry and drop out. What characteristics might distinguish between probable marriers and nonmarriers?*
5. *What characteristics might differentiate the salesman successful in selling furniture to the lower-middleclass from one successful with upper-middleclass customers?*
6. *If someone should be so foolish as to try to define the psychological requirements for success in college faculty positions, can he analyze all such positions together or should he use a narrower category. How narrow?*
7. *In view of the specificity of occupations, how can GATB be used effectively in guidance in grade 9? In grade 12 when the majority of students are entering the local job market?*

Choice of Tests for Tryout

Having tested characteristics presumed to be important in a job, the investigator must then find tests. He may seek one test that combines the many job requirements or he may seek a group of tests, each a pure and independent measure of one required ability. The former method usually requires the investigator to design a new test. As we have seen in considering mechanical, psychomotor, artistic, and academic aptitudes, the relatively complex test that comes close to the requirements of the job will generally give a higher validity coefficient than any one simple test, but tests of simpler abilities are likely to be equally useful when a number of them can be combined. Generally the latter plan is preferred because it can use existing tests and is flexible.

If the abilities the job seems to demand are already measured in published tests, such tests should be tried. Not every test with a relevant name will be suitable; the investigator must consider the difficulty of the test, its appropriateness to the intelligence and education of applicants, and the like. If the job calls for an ability that is represented only approximately in available aptitude tests, it is more desirable to make a new test to measure this ability than to obtain a pale image of it from an indirect measure. We can use MCT to illustrate this point. To select men for advanced electrical training, it is probable that Bennett's items dealing with electricity will serve better than his items on forces, motion, and buoyancy. Inclusion of the latter items dilutes the test so that it fails to select the best workers for a job requiring electrical comprehension only.

In addition to tests with predetermined scoring patterns, many selection studies try instruments that are no more than collctions of heterogeneous items. The most common of these is the biographical inventory. There is no commercially published inventory of this type, but it is a simple matter to prepare a suitable collection of items covering work and educational experience, hobbies, athletic background, social activities, and home conditions. The correlation of each item in the miscellaneous collection with success on the job is examined. Each job will show significant correlations with some of the responses, and a score is formed by counting just those answers that predict success in that job. (For example, it may be found that among male applicants those who have had 1 to 2 years of post-high-school education—not more—are the best prospects for office manager.) The same technique of keying can be applied to interest and personality tests. Inventories scored in this manner have often predicted job success as well as ability tests do. An Air Force Biographical Data Blank correlated 0.30 with pilot success (the responses scored being those that distinguished successes from failures in the first group studied; Guilford, 1947. See also p. 428).

Experimental Trial

The crucial step is experimental trial. One gives the tests to typical *applicants* and observes the correspondence of test scores to success. In practical work there is much pressure to omit the experimental study. When the psychologist reports to his boss that he believes test X will eliminate poorer employees, the boss is far more anxious to install the test and benefit from it at once than to withhold judgment during weeks or even years of investigation. It is hazardous to install a program without full experimental trial. There have been many instances in which "likely" tests proved to be of no value in selection. Indeed, half the tests in a trial battery usually prove to be worthless, either because they are irrelevant or because they duplicate other information.

The nonpsychologist may propose to use the tests to eliminate poor prospects and to study the survivors to determine the relation between test and performance. This plan is severely limited. A test may not predict which of the acceptable men would do well on the job even though it can weed out failures. (Example: A hearing test would rule out some people as music students; but within a selected group, all of whom can hear, it would not predict success.) Trial on an unselected group establishes more accurate critical scores and combining weights. Air Force psychologists thought trial on an unselected population so important to validate selection methods that they went to the trouble of sending through training a 1300-man random sample of all eligible recruits, even though they knew in advance that the majority would fail (DuBois, 1947).

Preferably, subjects in a selection study take the tests with the same motivation that will be present when the tests are used thereafter. The investigator will try more tests than he can use in his final prediction battery, since some will probably not be helpful. This makes the trial battery long, and special attention must be paid to maintaining cooperation from the subjects.

The legal requirement that employment practices be demonstrably fair is one important reason for full experimental trial. It is not enough to show, for example, that furniture salesmen now doing well in a certain store score high on a test of "culture and taste." Perhaps men who score low would be adequate salesmen if they could get past the employment office. Perhaps on-the-job training would quickly give them the abilities needed. The employer can convincingly meet a charge of unfair practice only by showing that the persons who fail his test are poor on the job after a reasonable training effort has been made.

On the other hand, experimental trial has practical limits. The Air Force took costly risks in sending an unselected group into training. Neither the employer nor the public wants to see unscreened men in responsible positions. The employer tied by seniority rules may properly refuse to hire low scorers that he will be unable to get rid of. All the costs, obvious and hidden, must be weighed in deciding on the proper scale and duration of a tryout.

It is natural to stress the role validation plays in improving prediction schemes and in making sure they really do what is claimed for them. There is an important side benefit: a clear-cut validation makes it a good deal more likely that the procedure will be put into use. A personnel department often encounters difficulty, for instance, when the conclusions it reaches about candidates for promotion conflict with the impressions of the men's supervisors. The sales manager cannot believe the report that one of his star salesmen is unlikely to fit a management assignment. If there is presentable evidence that assessments by the personnel staff do reduce the rate of failure, its recommendations will get a hearing. If not, they very likely do not deserve a hearing.

8. *What is meant by this statement? "When one diagnoses a clinical patient one is measuring his aptitude for various treatments."*
9. *What practical conditions would a department store consider in deciding whether to make a special test for each type of clerk or to use a published test for salespeople in general?*
10. *Suppose an employer puts a test in use without tryout. What harm can result from this, assuming that the validity of the test is zero or low positive?*

The Criterion

After giving his tests, the experimenter waits for evidence of good and poor job performance. The experimental group is treated in the same way as other workers, being given normal training and duties. After a suitable interval, data on success are obtained. Among the criteria used are quantity of production, quality of production, turnover, and opinions of superiors. As was explained on p. 127, it is important that the criterion possess a high degree of validity. A test that can predict quality of work will seem to be a poor test if it is judged by a criterion that does not fairly indicate quality of work. The criterion (or set of criteria) should cover all important aspects of the job.

Criteria may be based on measured output, observations, or ratings. An adequate number of observations representative of normal performance is required. If a proficiency test is the criterion, it must meet the usual requirements of objectivity, stability, and validity. Ratings are particularly common—and troublesome—criteria. Methods of making ratings more dependable are discussed in a later chapter (pp. 571 ff.).

There is always a risk that judgmental criteria will be contaminated by the judge's knowledge of predictor data. Thus a foreman may rate a man higher than his performance warrants because he knows the man has considerable experience. A therapist may be quicker to note signs of progress in a patient whose intake record included a favorable test report than in another patient whose behavior is much the same. Such influences spuriously raise the validity coefficient and sometimes cause a measure to appear valid even though it is irrelevant to job performance. Even strictly objective criteria become contaminated. For example, a teacher may give extra attention to a C student known to have a high IQ and so help him to prepare better for an achievement test, while neglecting another C student whose aptitude-test score is low. This artificially raises the IQ-achievement correlation. The only way to eliminate contamination is to keep predictor data secret until all criterion scores have been collected.

If the investigator picks the wrong criterion, he is likely to pick the wrong selection tests. We have already seen (p. 387) that the relevant predictors change when quality rather than speed of production becomes important. A Navy study (Figure 13.1) shows the effect of changing criteria for a mechanical job. Grades

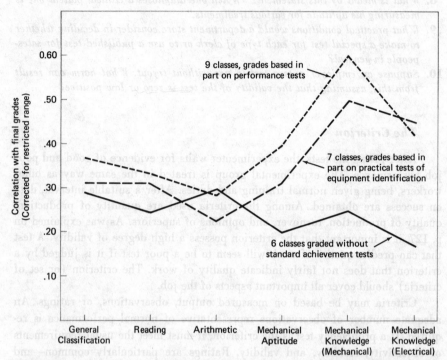

Figure 13.1. Correlations of Navy classification tests with grades in Basic Engineering School, before and after introduction of standard achievement tests. *Stuit, 1947, p. 307.*

in ship's engine operation, based only on instructor's judgments, correlated little with predictor tests. But when highly valid achievement tests were used in allotting school grades, the classification tests were satisfactory predictors. The subjective judgments were most related to academic and intellectual abilities. The valid criterion of job knowledge and skill was predicted best by Mechanical Knowledge and Mechanical Aptitude. The tests that predict a valid criterion may be different from those that predict a biased or incomplete criterion. Ghiselli (1966) finds that in hundreds of studies of occupational success the tests that predict training criteria differ from those that best predict on-the-job performance. The former relate much more to verbal and reasoning abilities.

Temporal relationships are puzzling. Sometimes tests predict a criterion relatively close to the point of testing, but cannot predict a more distant criterion of the same sort. Thus Humphreys (1968) finds the usual substantial correlation between freshman grades and freshman aptitude tests, but little relation between junior- and senior-year grades and the earlier tests. (One might argue that some students "find themselves" after a poor start; or one might argue that grades in the smaller, more specialized classes of the upper years are less meaningful criteria.) Just the opposite trend is shown in some studies relating college success to career success. Men with good marks do no better than men with intermediate marks, until after 10 years of job experience; then the men who were good in college shoot ahead. One study of this sort is summarized in Figure 13.2, derived from records of the American Telephone Company. College grades of present employees were sorted into groups. Their salary after, say, 12 years of work was compared with the median salary of all men at the 12-year point. The tabulation suggests that differences among senior employees are moderately consistent with individual differences observed in college, and probably with conventional ability tests, even though the correspondence among employees in their junior years is less marked. To some extent, then, "the cream rises," and the college record has some degree of long-range forecasting validity. Arnold Roe (1963) presents other sets of data that give a similar impression. The studies are made harder to interpret by the fact that salary policies change from decade to decade, and that the data for earlier years compile the salary experience of present senior employees (who were juniors 20-odd years ago) along with men still in their junior years. Separate analysis by cohorts graduating in the same decade would be a valuable addition. But that is aside from the point of the present discussion. Here, we are only pointing out a difficulty in selection research that has been given too little attention: tests that predict short-term criteria may have limited long-run validity, and vice versa.

One might speak of a hypothetical "ultimate criterion" that fully represents the outcome the selector desires. The medical school would, if it could, judge the success of its students by their lifetime contribution to the health of the communities where they later practice. This probably depends more on personality

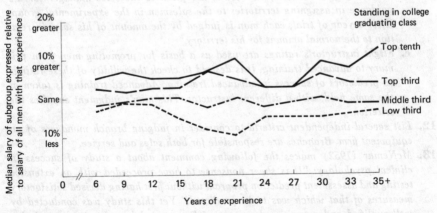

Figure 13.2. Salaries of employees at different levels of experience, as a function of college performance.
Arnold Roe, 1963.

attributes than on abilities; it certainly is not very closely related to grades in biochemistry. The student's grades, however, are likely to be the criterion in any selection research done by the medical school.

One extensive effort to get a near-ultimate criterion was made during the Korean war. Observers and interviewers went to the theater of combat to obtain information on performance; these data were supplemented by ratings from field commanders. The validity of an Army test battery developed to predict performance in training and in maneuvers was 0.27 against these peacetime criteria, but only 0.17 against a combat criterion. A battery designed to fit the combat criterion correlated 0.36 with both training and combat criteria. The important difference between the two batteries was the inclusion of a personality questionnaire in the combat-valid battery (Willemin *et al.*, 1958).

In place of the single "ultimate criterion" it is more realistic and more illuminating to think of multiple criteria of different kinds, which become observable at different times, and all of which shed light on selection policy. We shall illustrate multiple criteria later in the chapter.

11. *In each of the following situations, trace how contamination might occur, and suggest an improved procedure to avoid it.*
   a. *A psychologist administers aptitude tests to entering college freshmen and from the results predicts each student's success. Success is determined after two years by noting which students have been dropped from school by the school guidance committee for unsatisfactory work. The predictions are kept in a locked file and not made available until the two years have passed. The psychologist is a member of the committee but does not disclose the predictions.*
   b. *Tests for selecting salesmen are being tried experimentally. Because they are thought to be valid, the results are given to the sales manager for his guidance in assigning territories to the salesmen in the experimental group. After a year of trial, each man is judged by the amount of his sales in relation to the normal amount for his territory.*
   c. *Flight instructor's ratings are used as a basis for promoting men from primary to advanced training. It is desired to check the validity of these ratings as predictors of success in advanced training. Advanced training is taken at the same field, with a different instructor. This man's judgment supplies the criterion.*
12. *List several independent criteria to consider in judging branch managers of an equipment firm. Branches are responsible for both sales and service.*
13. *McNemar (1952) makes the following comment about a study of success in clinical psychology: "It is sheer nonsense to have proceeded with an extensive testing and assessment prediction program without first having devised satisfactory measures of that which was to be predicted." Yet this study was conducted by well-qualified and experienced persons and supported by a large appropriation from equally responsible psychologists in the Veterans Administration. What arguments can be given on each side of this controversy?*

14. *In industry, does one wish to predict an employee's maximum performance (proficiency) or his typical behavior? Give illustrations to show that criteria of both types are in use.*

Development of an Aptitude Test
for Computer Programmers

A realistic idea of test development can be given by a brief account of the evolution of the Computer Programmer Aptitude Battery (SRA, 1967; the author is indebted to Jean Maier Palermo for unpublished information). The validation research did not conform to all the recommendations we have made and will make later in this chapter; under practical conditions one must make compromises, and in that respect this study is quite typical.

Some persons have great difficulty in learning to write computer programs, which makes it important to select good prospects for basic training and advanced assignments. Ability to learn routine programming is not enough. One wants programmers who can cope with novel problems and can write programs that use expensive computer time efficiently. The original impetus for the CPAB was the desire of certain firms making computers to help their customers establish efficient installations; a bad programmer can make the best system look bad. Two tests were ultimately prepared: one supplied through private channels to customers of a single company, and one more generally distributed.

The first step was a job analysis that relied in part on earlier studies of abilities correlated with success in programming. This led to a fairly long list of possibly relevant abilities. Since it was not practical to try out all the kinds of test suggested, the list was reduced to seven kinds of task. For each task, a large set of trial items was prepared.

Active experimentation began with the following:

● Verbal meaning. This was tested by fairly difficult synonyms items. The following sample item indicates the lowest level of difficulty in the test:[1]

RECIPIENT   donor   owner   performer   receiver   borrower

Words used were taken from material advanced programmers have to read, in fields such as business management and systems engineering. While the programmer's job is not particularly verbal, it was noted by the test developers that he does have to communicate with specialists in these related fields.

● Letter Series. This is an analytic task, with items as difficult as this:

s c a g s c d j _____   g s c e p

This test is speeded.

● Number series. Another reasoning task.

[1] This item copyright © 1964, Science Research Associates, Inc. Reprinted by permission of the publisher.

● Number ability. This is a straightforward test on computation, except that a good many of the items ask the person to select the answer that is approximately correct, so that judging of order of magnitude rather than precise arithmetic is stressed. The test is speeded in order to encourage subjects to make estimates.

● Reasoning. A quantitative reasoning test emphasizing use of symbols. Items are generally harder than this specimen:[2]

> An office manager ordered a conference table which cost S dollars, a dozen chairs which cost P dollars each, and three book shelves which cost Y dollars apiece. The total cost of the order in dollars is

$$S + P + Y$$
$$SP + 3Y$$
$$S + 12P + 3Y$$
$$S + \frac{(P + Y)}{4}$$
$$S + P + 3Y$$

● Ingenuity. A version of the Ingenuity section of a battery prepared by Flanagan. A specimen item is the following:

As part of a manufacturing process, the inside lip of a deep, cup-shaped casting is machine threaded. The company found that metal chips produced by the threading operation were difficult to remove from the bottom of the casting without scratching the sides. A design engineer was able to solve his problem by having the operation performed

i _____	p	h _____ h
m _____	n	c _____ e
f _____	r	w _____ l
i _____	d	b _____ k
u _____	e	d _____ n

The subject can only answer correctly by imagining the solution and then locating the letters that identify the descriptive phrase. Most items describe problems involving concrete objects and machines.

● Diagramming. The programmer must analyze a complex process into a sequence of decisions or operations. To test the ability to think systematically about such details, the test items employ flow diagrams similar to Figure 13.3. (Actual test items are more complex.) The subject must decide what order or question to insert in the numbered cells. Cell 1, for example, requires the question: Is it in the range 3.5 to 4.4 ounces? An introductory problem is used to acquaint the subject with the code employed (e.g., Y implies a "Yes" answer), so that persons who have not used this scheme before will have little disadvantage.

In this account we shall intermingle data from the two forms of the test. A number of validation studies were carried out, almost invariably examining a

[2] This item and the specimen ingenuity item copyright © 1957 by John C. Flanagan. Reprinted by permission of the publisher, Science Research Associates, Inc.

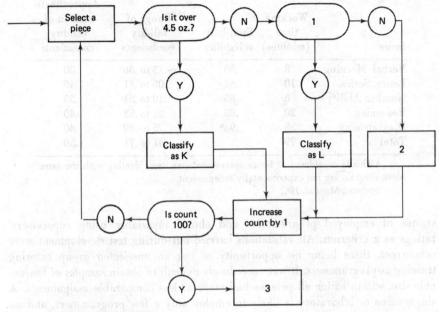

Problem and conditions

A. A company inspects and classifies its products in lots of 100.

B. It is necessary to classify the individual pieces within each lot of 100 into three classes by weight:

Class K—4.5 oz. or over
Class L—3.5 to 4.4 oz.
Class M—less than 3.5 oz.

Cell 1.
A. Is it less than 3.5 oz.?
B. Select a piece.
C. Is it 3.5 to 4.4 oz.?
D. Classify as M.
E. Classify as L.

Cell 2.
A. Classify as K.
B. Classification of lot complete.
C. Select a piece.
D. Classify as M.
E. Classify as L.

Cell 3.
A. Select a piece.
B. Classification of lot complete.
C. Classify lot as K.
D. Classify lot as L.
E. Classify lot as M.

Figure 13.3. Diagramming item to test aptitude for computer programming.
A specimen item from the Computer Programmer Aptitude Battery. © 1964 by Science Research Associates, Inc. Reprinted by permission of the publisher.

Table 13.1.   Validity coefficients for Computer Programmer Aptitude
Battery for small samples

Score	Working time (minutes)	Split-half reliability	Range of validity coefficients	Approximate median of validity coefficients
Verbal Meaning	8	.86	−.13 to .36	.30
Letter Series	10	.67	.08 to .61	.40
Number Ability	6	.85	.10 to .61	.30
Reasoning	20	.88	.21 to .52	.40
Diagramming	35	.94[a]	.25 to .69	.40
Total	79		.31 to .71	.50

[a] This is considered to be an overestimate, as items dealing with the same
block diagram are not experimentally independent.
SOURCE: Manual, 1967.

sample of employed programmers and almost invariably using supervisors'
ratings as a criterion. All validations carried out during test development were
concurrent, there being no opportunity to test an unselected group entering
training as programmers. It was exceedingly difficult to obtain samples of reasonable size, within which all persons had more or less comparable assignments. A
single office or laboratory is likely to employ only a few programmers, and no
one supervisor knows very many of them.

In one key study the set of seven tests was given to 186 programmers working at different installations within the same corporation. This provided fine
data for studying test intercorrelations and split-half reliabilities. But to get a
good criterion it was desired that each subject be known to at least four supervisors. This requirement reduced the number of cases to 46. Two decisions were
made at this early stage. The Ingenuity subtest correlated zero with the criterion
(confirmed in other samples); it was dropped. In retrospect, it seems that the
concrete problems of that test do not resemble the tasks of the programmer.
Number Series showed some validity, but it correlated substantially with other
subtests. Therefore it could add little and was dropped. Four of the remaining
tests looked promising by both standards: validity and independence. Verbal
Meaning did not correlate with the criterion in the 46-case sample, but this was
thought to reflect the use of a highly select, well-educated group. These five subtests, then, went into the experimental forms of the test and eventually into the
published test.

Table 13.1 gives some impression of the validity data reported in the test
manual. Subtest intercorrelations add further insight. They imply that the principal factor running through the test is the ability measured by Reasoning and
Number Ability. The Diagramming test, which to some extent simulates the programmer's work, is a specialized ability. As this appears to be a good subtest, one
might wish to use more problems of this type in a future edition of the test.

From the data one concludes that the test seems to be worthwhile, but there is no way to form a clear impression as to the validity the test would have in actual use. The manual fails to report the test means and standard deviations, or the level of education, in the validity samples, so that one cannot judge how much preselection had taken place or how these samples might compare with an applicant population. Did computer training increase the test scores of the subjects? One cannot be sure. Some of the criteria are seriously faulty. In one group of slightly over 40 subjects, the test correlated 0.03 with a supervisor's rating, but correlated 0.46 with grades assigned during an advanced training course. One is inclined to discard the rating criterion, especially when one learns that older workers received higher ratings (r of age with rating is 0.65) and lower test scores ($r = -0.31$). Because this study used employed programmers, the older workers were highly experienced and were taking more responsibility; this did not mean that they were superior as programmers.

The test manual properly urges a continued program of validation, including validation by each prospective user in his own situation. There will ultimately be a revised manual making use of data now being accumulated by users. One reported study (Perry, 1967) provides data considerably better than those available during the test development, and brings additional interesting facts to our attention. System Development Corporation trains a large number of programmers. Of trainees who passed the screening procedures normally in use, 114 were measured on 19 variables, including the Number Ability, Reasoning, and Diagramming scores of CPAB; Verbal Meaning and Letter Series were covered by somewhat similar PMA tests included in the previous selection program. Course marks in programming were used as a criterion. Correlations were corrected statistically to obtain validities for the unrestricted applicant population (see p. 431). Age, education, and college grades had essentially no predictive value. There were coefficients in the range 0.50–0.70 for CPAB Reasoning and Diagramming and PMA Reasoning. CPAB Number, PMA Verbal, and several other verbal and reasoning tests (including Matrix) correlated about 0.40 with the criterion. To check on a proposed selection plan using PMA Verbal and Reasoning plus CPAB Reasoning and Diagramming, a cross-validation study (see p. 433) was run on another 88 cases the next year. Perry concluded that the battery has a validity of about 0.67 for an applicant population, and a validity of 0.56 even within a group that has been screened. It appears that CPAB itself would have worked as well as the CPAB-PMA combination.

Drawing Conclusions from Selection Tests

Strategy of Decision Making

The test scores, once obtained, are translated into decisions according to some plan. The plan describes how scores from various tests are to be combined,

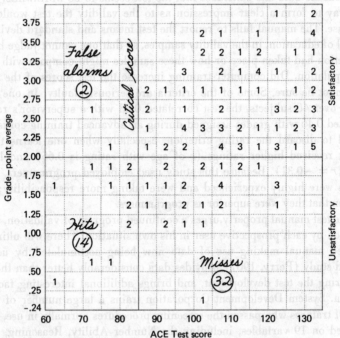

Figure 13.4. Scatter diagram for the ACE test as a predictor of engineering grades.
Sessions, 1955.

how they are to be combined with nontest information, and what decision will be made for any given combination of facts.

For the moment, we consider only decisions based on a single test score. When the number of vacancies to be filled is fixed, the obvious strategy is to rank individuals and fill vacancies from the top of the list. If there is no limit on the number of persons to be selected, one sets a "cutting score" and rejects all persons below this score.

The cutting score is determined from the scatter diagram or expectancy table. The validation data indicate what degree of success is to be expected from persons at each score level. The decision maker decides what level of risk he is willing to accept and fixes the critical score accordingly. The expectancy table in Figure 13.4 shows how engineering marks at the University of Idaho in a certain year corresponded to aptitude scores. A grade average below 2.0 is regarded as unsatisfactory. The investigator, after examining the successive columns of the table, set 85 as his critical score. In later classes, any applicant scoring below 85 was discouraged from entering the School of Engineering.

A follow-up study divides the predicted failures into "hits" (actual failures) and "false alarms." Among those who are cleared by the test, the persons who

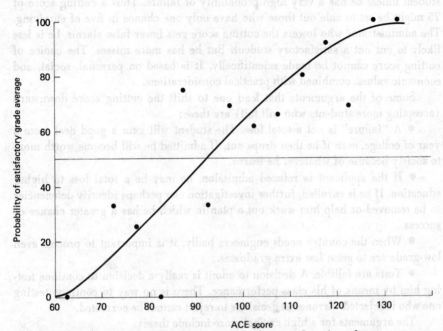

Figure 13.5. **Probability of success in engineering as a function of test score.**

should have been identified as failures are called "misses." Finally, there are those who succeeded as predicted, ordinarily much the largest fraction of the sample. Among the 147 cases in the engineering study, there were 16 predicted failures. Of the 16, 14 were hits and 2 were false alarms. 32 misses slipped past the test into the engineering school.

It is generally unwise to set a cutting score directly from the raw data. In the engineering scatter diagram, there seems to be a marked difference between persons scoring 85–89 and those scoring 80–84. Three-fourths of one group pass, whereas none of the others pass. This abrupt decline is almost certainly an accident of sampling. With more cases, there would be more misses in the 85–89 column and some false alarms in the 80–84 column. Figure 13.5 estimates what will happen in a large population. The dots in that figure show the proportion of failure in each five-point interval. The line fitted to the points estimates the trend in the population of which these 131 cases are a sample, i.e., of the trend to be expected in other samples. Estimating from this line, the failure rate at 85 (the cutting score originally proposed) is about 62 per cent.

Setting a cutting score requires a value judgment. If we set a cutting score of 85, it means we wish to reject persons who have less than a 62-per cent chance of passing. One college administration might decide that it cannot afford to admit applicants with less than a 70-per cent chance for survival; if so, the cutting score will be 105. Another administration might leave the choice to the

424 0 Essentials of Psychological Testing

student unless he has a very high probability of failure. Thus a cutting score of 75 might be set to rule out those who have only one chance in five of surviving. The administrator who lowers the cutting score gets fewer false alarms, he is less likely to cut out a satisfactory student. But he has more misses. The choice of cutting score cannot be made scientifically. It is based on personal, social, and economic values, combined with practical considerations.

Some of the arguments that lead one to shift the cutting score downward (accepting more students who will fail) are these:

● A "failure" is not a total loss. The student will gain a good deal from a year of college, even if he then drops out. If admitted he will become worth more to society because of whatever he learns.

● If the applicant is refused admission, he may be a total loss to higher education. If he is enrolled, further investigation can perhaps identify deficiencies to be removed or help him work out a plan in which he has a greater chance of success.

● When the country needs engineers badly, it is important to process even low-grade ore to get a few extra graduates.

● Tests are fallible. A decision to admit is really a decision to continue testing him by means of his class performance. There is no way to continue testing one who is rejected. Erroneous decisions to reject cannot be corrected.

The arguments for a high critical score include these:

● Accepting someone who is unlikely to succeed wastes educational resources. He takes staff time that might better be spent on more promising students. His presence in the group lowers the level of discussion and thus robs the better students.

● The young man who is going to fail is better off facing the fact at once, rather than after he has wasted a year. He can use the year to get started in a more suitable trade or course of study.

Expectancies and critical scores change as institutions change. One striking example of such change is the report of grades of students entering medical school summarized in Table 13.2. The 1955 admissions were strikingly poorer than those in 1950. The schools evidently were able to hold to the same entry score, but they attracted far fewer "A" applicants. For the college counselor and his client considering medical school in the mid-1950s, the change was of great importance. An undergraduate with a B+ average would have been only an average medical student in 1950, but in 1955 he would have been near the 75th percentile of his class. (Recent data are not available.)

15. *The following is taken from a letter to the* New York Times:

"I submit that 'slaughter on the highway' will continue until state licensing authorities recognize some simple facts: To drive a car on today's highways demands a rather complex set of sensori-motor skills. These skills are 'normally' distributed; i.e., some folks have them, some do not. Instruments are available

Table 13.2.   Caliber of first-year medical students in successive years

	Percentage having an undergraduate grade average of		
	A	B	C
1950–1951	40	43	17
1951–1952	30	55	15
1952–1953	18	68	14
1953–1954	21	69	10
1954–1955	17	69	14
1955–1956	16	71	14

SOURCE: Anon., 1956.

to measure these skills. Authorities have some remote responsibility here to see that such instruments are used before licensing."

a. *What degree of validity should be required before tests are used as proposed?*
b. *If scores are normally distributed, how should the cutoff score be fixed?*

16. *In Figures 13.4 and 13.5, what cutting score would be used to eliminate students with one chance in three of failing?*

17. *What assumptions are made if the cutting score of 85 on the ACE, proposed for the University of Idaho, is applied in other engineering schools?*

18. *A screening test is applied to school children to identify those in poor mental health so that they can be given intensive study by the school psychologist. What factors argue for a high cutting score? What factors argue for a low cutting score?*

19. *A large office has about ten vacancies a month for clerk-typists. It places accepted applicants on a waiting list, and when a vacancy occurs offers the job to applicants in order of their application. Is the personnel department free to set a cutting score which insures that 95 per cent of the girls hired will be successful?*

20. *Which is to be preferred, false alarms or misses, in each of these situations?*

a. *Patients entering a hospital are given a reasoning test that gives a rough indication of organic brain damage. Suspect cases are given a thorough neurological examination.*
b. *Candidates for admission to teacher training are screened for ability.*
c. *It is important to hire skilled sheet-metal workers to fill vacancies, during a time of tight labor supply. Men cannot be trained on the job.*
d. *In inducting soldiers, a mental test is used to determine which men are too dull to be useful to the service.*
e. *A company wishes to hire mechanics and put them through an expensive training program; success cannot be observed until the end of the course.*

Combining Predictor Data

From the tryout results one must decide which tests to use and how to combine them. If only one test is to be used in selection, that with the highest validity

Table 13.3.   Effect on multiple correlation of adding tests to a battery

Tests	Correlation with criterion (shop performance of junior-high-school boys)	Multiple correlation of criterion with first test, first two tests, first three tests, etc.
Paper Form Board	.43	.43
Stenquist Assembly	.26	.44
Steadiness	.29	.53
Card Sorting	.27	.563
Tapping	.18	.580
Spatial Relations Formboard	.36	.594
Packing Blocks	.28	.5953

SOURCE: Paterson *et al.*, 1930, p. 83.

is chosen. An exception to this rule occurs when the best test is expensive to apply and some cheaper test yields nearly as good a correlation. A second exception occurs when the tests tried out have quite unequal reliabilities. If a reliable test has the best validity, and the runnerup is notably unreliable, the best procedure may be to lengthen the latter test to increase its validity (cf. p. 172). Prediction is ordinarily improved by combining several tests that cover different relevant aptitudes.

It is customary to employ multiple-correlation techniques to select and weight tests. Formulas for computing the multiple correlation R are given in most statistics texts.

To obtain a high multiple correlation one searches for tests that have a positive correlation with the criterion and low correlations with each other. Combining tests of the same sort usually improves prediction only slightly. A second test that measures a component of the job not covered by the first test will improve the multiple correlation appreciably. The example in Table 13.3 shows how prediction improves when we combine several tests with low validity. It also shows that the multiple correlation reaches a ceiling very rapidly; adding tests beyond the first three or four rarely is valuable.

Little is gained from extending a battery by adding tests that duplicate abilities already well measured, as seen in the following correlations of predictors with elimination from flight training (DuBois, 1947, p. 194):

Pilot stanine (i.e., composite score on selection battery)   0.653
Stanine plus Qualifying examination   0.655
Stanine plus Qualifying plus General Classification Test   0.655

Elaborate prediction batteries are worthwhile when each added test measures a new factor, when combining weights are based on a large sample, and when the conditions of work are standardized and unlikely to change.

The multiple-correlation procedure starts with the test validities and test intercorrelations. Customarily, one selects the test having the highest validity as the first member of the composite predictor. Then the intercorrelations are examined systematically to determine which test predicts the criterion and at the same time least duplicates the test already chosen. The third test, in turn, will be one that overlaps little with the first two. Out of the computations come a set of *regression weights*. Weights are heavy for the tests first selected for the battery and smaller for the others. A cutting score for the weighted composite is established in the same manner as for a single test.

Table 13.4 shows how tests were weighted to predict graduation from pilot, bombardier, and navigator training during World War II. A different combining formula was required for each job. In selecting bombardiers, Discrimination Reaction Time and Finger Dexterity counted heavily, whereas Reading and Arithmetic had very little weight. The navigator composite, on the other hand, depended primarily on these intellectual abilities. The jobs have been redefined as new planes and tactics altered crew duties; weights have changed accordingly.

Combining tests works best when the battery contains independent tests measuring quite different factors. One of the major claims of factor analysis is that "pure" tests can be put together in whatever proportion a given criterion demands, whereas an impure test puts both wanted and unwanted factors into the composite. While GATB comes close to this ideal, nonoverlapping tests have not been easy to devise.

One cannot assume that the regression weights constitute an explanation of criterion performance. Which variables happen to pick up weights is complexly determined. Several examples can be found in a study of prediction of high-school marks from GATB (Ingersoll & Peters, 1966). Marks in English are predicted ($R = 0.633$) by a combination of V, N, Q (clerical perception) and K (mark making). Since the sample consists of 1673 cases, crossvalidation would surely give the same result. But why no weight for G? Is it irrelevant? In the original r's, G correlated 0.55 with the criterion while V and N correlated 0.54 and 0.54. There is no weight for G in the formula because the formula covers the G information when it uses V and N as a pair. Although K correlates only 0.27, it gets into the formula; P, with an r of 0.31, does not. Does this mean that English requires speedy mark making? Surely not. If a rationalization must be sought, it probably has to do with willingness to perform an uninteresting task. Whatever relevant attribute P measures is covered in other scores, so it gets no weight. The predictor for Latin gives weights to G, Q, and N, and not to the "obviously relevant" V. But very likely counselors keep low-V students out of Latin classes, which restricts the range on that variable so much that N is left as a slightly better predictor.

In academic prediction, previous school marks play an important part, since they invariably correlate well with success at the next level of education. It is well known, however, that A's are easier to earn in some schools than others, and

Table 13.4.   Validity data and combining weights used in an Air Force classification program

Test	Correlation with criterion Bomb.	Nav.	Pilot	Relative weight Bomb.	Nav.	Pilot
Printed tests:						
Reading Comprehension	.12	.32	.19	8	2	—
Spatial Orientation II	.09	.33	.25	—	10	5
Spatial Orientation I	.12	.38	.20	—	9	6
Dial and Table Reading	.19	.53	.19	14	18	4
Biographical Data—pilot	—	—	.32	—	—	15
Biographical Data—navigator	—	.23	−.03	—	9	—
Mechanical Principles	.08	.13	.32	—	—	8
Technical Vocabulary—pilot	.04	.10	.30	—	—	13
Technical Vocabulary—nav.	.04	.22	.09	—	—	—
Mathematics	.10	.50	.08	—	18	—
Arithmetic Reasoning	.12	.45	.09	8	12	—
Instrument Comprehension I	—	—	.15 ⎫	—	—	9
Instrument Comprehension II	—	—	.35 ⎭			
Numerical Operations, front	.13	.26	.01			
Numerical Operations, back	.11	.28	.02			
Speed of Identification	.09	.19	.18			
Apparatus tests:						
Rotary Pursuit	.14	.10	.21	12	—	4
Complex Coordination	.18	.24	.38	12	—	17
Finger Dexterity	.16	.20	.11	19	6	—
Discrimination Reaction Time	.22	.36	.22	27	6	4
Two-Hand Coordination	.12	.26	.30	—	11	4
Rudder Control	—	—	.42	—	—	12

Note: The criterion for the various validity coefficients is graduation or nongraduation from training.

SOURCE: DuBois, 1947, pp. 99, 101.

the person who ranks at the median in a select school is much better than the median student in most schools. With these facts in mind, various correction procedures have been proposed. The most satisfactory procedure would be to follow graduates of each school, to determine just how much the usual formula underpredicts or overpredicts their success, and then to apply a correction. Linn (1966), reviewing all these proposals and the data arising from trials of such procedures, concluded that validity is improved very little by such corrections, particularly where standardized tests can be combined with the marks to make the prediction. Only under unusual circumstances can beneficial corrections be made.

21. *The manual for a multiscore battery offers weights for estimating relative score on CTMM, a general mental test. Interpret this equation:*
    Estimated CTMM standing $= 7.5\,V + 0.3\,S + 0.9\,N + 1.3\,R$
22. *Why are different weights assigned the first two tests in Table 13.4 for navigator prediction, when their validity coefficients are similar?*
23. *Which of the three aircrew jobs has the smallest psychomotor component, according to the prediction weights?*

Interpreting Selection Studies

What Is an Acceptable Validity Coefficient?

As validity coefficients for various tests have been presented in past chapters, the reader probably has been classifying them mentally as "good" or "poor." Many tests, particularly those of special abilities, do not seem very satisfactory at first glance. But the fundamental question is, Does the test permit a better judgment than one could make without it—sufficiently better to justify its cost?

Coefficients as low as 0.30 are of definite practical value (see Table 13.4). In discussing this point, E. K. Strong (1943, p. 55) commented that the test critic who is contemptuous of low positive correlations is quite willing to accept information of no greater dependability when he plays golf or employs a physician. The correlation of golf scores between the first and second 18 holes in championship play is, he said, about 0.30, and the reliability of medical diagnosis is near 0.40. The personnel psychologist can evaluate a selection program by comparing selected and unselected men with respect to number of failures in training, average length of training required, rate of turnover, average production, and so on. Such analyses show that tests with validities in the range from 0.30 to 0.50 make a considerable contribution to the efficiency of the institution, though they forecast wrongly for many individuals. The cost savings from testing may at times be startlingly large. Dunnette (1967, pp. 175 ff.) shows how a simple personality questionnaire could save four million dollars every month in military screening, and how an instrument for selecting office workers could save about $125 per productive employee.

The best single rule of thumb for interpreting validity coefficients in selection is Brogden's (1949). Making certain reasonable assumptions, he showed that the benefit from a selection program increases *in proportion to the validity coefficient*. Suppose 40 applicants out of 100 are hired. We can consider the average production of randomly selected men as a baseline. An ideal test would pick the 40 men who later earn the highest criterion scores; the average production of these men is the maximum that any selection plan could yield. A test with validity 0.50 will select men whose production averages halfway between the base level and the ideal. To be concrete, suppose the average, randomly selected

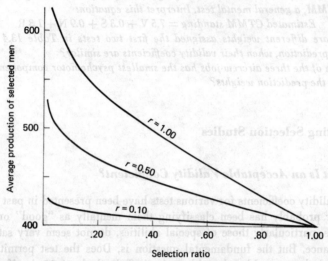

Figure 13.6.   Benefit from a selection program as a function of validity and selection ratio, under Brogden's assumptions.

worker assembles 400 gadgets per day, and the perfectly selected group of workers turns out 600, on the average. Then a test with validity 0.50 will choose a group whose average production is 500 gadgets, and a test of validity 0.20 will select workers with an average production of 440 gadgets. The assumptions underlying Brogden's rule are these:

The job to be performed remains the same, whether men of high or low ability are selected.

Production (or other measure of benefit) has a linear relation to test score.

The benefit derived from a selection plan depends on the selection ratio, as well as on the validity of the test. The *selection ratio* is the proportion of persons tested who are accepted. If there is a large labor supply, the selection ratio can be very low, but when applicants are scarce the selection ratio is forced up toward 1.00. Even an ideal test does not raise the quality of workers when every applicant must be hired. If the employer can pick and choose, average output can be much improved. Figure 13.6 shows the relation of production to selection ratio for the gadget assemblers of our illustration. It is assumed that among unselected workers the average production is 400 gadgets, and the standard deviation is 100. Tests of low validity have considerable value when the selection ratio can be very low, when individual differences in job performance are large, and when small increases in production have a large dollar value.

In evaluating validity of a selection test one must ask the following questions.[3]

_____

[3] The questions are so worded that an answer of "no" indicates that tests of relatively low validity are likely to be helpful.

Are individual differences in job performance or other outcomes fairly small?

Can we afford to discharge or transfer to other duties men who prove to be unsuccessful? That is, can we tolerate "misses"?

Is it important to hire every applicant who will be satisfactory, even though this also involves hiring many men who will fail? That is, must we avoid "false alarms"?

Does this test measure an ability that is already fairly well measured by other tests or procedures already in use?

Is it possible to modify the job so that it makes less demand on the aptitude tested?

Is the validity coefficient much lower than the coefficient of generalizability of the test? (If not, taking a larger sample of test behavior should raise validity.)

Is administration of the test difficult and costly?

Restriction of range. Tests predict individual differences poorly, within a homogeneous group. Validity coefficients are largest in a group with a wide range of ability, and tend to be small in a restricted, preselected group. A shorthand aptitude test is likely to be tried on girls already planning to take the course. Girls of low aptitude would be excluded, since normally those entering a shorthand course have successfully completed some work in typing. If the test were tried on an entirely unscreened group, a higher coefficient would result. (D. A. Peterson & Wallace, 1966.)

How screening reduces the coefficient is illustrated by the Air Force study referred to earlier. The validity coefficient of the battery for pilot selection was in the neighborhood of 0.37 for men who met standards for flight training. When, for experimental purposes, a completely unscreened group was sent into pilot training, the failure rate was very great, and in this unrestricted group the validity coefficient rose to 0.66 (DuBois, 1947, pp. 103, 193).

Investigators are frequently perplexed when a variable listed in the job analysis fails to predict the criterion of success. The job analysis may have been correct in listing the ability as essential to the job, yet preselection may have reduced its significance as a predictor. If future applicants are preselected on this ability (e.g., by having survived in related training), this variable will not help in prediction. If applicants are less select than the validation sample, this variable may turn out to be a good predictor. For example, intelligence tests have consistently been poor predictors of success in teaching. The explanation is obvious: Nearly every teacher has survived years of schooling with adequate grades, which ensures a fair to superior degree of academic ability (Figure 13.7). Among those so selected, differences in tested intelligence play little part in determining teaching success. Granted that a scholastic-aptitude test will not help a school system hire teachers, such a test is still a major factor in advising a girl in high school whether she is likely to be able to complete a teacher-training course.

Failure to recognize a range effect sometimes leads to discarding useful tests.

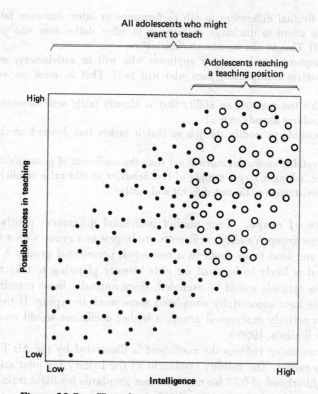

Figure 13.7.   Hypothetical data illustrating the effect of preselection upon correlation.
Data show scores to be expected if every ninth-grader interested in teaching later enters the profession. Circles show scores of persons likely to survive gradual elimination as a consequence of low school marks.

In 1930, F. Moss developed a test for selecting medical students that, in tryout studies, had good correlations with grades. When schools selected students on the basis of the test scores, the predictive coefficients calculated for students accepted into medical school were quite low. Ultimately, in 1946, the Moss committee was discharged and the test was abandoned. Then, when the test was no longer used to select students so that student scores again covered the full range, research studies began to find high coefficients again!

Random error in the criterion.   Criterion measures are often inaccurate, especially when they are based on judgment or brief observation. Any sampling error (e.g., drawing a lenient rater for some men) will lower the validity coefficient. If the extent of such errors can be determined by a suitable study of generalizability of the criterion, a correction formula can be applied to determine how well the tests would predict an accurate criterion score. This will often indicate that faulty prediction is not due to inadequacy of the test battery.

24. *In one study, the predictive validity of pencil-and-paper tests for selecting pilots was 0.64 against an elimination-graduation criterion. The coefficient rose to 0.69 when apparatus tests were added. Is such a small increase worthwhile?*

25. *State employment offices use tests to guide workers into appropriate positions. A very low selection ratio may be used, since a particular unemployed worker may be directed into any one of hundreds of job families. In a particular insurance agency, on the other hand, it is necessary to employ about 60 per cent of those who apply for clerical jobs. Are the same tests equally suitable in both situations?*

26. *In which of these situations is there likely to be a fixed number of vacancies, and in which can the decision maker set the critical score as high or low as he likes?*
   a. *A parole board decides which prisoners may be released.*
   b. *An engineering school admits well-qualified applicants.*
   c. *A school psychologist identifies mentally handicapped children to be placed under a special teacher.*
   d. *A college counseling bureau identifies clients likely to profit from psychotherapy.*

27. *If one were considering the probable success in industrial jobs of graduates from an engineering school, what characteristics would have a restricted range owing to preselection? What characteristics would probably not have been restricted?*

Necessity for Confirmation of Findings

When an investigator has once obtained a satisfactory validity coefficient, he tends to install his program and stop research. Other workers, reading his report of the study, may accept his test as valid and put it to work in their own situations. This practice is unsound.

Correlations fluctuate from sample to sample. Consequently the test best in one sample may not be the best predictor in a similar sample. Even when the sample is sizeable, the particular critical score or the weights that give the very largest multiple correlation are certain not to be best in a second group. The weights or the critical scores are determined so as to get the best possible prediction in the sample studied. To estimate properly the validity of such a formula one must crossvalidate by trying it on a sample *not used* in selecting tests and establishing scoring weights. In this *crossvalidation* sample, the formula is expected to have lower validity than in the sample to which weights were fitted. We speak of this as "shrinkage" of validity. Shrinkage is relatively small when the predictors are chosen initially on the basis of substantial past experience and theory, and relatively large in a "shotgun" study where miscellaneous predictors are tried with no particular rationale or when the tryout sample is small. A sample of 100 cases justifies weighting at most three predictors; with 250 cases, one can perhaps weight four predictors without undue shrinkage (Burket, 1964; Goldberg & Hase, in press).

Although the investigator is using sound mathematics when he calculates regression weights, the weights so established are often not truly "best." A simpler weighting system—perhaps simply assigning equal weight to all relevant tests— often works just as well in the next sample (e.g., Trattner, 1963; see also Madden & Bottenberg, 1963). The investigator should be particulary skeptical of weights that make little psychological sense, since they are likely to have come from sampling errors.

A crossvalidation is a second study under essentially the same conditions, carried out in the same factory or school as the original study. But the supply of men and the conditions of training change from time to time, which may change the relevance of the predictors. Also, questions arise about the selection of employees in other plants or for "similar" jobs. These are questions about *validity generalization*. Even when a procedure continues to be used in the same plant, periodic checks on validity should be made to verify weights and cutting scores. In a fresh situation, a complete validation study is called for. Unless there have been so many reports of consistent results in different companies that a firm generalization can be made, one would want to complete such a study before installing the selection program. Even if one has enough confidence to start using some selection rule, follow-up studies are a necessary precaution.

Unconventional Handling of Selection Data

Our discussion to this point has concentrated on the classical procedure in selection studies, in which there is a single accepted criterion and the cutting score is established for one predictor or a linear composite of predictor scores. Sometimes the decision is based on the patterning of predictor scores instead. Sometimes predictions are made for several aspects of criterion performance, each prediction resting on different tests or composites.

Nonlinear Treatment of Predictors

Whether prediction is made from a single test or a score derived by combining several tests, the most common formula assumes a straight regression line such as was introduced in Figure 5.3. This is a linear function. In a linear interpretation we assume that the expected increase in grade average when SAT goes from 500 to 600 equals the further increase in going from 600 to 700. A nonlinear assumption would allow for the possibility that the second increase is larger or smaller than the first. The linear-nonlinear distinction also applies to combining formulas. If one simply adds up predictor scores, with or without

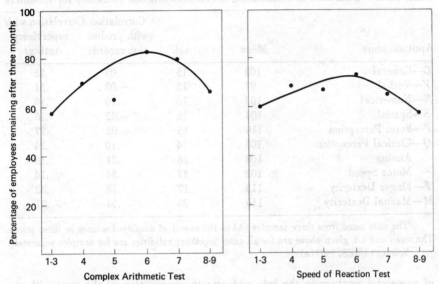

Figure 13.8.   Curvilinear relations between predictors and turnover of taxi drivers.
C. Brown & Ghiselli, 1953.

weights, then the composite is linear. But a complex rule—e.g., add a point to the composite score for every SAT point up to 600, and half a point thereafter—is nonlinear.

Multiple cutting scores.   The conventional approach assumes that the higher the predictor score the better. Yet sometimes an intermediate degree of a trait is optimal. This is most likely to be true for a personality trait—e.g., perhaps the best supervisor has an intermediate degree of criticalness. One might think that superior ability is always to be preferred, but that is not true where turnover is costly. In some jobs, men of very low ability and very high ability are most likely to quit, as seen in a study of taxi drivers (Figure 13.8). Seven out of ten tests of discrimination, motor speed, and reasoning showed this curvilinearity. It is reasonable to suppose that the poorest men drop out because of difficulty on the job, while the best men move to more satisfying or better-paid work. When one has data such as these, the selection strategy might be to use two cutting scores, rejecting both very low and very high men. Rejecting men who are "overqualified for the job" is hard to defend as a fair employment practice, however.

When there are several predictor scores, each thought to be relevant, a common practice is to establish a cutting score for each predictor, accepting only men who pass all the hurdles. The USES rules for applying GATB are of this type. Occupational standards are established by considering the average score

Table 13.5.   Data used in establishing GATB occupational standards for mounters

Aptitude score	Mean	s.d.	Correlation with production records	Correlation with supervisory ratings
G—General	102	15	.03	.26
V—Verbal	97	13	−.02	.31
N—Numerical	103	16	.10	.19
S—Spatial	104	16	−.02	.16
P—Form Perception	110	16	−.02	.27
Q—Clerical Perception	105	14	.10	.24
Aiming	108	16	.21	.18
Motor Speed	102	17	.34	.14
F—Finger Dexterity	113	17	.18	.32
M—Manual Dexterity	110	20	.54	.21

The data come from three samples (43 to 100 cases) of employed women in three states. The mean and s.d. given above are for all cases together; validities are for samples separately. SOURCE: USES, 1967(a).

of successful workers in the job, and also the correlation of the tests with the criterion and with each other. An example is the standard for the job of "mounter." A mounter assembles bases for radio tubes and connects very small parts and wires, spot-welding them in place. The passing standard for this occupation is Form Perception (P) 85, Motor Coordination (K) 85, Finger Dexterity (F) 85, and Manual Dexterity (M) 80. The cutting score eliminates perhaps a third of the women who would otherwise be employed.

Table 13.5 summarizes the data from which the standard was derived. Data were collected with an older form of the test which used Aiming and Motor Speed tests that have now been replaced by score K. The authors looked particularly at four factors. K, F, and M were thought to be relevant because of the small movements, with and without hand tools, that the job requires. The validity coefficients, though modest, supported this. The P score was also expected to be relevant because the job requires visual inspection and eye-guided movements, but the validity coefficient against the production criterion was negligible. Nonetheless, P was included in the standard, as the relatively high mean on this score implied that poor perceivers had already been removed from the employed group.

Mention may be made of the remarkable consistency of the results for two samples in which production records were used as a criterion, even though the data come from two different companies in different states. Supervisory ratings seemed to relate to a rather different set of tests than the production records; the shift in the coefficient for V is notable.

The most useful statement on the validity of the screening procedures comes from a later study that used a "longitudinal" or predictive design in which the tests were given before employment and criterion performance was measured

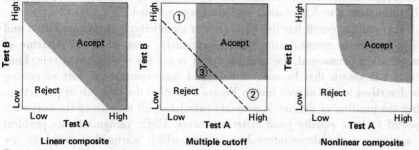

Figure 13.9.   Three selection rules.

after training. Workers were not selected on the basis of the tests, and 19 per cent of them failed to reach a satisfactory level of production. If those whose GATB scores were below the standard for mounter had been eliminated, there would have been only 10 per cent unsatisfactory on the job. What we do not know is how much better or worse the result would have been if the K, F, and M scores had simply been weighted into a linear composite, and a single cutoff score established. One suspects strongly that in this case the linear procedure would be at least as good, though perhaps the multiple cutoff is easier for interpreters in State employment offices to apply.

The multiple cutoff eliminates persons who are low on any test. In the composite score, a person who is very low on one test may make up for this by a very high score on another. Figure 13.9 compares these two plans. The essentials difference is that the weighted composite acts on the assumption of compensation among abilities. A person weak in dexterity may be accepted if he has exceptional perceptual ability; strength in the one is presumed to make up for weakness in the other. In most predictions this assumption is justified, but not in all.

At one time during World War II the Navy desired to train men to operate antisubmarine listening gear. By the usual correlation procedure, psychologists established a prediction formula: men were screened on general intelligence, and within the surviving group, predictions were based on the average of the Bennett MCT and several Seashore tonal tests. Following standard Navy procedure, acceptable men were sent to training school, and those who failed in school were assigned to general sea duty. It was therefore a serious matter when a man of good intelligence was sent to a school for which he was unqualified, since his ability would not be properly used. Many men who failed in sonar school did so because of very poor tonal judgment, which made them unfitted for listening duty, How had they happened to be sent to sound training? Their high mechanical comprehension (many had studied college physics) raised their composite enough to conceal their weakness. Such men, despite an adequate "average" ability, were doomed to fail in sound training whereas they would have been excellent in engineering, radar maintenance, or navigation. In fact, a few were salvaged by school officers and sent to other training, where they did well. Ultimately, a multiple-cutoff procedure was adopted.

The multiple cutoff has the advantage of simplicity, both in calculation and in explanation to nonprofessionals. Unfortunately, even when the doctrine of compensation is unsound, the multiple cutoff is not the most efficient rule. Lord (1962) has shown that because of errors of measurement the sort of cutting rule described by the curved line in Figure 13.9 does the best job of prediction. When the position of the line is properly calculated, all men along the curve are expected to have equally good criterion scores. USES recognizes this problem by applying a confidence-interval technique, which warns that decisions are risky for any case that falls into a region close to an occupational cutoff line on GATB.

We have discussed the cutoff rule as it can be developed in a specific institution. USES supplies its cutoff rules, however, for use in decisions all across the country. While no better plan can be suggested for a mass operation, the procedure has a serious fault that school counselors should be aware of. For men given the same job title, levels of acceptable performance vary from company to company and sometimes from department to department in the same factory. While validity data can show that abilities are relevant—if a job has been well-defined —one cannot set a universal cutoff rule any more than one can set a single IQ level as implying "ability to succeed in college."

Configural prediction. The conventional method of combining scores is simple weighted addition. This linear assumption does not always give the best prediction. A certain amount of manual dexterity may be required on an assembly line, but dexterity above the minimum makes little or no difference if the assembly line moves at a fixed speed. A worker who keeps ahead of the line produces no more than one who can just comfortably keep up. His superior dexterity does not compensate for weakness in some other ability.

We are always interested in drawing the cutoff line so that men at different points along the cutting line are equally acceptable. Three possible relationships between predictor score and expected criterion score are diagrammed in Figure 13.10. One would establish such relations by calculating the average criterion score for men with each combination of predictor scores, and then smoothing the result as we did in Figure 13.5. Panel (a) shows the compensatory situation for which the linear combination is ideal; the cutting line identifies persons with an expected criterion score of 11 or better. (Note that as X increases the rate of increase in criterion score is the same at all Y levels.) Panel (b) again shows a cutting rule that selects persons expected to reach 11 or better on the criterion, but the relation is nonlinear. When Y is high, the criterion score is strongly related to X. When Y is low, there is only a slow increase in the criterion with increases in X. Panel (c) shows a somewhat similar situation. The criterion is related to X when Y is large and not when Y is small. Patterns (b) and (c) are

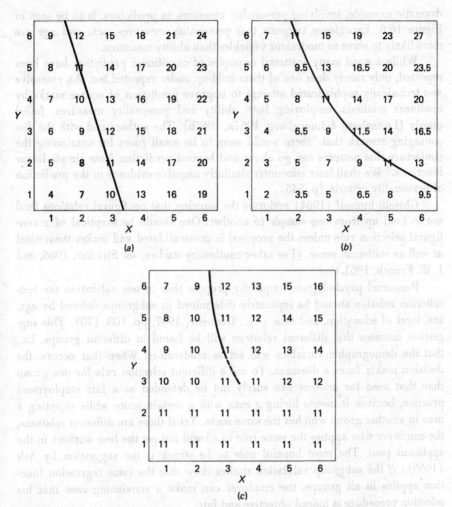

Figure 13.10.   Expected criterion score as a function of two predictors.

said to be configural, because the implications of an X score depend upon the level of the Y score. In such a case, one may speak of Y as a moderator variable, because it modifies the X-to-criterion relationship (or, equally, of X as moderating the Y-to-criterion relationship).

Ghiselli (1960) has referred to the situation in panel (c) as a case in which we can "predict predictability." That is, if Y is high we predict that X will be a valid predictor of the criterion score; but X cannot predict for the subjects whose Y is low.

The example of sonar selection indicated a configural relationship. Another dramatic example, involving personality measures as predictors, is to be seen in Figure 16.6. Experience suggests that personality measures, sex, and age are more likely to serve as moderator variables than ability measures.

While a good many scattered examples of curvilinear prediction have been reported, only rarely does one of them hold up under repeated test. An extensive and technically sophisticated attempt to improve prediction of course marks by nonlinear methods, employing both ability and personality measures, failed utterly (Lunneborg & Lunneborg, 1967a, 1967b). The authors end with the discouraging remark that "there would seem to be small room for continuing the conjecture that patterns can go above and beyond prediction from simple linear functions." We shall later encounter similarly negative evidence in the prediction of personality criteria (p. 545).

Ghiselli himself (1964) endorses the warning that configural relations tend not to hold up from one sample to another. One should be skeptical of a configural selection rule unless the proposal is crossvalidated and makes theoretical as well as statistical sense. (For other cautionary studies, see Stricker, 1966, and J. W. French, 1961.)

Personnel psychologists frequently propose that in test validation the test-criterion relation should be separately determined in subgroups defined by age, sex, level of education, and race (e.g., Dunnette, 1967, pp. 108, 170). This suggestion assumes that different relations will be found in different groups, i.e., that the demographic variables will act as moderators. When that occurs, the decision maker faces a dilemma. To use a different selection rule for one group than that used for another can surely not be defended as a fair employment practice, because it means hiring a man with a certain score while rejecting a man in another group who has the same score. Yet if there are different relations, the employer who applies the same rule to all will not get the best workers in the applicant pool. The most hopeful note to be struck is the suggestion by Ash (1966): *if* the subgroup validation studies show that the same regression function applies in all groups, the employer can make a convincing case that his selection procedure is indeed objective and fair.

28. *In a configural scoring formula, weights may be assigned to every variable and to every pair of variables. How many scores are weighted (or considered for possible weighting) when a configural method is applied to a set of ten subtests? What does this imply about the shrinkage of configural validities?*

29. *In a later crossvalidation in a new locality, production of mounters again showed significant correlations for K, F, and M; P again showed a zero correlation. In this sample the mean for P was 95. Apparently using P as part of the standard is not justified. Is any harm done by including it in the standard? Is there any benefit?*

30. *Consider the weights in Table 13.4. In view of the apparent psychological requirements of each job, which weights are open to suspicion?*

31. *If it is unfair to reject an applicant because his ability scores are very high, what legitimate use can be made of findings on turnover—such as those of Brown and Ghiselli?*

32. *Suppose it is found that for young persons just out of school, a measure of arithmetic and reading proficiency predicts success on a job, but that for older applicants a measure of learning ability is the best predictor. Can one defend as fair practice the rejection of a young worker whose scores on the tests are identical to those of an older worker, or vice versa?*

Sequential Strategies

In the multiple-cutoff or composite-score plan, all the tests are given at once and the decision is then made. For many decisions a more economical procedure is sequential, testing being divided into several stages. After each stage, a decision is made to reject some men, to accept others, and to continue testing those close to the borderline.

The decisions in the first stage of a sequential plan are based on a short and incomplete test, and the method makes somewhat more wrong decisions than a plan in which every man takes all tests. The plan reduces costs, however, because relatively few men take the second and later sets of tests. Especially when the later stages include expensive tests or interviews, the saving can be considerable, at the price of a very small reduction in the correctness of final decisions (Cronbach & Gleser, 1965, pp. 83 ff.).

An ingenious example of sequential testing under everyday circumstances is found in the Junior College Placement Program of SRA. There are three levels of mathematics test, for example. The student begins with three fairly hard high-school algebra problems. He responds by scraping an opaque patch opposite the answer he prefers; a right answer shows a Z, a wrong answer a V. If two or three V's show he is sent to the easy level of the test. Further questions sort out those who should go to the hardest part of the test, and those who should take the middle level. The student thus spends most of the testing period on items that truly test him. (See also p. 172.)

Nonstatistical Combinations of Scores

All the procedures discussed so far involve an experimental determination of the selection rule, and objective application of it. The psychologist with a clinical orientation often complains that such a mechanical method is insensitive to the unique characteristics of the particular case and cannot possibly be as wise as a psychologist.

It seems that a competent professional interpreter, bringing reason to bear on the data, should do no harm and might well improve decisions—but this expectation is contradicted by experience. In the Navy, for example, trained classification specialists interviewed each man, having at hand his test scores, a life history, and other data. The interviewers gave a final rating as to the man's probable success in the training to which he was assigned. A mechanical prediction formula combining two tests (Electrical Knowledge and Arithmetic Reasoning) correlated 0.50 with success in training of electrician's mates. The interviewer's rating based on these tests *plus judgment* correlated only 0.41 with success. In other words, where judgments departed from the statistical formula, they reduced the correctness of prediction (Conrad & Satter, 1945). P. E. Meehl (1954) made a major comparison of "clinical vs. statistical prediction" in which he examined every study in which predictions made by judges could be compared with predictions made from the same data by statistical formula. In some twenty studies in which such a comparison could be made, the actuarial, cookbook prediction was equal or superior to the judgmental prediction in every case save one. The statistical method (which is obviously cheaper to apply) beats the judge time after time, whether the judge be a counselor, a clinical psychologist, or an industrial personnel manager. Other data will appear in later chapters (pp. 236; 289 ff.).

Why does the judge do so poorly? The foremost reason is that he combines the data by means of an intuitive weighting he has not checked. The statistical formula, on the other hand, has been carefully checked on subjects like the one for whom the new prediction is made. The judge can beat the formula only by bringing in additional data and interpreting them correctly. In particular, he must not give the extra data too much weight, so that they override valid information the formula uses.

It is very difficult for a judge to function efficiently. In the first place, he does not know what weights he uses to arrive at a decision. He looks at the man from various angles and finally comes to an intuitive conclusion. Almost certainly, he gives greater weight to some factors than they deserve, and changes his weights from one case to the next. The clinician might judge the same case differently on different days, whereas the formula never varies. The validity of a single judge is less than that of formula predictions. If judgments of many counselors had been averaged to even out inconsistencies, their judgments would have been as valid as formula predictions; but this does not imply an advantage for the clinician, since judgment is an expensive process.

There is some reason to think that judges give too much weight to whatever supplementary facts they have, and too little to the key data (Bartlett & Green, 1966). Judges have stereotypes and prejudices; for example, they make different predictions for women than they do for men who have similar scores, even when there is no evidence that men and women perform differently on the job.

In one of the most interesting studies of error of judgment, it was found that the judges had gone wrong by applying a well-confirmed generalization in a situation in which for some unknown reason it failed to hold. Sarbin (1943; see also Cronbach, 1955) asked counselors to predict grade averages of students at Minnesota from their high-school records, aptitude test scores, and a whole dossier of information on interests, experiences, and motivations. The statistical formula combining aptitude and high-school rank had a validity of 0.45 for men, 0.70 for women. The counselors did a little worse: 0.35 for men, 0.69 for women. When we examine the weights used, we find that the formula placed almost its entire weight on high-school rank; it paid no attention to test scores because in the three preceding classes at Minnesota the test had made no independent contribution to prediction. The counselors, however, gave about equal weight to high-school marks and to test scores. Such a weighting had been found best in most of the reported investigations of college success, and is quite consistent with experience of colleges generally. For some reason, the Minnesota situation during the period of this study was exceptional; quite reasonable weights used by the counselors were wrong for this situation. The statistical formula was custommade for the Minnesota situation and of course it did better than the counselors who worked from general psychological lore.

What does this imply? It implies that the counselor, personnel manager, or clinical psychologist should use a formal statistical procedure whenever he can develop a combining formula for his own situation. He should be extremely cautious in departing from recommendations derived from the statistics, modifying them only when he is convinced that the additional information he brings in is a valid basis for decision. When he does use judgment, he should make followup studies, comparing the number of hits with the number of hits the formula would have yielded.

The proper province of the statistical formula is the institutional decision, in which a definite and irreversible decision is required to carry out the purposes of the institution, and the decision is recurrent so that a file of pertinent data can be cumulated to form a rule. The admissions officer who has to choose the applicants for a limited number of openings should certainly make decisions in whatever way will be most accurate. In counseling, on the other hand, decisions are personal decisions of the client and can be guided but not dictated by an experience table.

Multiple Criteria

Success is never unidimensional. Particularly in high-level positions, there are many patterns of success. Teachers, for example, may excel in different ways: one develops into a friend and counselor for youth, one stimulates independent thinking in the few brightest students, one overcomes the blockings that cause failure among weak students. To try to score these types of performance on a single scale is pointless—one loses information *and* predictability.

When multiple criteria for the same occupation are collected, the correlations between criteria are frequently low. Sometimes this is simply because one criterion or the other is a bad measurement. One can make no other interpretation of E. L. Kelly's finding (1964), for example, that grades on a State Board examination to license physicians correlate less than 0.20 with a National Board examination in the same subject, or with the grades earned in that subject the previous year. At other times, the criteria reflect psychologically distinct aspects of job performance. A rating of probable success as Hospital Administrator might reasonably have little to do with promise as Pediatrician. Kelly finds that premedical grades and aptitude measures correlate modestly with all types of criteria, but only the medical-school grade average and the national examinations are predicted well enough for decision making. The tests and premedical grades correlated low with ratings by senior-year classmates as to who would reach the highest income and who would be best satisfied as a family doctor in general practice, and with faculty ratings during internship on diagnostic competence, sensitivity to patient's needs, and overall promise. This is a frequent finding: the closer the criterion is to book work, the better the tests predict it; the closer to the duties of the job, the more chancy the prediction.

The only solution appears to be more persistent and more analytic research, starting with the development of limited, well-measured criteria. The National Board of Medical Examiners, for example, is supplementing its tests of book learning with a pencil-paper test that simulates the task of diagnosing a patient from the information available in a clinical record, bedside chart, laboratory tests, and a motion picture of the patient. The test of diagnostic competence measures something different from the usual test—the two correlate only moderately even after correction for errors of measurement (Hubbard, 1964; Hubbard et al., 1965). Follow-up studies are needed to be sure that the test measures a skill of medical practice and not just ingenuity in test taking.

Once diverse and dependable criteria of job performance are available, it is profitable to find the predictors for each. This is valuable as a way of understanding the nature of success on the job. It may, as in Table 12.5, suggest giving special weight to certain of the criteria. It may suggest a way of altering the training so as to save men who have trouble in the present training but can do well on the job. It may be useful in assignment of responsibilities to fit an employee's pattern of competences. The pattern is also useful in counseling to increase self-understanding.

Information about multiple predictor-criterion relationships is hard to use in selection. One can form an arbitrary composite of the criteria and apply the usual analysis to get a selection rule. If the criteria are truly diverse, however, different ways of combining them will select men of entirely different types.

Some industrial psychologists defend a procedure labelled "synthetic validity." The investigator identifies distinct elements in job performance (e.g., accuracy in checking entries in records) and looks for tests that have been previously shown to predict each element (e.g., DAT Clerical). Then he judges the importance of each element in success on this job in this company and combines the tests accordingly. This approach has all the faults of methods based on judgment. The one safeguard is that a follow-up study to check the soundness of the selection rule is recommended. The method is well adapted to the needs of the small firm that hires only a few workers for a certain job, and therefore cannot carry out a statistical study of the traditional type to decide on predictor weights (Balma, 1959).

Classification Decisions

The employment manager and the college admissions officer hire or admit some applicants and have nothing further to do with those they reject; these are true selection decisions. Classification decisions are far more numerous than selection decisions, and many so-called selection programs really lead to classification. A classification decision is one in which persons are assigned to different jobs, courses, therapeutic treatments, etc. Employee classification aims to assign each person to the job on which he can do best—subject to limits imposed by the number of vacancies in each job category. The decision maker is concerned about the subsequent performance of everyone, rather than just the persons assigned to one treatment. Air Force "pilot selection" is really a classification program, because men who do not pass the tests are retained in the service and assigned to other duty.

The theory of classification testing must probe into the same questions as the theory of selection. There are methods of combining scores for classification purposes, strategies for assigning persons to fill quotas, and so on. The methods differ quite a bit from those appropriate in simple selection. We shall not attempt to summarize these methods and the related theoretical principles, except to comment on the relation between test validity and classification efficiency.[4]

Differential Validity

A test that predicts success within many jobs is a poor instrument for classification because it does not tell which job the person can do best. Thus a general mental test is of little value for deciding which curriculum a college student should enter, even though it correctly indicates that he will do well in academic work. The ideal classification test has a positive correlation with performance in one job and a zero—or better yet, negative—correlation with performance in other jobs.

When we apply Brogden's assumptions to classification, we find that the value of a test used to assign persons to one of two treatments is proportional to its *differential validity*. Differential validity is expressed by the formula

$$s_1 r_{1t} - s_2 r_{2t}$$

Here s_1 and s_2 are the standard deviations of criterion scores for the two treatments for randomly selected men, the two criteria being expressed in comparable

[4] For a summary of much of the theory, and further references, see Cronbach and Gleser, 1965, especially Chapters 6 and 9.

units such as dollar value of the worker's production. r_{1t} and r_{2t} are the usual predictive validity coefficients for test t (Brogden, 1951). For differential validity one must look at the regression line relating treatments to criteria. Comparing correlations is not enough, if s_1 and s_2 differ. To simplify, however, let us assume that the criterion standard deviations for pilots and navigators are about equal— that is, that the difference in value to the Air Force between an ace pilot and a borderline pilot is equal to that between an outstanding and a mediocre navigator. Then, looking back at Table 13.4 (p. 428), we see that the Two-Hand Coordination Test has a validity of 0.26 for navigator and 0.30 for pilot. Therefore, it has no differential validity. Numerical Operations has a validity of 0.26 for navigator and 0.01 for pilot. It is therefore a good classification test. The Mathematics test, with validities 0.50 and 0.08, is even better.

Differential predictors make much better use of a pool of manpower than a general predictor can. Suppose we have three tests, A, B, and C. Test A, a general test, has validity 0.40 for job 1 and job 2. If we want to rule out below-average performers, we accept the best 50 per cent of the men. We must divide them randomly between the two jobs because test A has no differential validity. Test B has validity 0.40 for job 1, 0.00 for job 2, and zero correlation with test C. Test C has validity 0.00 for job 1, and 0.40 for job 2. Now we can accept all men above average on *either* B or C and assign each one according to which test he does better on. With these differential tests, 75 per cent of the men can be used, yet each one is average or better in aptitude for the job in which he is placed (Figure 13.11).

There are no quotas in clinical diagnosis; every person tested can be called "normal" or every one called "schizophrenic" if such uniform classification appears correct. When the clinician is trying to identify a rare condition, uniform classification is often the best strategy—even when there is a test with significant validity. Meehl and Rosen (1955) take prediction of suicide as an example. If a test identifies a person as having a high probability of suicide, the clinician will probably recommend that he be given closer attention and more intensive treatment than a probable nonsuicide. Suppose that 5 per cent of those tested in a certain clinic later attempt suicide. A person with a low test score (on a hypothetical test) has probability 0.001 of a suicide attempt, and one can confidently place him in the nonsuicide category. With higher test scores, probability of suicide increases, so that the test has undoubted validity. The highest score in the clinic sample, however, may indicate only probability 0.20 of a suicide attempt. Such a person cannot be called a "probable suicide." If we diagnose such persons as probable suicides, we make four errors (false alarms) for every correct decision. To put a special watch on a probable suicide is a great drain on the resources of a clinic. Perhaps it cannot invest this effort in four false alarms in order to forestall one suicide. To be sure, the clinic may argue that one person saved far outweighs the cost of guarding all five, in which case persons with the highest test score will be placed in the risk-of-suicide category. The principle

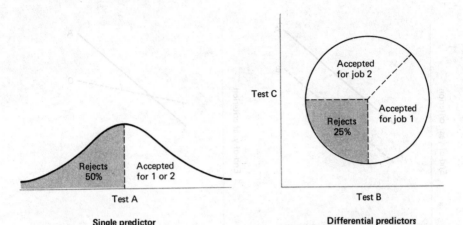

Figure 13.11. Superior use of manpower by means of differential predictors.

still holds: a valid classification test is not worth using if the cost of false alarms outweighs the benefit from hits.

Aptitude-Treatment Interactions

When a choice between treatments is being made on the basis of a test, the differential validity of the test must be demonstrated. It is not enough to know that the test predicts outcome; indeed, a test that predicts outcome under both treatments has no value (Cronbach, 1957).

A school teaching history by method A may be disturbed by the fact that some students do badly. When it is found that a reading test predicts success, it seems natural to assign poor readers to a class that uses another method. But that is not a sound strategy if the relations are as pictured in Figure 13.12a; the test predicts performance in Treatment B as well as A, and since B has a lower mean the poor readers are actually worse off than in A. Figure 13.12b introduces a Treatment C that is almost unrelated to the reading test. The test and treatment *interact*; we cannot predict whether a student will rank high, average, or low until we know both his score and the treatment he is assigned to. It is evidently wise to assign low scorers to C and high scorers to A.

Most aptitude tests used by schools have been accepted simply on the basis of predictive validity. But if the tests are used to choose instructional treatments rather than merely for selection there must be evidence that the aptitude interacts with the alternative treatments.

A study carried out 30 years ago by G. L. Anderson (1941) showed that interactive effects can be found in large-scale, classroom experiments. A conventional drill method for teaching fourth-grade arithmetic was contrasted with

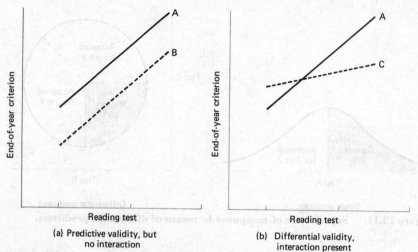

Figure 13.12.   Test-criterion regression under treatments A, B, and C.

a more meaningful method. Both methods had similar effectiveness on the average, the advantage shifting according to the kind of outcome measured. There was a consistent tendency for one group of children to do better on the drill method—these were the ones who had developed strong crystallized ability in arithmetic, as shown on a pretest, but who had somewhat lower standings on a general mental test. Conversely, the meaningful method produced superior results with bright children who had not mastered arithmetic taught previously by conventional methods.

Figure 13.13 illustrates the direction in which research on this problem is moving, with the introduction of complex instructional variations and consideration of some novel aptitudes. Koran (1968) taught teachers to ask "analytic" questions of their classes; in the training they observed this skill being applied by a master teacher. One group observed that teacher on videotape, so that they saw and heard what was said. Another group received a written transcript from the sound track of the videotape, and did not view the interaction. The aptitudes measured prior to the experiment were fluid ability (by a version of EFT) and film memory. In the film-memory test, a silent movie of humans in interaction is presented and the person is asked at the end to recall as much of the action as he can. The outcome measure in the experiment was a count of the number of analytic questions the student teacher asked as he taught a small class. Figure 13.13 comes from an unpublished analysis of the data made by Koran and R. E. Snow. There is no question that an interaction exists, but the reader is reminded that results such as this require confirmation in a variety of situations before firm conclusions can be drawn.

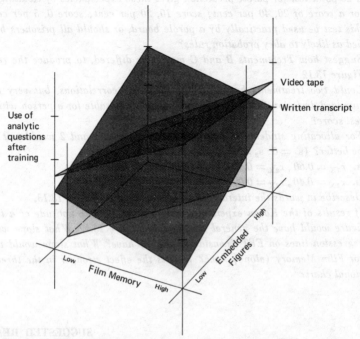

Figure 13.13. Ability of student teachers to ask analytic questions as a function of aptitude and kind of training.
Unpublished figure prepared by R. E. Snow from data of M. L. Koran (1969).

33. *A complex study investigated alternative ways of predicting achievement-test scores in four kinds of courses (Guilford, Hoepfner, & Peterson, 1965). Interpret the results in the light of the concepts of this chapter. (Only a fraction of the results are mentioned here.)*

The average multiple correlation for the four courses, using four DAT scores as predictors, was 0.53. When weights were assigned to twenty factor scores (derived from 25 Guilford tests), the average multiple R was again 0.55. When only 13 weights were assigned R dropped to 0.53. The factor battery (including tests that did not predict) required more time than the DAT tests. The regression formula for prediction from factor tests varied considerably from one course to another; different tests were given heavy weight. The formulas for predicting from DAT were much the same from one course to another.

34. *Suppose that pilot performance is judged to be three times as important as navigator performance ($s_1 = 3s_2$). Then what tests have greatest differential validity for these jobs? (Use Table 13.4.)*

35. *What tests had greatest differential validity for distinguishing pilots from bombardiers, according to Table 13.4?*

36. *A 20-point test for parole prediction gives these expectancies of violating parole: for a score of 20, 40 per cent; score 10, 20 per cent; score 0, 5 per cent. Can this test be used practically by a parole board, or should all prisoners be classified as likely to obey probation rules?*

37. *Suggest how Treatments B and C may have differed, to produce the results in Figure 13.12.*

38. *Could two treatments have equal test-outcome correlations, but very different standard deviations? If so, which treatment is advisable for a person with a high test score?*

39. *For allocating students to instructional treatments 1 and 2 would test X or Y be better? ($s_1 = 6$; $s_2 = 4$)*

    a. $r_{1X} = 0.60$, $r_{2X} = 0.30$; $r_{1Y} = 0.30$, $r_{2Y} = 0.60$.

    b. $r_{1X} = 0.40$, $r_{2X} = 0.00$; $r_{1Y} = 0.40$, $r_{2Y} = -0.40$.

40. *Describe in words the interactive effect displayed in Figure 13.13.*

41. *If results of the Koran experiment were plotted for one aptitude at a time, the figure would have the general structure of Figure 13.12. What slope would the regression lines on EFT (considered alone) have? What slope would the lines for Film Memory (alone) have? Why is the effect stronger in the three-dimensional chart?*

SUGGESTED READINGS

Dunnette, Marvin D. Decision making in personnel selection and placement. In *Personnel selection and placement.* Belmont, Calif.: Wadsworth, 1967. Pp. 160–199.
  Defends unconventional approaches to the use of personnel data as the only reasonable way to cope with industrial realities. Of special interest are the estimates of benefit from selection and the demonstration of detailed procedures in classifying young ladies for four jobs in a Las Vegas casino. While this example is hypothetical, Dunnette's next chapter summarizes real studies using unconventional procedures.

Fleishman, Edwin A., and Berniger, Joseph. One way to reduce turnover. *Personnel,* 1960, *37,* 63–69. (Reprinted in Fleishman, 1967.)
  Outlines from start to finish a simple study in which information from a routine application blank was weighted into a selection formula. The reader should raise two questions: Do the weights assigned make psychological sense? What use did the crossvalidation study have?

Goldman, Leo. Evaluation of statistical and clinical approaches. In *Using tests in counseling.* New York: Appleton-Century-Crofts, 1961. Pp. 197–211.
  A balanced account of the evidence on statistical and judgmental approaches to decision making. Distinguishes situations in which judgment may be used advantageously, and discusses how to make judgment more accurate.

Harker, John B. Cross-validation of an IBM proof machine test battery. *Journal of Applied Psychology,* 1960, *44,* 237–240.

A follow-up study of a multiple cutoff formula for selecting clerical workers in a bank. Illustrates the practical value of a cutoff procedure, and also the difference between initial and crossvalidation results.

Kelly, E. Lowell. Alternative criteria in medical education and their correlates. In *Proceedings, invitational conference on testing problems, 1963*. Princeton: ETS, 1964. Pp. 64–85. (Reprinted in Anastasi, 1966).

Extended studies with a variety of tests and criteria show that the use of tests in a selection policy involves serious value judgments. Conventional studies that use a single criterion such as grade average are unlikely to select persons outstanding in other respects.

Krug, Robert E. Some suggested approaches for test development and measurement. *Personnel Psychology, 19,* 1966, 24–35.

Argues for the validation of employment tests within narrowly defined groups (e.g., female Negro high-school graduates) and setting up different selection rules for each group. The critical question is whether this will be regarded as a "fair" employment practice.

Newman, Sidney H., Howell, Margaret A., and Cliff, Norman. The analysis and prediction of a practical examination in dentistry. *Educational and Psychological Measurement,* 1959, *19,* 557–568. (Reprinted in Jackson & Messick, 1967.)

Careful observations of job performance are used to validate information from a variety of tests. A good demonstration of multiple-correlation technique and of the use of factor analysis to understand criteria.

Tiffin, Joseph, and McCormick, Ernest J. General principles of personnel testing. *Industrial psychology.* (5th ed.) Englewood Cliffs, N.J.: Prentice-Hall, 1965. Pp. 115–151.

Procedures used in validating tests for industrial selection are described. Particular emphasis is placed on the difference between studies on present employees and studies conducted on new applicants tested at the time of hiring but not screened on the basis of test performance. The importance of the selection ratio as a factor determining the usefulness of a test is fully explained.

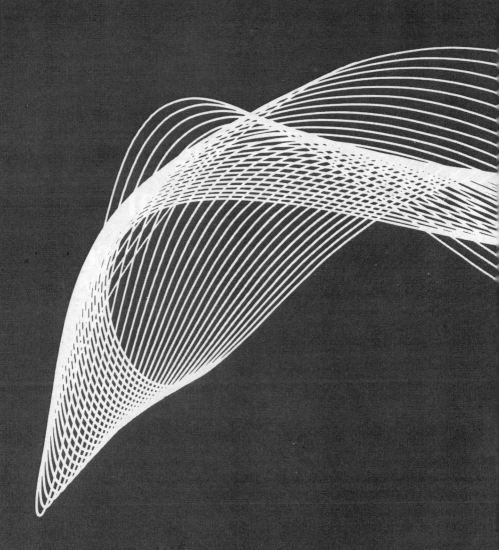

part III

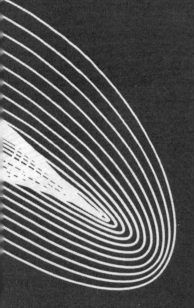

Testing
of Typical
Performance

14

Interest Inventories

We now turn from the study of tests that try to elicit the person's best performance to procedures for investigating typical behavior. We begin with interest inventories. After these concrete examples are before us, Chapter 15 will discuss the general problems of personality and attitude testing.

Functionally, interest inventories are closely related to the aptitude tests considered in preceding chapters, since their main use is in vocational and educational guidance. An interest questionnaire applies the "self-report" technique, having the individual describe his own characteristics. The questionnaire or inventory may be regarded as a written interview; since it uses a great number of rather indirect questions, it is in some ways more satisfactory than the direct oral interview. The single question, "Would you like to be a teacher?" does not give adequate information for guidance because the person may not answer wisely. A girl may reject teaching for no better reason than that she thinks correcting papers would be tedious, and is little aware of the other activities in a teacher's day. A boy may choose law because it calls for public speaking, ignoring its long hours of isolated research and thinking. The indirect, comprehensive, objectively scored inventory gets better information than the blunt question. As an additional advantage, the standardized inventory allows comparison of the person with reference groups.

Three starting points for inventory construction may be distinguished: sampling from content categories, forming clusters of correlated items, and assembling miscellaneous items for actuarial keying. All approaches enter into the development of the usual instrument; as the instrument evolves, the investigator shifts from one technique to another. Even though this blending tends to make instruments similar, the way any instrument has been assembled needs to be understood by its interpreter.

Construction from Content Specifications

The most primitive approach is analogous to that of the achievement tester: a category of content is defined and items are written that fit the definition. A measure of reading interests can be constructed by defining categories—adventure, business, science, romance, etc.—preparing sentences to suggest the plots of a dozen stories in each category, and arranging them in haphazard order. The pupil checks stories he thinks he would enjoy reading. This approach is quite suitable for simple inquiries, such as a study of sex and age differences in late childhood and adolescence. The commonsense, face-valid categories give results that are readily understood, at a nontheoretic level. With such data the teacher can suggest supplementary reading or an individual project a pupil is likely to enjoy. The curriculum evaluator can use this type of device to learn whether a course increases interest in reading about historical events. (He should administer the interest inventory in the homeroom or the English class, not in the history class, to reduce the likelihood that the pupil will respond as he thinks the history teacher wishes.)

The California Occupational Preference Survey illustrates the building of an instrument along content lines. Eight interest categories were used: science, technical, outdoor, business, clerical, linguistic, aesthetic, and service. Items were collected by sampling descriptions from the *Dictionary of occupational titles*; for example, the linguistic category includes "Compile and edit for publication the diary and letters of a famous literary person" and "Proofread typeset against original copy." These categories remained in the final instrument, but there was one departure from representative sampling. Any item that failed to correlate with the total score over all trial items in the category was discarded. This "purification" was a step toward the homogeneous-cluster type of instrument.

A second feature of the original design was a search for items at five levels of responsibility and skill: the two linguistic items quoted above represent the highest and lowest levels, respectively. The scheme would have mapped interest onto a two-way grid of content and level. It assumed that some people are interested in high-level linguistic work and not low-level linguistic work, etc. It was found, however, that persons tend to like—or to dislike—activities that range widely in level. In the final test, all outdoor items were collapsed to ignore level; the same was done for clerical items. In the other categories only two levels were distinguished: professional and skilled. Unnecessary a priori categories were thus abandoned.

Construction with Homogeneous Item Clusters

A commonsense interest category represents a working hypothesis about activities that in some way appeal to the same interest. Internal-consistency studies and factor analyses check and modify such hypothesis. While "adventure stories" seems to be a sensible category, a close examination might show that boys who like desert-island, man-against-nature stories do not particularly care for tales of villainy, man-against-man. This (hypothetical) finding would suggest substitute categories: endurance stories and aggression stories. If the two category scores have a low correlation but high internal consistency, the proposed categories would be a useful basis for reorganizing the test.

Kuder Inventories C and E

G. F. Kuder has been responsible for much instrument development and research on vocational interests. His inventories are of different types, and successive versions of the same instrument have been given different names. In the present section we shall give attention to Form C (or CM or CH), Kuder Preference Record-Vocational, and Form E, the General Interest Survey. These tests are essentially the same. Form E uses a simpler vocabulary and has norms for junior high school as well as high school. We shall speak most often of the older Form C because there has been much research on it; very likely similar results will be obtained for E.

Kuder demonstrated reasonable homogeneity and independence for the following ten categories: Outdoor, Mechanical, Computational, Scientific, Persuasive, Artistic, Literary, Musical, Social Service, and Clerical. His inventories employ a preference (forced-choice) format. Three activities are listed together, for example:

a. Develop new varieties of flowers.
b. Conduct advertising campaign for florists.
c. Take telephone orders in a florist shop.

The subject selects which he likes most and which least, leaving the third unmarked. A person who chooses "a" as most liked receives credit under Scientific and Artistic; choice of "b" is scored as Persuasive; and choice of "c" is counted as Clerical. These scorings are not arbitrary; the items are counted in whatever key they correlate with.

One popular feature is Kuder's self-scoring answer booklet. The student responds by punching holes into suitable spaces on the face of the booklet. At the end of the test, when he opens the booklet, the responses appear as pinholes on each page, one page for each key. On one page, for example, there is a printed circle for each response in the Outdoor key, and the student simply counts how many circles contain pinholes to get his own Outdoor score.

Attempts at occupational keying. When Kuder published the first form of his instrument in 1940, he suggested interpretation on the basis of the face validity of the categories. He listed occupations corresponding to each type of profile. This required assumptions about the interests fitting the occupations, and studies were needed to validate those assumptions.

Form C occupational data, gathered more or less as opportunity permitted, did not necessarily sample the various professions adequately. To get psychologist norms, for example, 260 Fellows in four divisions of the American Psychological Association were asked to fill out the scale; 111 (46 per cent) provided data (Baas, 1950). The median of the psychologists fell at the 84th percentile (of men in general) in Scientific and Literary, between 60 and 70 in Computational and Social Service, and at or below 30 in Clerical, Mechanical, and Persuasive. Some of these differences are consistent with the usual concept of the psychologist but the high Literary score is a surprise.

Other results also tend to agree with occupational stereotypes. The profile for accountants peaks in Computational and Clerical. Authors, editors, and reporters peak in Literary, chemists in Scientific, musicians in Music. These, however, refer to averages. Many men in an occupation fall below the median on a scale that "fits" the occupation.

A regression equation can combine Form C scores into an occupational score intended to identify people who resemble men in a certain occupation. A formula for identifying carpenter interests counted Mechanical positively and gave *negative* weights to Scientific, Literary, and Clerical. The formula had some power to distinguish carpenters from men in general and from men in other trades (Mugaas & Hester, 1952). Over a period of time, however, Kuder decided that this approach was not very powerful, because there were many misses and false alarms. Only ten weights can be assigned when one is working with ten pre-scored scales. Weighting each item in turn should permit sharper separation of occupations. There would be no advantage in weighting homogeneous items, however, because strongly correlated items get similar weights. It was for this reason that Kuder developed the heterogeneous Form DD (see below).

Interpretation. Kuder now urges users of Forms C and E to interpret the direct surface meaning of scales rather than attempting to match profiles directly with occupations. Even content-based interpretations sometimes have to be hedged; a high literary score may arise from a passive interest in reading, implying no interest in writing.

The pertinence of the descriptive profile (Figure 14.1) is seen in the case of Mary Thomas, who was majoring in child development in college at the time she filled out Form C. Her grades were mediocre, and her work with children

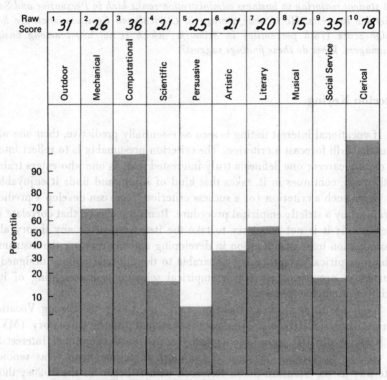

Figure 14.1. Kuder profile of Mary Thomas.
From the Profile Form of Kuder Preference Record, Form C by G. Frederick Kuder. Adapted by permission of the publisher, Science Research Associates, Inc.

was not especially successful. When questioned regarding her choice of major, she explained that she had set her heart on work in an orphanage. This desire had arisen in childhood when she read a book about a woman who helped orphan children—a "wonderful" thing to do as a lifework. The low Persuasive and Social Service scores suggest a somewhat withdrawn personality, while the high Mechanical, Computational, and Clerical scores suggest a liking for routine, uncreative activities. When questioned about office work, Mary enthusiastically described her previous summer's work as a file clerk; her duties apparently consisted solely of alphabetizing folders; yet she had "just loved it." Moreover, she had done well in secretarial training courses. Evidently both ability and interest fell in an area she had not considered as a vocational goal.

1. *A high-school boy has the following percentile scores: Outdoor, 60; Mechanical, 50; Computational, 30; Scientific, 70; Persuasive, 98; Artistic, 70; Literary, 90; Musical, 50; Social Service, 40; Clerical, 15. Interpret.*

2. *A student majoring in business administration ranks high in Persuasive and Social
Service interests. He is near average in Clerical and Computational. He has a
high score (78th percentile) in Scientific, which is not usual among business
managers. What do these findings suggest?*

Criterion Keying

If vocational interest testing is seen as essentially predictive, then one wants
scores that will forecast a criterion. The criterion presumably is to reflect interest
in a certain career; one defines a truly interested man as one who enters training
for the field, continues in it, takes that kind of a job, and finds it enjoyable.

Given such a criterion (or a success criterion), one can develop a predictive
instrument by a strictly empirical procedure. Items are chosen that correlate with
the criterion; it is not necessary to take the item content or any theory about
the occupation into consideration in developing and interpreting the instrument.
Such an empirical inventory is comparable to the aptitude battery designed for
a particular occupation, in which empirical selection and weighting of items
maximizes predictive power.

There are three empirical instruments in use today, the Strong Vocational
Interest Blank (SVIB), the Minnesota Vocational Interest Inventory (MVII),
and Kuder Form DD, more often referred to as the Occupational Interest Survey (OIS). The Strong has been a landmark in testing history, as renowned
in its way as the Stanford-Binet. Research with it began in the 1920s; though
revisions have continued, it has not basically been changed since the first publication. MVII is constructed on the same principles as the Strong, so we shall not
consider it at length. The new OIS merits fuller discussion because its principle
of keying is quite different from that of Strong.

The Strong Blank for Men (SVIB)

SVIB consists of questions on hundreds of activities both vocational and
avocational. Most of the 399 items in the 1966 form for men require a "like-
indifferent-dislike" response to activities or topics: botany, fishing, being an
aviator, discussing the purpose of life, etc. (D. P. Campbell, 1966b). About 40
minutes are required to complete the questionnaire.

Assignment of scoring weights. Men in a particular occupation, Strong
supposed, tend to enjoy much the same sorts of activity. He went on to assume
that a young person having the interests found in an occupational group will
probably enjoy work in that occupation. High-school seniors who enjoy what
engineers enjoy, be it fishing or science fiction, are advised to consider engineering

Table 14.1. Determination of weights for SVIB Engineer Key (1966)

First 10 items on SVIB	Responses of "men-in-general" (%)			Responses of engineers (%)			Differences in percentages			Scoring weights for engineering interests		
	L	I	D	L	I	D	L	I	D	L	I	D
Actor (not movie)	28	33	39	9	31	60	−19	− 2	21	−1	0	1
Advertiser	31	40	29	14	37	49	−17	− 3	20	−1	0	1
Architect	46	36	18	58	32	10	12	− 4	− 8	0		0
Military officer	29	28	43	31	33	36	2	5	− 7	0	0	0
Artist	32	36	32	28	39	33	− 4	3	1	0	0	0
Astronomer	33	41	26	38	44	18	5	3	− 8	0	0	0
Athletic director	34	38	28	15	51	34	−19	13	6	−1	1	1
Auctioneer	8	26	66	1	16	83	− 7	−10	17	−1	−1	1
Author of novel	41	36	23	22	44	34	−19	8	11	−1	0	1
Author of technical book	41	36	23	59	32	9	18	− 4	−14	1	0	1

Data supplied by David P. Campbell.

as a vocation, and students with some other interest pattern are warned that they do not have the inclinations of the typical engineer.

The pattern for a profession is determined by tabulating item responses of satisfied members of that profession. This pattern is compared with that of a pool of "men in general" (MIG) from various occupations. Items on which the two differ are counted in the scoring key, as shown in Table 14.1. The percentage of MIG respondents giving each answer to a particular item is compared with the percentage of men-in-the-occupation giving the answer. Engineers, more than other men, say they dislike "Actor." Response "D" is therefore assigned a positive weight in the Engineer scale. The weight is in accord with the difference. Liking to be author of a technical book is especially common among engineers; it is given a weight of +1. Whereas engineers tend to dislike acting, 40 per cent of artists respond "L" to "Actor." The weights of "Actor" in the Artist scale are +1 for "L," 0 for "I" and "D."

Occupational scores are converted into letter grades. The A level is defined to include about 70 per cent of the successful men in the occupation. The C (lowest) level includes only 2 per cent of the criterion group for the occupation, but it includes something like half of men in the population.

The key embodies no psychological theory about engineers; it relies entirely on test data to define what engineers are like. Some of the weights fit our expectations. Other weights are unexpected and difficult to rationalize. One would not have guessed that being indifferent to "Auctioneer" is a negative sign of engineering interests, while indifference to "Athletic director" is a positive indicator. Equally puzzling, engineers differ little from the MIG on "Architect" and "Astronomer." Some of the puzzling weights may result simply from chance in selection of the occupational sample.

An empirical key is somewhat heterogeneous. Responses weighted for Engineer encompass technical interests (author of technical book, operating machinery), dislike for verbal activities (actor, author of novel, making speeches), liking methodical work, etc. Weights are also given to a few miscellaneous likes. These scattered items have much less influence on the score than the cumulative effect of the many highly correlated technical items, so that the key is dominated by a homogeneous core of obviously engineer-related items.

Keys are continually being added; there are keys for several dozen male occupations. The Strong items are so varied that they can be weighted to identify almost any interest combination. A key can be made for any distinct group. For example, Strong originally provided separate keys for accountants and certified public accountants. A later study found however, that only about 40 per cent of certain CPA subgroups scored A on CPA whereas 70 per cent of men in an occupation are expected to make A. Strong therefore prepared a new key for Senior CPA. The original scale seemed to apply well to owners or managers of accounting firms; it is now named CPA Owner. The Accountant scale seems to apply to junior accountants, and probably also to men who move from accounting into business management. The Owner scale stresses verbal interests; the Senior scale involves mathematical interests and correlates negatively with Lawyer and Advertiser (Strong, 1949).

The 1966 revision is based partly on Strong's data from 30 to 40 years back and partly on recent testing. Weak or dated items were dropped or replaced. A fresh sample of men-in-general was drawn from available cases, old and new. For most keys Strong's old occupational data were compared with the new MIG statistics to determine weights, weights being assigned only to the 300 items retained from the first edition. This use of old data is defended by citing evidence that men tested today have an average profile like that for men in the same occupation who were tested decades ago (D. P. Campbell, 1966c). The use of mixed old and new data has to be regarded as a stopgap; the partial updating probably has had benefits, but greater efficiency can be expected from keys and norms based wholly on recent data. Such keys will be developed as research continues. The most basic source of information on the instrument, as it stands today, and on the women's blank (see p. 484), is the *Handbook for the SVIB* (to be published in 1970 by the Stanford University Press).

Even though the 1966 revision is formally quite similar to the original, there is some evidence that the old and new keys, applied to the same test papers, give quite different results (Williams *et al.*, 1968). On many keys, a third of those who earn A in the occupation when scored by the old key drop to B or lower on the new one. One cannot, then, on the basis of old-form experience, take for granted that the new form will be equally satisfactory to counselors. Users should examine research results on the new form as they appear.

Strong keys are not confined to vocational interests. Scoring the answers that men give more frequently than women, for example, generates a masculinity-of-interests key. There is an "Academic Achievement" scale, prepared by contrasting college students with high and low grades. (This is to be distinguished from the type of scale developed in some other studies by contrasting *over*achievers and *under*achievers.) In principle, SVIB could be keyed against any external criterion; one could make an Embezzler key, or a key to correlate with financial credit rating.

Ordered relations among scales. Kuder set out in Forms C and E to describe interests with a minimum number of scales. Since his scales are independent (except for a few fair-sized correlations such as that of Scientific with Mechanical), the parallel-factor model applies and the profile form consists of parallel stalks. For SVIB also it has been customary to present a profile of parallel scales, but there have been repeated attempts to impose some structure on the set. Some occupational groups have much the same interests, and there is an orderly progression from occupation to occupation.

Neither the parallel-factor model nor the hierarchical model seems right for interest data. Most mapping attempts find that traits can best be displayed on a globe, with a more or less continuous transition from one type of behavior to another. Figure 14.2 represents many of the relationships among Strong scales by locating them on the surface of a split-open globe.[1] In general, scores for occupations near each other have strong positive correlations, and those on opposite sides of the globe have negative correlations. The artist, for example, dislikes what bankers like.

A number of clusters or constellations can be identified in the chart. The grouping that appears here is by no means the only possible one; several earlier proposals are reviewed by Super and Crites (1962, pp. 382 ff.). The most important is surely the following, derived from Strong's work. Approximately this grouping has been used in most discussions of the theory of interest development.

Group I, Biological science (e.g., psychologist, architect, physician)
Group II, Physical science-technical (mathematician, physicist, engineer)

[1] This scheme is modeled on a chart devised by Strong to display individual scores. Reports in such a form cannot be prepared by scoring machines and the chart is no longer published. The writer located scales in Figure 14.2 by extracting three principal components from the scale intercorrelations given in the manual and extending each vector of loadings to unit length. Scales not strongly loaded on these three factors (e.g., osteopath, policeman, CPA) are omitted from the diagram.

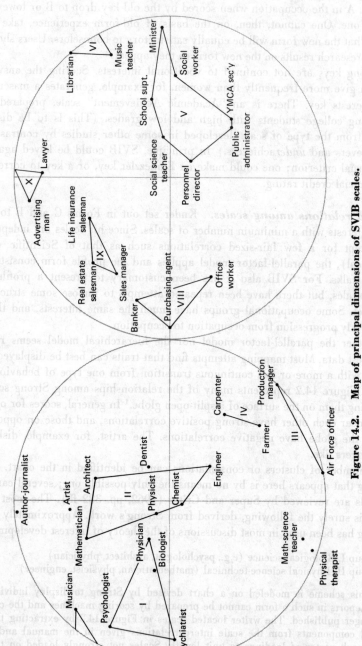

Figure 14.2. Map of principal dimensions of SVIB scales.

Group III, Technical supervision (production manager, Air Force officer)
Group IV, Technical concrete (farmer, carpenter, forest service)
Group V, Social service (public administrator, personnel director, social-science teacher, school superintendent, minister)
Group VI, Cultural (musician, artist, librarian)
Group VII, Systematic record keeping (CPA, accountant)
Group VIII, Business detail (office worker, purchasing agent, banker)
Group IX, Business contact (sales manager, real-estate salesman, life-insurance salesman)
Group X, Verbal (advertising man, lawyer, author-journalist)

One may suggest various names for dimensions in the chart. The front-to-back dimension separates scientific from nonscientific occupations. A line running from Group III up toward Musician could be interpreted as a masculine-feminine direction. Or a line running from Group IX downward toward YMCA secretary, and toward physical therapist on the other face of the globe, can be seen as a business-vs.-nonbusiness array. It is hard to defend one placing of the axes ("factors") as sounder than another. Anne Roe *et al.* (1966) have tried to arrange the occupations in a two-dimensional loop, but this simplification is not consistent with the SVIB correlations.

Homogeneous keys for SVIB.   For some uses—e.g., comparisons of groups in research—the occupational keys are cumbersome, and, because of their heterogeneity, they are hard to interpret psychologically. D. P. Campbell and others (1968) therefore collected items into homogeneous subsets, insofar as possible. There are 22 such subsets, or "basic scales"; they were not designed to be independent and some should probably be combined.

The scales generally contain no more than about 12 items, and thus represent their categories rather thinly. Such a set of items will correlate around 0.80 with another set representing the same category. But one obtains a correlation near 0.90 for a Kuder scale of 80 items. This reinforces the view that a set of items assembled on one principle is unlikely to serve all measurement functions. Kuder (in Form C) had many items, of a few kinds; he got a good descriptive profile and poor occupational identifications.

3. *Estimate the weights for the Chemist scale, of the item "Actor," if responses of chemists are as follows: 16 per cent "L," 34 "I," 50 "D."*
4. *Suppose you wished to make a key to measure interest in being a mother, i.e., to predict whether a girl will enjoy raising a family. Outline the steps you would follow to prepare the scale, with special attention to the persons you would use as a basis for the key.*
5. *Each of the following assumptions is implied in the construction or in some uses of SVIB and OIS. For each one, state a reasonable contradictory hypothesis.*
   a. *One is not likely to succeed in an occupation unless the work interests him.*
   b. *One is not likely to succeed in an occupation unless his interests are similar to those of most other men in the profession.*

    c. *Interest in the school subjects required to prepare for a profession is not an adequate basis for predicting satisfaction in the profession.*

    d. *The interests leading to satisfaction in a vocation in 1970 will also be associated with satisfaction in 1990.*

6. *"An A rating in psychologist with B+ in physician and dentist should suggest a different preparation and career than an A rating in psychologist with B+ rating in engineer, production manager, and carpenter"* (Strong, 1943, p. 54). *What differences in advice are justified in these cases?*

7. *Would Strong improve his Engineer key by discarding weights that do not seem logical even though the item in question shows a difference between Engineers and MIG?*

8. *D. P. Campbell (1965) published SVIB records for a number of psychologists. One record included is that of the author of this book, based on a test at age 32. Interpret the following information with the aid of Figure 14.2.*

    A's: Psychologist, *psychiatrist, personnel manager, public administrator, vocational counselor, social worker, school superintendent, music teacher, advertising man,* lawyer, *author-journalist.* (Highest scores in roman type.)

    Lowest scores: Carpenter, industrial-arts teacher, forest-service man, veterinarian.

The Occupational Interest Survey (OIS)

In preparing his Form DD, now more often designated OIS, Kuder adopted a method of criterion keying that, in his opinion, gives results vastly superior to Strong's. The Strong uses a general reference group and counts responses in which, for example, engineers differed from the general group. Kuder simply asks how similar the subject is to the engineer group. The Strong Engineer key (Table 14.1) allows -1, 0, and 1 for the responses "L," "I," and "D" to "Actor." Kuder would assign scores 0.09, 0.31, and 0.60—which tends to put more emphasis on the "D" response. Basically, points are assigned according to how many engineers agree with the subject. At first glance, the new keying seems to make little difference; the order and spacing of the Strong weights for "Actor" are proportional to Kuder's. If we examine all the -1 weights in Table 14.1, however, we find that the corresponding weights according to Kuder's scheme would range from 0.01 to 0.22.

Kuder describes his procedure as follows. It is as if we took the subject's paper as a key and scored the papers of all the engineers in the reference group. We could average those scores to see how similar the engineers are to the subject. We could do the same for each other occupational group. Then we would be in a good position to decide *which* occupational groups the man most resembles. Men-in-general do not enter the calculation.

The Strong procedure tells whether the man differs from the norm *in the direction* of the engineer group, but the size of the score does not indicate how similar he is to engineers. To clarify this, assume that engineers and physicists

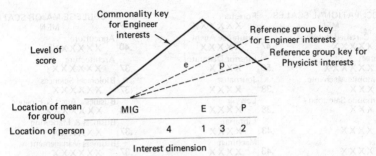

Figure 14.3. Schematic diagram to illustrate difference between Strong and Kuder OIS keying.
MIG, mean in general; E, engineers; P, physicists.

differ from MIG in the same direction (i.e., have similar kinds of special interests) but that physicists are more extreme, as charted in Figure 14.3. By Strong's method, all scores to the right of e would be given A on Engineer, because persons in that range are more like engineers than MIG. All scores to the right of p would get A on Physicist also. The solid line is like Kuder's similarity-to-engineers score. Consider man 1. By similarity scoring he is high on E, not very high on P. Strong scores support this, though the Engineer score is less extreme. Man 2 is far from MIG in the engineer "direction." Strong gives him a higher score on Engineer than on Physicist, whereas Kuder gives him a rather low E score.[2] If one is primarily measuring "similarity to engineers," Kuder's empirical keying seems to be logically superior. But low Kuder scores, implying dissimilarity, are ambiguous, as persons can differ from the engineer in many ways. Persons 2 and 4 would be given the same E score by Kuder. At the end of the chapter we shall return again to the logic of keying, and there we shall note some possibilities for further advances in technique.

OIS (see Figure 14.4) has keys around 80 male occupations, based on 200–400 men in midcareer who report themselves satisfied in their work. There are also 20 scales for college major fields (based on men). There are 36 keys for women, and Kuder recommends applying many of the male keys to them also.

9. *Discuss cases 3 and 4 of Figure 14.3.*
10. *Prepare a diagram like Figure 14.3 and work out scores for the case where M is between E and P.*
11. *The following descriptions of occupational criterion groups are given in Kuder's OIS manual. How satisfactory is each description as information to the test user? How satisfactory is the selection of cases itself?*
     a. *"Interior Decorator (190). Members of the American Institute of Decorators. Mean age 43.4; standard deviation 8.6. 100 college graduates, 83 high school*

---

[2] Compare the finding that, on MVII, food-service managers average higher on the Baker key (i.e., differ more from tradesmen-in-general) than bakers do (D. P. Campbell, 1966a).

OCCUPATIONAL SCALES MEN		Forester XXXXXX	.49	COLLEGE MAJOR SCALES MEN	
Acc't, Certified Public XXXXXX	.47	Insurance Agent XXXXX	.40	Agriculture XXXXXX	.49
Architect XXXXXXX	.50	Interior Decorator XXXX	.37	Architecture XXXXX	.49
Automobile Mechanic XXXX	.38	Journalist XXXX	.37	Biological Sciences XXXXXX	.49
Automobile Salesman XXXX	.38	Lawyer XXXX	.38	Business: Acc't & Finance XXXXXXX	.50
Baker XXXXX	.43	Librarian XXXX	.37	Business & Marketing XXXXXX	.47
Banker XXXXX	.43	Machinist XXXX	.37	Business Management XXXXXX	.46
Barber XXXX	.38	Mathematician XXXXX	.43	Economics XXXXXX	.48
Bookkeeper XXXXX	.42	Math Teacher, High School XXXXX	.43	Engineering, Chemical XXXXXXX	.55
Bookstore Manager XXXXX	.44	Meteorologist XXXXXX	.45	Engineering, Civil XXXXXXXX	.55
Bricklayer XXXXX	.40	Minister XX	.25	Engineering, Electrical XXXXXXXX	.56
Building Contractor XXXXX	.42	Nurseryman XXXXXX	.49	Engineering, Mechanical XXXXXXXX	.55

Figure 14.4.   Report for Kuder Occupational Interest Survey.
Specimen case from test manual. About half the form is shown here. *From Kuder Occupational Interest Survey by G. Frederick Kuder. Reprinted by permission of the publisher, Science Research Associates, Inc.*

graduates, 6 grade school graduates, 1 with less than a grade school education.

"Only subjects between twenty-five and sixty-five years of age who had been in the same occupation for at least three years and who met other standards of job satisfaction were used . . . selected from all parts of the country on the basis of geographical distribution of members of the occupation."

b. "Department store salesmen (200). Selected from 8 department stores . . . through the courtesy of . . . Director of Personnel, Allied Stores Corporation. Mean age 40.2; standard deviation 12.9. 17 college graduates, 137 high school graduates, 45 grade school graduates, 1 with less than a grade school education."

c. "Truck driver (185). Long-distance truck drivers working for several different companies. Subjects filled out blanks during stop in Charlotte, North Carolina. Mean age 36.7; standard deviation 6.4." (Educational tally also given: 2, 54, 106, 21 in respective categories listed above, plus 2 unknown.)

Validity of Interest Measures

Stability of Interests

In using interest tests for counseling the first assumption is that interests are stable, as the predictions have to do with satisfaction throughout a career.

Interests are moderately stable after age 17. According to Campbell's summary (1969 supplement to the SVIB manual, p. 21),

Test-retest correlations over 30 days average slightly over .90, dropping to about .75 over 20 years for adults and to .55 over 35 years for men first tested at age 16. Correlations over the four years of college usually are in the .60's. . . . When the SVIB is used for those below the age of 21, the possibility of future change must be recognized.

For original reports of research on stability see Strong (1955, p. 63), Darley and Haganah (1955, pp. 37, 53), Trinkhaus (1954), and Canning *et al.* (1941).

Another way of examining stability is to see whether, within the profile, the same scores remain as peaks. In Strong's 18-year follow-up, only about 6 per cent of all A ratings changed to C, 3 per cent of C's to A. Half the profiles were similar enough 18 years later to suggest essentially the same occupational advice. But cases did occur whose profile peaks and valleys were reversed in the interval (Strong, 1955, p. 64; see also Darley & Haganah, 1955, p. 43).

Long-range studies of Kuder C stability are rather few. From age 17 to 21, correlations for various scales range from 0.50 to 0.84 (Herzberg & Bouton, 1954). Stability during high school is perhaps as good as in college (Tutton, 1955; Rosenberg, 1953; Mallinson & Crumbine, 1952). An occasional study is quite discouraging; in a group of engineering students (atypical?) the retest coefficients over four years ranged from −0.22 (for Clerical) to 0.66 (Long & Perry, 1953).

Most research on childhood interests has merely tabulated interests at various ages. Individual scores, when obtained, were usually designed to reflect the "maturity" of interests—that is, whether the games and books a certain 10-year-old enjoys are those typical of 8-, 10-, or 12-year-olds. The one more analytic report is Leona Tyler's (1964). She reports that changes during the elementary grades are better seen as personality development than as interest formation. Aggressiveness, bookishness, and other broad styles are shaped in home, classroom, and peer group. Some actions bring reward and others prove chancy enough that the child comes to dislike them. The main structure of individual differences seems to be related to strength of sex typing. Some boys play the masculine role fully and reject activities suitable for girls; others do not. Among boys who later have scientific interests, masculinity tends to be pronounced in the early grades. Their activities take a specifically scientific turn between ages 10 and 14.

In junior high the pupil begins to form some picture of adult occupations and of the branches of knowledge. He also begins to form a conscious picture of how he differs from other persons. Science, shop, and other courses give him opportunity to discover what he enjoys, but his acquaintance with these areas remains superficial. As he pursues more specialized high-school courses, reads more adult magazines and indulges in hobbies, his interests become more definite. The boy who likes sports spends more time in them, increases his athletic proficiency, makes friends having the same interests, and so builds a little world in which this interest is reinforced. High-school activities also develop interests. The aim of vocational guidance prior to the senior year is to point out areas for exploration. A student who enters high school with greater-than-average liking for persuasive activities should enroll in courses and activities that will test and clarify that interest; he should not commit himself to become a lawyer or salesman. During college, according to Super and Crites (1962, p. 399), interest scores change only for a minority of students. But rather than argue that the "self" has become fixed, one can argue that failure of new interests to appear is a sign of failure of the college program.

The above paragraphs emphasize the boy. Girls' vocational interests have not been so well studied. It is suggested by the data of Matthews and Tiedeman (1964) that in a girl's development the resolution of the home-vs.-career question overrides formation of vocational interests. Interests that surface in early adolescence often fade away when, nearer to womanhood, the girl finds greater attraction in homemaking or for some reason decides to subordinate marriage plans to a career.

The shaping of a career is never finished. Certain doors close if a person does not get the right training at the right time, but whatever training he does get leaves many options. Opportunities to specialize, to turn to administration, or to learn new skills are constantly before the professional man and white-collar worker. The skilled worker likewise, long after he leaves school, continues to make vocational decisions—to change jobs, to acquire a new skill, or to go into business for himself. The worker in a routine factory job has less chance for vocational choice; change, when it comes, is usually forced on him by a layoff. Even retirement brings a need for self-knowledge and choice of activities.

Interests never become entirely fixed. While broad lines of interest remain unchanged, details are reshaped. The beginning psychologist may enjoy everything about the job: testing, directing an experimental laboratory, analyzing data, vocational advising, giving talks on occupations. After a while he finds his greatest satisfaction in advising, and he begins to leave the other tasks to someone else. If his greatest satisfaction comes from dealing with the kind of student whose vocational questions are part of an emotional conflict with his parents, we may find that he encourages only such students to return for extended counseling. No label tells what a person entering a professional field will do. Interests help a student choose between broad lines of training, but in that training and subsequent experience he will modify his interests and make further career decisions.

12. *L-I-D items on biology were applied to eleventh-graders twice, three weeks apart. The score correlation was 0.86; an internal-consistency (α) coefficient for one administration was 0.93. The investigator explains the drop: "It is expected that interests will exhibit some changes over even a 3-week interval." Suggest an alternative explanation.*

Correlations Across Inventories

One might suppose that scores having similar titles in various inventories would correlate highly, but this is not the case. When a fairly large sample of college men took SVIB, MVII, and OIS, the correlations of corresponding scores were often quite low. Median correlations for several seemingly similar scales were 0.25 for SVIB vs. OIS, and 0.19 for OIS vs. MVII. At one extreme, Sales Manager scales of two instruments correlated 0.07; at the other, the correlation for two Carpenter scales was 0.49 (Zytowski, 1968; see also R. Wilson & Kaiser, 1968). This cannot be fully explained. It may imply serious weakness in the instruments.

Surely the most basic reason is that keying procedures differ. Note, for example, in Figure 14.3, that the commonality key and the reference-group key for Engineer do not rank the individuals in the same order. As a person's score moves toward the right of the diagram, his reference-group score rises and his commonality score drops. This is perhaps sufficient to explain the discrepancy between Kuder OIS and Strong scores. MVII and SVIB both use reference-group keys; where their similarly-named scores correlate poorly, it may be because of the different makeup of the reference groups. Complications like this are inevitable when keys are empirical. In the end, one can only learn what a scale means by living with it; even then, he can have little confidence in interpreting profiles for persons who come from a population with which his experience is limited.

The much used Kuder C, which has homogeneous keys, has been compared with SVIB from time to time. The general impression is of modest agreement; correlations above 0.60 of scientific-technical Strong scores with Kuder Scientific, business detail with Clerical, and business contact with Persuasive. But Strong social-service keys correlate less than 0.40 with Kuder Social Service.

Prediction of Vocational Criteria

Overlap with claimed interests. Does the interest inventory give more information than could be obtained by asking the person what fields of work he would like? Evidently the answer is "Yes." Students were asked to estimate their own Kuder Preference Record profiles, i.e., to report the strength of their various interests. The average correlation between estimated interest and measured interest was 0.52 (Crosby & Winsor, 1941). In another investigation (Haganah, 1953; cited in Darley & Haganah, 1955, p. 67), roughly two-thirds of those who claimed interest in business detail, business contact, or a technical field had similar measured interests; but the test supported only a third of those who claimed dominant scientific, social service, and verbal-linguistic interests. (See also Super & Crites, 1962, p. 437–441.)

There are at least two explanations for disagreements between scores and claimed interests. A large number of items, many of them indirectly related to the job in question, provides a thorough sampling of interest, more reliable and more penetrating than the self-estimate. Second, the student who knows his own interests still cannot judge how his interests compare with those of other persons; the inventory places scores on a comparative basis and is logically different from self-estimates of "strength" of interest (see p. 486).

The counselor must not assume that inventory scores are more valid than expressed interests. When claimed and inventoried interests disagree, the counselor will want to make sure that the expressed interest is based on mature consideration, but he would be unwise to dismiss it as "wrong." And when the two agree, he cannot dismiss the possibility that the student has decided to be an engineer and so filled out the inventory to fit the stereotype of the engineer (Bordin, 1943).

Prediction of occupational choice and satisfaction.   Inventories do predict career choice. Strong's most impressive data (1955) are those showing that college interest scores predict the occupation the man will be engaged in 18 years later. Among men in an occupation, five times as many had A ratings in that occupation in college, three times as many had A− ratings, and one-fifth as many had C ratings as did men employed in other fields. Of college men with A in Engineer, one in three became an engineer, one in three entered a related occupation, and one in three entered an occupation having little resemblance to engineering. This indicates good validity, since the man may have A's in several fields yet can enter only one field of work.

Prediction is limited by the fact that subclasses within a profession differ in their interests, as Strong' accountant study illustrated. Dunnette (1957) tested three types of engineers employed in the same company. Interests strong in each group are plotted in Figure 14.5. The research group have scientific and technical interests. Dunnette developed keys to separate the engineers into types, and succeeded in classifying two-thirds of a crossvalidation group.

Interest tests can discriminate men satisfied in a job from those who are dissatisfied. Perry (1955) classified Navy yeomen (clerks) as satisfied and dissatisfied. On the Strong Office Worker key, the mean of satisfied yeomen was 48 while that of the dissatisfied men was 21. In another study, a guidance service that had given the Kuder Preference Record to high-school seniors and adults asked the subjects, a year or more later, what work they were doing and how well they liked it. The investigators then classified each person according to whether his tested interests were "suitable" for the job he held. A similar judgment was made regarding his measured mental ability. As Figure 14.6 shows, interests forecast satisfaction; interests and ability taken together give an excellent prediction.

Further evidence is found in Strong's studies (1943, pp. 114 ff.) of men who

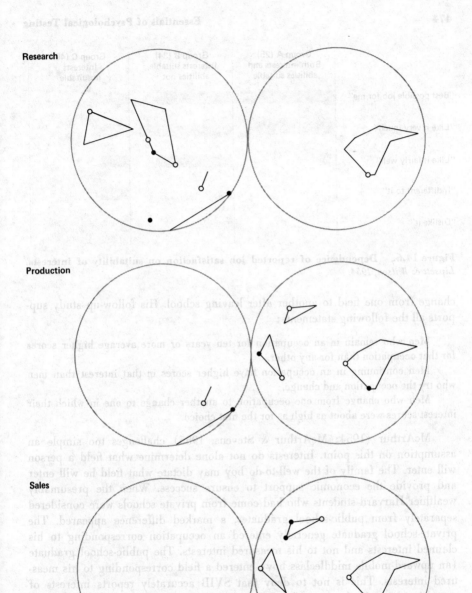

Figure 14.5. Interests shown by engineers performing different functions.
Dunnette, 1957. Each dot shows a Strong score in which the average score of these engineers was A or B+; each open dot shows an average of B. (For names of specific occupations, see Figure 14.2.)

● A or B+
○ B

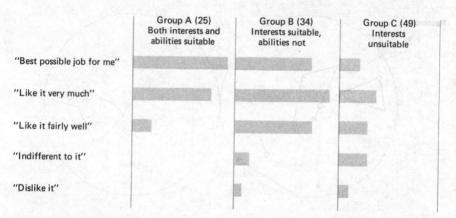

Figure 14.6.   Dependence of reported job satisfaction on suitability of interests.
Lipsett & Wilson, 1954.

change from one field to another after leaving school. His follow-up study supports all the following statements:

Men who remain in an occupation for ten years or more average higher scores for that occupation than for any other.

Men continuing in an occupation have higher scores in that interest than men who try the occupation and change.

Men who change from one occupation to another change to one in which their interest scores were about as high as for the first choice.

McArthur (1954; McArthur & Stevens, 1955) challenges too simple an assumption on this point. Interests do not alone determine what field a person will enter. The family of the well-to-do boy may dictate what field he will enter and provide the economic support to ensure success. When the presumably wealthier Harvard students who had come from private schools were considered separately from public-school graduates, a marked difference appeared. The private-school graduate generally entered an occupation corresponding to his claimed interests and not to his measured interests. The public-school graduate (an upward-mobile middleclass boy) entered a field corresponding to his measured interests. This is not to deny that SVIB accurately reports interests of upperclass boys. Darley says (Gee & Cowles, 1957, p. 26):

It is not that the Strong doesn't "work," it is that you don't need it when students' occupational choices are so completely determined by the subculture from which they come. The Strong may truly reflect another pattern of motivation which his subculture does not allow him to use, and this is the tragedy of that subculture.

For those entering professions or skilled jobs, interest measures are highly pertinent. But a large number of jobs are routine and offer little possibility of self-fulfillment. Probably only faint differences distinguish one unskilled occupation from another. The mounter, whose aptitudes we discussed earlier, spends hour upon hour fastening wires together; wherein lies his vocational satisfaction? If he is to be satisfied, his pleasure must come not from the work itself but from companionship, good working conditions, and freedom from responsibility. The very essence of interest is a changing environment, presenting new situations to be interpreted and dealt with. Thus, while some people can be content in a routine job, it probably cannot command active interest.

Prediction of job success. Only a few studies compare interest scores with excellence of job performance. Most adequate are Strong's investigations of insurance agents (1943, pp. 486–500). Men with A scores in sales interest wrote, on the average, $169,000 per year of new polices, whereas C men averaged only $62,000. A few C men reached the minimum level required to support themselves by commissions; none got much above it. The correlation is only 0.37, no doubt because most C men had dropped out of the sample during their first unproductive years. The dollar values above reinforce our earlier emphasis on the practical significance of tests whose correlations with a criterion are quite moderate (p. 429).

E. L. Kelly and D. W. Fiske (1951) tested students entering training for clinical psychology. Four years later they collected grades, scores on performance tests, ratings by training supervisors, etc. Particular interest attaches to the ratings on Overall Clinical Competence and Research Competence. With hundreds of predictive scores and a dozen criteria, no single coefficient is dependable, but several tentative findings regarding interest tests emerged. Except for Miller Analogies (a *v:ed* measure) no test predicted better than the Strong. Most of the larger correlations for the clinical and research criteria are summarized in Table 14.2. (The correlations may well have been reduced by restricted range in the group and by unreliability of the ratings.) Verbal interests and creative-scientific interests appear to be associated with rated success in clinical-psychology training. Later, information on extent of scholarly publication was collected as a further limited criterion. In one sample several SVIB scientific scales correlated at least 0.20 with the criterion, and office-banker interests correlated negatively. Nothing predicted this criterion, however, in a sample of men who were younger when they entered graduate school and at the time of follow-up (Kelly & Goldberg, 1959).

Inventories have not been good predictors of success in vocational training. The Air Force correlated interest scores with grades in 13 training schools. Almost all correlations were below 0.20 (Brokaw, 1956). K. Clark (1961, p. 87) got a correlation of 0.30 in a Navy electronics school. He suggests that perhaps interests predict grades of students in the middle range of the ability distribution, if not elsewhere. Interest cannot save the incapable; lack of interest cannot spoil the chances of those with high aptitude. In the middle range, perhaps interests matter more.

Table 14.2.   Correlations of SVIB scales with ratings of trainees in clinical psychology

	Correlations with ratings on	
	Overall clinical competence	Research competence
Group I: Biological science	.10 to .22	.22 to .34
Group II: Physical science-technical	—.04 to .09	.27 to .36
Group III: Technical supervision	—.25	—.10
Group V: Social service	—.03 to .06	—.15 to —.01
Group VIII: Business detail	—.24 to —.08	—.30 to —.25
Group IX: Business contact	.02 to .07	—.24 to —.21
Group X: Verbal	.24 to .35	.15 to .27
Psychologist keys (developed in 1949)		
Clinical	.26	.01
Experimental	—.08	.16

SOURCE: E. Kelly & Fiske, 1951, pp. 150–155.

Interest scores based on responses of typical men in the occupation cannot predict success as well as the "merit key" discussed below (p. 484). Ryan and Johnson (1942) show that this method of keying may have substantial predictive power.

Counselees are likely to misinterpret the interest profile as showing what they can do best. Interests tell nothing about abilities; the correlations between interests and more-or-less corresponding abilities (e.g., between Kuder Clerical and DAT Clerical) are close to zero. A high interest score indicates that *if* a person survives training and enters the occupation, he is likely to enjoy his work. Although interests imply motivation, their influence on success is rather small. Perhaps the most reasonable summary is this: a person with interests and abilities suitable for an occupation can and will do well in it, a person with suitable abilities but unsuitable interests can do well but may not, and a person with low aptitude will do badly.

13. *Barnette examined the question of whether men who planned to enter engineering continued in such training. The Kuder Mechanical score had no relation to continuance; it was high for those who dropped out as well as for those who continued. Computational had a marked relation to continuance. Explain.*

14. *Do you agree with the following statement?*

> *"Insofar as stated choice of occupation by groups of individuals (high-school girls) may be considered a true criterion of interest, the lack of relationship between statement of occupational choice and interest scores . . . may be considered evidence of the lack of validity of the interest inventories."*

15. *Production engineers average only B— and sales engineers average C on the Strong Engineer scale. What does this imply regarding the use of SVIB scores in guidance?*

16. *Assuming a normal distribution of Office Worker scores, and the same s.d. in both groups, sketch distributions for satisfied and dissatisfied yeomen in Perry's study. How well does the Strong distinguish these groups?*

17. *Expressed interests of private-school graduates predict what work these students will be doing as adults more accurately than inventoried interests. Does this mean that SVIB is an invalid indicator of their interests?*

18. *Do you agree with this opinion?*

> *Various criteria have been suggested in connection with vocational counseling. . . . Success is often employed as a criterion. It is more appropriate in connection with aptitude tests than with interest tests. But it is doubtful if it is as good as it seems. Fifty per cent of the people must always be less successful than the average. Counseling evaluated on such a basis must always appear rather ineffective"* (Strong, 1955, p. 11).

Prediction of Academic Criteria

Correlations of interests with grades in related fields are generally below 0.30, so interest tests add only a small amount to academic prediction. Interests sometimes predict who stays in training and who drops out. Of those with A and B+ scores on the Strong Dentist key, 92 per cent graduated from dentistry training, compared with 67 per cent of B's and 25 per cent of C's (Strong, 1943, p. 524; see also a study on Kuder scores of teachers in training by Stewart & Roberts, 1955).

It has been suggested that the profile will predict differences in grades between preferred and not-preferred areas. An extensive study by J. W. French (1962a, 1963) shows that prediction of this sort has too little accuracy to be of use.

No technique of using interest scores to predict marks has shown power to increase multiple correlations by much. Even if validity were high, one would hesitate to use questionnaire statements as a basis for admission decisions because faking is too easy. A case can be made for using past activities as evidence of interest and ability in admission decisions. A questionnaire on a high-school student's voluntary activities is unlikely to be faked because reports of projects, awards, etc., can be independently verified. For some evidence on the validity of biographical data of this type, see pp. 428, 479.

Interests and Personality

Interests give clues regarding adjustment and personality. While a person conceals many of his attitudes and feelings from a questioner, he is usually pleased to display his interests. When it is understood that the data will be used to lead him into activities he will enjoy, there is likelihood of honest report.

Liberty, Burnstein, and Moulton (1966) find that persons with a strong sense of mastery of their own fate tend to pick professions in which high competence is demanded (e.g., chemist) rather than high-prestige occupations (e.g., banker) that they see as demanding less competence. Narrow concentration on what one is best at, on the other hand, may be an attempt to evade challenges.

Some persons with conflicts arising from self-criticism find satisfaction in activities that others find monotonous. Bookkeeping appeals to some workers who need to be sure what they do is right. Having added a column of figures and checked themselves, they can feel an assurance they could never have in some more creative activity. There are others who can be satisfied only when imposing their own individuality upon their work. People who dislike routine or stereotyped activities may respond eagerly to tasks and instructional procedures in which originality is essential.

This suggests going beneath the interest profile in an attempt to infer personality. Because it relies on the insight of the interpreter, any such attempt is open to error. A good many empirical studies (Darley & Haganah, 1955, pp. 103–133; Gobetz, 1964) have found modest relations of interests to personality tests, but clinicians and counselors have not found these studies very illuminating because the personality scores themselves reveal little about stresses within the personality. Clinicians therefore fall back on cumulated experience with their own cases. Rarely is such experience collected and systematized; the most complete research of this character is that of Anne Roe (1952, 1957). A broader study (Anne Roe & Siegelman, 1964) suggests that interpersonal stresses in the home make or break early sex-role identification, and that this in turn is often expressed in the eventual vocational choice.

Conclusions about personality trends in groups are well illustrated by these comments on medical students (E. Kelly in Gee & Cowles, 1957, pp. 185–196):

As a group, the medical students [at the University of Michigan] reveal remarkably little interest in the welfare of human beings. For example, one of the sharpest distinctions I can find between a group of physicians at Michigan and a group of clinical psychologists whom we have been studying is [the physicians' higher] Farmer score on the Strong. . . . The Farmer key . . . is based on the modal interest pattern of highly successful graduates of scientific agricultural schools. . . . Such persons are not scientific in the sense that they want to discover new truths; their concern is rather the application of science toward the goal of increasing production. . . .

Another characteristic of medical students is reflected by their relatively high scores on the Aviator scale. . . . The one thing they [various kinds of pilots] have in common is maleness and a lack of interest in anything cultural.

Our data suggest that if you want to select the kind of lad who is going to be interested in public health, general practice, and so on, you should pick the person with a high Strong score on the Carpenter key. This is a person who has a relatively low upward mobile ambition in our society.

Kelly's data illustrate that interest scores shed some light on the role the person is likely to perform within his profession. Among other criteria, socio-metric ratings were obtained from the student's peers, indicating (1) his social relationships, likelihood of becoming a hospital administrator, and personal acceptability as a colleague, and (2) his likelihood of entering some public ser-vice role such as medical-school teaching, and willingness to sacrifice high in-come. Strong scores were used as predictors of these criteria. For Kelly's 112 cases, the Strong Mortician key predicted the social relationship rating ($r = 0.30$), and Mathematician and Chemist had negative correlations of -0.29 with the rating. The highest correlations with the rating on service orientation were Carpenter, 0.44, and Sales Manager, -0.42. Other scales having positive correlations between 0.30 and 0.39 were Industrial Arts Teacher, Math-Science Teacher, Physicist, and Dentists; Advertising Man, CPA, and the Strong keys for sales occupations had negative correlations. There are many pathways to success in medicine or any other profession; vocational self-understanding is not complete when the person is fitted into a broad occupational category.

Information on personality correlates of interest scores comes from a study of 100 Air Force officers assessed by many techniques (Block & Peterson, 1955; see Darley & Haganah, 1955, pp. 128–129). Clinical psychologists rated each man on an adjective checklist. A tabulation was made of the characteristics relatively common among men high on each Strong scale. It was found that the following descriptions tended to fit those with high Mathematician scores, for example: concerned with philosophical problems, introspective, lacking in social poise, lacking confidence in own ability, self-abasing, reacts poorly to stress, sympathetic; and not ostentatious, not aggressive, not socially ascendant. This does not, of course, imply that the mathematicians are a homogeneous group.

Some research with interest measures extends our knowledge about crea-tivity. Helson (1966) studied college senior girls known to the faculty for crea-tive achievements in art, science, etc. The creative girls were much more likely than others to recall that their childhood satisfactions came from creative writing, reading, putting on shows, etc. So strong was the relation ($r = 0.58$) that Helson made all her further comparisons *within* the group reporting such childhood interests. Comparing the creative girls with noncreatives who also had had artistic childhood interests, she found the creatives a bit higher on Strong group keys I, II, VI, and X. She found also that the true creatives were more persevering, more planful, less conformist—and better on SAT-Verbal. They did not differ on the Unusual Uses test of divergent thinking or on several other supposed indicators of creativeness.

Similar findings come from a retrospective study of male engineers well into their careers (S. Klein & Owens, 1965). The criterion (information on patents and research leadership) was predicted with validities 0.25 to 0.30 by a test of mechanical ingenuity given to the men in college 10 years before. Each item in this test depicts a power source (e.g., a turning axle) and a resultant motion (e.g., an up-and-down vibration) and asks the subject to sketch a mechanism for converting one motion to the other. He is to give several solutions; a quantity score was not as predictive as one that took quality into account. What is relevant in this chapter is that adding scores from a life-history questionnaire to the test score produced a multiple correlation of 0.41 in one group, 0.69 in a second. (The former is a crossvalidation; the latter would probably drop to around 0.55 if crossvalidated—still, a remarkable prediction for such a criterion.) The questionnaire shows the more productive men to have been more interested in science as children. Some of this "predictive" information is a reflection of professional success; a follow-up study, with the questionnaire given during college, is still needed.

Interest patterns are not to be called good or bad. Perhaps the reader is inclined to judge the mathematically oriented officers described above as being maladjusted. Such a value judgment can be made only on the basis of some theory of the good life—and such a theory is open to challenge. Contemporary psychological writing appears to assume that the ideal person is confident, interested in social contacts, and effective as a leader. Anne Roe (1952), however, points out that many distinguished, effective, apparently contented physical and biological scientists are not socially oriented. They care little for making friendships or for earning the good opinions of others. Eminent and effective psychologists (including laboratory experimenters), on the other hand, typically are concerned with having good relationships with others. Roe finds that men in both groups had difficulties with social relationships at some time in their preadult development, and believes that each group found a different method of adjusting successfully to these difficulties. The physical scientists became absorbed in tasks not involving other persons, while the psychologists made other persons their professional concern. This leads Roe to question whether psychologists, merely because their own personalities call for an active relationship with others, write a similar relationship into their definition of "adjustment." Quite possibly, says Roe (1953), the psychologists underrate healthy patterns of adjustment that do not coincide with their own. Conversely, if physical scientists were to define the healthy personality after studying all the data available to psychologists, their ideal might place little emphasis on warm friendships and ability to lead, and a great deal of emphasis on responsibility, freedom from suggestibility, and independence of group opinion. This argument is supported by the finding that clinical psychologists' ratings of "soundness" of personality depend strongly upon warmth in interpersonal relations. Eccentricity or deviation from the norm they regard with suspicion. When nonpsychologist faculty members rate the same students, however, "soundness" is judged almost entirely by effectiveness in getting work done (Barron, 1954).

In this discussion we have confined attention to the interpretation of personality from the usual inventory scores. It is possible to use interest inventories more directly as disguised personality measures. The empirical technique can construct an anxiety key for SVIB by counting responses of a criterion group of anxious persons, and indeed this has been done (Garman & Uhr, 1958).

Interest Inventories in Counseling

Historically, interest tests have always been a method for helping the individual attain satisfaction for himself rather than a method for satisfying institutions. As a result, the interest inventory is used almost entirely in academic and vocational counseling, and not for administrative decisions.

One may conceive such counseling as intended to arrive at a definite decision—a definite goal and a training plan—or one may conceive the counseling as intended to promote the client's continual growth in self-understanding. Counselors generally take the second point of view. As we pointed out earlier, vocational development involves new choices as new facts become available, as the individual matures, or as his social circumstances and opportunities change. The student and counselor in high school may set down a definite plan to study certain subjects, to enroll in a certain college curriculum, to complete training in a certain professional school, and to find an opportunity to enter a certain type of practice. This plan has small probability of being carried out. Somewhere along the line instructors will open new vistas to the student or arouse new interests. Somewhere along the line concrete experience will show him that he does not enjoy some aspect of the work and will reveal an unsuspected talent in another direction. Counseling should generate plans with many branches. The significant goal in counseling is to equip the student to make future decisions as choice-points are reached. The aim in counseling should be to give the student a more sophisticated view of the world of work, of the choices open to him, and of his own range of potentialities for achievement and satisfaction.

Interest inventories are highly suited to vocational counseling. The student expects his interests to be considered and is not threatened by the questionnaire as he may be by personality or ability tests. The interpretation, when given, carries considerable force, because the student can see that he is looking in a mirror, reflecting on what he himself has said. No psychological mysteries becloud the interest test as they do tests that involve esoteric constructs. The counselor hesitates to tell a student his aptitude and personality test scores unless there is ample evidence that he can accept and comprehend the findings, whereas scores on interest tests can be discussed freely. While they may require the student to examine discrepancies within his self-concept, they rarely challenge self-esteem.

The interest inventory can be given to entire classes or entire student bodies, and interpretation of profiles can be carried out in group discussions rather than in individual counseling (Layton, 1958, pp. 32 ff.). Such a process—leading each student to list several career possibilities suggested for him by the test—is an excellent preliminary to further group study of careers or to individual counseling.

The interest inventory assists counselors in other ways. A promise to interpret interest scores invites students to seek out the counselor. In the course of the discussion of vocations the student will talk about his family, his social relations, and his academic difficulties, and so may touch upon problems on which the counselor can provide assistance. The conference opens a natural opportunity for the student to express his desire for such help, a desire he might otherwise never have acknowledged even to himself.

In view of the aims described above, it is most unwise to concentrate the interview upon scores for a few specific occupations. This gives the student far too narrow a description of himself and leaves too many things out of consideration. It is absolutely essential that the student go beneath occupational labels and stereotypes, that he understand the variety of roles within the same occupation, that he understand the differences between demands of the training program and demands of the occupation, and that he recognize the shifting nature of occupations. He must consider his abilities and academic prospects, the pressures from his family, his motivations and values, his financial resources, and the probability that his present interests will shift.

Darley and Haganah (1955, p. 195), speaking from this point of view, sharply criticize some common practices in vocational counseling. They take as an example the student with peak interests in the social service group.

At some point in the counseling interview series, the counselor can make this bald statement: "You have the same kind of interests as successful personnel managers or Y.M.C.A. secretaries or school superintendents." With minor modifications, this is probably the standard approach to interpretation. It is also the least effective approach and the one most likely to lead the student and counselor into ever deeper morasses of interpretive difficulties.

Darley and Haganah give eight reasons for condemning the approach, most of which we have touched on already. Most specifically, such an approach causes the student to think in terms of occupational stereotypes, instead of trying to see what interests of his match activities in the job. Moreover, the counselee who sees himself as a business executive in an all-male world may attach a negative connotation to—let us say— "school superintendent." Then he may find it necessary to resist the test interpretation.

Instead of making a narrowly occupational interpretation, counselors should help the student identify the groups of activities in which he has expressed interests. Kuder scores C and E lead directly to this type of interpretation. A high score in literary interests, for example, can be amplified by questioning that will clarify whether this is an interest in reading, in writing, or in speaking; whether it is an interest in face-to-face communication or in isolative writing; and whether it is accompanied by any evidence of appropriate talent. The discussion will ultimately come around to specific vocations, as examples of ways in which the interests might be satisfied. Illustrative vocations should be consistent with the student's claimed interests, his probable ultimate level of education, and his abilities. It is more awkward, but not impossible, to generate such a discussion with OIS. With SVIB, according to the 1969 supplement to the manual, Campbell now recommends starting interpretation with the "basic" homogeneous scales, and supplementing them by examining selected occupational scales. This is a radical departure from previous practice in using SVIB.

One must help the student to an emotionally acceptable reconciliation of claimed and measured interests. To tell Mary Thomas, "You don't really want to work in child development; you want to be a secretary," would precipitate emotional conflict. No one can abandon a long-standing self-concept easily. An authority who bluntly contradicts firm beliefs invites the counselee to reject him as an authority. In Mary's case, it might be best to inquire as to the reasons for her choice of child development, to ask her to envision the activities she may be engaged in 10 years hence, and to compare them with the activities rated high in the interest blank. The fact that the inventory contains only her own ratings brings her to face self-contradictions. The psychologist is no longer the "authority"—he is merely holding the mirror.

19. *Campbell now recommends emphasis on the short, undisguised, descriptive "Basic Interest Scales" in counseling. All previous research with SVIB has dealt with the occupational scales. List specific questions future research should answer to determine whether the basic scales are a more satisfactory focus for counseling. Describe studies that would answer these questions.*

A List of Inventories

Among the interest inventories currently in use are the following:

• California Occupational Preference Survey; Robert R. Knapp, Bruce Grant, and George D. Demos; *EITS.*
One hundred sixty-eight relatively transparent items to be checked on a 4-point scale to indicate strength of liking or disliking. Items are clustered into scales such as Science—skilled, Aesthetic—professional, etc. Split-half reliabilities are high but there is no evidence on stability or validity at present.

• Minnesota Vocational Interest Inventory; Kenneth E. Clark with David P. Campbell; *Psych. Corp.*
For high-school students and adults. Forced-choice triads are scored by weights developed according to Strong's procedure, to indicate how closely one's interests resemble those of men in trades such as baker, plasterer, retail sales clerk, and milk-wagon driver. A second set of scales is based on homogeneous clusters (e.g., office work, outdoors, food service). Covers a portion of the occupational range for which SVIB is inadequate.

● Occupational Interest Survey, Form DD; G. Frederic Kuder; *SRA*.
100 forced-choice items keyed for various occupations and college majors on
the commonality principle. A new and promising empirical instrument. (See
pp. 466 ff.)

● Preference Record, Vocational, Form C and General Interest Survey,
Form E; G. Frederic Kuder; *SRA*.
For grades 7 upward. Ten scores show percentile standing in various interest
categories. Form E is the more recent; it has 168 forced-choice items and administration requires nearly an hour. (See pp. 457 ff.)

● Strong Vocational Interest Blank for Men; E. K. Strong, Jr., David P.
Campbell, and others; *Stanford*.
For high-school students and adults. (See pp. 460 ff.)

● Strong Vocational Interest Blank for Women; E. K. Strong, Jr., David P.
Campbell, and others; *Stanford*.
A 1969 publication. Emphasis is on professional and skilled occupations. The
original women's blank proved to have less predictive validity than the men's
blank, perhaps because women are less able to choose careers that particularly
interest them. Follow-up studies on the new blank will be needed to determine
whether it functions better than the old one.

New Directions in Interest Measurement

Alternatives in Keying

The Strong key is purely empirical. His keying procedure contrasts engineers (for example) with "men-in-general," most of them college graduates.
Another reference group could be used—e.g., all adult males, or a noncollege
group—and a different key would result. Kuder OIS shifts to a "commonality"
procedure, determining how closely the person's interests match those of engineers without taking any broader reference group into account. A further
possibility is to contrast "merit" groups, comparing successful engineers with
unsuccessful engineers. Figure 14.3 has already suggested that Strong's procedure is not the best.

To illustrate further how keys depend on the weighting system, Figure 14.7
displays hypothetical data for five groups; all adult men (M), male college
graduates (C), "successful" engineers (E), and two groups E+ and E— of
engineering graduates classified on the basis of merit on the job. One may
reasonably suppose that the E group is largely but not wholly made up of E+'s,
and that the E— group includes some who have left the field as failures. The differences on our illustrative items are, we hope, plausible, but there is no evidence
on them. We argue only that there must be *some* items that show patterns of this
sort. To simplify, we score every response +1, 0, or −1, and for the moment
ignore "I" and "D" responses.

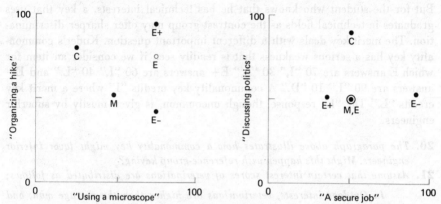

Figure 14.7. Hypothetical percentage of "L" responses in various groups.
M, men in general; C, college graduates; E, engineers; E+ and E—, engineers judged
good and poor.

We get one set of weights if we contrast E with M, and another if we contrast E with C:

REFERENCE GROUP

	Men-in-general	College graduates
Organizing a hike	1	0
Using a microscope	1	1
Discussing politics	0	−1
A secure job	0	0

The first key favors organizers, the second favors those without political interests. (One could obtain still a third key by comparing engineers with graduates in all scientific and technical fields. A fourth possibility is to compare one type of engineer with engineers-in-general.)

Contrasting E+ with E— to identify interests associated with merit produces a key favoring the man who likes to organize a hike and who does not call for a secure job. The microscope item, which entered the first keys, drops out; liking to use a microscope is, on this hypothetical evidence, common to good and bad engineers alike.

The commonality key simply credits whatever response the majority of engineers give: here, "L" on hike and microscope. On these items the key is the same as the men-in-general contrast key. But suppose the percentage of "L" responses is 10 for E and M instead of 50, and the percentage of "D" responses is 90. Then "D" would count in the commonality key and not in the contrast key.

Probably M is a poor reference group. To guide a student regarding occupations that require college training, using C as reference seems reasonable.

But for the student who knows that he has technical interests, a key that uses graduates in technical fields as the contrast group may offer sharper discrimination. The merit key deals with a different important question. Kuder's commonality key has a serious weakness that is readily seen if we consider an item for which E answers are 70 "I," 30 "L," E+ answers are 60 "I," 40 "L," and E– answers are 90 "I," 10 "D." A commonality key credits "I" where a merit key credits "L." The "L" response, though uncommon, is given mostly by superior engineers.

20. *The paragraph above illustrates how a commonality key might favor inferior engineers. Might this happen with reference-group keying?*

21. *Assume that certain interest scores of veterinarians are distributed as follows:*

> *In Outdoor interests, veterinarians are higher than the average man, and their success is positively correlated with the interest score.*
>
> *In Persuasive interests, veterinarians have the same average as men in general. Persuasive interests are positively correlated with success in the field.*
>
> *In Social Service interests, veterinarians tend to be below the average for all men, and the correlation between their interests and success is positive.*

What advice would a key of the Strong type lead to? What advice would be given if expectation of success within the field were considered?

Absolute Profiles

The psychologist has usually thought of his numerical scales as arbitrary. Making items on an ability test easier or harder would move scores lower or higher. Selecting more popular or less popular activities for an interest scale would likewise move the score up or down. But absolute, criterion-referenced scores are possible for ability measures (the decibel scale for measuring hearing, or a measure of typing speed in words per minute, for example). Perhaps directly interpretable interest scores can and should be developed.

Emphasizing norms is hard to defend. To tell a girl, "Your interest in raising a family is at the 30th percentile" suggests that her interest is low; this is quite the wrong conclusion, if 90 per cent of girls are positively interested in that responsibility. "Your interest in washing dishes is at the 90th percentile" is equally misleading, if 99 per cent of girls hate dishwashing. At most, the facts suggest that this girl hates dishwashing less intensely than others, and is not so wildly enthusiastic about raising a family as some. A percentile scale implies that one should seek out the field in which he *ranks* highest, not the field in which his interest is most intense. Strong assigns A to a score that falls above the 30th percentile in the occupational sample, which seems to assume that, no matter what the occupation, 70 per cent of job holders like their work. (Strong never tried to make a key for dishwashers!) As a minimum the interpreter should know what percentile standing on each dimension represents the point where liking shifts to indifference.

Table 14.3. **Popularity of occupations as a function of definition of response categories**

Occupational category	Percentage of occupations endorsed at each level of liking		
	T	PA	SO
Artistic	48	28	17
Clerical	52	27	9
Persuasive	60	38	26
Mechanical	68	48	33

SOURCE: Terwilliger, 1960.

Research by Terwilliger (1960) takes a step in this direction. He defined response categories much more carefully than usual, giving definitions (which we must abbreviate here) for the following degrees of liking.

SO: Would you make a great effort to *seek out* a job of this kind (taking special training, moving to another city, etc.)?

PA: Would you think quite seriously about an offer of this job and *probably* accept it?

T : Could you *tolerate* the work? Would you be willing to stay in such a job if you did not know whether you could get another job?

(We omit two intermediate levels.)

Job titles in four fields, with brief definitions, were sampled from the *Dictionary of occupational titles.* Each subject was assigned one of the response definitions to follow. High-school boys responding under SO directions endorsed 17 per cent of occupations in the "artistic" field and 32 per cent of "mechanical" occupations. Table 14.3 gives further results. The popularity of mechanical and persuasive work and the unpopularity of clerical and artistic work are clear.

One could use a procedure like Terwilliger's in measuring individuals, profiling the percentage of jobs judged acceptable. Figure 14.8 shows what two such absolute-score profiles might look like, and compares these profiles with a plot of the same data as percentiles. Person A is equally mild in his endorsement of all fields. The plot of percentiles suggests incorrectly that A likes artistic work and clerical work. B, who seems to lack any strong interest when percentiles are inspected, actually likes mechanical jobs much better than artistic and clerical.

Terwilliger had limited data and only a tentative procedure. A good deal of developmental research would be needed to make absolute profiling practical. Even so, the study is a clear demonstration that percentile standing does not indicate degree of interest, and is a basis for seriously criticizing the traditional mode of interpretation.

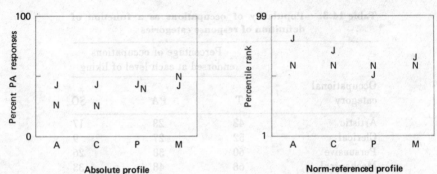

Figure 14.8.   Absolute and norm-referenced profiles for Jim and Nick (hypothetical data).

SUGGESTED READINGS

Callis, Robert, Polmantier, Paul C., and Roeber, Edward C. The case of Bill Davis. In *A casebook of counseling*. New York: Appleton-Century-Crofts, 1955. Pp. 77–103.

> Transcribed interview notes. A senior engineer student who expresses his lack of interest in engineering goes over his Strong and Kuder profiles with a counselor.

Darley, John G., and Haganah, Theda. The Strong Vocational Interest Blank in individual cases. In *Vocational interest measurement: theory and practice*. Minneapolis: University of Minnesota Press, 1955. Pp. 194–263. (Reprinted in Jackson & Messick, 1967).

> The authors explain how to proceed from the profile that shows primary interest areas to a discussion of specific occupational choices. Ten cases are described, showing how the use of SVIB information varies according to the client's aptitudes, maturity of self-concept, and background influences. Of particular interest is a history (Karl Brooks) that describes development from age 14 to 25.

Perry, Dallis K., and Cannon, W. M. Vocational interests of female computer programmers. *Journal of Applied Psychology*, 1968, 52, 31–35.

> A representative study that employs empirical methods to develop a key. Even though the study uses the 1966 Blank for men, it separates the women programmers from men and from women in general.

Super, Donald E., and Crites, John O. The nature of interests. In *Appraising vocational fitness*. New York: Harper & Row, 1962. Pp. 377–416.

> An authoritative review of findings on the development of vocational interests and their psychological and practical significance. Two following chapters compile further evidence, more closely tied to particular tests. The authors' admiration for Strong and his test, while warranted, generates an emphasis a bit different from ours.

General Problems in Studying Personality

We have suggested a rough division of tests between those that seek to measure what a person can do and what he "typically" does. Most personality measures can be thought of as attempts to assess typical behavior, but the notion has some limitations. In some ways, personality is an "ability"—there are some persons who simply cannot bring themselves to be aggressive, and others who cannot act submissively for very long. Some of the ability tests examined in Part II are interpreted as indices of personality; the special value of the Porteus maze (p. 237) may come from the fact that impulsive persons do badly. Another difficulty is that to identify personality with "behavior" is to ignore the importance of subjective mental states. As Part III develops we shall see that no single interpretation applies to all tests.

Types of Data

Observations in Representative Situations

The logical way to learn about a person's typical behavior is to observe him repeatedly on a random sample of occasions or, more efficiently, in selected situations likely to elicit the responses in which we are interested. To study interests, one would observe the person during his leisure. To evaluate a businessman's generosity, one would observe his responses to charitable appeals, his tipping, and his dealings with employees.

The first requirement is a sufficient number of suitable observations. No one act can be taken as typical. The act is influenced by the mood, by immediately preceding experience, by details of the surroundings, and by other factors. Behavior has cycles and trends. If a subject appears quarrelsome on several occasions, quarrelsomeness seems typical of him. Perhaps, however, he is in a continuing state of irritability because of some worry, and some months earlier or later he would appear to be well adjusted. One who thinks of personality as the person's "nature" will argue that we took too few observations or made too little allowance for the disturbing element. What we observed, he calls a mere temporary deviation. Yet the deviation was real, and the behavior reported was typical for the subject during that time. Ups-and-downs may be of as much interest as the evened-out average.

What is a "suitable" observation needs to be defined. One cannot guess what a report of typical behavior means unless the observer specifies directly or indirectly the time span of the data, the range of situations, the range of incentives before the subject, and the actions taken into account by the observer.

The second procedural requirement is that the act of observing must not alter the behavior observed. The presence of a traffic cop at an intersection raises drivers' performance above their habitual level. The presence of the psychological observer may cause the subject to try harder. This seems to occur even when there is no direct threat or possible benefit. Roethlisberger and Dickson (1939) attempted to compare work output under various conditions at a manufacturing plant. Relay assemblers were placed in a small room where they could be observed. Their output was recorded in great detail, as various experimental rest pauses and privileges were introduced. As changes continued, no matter what they were, production climbed. Finally the rest pauses and privileges were removed, and production per hour still remained as high as under the "best" working conditions. Absenteeism dropped from 15.2 days per year per worker before entering the study to 3.5 days per year in the test room. The heightened morale of the workers—as a result of being singled out for study, of being better acquainted with their supervisors, and of feeling personal responsibility for their rate of output—changed their performance so that it was no longer comparable to that in the regular workroom. (This morale effect, important in educational and social research, is often called the Hawthorne effect, after the Hawthorne, Illinois, works of the Western Electric Company, where the study took place).

Distortion is less when the judging is a regular part of the work procedure. Ratings by foremen can reasonably be regarded as reports of typical behavior in the plant, for the foreman is usually present; how the man would act if no foreman were provided is not of interest.

An ideally random sample of total behavior can never be observed. Those moments of life open to the psychologist's inspection are by no means typical. Tabulating the businessman's responses to charitable appeals is a fantasy; these private moments are not open to our observation. Observation in representative situations can be used to learn about the individual's typical *public* behavior: in classrooms, on playgrounds, and in certain work situations. Because it is so costly, sampling of "natural" behavior is used almost exclusively for research, particularly research on children young enough to ignore the presence of the observer.

1. *Define the range, in time and situations, of the behavior one should study to answer these questions:*
   a. *How well does this supervisor handle grievances?*
   b. *Does study of philosophy make one more rational in his adult life?*
   c. *Does viewing a film on nutrition improve housewives' practices in menu planning?*
   d. *Do graduates of the modern elementary school write legibly?*
   e. *How anxious is this patient at this point in therapy?*

Reports from Others and from the Subject

When the precision and detachment of the scientific observer is not required, information can be elicited from the subject's acquaintances and coworkers. The rating by a foreman is more nearly a general impression than a record of typical behavior, but it is nonetheless useful. Similarly, mothers give information about children, nurses about patients, patients about ward attendants, and so on.

It is common to regard ratings and descriptions as information given by a competent authority who is a professional ally of the psychologist. Any report, however, is one individual's perception of another, subject to as much distortion as any perception of a fluctuating, ambiguous stimulus. Indeed, such reports often serve as information about the personality or motivational state of the rater.

Sociometric techniques obtain reports from participants in a common situation. Children rate other members of their school groups, college girls rate other members of their sororities, officer candidates rate classmates, pupils describe the practices of their teacher. Students describe events that add up to a picture of the "climate" of their college. The interpreter who does not assume that such a report is a valid accounts of the facts may still be interested in the impression the person or the institution has made.

Similar comments are to be made about the self-report. The subject is informed about his own behavior, but there are distortions in his perception of himself and in his report. We shall discuss the interpretation of self-reports at some length below.

Performance Tests

In principle, reports from others and self-reports can shed light on corners of the subject's life where the observer may never go, can cover past behavior that is no longer observable, and can take into account far more incidents than could be observed directly. Moreover, they record information on mood and feeling. But subjective impressions, however significant they may be, are not dependable accounts of behavior. Performance tests are intended to get distortion-free information on overt behavior.

The performance tester gives up the attempt to observe in typical situations. His technique is to offer a provocative stimulus that will elicit especially significant behavior. As in a measure of aptitude or achievement, the tester puts before the individual a standardized task, and assigns an objective score to what the person accomplishes or records information on the way he responds. Inferences are then made about the personality "behind the behavior."

Various techniques fall in this category. One might measure interests, for example, by a test on knowledge of current developments in science, engineering, music, public affairs, and so on, assuming that knowledge to some degree follows interest. One might allow the subject a supposed "rest period" midway in a battery of tests and let him browse in a library; the books that attract his attention might be presumed to represent his interests. A third technique is to require him to make up stories about pictures showing people at work in settings such as a hospital operating room. The ideas and feelings he attributes to the characters in the pictures may indicate his attitudes about various types of work.

There is no accepted classification system for performance tests. R. B. Cattell applies the term *objective test* to devices that yield a direct measure of performance, unmodified by any subjective report or clinical interpretation. This name, however, is not commonly used because even a questionnaire is "objectively" scored. The name *situation test* has been applied to tests of performance in complex, lifelike situations. It was first used for worksamples of leadership, in which the candidate for a leadership position was given a crew of men, assigned a task, and observed as he directed the crew. Another subcategory is the *projective technique*. In it, the tester presents a picture or other ambiguous stimulus and asks the subject what he sees in it or what he thinks will happen next. Instead of scoring the number and quality of responses, the interpreter may assume that responses are projections of the subject's unconscious wishes, attitudes, and conceptions of the world, following the model of Freudian interpretation of dreams.

The great advantage of the performance test is that it permits fair comparison of individuals. A rating of leadership may reflect differences in opportunity rather than differences in readiness to lead, but a performance test gives each candidate the same opportunity to lead. Individual differences in use of that opportunity somehow reflect personality.

Behavior in the standardized situation cannot be considered "typical." It is a sample of response to a very special stimulus—namely, a-leadership-opportunity-when-being-tested-by-a-psychologist-whose-good-opinion-will-have-certain-consequences. The performance test gives neat data, but interpretation is far more difficult than interpretation of observations in representative situations or reports from others.

For research, on the other hand, the standardized performance test is a preferred technique. An investigator who wishes to understand an aspect of behavior (e.g., persistence) will devise a test by which that tendency can be observed. He and other psychologists can carry out comparable experiments. Questionnaires are also used in this way. Too often an investigator confines his study to a single instrument. It is much more desirable to develop two or more dissimilar techniques to measure the same trait—e.g., a performance test and a questionnaire, or a task that uses motor response and a verbal task. If these tests correlate, and if they give similar results in an experiment, one can have greater confidence that the findings deal with a broadly significant trait.

2. *How well can the four procedures—observation in representative situations, report from others, self-report, and performance tests—satisfy the following requirements? Rank the procedures from best to poorest in each respect.*

  a. *The data reflect differences in personality rather than differences in environment and opportunity.*

  b. *The data reflect the individual's behavior, undistorted by the perceptions of those who provide data.*

  c. *The data provide a summary or estimate of the individual's behavior during all moments of his life.*

  d. *The results are the same, regardless of whether the subject wishes to make a good impression on the psychologist.*

The Self-Description: Report of Typical Behavior?

The simplest view of the self-report is to treat it as a record of typical behavior, which the subject is in a uniquely excellent position to observe. There is some justification for so interpreting the interest inventory, since the person seeking guidance wants his interests to be satisfied in the work he selects. Likewise on an opinion questionnaire, faking is rarely a problem. Since "every man has a right to his own opinion," candid answers are usually expected. "The respondent's understanding of the purpose of the test and the psychologist's understanding are in agreement. Were the respondent to read the psychologist's report of the test results, none of the topics would surprise him" (D. T. Campbell, 1957). Views are misrepresented, of course, if the questionnaire asks about topics subject to social taboo. And even an interest inventory used for counseling may be distorted by the student who wants to display high aims so as to win the counselor's approval.

Various distortions prevent us from accepting personality questionnaires as frank and valid self-descriptions. The first difficulty is that items are ambiguous. "Do you make friends easily?" seems to be a straightforward question, but it is hard to say just what behavior the question refers to, and what the tester means by *easily*. The subject, reflecting upon his past behavior, is unable to count up positive and negative incidents. If he could, his report would be a simple factual statement. But he will recall some people who became warm friends quickly and other acquaintances who remained somewhat distant for months. If he tries to push for a more literal interpretation of the question, he soon bogs down. What does *friend* mean—intimate companionship? pleasant interaction without emotional involvement? or something in between? The subject responding to a questionnaire does not ask such fussy questions (though a scientific observer would have to). The subject answers the question in terms of an inarticulate self-concept. If he regards himself as being the type who makes friends easily—hang niceties of definition!—he says "Yes" to the question. Another equally popular boy may have a different self-concept and respond "No."

Similar difficulty arises because most questionnaires ask about the hypothetical "typical" situation, instead of asking about well-defined situations. "Do you seek suggestions from others?" is a fairly clear question, but most people would have to answer, "Sometimes I do, but not always." This might be further qualified: "I do on difficult problems"; "I do if someone is around whose ideas are especially good"; "I don't if I'm supposed to make the decision myself." These qualifications would have to be stated if the subject tried seriously to report typical behavior. Since he cannot average his memories to determine what percentage of the time he has sought suggestions, the question will be answered offhand. When one person defines "Yes" to mean "With very few exceptions," and another defines it as "Fairly often; at least in difficult situations," they are answering different questions and their responses are not comparable. Another example is the apparently clear item: "Do you like to operate an adding machine?" Many students say that they enjoy this but would be dissatisfied with a job in which they had nothing to do *but* operate an adding machine.

Many self-report tests ask for responses "Always," "Frequently," "Never," or the like. Simpson (1944) examined what such ratings might mean quantitatively. He asked students what they meant by saying they "usually" did something. Twenty-five per cent of them applied "Usually" only to responses made at least 90 per cent of the time; another 25 per cent said that "Usually" included frequencies below 70 per cent. The quantitative interpretation of other words is shown in Table 15.1. It is evident that subjects with identical behavior choose very different adverbs to describe what they do.

We shall devote most of our attention to complicated inventories with long lists of questions. But we should not lose sight of the fact that the subject can often give us good information on a simple one-item self-rating. Considering the saving in time and effort, a few such questions may indeed be preferable to a "test." The advantages of the inventory are in allowing more precise comparisons

Table 15.1.   Range of meanings assigned to response
terms commonly used in personality
inventories

	What percentage of all occasions is indicated by the word at left?	
	Median answer	Range of answers of middle 50 per cent of subjects
Usually	85	70–90
Often	78	65–85
Frequently	73	40–80
Sometimes	20	13–35
Occasionally	20	10–33
Seldom	10	6–18
Rarely	5	3–10

SOURCE: Simpson, 1944.

between persons and in bringing norms to bear; neither of these factors may be
of first importance in, for example, opening up counseling.

Response Biases

A person approaches the test with a certain attitude and with a certain
interpretation of whatever ambiguities there are in the directions. This influences
his score. If we change his interpretation, the score will change. The tendency of
some subjects to say "True" when in doubt dilutes the validity of true-false tests
as measures of knowledge. In a personality test, similar response biases enter.
Some persons taking the SVIB use the "L" response very frequently; we have no
way of knowing whether they truly have unusually broad interests, or simply
respond "L" to any activity they do not find unpleasant. Some people are evasive,
using "Indifferent," "Cannot Say," or some other intermediate response with
great frequency. And—perhaps most important—some people deliberately try to
paint a self-serving picture of themselves.

Faking.   The tester may view his inquiry as a scientific project to which the
subject is willing to contribute valid information, but the subject sees it differently. In the clinic, he may want to avoid certain threatening diagnoses. In
employment testing, his first concern is to land the job. In vocational guidance,
he may set out to convince the counselor that he should enter a certain occupation rather than to learn the truth about his suitability for it. When industrial
workers filled out identical health questionnaires under two conditions, the results
were strikingly different. One questionnaire was turned in to the company medical department, as a preliminary to a medical examination designed to improve

the worker's health. The other questionnaire was mailed directly to a research team at a university. The workers listed far more symptoms on the research questionnaire (which would not help them) than on the other, despite the fact that an honest report to the company physician might bring them medical help.

The majority of subjects pick the "socially desirable" (SD) response to any item. Some tests have SD keys that count how often the person gives the response socially accepted as desirable. A high SD score may mean that the person truly has an admirable personality, but it is also possible that he has been less than frank in filling out the questionnaire. Nor can one dismiss the possibility that he is deceiving himself and has never realized some of the faults in his behavior.

Some subjects deliberately paint an unfavorable self-portrait. A draftee may report an impressive array of emotional symptoms if he thinks it will get him a discharge. In an ordinary clinical test, exaggerating symptoms may be a gambit to enlist sympathy and attention. The subject may prefer to have the tester believe that his troubles as a student are caused by emotional disturbance than to be thought stupid or lazy.

A so-called "hello-goodbye" effect confounds evaluation of psychotherapy. Upon entering the clinic, the client tends to present the worst side of himself. He probably does not lie outright, but when either of two responses could be defended he selects the unfavorable one. His symptoms are at such a peak that they have brought him to treatment. They are very much on his mind, and his full display of them bids the clinic to take his problem seriously. Just the opposite is noted when the client is discharged after treatment. Now the self-description glows with the psychological counterpart of "Thanks, Doc. I feel fine." The passage of time alone is likely to have reduced the intensity of distress. The favorable report may involve some self-deception, to prove that the sacrifice of time, money, and privacy was not foolish. One motivation of faking good, Hathaway suggests, is the client's desire to repay the therapist by letting him see how much help he has given. It would be ungrateful indeed for the departing client to dwell on the symptoms the therapy left untouched. On his exit questionnaire the client may be disposed to give himself (and his therapist) the benefit of all the borderline decisions. The number of symptoms is thus below the number reported at intake. True improvement is not easily distinguished from change in test-taking attitude.

Various devices have been used to make it hard to falsify scores; we shall discuss some of them below. To test whether they are effective, the investigator asks some subjects to fill out the questionnaire honestly and others to try to give a false picture—a socially desirable report, a socially undesirable one, or one that fits a particular role. Longstaff had students take the Strong and Kuder (a forerunner of Form C) in the normal way, and then to take them again, trying to show a certain pattern of high and low scores. Table 15.2 shows some of the results. While both tests are fakable, it is perhaps easier to fake high interests on the Strong and easier to fake aversion on the descriptively scored Kuder. Wes-

Table 15.2.   Percentage of male students able to fake Strong and Kuder scores successfully

Scores "Faked Upward"							
Percentage reaching A on Strong keys	Carpenter	9	Chemist	91	Artist	86	Author 83
Percentage reaching 75th percentile on Kuder keys	Mechanical	32	Scientific	5	Artistic	83	Literary 51
Difference		−23		86		3	32
Scores "Faked Downward"							
Percentage reaching C on Strong keys	Accountant	26	Life insurance sales	20	Personnel manager	37	Office man 54
Percentage reaching 25th percentile on Kuder keys	Computational	30	Persuasive	70	Social service	70	Clerical 41
Difference		− 4		−50		−33	13

NOTE: The Kuder scale used was a forerunner of forms C and E.
SOURCE: Longstaff, 1948.

man (1952a) gave a personality inventory with the instructions: "I want you to pretend that you are applying for the position of salesman in a large industrial organization. You have been unemployed for some time, have a family to support, and want very much to land this position. You are being given this test by the employment manager. Please mark the answers you would give." The next week, the same inventory was filled out "as if you were applying for the position of librarian in a small town." The scores on the two occasions differed spectacularly (Figure 15.1). Probably most applicants give more honest answers than the students in these experiments did, but the fact remains that the applicant can beat the test. Moreover, faked scores have no predictive validity (Dunnette *et al.*, 1962).

Acquiescence.   We have no doubt that acquiescence is a nuisance in true-false tests of knowledge. The apparent ability of the high-acquiescent rises or falls, depending on whether the testmaker presents more true statements than false or vice versa. The personality tester can also see tendencies to say "Like," "Yes,"

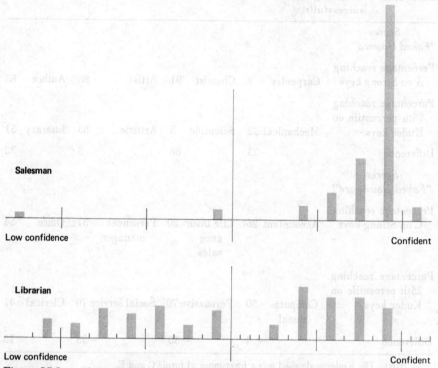

Figure 15.1. "Self-confidence" scores of the same students when playing the role of applicant for sales and library positions.
Wesman, 1952a.

"Often," etc., as nuisances. Two people who enjoy identical activities will reach different interest scores if they use the "L" response differently. A test developer who sees response biases as casual consequences of the subject's interpretation of directions will try to eliminate or reduce their influence. He may, for instance, try to arrange matters so that there are as many items keyed "L" as there are items keyed "D," in any particular scale.

Another school of thought argues that response biases express significant personal styles. The acquiescent person, it is said, is submissive and conformist at heart; the one who evades the questions with "Cannot Say" also withdraws from challenges in his daily life. Some writers suggest even that the style of response tells more about the man's true characteristics than the content of his responses does. Styles have some significance. We know this from the finding that when data are collected for an empirical key the responses of the criterion group usually show a consistent bias. Suppose that a Strong key for Public Relations men, constructed in the usual manner, assigns positive weights to 200 "L" responses and 50 "D" responses. Then perhaps an indiscriminate set-to-like-everything is common to men in that profession. The counselee who gives mostly "L" responses is thereby telling us something about his readiness to enter such a "keep-smilin' " profession.

There is plentiful evidence that the maladjusted respond "Disagree" more often than "Agree" on attitude or self-descriptive items half of which are worded so that "Agree" is a liberal or desirable response (Rundquist, 1966). Hence a tendency to disagree is a diagnostic indicator of sorts.

The debate about the importance of acquiescence has attracted undue research attention, perhaps because it is so easy for any psychologist with a drawerful of test data to count the number of "Yes" responses and correlate them with every other score he has on file. While we shall discuss below the practical residue from these studies, we refer the reader interested in details of the controversy to the bibliography and review offered by J. Wiggins (1968, especially pp. 296–308). An interpretation can be offered for an "acquiescence" score or a "social desirability" score just as for a score on items grouped by content. Validation is required for each such score and for each facet of the interpretation.

3. *What sort of personality would you try to show if "faking good"*
   a. *in a test to select Boy Scout leaders?*
   b. *in a test to select scientists for advanced training?*
   c. *in a test for psychiatric ward attendants?*

Taking Biases and Distortions into Account

Subtlety in inventory construction. If the inventory is transparent, the subject can see what he is disclosing and can decide whether to censor his responses. This presents little problem for the tester who views the questionnaire as a simple communication device through which the client records what he would be equally willing to say face-to-face. Such a tester expects to start his counseling or therapy by conversing on matters the client is ready to talk about, not his secrets and self-delusions. The tester who regards it as his job to get at "the truth" regardless of whether the subject wants the information known must plot a way around the subject's defenses. This tester masks his inquiry somehow so that the person cannot judge how a response will be interpreted.

One masking device is to use "subtle" items that seemingly have little relevance to the decision being made. Empirical keying for SVIB assigns weights to any answers engineers tend to give. Some are transparent—for example, "like to be author of technical book." This is said by genuine engineers and also by persons who are trying to masquerade as prospective engineers. But "red sports cars" is a subtle item, since the subject has no way of knowing how it counts, if at all, in his Engineer score. The working assumption of empirical test construction is that a response has the same significance whether given with intent to deceive or given honestly. But surely an honest report of liking to write technical books has a different psychological significance from a sham report. So the assumption is plausible only with regard to the subtle items.

Garry (1953) showed that when subjects attempt to fake interest in a particular field on SVIB they answer the "obvious" items correctly. Most of them are unable to fake successfully on the items whose correlation with the criterion is lower and less obvious. While a score derived wholly from subtle items may be nearly fakeproof, the majority of empirical scales are loaded with transparent items. One worthwhile proposal (D. Wiener, 1948; Seeman, 1952) is to score separately the subtle and transparent items. When the two scores agree, we can have some confidence in the result. If they disagree, we need data on their separate validities.

Weiner developed such keys for five MMPI clinical scales. No direct validity studies were carried out on them, but there is evidence that the subtle and transparent keys differ in their susceptibility to fake-good effects and response sets. Subtle keys are probably less reliable than transparent keys of the same length. Potentially more valid?—who knows?

Another way to control response bias is to employ forced-choice items, as in the Kuder inventory. Like multiple-choice achievement items, they invite the subject to give the best answer; the question cannot be evaded, and acquiescence has no effect. If all the choices in an item have the same level of social desirability, there is no obvious way to fake good. The subject has to say *which* good statements are most characteristic of him, and *which* faults he suffers to the greatest degree. Navran and Stauffacher (1954) asked student nurses to rank fifteen needs (e.g., deference) in order of their social desirability. Each nurse also ranked the needs from most to least characteristic of herself. The correlation between these two rankings for any nurse would indicate her tendency to give a favorable picture of her own needs. The correlation was higher than 0.44 for the majority of nurses. A quite different result was found on the Edwards forced-choice inventory. In not one case did the rank order of needs given by Edwards scores correlate as high as 0.44 with the desirability ranking.

While the forced-choice item gets more information than the simpler items, it remains somewhat open to faking. In the first place, matching of alternatives is imperfect, and the person who wants to give a favorable picture can usually recognize one of the alternatives as most likely to win approval (Feldman & Corah, 1960; Dunnette *et al.*, 1962; Hofstee, 1963). Even if matching on general desirability were perfect, the person could fake a particular image such as the "librarian" stereotype of the Wesman study above (Saltz, Reece, & Ager, 1962; N. Wiggins, 1966). Forced choice has other defects. It requires more time to obtain an equal number of responses. Subjects object to its "Have you stopped beating your wife?" character. This objection has merit: imagine yourself deciding what response to give an authority figure, perhaps one with power over a job or parole, who asks you to say whether you are better described by

I feel like blaming others when things go wrong for me; or,
I feel I am inferior in most respects.

(Cited by Westin, 1967, p. 261.) Moreover, the forcing of choice may reduce validity of criterion prediction, for reasons discussed below.

When a test is to predict one well-defined criterion, refined forced-choice methodology can probably improve validity. Even the older methods of constructing forced-choice instruments give more valid prediction than single-item formats if the test is long (Osburn et al., 1954). Norman (1963) has devised keying procedures that seem to have superior predictive validity, at least in the institution for which keys were developed. His forced-choice technique is quite open to faking, but any faked report is readily identified as such. Since strictly empirical use of personality tests as predictors is not much recommended today (see p. 548), this technical advance will not serve the average tester.

Evaluative research in education often requires a measure of interest, to assess the effect of instruction or a persuasive communication. A new science course, for example, was supposed to make pupils interested in theoretical explanations, rather than solely in practical uses of science. To test its effect, Heath (1964) developed a Cognitive Preference Test. Pupils were directed to indicate which of four comments on each scientific statement they preferred, when given an item such as the following:

The pressure of a gas is directly proportional to temperature.

(a) The statement, as given above, fails to consider the effects of volume changes and changes of state.

(b) Charles' or Gay-Lussac's Law.

(c) The statement implies a lower limit to temperature.

(d) This principle may be related to the fact that over-heated automobile tires may "blow out."

The options are credited, respectively, to preferences for questioning, memory for specifics, fundamental principles, and practical applications. While Heath's results showed that during the course pupils' choices moved in the "theoretical" direction, the finding is not convincing because the course preached the importance of theory. By the end of the course the pupils surely knew which answer their teacher wanted them to "prefer."

A sophisticated change in technique was made by Greenwald (1965), for a social-psychological experiment. He designed a behavioral measure of preference, in the hope that choices the subject had to "live with" would not be falsified. He needed to measure preference between two types of assignment, vocabulary and history. He used a ranking technique, with these two categories listed among others, to get a self-report of preference. But he also presented pairs of exercises (one on vocabulary, one on history), and directed pupils to complete one exercise of each pair, whichever they preferred to work on. The score was the proportion of vocabulary tasks the pupil chose, before and after exposure to propaganda about the educative value of vocabulary development. An experiment does not require an accurate score for each individual, and Greenwald's measures were precise enough to show group effects. The finding important for us is that the two measures gave different results, the behavioral measure showing a significant effect of the experimental attempt to change preferences and the verbal report showing none. Some differences on the latter (nonsignificant) were opposite to results on the behavioral test. Even though the behavioral measure seems superior in validity, it can of course be faked by the subject who is willing to take pains to make a good impression.

Concealing the purpose of the test. Some questionnaires openly call themselves measures of adjustment. More commonly, the title is unrevealing: for example, "The California Psychological Inventory." The subject does not know what scores will be recorded or what interpretations will be made. He may guess something from the item content, but he is unlikely to suspect that one of the scores will estimate his tendency to delinquency, and another his probability of moving to a higher level in society. To be sure, when the subject does not know what the tester is looking for, he may become even more suspicious and defensive in his responses. But let us not overstress this. Most people enjoy talking about themselves—Dr. Gallup's door-to-door interviewer finds getting away one of his hardest problems!

The tester may state a plausible but false purpose for the test. The *F* scale, for instance, is on the surface an inventory of opinions, but it is used to draw conclusions about the underlying personality. If the test content is such that subjects regard it as a measure of ability, faking can be reduced or even eliminated. Measures of knowledge or reasoning ability can be designed for disguised measurement of attitude when group comparisons rather than individual assessment is the aim (D. T. Campbell, 1957). Another disguised test asks for opinions, but the scoring has little or nothing to do with the opinions stated. Thus one investigator asks boys to check titles of books they have read, seemingly to measure reading interests. He inserts fictitious titles in the list, and the number of such titles checked is taken as one indicator of deceit or boasting.

Any effective disguise skirts the edge of unethical practice. To try to outsmart the deceptive subject by becoming deceptive oneself merely lends credence to the view that psychologists are tricky. In the long run, it drives subjects to even greater evasiveness.

Perhaps the subtlest procedure is the most legitimate one: to establish the sort of rapport through which the subject wants to give the best information he can. But rapport is a complex interpersonal relationship, depending on many factors other than the tester's technique. Never may the tester safely assume that he has the ideal relationship in which the subject wants to tell "the whole truth." The subject may shift back and forth between concealing and confessing, but there is little chance that he will come to rest at "objectivity."

Verification and correction keys. Some subjects are too little motivated to make hundreds of judgments seriously. There are even some who mark at random toward the end of the inventory.

Kuder Forms C and E have a special verification score, such that a high count implies that the person answered without proper concentration. The Edwards inventory uses 210 forced-choice pairs of statements. Fifteen of the pairs reappear at random intervals within the test. The verification score indicates how often the subject repeated an answer. Some inconsistencies are to be expected, but a large number of them suggests an invalid self-report. Other inventories use a variety of check scores, including façade keys and keys to detect response biases (see p. 530).

The check score may be used to eliminate suspect records. Statistical formulas make it possible also to partially correct the score to compensate for an abnormal response style.

4. *If a high-school senior earns a suspiciously high verification score on Kuder Form C, what should the counselor do?*

Alternative Interpretations of Response Content

No matter what special procedures are used to reduce distortion, inventory responses depend upon how much of the truth the subject is willing and able to report. Interpretation must take this fact into account.

Simplest but most hazardous is to interpret the responses as a frank report of typical behavior. If the relationship between tester and subject makes this a reasonable expectation, then no subtleties of test design are required.

Complete frankness cannot be anticipated if certain responses will gain reward or approval. Some degree of promise or threat is implicit in any institutional use of tests, such as clinical diagnosis or employee selection. Honest self-examination can be hoped for only when the tester is helping the subject to solve his own problems—and even then the subject may have a goal for which he wishes the support of the counselor's authority, which biases his response.

Interpretation as "Published" Self-Concept

It is more reasonable to interpret the report as a "public" self-concept than as a statement of typical behavior or a private self-concept. To be sure, one's public self-concept should correspond in some measure to his behavior, but the ambiguity of test items and the inevitable distortion in self-description reduce this correspondence (Combs, Soper, & Courson, 1963; Parker, 1966).

A historian, examining the diary of a statesman, refuses to assume that the statements made therein are true reports of the man's beliefs and feelings. Unless it is clear that the document was a private one intended never to see the light of day, the safest assumption is that the statements represent the image the man wished to leave in history. The psychologist, likewise, can regard the responses of his subject as a "published" self-concept, a statement of the reputation the subject would like to have.

This edited information may be of considerable value. The fact that an individual is unable to admit certain kinds of tabooed impulses may be highly diagnostic. A person who presents too perfect a picture of himself may be expressing his fear that others are critical and punitive, and that he can maintain their respect only by keeping his halo bright. Unless there is some obvious motive for deceit, the psychologist should suspect that the person who presents so perfect a façade on the test maintains a similar façade in all his social relations. The façade of perfect control and freedom from impulse is a brittle one and can be maintained only at considerable emotional cost. Hence the façade itself has diagnostic and prognostic significance.

The person who admits to certain emotional problems may also be building up a public image. These may not be the most important problems of which he is conscious. It is commonly observed in psychotherapy that people do not bring out their main problems until several interviews have passed. When a person admits to problems that call for counseling, his report is an invitation to open counseling with an examination of the area mentioned. He is saying, first of all, that he is willing to be counseled; second, that this area is one that concerns him but is not too sensitive to be discussed. His most serious conflicts may be completely concealed by his questionnaire responses, but if he is unwilling to admit these conflicts he is probably also unwilling to deal with them immediately in psychotherapy.

Dynamic Interpretation

The clinical psychologist is unwilling to reduce personality to a statistical report of overt behavior. The clinician is concerned not with the number of times a person becomes emotionally upset but with the conditions under which this happens and the forces, internal and external, that lead to it. An individual who now becomes upset about once a month might become chronically disturbed if conditions changed in a cetrain manner. In this event, a statistical average of his past behavior would have almost no predictive value. A "dynamic" picture of an individual is a picture of the forces altering his responses as situations change. Important in such a picture are his perceptions of the people he deals with, his feelings about himself, and the needs he is trying to satisfy. If the clinician has insight into these characteristics, he has some hope of predicting reaction to opportunities and stresses.

Drawing conclusions about personality dynamics even from an extended series of interviews is difficult, and questionnaires can only offer hypotheses of questionable validity. Questionnaires are a common basis for dynamic interpretation, however. The working hypothesis of dynamic interpretation is that every act is meaningful, even when inconsistent with other observations. The task of the interpreter is to seek some underlying unity that resolves as many of these contradictions as possible.

Dynamic interpretation requires extensive data about the individual's environment and difficulties as well as his test score, and considerable knowledge of personality theory. It can be demonstrated in a brief example, using an analysis by a University of California counselor. Barbara Kirk (1952) describes the pattern often found among academic failures or near-failures who had done well on aptitude tests given at the Counseling Center. (This summary is drastically condensed.)

The explanation and the excuses for the academic deficiency are unrealistic, superficial, and largely implausible. The counselee demonstrates no real recognition or admission of the reasons for this deficiency, but, on the other hand, he evidences no surprise at the results of the tests. He may be surprised that he was not tense or bothered on tests administered to him during counseling because he frequently has been tense or bothered during academic examinations. The impressions regarding the Minnesota Multiphasic Personality Inventory records in these cases are:

Most frequent is "psychoneurosis with compulsive and depressive features." Such [persons] tend to be pervasively resistant on an unconscious level to any externally imposed task. Since childhood, however, they have concealed such resistances from themselves and others by a façade of hard-workingness, meticulousness, and earnest dutifulness. In the unstructured environment of a university, the loss of the continued external pushing of teachers and parents permits the overthrow of the process of grudging achievement, and the resistances then manifest themselves in nonperformance.

The academic failure probably has meaning in terms of unconscious satisfaction of the hostility usually directed towards some member of the family who demands success, while the excellent scores on tests taken in a counseling situation may be interpreted also as hostile gestures. Because no importance is attached to these tests, the counselee is free to do with them as he wishes. It is a declaration, perhaps, of the lack of significance of his academic failure.

Whether derived from a single test or from several months of therapeutic interviews, such interpretations involve considerable speculation. Nonetheless, they guide the counselor in planning a trial strategy for next steps in treatment.

Attempts to explain the person in terms of his covert motivations may be contrasted with another, equally individualized approach used in what is currently called "behavior therapy." The attempt here is to identify precisely the stimulus situations that trigger an unwanted response, and then to recondition the person so that the response is replaced by a better one. This perhaps requires a careful individual analysis, ordinarily by interview and by observation in controlled situations rather than by tests of the customary sort. A study by Emery (see Emery & Krumboltz, 1967) suggests that the individual analysis is not especially valuable, however. The analysis used in behavior therapy is conservative rather than speculative, making little claim to "understand" the person. We shall give some further attention to this approach in Chapter 18.

5. *Distinguish in each of these cases whether the investigator is assuming that self-reports are truthful:*
   a. *The clinical symptoms of condition x are determined by observation. A list of symptoms (swollen feet, rash, etc.) is prepared. This list is used to determine how frequent condition x is in several localities. Each subject is asked to check whatever symptoms he has.*
   b. *There are three general stages in social development in which a child names as favorites (1) other children without regard to sex, (2) persons of his own sex exclusively, (3) persons of the opposite sex. The investigators ask a child to name his favorite playmates as a means of determining his level of development.*
   c. *A psychologist administers to a group of applicants a checklist in which each marks the adjectives that describe him. The success of these men is observed, and a record is made of the characteristics checked by the successful applicants but not by the others. This checklist is then given to further applicants, and those who check the same characteristics as the previously successful men are hired.*
6. *A questionnaire is filled out by all parents belonging to a study group, as a means of identifying problems to be taken up in group discussion. Mr. Smith checks many problems having to do with developing the child's honesty, respect for the property of others, and care for his own property. The school counselor knows, however, that his son has been in difficulty several times because of aggressive fighting on the playground, window breaking, and other aggressive offenses that have been called to Mr. Smith's attention. Can the counselor draw any useful conclusion from Mr. Smith's self-report?*
7. *An attitude test for foremen presents hypothetical problems that might arise on the job and asks the subject to indicate what action he would take if he were foreman. Scores are based on response patterns (e.g., "takes quick action," "seeks facts," "emphasizes morale," "emphasizes cost-cutting"). What use can be made of the responses, in view of the obvious temptation to give a desirable picture?*
8. *On a certain inventory each scale has a possible score range from zero to 30. A person who scores 15 points on Irritability falls at the 80th percentile; a person who scores 15 points on Punctuality falls at the 15th percentile. Suppose a person earns 15 points on each scale; is it correct to say that he is more irritable than punctual? Can any meaning be given to score-to-score differences in a personality profile?*

Actuarial Interpretation of Responses as Signs

The risky assumption that the subject is telling the truth can be avoided if we interpret his response, not as self-description, but as an act of verbal behavior that is correlated with his inner nature. These two approaches have been characterized as the "sample" and "sign" approaches. If self-reports are seen as frank reports of an observer, we present transparent items sampling various content areas and pay primary attention to the content of the responses. We are at the mercy of the subject who wants to mislead us. But if responses are signs, we can use items the surface content of which is irrelevant to our concern. Even distorted responses may have significance.

The Strong blank, as originally employed, used the "sign" principle. Strong did not restrict his Engineer key to activities that are part of the engineer's work; he asked only whether the response was statistically associated with being an engineer. Counting dozens of such "signs," he separated men who resemble the typical engineer from those who lack the usual signs. The person is placed in a category on a strictly actuarial basis. Strong can say, "Persons with this combination of responses tend to become engineers" in the same way that an insurance examiner can say, "People with this combination of weight, blood pressure, and heart condition rarely live beyond 70." In strict actuarial interpretation, the tester makes no pretense of a rational connection between the response and the criterion. If engineers have greater than average liking for wire-wheeled sports cars, the statement that a counselee resembles engineers can be based (in part) on this fact regardless of whether any psychological significance can be attached to it.

The actuarial approach eliminates the assumption of honest self-report. The question "Is your health better or poorer than average for your age?" does not obtain valid facts about health. One person overrates his health in reporting; another exaggerates minor ills. If neurotics reply "poorer" more often than normals do, this answer may be diagnostic even when false-to-fact—in fact, it may be diagnostic just because it is false. Scales with empirical keys are not seen as self ratings. They are seen as a summary of observations of behavior in a standard situation. The behavior is verbal, to be sure; but the words as such are not taken seriously.

Empirical keying can be used for purposes the subject never suspects. SVIB ostensibly assesses vocational interests, but one key counts items men answer differently from women for a "masculinity-femininity" score. It is presumably possible to make keys that distinguish, at better than a chance level, communists from noncommunists, girls who are likely to marry and stop working from those likely to remain on a job, and future suicides from nonsuicides. The key capitalizes on the fact that any group that has one distinctive psychological quality differs from the population on other qualities.

The soundness of an empirical key depends entirely on the adequacy of the data used to establish weights. Some weights assigned to items are so inexplicable as to seem absurd; then the original validation was very likely based on an inadequate sample. Can one really take seriously a key that counts saying "green" in response to the stimulus "grass" as a sign of "loyalty to the gang"? Loyal boys very likely gave this response more often than disloyal boys in the sample tested, but it is implausible that the same result would be found in further studies. Large, reasonably up-to-date samples, representative of the subjects to whom the test

Table 15.3.   **Comparison of three styles of interpretation**

	Test taken as self-description	Dynamic interpretation	Actuarial interpretation
Kinds of items emphasized	Transparent statements on actions and feelings.	Any type. Items that allow rationalizations and denial of symptoms important. May ask what stimuli elicit a response rather than how often the response occurs.	Any type. Subtle items are favored in theory, but rarely predominate.
Grouping of items into keys	Correlated items or items logically fitting a category are treated together.	Any type of key may be used.	Items are grouped according to correlation with a criterion. Internal homogeneity is not sought.
Assumption as to subject's attitude in taking test	Answers are assumed to be as honest as an interview would elicit.	Distortions, conscious and unconscious, are expected.	Subject is assumed to take the attitudes of persons in the keying or weighting sample.
Use made of face content of items	Statements taken at face value as descriptions.	Content of statement is often seen as an expression of defense mechanisms.	Content ignored.
Use made of personality theory	Only a superficial sampling concept is required.	Interpretation relies on complex theory, usually derived from psychoanalytic concepts.	Theory plays no part.

will be applied, are crucial for empirical keying. Moreover, criterion validity must be high; it simply will not do to have a predictor of delinquency that counts responses common to *all* lowerclass boys just because lowerclass boys made up the delinquent sample. At best the validity of empirical keys is only moderate, since they rely on indirect information. Because they are indirect they are less readily explained to clients than are tests relying on content interpretations.

Comparison of interpretative approaches. Table 15.3 summarizes the chief types of interpretation we have discussed. The table overemphasizes differences. A particular test may be used in all three ways, and even in dealing with a single case or a single research study the interpreter may shift from one point of view to another.

The actuarial style is perhaps hardest to comprehend because it enters test operations in various ways. The basic logic is that of predictive validation against a criterion, comparable to the insurance actuary's prediction of mortality. No "psychological" interpretation is offered or required. But the empirically keyed test is usually used descriptively rather than predictively. As we saw in Chapter 14, the counselor uses the Strong profile to help the client understand what kind of person he is. As experience with a key accumulates, the criterion used in keying is forgotten. An instrument keyed on categories of psychiatric patients may be used to describe normals, as soon as there is sufficient knowledge about the traits of high scorers. As an example, recall Kelly's statements about medical students—that high Farmer scores on SVIB show a lack of interest in scientific discovery, and high Aviator scores a lack of cultural interests. This is a relatively conservative descriptive form of interpretation.

But the actuary, having abandoned his original criterion, may come back with a new formula-scoring procedure. He may develop a formula combining several of the original keys to predict a new criterion, or even to predict one of the original criteria in a new kind of sample. And, as we shall see in the next chapter, he may even develop a descriptive interpretation of the test on the basis of statistical rather than psychological inference.

9. *In developing an empirical scale for college students one might develop a key consisting of items that distinguish campus leaders from nonleaders. Suggest other criteria that might mark important personality dimensions.*

Ethical Issues

Practical personality testing has flourished in two contexts, one institutional, the other individual. Valid information about personality would presumably be of great value to employers, college admissions officers, and others who make decisions to carry out institutional policies. In fact, personality questionnaires were first applied to screen potentially neurotic soldiers. Institutional testing tries to determine the truth about the individual, whether he wants that truth known or not. In noninstitutional testing, tests are applied for the benefit of the person tested. Here also the tester believes that learning the truth will be valuable but he does not feel free to violate the person's wishes. The client who comes with an emotional difficulty wants the psychologist's assistance, but he may be quite unprepared to pay the price of unveiling his soul.

Any test is an invasion of privacy for the subject who does not wish to reveal himself. While objection may be encountered in testing knowledge and mental ability of persons who have left school, the personality test is much more often regarded as a violation of rights. Every man has two personalities: the role he plays in his social interactions and his "true self." In a culture in which, for example, open expression of emotion is discouraged and a taboo is placed on aggressive feelings, there is certain to be some discrepancy between these two personalities. The personality questionnaire or the projective technique obtains its most significant information by probing into feelings and attitudes which the individual normally conceals. One test purports to assess whether an adolescent boy resents authority. Another tries to determine whether a mother really loves her child. A third has a score indicating the strength of sexual needs. Virtually all measures of personality seek information on areas that the subject has every reason to regard as private, in normal social intercourse. He is willing to admit the psychologist into these private areas only if he sees the relevance of the questions to the attainment of his goals in working with the psychologist. The psychologist is not "invading privacy" when he is freely admitted and when he has a genuine need for the information obtained.

While some candid discussions of questionable usage of personality tests had previously appeared (Otis, 1957; Cronbach, 1960, p. 460), psychologists were shocked during the 1960s to find themselves accused of wholesale violations of human dignity. Congressional investigators and editorial writers pilloried the psychological tester alongside the industrial spy who planted microphones in cocktail olives. At one point in 1963 Senator Goldwater persuaded the Senate to add to a bill extending Federal support for guidance services a provision that "no such program shall provide for the conduct of any test . . . to elicit information dealing with the personality, environment, home life, parental or family relationships, economic status, or sociological and psychological problems of the pupil tested." While attacks came first from the spectrum of political opinion that holds suspect all efforts to provide social services, liberals and civil libertarians led some of the later and more penetrating attacks (Freedman, 1965a,b; Westin, 1967). Pressure from critics has at times forced reputable investigators to destroy research questionnaires before tabulating them and to abandon their lines of inquiry (Nettler, 1959).

The central question is whether it is objectionable to use personality questionnaires when they are soundly interpreted. But first let us dispose of some contentions that are *not* central.

● "Psychologists have made indefensible claims regarding the validity of their tests." True, and claims that go beyond demonstrated validity are unethical. But most test developers and users are reasonably conservative in their claims today. Many violations come from inadequately trained testers. Some come from nonprofessionals—anyone with a printing press can go into the testing business.

● "Inventories have low validities." True, for many purposes. But this is not a matter for ethical objection; valid tests would be more objectionable. A test with nearly perfect validity for forecasting treason, embezzlement, or sexual offenses would be unthinkably dangerous—a clear invitation to cast a man out of society when he has committed no objectionable act.

● "Inventories award high scores to conformers." This is an attack on the values of decision-makers in schools and business, a proper enough matter for debate. Inventories, however, are an expression of the values, not a cause. An employer who wants yes-men will get them, with or without the inventory. Personality tests find it no harder to identify the independent-minded than to pick callow conformers. Admittedly, some interpreters have been too quick to define "the healthy personality" as one free from emotional conflict. Conflict is a price one pays for independence.

● "Merely asking a young person whether he has committed some act suggests the act to him" (e.g., have you ever taken candy from a store without paying for it?). It is hard to accept the idea that character is destroyed by such casual influences, especially in an age in which the mass media display every type of deviance. Such a contention as this can never be disproved, however.

● Closely related is the fear of some clinical psychologists that anxieties may be heightened just by probing into areas of conflict—e.g., by asking certain questions of latent homosexuals or boys who have passed through a homosexual experience. An even more serious question arises in some "entrapment procedures," as Kleinmuntz (1967) calls them. These are performance tests in which the child is given an opportunity to steal, not knowing—before or after—that he has been observed. Has the psychologist the right to create guilt? (Kelman, 1967). These are most serious matters, but they do not bear on the questionnaires that have been the center of criticism.

Now, to the central issues, the first of which is dignity.

Respecting the Dignity of Persons Tested

Has an employer the right to question an applicant about any aspect of his life not directly related to his work? Has a teacher any right to ask children about their fears, hatreds, and home life? Affirmative answers can be defended on various grounds. Unacceptable is the autocratic "I own this business, and if I want to hire only men with exemplary home lives why shouldn't I?" Milder is the claim that a man's private life affects his usefulness as an employee: it is not good for the bank if its teller is seen regularly at the race track (but is that *private* behavior?). As for the school, the justification lies in the institution's use of the responses. If the maladjusted pupil will be singled out for help, the community interest is served. On the opposite side of the argument is the principle that no one should be forced to testify against himself. And there is the parent's right not to have *his* privacy invaded by such questions as "Do your parents quarrel frequently?"

Rather than attempt to defend a fixed position, we can put this matter simply in terms of practicality. Paternalism is out of style today—in business and in education. No one can get by for long with intrusive questions unless he can convince the educated public including the students that his questions are fully in the public interest. A balance is to be struck between the intrusiveness of a question and the benefits that can come from asking it. Even the sex life of a man being hired as a CIA agent can be a matter for inquiry (though for mysterious reasons an interview raises fewer objections than a questionnaire). In general, the employer had better be able to demonstrate in a "fair employment" hearing that every question he asks has genuine relevance to a man's ability to perform the job in question. A school board ought to favor use of adjustment inventories when there is a responsible program for making constructive use of the information. It ought to veto them if the aim is only to get data on file. And it ought to be outraged by a proposal to test so as to detect troublemakers in advance.

The tester can remove a good many objections simply by checking the acceptability of items and discarding those his public finds objectionable. Employees in a manufacturing firm were asked to check items about which they would "feel personally offended" if asked to respond (Winkler & Matthews, 1967). In a typical questionnaire, the usual person objected to no more than one per cent of the items. The items arousing most frequent objection included these:

> Do you feel strongly against kissing a friend of your own sex and age?
> Does the sight of pus disgust you?
> Have you ever kept a personal diary on your own accord?
> Do you cry rather easily?

The first drew 34 per cent objections, the others, from 13 to 22 per cent. Such unacceptable items could be dropped with little loss. To be sure, some persons objected to a third or more of the items, and one objected to 80 per cent! It seems best to allow applicants to leave items unmarked and to discard scores of those who ignore enough items to spoil the test. For those persons, there may be no recourse but to fall back on an interview.

No one knows just how much validity would be lost if the objectionable items were sacrificed. Starke Hathaway, an author of the MMPI, fears serious loss. Use of MMPI in selecting government employees was criticized because some items deal with religion, and the Constitution does not allow screening for public office on the grounds of religious belief. Hathaway attempts to answer this as follows (1964, pp. 206–207):

> If the psychologist cannot use those personal items to aid in the assessment of people, he suffers as did the Victorian physician who had to examine his female patients by feeling the pulse in the delicate hand thrust from behind a screen. . . . It is obvious that if we were making a new MMPI, we would again be faced either with being offensive to subgroupings of people by personal items they object to or, if we did not include personal items and were inoffensive, we would have lost the aim of the instrument.

While Hathaway has a point, the most zealous search for valid predictors must turn aside in the face of a Constitutional prohibition.

Although the public outcry has centered on questionnaires, the same objection can be raised to observations and performance tests, so long as the person is unaware of the observations or believes that he is revealing less than he is. Hence the same defenses of relevance to the public interest must be prepared, and again they must be very strong defenses if the procedure intrudes into very private areas.

How Permissible Is Deception?

This brings us to the second issue: deceit. We have described many ways in which test constructors try to outwit the subject so that he cannot guess what information he is revealing. The psychologist trying to extract the truth from unwilling subjects can put himself into an indefensible position. A diagnostic procedure the subject does not understand is acceptable, if the information obtained is what the subject would willingly allow others to know; it is this that justifies the mysterious and sometimes intrusive procedures of medical diagnosis. Also, when the public interest overrides the individual interest a strictly objective look at the person can be justified; one notes, for instance, the proposal for sanity examinations of persons in charge of powerful weapons (Rogow, 1963).

The psychologist should ordinarily introduce procedures with as frank an account as possible. The person seeking therapeutic help can readily understand the aim of diagnosis. To make diagnostic questions transparent would be simply to invite him to choose his own diagnosis; the necessity for subtle questions can be made clear. An interest test is easy to explain. It is hard to give a frank account of a test that observes the person's style of work (e.g., impulsiveness) because the person, knowing that style is observed, will try to display the style considered good. Except with cooperative volunteers, the uses of disguised procedures are extremely limited.

To keep matters open and above board in testing candidates for therapy, the psychologist can introduce matters in this manner (see also pp. 376–380): "It should help to solve your problem if we collect as much information as we can. Some of our tests use straightforward questions whose purpose you will readily understand. Others dig more deeply into the personality. Sometimes they bring to light emotional conflicts that the person is not even conscious of. Few of us admit the whole truth about our feelings and ideas, even to ourselves. I think I can help you better with the aid of these tests."

The client may refuse to take disguised tests if he is not ready to trust the psychologist with full knowledge of his personality. If this is the case, the information probably could not be used constructively in counseling him. In counseling it is both advantage and disadvantage that direct, unsubtle tests do no more than tabulate statements made by the person about himself. While they uncover no secrets, they can accelerate the counseling process because they tell what the client is ready to discuss.

Perhaps the basic fault in personality testing is that on occasion tests have been used for no constructive purpose. Some personality testing has been done with only the vague motivation of finding out about the person. There is no point in describing or diagnosing the person unless something constructive can be done. A defect in personality is worth knowing about when there is a remedy to apply. Clinical diagnosis is pointless unless there is valid evidence that persons with a given diagnosis are best served by a certain treatment. There has been very little research on how treatments fit particular personalities—whether we are talking about therapy, adapting schooling to the child, or fitting supervision to the worker. Until this step is taken, much personality testing is unwarranted nosiness.

Limits on Freedom of Scientific Inquiry

A third issue is freedom of research. It is in the public interest to understand what sorts of persons break under stress, what sort become delinquent, and what influences during development create a Lee Oswald or, for that matter, a John Kennedy. Citizenship education is bound to remain impotent unless the effect of each innovation on typical behavior is verified. Social scientists have a high sense of social purpose and are puzzled by the vehemence of public objections to some of their probings. When *they* know that their intentions are pure and that their data will be safeguarded, they are inclined to stress their right to inquire. If their probings threaten to expose weak spots in the society, they go further, insisting on their *duty* to inquire.

This is as it should be. As a committee appointed by the President's Office of Science and Technology (*Privacy and behavioral research*, 1967) rightly states, "Behavioral science is representative of [a] value vigorously championed by most American citizens, the right to know anything that may be known or discovered about any part of the universe. Man is part of this universe. . . . If society is to exercise its right to know, it must free its behavioral scientists as much as possible from unnecessary restraints." The social scientist must accept some restraints, if only to keep his study from being shot down in midflight. Patiently explaining the study to the participants or, in studies of children, to all segments of the community, is one of the costs of doing business as an investigator. Testers too often assume that using volunteer subjects or unsigned questionnaires removes all difficulty. If a question is offensive, however, or if it exposes information the volunteer did not know he was going to reveal, objections have some justification.

There are other threats. Research data are not proof against subpoena. "Good data" for a study of adolescent rebellion might be telling evidence against a subject's character in a later trial for some alleged offense as an adult. Coding of records is not a full safeguard. Identity can be detected by matching facts from the coded questionnaire with other facts that are openly recorded. There are enough anecdotes of malign detective work of this kind from the precomputer days of Nazi Germany to justify sober thought on the risks inherent in data banks.

10. *Would it be proper for a psychologist working in a government intelligence agency to develop a key for scoring the Strong or MMPI so as to detect communists among college students?*

11. *The Minnesota Teacher Attitude Inventory attempts to identify teachers who have the attitudes that lead to high ratings from principals. Which would be best in a school staff: uniform attitudes or variety?*

12. *Can there be ethical objections to requiring newly employed engineers to fill out a questionnaire to aid the personnel manager in deciding whether to assign them to sales, research, or other responsibilities?*

13. *Which of the following positions is "sensitive" enough to justify the imposition of a disguised personality test?*
    a. *Peace Corps volunteer going to an isolated post to work under harsh conditions.*
    b. *Peace Corps volunteer going to an area where there is active left-wing insurgency.*
    c. *Chief of police in a community where there is tension.*

14. *Discuss the following advice from an older textbook. Is it acceptable today? "Whether serving an institution or serving an individual client, the tester should not use indirect and misleading techniques unless the subject clearly understands that anything he says may be used against him. To be sure, an employer may regard his refusal to submit to tests as grounds for denying him employment, but this is ethically preferable to obtaining deceitfully information he does not wish to give."*

15. *Investigators sometimes ask the subject to fill out a questionnaire on beliefs to indicate the responses the majority of people would give; i.e., they present a task of social insight rather than of self-description. Scores summarizing the beliefs he attributes to others perhaps correlate with independent evidence on the subject's traits (e.g., conformity) better than his self-description does (Goldberg & Rorer, 1966). Suppose that this indirect and disguised technique is valid. For what purposes would you consider it a proper way to measure beliefs, fears, etc.?*

16. *In premarital counseling, a questionnaire is given separately to both engaged persons to determine their suitability and probable success as marriage partners. Should it use direct or subtle questions?*

17. *To find out if questionnaires "would have utility for screening and selection decisions," an investigator gave anxiety and ego-strength questionnaires to Peace Corps volunteers during training. He did find that the correlations with criteria of performance in Nigeria were higher than correlations of faculty ratings with the criteria (Mischel, 1965). Comment pro and con on his decision to make clear to the subjects that the questionnaires were being given for research use only and would play no part in Peace Corps decisions. (He did adhere to this promise.)*

Questionnaire Data as a Source for the Theorist

While there has been some decline in the use of personality questionnaires for decision-making, their use in theoretical research has been steadily increasing. This use is not confined to research on "personality." On the contrary, investigators of conditioning, probability learning, signal detection, and many other processes find that personality measures provide a useful control in their experiments and sometimes contribute to theoretical explanations.

Traffic between personality testing and the experimental laboratory was greatly encouraged by the work of H. J. Eysenck in London and Janet Taylor Spence in the United States, among others. Eysenck separated various groups of subjects by means of a simple inventory, and proceeded to demonstrate differences between the groups on such phenomena as reminiscence (recovery after rest) on a motor-skill task, response to depressant drugs, and conditioning. The Taylor Manifest Anxiety Scale was developed to test hypotheses about the role of drive level in laboratory learning. Following the initial work, studies on such hypotheses have multiplied endlessly—with the original inventory or with special forms for children. While studies are not entirely consistent, a large body of significant findings have appeared. For summaries and critical comments, see Spielberger (1966), Spence and Spence (1964), and Eysenck (1965, 1966).

In research of this type, the usual faults of the inventory are not serious. Some subjects are more candid than others, but there is no incentive for gross faking. Stability over long periods of time is not required; the data are collected within a short time span. Any errors or distortions should be equally common in experimental and control groups. The instrument, however, is contaminated to some degree by unwanted variables. Therefore, in testing an hypothesis about a construct, it is highly desirable to use two or more techniques of measurement having different forms, which presumably will be contaminated in different ways. Thus in the same study anxiety might well be appraised by the Taylor questionnaire, by a measure of palmar sweat during stress, and by a projective technique that requires interpretations of potentially threatening pictures. Only if the outcome of the experiment (e.g., speed of conditioning) relates in the same way to all three measures can a simple generalization about "anxiety" be accepted (Franks, 1963).

The study that establishes a generalization is usually designed to show a trend—one strong enough that it cannot be dismissed as a chance result. A procedure need not measure individuals precisely. Many reports on group trends fail to remind the reader that only a small fraction of the variance in outcome has been accounted for. This is to be expected, since almost always there is more than one influence at work.

A common strategy is to select from a population the persons with extremely high or low scores on the trait and then to study this small number of subjects in laboratory situations. This procedure magnifies relationships that would be hard to detect in subjects who are less strongly contrasted. The result moves the theorist forward even if the effect is very weak among more representative subjects.

The program of research on internal-vs.-external control is illustrative. Several sociologists have suggested that an important difference among people is their feeling of control. The internals feel responsible for what happens to them and their world, while the externals think fortune depends on fate, "the breaks," or uncontrollable events. Among psychologists the most extensive work has been done by Rotter and associates. They have developed several I-E scales and have established a considerable number of correlates. The person scored as "internal" tends to be more alert to pick up information useful in decision-making, to take steps to better his condition, to be more concerned over failures, and to be less suggestible (Rotter, 1966). These conclusions are based on laboratory behavior and everyday behavior.

Such a program must also demonstrate that the "feeling-of-control" dimension is a distinct trait and not a new name for some other construct. Support for this claim comes from low or zero correlations of the I-E scales with questionnaire measures of anxiety, social desirability, scholastic aptitude, etc. (The same or similar constructs are, however, discussed by other investigators under such names as risk taking and motive for achievement; the structure of traits within this family is as yet unclear.) Rotter's program of construct validation gives support both to the test and to the "social learning" theory it derives from. But validation of this sort—resting on group differences that are often fairly weak— is not in itself a basis for employing the test to make decisions about individuals.

Mischel (1968, p. 100) properly emphasizes that constructs are not an end in themselves. Personality theory has the function of generating understanding that will permit parents, schools, clinics, informal groups, etc. to act more wisely. This will require the demonstration of aptitude-treatment interactions (p. 447), i.e., verification that persons described as different by the tests respond differently to different treatments.

Practically oriented personality research has been dominated by simple-minded goals of prediction and classification. But the point is not to predict that a boy has high probability of becoming a delinquent; the point is to suggest a treatment that will reduce that probability. The point is not to class a patient as "Type Q"; the point is to prescribe a treatment that will have a better effect on him than other treatments. There are many hints that treatments do interact with personality dimensions. Typical is Figure 3.3, in which work output of anxious and nonanxious persons was seen to differ as a function of ego-involving pressure. We may ask what any construct such as Rotter's internal-external control dimension implies for treatment. One hypothesis is that the high externals will profit from highly structured instructional systems such as programmed instruction, and from an operant-conditioning type of therapy, whereas the High internal will resist either of these methods. But the evidence at this time is so fragmentary, and based on such short-term experiments, that no well-validated links between construct interpretations and treatment recommendations can be made.

Aims and techniques of personality measurement are in flux, and the privacy issue is just one of the forces turning the flow in new directions. There is a general dissatisfaction with many of the personality theories that were dominant at the time most tests were devised. Freudian theory is more a part of cultural history than a living, growing psychological theory. The psychiatric classification system, whose origins are even more remote, is ripe for retirement. A simple lexicon of traits—dominance, anxiety, sociability, etc.—has proved insufficient. The research of the past decade has made some use of all these, along with various newer concepts such as coping strategies and information-processing techniques. On the atheoretic side there are superactuarial studies made possible by the computer, by automated apparatus, etc.

Each psychologist has his preferences among techniques and theories. Nearly all those now in existence have some usefulness, but at this time the profession is strongly aware of the limitations of personality testing and personality theory. In the following chapters, we shall try to extract lessons from experience with obsolescent techniques and to sample the novel techniques that are not yet established. Work with these methods must establish the research base for the theoretical breakout that personality study needs. In the writer's opinion, the solution must be one that accounts for the interaction of person with situations. Traits and type-descriptions that try to say "what the person is like" cannot account for his acting differently as the situation changes.

18. *In a conformity test, a person is asked to judge the length of a line after other "subjects" who speak first have given a uniform implausible estimate. Tendency to yield did not relate to I-E scores. Then the test was given with the added feature that the subject could, if he wished, bet money on his judgment. Under this condition the internals less often went along with the group, and more often bet on their judgments, than the externals (Crowne & Liverant, 1963). Do the results of this study support or cast doubt on Rotter's hypotheses?*

19. *For a theory involving a personality variable to be considered a worthwhile achievement, about what percentage of variance in outcome (say, in a conditioning experiment) should it account for?*

SUGGESTED READINGS

Freedman, Monroe H. Testimony. *American Psychologist*, 1965, *20*, 923–931.
   A no-holds-barred attack, by a lawyer and civil libertarian, on the use of personality tests in selecting for the Peace Corps and other government employment. Other witnesses in this set of Senate hearings present more balanced views.

Lovell, Victor R. The human use of personality tests. *American Psychologist*, 1967, 22, 383–393. (Abridged in Barnette, 1968.)

A counseling psychologist argues that the tester necessarily enters into a contract with the subject, and that this contract has to be based on reciprocal honesty. This leads him to the strong conclusion that "tests of character" (essentially measures of typical behavior) should never be used for any kind of personnel decision.

McClelland, David C. Roles and role models. In *Personality*. New York: Holt, Rinehart and Winston, 1957. Pp. 289–332.

Describing personality in terms of typical behavior is not completely satisfactory because behavior varies with the situation. McClelland illustrates and accounts for such inconsistency in terms of changing social roles.

Meehl, P. E. The dynamics of "structured" personality tests. *Journal of Clinical Psychology*, 1945, 1, 296–303. (Reprinted in various books of readings.)

Reflecting the concepts operating when MMPI was constructed, Meehl argues that self-report is undependable and uninterpretable if taken at face value, and defends actuarial keying as the only suitable method of obtaining useful insight from questionnaires. (His position in later writings is not so one-sided.)

Vernon, P. E. "Measurement of traits and factors." In *Personality assessment*. London: Methuen, 1964. Pp. 179–200.

In this book, Professor Vernon, who has been deeply involved in personality testing of all types since the 1930s, on both sides of the Atlantic, candidly surveys disappointments, problems, and possibilities. This chapter discusses the trait model, supplementing our treatment with a balanced review of the proposals of Eysenck and R. B. Cattell. Other chapters of the book are also worthy of attention. Vernon favors interpretations that stick close to common sense, in present-day use of tests for counseling and clinical work; the self-report and reports from acquaintances are significant, even when in some way "biased."

16

Personality Measurement Through Self-Report

History of Personality Inventories

In introducing personality measurement we have spoken of it as an attempt to assess "typical behavior." This phrase, which has served our purposes to this point, echoes behavioristic psychology, which directs attention to overt, observable responses. The behavioristic outlook is somewhat limiting, however, and we can understand personality assessment better if we recognize in it the influence of *phenomenological psychology* (Wann, 1964). Phenomenological psychology is concerned with the way the world appears to the individual, with his so-called private world. Such expressions as *self-concept, feelings of hostility,* and *attitude toward authority* refer to perceptions and reactions that occur within the individual. It can be argued that crises of adjustment are shaped more by the individual's perception of events than by the events themselves.

The first personality questionnaires were developed in an attempt to study the inner world of perception and feeling. Galton devised the technique in the 1880s when he needed a standard procedure for studies of mental imagery. Use of questionnaires, again for research purposes, was extended later in the 19th century by G. Stanley Hall in his studies of adolescent development. He used information given by large samples of adults to delineate normal trends in development.

Adjustment Inventories

The first inventory primarily concerned with the individual was the Woodworth Personal Data Sheet. At the beginning of World War I, the U.S. Army wanted to detect soldiers likely to break down in combat, but individual psychiatric interviews were not practicable when recruits were processed by the thousands. Woodworth made a list of symptoms such as psychiatrists would touch upon in a screening interview. His pencil-and-paper version of the interview presented questions a psychiatrist might ask, such as: "Do you daydream frequently?" "Do you wet your bed?" The sensitivity of individual questioning was sacrificed for speed. Men who reported numerous symptoms were singled out for further examination. The test had appreciable power to detect maladjusted soldiers.

The Woodworth scale was a forerunner of a number of "adjustment inventories" that list problems, symptoms, or grievances to be checked. These instruments are not descriptive; they often yield only a single score representing level of adjustment. Sometimes only one type of symptom is covered, as in an inventory of psychosomatic complaints. Sometimes the items are grouped by logical categories, as in the Bell Adjustment Inventory, which has scores for home adjustment, health adjustment, submissiveness, emotionality, and hostility, based (respectively) on transparent items[1] such as

Is either of your parents very easily irritated?

Are you subject to attacks of influenza?

If you were a guest at an important dinner would you do without something rather than ask to have it passed to you?

Do you get angry easily?

Do you often call attention to "dumb remarks" made by some of your associates?

The adjustment inventory usually consists of items on which subjects known to be maladjusted respond differently from subjects judged normal.

Adjustment inventories are screening instruments. They single out persons who freely check symptoms and self-criticisms. They are not focused measures of any clearly defined trait. While the information they provide is superficial, their very transparency may make them easier to justify in school settings.

The inventories may be used to identify persons who should be offered counseling. While "problem cases" who cause trouble are easily recognized, children and adults who are withdrawn and insecure may not attract the attention of observers. An adjustment inventory draws attention to many of these cases.

Table 16.1.   Intercorrelations of Bernreuter scores for adolescent boys

	Neurotic tendency	Self-sufficiency	Introversion	Dominance
Neurotic tendency (low adjustment)		—.39	.87	—.69
Self-sufficiency			—.33	.51
Introversion (low extroversion)				—.62

SOURCE: Flanagan, 1935.

Trait Descriptions

During the period from 1920 to 1945, most psychologists were behavioristic in outlook. The inventory was thought of as primarily a substitute for observation, and the questions placed more emphasis on what the individual did than upon how he felt or what he thought. The questionnaire was broadened to describe separate aspects of behavior in a trait profile. Personality was conceived during this period as a bundle of pervasive habits. The individual was described by the strength of his friendliness, confidence, persistence, and the like —that is, by the frequency with which he made such responses.

Dozens of instruments were produced, each taking items from its predecessors, adding a few new ones, and scoring them in new combinations. The best-known instrument of this period was the Bernreuter Personality Inventory, scored for Neurotic tendency (i.e., adjustment), Self-sufficiency, Introversion, and Dominance (see p. 117).

Flanagan attempted to define key dimensions of this scale by factor analysis, an effort that still continues. Flanagan adopted the principle that to deserve separate names, traits must have low correlations. He intercorrelated the Bernreuter scores of 305 adolescent boys (Table 16.1) and found much overlap. "Introversion," as there measured, is little different from "Neurotic tendency," since items on social isolation and daydreaming carry weight in both scales. Flanagan concluded that *Confidence* and *Sociability* factors could account for the information carried by the four original keys, and he developed scoring keys for these traits. These two scores correlate negligibly and thus do represent independent aspects of the self-report.

There followed a period when personality theory was wholly subordinated to a statistical search for dimensions. Guilford divided introversion into Social introversion, Thinking introversion, Depression, Cycloid tendencies or frequent shifts of mood, and Restraint; later he added eight more scales. Other investigators rearranged them into patterns that they regarded as more efficient. Thur-

Table 16.2.   **Three current lists of personality traits**

Eysenck[a]
    Neuroticism
    Extraversion[b]—Introversion

Norman, following Tupes & Christal
    Extroversion
    Agreeableness
    Conscientiousness
    Emotional stability
    Culture

Cattell[a, c]

Outgoing	Happy-go-lucky	Suspicious	Liberal
Intelligent	Conscientious	Imaginative	Self-sufficient
Emotionally stable	Venturesome	Shrewd	Controlled
Assertive	Tender-minded	Depressive	Tense

[a] The Eysenck scores appear in the Maudsley (or Eysenck) Personality Scale. The Cattell scores appear—sometimes with altered names—in several inventories, the most prominent being the 16 PF Test.

[b] British spelling.

[c] The full description includes several additional near-synonyms for each trait, and several labels for the opposite pole.

stone, for instance, accounted for much of the information in Guilford's thirteen scores by seven factors: *Sociable, Reflective, Emotionally stable, Vigorous* (or masculine), *Dominant, Active,* and *Impulsive.* This game is interminable. One psychologist classifies the items finely, the second puts some of the small bundles together, the third redivides the large bundles in a new way—and each gives his own names to the factors. Until trait lists can be tied down to a definite theory or to external criteria, choice can be made only on aesthetic grounds. There is less consensus as to the number of personality factors reliably identified, the best organization of them, or their most appropriate names than there is regarding ability factors. Table 16.2 represents the current state of the art, offering the trait lists of the investigators who are most vigorously pursuing factor analysis of personality.

    It is evident that trait systems vary in content and complexity. Most systems contain a variable having to do with anxiety or emotional stability or neurotic tendency; most contain a variable relating to energy level or activity. Dominance and sociability are also prominent. Osgood's research on the structure of language suggests that adjectives usually connote particular degrees of goodness vs. badness, strength vs. weakness, and activity vs. passivity. In considering systems of traits, the reader will often detect this simple three-dimensional structure.

Many personality traits given specialized names by investigators can be adequately characterized in the Osgood scheme, which is not a personality theory at all (see p. 566).

Trait names are a source of serious confusion. Cattell decides (Cattell & Warburton, 1967, pp. 199–200) to separate *Neuroticism* ("regression") from *Anxiety* ("maladjustment"), and argues that Eysenck's *Neuroticism* is a mixture of the two. Eysenck (1963) says that his use of *Neuroticism* and *Anxiety* is exactly the opposite of Cattell's. The meaning of "introvert" is twisted and turned so that it represents for one author a brooding neurotic, for another anyone who would rather be a clerk than a carnival barker. "Ascendance" ranges from spontaneous social responsiveness, in one theory, to inconsiderate and overbearing behavior in another. The verbal coinage has been so debased by popular usage and by questionnaire makers that none of the abstract terms is a useful way of exchanging ideas. Personality theory needs a set of constructs on which many investigators agree and which they interpret similarly; and for each such construct there should be several indicators derived from various sorts of data. We are far from that state at present.

In the present Babel of trait names, the only useful way to discuss personality data is to speak of "the Edwards Need for Achievement score," "the Atkinson TAT *n* Achievement score," "the CPI Achievement-through-Independence score," "the Rotter Internal Control score," etc., according to the measure used. Sometimes scores with similar names have zero correlations and entirely different meanings. Even within the same investigator's system, it sometimes appears that measures given the same name are psychologically quite different, especially when one comes from self-report and one from ratings or performance tests (D. R. Peterson, 1965).

1. *Which of these problems or topics of research falls within behavioristic psychology, and which within phenomenal psychology?*
   a. *How frequently does mood change in the typical woman?*
   b. *How much does speed of reading decline in the presence of loud, continuous noise?*
   c. *Do managers and workers describe the company policy on selecting workers for promotion in the same way?*
   d. *What is this child afraid of?*
2. *Does the Woodworth inventory employ the "sign" or the "sample" approach?*
3. *Some testers have treated Flanagan's two scoring keys as supplements to the four supplied by Bernreuter, reporting all six scores to describe an individual. Discuss the advisability of this practice.*
4. *What is a desirable score on a test such as the Bernreuter?*
5. *What does it mean to say that Henry falls at the 50th percentile in Sociability?*
6. *In the three trait lists of Table 16.1, what possibilities for hierarchical reorganization do you see?*
7. *Characterize each adjective in Table 16.1 as +, 0 (intermediate), or − with*

respect to its connotations of goodness, strength, and activity. For example, perhaps an assertive person is ordinarily neither good nor bad [0], is strong [+], and is active [+].) When you have finished, identify pairs of traits you have rated the same. If they are not synonyms, in what respect do they differ?

Criterion-Oriented Scales

Construction of personality questionnaires according to the "sign" principle used by Strong was slow to develop, chiefly because criteria for personality are disputable at best. One obvious point of departure is psychiatric classification. Following explorations by the industrial psychologist D. G. Humm, the Minnesota Multiphasic Personality Inventory (MMPI) was published in 1942 by a psychologist-psychiatrist team. This scale was rapidly accepted and remains today the most widely used and most widely investigated of questionnaires. Although strictly empirical in its original conception, it proved to be ineffective in allocating patients to diagnostic groups. The inventory grew in prominence, however, because accumulated research and clinical experience gave a basis for other types of interpretation. Results on differential diagnosis with questionnaires other than MMPI have in general not been encouraging, and all competing questionnaires for this purpose have disappeared. MMPI is rather unsuitable for normal groups, particularly younger ones. The California Psychological Inventory (CPI) and Minnesota Counseling Inventory (MCI) are descendants of MMPI that are designed for relatively normal high-school and college students. Both are criterion-keyed. The MCI keys are labeled Family Relationships. Emotional Stability, Conformity, Adjustment to Reality, Mood, and Leadership. Some of these keys are closely related to MMPI clinical scales. CPI has emphasized criteria of everyday social and intellectual effectiveness in forming scales (e.g., responsibility, social presence, and femininity).

Tests Derived from Theory

Whereas both the factor analysts and the empiricists developed tests by blind groping to find what-correlates-with-what, the more recent trend in personality measurement is to define constructs on the basis of personality theory and to prepare items specifically to elicit information about those constructs. This is not wholly new; indeed, the earliest work on introversion was stimulated by Jung's personality theory. The long-lived Allport-Vernon-Lindzey *Study of values* (see Allport, 1966) derives from Spranger's typology; the Taylor Manifest Anxiety Scale was designed for research on Hull-Spence behavior theory, and Eysenck's scales are interpreted in neo-Pavlovian terms. Few of the theoretically based scales are put to practical use. Most of them were created for the sake of research and their authors have not studied how they might be used in decision-making.

The construction of inventories for practical use has tapered off in the last decade. Partly, competitors in the clinical field were crowded out by the flourishing of MMPI. Partly, the rise of psychotherapy as a prestigeful activity reduced the interest of clinical and counseling psychologists in diagnostic problems. An instrument that describes a person in terms of broad traits such as "tense" and "introverted" is of no value in directing therapy. Lines of testing that might have been developed to serve the therapist were not exploited. Indeed, many psychologists practicing therapy seem to have rejected tests as a hateful reminder of the "old slave days" when the clinical psychologist's job was to do diagnostic workups as the psychiatrist called for them. There have been new tests for use with normals, but their authors have made little attempt to justify using them practically.

The psychologists sophisticated in personality measurement have increasingly concentrated on theoretical research. Construct-oriented personality tests, of both the self-report and performance varieties, have made possible far-reaching inquiries into social relationships, character, learning, effects of drugs, economic behavior—indeed, have reached into nearly all branches of psychology and social science.

Emerging Trends

Those who design computers, jet airplanes, and other technological devices speak of "generations"; the current "third-generation" computers are radically different in design and performance from those of 15 years ago. There are generations in testing also; the second generation of personality questionnaires, which appeared in the years following 1940, were vastly more sophisticated than the questionnaires of the first generation. Developments in inventories since the 1940s have been changes in detail rather than radical new developments. It is tempting to think that some of the current criticism, both of personality theory and of the measuring techniques, is paving the way for a third and distinctly different generation of inventories. The main-line efforts in the first generation conceived of the instrument as a content-valid self-report; the second generation was, by and large, criterion oriented, preoccupied with actuarial interpretation. If there is to be forward movement, the third must be a generation of construct development and validation.

If the writer were to hazard a guess as to the direction further evolution will take, he would call to mind the Campbell-Fiske demand that any trait be measured by two or more diverse methods (p. 296) in the ability domain. It is now usual to concentrate on variables that influence more than one kind of task—thus, we are interested in fluid ability just because tasks as different as Block Design, Embedded Figures, and Matrices all call for it. One suspects that measures of personality traits will move toward distinctively greater meaningfulness when attention focuses on traits for which we have two or three strongly convergent indicators. If the same trait can be measured by inventories and by other techniques, or by clearly different kinds of inventory content, it is surely significant. The other line of evolution will be away from attempts simply to classify persons or to describe their present response tendencies, and toward the study of responses to distinct types of situations. Just as there is a growing concern for the interaction between abilities and alternative instructional treatments, which, when understood, will permit us to place the individual in the kind of instruction best for him, so information about personality becomes useful when we understand the interaction between person and situation. Therapy, or personnel management, is concerned with placing the individual under those conditions where he will prosper. This calls for an entirely different kind of research from the old predictive studies that simply try to assess who is a "good risk."

8. *An investigator believes that teachers can be characterized by the trait "content-centered" vs. "child-centered." Outline the procedure needed to make a self-report test by means of criterion keying.*

9. *How many scores would you consider necessary to give a complete picture of personality?*

10. *The following items are taken from personality inventories. Is any apparent purpose served by the alterations in form and wording?*

    Did you ever have a strong desire to run away from home?

    > *Yes   No*

    At times I have very much wanted to leave home.

    > *True   False   Cannot Say*

11. *Is any apparent purpose served by these changes of form and wording that appear in different scales?*

    I am a good mixer.

    > *True   False*

    Do you like to mix with people socially?

    > *Almost always   Frequently   Occasionally   Rarely   Almost never*

Description of MMPI

The Minnesota Multiphasic Personality Inventory (MMPI) holds a place among personality questionnaires comparable to that of the Strong among interest measures. It was constructed in a similar empirical manner and was subjected to considerable research by its authors. It appeared at an opportune time, and great reliance was placed upon it during the rapid expansion of clinical psychology in the years 1940 to 1955. It has contributed to and benefited from the interest in clinical research. Published research on MMPI accumulates at a rate of 100 or more studies per year.

MMPI was originally constructed by Starke Hathaway and J. C. McKinley to aid in diagnosis of psychiatric patients. A collection of 500 items was prepared

Table 16.3.   Content of MMPI items as classified by Marks and Seeman

Category	Representative item	Number of items
Attitudes		122
Social	I like parties and sociables.	(12)
Religious	I believe in the second coming of Christ.	(19)
Sexual	Children should be taught all the main facts about sex.	(16)
Test-taking	I do not always tell the truth.	(15)
General health	I am seldom troubled by constipation.	81
Mood	I am happy most of the time.	56
Masculine-feminine	I very much like hunting.	55
Preoccupations	Someone has control over my mind.	46
Morale	I am entirely self-confident.	33
Phobias	I am afraid when I look down from a high place.	29
Occupations	I would like to be a soldier.	18
Educational	I was a slow learner in school.	12
Miscellaneous	I like to read newspaper editorials.	98

SOURCE: Adapted from Marks & Seeman, 1963, p. 24. Items from the Minnesota Multiphasic Personality Inventory are copyright 1943 by the University of Minnesota. Published by The Psychological Corporation, New York, N.Y. All rights reserved.

by borrowing from older inventories and rephrasing diagnostic clues used by psychiatrists. As Table 16.3 shows, some items refer to observable behavior, some ask about feelings that could not be observed from the outside, and some ask about beliefs. Some items frankly ask about abnormalities, whereas others appear to have no favorable or unfavorable connotations. Items are to be answered "T," "F," or "?."

Scoring Procedures

Psychiatric discriminant keys. The scoring keys were developed with the initial intention of identifying patients having various psychiatric disorders. Patients of each type were compared, item by item, with a so-called normal group drawn from visitors to a large city hospital. Items on which paranoids differed statistically from normals were counted in a *Pa* (paranoid) key. The contrast between the MMPI "sign" approach and the content orientation of its predecessors is illustrated by the fact that certain items of the MMPI are also found in the Guilford scales but are scored in the opposite direction.

For example, to say that most people inwardly dislike putting themselves out to help others, that most people would tell a lie to get ahead, . . . are responses scored as paranoid on the Guilford-Martin; whereas it is found empirically that these verbal reactions are actually significantly *less* common among clinically paranoid persons than they are among people generally. This kind of finding suggests that paranoid deviates are characterized by a tendency to give two sorts of responses, one of which is obviously paranoid, the other "obviously" not. [Meehl & Hathaway, 1946.]

The basic scales are as follows:

1 (*Hs*)—hypochondriasis ⎫
2 (*D*)—depression   ⎬ the so-called "neurotic triad"
3 (*Hy*)—hysteria   ⎭
4 (*Pd*)—psychopathic deviate
5 (*Mf*)—masculinity-femininity
6 (*Pa*)—paranoia
7 (*Pt*)—psychasthenia
8 (*Sc*)—schizophrenia
9 (*Ma*)—hypomania
0 (*Si*)—social introversion

Data for the reference group of normals provide a standard-score conversion so that results can be plotted on a profile sheet. Primary significance is attached to scores greater than 70 (50 being the average for the reference group). This cutoff is somewhat arbitrary, and interpreters examine the subject's three or four highest scores regardless of whether they cross this line.

Control keys. MMPI is provided with several keys intended to identify exceptional response styles. The *?* score is the number of times the person replies "Cannot say." *L* (lie) counts answers that deny reality, e.g., responding "False" to "I sometimes put off until tomorrow what I ought to do today." The *F* (false) score consists of responses given extremely rarely. A high count reveals carelessness, misunderstanding, or otherwise invalid answers.

K, the fourth control key, was designed on an empirical basis. It was found, early in the test development, that some quite normal individuals earn scores above 70 on one or another scale because of what have been called "plus-getting" attitudes. These persons reply with such complete frankness, to the point of self-depreciation, that their response distribution is abnormal. A large number of patients, on the other hand, have scores below 70 because they defensively deny symptoms. In order to reduce the number of such misses and false alarms, the *K* key was made, counting items commonly marked by clinical subjects whose profiles were less deviant than they should have been. The items express a bland "all is well" façade—for example, responding "False" to "Criticism or scolding hurts me terribly."

Whereas most control scores are used simply to signal untrustworthy profiles, the *K* scale is employed to adjust the regular scores. Thus *Hs* can be replaced by *Hs* + 0.5 *K*. The effect of the correction, when it operates properly, is shown by a comparison of normals with hypochondriacal patients. Five per cent of the normals and 62 per cent of the patients had an *Hs* score above a certain level. After correction, a cutting score that picked off 5 per cent of the normals picked up 72 per cent of the patients (McKinley *et al.*, 1948). The "misses" were thus reduced from 38 to 28 per cent. In subsequent validation studies, the *K* correction has not been found consistently valuable (Dahlstrom & Welsh, 1960; Ruch & Ruch, 1967).

The impossibility of providing a single correction that will enhance validity in different subpopulations has been increasingly recognized (Dicken, 1963). An even stronger point against the formal correction is made by Yonge (1966), who correlated the original and the *K*-corrected scales with scores on a second inventory. The change is dramatic; a correlation sometimes drops from 0.70 to 0.20 and sometimes shifts from a significant negative value to a significant positive one. Adding in *K*, instead of "correcting" a score, makes the score a measure of a distinctly different quality. In effect, *K*-corrected MMPI is a different instrument from MMPI. As Yonge says:

> When there is evidence that a person's scores are influenced by test taking attitudes, it is difficult to see how intratest manipulation of these biased scores will somehow rid them of their bias. Rather, it would seem more reasonable to assess the person's personality, attitudes, etc., by some *other* measurement operation.

Or, to put it more bluntly, if the subject lies to the tester there is no way to convert the lies into truth.

Profile coding. MMPI interpreters classify profiles so that subjects previously seen who resemble the case now under study can be located in the file. To code a profile the scale numbers are listed in order, starting with the one where the person's standard score is highest. The profile in Figure 16.1 is coded *49'83 . . . 50*. The prime separates scores over 70 from lower scores. Other details of the coding need not be discussed here. Among other advantages, use of the numbers eliminates some of the invalid connotations that creep in when verbal labels such as "paranoid" are applied to the profiles of normals.

Supplementary keys. More than 100 supplementary keys have been prepared: scales for socioeconomic status, ego strength, dominance, prejudice, etc. Few of these scales are used widely.

One scale that attained great prominence was, oddly, not intended for practical use. Spence and Taylor wished to test the effect of anxiety upon learning, in an extension of Hull's theory of drive (Spence, 1958). They presumed, from previous theory, that persons with marked, admitted anxiety symptoms have higher levels of drive and thus acquire a conditioned defense reaction more quickly. To get a simple, unsubtle measure, Taylor requested experienced counselors to choose MMPI statements that constitute overt admissions of anxiety.

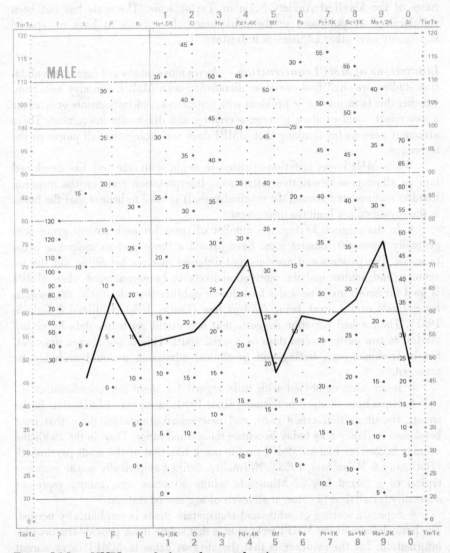

Figure 16.1.   MMPI record of a male mental patient.
Data from Marks and Seeman, 1963, p. 179. Profile form copyright 1948 by The Psychological Corporation, New York, N.Y. All rights reserved. Reproduced by permission.

The items so selected were combined into a short questionnaire and used for the laboratory studies. When a puff of air onto the eye was associated with a bright light, eyeblink responses to the light stimulus were far more numerous among the "anxious" subjects (J. A. Taylor, 1951). The questionnaire was subsequently adopted by many investigators and clinical counselors, under the name of the Manifest Anxiety Scale or Taylor scale. The scale has not been standardized or published in the usual sense. It appears to have no special superiority over other adjustment indicators.

Limitations of MMPI construction. As we move on toward results of validation studies, we shall find ourselves dissatisfied with MMPI. We may ask, then, whether this is an inevitable problem with criterion-keyed instruments or whether a new effort could produce a better screening and diagnostic instrument. There are many reasons for thinking that MMPI does not exploit the full power of the technique.

While MMPI was criterion-oriented to begin with, the test has developed into an all-purpose descriptive instrument. Interpretation rests on the meaning that has accumulated around the original keys. It is hard to believe that the faults in the keying do not limit the instrument.

● In the original keying, the number of cases for each patient group was generally below 50; chance must have played a large part in assigning items to scales. The patients and normals had different motives for filling out the inventory, and neither had the motivation likely to be encountered when MMPI is used for screening. The scales have lower stability than desirable, the median for normals over 1 week being 0.80 or less (Cottle, 1950; Gilliland & Colgin, 1951). The marked variation suggests that one would get better data by giving the test in two parts, several days or a week apart. This is not always practical, but in freshman-week testing and in clinical admission it could probably be managed.

● Items were combined with little regard for their intercorrelations.

● Items have changed in meaning since 1940; in an era of LSD, riots in the streets, the ubiquitous credit card, and new sexual standards, items that once betokened deviancy may today be within the normal range. Even in the 1940s the average adolescent had an MMPI profile much like that of the adult psychopath (Hathaway & Monachesi, 1953). Normality, defined empirically as the response typical of a mixed bag of Minnesota adults 30 years ago, cannot represent normality for all time to come, at all levels of age and education.

● Separate scoring of subtle and transparent items is emphatically needed. The basic defense of the MMPI technique is that subtle items provide trustworthy information, but the evidence is that the obvious items in MMPI carry almost all of the discriminating power in the present keys (McCall, 1958; Duff, 1965). With this finding, the whole empirical approach is called into question. Separate, separately validated subtle and obvious keys would be trustworthy in cases where they confirm each other, and a warning to the interpreter where they do not. And if the subtle keys prove invalid, making the test 100 per cent obvious improves it.

● Prerequisite to the development of a significantly better diagnostic instrument is the development of better psychiatric categories. Criticisms of the categories now standard are reviewed by Lorr, Klett, and McNair (1963, Chapters 2 and 9). The inadequacy of present psychiatric criteria is suggested by a detailed study of the reasons for disagreements in diagnosis. Among the cases reviewed, 5 per cent were attributed to inconsistency of the patient, 32.5 per cent to variability of the diagnostician, and 62.5 per cent to faults of the classification system (Ward *et al.*, 1962).

Interpretation of Profiles

Judgment of pathology. When MMPI is used as part of a general examination of a subject, the first important question is whether the person is emotionally disturbed. This is not indicated simply by the presence or absence of scores above 70. College students show those scores rather often, not because they are abnormal but because they come from a different social and age stratum than the norm group. Response biases also affect the likelihood that scores will be elevated.

The clinician, therefore, studies the whole profile. The process is impressionistic, but the impressions are guided by rather explicit generalizations. Kleinmuntz (1963) persuaded an experienced clinician to sort a pack of student profiles into two categories, reporting his thinking as he proceeded. The character of clinical thinking is reflected in the following excerpts (covering only the early part of the sorting process) :[2]

Now I'm going to divide these into two piles . . . on the left [least adjusted] I'm throwing all mults with at least four scales primed.

I'll throw all mults to the right [most adjusted] if there's no clinical scale above a *T* score of 60. I'll let *Ma* go up as high as 80 . . . maybe a raw score of 10 on *Mt* would be playing it safe . . . so I'm looking at three things now and sorting according to these conditions.

If either *Pd*, *Pa*, or *Sc* is primed, I'm putting it on the left side . . . it would also be nice to have all of the *P* scales slightly more elevated than the others.

If the elevations [high scores] are lopsided to the right with the left side of the profile fairly low, I'm throwing the mults to the left.

Here's a paranoid character. I wish his *K*-score were not quite so high and he could use more *Mt* . . . when that *Mt* score is less than 10, I figure something must be stabilizing him. I like an inverted V . . . on the validity scales [as evidence of paranoid maladjustment].

These rules are so clear-cut that Kleinmuntz (1969) was able to turn them into orders by which a computer could sort profiles; the computer classified with accuracy comparable to that of the human judge. Kleinmuntz does not propose to let the computer *decide* that a student is maladjusted, but he does regard it as feasible to process profiles mechanically to pick out suspect cases. These results are reviewed by a clinician; a judgment of probable maladjustment then leads

[2] Translations of jargon: "mult" = MMPI; "primed" = score above 70; "Mt" = scale to identify maladjustment of college students (Kleinmuntz, 1960) ; "inverted V on validity scales . . ." = pattern with *F* higher than *L* and *K*.

to an invitation to a counseling session. The advantage of the machine is quite simple: "When confronted with the task of screening several hundreds of thousands of MMPI profiles, the machine will gallop along its merry way without even a grumble or a thought about where it might more profitably be spending its time" (1963, p. 18).

Descriptive interpretation. Although MMPI scores were derived from psychiatric diagnosis, the diagnostic categories per se are no longer emphasized. After a decade of validation and clinical experience, one of the Minnesota investigators (Meehl, 1951) was ready to say:

> These days we are tending to start with the test, sort people on the basis of it, and then take a good look at the people to see what kind of people they are. This, of course, is different from the way in which the test was built, and different from the usual psychiatrist's notion of a test where you start with groups of people sorted out on some basis—for instance, by formal psychiatric diagnosis—and you try to build a test which will guess or predict or agree with that . . . criterion. . . . The primary function of psychometrics is [not] . . . to prophesy what the psychiatrist is going to say about somebody.

For descriptive purposes, any set of reasonably uncorrelated scales would presumably have been at least as appropriate as the keys of MMPI, but by the time the descriptive use emerged, it was the psychiatric scales on which experience had accumulated. The subsequent work on the test can only be described as an attempt to improve interpretations of obsolete scales.

Information on characteristics of persons with each profile type are accumulated in a number of "atlases" (e.g., Hathaway & Meehl, 1951; Gilberstadt & Duker, 1965; Drake & Oetting, 1959). To take one example, the admission profile a 50-year-old patient was *2'3 . . . 96*. The staff diagnosis was "psychosis, manic-depressive, depressed state." After a month of treatment in a hospital, the profile was *89' . . . 2*; but high *L* and *F* made the record suspect. At this time the staff changed the diagnosis to "paranoid" because the symptoms had changed. A third test came two years later, upon a readmission. This test showed a return to the 23 pattern, with no very low scores. The diagnosis was again manic-depressive, depressed. The case history follows (Hathaway & Meehl, 1951, p. 120):

> The admission of this patient with severe depression of about two months' duration was the latest of several such episodes, with seclusiveness, poor memory, inability to work, and somatic complaints the outstanding characteristics of the depression. When he was working, he misplaced tools; and he was convinced that people watching him noticed the poor quality of his work. He complained of failing memory; he slowed down physically and mentally; he suffered from insomnia; there was loss of appetite; and in general he lost contact with his surroundings. Lacking energy, he found it very difficult even to dress himself or go to meals. His speech was retarded and incoherent at times.

A year before admission there had been a similar attack from which he had recovered after six electroshock treatments. Until this first attack, his behavior had always been normal. His intelligence was average. A shy person, not socially aggressive, withdrawn, and moderately religious, he had always been kind and had never lost his temper. A premarital dependency on his mother was later transferred to his wife. His general adjustment to society was adequate although he was known as a "drifter," and at best he held only semiskilled jobs. Throughout his life there had been a history of cyclic mood swings in which he moved from periods of elation to periods of depression.

On admission he showed rather severe psychomotor retardation. He did not appear to be delusional. He had no paranoid ideas, nor was he suicidal. His sensorium and intellect were intact, and he had some insight into the depression. There was marked apathy, but he was cooperative and expressed the hope that he might be "well again." After shock therapy, which brought about rather marked change, he became more disoriented, careless, and talkative. He showed some regression, answered questions foolishly, and was occasionally euphoric, uncooperative, loud, and demanding. With the continuation of the shock treatments his behavior became more acceptable and five days after the last of the eleven treatments he was discharged with almost complete remission of his symptoms. At that time it was felt that he would probably have another depression. Twenty months later the patient returned to the hospital. Following his first discharge, he had been euphoric and unstable for about three months, then had begun to slip into another depression which persisted until the second admission. He was discharged after seven shock treatments and was to return to the outpatient clinic for supportive care. The prognosis about a further relapse was very guarded.

In this account we may note several points, the first being the essential consistency of the first and third records, 2 years and 11 shock treatments apart. The intermediate record was radically different, but it was challenged by the control scores. High D (2) in the admission profiles is consistent with the clinical picture, and high Hy (3) is consistent with the patient's "withdrawn, kind, dependent" exterior. The inadequacy of his defenses, however, led the psychiatric staff to classify him as psychotic rather than neurotic.

Meehl, having demonstrated that judgment is frequently inaccurate (see p. 442), proposed that a standard interpretation be worked out for each type of profile. It was demonstrated that for at least certain codes a prepackaged interpretation was more valid (i.e., better matched the impressions of the therapist) than the report made by an experienced psychologist interpreting the profile (Meehl, 1956b).

The Marks-Seeman *Atlas* (1963) provides standard interpretations for 16 profile types, including the *49* profile of Figure 16.1. The authors searched clinical files to find records of each type. They found 18 males and 26 women with *49* profiles. Qualified professionals read the case history folder (*not* including MMPI) for each case and prepared a description with the aid of *Q*-sort cards (see pp. 585 f.). The patient's therapist also gave such a description. Then a composite description was compiled for patients in the category. Finally, descriptive statements and objective data were compared so that the *Atlas* could report how the selected group differs from the sample as a whole. For the *49* group, Marks and Seeman give six pages of information, of which the following is representative:

> Undercontrols own impulses
> Is egocentric; self-centered; selfish
> Avoids close interpersonal relationships
> Has inner conflict about emotional dependency
> Mean age of onset of illness: 22.6 (range 16–31)
> 80% are classed as personality disorders
> Symptoms: sexual difficulty, 89%; dependent, 67%;
>   amorality, 39%; drug usage, 22%.
> Prognosis in treatment: good, 0%; fair, 36%; poor, 64%.
> Mean WAIS IQ 118 (range 103–125)

As there are 24 statements describing this type of personality, the report is almost as full as the "dynamic" report a clinician might write. The final step in automatization is to store something like the Marks-Seeman book in the computer memory, and have the computer print the interpretation on call. Indeed, matters have been carried to the point where the clinician can send the test result to a scoring center and receive a descriptive report from the computer, like that shown in Figure 16.2. (Similar service is becoming available for other complex tests.) The MMPI interpretation in Figure 16.2 is based on the experience of the Mayo Clinic and its consultants; the description corresponding, for example, to a male's score on scale *4* in the range 37 and above is pulled from the computer memory. Unlike the Marks-Seeman scheme, this interpretation considers scores in turn rather than in combination.

The actuarial method is sure to be right, if the stored report is based on patients who are truly "just like" the subject in hand. But when the Marks-

-NUMBER OF PHYSICAL SYMPTOMS AND CONCERN ABOUT BODILY FUNCTIONS
FAIRLY TYPICAL FOR MEDICAL PATIENTS.
-VIEWS LIFE WITH AVERAGE MIXTURE OF OPTIMISM AND PESSIMISM.
-HIGHLY REBELLIOUS AND NONCONFORMIST. UNRELIABLE. SHALLOW FEELINGS
AND LOYALTIES. POOR FAMILY AND SOCIAL RELATIONSHIPS.
-NORMAL MALE INTEREST IN WORK, HOBBIES, ETC.
-SENSITIVE. ALIVE TO THE OPINIONS OF OTHERS.
-HAS SUFFICIENT CAPACITY FOR ORGANIZING WORK AND PERSONAL LIFE.
-TENDS TOWARD ABSTRACT INTERESTS SUCH AS SCIENCE, PHILOSOPHY,
AND RELIGION.
-RESTLESS AND IMPULSIVE. SCATTERED INTERESTS AND ENERGIES.
PROBABLE SUPERFICIAL GAIETY AND GREGARIOUSNESS.
-HAS CAPACITY TO MAINTAIN ADEQUATE SOCIAL RELATIONSHIPS.

Figure 16.2. A computer interpretation of the MMPI profile of Figure 16.1.
Statements reproduced from Pearson et al., 1964.

Seeman or the Mayo tabulation has to be applied without regard to age, sex, education, geographic origin, ethnicity, years since onset of illness, etc., the next case cannot be just like the defining pool. The clinician can consider such facts, and also can consider scores other than 4 and 9. The machine cannot; collecting a file of cases for every subgroup within the 49 type would take forever. But the burden of proof is on the clinician to show that when he uses extra facts he does so validly. On the strength of the evidence regarding the judgments of present-day clinicians, one has to bet on the computer, leaving the clinician only the task of translating the printout into recommendations. These decisions have to fit the patient's unique family situation, the resources of the clinic, etc.; no computer prescription will work.

The present state of the art of automated interpretation is summarized by several leading investigators in a volume edited by J. Butcher (1969), which includes a statement by Carson considering in detail the limitations noted above.

MMPI interpretations may be made for subjects in the normal range, though fewer criterion data have been collected to guide such thinking. Black had each of 200 women students at Stanford rate other girls residing in her dormitory by checking adjectives to describe her. The girl also described herself on the

Table 16.4. Reputations and self-descriptions associated with MMPI scores of college women

Scale or pattern with high score	N	Description by dormitory mates	Self-description
2 (D)	16	Shy, not energetic, not relaxed, not kind	Shy, moody, not energetic; not relaxed, not decisive
3 (Hy)	25	Many physical complaints, flattering, not partial, not clever	Trustful, friendly, not emotional, not boastful
4 (Pd)	26	Incoherent, moody, partial, sociable, frivolous, not self-controlled	Dishonest, lively, clever, not adaptable, not friendly, not practical
5 (Masculinity)	15	Unrealistic, natural, not dreamy, not polished	Shiftless, not popular, unemotional, not having wide interests
5 low (Femininity)	68	Worldly, not energetic, not rough, not shy	Self-distrusting, self-dissatisfied, sensitive, shy, unrealistic
6 (Pa)	24	Shrewd, hard-hearted	Arrogant, shy, naïve, sociable
7 (Pt)	20	Dependent, kind, quiet, not self-centered	Indecisive, soft-hearted, depressed, irritable
9 (Ma)	52	Shows off, boastful, selfish, energetic, not loyal, not peaceable, not popular	Enterprising, jealous, courageous, energetic, popular, peaceable, self-confident

Source: After Black; see Welsh & Dahlstrom, 1956, pp. 151–172.

checklist. The statistical tabulation then showed which adjectives were applied to girls with high scores on any MMPI scale. Table 16.4, based on a portion of the results, shows what reputation and what "published" self-concept goes with each MMPI score in this sample. The various MMPI scales do seem to depict different types of personality. A high score need not be pathological; a High *9*, for example, marks a colorful, self-assertive person.

The difference between the self-ratings and ratings by others is striking. The girls frequently use favorable adjectives to describe characteristics others disapprove in them. High *9*'s say they are enterprising and courageous; others call them boastful and selfish. This strongly reinforces the view that the self-description tells what the person believes about himself or wants others to believe. It also shows that ratings carry information on the judge's frame of reference (see pp. 576 and 598).

12. *A client coming to a social agency has these MMPI scores:*

Scale	1	2	3	4	5	6	7	8	9
Score	43	45	50	50	50	68	42	67	69

How would the interpretation be affected if the "control scores" were as follows:
a. *?, 72; L, 50; K, 50; F, 50.*
b. *?, 50; L, 73; K, 50; F, 50.*
c. *?, 50; L, 50; K, 72; F, 50.*
d. *?, 50; L, 50; K, 35; F, 50.*

13. *To what extent do the two actuarial descriptions based on the profile of Figure 16.1 give the same impression?*

Validity of Inventories for Decisions About Abnormality

Screening of Deviant Personalities

Separating patients from normals. The authors of MMPI early abandoned hopes that the test had great power to detect the mentally disordered. Some of the scales were regarded as questionable even at the time of publication. In papers by the test authors one finds many remarks such as: "The evidence for the validity of *Ma* [9] is certainly not conclusive." The published version of scale *8* is "only slightly better than the ones that were rejected." "The *Pt* [7] scale has never been considered very satisfactory." And for *6*, "Cross-validation was always disappointing." This frankness is in welcome contrast to the glowing accounts of test developers who have made less effort to validate.

Under favorable conditions, most of the scales have more or less the same discriminating power. A cutting score that yields 5 per cent false alarms among

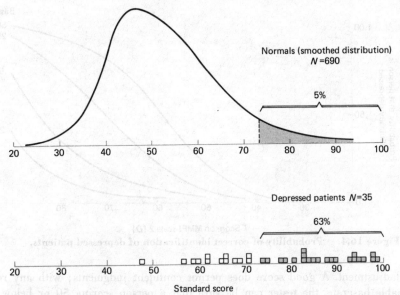

Figure 16.3.   Distributions of normal and patient groups on MMPI scale 2 (D).
From Hathaway & McKinley, 1942.

normals will identify some 70 per cent of the patients in the category from which the scale was derived. The precise character of the data is indicated in Figure 16.3, which shows the distributions on scale 2 (D) of 690 normals and of 35 patients who had previously been identified as clinically depressed. The patient group has a distinctly higher mean. This information alone does not tell whether the screening validity is high enough to be useful. In order to face this question, we must take into account the number of true depressive cases in the population to be tested (Meehl & Rosen, 1955).

As an illustration, let us assume that among the persons coming to a clinic 50 per cent are depressed. Then let us change this figure to other baserates; 20 per cent, 5 per cent, and 2 per cent. Figure 16.4 plots the probability that a person with each score is indeed clinically depressed, using the distributions of Figure 16.3 with each baserate in turn. Again, we see the clear relation between score and probability of being properly called a depressed patient. The value of the test in diagnosis depends heavily on the baserate. The psychologist is right 80 per cent of the time in classifying a person with a score of 70 on scale 2 as depressed—*if* such patients constitute half of the sample he sees. If depressives are a fifth of the population, the cutting score must be 83 to permit the same confidence in a borderline diagnosis. Such a shift, however, leaves more than half the depressives undetected. A poor score is not a dependable indicator of

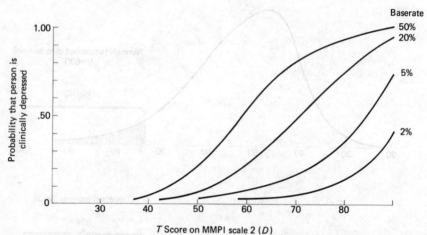

Figure 16.4.   **Probability of correct identification of depressed patients.**

maladjustment. A good score does permit confident judgments; with any reasonable baserate, the tester can be sure that a person scoring 50 or below is very unlikely to be depressive. If these low scores are passed over while the remaining subjects are submitted to further interviewing or testing, virtually no depressives will be overlooked.

Identifying suspect cases for intensive examination.   Short, undisguised questionnaires have been of distinct value for screening military populations (W. Hunt & Stevenson, 1946). An inventory of only 20 items was profitably used to determine which Navy recruits should be seen by psychiatrists for examination and possible discharge as unfit. With a cutting score set to allow 5 per cent false positives, 53 per cent of the discharge cases could be identified. A questionnaire given 2081 Seabees successfully identified 281 persons later judged by psychiatrists to present neuropsychiatric conditions; it missed 16 who came to the psychiatrists' attention through difficulty on duty and falsely picked up 244 men judged normal upon further study (D. H. Harris, 1945). This means that the test permitted psychiatrists to omit individual interviews with 1540 men—not a trifling saving.

Attempts to screen students to find those who should be counseled have been disappointing. In a study with an especially good criterion, more than 800 college students were interviewed repeatedly during the year by counselors who then made a diagnosis regarding the kind and extent of maladjustment (Darley, 1937). The Bell inventory had been given at the start of the year. A certain cutting score identified 40 students truly having problems relating to home adjustment, missed 41, and produced 73 false alarms. On emotional adjustment, there were 32 hits, 75 misses, and 42 false alarms. In a similar study of the Bernreuter, among 16 girls scoring at the maladjusted extreme (out of 81 subjects), only 6 were considered actually maladjusted. Two of those least maladjusted according to the test were rated maladjusted on the criterion. Confidence ratings agreed with test scores for all 10 girls who showed extremely low confidence on the test, and for 6 of 8 whose test scores showed high confidence (Feder & Baer, 1941). While the fit between scores and criterion reports is "better than chance," errors are too frequent to warrant trust in questionnaires to detect maladjusted students.

Identifying problem cases from self-reports at earlier ages is also very difficult. Investigators who compare known delinquents with normals find some differences in scores, but the overlap discourages reliance on the tests. On the Heston Personal Adjustment Inventory, 30 to 48 per cent of delinquents (compared with 8 to 16 per cent of a matched control group) fell below the 20th percentile on Emotional Stability, Confidence, and two other scales (Hathaway & Monachesi, 1953). This is far poorer than the level of discrimination achieved by psychiatric interviewing of such cases.

An exceptional study tested all ninth-graders in Minneapolis and followed the 4000 subjects for 4 years. Predictive validity was examined by comparing those who later became delinquents with the remainder. Among boys the significant differences were those indicated in Table 16.5. High scores on control scales and on scales related to excitability were prognostic of delinquency, and high scores on scales related to inhibition were relatively rare among delinquents. The *F* scale (rare, probably careless responses) proved to be the most indicative of potential delinquency. High *4*'s are acting-out, impulsive personalities, insen-

Table 16.5. Rate of juvenile delinquency for various MMPI profile types

Profile type	High score	Per cent of all boys who fall in code class	Per cent of boys in code class who become delinquent
Invalid	F or L	7	36
Excitable	4 (Pd)	19	24
	8 (Sc)	14	24
	9 (Ma)	22	22
All boys		100	21
Inhibited	0 (Si)	6	11
	2 (D)	4	13
	5 (Mf)	6	11

SOURCE: Monachesi & Hathaway, 1969.

sitive to social controls. Among girls, delinquency is rare, but the direction of scale validities is the same and the relations are strong (Monachesi & Hathaway, 1969).

Limitations of validation studies.   One can always make somewhat valid predictions by the simple rule that persons who have displayed symptoms in the past are more likely than others to display symptoms in the future. One bit of evidence for this is provided in results to be presented below. (See Table 16.6.) Another is a large study of parole violations (Gough, Wenk, & Rozynko, 1965). More dramatic is the report (Lasky *et al.*, 1959) that the thickness of a mental patient's file folder correlates 0.61 with his chances of being hospitalized again after release!

Inventories are considerably less potent as predictors of deviant behavior than are records of past deviant behavior. Prediction may be enhanced by the "Give-a-dog-a-bad-name" effect. Moreover, conflict with one's environment breeds future conflict, unless someone helps the person resolve the initial conflict. These findings are precisely like the findings in the intellectual field: the best way to predict who will do well in schooling is to find out who has been doing well in school.

But this argues for rather than against the importance of tests. To predict from life history is a conservative strategy: good is expected of those good in the past, and the worst is expected of those with bad past records. Prediction from past records is far from perfect. The proper function of psychological methods is to locate the seemingly adjusted people who are in danger of developing emotional disturbance, and the persons with histories of maladjustment who might be salvaged. And this implies a need to measure not level of adjustment but probability of responding favorably to one or another treatment. (Compare with our interest in fluid ability as a possible predictor of achievement; p. 293).

Validation research has rarely come near to this problem. Few studies ask which tests can predict adjustment *within* a sample of persons with bad records, or within a sample with good case histories. One suspects that quite different scales might be predictive in the two groups. The prediction formula ought also to be derived within a group of uniform ability. The incompetent student or recruit will have problems of adjustment, and it is no brilliant achievement for a "personality" test to predict this. Within the incompetent group, some will develop emotional symptoms and some will not; the personality characteristics associated with breakdown in this group may be different from the characteristics associated with breakdowns within the high-ability group. Once controls for past history and ability are introduced, one suspects that present scales will show negligible validity for screening.

The studies above consider only one score at a time. Writers on MMPI have urged that judgment be based on all scores together. It is well established that a deviant group has high averages on several scales, not just on the one "appropriate" to its diagnosis; this is a reasonable finding, since a disorder often involves many types of symptom. The argument is made, therefore, that screening should take into account many scores at once. It is difficult to locate evidence about the accuracy of multiscale screening, the statistical studies of it being few and inadequately reported. Some evidence on the use of MMPI patterns to distinguish between types of patients is presented below.

Before trying to explain the generally poor performance of inventories as screening devices, let us emphasize certain aspects of the design of validation studies. These points are important because some articles report striking success in prediction, though the apparent success results merely from improper analysis.

● Validation of a key or formula on the cases used to select items and establish weights proves nothing. Crossvalidation (p. 433) is essential to avoid giving credit to a screening rule that fits only the first sample.

● To demonstrate significant differences (e.g., between delinquents and normals) without examining the baserate is misleading. The usefulness of a screening instrument depends upon the count of misses and false alarms at the proposed cutting score. Given enough cases, "highly significant" differences can be established with instruments of no practical value.

● Comparisons of extreme groups show the presence of a relationship, but one wants to know how strong the relation is in the intact population. Significance levels are not evidence on strength of relations, and a correlation for extreme groups is false evidence. There is a significant difference, on a CPI scale, between boys nominated by principals as most and least self-accepting. This comparison is based on 114 boys from six high schools. For the test manual the author computed a biserial correlation of 0.46 from these data. But, as can be seen in Figure 5.3, there can be a large difference between extreme groups when the correlation for the entire population is very low. A correlation coefficient must be computed on (or estimated for) the whole population to whom the test will be applied. If, as the manual seems to indicate, the principals nominated the extreme 1 per cent of their student bodies, a recomputation indicates that the validity of the CPI score is approximately 0.15, not 0.46.

Correlations with criteria are often low. The defender of an inventory will argue that the evidence on screening and diagnosis is, on the whole, favorable. The defender points out that the criteria are themselves invalid, and, indeed, that a test that did predict psychiatric diagnosis perfectly would give imperfect information on personality. While the attack upon the diagnosis is legitimate, one must be wary of any implication that when test and psychiatrist disagree the test is dependable. Evidence to support this type of claim has not been developed.

A second pertinent defense is that many a criterion is crude. Thus the data on depressives (above) are probably unfair to the MMPI. The patient group perhaps included some cases who had recovered from their depressive phase before testing, and the normal group, including as it did unhospitalized relative of patients, may well have included numerous undetected depressives. More generally, nonpatient status is no guarantee of sound personality; many persons in the community have serious maladjustment that remains undetected so long as they are exposed to no exceptional stress. The fact that the pressures of life are not the same for all persons greatly reduces the prospect of predicting behavior from personality measures.

One favorable final statement can be made. In dealing with large populations (military recruits, college students, etc.) in which individual attention cannot be given to everyone and in which case histories are not available, questionnaires validated on that type of population are of value as a preliminary screen. Persons with better scores can be passed over while the remainder are systematically examined. The number of deviant cases missed is reduced by control keys. It is never proper to assume that a person who earns a poor score on a questionnaire is maladjusted; the number of false alarms makes it imperative to regard the test as only a first stage of investigation.

14. *What does Table 16.5 indicate about the practical value of MMPI for screening potential delinquents?*

15. *Is concurrent or predictive validity the primary concern in screening studies?*

16. *What importance can be attached to the finding that Pd (4) scores decrease markedly with age?*

17. *In view of the cost to society of care for persons who have neglected their bodies, and the cost of institutional care for mental patients, what would you think of a proposal that everyone be required to have an annual medical checkup, one part of which would be a questionnaire more or less like MMPI?*

Classification of Patients

The second original aim of MMPI was to distinguish one type of psychopathology from another. Mental hospitals and outpatient clinics often need to make a rapid decision as to the probable nature of the patient's disorder.

Profiles for diagnostic groups differ significantly, and experienced MMPI users can classify profiles with some success. Guthrie (1950) asked such clinicians to classify records into six piles (paranoid, anxiety state, depressed, etc.); the judges made 36 to 54 correct placements out of 89. Though substantially better than chance, this is low for diagnostic purposes. Sullivan and Welsh (1952) found eight "pattern" characteristics (e.g., score *1* higher than *3*) that, in combination, differentiated ulcer patients from unselected neuropsychiatric patients with modest success (70 per cent of ulcers correctly identified at a cost of 37 per cent false alarms). Rules for other disorders had similar success. MMPI is at best a source of hypotheses about the person's diagnosis that must be checked by other methods.

This topic permits us to return once more to two much vexed questions: configural prediction, and clinical prediction. Claims on these matters appear in print so often, and are so appealing to psychologists who want to be optimistic about their techniques, that the discouraging evidence must be faced. The highly experienced Professor Meehl insisted (1956a, 1959) that configural methods ought to be indispensable for discriminating neurotics from psychotics.

I expect the discriminant function [a linear formula, to outdo] . . . the fledgling cliniker, but I expect the skilled cliniker to do still better. Better than all three . . . will be an objective set of complex-pattern rules. . . . The student clinician follows a near-linear and unconfigured function, non-optimal weights, and low diurnal reliability for identical profiles. The discriminant function eliminates the unreliability and non-optimal weights. The skilled cliniker employs a configural function, and in the case of the MMPI this is so important that the superimposed errors of non-optimal weights and unreliability do not wash out the configural gain. Finally, the objective pattern-criteria are configural and the decision is consistent from case to case. (Meehl, 1956a, pp. 140–141.)

To test this hypothesis, 861 subjects were collected, about half of whom had been finally classified as psychotics, and half as neurotics, in the clinics where they were treated. Judgmental classifications were made by experienced and inexperienced clinicians, and by a great variety of statistically derived formulas, linear and nonlinear. Without going into detail, we may quote from Goldberg's summary (in press) of a decade of attempts to find the best classification procedure:

A simple linear composite of five single scales . . . outperformed all of the 29 diagnosticians. A . . . [weighted linear composite], utilizing the 11 single scales, yielded a cross-validity no greater. . . . Configural actuarial techniques do not display greater relative validity than linear techniques for this diagnostic problem. . . . While psychologists should certainly not give up the search for more powerful configural techniques, they are likely to need sample sizes as much as a hundred times as large as are found in most studies and at least 10 times as large as the total sample analyzed in the present study.

Perhaps the suggestion of collecting samples of 10,000 cases is too desperate; configural relations do show up in studies guided by theoretical constructs, in relatively small samples (e.g., p. 563). But these have little to do with practical classification problems.

If the current best hope in diagnosis is linear, simple rules, and if MMPI is the best instrument in hand, it is worthwhile to look at Rosen's (1966) improvements on MMPI diagnosis. He recognized that scales weighted so as to separate patients in a particular diagnosis from men in general are not logically suited to distinguish between groups of patients (cf. Figures 14.3 and 14.7). He formed five keys by weighting items that separate patients in a particular diagnosis from *patients in general*. Rosen's Cr score, keyed on "conversion reaction" (hysteric) cases, differs strikingly from the original Hy key; in fact, the two correlate only 0.24. Cr correlates 0.91 with the original key 7 based on "psychasthenic" anxiety cases. The new keys seem to correspond better to the patients' diagnoses than the original keys. There are no data as yet on the usefulness of the Rosen keys for screening patients from normals or on their usefulness in descriptions.

Although enormous effort has been expended in attempts to classify patients and to validate the assignments to categories, this is regarded by many clinicians as at best a start toward the analysis of the case. Holt (1968, pp. 10 ff.), in revising a classic book on "diagnostic testing," insists that the job to be done is one of analysis and description.

> Diagnosis is after all a medical term, meaning the art or act of identifying a disease from its signs and symptoms. . . . The ideal conception of disease was one of a clearly identifiable, unique pattern of symptoms arising from the deleterious effect of an external agent upon a healthy organism. . . . A diagnosis is not a sufficient classification but a necessary constituent of a personality description. . . . From clinical data such as tests provide, one can proceed by means of what I call primary inference only to variables [of intellect, defense, affect, motivation, etc.], not to diagnoses. . . . Typological concepts such as . . . pathological syndromes are standard forms of organization, simplified paradigms of ways people tend to be put together, but good diagnostic work uses them in a differentiated way as starting points of the construction of individualized models of personality.

That is how a writer who favors dynamic interpretation speaks. One who rejects the Freudian-Kraepelinian tradition, and swings nearly to the behaviorist extreme, says almost the same things:

> The only legitimate reason for spending time in clinical assessment is to generate propositions which are useful in forming decisions of benefit to the persons under study.
>
> The main difficulty with the typological, disease-oriented approach to the study of human problems is simply that we are not dealing with disease types in the assessment and modification of disordered behavior. A child who strangles kittens or spits at his mother does not have a disease. He *does* have something somebody defines as a problem. . . . The therapeutic need is to get the client to change his behavior, not to cure his illness, and the vital diagnostic need is for information contributory to the behavior changing enterprise. (D. R. Peterson, 1968, pp. 4–5, 32).

A psychotherapist who applies a uniform approach to all patients gains almost nothing from diagnosis; at best, tests serve him by screening out the kinds of patient he does not think his method can help. The agency administrator who is concerned with finding the best treatment for every patient, and with allocating expensive resources so that they will do the most good, has to ask whether a diagnostic procedure has practical value. The agency applies some decision rule to convert the diagnosis into a recommendation regarding treatment. It is not sufficient to "validate" the tester's diagnosis by checking whether it agrees with a diagnosis based on thorough study of the case. One ought to validate the diagnosis and the decision rule together, in terms of their ability to improve outcomes of treatment.

This requires a quasiexperimental study in which persons with the same diagnosis are assigned to alternative treatments. The outcomes (e.g., per cent who are discharged and remain out of the hospital) have to be tabulated for each diagnosis-treatment combination. If a treatment works better for some patient categories than others, there is an interaction between personality and treatment, and the diagnostic scheme has utility.

Full-fledged experiments on diagnosis-treatment interaction are impossible. One cannot ethically apply the treatments an institution offers to a random selection of patients. But for most patients there are reasonable options, and experimental studies limited to these alternatives can tell whether the diagnosis provides a sound basis for decision.

Validity of Decisions About Normal Subjects

To this point we have concentrated on MMPI and on clinical problems. We now broaden the discussion.

Prediction of Vocational Criteria

Inventories are poor predictors of employee performance. Ghiselli and Barthol (1953) located 113 correlations between job proficiency and presumably relevant inventory scores. Nearly all correlations were positive. The average correlation was as high as 0.36 for sales personnel but only 0.14–0.18 for supervisors and foremen. There was a wide range among coefficients for the same occupation. One gets much the same impression from a later compilation by Guion and Gottier (1965). The Ghiselli-Barthol averages are probably unreasonably high, since investigators tend to file and forget studies that show negligible relations.

No recent work has overcome the difficulties reported 30 years ago by Wonderlic and Hovland (Moore, 1941, p. 60):

We were unable to find any test in which the total score was significantly prognostic of success in our organization to warrant its inclusion as part of a selection program. In the cases of many of the purchasable personality tests, results were obtained which ran counter to expectations. Clerical workers seemed to be more aggressive than salesmen, salesclerks were higher than managers.

Just as "everyone knows" that extraverts make the best salesmen, so one would expect the rigid, conservative, nationalistic authoritarian to be the worst of candidates for the Peace Corps. M. B. Smith (1965) validated preinduction questionnaire measures of this trait against adaptation as a schoolteacher in Ghana, with the hunch that high scorers would make poor cultural ambassadors. The tests did not predict performance in the field. Smith tries to account for the near-zero correlations, noting first that the true authoritarian does not volunteer for the Peace Corps. Very likely the extreme Lows are too unruly and impulsive to adapt as the moderates (who within this select population rank as Highs) do. Then he notes that the Ghanaian school system is organized rigidly. Success on the job means fitting the demands of the system, even if one never gets around to making friends with the populace. As one reads Smith's post-mortem on the once-lively hypothesis, the only wonder is that authoritarianism failed to correlate *positively* with success.

Inventories can inquire only about one's general style, not about what he does in particular situations. Regardless of what a person is prone to do when choosing freely, he adapts to demands. He can be assertive as a parent, submissive in reporting to his commanding officer, boisterous at a party, decorous in church. People vary in their ability to assume roles, but one does not have to be an actor to assume convincingly a role far from his typical behavior. In this sense, personality is like posture: the young man who slouches habitually can be placed in uniform and trained to hold as rigid a military bearing as anyone else, so long as he is on duty. Personality, as commonly measured, probably has much to do with the sort of work and personal relations a person *seeks*, but little to do with his ability to perform a role when he is thrust into it. The adjusted person is able to adapt his style to role demands; let Shakespeare's Kate be our reminder that sometimes one relishes the new role enough to make *it* his personality.

Personality inventories should not be directly used for employee selection. This strong conclusion can be weakened to acknowledge (a) that such instruments may play a part in assessment in which decisions in the end rest on a professional's judgment (see Chapter 19), and (b) that a long program of research in a single establishment can establish a valid "merit key" (see p. 485).

Such a key has to consist of responses characteristic of successful employees in this job in this firm. The most successful device of this nature is the Aptitude Index designed for use in life insurance agencies. It is a combined personal history and personality questionnaire; most of the items are of the sort usual in an application blank, and thus are inoffensive. Moreover, agents who will be paid on commission have as much to gain as the company from a valid prediction of their promise. The applicants cannot be shown the key, but they can be told that it predicts earning level and is empirically derived from a large sample of agents. The correlation with sales volume is 0.40. Although this prediction is crude, selection by means of the Index leads to considerable gains in average sales per agent. Ignoring those men who quit in their first year, it was found that agents rated A on the Index produced twice as much business as the average agent, while those rated E produced only half as much as the average (Kurtz, 1941).

One cannot dismiss entirely the hope that personality information will contribute to an understanding of job performance. Guidance should be able to make good use of theoretical understanding of personality, as that develops. Modern descriptive questionnaires have rarely been compared with job performance. There are scattered instances of practically important correlations. The notable example is the prediction of a Korean-combat criterion by personality information (see p. 416). But all we have said about variation in criterion situations and the need for local validation applies with special force to the use of personality measures for selection.

The fact that individuals adapt to role demands has suggested to some writers that one should base prediction not on typical behavior but on aptitude for taking a role (J. Wallace, 1966). One might well use an ability test, in which the task to be performed and the style to be adopted are made quite clear to the subject. An occasional performance test of personality does take this form, although playing a role for half an hour in a test is not the same thing as playing it for half a lifetime. It seems unlikely that a questionnaire could contribute to the measurement of ability to play a role.

Prediction of Academic Criteria

In general, attempts to predict academic performance from personality inventories have been disappointing (Freeberg, 1967). Against the many failures (and the strikingly high correlations that never get replicated) there is one solid positive result. The study has a good sample size and is crosschecked in several high schools. In these schools, IQ predicts marks with $r = 0.60$. Several keys of the California Psychological Inventory having to do with self-reported responsibility and success raise the multiple correlation to 0.68 (Gough, 1964). There is no report on whether the inventory adds to the prediction that can be made from previous grades (which are perhaps a more direct indicator of responsibility and success).

After reflection on the published literature and after sponsoring studies of its own, the College Entrance Examination Board (1963) made a noteworthy official statement to member colleges, warning "of very serious risks that would certainly attend the actual use of [any existing personality] tests in making admissions decisions." The problems mentioned include possible misunderstanding by the public, faking and coaching, absence of parallel forms, overemphasis on scales that correlate only slightly with marks, and inability to allow for the fact that adolescent personalities are changing.

Relations of personality variables to academic performance have theoretical interest even when they do not lead to practical uses of the tests. Much attention has been given to the relation of anxiety to intellectual performance. The results are far from consistent because the relations are complex and simple analyses do not bring them out. In one type of study a college student takes two equivalent examinations, one under the usual pressure and one under relaxed, "this-will-not-count-on-your-record" conditions. The second score may be higher or lower. An investigator who simply correlates the change with anxiety will find no clear relation. But if he eliminates from the sample students with very high or very low scholastic aptitude, the remaining cases show a statistically significant effect. Highly anxious students improve under the relaxed condition while the non-anxious are likely to do worse (Spielberger, 1966; Paul & Eriksen, 1964). This ties to the theory that there is an optimal level of tension. Putting stress on the low-anxious person may bring him to his peak, whereas it disrupts the person who is already tense (see p. 62).

We directed attention earlier (p. 447) to the possibility of interactions between individual differences and treatments. There are many hints that personality variables enter into such relationships. Domino (1968), for example, separated college courses according to whether the instructor demanded conformity or independence, demand for independence being indicated by emphasis on ideas rather than facts, emphasis on student presentations and independent work rather than examinations, and latitude with regard to attendance and assignments. He compared students high and low on a CPI scale labeled "achievement through independence" (Ai), with results that can be summarized as follows:

High Ai, grade average	in conforming situations	2.7
	in independent situations	3.0
Low Ai, grade average	in conforming situations	2.5
	in independent situations	2.2

The less structured instructional procedures are significantly advantageous for Highs and significantly disadvantageous for Lows. The difference is not great, however, even among the extreme Highs and Lows selected by Domino for his research. Other evidence supporting the hypothesis that personality variables indicate readiness to respond to a particular type of instruction is cited on p. 664. Further refinement of tests and better classification of instructional procedures may ultimately bring us within sight of practically useful relations. It should be noted that use of personality measures for this purpose is not open to the ethical objections that enter when they are used for selection, since if one can match the student to the style of instruction best for him, everybody wins.

18. *Should inventories be used to advise students about their probable vocational success?*

19. *What advantages does a biographical inventory have over a personality questionnaire in employee selection?*

20. *What differences among clerical jobs might account for variation in the validity of personality tests?*

21. *How might lack of self-confidence help one student to attain high marks, yet be a drawback to another?*

Validity of Inventories for Trait Description

The Score Profile as a Mirror

In counseling, the personality inventory is used like the interest inventory, as a mirror to help the individual examine his view of himself. He knows what he has said, but the test permits him to compare himself with others. His raw scores and percentile standings in various traits form an appropriate initial topic in counseling. It is probably wise not to use subtle scales, or scales the meaning of which is difficult to communicate. To show a counselee his MMPI profile could lead only to difficulties in explaining the meaning of the categories, and possibly to his rejection of the indirect interpretations.

What inventory is preferred will depend upon the nature of the counseling. Adjustment inventories or other single-score instruments are of little use in counseling because they pose few questions for discussion. A descriptive scale that reports introversion, impulsiveness, and so on is of potential value in vocational guidance and may open discussion of traits the client regards as faults. (To advance such thinking, the client may be asked to fill out the scale a second time, "as he would like to be.") Descriptions in terms of preferred activities and values (Allport-Vernon-Lindzey, Gordon) are somewhat better suited to vocational guidance than scales that describe emotional reactions. A problem checklist is of value because it draws attention to specific concerns the client is ready to talk about and wants help with; it is more a preliminary interview than a measuring device.

Edwards' descriptive inventory (EPPS) is useful in initiating counseling of college students. The profile describes fifteen "needs" or concerns that presumably direct the subject's actions. Some of the needs, and items related to them are:

> Abasement—to accept blame when things do not go right.
> Achievement—to be a recognized authority.
> Affiliation—to be loyal to friends.
> Aggression—to attack contrary points of view.
> Autonomy—to be independent of others in making decisions.

The interpretation of the scales clings to the explicit content of the items, which aids communication, and yet the summary in terms of needs may add to the subject's insight into himself. The counselor can help him examine how his major needs are currently being frustrated, how well his future plans will satisfy these needs, or how factors in his earlier development caused certain needs to develop.

When a questionnaire reflects the client's remarks, several questions related to validity are of interest. Only partial and rather general answers can be given here; much further information can be obtained from Wylie's book (1961), which summarizes research on the self-concept.

• Are the scores adequate measures of the published self-concept? Would another set of items give the same profile? This is to be answered by parallel-form or internal-consistency reliabilities, or by correlations between inventories having similar scales. The better inventories show reliabilities of 0.80 and above, which is sufficient for picking out salient characteristics. But scores with the same name in different inventories may not agree.

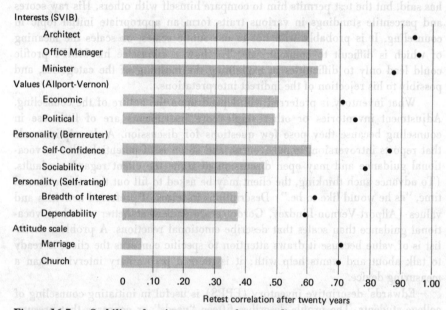

Interests (SVIB)
    Architect
    Office Manager
    Minister
Values (Allport-Vernon)
    Economic
    Political
Personality (Bernreuter)
    Self-Confidence
    Sociability
Personality (Self-rating)
    Breadth of Interest
    Dependability
Attitude scale
    Marriage
    Church

0   .10   .20   .30   .40   .50   .60   .70   .80   .90   1.00

Retest correlation after twenty years

Figure 16.5.   Stability of various aspects of personality.
E. L. Kelly, 1955. The dot indicates the reported correlation for a retest after a short time
interval (usually a week).

● Do scores reflect lasting characteristics? Kelly questioned 300 students
during the years 1935–1938 and retested nearly all the subjects again in 1954.
The self-report instruments used measured interests, attitudes, and traits. Figure
16.5 shows the similarity of self-descriptions 20 years apart. Interests and values
are most stable (when we allow for the inaccuracy of the measure of values).
Trait scores are slightly less stable, and attitudes are quite changeable. While
the self-concepts of most persons seem to change little, the meanings attached to
the rest of the world change greatly.

Data from studies of children may also be mentioned even though they do
not come from self-report. Trained interviewers asked mothers about children's
lack of appetite, nailbiting, quarrelsomeness, etc. A total score indicating severity
of problem behavior was derived. The procedure was repeated each year from
infancy to age 14. The correlations in Table 16.6 should be compared with the
correlations for repeated mental tests (p. 232), which come from the same longitudinal study. In both tables, we find that correlations from year to year are
much higher at later ages. The stability of the adjustment score is lower than that
of mental tests, but not much lower. Even when a surface trait is inhibited by
further socialization, there may be consistency between the adult and child personality. The aggressive girl does not usually become an overtly aggressive
woman, but as an adult she is likely to strive for intellectual mastery and to be
competitive (Kagan & Moss, 1962).

Table 16.6.   Correlation of problem behavior score of boys with score
               at a later age

Approximate age at first rating	Years elapsed between first and second score			
	1	3	6	12
1¾	.38	.40	.27	−.01
3	.50	.31	.35	.47
4	.56	.57	.54	—
6	.67	.70	.81	—
7	.73	.55	.51	—
9	.70	.75	—	—
11	.86	.80	—	—

SOURCE: Macfarlane, Allen, & Honzik, 1954.

A trait-by-trait analysis of the follow-up data treated in Table 16.6 is offered
by Bronson (1966). Here we can recount only a few main findings. There is a
persistent central difference in styles, described as expressive-gay-outgoing
(= active, strong) vs. reserved-somber. For boys, a measure of this at age 6
correlates 0.69 with a measure at age 15. Stability is less for girls: 0.70 over a
3-year span but 0.50 for a longer interval. A second style, placid-compliant
(= good, passive, weak) vs. explosive-resistant holds up over 3-year periods. Each
style shapes action differently at different ages. In early childhood, the reserved
style tends to go with low physical vitality, in late childhood with cautiousness
and emotional vulnerability, and in adolescence with a sense of inferiority. Thus,
while "personality" is somewhat stable, "behavior" is not. Indeed, a score
describing a single kind of action often shows zero correlation of age 6 with
age 15.

● Do the descriptions agree with external evidence of typical behavior?
Research comparing self-descriptions with objective records of behavior is lacking. There have been numerous comparisons of scores with judgments. In the
study reported in Table 16.7, children's self-reports corresponded poorly with
the way their teachers and peers rated them, but some studies obtain values as
high as 0.50 (see Wylie, 1961, pp. 30 ff.). With college students, somewhat higher
agreement has been reported. For example, the manual for the Gordon Personal
Profile (*Harcourt*) reports correlations of 0.47 to 0.73 of students' scores with
ratings given concurrently by dormitory mates. (See also Table 16.4.)

● Do the descriptions agree with the true self-concept? A criterion could be
obtained by asking a therapist well acquainted with the person's inner attitudes
to describe him. Evidence of this sort, however, is rare.

Descriptions in Aid of Institutional Decisions

The second major descriptive use of inventories is to provide others (clinicians, teachers, etc.) with insight into the individual.

Table 16.7.   Correlations between three types of adjustment measures for ninth-
               graders

	Teacher rating	Peer judg- ments	Self-reports		
			Self- Adjust- ment	Social Adjust- ment	Basic Difficulty
Teacher rating: Adjustment		.56	.30	.33	.22
Peer judgments:					
Nominations on desirable traits	.56		.28	.28	.16
Self-reports:					
California Test of Personality Self-Adjustment	.30	.28		.73	.61
California Test of Personality Social Adjustment	.33	.28	.73		.47
SRA Youth Inventory, Basic Difficulty score	.22	.16	.61	.47	

Note: Correlations between distinct methods are in boldface type.
Source: Ullmann, 1952. Cowen et al., 1965, report very similar figures for 9-year-olds.

The validity of descriptive interpretations is difficult to assess, especially when the construct employed cannot be equated with any one observable action. The MMPI scales have been given meaning by integrating evidence from all manner of studies, gradually formulating a psychological hypothesis about the meaning of each score. Meehl's remarks on scale 4 (Pd) illustrate the process (Cronbach & Meehl, 1955) :[3]

The Pd scale of MMPI was originally designed and cross-validated upon hospitalized patients diagnosed "Psychopathic personality, asocial and amoral type." Further research shows the scale to have a limited degree of predictive and concurrent validity for "delinquency" more broadly defined. . . . For example, a recent survey of hunting accidents in Minnesota showed that hunters who had "carelessly" shot someone were significantly elevated on Pd when compared with other hunters. . . . The finding seems to lend some slight support to the construct validity of the Pd scale. But of course it would be nonsense to *define* the Pd component "operationally" in terms of, say, accident proneness. We might try to subsume the original phenotype and the hunting-accident proneness under some broader category, such as "Disposition to violate society's rules, whether legal, moral, or just *sensible*." But now we . . . are using a rather vague and wide-range class. . . .

We want the class specification to cover a group trend that (nondelinquent) high school students judged by their peer group as least "responsible" score over a full sigma higher on Pd than those judged most "responsible." . . . Again, any clinician

[3] References for the studies described are given in the original.

familiar with MMPI lore would predict an elevated Pd on a sample of (nondelinquent) professional actors. Chyatte's confirmation of this prediction tends to support *both:* (a) the theory sketch of "what the Pd factor is, psychologically"; and (b) the claim of the Pd scale to construct validity for this hypothetical factor. [Then there are] Hovey's report that high Pd predicts the judgments "not shy" and "unafraid of mental patients" made upon nurses by their supervisors; Gough's report that *low* Pd is associated with ratings as "good-natured"; and Roessell's data showing that high Pd is predictive of "dropping out of high school."

This body of consistent evidence leaves no doubt that score *4* has some relation to internal personality structure. The correlations cited are not strong; if they were, we would find the same person dropping out of school, being rated ill-natured, becoming a Broadway actor, and shooting a fellow hunter. Circumstances dictate much of behavior. Personality structure, even if perfectly measured, represents only a predisposition rather than a determining force.

Granting that score *4* and the others have some validity, we are still uncertain as to the closeness of correspondence between the scores and the personality. Before interpretations can be used with confidence, we require evidence as to how often we go wrong in assuming that a high *4* has this vaguely defined pattern of arrogant, unruly attitudes. Facts of this sort are distressingly incomplete, and many of the findings strike a pessimistic note. Gough correlated a number of CPI scores with ratings of students made by a staff of psychological assessors (manual, 1957). These ratings are based on comprehensive psychological study and provide a reasonable criterion to test the statement that persons with certain scores tend to be seen in certain ways. The correlations of CPI scores with the ratings to which they supposedly relate range from 0.21 to 0.48—positive but very weak.

This finding argues only against the attempt to interpret one dimension in isolation. A way of describing the person as a whole is to sort out a pack of descriptive statements to indicate which ones fit him (see p. 586). This sorting can be compared with a "criterion" sort made by someone who knows him well. The degree of agreement is expressed as a correlation, there being one correlation for each subject. One study of this kind reports *r*'s of 0.36 to 0.88, showing respectable agreement between MMPI interpretations and a therapist's concept of his patients. There is no similar study of normals.

The evidence now available requires us to regard descriptive interpretations for normal subjects as generally undependable. For patients, results tend to be better (e.g., Goldstein & Jones, 1964). Inventories do measure individual differences reliably and those differences have some relation to personality as observed in other ways. When the description from the test is a point of departure for further study of the individual, errors of interpretation can be corrected. Under no circumstances should a description be passed on to a school principal, an employer, or any other decision-maker who is not trained to check the interpretation critically against other evidence.

22. *In counseling with the Edwards inventory, should raw scores (ranging 0 to 15 on each scale) or percentiles be used to plot the profile?*

23. *A leadership score identifies pupils whose responses resemble those of other pupils who have become leaders. What characteristics other than leadership ability and interest are likely to distinguish student leaders in high school from the students who take little part in student affairs?*

24. *If school officials make use of leadership scores in encouraging certain pupils to take leadership responsibilities, will this tend to increase or decrease the correlation between the original scores and leadership record by the end of high school?*

25. *Scores on certain instruments purport to identify students likely to be trouble-makers and potential delinquents. Assuming that such a score has very high stability and validity, what use might be made of such a test by high schools? If, as is the case, the validity coefficients are quite low, what undesirable ef-fects may follow if such scores are collected by principals?*

26. *The restrictions on use of personality inventories suggested above are admittedly conservative. Some psychologists argue that it is unwise for counselors to "imi-tate the secrecy of the medical profession" in withholding scores from teachers and other laymen. These psychologists argue that laymen continually make judgments about personality, and that if discouraged from using inventory scores they will base their judgments on casual observations that have even less validity. What do you think?*

27. *The basic MMPI principle (as it has emerged) is to form several scales, and collect information on persons having each kind of score profile as a basis for descriptive interpretation. If you were to construct a new instrument today, for normal persons over 18, how would you proceed? What scores would you form? What interpretative information would you collect?*

Representative Personality Inventories

The following inventories illustrate procedures now in use but by no means exhaust the field.

- Adjective Checklist (ACL); Harrison G. Gough and A. B. Heilbrun, Jr.; *CPP*.

Adults. Adjectives (e.g., "arrogant," "calm," "defensive") to be checked. An objective means of securing reports of impressions of others. One can explore the meaning of a new instrument by seeing what adjectives the scores correlate with. ACL may be used as a simple self-rating technique. Keys have been prepared for obtaining summary scores on various styles and "needs." The manual reports validity studies in obscure ways; apparently an ACL self-report score rarely correlates with a related score on a conventional inventory higher than 0.40. Primarily useful in research.

- Adjustment Inventory; Hugh M. Bell; *CPP*.

High school and college. A successor to one of the oldest and simplest of questionnaires, intended to screen students who need counseling or to obtain information preliminary to a counseling interview. Requires 30 minutes or less. Keys for masculinity, hostility, emotionality, sociability, and home and health adjustment. Not subtle; favorable self-reports cannot be taken seriously. Manual inadequate to enable unsophisticated users to make properly cautious interpretations.

● California Psychological Inventory (CPI); Harrison G. Gough; *CPP*. High school and college. A lengthy inventory with sixteen principal scores covering Sociability, Tolerance, Intellectual Efficiency, etc. The instrument has been used in an extraordinary amount of research on groups. The traits it measures seem significant though validity coefficients are often low. Used by trained and cautious counselors, serves screening and descriptive purposes as well as any questionnaire.

● California Test of Personality; Louis P. Thorpe, Willis W. Clark, Ernest W. Tiegs; *CTB*.
Primary, elementary, secondary, and adult forms. Percentile scores on personal adjustment and social adjustment. Such subscores as Sense of Personal Worth, Nervous Symptoms, and Family Relations have skewed distributions and give meaningful information about patterns of adjustment only in rare cases. The evidence on validity presented in the manual is incomplete, and misleading in places. Acceptable as a screening instrument where a well-qualified school psychologist will oversee a constructive program for using information obtained; otherwise should not be made available to teachers.

● Edwards Personal Preference Schedule (EPPS); Allen L. Edwards; *Psych. Corp.*
College. To eliminate opportunity to show a "good" pattern, subject has to choose between paired statements of equal overall desirability. He can, however, fake a particular pattern of virtue, such as curiosity and initiative. Instrument is scored in terms of "needs" for achievement, affiliation, etc., but does not necessarily agree with the more subtle projective techniques. Might prove useful to counselors in promoting student self-understanding; avoidance of psychiatric constructs and of subtle keying reduces misconceptions. There has been little research on individual interpretation of the scale, however.

● Edwards Personality Inventory; Allen L. Edwards; *SRA*.
High school and college. A recent instrument organized in four lengthy booklets, yielding scores on 53 (!) scales: plans and organizes things, intellectually oriented, persistent . . . , shy, informed about current affairs, virtuous. Items are in true-false form and subject is to report how others would describe him rather than to give his self-concept. All items are in the third person, e.g. "He seldom gets bored. . . ." Reliabilities of many scales are low. There is no validity information and no statement regarding intended uses of the instrument. Should be restricted to research use at this time.

● Eysenck Personality Inventory; Hans J. Eysenck and S. B. G. Eysenck; *EITS*.

Adult. A version of the Maudsley Personality Inventory, much used in England. A short scale measuring two broad traits, Extraversion and Neuroticism. The validation available connects the test with many psychologically interesting variables, but not with practical criteria. Eysenck's theoretical views, and American research on the same domain, need to be integrated; research with this scale in the United States is likely to increase.

● Minnesota Counseling Inventory (MCI); Ralph F. Berdie and Wilbur L. Layton; *Psych. Corp.*

High school. An instrument combining features of MMPI and conventional adjustment inventories, with items chosen and scored to fit the normal range of personality. Keys include emotional stability, family relations, conformity, etc. Validity against criteria of overt behavior appears to be modest. Suitable for use by trained high-school counselors, but recent work on validity is not readily available.

● Minnesota Multiphasic Personality Inventory; Starke R. Hathaway and J. C. McKinley; *Psych. Corp.*

Late adolescents and adults. (See pp. 527 ff.)

● Mooney Problem Check Lists; Ross L. Mooney and Leonard V. Gordon; *Psych. Corp.*

Forms for junior high through college, and adult. Subject checks his problems in eleven fields: morals and religion, finances and living conditions, adjustment to schoolwork, social relations, etc. High scores identify those who should receive counseling, and items checked provide a basis for individual or group discussion. Simplicity makes it relatively useful in the hands of users with limited training.

● Omnibus Personality Inventory; Paul Heist and George Yonge; *Psych. Corp.*

College. A collection of 385 true-false statements, most of them taken from older instruments, organized to lead to scores reflecting temperament and attitudes. The scales relate to such matters as autonomy, impulse control, intellectual interests, masculinity, and social introversion. Has been used extensively to study reactions of students of different types to college programs. May or may not prove valuable in the clinical study of individuals.

● Orientation Inventory (ORI); Bernard M. Bass; *CPP*.

Adult and child forms. Classifies persons as self-oriented, task-oriented, or oriented to interpersonal interaction (Bass et al., 1963; Bass, 1967). Scores have modest correlations with persistence, volunteering, and other indicators of motivation. Only moderately reliable, but quite suitable for research to determine how leaders and managers can modify situations to fit each type of individual.

● Personality Research Form; D. N. Jackson; Research Psychologists Press.

College students and adults. A questionnaire yielding scores for some 20 dimensions. The chief claim to validity is the substantial correlations of these self-report scores with ratings given by peers. Parallel forms are an advantage in research.

● 16 P.F. Test; R. B. Cattell, and others; *IPAT*.
Various versions for school ages and adults. Sixteen scores (see Table 16.2).

The scales, as they stand on any single form, have extremely low reliability; combination of two forms is generally recommended. In a technically brilliant advance over conventional methods of obtaining profiles, Eber and Cattell (1966) employ a multiple-regression method in the course of computerized scoring, to obtain an improved estimate of each score. The description of the results is misleading, however. It is said that the validity of score A, for example, when obtained from Forms A and B combined, is 0.86 by the usual method, and rises to 0.90 when the regression method is used. What is here referred to as a validity coefficient is actually much more like the square root of a reliability coefficient. Hence it has really been shown that the new method raises the reliability of the score from 0.74 to 0.81. This improvement is welcome. The authors fail to report the correlations between the improved scores; almost certainly they will be larger than for the conventional scores. Higher intercorrelations indicate that the scale has less differential validity than previously supposed.

● Study of Values; Gordon S. Allport, Philip E. Vernon, Gardner Lindzey; *Houghton.*
Later adolescence and college. Forced choice between preferred activities and beliefs. Scored to indicate relative emphasis on Theoretical, Economic, Political, Aesthetic, Social, and Religious values. Of some value as a supplement to interest inventories in vocational guidance; much used for research in social psychology.

● Survey of Personal Values; Leonard V. Gordon; *SRA.*
High school and adult. A very short forced-choice instrument. Scored for six preferences: for variety, for difficult tasks, for definiteness of assignment, etc. Conceivably useful in counseling or employee placement, but no pertinent validity information has been reported. Proposed use in selection is questionable; author properly insists on local validation prior to any such application. There is a companion Survey of Interpersonal Values.

● Survey of Study Habits and Attitudes; Wm. F. Brown and Wayne H. Holtzman; *Psych. Corp.*
High school and college forms. Covers study behavior and attitudes (e.g., "Whether I like a course or not, I still work hard to make a good grade"). Keyed items distinguish students with good marks from those who do poorly. This score correlates about 0.45 with grades and, combined with an ability test, has a predictive validity of about 0.60. The test is fakable and is not recommended for use as an admission test. Both the total score and the item responses are useful in counseling and in how-to-study courses.

● Vocational Preference Inventory; John L. Holland; *Educational Research Associates.*

Adolescent and adult. A list of occupational titles to be checked. Yields six scores: Realistic, Intellectual, Social, Conventional, Enterprising, and Artistic. Primarily a research tool for studying adaptations to various environments. (Holland has classified environments with respect to the six dimensions, according to the encouragement they provide for each type of behavior; see Holland, 1966.)

Structure of the Individual Personality

Criticisms of the Concept of "Trait"

If a test is to rank or score the individual, there must be a scale. The desire for scales analogous to those for size, temperature, and reaction time led psychologists to postulate that personality has dimensions or traits. A *trait* is best described as the probability that one will react in a defined way in response to a defined class of situations. Traits are deeply embedded in Western languages; nearly all the adjectives that apply to people are descriptive of traits: happy, conventional, stubborn, and so on. These adjectives seem to imply a response to be expected in all situations; more restricted traits—"stubbornly defends his political views"—are envisioned by our definition. The trait postulate is threefold:

● Behavior is consistent; a person tends to show the same habitual reaction over a range of similar situations.

● People vary in the degree or frequency of any type of behavior.

● Personalities have some stability.

These premises lead one to consider a personality trait as a habit capable of being evoked by a wide range of situations. It would be tedious to catalog a series of traits such as "habit of bowing politely when meeting a pretty woman of one's own age on the street on Sunday," "habit of bowing politely when meeting a not-pretty woman . . . ," etc. Therefore, broad traits are sought. The trait approach to personality hopes to describe economically the significant variations of behavior while neglecting unduly specific habits. With 17,000 or more adjectives in the dictionary that refer to different styles of behavior, the problem of economy is serious.

We cannot let pass the opportunity to mention Fancher's sparkling finding (1966) concerning the number of traits the psychologist should use. The study has a tiny N and involves some indirect inference. It is nonetheless fascinating that people who construe others by means of a few broad traits—i.e., who use a simple personality theory—did best ($r = 0.75$) in understanding the personalities of others. That is, they did *if* they were superior in mathematical reasoning. But for persons high in verbal abilities it was the other way round; among the verbally talented, the best predictions ($r = 0.54$) were made by those who construct highly individualized, multiple-attribute explanations. What does this tell us about the factor analyst and the novelist, and about their disrespect for each other's methods?

A trait description is a statistical summary of behavior over many situations. If we could say that a boy is *perfectly* honest, the adjective would really tell us about him. But no one is 100 per cent or zero per cent honest; whether he acts honestly or dishonestly depends on the situation. The score "50 per cent honest" ignores and so conceals the fact that the person is perfectly honest with money and perfectly dishonest when grades are the reward (Burton, 1963). A trait scale permits faultless inference only if the person does the same thing whenever the opportunity to display the trait arises, i.e., if he scores 100 per cent or zero.

"The normal personality" presents troublesome problems of measurement. The person at either extreme of a trait distribution is well characterized. He exhibits the trait in unusual degree and in a large number of situations. A middle-level score tells little. A flat profile implies no lack of individuality. While the person is average on the traits reported, he departs from the norm on some traits we omitted to measure.

Situational specificity. The entire trait approach has been criticized on such grounds (Allport, 1937, pp. 248–257; Yinger, 1965, pp. 583 ff.; Mischel, 1968). One man may act from need; he will take money to feed his family, but will not cheat or lie. Another may be prudent rather than honest; he will be as honest as he must to avoid being caught. Another may define honesty in a limited way; he would never steal, but he thinks it right to operate a business on the principle of "buyer beware." These men are all honest to an intermediate degree; statistically, their honesty is in the average range.

Most inventory scores define traits as general, ubiquitous styles. To say that a person "typically is anxious" or that he "has high anxiety" is to describe responses in the abstract. But some situations are more likely to evoke an anxious response than others, and the situations that threaten Pat may not be the ones that disturb Mike. To be a useful basis for prediction and understanding, traits need to be defined in terms of situation classes to which the person will respond consistently (G. Patterson & Bechtel, in press).

One line of advance is the "crossed" inventory design explored by Endler and Hunt (see Endler, Hunt, & Rosenstein, 1962; Endler & Hunt, 1966, 1969; J. Hunt, 1965). Endler and his colleagues prepared a list of phrases describing possibly disturbing situations—for example, "making a speech before a large audience." Then they prepared a list of anxious responses (e.g., "heart beats faster," or, "want to avoid situation"). Pairing each of 14 situations with 11 responses gave 154 items. Subjects are asked to report how strongly each response occurs in each situation; this is, then, a 154-item test. It is scored across responses to get a score for anxiousness in each situation, and scored in the other direction to get a measure of tendency to use each response. There is clear evidence of person-situation interaction; profiles have distinctive shapes. Likewise, the self-reported response profiles have various shapes. The full set of $11 + 14 = 25$ scores is unnecessarily complex. Situation-to-situation correlations show a general self-report anxiety factor, with subgroupings for interpersonal threats and threats from physical, inanimate situations. Responses show no general factor; the groupings are distress, exhilaration, and autonomic responses. Further explorations along this line could produce a new type of practical instrument.

This exploration leads toward something like a hierarchical structure in personality, though it apparently will take the hard-to-imagine form of a stimulus hierarchy and a response hierarchy, crossing in a multiplex of possibilities. Just as microabilities need to be inventoried in planning remedial instruction (p. 351), so microhabits low in the hierarchy may be crucial in planning therapy (Mischel, 1968, Chapter 8). But broader trait descriptions can be useful in setting general policies about the handling of a person.

Another possibility is a wholly personalized approach. Sometimes John asserts himself, sometimes not. If we can learn what situations bring out assertive reactions—i.e., are equivalent for him—we can then hope to predict his behavior with some exactness. A personalized description would define traits as needed to fit the individual (e.g., "shy with women of his own age in nonbusiness relationships"). The list of truly characteristic traits would be different for each person. The difficulties that such efforts face are enormous, but some initial steps have been taken. There are techniques for studying the person's perception of the other individuals significant in his life (p. 598). These others are an important part of the person's world, and many reactions are determined by his perception of them.

Many persons concerned with patients are now emphasizing that the planning of therapy requires one to understand what class of stimuli will elicit a desirable response, or an undesirable response, from the patient. Such writers as Kanfer and Saslow (1965) do not reject tests, but they argue that

an assessment of the patient's behavior output is insufficient unless it also describes the conditions under which it occurs. This view requires an expansion of the clinician's sources of observations to include the stimulation fields in which the patient lives, and the variations of patient behavior as a function of these various stimulational variables.

Patterning of traits. Virtually all systematic research on traits deals with one trait at a time, yet the meaning of one trait depends on the level of another. Low confidence, for example, has a different significance in a bright, capable, and successful person than in a person who has frequently failed. To speak of "patterning" is to suggest that some effect is accounted for by the traits considered as a pair but not by the weighted sum or difference alone. Validation of such interpretations has rarely been offered.

One example of true pattern validation is a study of popularity and defen-

**Self-report
admits im-
perfections**

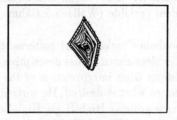

. . . quiet, works on
independent projects,
stays in background

. . . sparkling, sociable
enthusiastic, happy

**Self-report
denies having
any faults**

. . . apprehensive,
craves attention

. . . friendly,
worries about risk
of failure

Not chosen   **Popular**

**Figure 16.6.   Representative drawings and teacher characterizations of four types
of first-grade girls.**
Wallach et al., *1962, pp. 15–17.*

siveness, the latter being defined as giving inventory responses that picture oneself as perfect (Wallach *et al.*, 1962). First-grade girls were divided at the median
on each dimension to form four groups; it will be convenient to identify this as
a "2 × 2 design." The investigators hypothesized that the four types of children
will express themselves in different styles. They collected free "scribble" drawings, some of which are displayed in Figure 16.6. The investigators regard a
tight drawing as an indicator of timidity, inhibition, and tendency to withdraw.
In Figure 16.6 we characterize each kind of child with an extract from descriptions of children in that category given by teachers. (A count of adjective checklist data would be more dependable than this impressionistic extract from essay
descriptions.) It is clear that the four types differ, and that neither trait *alone*
identifies the personality type. Quite similar findings on an adult sample were

obtained with questionnaire measures of extroversion and anxiety, again with area-of-drawing serving as dependent variable (Wallach & Gahm, 1960; see also Taft, 1967).

While the various MMPI cookbooks make use of patterns, the research is never reported in a form that makes clear exactly what descriptive information is gained from the patterning, as distinct from interpretation of the traits in turn. Gough's studies of CPI come closer to what is desired. He sorts subjects on two dimensions and isolates four extreme groups: High-High, High-Low, Low-High, Low-Low. Then he tabulates adjective-checklist ratings given by acquaintances to persons in each group. He finds many significant differences (Gough, 1968). Here are adjectives associated with each pattern of CPI Dom and Re (each list starting with the strongest association):

High Dom, High Re: dominant, ambitious, responsible, progressive, conscientious, stern, formal, wise, alert. (In Osgood terms: *strong, good*).
High Dom, Low Re: touchy, dominant, robust, strong, cynical, tough, hardheaded, aggressive, temperamental, opinionated (*strong, active, bad*).
Low Dom, High Re: quiet, calm, peaceable, mild, modest, gentle, reserved, thoughtful, cooperative, honest (*good, passive*).
Low Dom, Low Re: irresponsible, suggestible, careless, foolish, unstable, pleasure-seeking, apathetic, changeable, confused, lazy (*bad, weak, passive*).

There are two chief questions to consider, First, just how strong is the set of relations? This is impossible to infer from a report on extreme groups only. Second, is the effect a true pattern relation such as Wallach had, or could we make the same interpretation merely by combining interpretations of the two scales separately? We present below the adjectives associated with the extremes on one scale at a time, and leave the reader to decide how much change in meaning emerges from the "pattern" table. (The reported single-scale analysis treats sexes separately, whereas the analysis above was made for both sexes together. That unwise decision makes comparison awkward.)

High Dom: dominant, forceful, optimistic, self-confident. Men, resourceful; women, conceited.
High Re: conscientious, reasonable, reliable, responsible. Men, capable; women, discreet.
Low Dom: submissive. Men are called indifferent, interests narrow; women, gentle, shy. (Dom is seen as good in men, bad in women. In the top ten adjectives for each sex, only "submissive" appeared for both sexes.)
Low Re: careless, lazy. Men, forgetful, showoff; women, arrogant.

A psychologist who uses a particular test a great deal may accumulate impressions as to how one score qualifies the meaning of another, but he will rarely have enough subjects with one pattern to validate such an inference. To validate interpretations for all patterns of traits is impossible. Suppose we class subjects as H, M, or L on each trait. Then for two traits (a 3 × 3 design) there are nine patterns. For a 10-score profile, taking two traits at a time, there are 336 patterns. One would have to search through more than 10,000 cases to get 30 of each kind, a minimum validation sample.

The significance of a trait pattern is likely to vary with age, sex, and educational or cultural background, which complicates matters further. Shotgun validation is out of the question. Only a few hypotheses at a time can be thoroughly studied, and these must be the ones that make theoretical sense. And yet theory arises only out of validation studies.

28. *A person may be "stubborn" in some situations and not in others. Both actions may be typical for him. Illustrate and suggest a rational explanation for his consistency.*
29. *For studying the relation between anxiety and eyeblink conditioning, to advance learning theory, would use of the Endler-Hunt type of instrument be advantageous?*
30. *Criticize the trait "responsibility" from the situational standpoint. Suggest a type of inventory that might satisfy the criticism to some extent.*
31. *List several types of validation study appropriate for an instrument of the Endler-Hunt type.*
32. *Much research supports Gough's observation that the correlations of a trait differ from sex to sex. Should personality testers take sex differences into account in assembling items into scales, or in providing separate norms, or in providing separate within-sex validity studies? Relate your answers to earlier discussions of "fair employment practice."*

A Semantic Differential Case Study

Osgood's Semantic Differential was developed for research on perception, meaning, and attitudes, rather than as a personality test (Osgood *et al.*, 1957). It measures indirectly the connotations of words or phrases. The stimulus is rated on a 7-point scale, various scales and stimuli being mixed in random order. Successive items might appear as follows:

My Father	soft	____:____:____:____:____:____:____	hard
Fraud	rich	____:____:____:____:____:____:____	poor
Confusion	fair	____:____:____:____:____:____:____	unfair
My Father	deep	____:____:____:____:____:____:____	shallow

In most studies Osgood and his students have been interested in specific concepts (e.g., "physicians," "Presidential Candidate A") as perceived by a large group. For examining an individual, Osgood employs concepts of personal significance, e.g., "my father."

The subject is to check the scale rapidly, recording his first impressions. Naturally it is difficult to defend any single response as "right" when judging

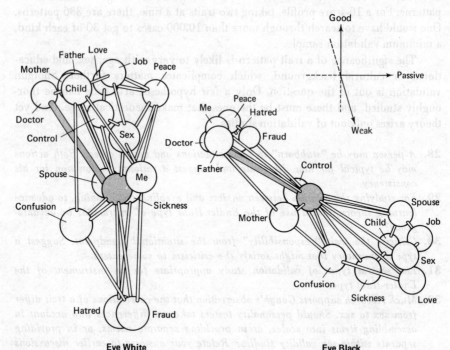

Figure 16.7.   Meaning systems of Eve White and Eve Black on the Semantic Differential.
Osgood & Luria, 1954.

communism on the scale *thin-thick*, but subjects have little difficulty in checking associations. The scoring can be accomplished in two ways. The scales can be grouped into *good-bad, strong-weak,* and *active-passive* keys. Average scores can be assigned for each stimulus. Thus we could say that a subject has indirectly described his father at +1 on good (on a scale from +3 to −3), 2.4 on strong, −0.4 on active. The other scoring method compares stimuli two at a time, converting the differences between their ratings into a "distance score" that measures the degree to which the subject perceives the stimuli as similar.

The best illustration of the technique is its application to a case of triple personality. A dissociated personality is one in which the person possesses two or more different "selves" and shifts back and forth between them (a bit like Dr. Jekyll and Mr. Hyde). Eve White had three such identities who "took possession" at various times, and her therapists were able to administer the Semantic Differential to each self in turn (Thigpen & Cleckley, 1953, 1957). In Figure 16.7 we present the configurations from two of the tests. The black ball represents the midpoint on all scales. "Good" is at the top, "active" at the left, and "weak" toward the viewer. The solid line connecting the black ball with "doctor" (who is always good, strong, very active) helps to orient the figure. Note our comment (p. 575) on the meaning of "good."

Two psychologists interpreted the patterns "blindly," i.e., with no further knowledge of the case. Indeed, they thought they had records of two distinct persons. They pointed out in Eve White's record the separation of love and sex, the meaninglessness of the spouse, the weakness of "me." Eve Black seems to place hatred and fraud in a favorable cluster with "me" and rejects spouse, love, job, and child. (The third self, Jane, is normal; love and sex are closely linked and favorable.) An impressionistic "guess" led to this summary of the first two personalities (Osgood & Luria, 1954):

> Eve White is the woman who is simultaneously most in contact with social reality and under the greatest emotional stress. She is aware of both the demands of society and her own inadequacies in meeting them. She sees herself as a passive weakling and is also consciously aware of the discord in her sexual life, drawing increasingly sharp distinctions between love as an idealized notion and sex as a crude reality. She maintains the greatest diversity among the meanings of various concepts. She is concerned and ambivalent about her child, but apparently is *not* aware of her own ambivalent attitudes toward her mother. . . . Those psychoanalytically inclined may wish to identify Eve White with dominance of the *superego*: certainly, the superego seems to view the world through the eyes of Eve White, accepting the mores or values of others (particularly her mother) but continuously criticizing and punishing herself. . . .
>
> Eve Black is clearly the most out of contact with social reality and simultaneously the most self-assured. To rhapsodize, Eve Black finds Peace of mind through close identification with a God-like therapist (My Doctor, probably a father symbol for her), accepting her Hatred and Fraud as perfectly legitimate aspects of the God-like role. Naturally, she sees herself as a dominant, active wonder-woman and is in no way self-critical. She is probably unaware of her family situation. . . . Like a completely selfish infant, this personality is entirely oriented around the assumption of its own perfection.

The pattern corresponds well with the therapists' picture of Eve. The therapists described the same personalities in these phrases, among others:

> Eve White: demure, almost saintly, seldom lively; tries not to blame her husband for marital troubles; every act demonstrates sacrifice for her little girl; meek, fragile, doomed to be overcome.
>
> Eve Black: a party girl, shrewd, egocentric; rowdy wit; all attitudes whimlike; ready for any little irresponsible adventure; provocative; strangely secure from inner aspect of grief and tragedy.

The correspondence of the portraits is remarkable. A single brilliant hit, however, is not adequate to substantiate a method.

Mapping stimulus equivalences gives a different type of information from that of the trait-oriented questionnaire, but the semantic map does give information about traits. Eve White is unquestionably dissatisfied with herself, perfectionistic, unwilling to express emotion—any questionnaire would show a high score on introversion and hysteric tendencies. The Semantic Differential adds information about specific sources of conflict: lack of acceptance of spouse and sex, and her child's weakness and need for protection. (Indeed, Mrs. White's feeling that she could not give her child adequate protection was a precipitating cause of her illness.) Eve Black is shallow, uncontrolled, self-centered—extrovert on any questionnaire and on MMPI surely extreme on 4 and 9. This is apparent in the Semantic Differential association of me, hatred, and fraud as "good and strong." But the map gives the additional picture of strong identification with men and rejection of child and spouse. One can judge what persons and treatments are likely to win her respect and cooperation, and what rewards she is likely to work for. Such information goes far beyond what one can get from even the most valid description of her general style. The rewards that a therapist might ordinarily offer—opportunity to hold a job, restoration of marriage—were spurned by Eve Black. The cooperation that eventually permitted some success in therapy came only when the therapist appealed to Eve Black's fear of sickness.

33. *Is the Semantic Differential fakable? Can one argue that it assesses unconscious attitudes?*

34. *How might the Semantic Differential be used to study transference relations during psychotherapy?*

35. *Osgood finds only three predominant factors among his scales. Do three dimensions appear adequate to describe one's perception of others?*

36. *Is Osgood's test primarily behavioristic or phenomenological in outlook?*

Traits and States

Throughout this chapter, we have concentrated on the interpretation of instruments as measures of typical behavior or personality. From this point of view, day-to-day variation is a source of error. A psychologist may have good reason for wanting to know how the subject feels at a given moment, however, and then he wants an instrument that is sensitive to changes in mood. Explicitly, the usual inventory asks the person about his life style or his typical behavior; that is, it calls for a report on a trait rather than on present state. But present state does affect the report, particularly by altering response bias.

A more direct way to obtain information on the subject's *state* is to frame the question in terms of the present moment: e.g., "Are you tense?" There has not been much systematic research on devices of this sort because the need for them usually arises in the midst of a substantive research program on the effects of mood-altering drugs or on session-to-session response to counseling. Some simple, face-valid rating procedure is likely to be used. One may also use an adjective checklist, with directions to report "the way you feel *now*" (McReynolds, 1968b, p. 249).

The research on "state" scales is somewhat bewildering as it now stands. Zuckerman and Lubin have developed a Multiple Affect Adjective Checklist (*EITS*) to be taken either with "today" or "general" directions. Responses under either condition are scored by the same keys, to arrive at measures of anxiety, hostility, and depression. For a small sample, the 7-day retest correlation is 0.31 for Today Anxiety and 0.68 for General Anxiety; this makes sense. The two scores on the same day correlate 0.43. The Taylor Anxiety Scale is a measure of trait anxiety, not state. According to the MAACL manual, it correlates with MAACL as follows in various small samples:

Sample	1	2	3	4	5
General set	.18	.58	.56	.62	.47
Today set	.29	.32	.54	.52	.32
Today, several days' responses pooled	—	.52	.58	—	.69

One would expect high correlations in the top and bottom rows, and fairly low correlations in the middle row. These and other findings (Herron, 1969) are so far from expectations that one can only hope that systematic research on larger samples will ultimately make clear the extent to which state scores differ from those collected under trait instructions.

SUGGESTED READINGS

"A statement on personality testing." *College Board Review*, Fall, 1963, No. 51, pp. 11–13.

An official statement advises colleges as to the limitations of practical personality testing and at the same time expresses optimism about the value of further research in the area.

Gough, Harrison G., and Hall, Wallace B. Prediction of performance in medical school from the California Psychological Inventory. *Journal of Applied Psychology*, 1964, 48, 218–226.

A successful effort to combine personality data to forecast academic performance. Peer ratings are used to learn more about persons who score high and low on the predictor scale.

Holt, R. R. Individuality and generalization in the study of personality. *Journal of Personality*, 1962, 30, 377–404. (Reprinted in Byrne & Hamilton, 1966.)

Reviews, from an historical and philosophical viewpoint, whether a scientific method can produce an understanding of the uniquely organized individual.

Mischel, Walter. Traits and states as constructs. In *Personality and assessment*. New York: Wiley, 1968. Pp. 41–72.

Mischel attacks all conventional personality testing, both trait-oriented and psychodynamic. In this chapter he argues that traits are not "patterns of

behavior" but the conceptions of the observer or personality theorist; he believes
that behavior is much too variable from situation to situation to be usefully
described in terms of traits.

Schiele, B. C., and Brozek, Josef. "Experimental neurosis" resulting from semi-
starvation in man. *Psychosomatic Medicine*, 1948, *10*, 31–50. (Reprinted in Welsh &
Dahlstrom, 1956, pp. 461–483.)

In a study of MMPI changes during experimental stress of 6 months' duration,
9 cases are described in detail, showing the relation between MMPI profiles and
behavior patterns.

Ullmann, Charles A. Teachers, peers, and tests as predictors of adjustment. *Journal
of Educational Psychology*, 1957, *48*, 257–267.

Evidence is given on the difference between information contained in teacher
ratings and in self-report questionnaires. Attention focuses on pupils who drop
out of school or who perform poorly in school. Items capable of identifying
such students are listed.

17

Judgments and
Systematic Observations

Regardless of whether an individual deserves the reputation he has, reputation is unquestionably significant. A person who impressed his former teachers as imaginative is favored by a college admissions committee. Business and military organizations file supervisors' opinions and use them in deciding whom to promote. Teachers find out what children think of each other in order to understand relationships in the classroom and to identify social misfits. Ratings provide criteria for studying job performance, progress of patients in mental hospitals, and educational development of the sort examinations cannot reveal. In this chapter we consider techniques for eliciting the impressions of responsible observers and of the subjects' associates. We also consider the collection of rating information on home and school environments. We then turn to systematic observations of behavior.

Ratings by Supervisors and Professional Observers

Descriptions by supervisors (foremen, teachers, superior officers, etc.) are hard to compare because styles of writing vary. Even when information is collected from trained observers, it has to be put into a standard form to permit formal analysis. Rating scales usually list traits to be rated, or descriptions to be checked. Before examining various kinds of rating scale, let us consider the chief difficulties to be overcome.

Sources of Error

Ratings can be ambiguous. Just as a self-report question on leadership can be variously interpreted, so a rater may define leadership in many ways. To one judge, "leadership" suggests conscious wielding of authority, crisp decisions, and general dominance. A person rated high by this judge would receive a lower rating from a judge who looks for a leader to encourage subordinates, bring out cooperative decisions, and subordinate his own views to the decision of the group. Ambiguity can only be overcome by clear definition of traits to be rated.

The response alternatives may also be ambiguous. In some of the early rating scales the respondent was asked to rate "friendliness," for example, on a scale from 0 to 100. With no definition given for numbers of the scale, a particular number is used by different raters to indicate quite different behavior. *Average, excellent,* etc., are equally indefinite. They should be replaced by specific descriptions of behavior.

Among errors introduced by the judge, the most serious is generosity, the tendency to give favorable reports. The teacher, asked to indicate on a report card whether the pupil is cooperative, is likely to rate all but the most troublesome pupils at the highest point on the scale. Company commanders rate 98 per cent of their junior officers in the top two categories (out of five) on efficiency reports. Such ratings provide little information. There are several reasons for excess generosity: the rater may feel that he is admitting poor leadership if he says that his subordinates are not performing well; he tends to feel kindly toward his associates; he thinks he may have to justify any implied criticism; and he often finds it easier to say good about everyone than to discriminate.

Some judges are more generous than others. There are additional constant errors—that is, individual peculiarities of response. The response styles mentioned in connection with achievement tests and personality questionnaires are observed in ratings. One judge, for example, rarely uses the extremes of the scale in describing subjects, whereas another describes most persons in black-and-white terms.

Judges disagree because each has limited information. The physical education teacher and the English teacher see different sides of a student. Even when the observer sees an individual in a variety of situations, his sample of behavior is limited. The supervisor can base his ratings only on what the man does under his supervision, and this may not be representative of all his work.

A "halo effect" obscures the pattern of traits within the individual. The observer's general opinion about the person's merit strongly influences ratings on specific traits. Even something as tangible as the worker's production may be rated too high if he is well-liked. Halo is responsible for the substantial correlations shown in Table 17.1 among ratings given to 1100 industrial employees. The ratings on quite dissimilar traits show a marked general factor, apparently corresponding to the foreman's opinion of the employee's industriousness and productivity.

These sources of error have four undesirable consequences.

Table 17.1. Intercorrelations of ratings given 1100 industrial workers

Traits	Safety	Knowledge of job	Versatility	Accuracy	Productivity	Overall job performance	Industriousness	Initiative	Judgment	Cooperation	Personality	Health
Safety	**.35**	.61	.52	.63	.55	.60	.49	.54	.62	.61	.55	.25
Knowledge of job	.61	**.46**	.81	.85	.79	.82	.78	.78	.80	.67	.67	.52
Versatility	.52	.81	**.47**	.80	.72	.80	.71	.78	.82	.68	.63	.50
Accuracy	.63	.85	.80	**.45**	.81	.67	.80	.78	.84	.74	.70	.84
Productivity	.55	.79	.72	.81	**.46**	.86	.86	.80	.81	.81	.73	.45
Overall job performance	.60	.82	.80	.67	.86	**.46**	.85	.83	.88	.80	.74	.60
Industriousness	.49	.78	.71	.80	.86	.85	**.47**	.82	.84	.80	.67	.53
Initiative	.54	.78	.78	.78	.80	.83	.82	**.48**	.86	.72	.72	.77
Judgment	.62	.80	.82	.84	.81	.88	.84	.86	**.45**	.76	.75	.43
Cooperation	.61	.67	.68	.74	.81	.80	.80	.72	.76	**.37**	.80	.52
Personality	.55	.67	.63	.70	.73	.74	.67	.72	.75	.80	**.39**	.71
Health	.25	.52	.50	.84	.45	.60	.53	.77	.43	.52	.71	**.36**

Note: Boldface figures show correlations of two raters' judgments on each worker, i.e., reliability of judging.

Source: Ewart et al., 1941.

● Ratings that pile up at the favorable end of the scale do not reveal important individual differences.

● Ratings may be seriously invalid, representing chance effects or traits other than the one supposedly rated. Psychologists rating "intelligence" on the basis of observation, for example, overrated the men with more introspective, less outgoing personalities (Barron, 1954).

● Halo bleaches out descriptive details.

● Judges disagree, as can be seen in Table 17.1. Reliability of rating is greatest for kinds of behavior that are clearly specified and for traits that are descriptive rather than interpretative. Traits reliably rated include "talkative," "assertive," "bashful," and "cultured." Reliability is lowest for vaguely stated attributes such as "adaptable," "sensitive," and "kindly" (Hollingworth, 1922; Mays, 1954).

Validity. It is extremely difficult to state whether, in a given situation, ratings by superiors will be valid summaries of behavior. One might expect supervisors to rate job knowledge accurately. The trait is well defined, the behavior is observable, and the supervisor has ample opportunity to observe. Nonetheless, supervisors' ratings on job knowledge usually correlate only about 0.35 with the knowledge measured by a formal test. Ratings in one department did reach a validity of 0.55 (Peters & Campbell, 1955; Morsh & Schmid, 1956). In another study department heads rated foremen. The rating correlated only 0.22 with an objective record of the work performance of each crew. The rating supposedly reflected productivity—but it correlated 0.59 with how long the rater had known the foreman, and 0.65 with his liking for the foreman (Stockford & Bissell, 1949).

Even more discouraging is a report from the Korean war, where ratings on effectiveness of bombing teams were collected. There was substantial agreement among the officers and men as to which teams were most effective. But an observational study demonstrated that bombing accuracy was entirely inconsistent from day to day, was essentially unpredictable, and could not truly be judged. Evidently legends built up as a consequence of random incidents; the raters could report reliably on the teams' reputations, but these had nothing to do with the facts (Hemphill & Sechrest, 1952). Such findings are particularly distressing in view of the wide use of ratings as criteria.

Ratings are sometimes excellent sources of data. A striking example is a study where ratings of "ascendance" by nursery-school teachers correlated 0.81 with a score derived from objectively recorded observations on the playground (Jack, 1934).

1. *Why might integrity and kindness be especially hard to rate reliably?*
2. *Which of the following traits would probably be hardest to rate reliably after observations: "skill in self-expression," "freedom from tension," "freedom from anxiety," "leadership" (Hollingworth, 1922, p. 32)?*
3. *Ratings on leadership made at Officer Candidate School correlated only 0.15 with ratings on efficiency of combat leadership by superior officers observing the men in combat (Jenkins, 1947). Why is the correlation so low?*
4. *In Table 17.1, explain why the intercorrelations of traits are higher than the coefficients in the diagonal which show rater agreement.*
5. *School marks may be regarded as ratings. Which sources of error discussed above affect marks?*

Number of Dimensions To Be Considered

A great deal of self-report information can be captured in three dimensions: good-vs.-bad, strong-vs.-weak, and active-vs.-passive. This is also true of ratings. Ratings of patients by their therapists, and of normals by their acquaintances, consistently exhibit an order of traits such as that shown in Figure 17.1. The order is fully circular if one disregards "deference" and "abasement." The spherical diagram, however, quite reasonably displays "abasement" as a weak submissiveness and "deference" as a weak agreeableness. While one might obtain some further insight from the full report on fourteen traits, scores on three dimensions carry 70 per cent of all the information, and the fourth and later factors are small. One finds essentially the same two or three dimensions in studies of ratings of child behavior (Becker & Krug, 1964; Digman, 1965; Bronson, 1966). Tupes and Christal (1961) extract five traits from Air Force

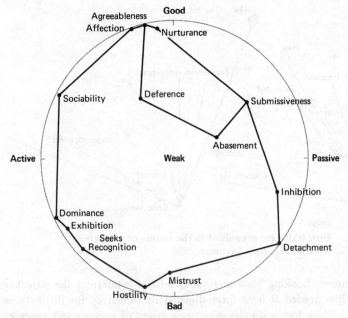

Figure 17.1.   Ordered array of personality traits.
Configuration derived from ratings of acquaintances. The "front-to-back" dimension of the spherical plot represents a weak-to-strong dimension; all traits in
this sample fell in the weak sector. *Data from Lorr & McNair, 1965.*

peer ratings. Their list has a good-bad factor (*Agreeableness*) and an active-
passive factor (*Surgency* or *Extroversion*). The other three are *Dependability*,
Emotional stability, and *Culture*.

The reader should not blindly treat scores high on the so-called good-bad
axis as desirable. In this as in other research, the axis coincides more with
pleasantness than with effectiveness. A person cannot be effective as a decision-
maker, for example, if he is always agreeable.

The collapse of ratings and self-reports into a few dimensions is primarily
a finding about the nature of everyday language (Norman & Goldberg, 1966;
d'Andrade, 1965). Nearly every trait name implies a level of goodness, activity,
and strength. Thus "aggressive" connotes "bad," "active," and "strong." While
"aggressive" does not have precisely the same meaning as other bad-active-strong
labels (e.g., "destructive"), a rater rarely needs to make a distinction between
the two. How often, among a thousand cases, would one have occasion to say,
"He is destructive, not aggressive"? Our language is rich in adjectives and trait
names—but most of the distinctions they allow are rarely needed, and hard to
make validly.

The studies just described deal with the pooled judgments of many raters;
it is a composite of their conceptions of trait meanings. But judges have indi-

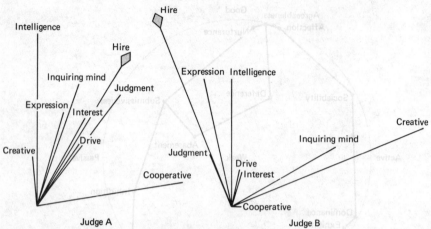

Figure 17.2.   How traits are organized in the minds of two raters.
Cronbach, 1958; based on data from Sternberg, 1950.

vidual structures. Looking back at p. 566, we can reinterpret the structures of
Eve. Eve White needed at least three dimensions to convey the distinctions she
saw. But Eve Black had a simpler view: one group of persons and concepts she
saw as very good-strong-active (extreme halo), and the others were spaced out
in a chain. Seen from above, the configuration would resemble that of Figure
17.1, but with a queer order. We see the same thing in a study of two interviewers
employed by a company. For research purposes these men rated the same applicants, marking eight scales and then recommending that the man should or
should not be hired for training as an executive. Judge A seemed to recognize
two independent factors of ability and cooperation; the two counted almost
equally in his decision to hire. (In this chart, derived by factor analysis, a short
line indicates a trait on which the judge tends to rate most men the same.) For
Judge B the decision to hire depended strongly on judged intelligence. Creativity
and cooperation counted for nothing. Indeed, among men he saw as equally
intelligent, he would prefer the less creative, less inquiring one. These two men,
then, were employing markedly different policies—or prejudices—in their advice
to the company.

While global impressions in clinical work can usually be reduced to a small
number of dimensions, more detailed checklists of diverse symptoms are often to
be preferred in research. Gleser (1968) is severely critical of studies of drug
treatments that draw conclusions from the psychiatrist's simple rating of the
subject on a health-to-sickness continuum. If symptoms can be specified
precisely, a catalogue of symptoms captures definite information that is not distorted by the judge's personal concept of mental health. But sometimes symptoms
are described only as, for example, "depression" or "anxiety." Then, says Gleser,

psychiatrists differ considerably in the concept they have in mind when asked to rate such symptoms. Thus, one doctor might think of bound anxiety and consider certain somatic symptoms as evidence of anxiety. Another might pay attention only to anxiety manifested in the interview in the form of restlessness, tremor, perspiration, etc.

6. *Becker and Krug at one point extracted five factors from reports on children: Calm (vs. emotional-rebellious), Submissive, Sociable, Loving (vs. distrusting), and Cooperative. Exactly what information carried in the five dimensions is not carried in the good-strong-active dimensions?*
7. *Name two adjectives that both would fall in the good-strong-passive sector. Do the two really have distinct meanings?*
8. *Do the same for the good-strong-active sector.*

Improvement of Ratings

Efforts to improve ratings encounter the same obstacles as efforts to improve self-reports. Again, the tester must assume that the respondent will give false information if he thereby gains psychological rewards. While the information affects the subject's future rather than the rater's, this does not mean that the rater is uninvolved. We have mentioned the rater's inclination to interpret reports on the subject as a reflection on his own teaching or supervision. Bias is even more probable when the therapist's ratings are a criterion of personality change during therapy. Sometimes a rater gives a low rating because he wishes to retain an employee who might otherwise be promoted. A teacher rating a scholarship applicant may enlarge upon his merits nearly to the point of perjury in order to help the student.

Selecting qualified raters is the place to start to improve ratings. Raters cannot give valid information unless they know the subject well. Other things being equal, those in immediate contact with the subject give better information than those who rely on hearsay. A teacher is better informed about a pupil's work habits and social behavior than the principal.

One elementary precaution, often overlooked, is to ask the rater how well he knows the subject, and in what kinds of situation he has observed him. There should be a place where the rater can indicate "insufficient opportunity to observe" instead of estimating a trait from inadequate information. If a judge is directed to mark every trait, some ratings are little better than guesses. Conrad (1932) directed raters to star traits which they regarded as especially important to the child's personality. Interjudge correlations on all traits ranged from 0.67 to 0.82. But for the traits three judges agreed in starring, the ratings correlated as high as 0.96.

When the same judge is used repeatedly, it may be possible to record his ratings and ultimately to estimate his constant error. Thus a college learns to allow for the fact that one high school has a "tough" grading or rating policy, whereas another school is lenient. It is rarely practical to make exact statistical corrections for differences between raters.

Even when a scale is carefully edited, Judges may interpret their instructions differently, and so be rating rather different aspects of the person. Gleser (1968), for example, recounts an instance where two psychiatrists differed radically in rating the current degree of illness of schizophrenic patients. Questioning disclosed that one psychiatrist was reporting typical behavior while the other was basing his rating on the most extreme deviant behavior shown by the patient. The remedy for such difficulties is to train the judges. It is often necessary for the judge to rate a series of trial cases and to discuss those where his ratings differ from a standard set by the investigator. In some kinds of research, the training can make use of videotape recordings, so that the same stimulus is presented to every rater being trained.

Combining impressions of several judges reduces error. If, as in Table 17.1, the interjudge correlation is about 0.45, averages from two pairs of independent

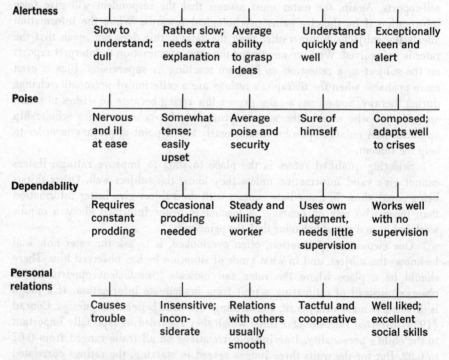

Figure 17.3. Descriptive graphic rating scales.
These scales for rating applicants or workers are adapted from the following sources: A General Foods Corporation form (National Industrial Conference Board, 1942), a Mutual Life Insurance Company of New York form (Marting, 1967), and a form from the National Retail Merchants Association (1968).

judges will correlate 0.60. Averages of five judges correlate 0.80. In the average the bias of one judge tends to cancel the bias of another, and each adds information the other had no opportunity to observe. Reliability may be lowered rather than raised, however, when an added informant who knows little about the subject is averaged in.

Scale formats. When a rater is to record his impression just once for each trait, the *descriptive graphic rating* form (Figure 17.3) is generally best. The scale is descriptive, since each point corresponds to a recognizable behavior pattern. It is graphic, in that the rater is allowed to mark at intermediate points if he does not find any one of the descriptions entirely suitable. In general, 5- to 7-point scales seem to serve adequately. With informed and serious professional judges, much finer subdivisions of the scale prove profitable (Champney & Marshall, 1939).

The 5-point scale obtains more discrimination than the "yes-no" checklist. A judge will ordinarily say "Yes" when asked "Does the subject have good judgment?" but if given graded alternatives he may check "Sometimes overlooks relevant facts in making decisions." The 5-point scale has the further advantage of drawing attention to various kinds of deviation. A simple "yes-no" question, "Does he accept authority?" would not distinguish the respectful, obedient child from the slavish, spiritless conformer.

A relatively elaborate technique for obtaining an opinion from a conscientious professional observer, is the Fels Parent Behavior Rating Scales, developed to study the preschool child's family. Trained observers visited each home periodically and wrote a descriptive report; to provide systematic data that could be treated statistically, the observer also gave ratings on thirty scales. These scales were designed to cover emotional relations, disciplinary methods, and values of the home.

The directions for one scale, for example, are as follows:

Quantity of Suggestion (Suggesting—Non-suggesting)

Rate the parent's tendency to make suggestions to the child. Is the parent constantly offering requests, commands, hints, or other attempts to direct the child's immediate behavior? Or does the parent withhold suggestions, giving the child's initiative full sway?

This does not apply to routine regulations and their enforcement. Rate only where there is opportunity for suggestion. Note that "suggestion" is defined broadly, including direct and indirect, positive and negative, verbal and nonverbal, mandatory and optional.

—Parent continually attempting to direct the minute details of the child's routine functioning, and "free" play as well.

—Occasionally withholds suggestions, but more often indicates what to do next or how to do it.

—Parent's tendency to allow child's initiative full scope is about equal to tendency to interfere by making suggestions.

—Makes general suggestions now and then, but allows child large measure of freedom to do things own way.

—Parent not only consistently avoids volunteering suggestions, but tends to withhold them when they are requested, or when they are the obvious reaction to the immediate situation.

The course marks that instructors assign are essentially like ratings, unless they are determined mathematically from examination scores. Any judgment based on observation of the student's work or review of products he turns out is a rating. The marking process may be improved by defining standards clearly. It is often advantageous to define separate aspects of good performance and prepare a rating scale for each one. A weighted combination of the several scales provides an overall mark. The marks so generated often differ from the marks instructors assign when they give a direct overall judgment. Oaks, Scheinok, and Husted (1969) demonstrate this with data from a clinical course for medical students and discuss some of the errors that the piecemeal rating process overcomes.

Lengthy scales requiring thoughtful discrimination contrast markedly with the simple rating scales used in obtaining recommendations from past employers and teachers. The fine distinctions of this scale permit a much more reliable and comprehensive picture of the home than a simple form would. Rater-agreement correlations range from 0.50 to 0.90 on single traits. The scale is designed to be used by a qualified professional observer who has a substantial amount of information to record, information that could not be communicated fully in a coarse scale. An elaborate scale is unnecessary when the rater has only casual impressions to convey.

The Fels scale is organized around factors of *Warmth* (first five variables in Figure 17.4), *Adjustment, Restrictiveness, Clarity of Policy,* and *Interference.* The detailed picture of five areas that are themselves further differentiated forestalls any tendency to characterize homes as simply good or bad. The data show that democratic homes can be cold and conflictful, orderly yet affectionate, or warm and still maladjusted. The Stones (Figure 17.4) are warm, protective, rather coercive—giving, the authors say, a picture of "restrictive indulgence" (Baldwin, Kalhorn, & Breese, 1949, p. 29; see also Baldwin *et al.,* 1945).

The rating of readiness of enforcement contributes a definite flavor to the interpretation. The mother is restrictive, but lax in enforcement and also, we see, mild in her punishments. The home begins to appear verbal and nagging, but without any core of enforced disciplinary policy. When ratings of low adjustment, high discord, low effectiveness of policy, and high disciplinary friction are added, the suspicion arises that Ted does not conform to his mother's standards. She talks and nags, but achieves little. The fact that approval is still high in spite of all this conflict and discord might be interpreted as a determined effort by the mother to see the boy in the best possible light. . . . A low rating on understanding makes it clear that the mother has little insight into what Ted wants and needs but instead is projecting on him her own motivation.

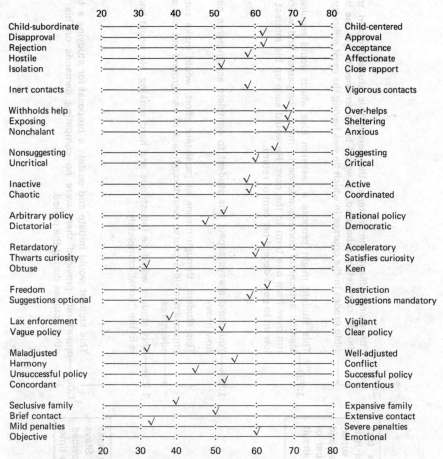

Figure 17.4. **Rating of the home treatment of Ted Stone.**
Baldwin et al., *1949, p. 28.*

This rating pattern fits the clinical description given by the visitor. Could elaborate ratings accomplish all that a clinical description does? An attempt to reduce individuality to a list of dimensions loses some idiosyncratic features. The ratings characterize the Stone family in terms of qualities on which all homes can be judged, not in terms of its own recurrent themes and conditions. From the clinical notes we learn that Mrs. Stone has had lifelong trouble in forming emotional ties, with the significant exceptions of her mother and her son, and that she is contemptuous of her husband. She thinks that no one, not even her husband, understands that she has "sacrificed her life for Ted." "Having identified herself completely with her product, it was necessary that the child himself be immaculate, perfect in behavior, precocious intellectually." Ted is prone to respiratory infections and subject to allergies. These ailments intensify his

Persistence and drive

Capable of prolonged attention to a task whether self-initiated or assigned, until it is completed, without requiring constant supervision. Works energetically, without delay and procrastination. May undertake a number of different activities simultaneously in pursuit of a single goal.

↑ 2.00

The more difficult the material the harder this student would try. Even though completely exhausted, he would be determined to get the best possible grades in the courses in which he was having the most difficulty.

1.75 ←— This student might propose a research idea which would require a substantial amount of correspondence to many companies and which would run over from one term to the next. He would keep up his interest and follow up to get a decent per cent of return.

1.50 ←— You could always expect this student to complete assignments no matter how heavy.

This student, through means of persistent effort, would make substantial improvement in a course even though lack of background put him at a disadvantage.

1.25 ←— This student would be industrious and hard working. He would know what is in the "book" completely.

1.00 ←— This student would initiate and sustain a proposal for studying a business opportunity provided there were no competing demands on his time in other courses during the period.

Capable of prolonged attention to a few tasks which are of special personal interest. Stays with a task until it is completed provided there are no conflicting demands on his time.

0.75 — If a problem is of particular interest to this student he would stick with it and examine all aspects of it. If it does not interest him, he would be likely to give it only superficial attention.

This student would finish work that interests him, but procrastinate on other tasks.

0.50 — In a library research paper, you could expect this student to find a few references, but not to pursue the literature sufficiently to find the most pertinent material.

0.25 — If unable to solve a problem in probability theory by application of formulas discussed in class, you would expect this student to give up after a few minutes even though he knew he could solve the problem by using a tedious method of enumeration.

0.00 — You would expect this student not to stick with his attempt to pass the course.

Stays with any task for only a limited time. Unable to pursue several tasks concurrently to completion.

Figure 17.5. Anchored scale for collecting criterion ratings from faculty members on the basis of remembered incidents. *Research in process under the direction of the Policy Committee for the Admission Test for Graduate Study in Business. Copyright © 1968 by the Educational Testing Service and reproduced by permission.*

mother's anxiety. Discipline is pulled in opposite directions by Mrs. Stone's desire for perfection and by her identification with Ted. "On one occasion when he was sent to bed an hour early as a punishment, Mrs. Stone decided she had been overly severe and went to the bedroom to read to him for the extra period." Such descriptive color and texture, of no use for statistical reports, is informative to the psychologist trying to understand the situation.

Ratings often serve as criteria, and one can use a more elaborate procedure than would be tolerable in an operational rating scale. How far investigators may go is illustrated by the Smith-Kendall technique (1963), as it is being used to get criteria in a business school. Figure 17.5 displays one of seven scales faculty members are asked to use. The faculty member is to think back over recent interactions with the student, recall a relevant incident, jot down a brief summary, and assign a scale value to the incident with the aid of the printed "anchor" incidents. The incident "Came to a conference without having completed readings he was to discuss; explained that work on a class project had absorbed his time," for example, would perhaps be scored at 1.10. Next, the faculty member is to look back over the set of incidents for this student and this scale—perhaps four in number—and to assign a scale value to the student's characteristic behavior. This is not a straight average of the original scale values; the faculty member is told to give less weight to unrepresentative occurrences. The procedure is well designed, insofar as the report is very likely to be the best information the faculty member can give. But the complexity of the procedure is sure to generate resistance.

Another set of anchored scales, for recording judgments of clinicians, is discussed by James B. Taylor (1968). Rater agreement was very much higher than for ordinary graphic rating scales; the accuracy approached a level only the average of *four* raters could attain with the ordinary scale.

Scorable inventories and checklists. Whereas most rating procedures attempt to capture gross judgments, the technique can be elaborated into something like a test: the informant reports on rather unambiguous acts or stylistic elements, and these "items" are accumulated into scores. Perhaps the best example is the Inpatient Multidimensional Rating Scale, which records impressions of the psychiatric interviewer. The principles that guided the construction are probably widely applicable (Lorr, Klett, & McNair, 1963, pp. 26, 28, paraphrased here):

● Each scale should refer to a single variable. Too often, scale labels entangle two or more traits or kinds of behavior.

● There should be related but nonequivalent scales. Clinicians often seek to record information on a major concept with a single rating scale. This is like trying to determine ability in arithmetic by administering just one problem.

● The scale should be unidirectional, running from zero degree of a characteristic to a maximum. Scales with two poles are treacherous because logical opposites may not be psychological opposites; the opposite of "exhibitionism" could be self-effacement but it could also be indifference to attention.

• The scales should differentiate between persons. There should be some persons rated at all scale positions.

• Scales should be as free as possible of theoretical preconceptions. One should avoid words such as "regression," "mannerisms," and "acting out," sticking to everyday language.

The IMPS (*CPP*) has 75 items, each of which belongs to one of ten subsets, e.g., Excitement, Hostile Belligerence, Paranoid Projection, Grandiose Expansiveness. The interviewer records his impressions from the interview, ignoring other data in the record, in response to nine questions such as:

COMPARED TO THE NORMAL PERSON TO WHAT DEGREE DOES HE . . .

7. Express or exhibit feeling and emotions openly, impulsively, or without apparent restraint or control?
   Cues: Shows temper outbursts; weeps . . .
9. Manifest speech that is hurried, accelerated, or pushed?
40. Try to dominate, control, or direct the conduct of the interview?
   Cues: Number of times he interrupts, . . .

These items all count in the Excitement score. Responses are made on a 9-point scale: not at all, very slightly, a little, . . . markedly, extremely. The authors believe that this demand for fine discrimination adds to the power of the instrument. Note that the excitement items are scattered among items on other qualities, so that the rater is not conscious of the trait to be scored. While the use of multiple items has a clear advantage, one must not increase the rater's task to the point where he makes hasty judgments or fails to return the rating form.

The authors' studies indicate that persons observing the same interview agree well but not perfectly ($r = 0.88$ for Excitement); most errors of judgment have been eliminated by the refined technique. Also, internal-consistency analysis is favorable; the coefficient for Excitement is 0.90—remarkable for a 9-item scale. What is lacking is evidence of consistency over interviews during a period of time, and of stability (in the absence of radical treatment). Klett (1968) reviews this and other rating procedures used to assess change during psychotherapy.

Interviewers and observers arrive at a complex impression of the subject. Much of this information is lost if one collects only a few numerical ratings. A written description often includes vague remarks applicable to any subject and fails to touch on some important characteristics. Moreover, descriptions in essay form are hard to compare.

The Q sort is the best way to capture such impressions of personality (Stephenson, 1953; Block, 1960). A standard set of phrases is prepared, covering the aspects of personality or performance important to those who will use the report. The statements are written on separate cards. The rater is told to sort the cards into, say, 9 piles, with statements most descriptive of the subject in the first pile and those least descriptive in the ninth. Investigators generally direct the sorter to put a specified number of cards in each pile. He might be told to distribute 100 statements in this manner:

	Most descriptive							Least descriptive	
Pile	1	2	3	4	5	6	7	8	9
Number of cards	5	8	12	16	18	16	12	8	5

(The number of statements, piles, and sorting rules may, of course, be different from this.) Asking the rater to fill out a standard personality questionnaire so that the responses describe the subject has similar advantages, so long as the items refer to overt behavior and not to feelings. Q-sort decks can be used to obtain self-descriptions (Wylie, 1961, pp. 41–64).

The sorting procedure has some advantage over the rating form or printed checklist, since the sorter can shift items back and forth as he proceeds. One's definition of a category such as "Definitely true" may shift while he is working down a list, but in a Q sort we may expect the items placed in the same pile to be equally descriptive of the subject as the rater sees him. The fixed distribution eliminates rater differences in response style. It cannot eliminate rater bias, as the rater can easily arrange the items to describe the subject favorably.

The report on a subject may be examined impressionistically or may be processed formally. One may compute the median position of statements representing a single dimension of personality, just as a personality questionnaire is scored for anxiety or dominance. One may develop a key that weights items relevant to a criterion. One may compute a correlation showing how similar one subject is to another—but this and some other elaborate techniques used with Q sorts are open to serious misuse (Cronbach & Gleser, 1954; Cronbach, 1958). Some Q decks are filled with evaluative items; the data obtained are then primarily a reflection of halo or approval, and the elaborate sorting procedure contributes nothing.

For use by professional psychologists who have formed an impression of the subject through observation, during therapy, or from a complex testing procedure, the California Q-set (Block, 1960, pp. 138–139; CPP) is suitable. The items have been carefully screened and annotated for clarity, and have been evaluated to make sure that no commonly wanted information is omitted. The items range from favorable to unfavorable, but about half are neutral in implied merit and adjustment, or such that the value attached to the behavior depends on the context in which it is exhibited. Illustrative items are seen in Table 17.2.

This table illustrates use of the Q-sort in research. Ravenna Helson arranged for women outstanding in mathematical research to be interviewed and tested

Table 17.2. Personality characteristics associated with creativity in women mathematicians

Correlation with criterion	Statement from California Q-set
+0.64	Thinks and associates ideas in unusual ways; has unconventional thought processes.
+0.55	Is an interesting, arresting person.
+0.51	Tends to be rebellious and non-conforming.
+0.42	Is self-dramatizing; histrionic.
+0.36	Expresses hostile feelings directly.
−0.37	Prides self on being "objective," rational.
−0.40	Favors conservative values in a variety of areas.
−0.43	Behaves in a sympathetic or considerate manner.
−0.45	Is a genuinely dependable and responsible person.
−0.62	Judges self and others in conventional terms like "popularity," "the correct thing to do," social pressures, etc.

SOURCE: Block, 1960, pp. 25–26. See also Helson, 1967.

by psychologists who recorded their impressions with the Block cards. Independently, she obtained criterion ratings indicating the degree to which these women were original and creative, as distinct from merely competent and productive. Each single statement in the Q-set was then correlated with this criterion. A statement often used as "most descriptive" in rating the more creative women would correlate with the criterion. The correlations for the items listed in Table 17.2 are remarkably high when we realize that single items correlate less than test scores, and that the subjects are highly select.

The choice among reporting schemes depends upon the purpose of rating, the qualifications of raters, the information they have about the subjects, and the likelihood of distortion—deliberate or unconscious. The short, unsubtle, but carefully prepared descriptive graphic rating scale is probably best when each subject is rated by different individuals and one may assume a reasonable degree of honesty in rating. Ranking (see below) is advantageous when a single judge gives information on the complete group or a representative sample of the group. The Q sort is of greatest value when a comprehensive description of a single individual is desired and an informed rater can be expected to give patient consideration to a long list of questions.

Empirical scales. To predict an external criterion, traits for rating can be selected empirically. The old Haggerty-Olson-Wickman scale was designed to screen maladjusted pupils for psychological study. A direct interpretation might be made by scoring socially desirable behavior. But behavior that on its face seems desirable may actually be a sign of maladjustment, more common among problem children than among pupils in general. For example, "wide-awake" is a favorable description, characteristically applied to adjusted children, but "keenly alive and alert" describes children who get into trouble as much as it does adjusted ones.

Perhaps we can conceal the scoring plan to outwit the rater unwilling to give an unfavorable report. We might count only those ratings that correlate with the criterion. For example, in selecting salesmen one might give credit for ratings as "energetic," "ambitious," and "friendly" (if these traits correlate with success in the job) and no credit for "hard-working," "well-adjusted," and "cooperative" (if these traits have no predictive value). Indeed, we may go further, and assign a *negative* weight to these irrelevant favorable ratings to compensate for rater generosity.

This idea underlies the forced-choice method of merit rating. Periodic ratings of Army officers are required for use in promotion and reassignment. The tradition of giving favorable ratings, however, means that conventional rating forms bring in almost no information. Psychologists therefore invented a forced-choice scale. Phrases are classified on the basis of preliminary studies into four types. A favorable-valid item is one that raters apply frequently and that predicts an independent criterion: an unfavorable-valid item is rarely applied, and correlates negatively with the criterion. Invalid items are those not associated with success or failure. The rater is directed to choose the statement that best describes the man. The choices might be

> Wins confidence of his men   (Favorable-valid)
> Punctual in completing reports   (Favorable-invalid)

or

> Has weak tactical judgment   (Unfavorable-valid)
> Inclined to gripe about conditions (Unfavorable-invalid)

A plus credit is given for each favorable-valid choice and a minus credit for each unfavorable-valid choice. Another technique, possibly more effective, is to provide four favorable items in each set (Zavala, 1965).

Raters are antagonistic to forced-choice techniques. They want to know how their reports will be interpreted and want to be free to give an entirely favorable impression of the man rated. Whether a forced-choice scale can be used in a given situation depends upon the cooperation the data gatherer can anticipate or upon the authority he can bring to bear. The Army, after developing the technique and establishing its superior validity (e.g., Highland & Berkshire, 1951), concluded that resistance from officers was too great to justify continuing its use in efficiency reports. In industry, forced-choice merit ratings have had considerable application.

A request for ranking encounters less opposition. When many men are to be judged, the instructions may call, not for complete ranking, but for grouping the top 5 per cent, next 20 per cent, middle 50 per cent, etc. This forced distribution may give more differentiation than the graphic scale. Ranking presupposes that the judge is considering the proper trait. Ranking on merit will be misleading if the rater stresses obedience and dependability when the institution wants initiative and imagination. The chief limitation of ranking is that groups are rarely comparable. A top man in one group might rank tenth in another.

9. *Would use of an elaborate rating instrument such as the Fels scales be advantageous when obtaining ratings of a child by his teacher?*
10. *How much of the information quoted from the caseworker's notes on the Stones could have been covered by adding additional traits to the rating scale?*
11. *Relate the Fels scales of parent behavior to the Osgood good-active-strong dimensions. What traits do not fit the three-dimensional scheme? If two traits fall at the same point in the Osgood space, do they differ?*
12. *Describe a suitable rating technique for each of these purposes.*
    a. *Obtaining ratings from principals to be used in deciding which teachers should receive salary increases for special merit.*
    b. *Obtaining information for school records regarding parents' impressions of their children's personalities.*
    c. *Maintaining weekly records of ward behavior of patients as seen by attendants.*
    d. *Recording teacher characteristics as judged by an observer in research evaluating teacher-training methods.*
    e. *Obtaining reports from supervisors of student teachers, to be used by campus instructors in helping the student to improve.*
    f. *Obtaining reports on pupils to be used in awarding college scholarships to the most deserving graduates in a state.*
13. *To what extent does the information in the California Q-set appear to go beyond the good-active-strong scheme? beyond the Tupes-Christal traits?*

Reports of Participants

Peer Ratings

Ratings of group members by their associates may give useful information. Such reports are often called "peer ratings" (a peer is an individual who has the same status within the organization as the person rated). Black's study in which girls rated others living in the same college dormitory is one example. Another is the rating of officer candidates by their classmates.

Whereas only one or two superiors know a subject well, 10 to 30 raters may give ratings in a class or dormitory. As a consequence, the average rating on any trait is precisely determined. Indeed, for well-defined traits, in a group that has had reasonable opportunity to become acquainted, composite peer ratings generally have reliabilities in the neighborhood of 0.90.

Peer ratings and ratings of superiors give different information. A child who impresses his peers as being a leader may not be the one the teacher regards as a leader; the peers, for example, may consider popularity whereas the teacher notices originality and initiative. It helps for the teacher or counselor, however, to know which persons are regarded as leaders by their own group. The information may be most significant in just those cases where the superiors and the peers have different impressions. The peer rating is an objective statement about the individual's reputation. Reputation is based to some extent on behavior, but the social pattern and role relations in the group introduce biases of various sorts. Among adolescents, correlations between reputations and observations of corresponding behavior range from 0.45 to 0.70 (Newman & Jones, 1946).

To obtain peer ratings it is usually necessary to simplify the task. Raters are untrained, and we desire each rater to describe many individuals. The adjective checklist (see p. 556) can be marked quickly and can cover many aspects of behavior. To score it, related adjectives are classified into groups and a count is made of the frequency with which adjectives in each category are checked for each subject. This leads to a descriptive profile.

If 30 persons in a group rate each other on 20 traits, each person is being asked to give 600 responses. Carelessness and halo may be expected. A nomination technique reduces the labor without reducing the amount of significant information. Each member of the group is asked to name persons outstanding in a particular respect, such as leadership. A similar nomination of persons lacking in leadership may also be solicited, but this arouses anxiety because subjects know that they are being considered for unfavorable nominations and because, as raters, they are reluctant to speak unfavorably of associates.

For young children, the technique may be put as a guessing game, or as a matter of naming pupils to fill parts in a play. Each member of the group names the pupils the description seems to fit. Typical descriptions are (Hartshorne & May, 1929, p. 88):

Here is the class athlete. He (or she) can play baseball, basketball, tennis, can swim as well as any, and is a good sport.
This one is always picking on others and annoying them.

One counts how often each child is mentioned for each description.

The *sociogram* takes a further step to study the social structure of a group; it identifies cliques, hierarchies of leadership, and other groupings. (Moreno, 1934). The best procedure is to request members of a group to indicate their choices for companions in a particular activity. Gronlund (1959) suggests the following directions for use in the upper elementary grades.

During the next few weeks we will be changing our seats around, working in small groups, and playing some group games. Now that we all know each other by name, you can help me arrange groups that work and play best together. You can

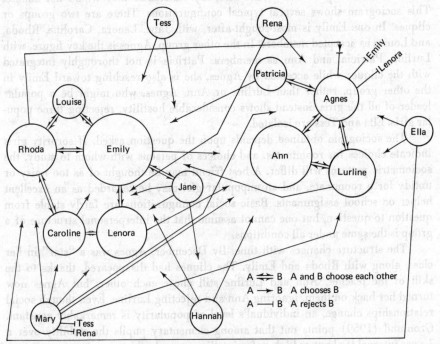

Figure 17.6.   Sociogram for a class of fourth-grade girls.
Adapted from Staff, Division on Child Development, 1945, p. 297.

do this by writing the names of the children you would like *to have sit near you,
to have work with you,* and *to have play with you.* You may choose anyone in this
room you wish, including those pupils who are absent. Your choices will not be
seen by anyone else. Give first name and initial of last name.

Make your choices carefully so the groups will be the way you really want
them. I will try to arrange the groups so that each pupil gets at least two of his
choices. Sometimes it is hard to give everyone his first few choices so be sure to
make all five choices for each question.

Directions should be concerned with real activities. The data are not obtained in a test setting; instead, they are obtained as a means of dealing with
the group. If data are obtained from a less real question, such as "Who are
your friends?" there is more likelihood of answers given to make a good impression. Subjects must know that their reports will be treated confidentially.
The sociometric data should be used as promised to set up work groups, com-
mittees, homeroom seating, or whatever; this permits one to obtain cooperation
when the technique is used again at a later date.

The choices are plotted in a sociogram (Figure 17.6) of a class of
fourth-grade girls early in the school year. Pupils indicated one to three

choices and were permitted to list also any classmates they would not choose. This sociogram shows several typical configurations. There are two groups or cliques. In one Emily is most-sought-after, with Jane, Lenora, Caroline, Rhoda, and Louise as accepted members. In the other group, Agnes is the key figure, with Lurline, Patricia, and Ann as members. Patricia is not thoroughly integrated with the clique; while accepted by Agnes, she is also reaching toward Emily in the other group, rather than Lurline or Ann. Agnes, who might be a popular leader of all the girls, instead shows considerable hostility, rejecting three popular girls. Ella and Tess are isolated.

The sociogram obtained depends upon the question asked. If sorority girls indicate choices for roommates, and choices of persons with whom to study, the sociometric patterns will differ. A best friend may be thought of as too noisy or untidy for a roommate, and an unpopular girl may be regarded as an excellent helper on school assignments. Basic social configurations are fairly stable from question to question, but one cannot assume that the interpersonal structure of a group is the same under all conditions.

The structure changes with time. By December, Agnes was a "star" in her class, along with Rhoda and Emily. The cliques had disappeared, thanks to the skill of the teacher. Ann and Lurline still chose each other, but Agnes now turned her back on them, ignoring Ann and rejecting Lurline. Even though social relationships change, an individual's level of popularity is remarkably constant. Gronlund (1959) points out that among elementary pupils the stability over a 1-year interval is about as high as for intelligence and achievement.

Value of peer ratings.   The term *sociometric rating* is applied to all methods of identifying social relationships among group members. No sharp distinction is to be made between the descriptive peer rating and the sociometric rating, but in general the latter is restricted to questions about whom the rater likes best or would prefer to work with, and thus is as much concerned with the rater's reactions as with the ratee's personality. When given willingly, peer ratings may be much more dependable than other sorts of ratings, as Lindzey and Borgatta point out (Lindzey, 1954, vol. I, p. 406):

> There is no need to train raters to engage in sociometric ratings. The difficult and time-consuming task of attempting to produce common frames of reference and homogeneous criteria in terms of which ratings shall be assigned is avoided. The rater is asked to apply exactly those particular, unique, and sometimes irrational criteria he has spent a lifetime developing. Everyone is an experienced or expert rater when it comes to sociometric judgments. Each of us has a vast body of experience in deciding with whom we wish to interact and whom we wish to avoid. Liking and disliking, accepting and rejecting are part of the process of daily living. . . . One might say that the individual who uses these techniques is taking advantage of the largest pool of sensitive and experienced raters that is anywhere available.

Peer ratings gain validity from the fact that a person's acquaintances collect data over many more hours than a supervisor or professional observer, including some of his less guarded moments. Moreover, in most studies one can average the reports of a larger number of peer informants. It seems that peers are generally willing to give truthful information about their impressions. The impressions may or may not be valid accounts of behavior. One bit of evidence is that choices stated by pupils as to preferred fellow actors in a class play correlated about 0.80 with actual choices when an opportunity to present impromptu plays was given (Byrd, 1951).

One might suspect that peer ratings reflect fortuitous events within the group, which put one person in the limelight rather than another of equal merit. But leadership ratings by fellow enlisted men in one squad correlated 0.80 with ratings given to the same men after all had been shuffled into new squads and new barracks, and had worked with their new companions for four weeks (Gordon & Medland, 1965). This compared rather well with the correlation of 0.90 between ratings four weeks apart in squads kept intact.

Information about reputation or status in the group can be used in many ways. The group worker uses it to identify individuals who require special attention and individuals who can be developed into leaders, or perhaps to reorganize a group so that it will function better—for example, to organize factory workers into congenial teams, or to assign delinquent girls in an institution to small living groups.

Peer ratings can be a basis for selection and classification. Among officer candidates, for example, the impression a man makes on his companions during the early phases of training forecasts his ability to win confidence and acceptance as an officer. Composite peer ratings of officer candidates correlate about 0.50 with later ratings by superiors in duty assignments—extremely impressive, in view of the criterion reliability of about 0.50. The rated traits that predict the criterion are in the good-strong-active sector, but "agreeableness" and "sociability" do not predict (Tupes, 1957). This then, is a case when it is helpful to separate at least four factors. Ratings of management trainees by their fellows forecast rate of promotion within a corporation (Roadman, 1964). Even patients in a ward can give valid information on their associates. They predict which persons will be rehospitalized, for example, as well as the professional staff can (Lasky et al., 1959). Barclay (1966) suggests comparing a mean rating of pupils by their classmates with a teacher rating; the probability that a pupil will drop out of school is very high when both ratings are low.

When a peer rating or nomination method is proposed, its acceptability and its propriety need to be considered. Among adolescent girls, in whom popularity is a matter of great concern, rating and being rated may generate anxiety. Students will object to questions that seem to make them spies for a school administration. Frankness regarding the uses to which the data will be put is imperative. Modern opinion would criticize use of the "Guess Who" format with young children if it misleads the children about the purpose of questioning.

Sociometry came to prominence in two contexts. In one, classification of military officers, some disregard of individual sensitivities is expected and can be justified. The other is the educational movement that in the 1930s began to emphasize the school's responsibility to promote emotional and social adjustment. At that time, in such a context, collecting data from peers was a wholly good-hearted and defensible endeavor. In the past decade, with an academic emphasis supplanting the adjustment emphasis (which never took root deeply), with students in open revolt against paternalism on campus, and with recognition that adjustment is readily confused with conformity, the whole matter invites renewed examination. There are times when data from peers can be used legitimately and constructively, and there are also illegitimate uses. Defensible practice does not remain the same from decade to decade.

14. *What children besides Tess and Ella are fringers? (Figure 17.6).*
15. *What interpretations of Agnes' hostility can be suggested?*
16. *Prior to this study, the teacher had characterized Tess as hard working, interested in accomplishing tasks, "fits in nicely with the group." Tess helps others with their sewing, at which she is superior. How would the teacher's outlook and treatment of Tess be affected by the information from the sociogram?*
17. *The following choices were made in a group of 10th-graders. Plot a sociogram and discuss the interactions shown.*

> *Shirley chooses Charles, Jim, and Sam.*
> *Charles chooses Shirley, Sam and Jim; rejects Tom.*
> *Phil chooses Jim, Charles, and Shirley; rejects Wallace and Tom.*
> *Wallace chooses Phil and Jack; rejects Tom.*
> *Jim chooses Jack, Sam, Charles, and Shirley; rejects Tom.*
> *Jack chooses Jim and Tom; rejects Phil.*
> *Shirley is chosen by several girls whom she does not mention. Sam and Tom were absent.*

18. *In a group of sorority girls, the sociometric question "Whom would you choose as a roommate?" is asked; will results be the same if the question is changed to "With whom would you choose to go on a double date?"*
19. *What would be the best way of studying the generalizability of sociometric data?*
20. *Surgency (i.e., energetic, talkative, enthusiastic behavior) correlates very little with leadership behavior as rated by observers, but correlates substantially with frequency of election as leader. Explain this finding. What does it imply regarding the use of peer ratings as criteria?*
21. *When sociograms were made of squadrons of Navy fliers on combat duty, it was found that the "administratively designated leaders" were often not the ones named as preferred work leaders by the men (G. Kelly, 1947, p. 133). What practical suggestions follow from this finding?*

Measures of Environment

Information from participants is increasingly being used to study the situation as well as the individual. This arises in part from increased awareness that behavior is the joint product of personality and situation, and not a reflection of personality alone. It arises also from practical and research concerns. When one is trying to understand why a certain type of student persists in one college and tends to drop out of another, one wants to know how the colleges differ, and, more particularly, how students *think* they differ. To investigate successful and unsuccessful teachers, one wants to know how they differ in their style and emphasis, and how the pupils perceive their style.

One could send a trained observer to form impressions or to tabulate exactly what happens during scheduled observation periods (see below). A less extensive report can be obtained simply by having the students or other participants record their impressions. The information is a mixture of a factual report on the way the situation really is and a phenomenal report on the way the situation looks or feels to the participant. Hence the information is ambiguous, but significant.

The technique commonly used in research of this kind is to prepare a descriptive questionnaire rather like the personality questionnaire in format. The respondent marks statements "True" or "False." A count of "True" responses for any item, over the whole sample of participants, gives a rather reliable report. Items may be recombined in clusters or dimensions.

The best known instrument of this kind is CUES, the College and University Environment Scales (*ETS*), developed by C. Robert Pace. George Stern (1962), who collaborated with Pace in the pioneering work, has also reported studies involving a slightly different procedure. The nature of items and scales in such instruments is illustrated below and in Fig. 17.7. A profile can be prepared for a college, for a curricular grouping within the college, for students living in a single dormitory, or for students at the start and end of their freshman year, for example.

Use of CUES information is exemplified in the *Indiana Prediction Study* (1965), a handbook prepared to help high-school students and their parents decide what colleges to apply to. In addition to facts about curriculum, admission requirements, and experience tables relating college marks to standard ability tests, the handbook presents a thumbnail sketch derived directly from the CUES profile. The pictures are far more realistic and more differentiated than the propaganda that normally appears in college catalogs. On the basis of score profiles such as appear in Figure 17.7, and examination of frequencies of response to single items, descriptions are prepared. One Indiana college is characterized as follows:

The college environment at ———— is one that encourages scholarship, strong fellowship, and an awareness of the deeper issues of life. . . . a high degree of respect for students who are serious about their work. . . . Students exhibit a sense of propriety that is indicative of the high standards of personal conduct expected. . . . The extracurricular aspects of college life are not ignored but are kept in proper perspective. Parties, sports, and publications are popular but reflect the restraint and good taste of the student body.

Another college located not far away is described quite differently:

> The climate . . . encourages students to seek the practical benefits of education in a structured environment. . . . Relationships between students . . . are friendly and informal. The college provides supervision of extracurricular programs. . . . Casual modes of dress are accepted by the students. Bermuda shorts are a regular part of campus dress; and spur-of-the-moment activities, including an occasional student prank, are not uncommon. . . . The interests and efforts of the students are directed toward the formal academic program rather than toward activities in cultural, creative, or esthetic fields.

The data make it clear that a college education is a very different experience at different places or in different programs. Stern (1962) has reported marked contrasts between liberal arts programs and business-administration programs:

Liberal arts	Business	
14.1	56.0	The school administration has little tolerance for student complaints and protests.
32.2	83.0	Professors usually take attendance in class.
75.3	17.9	When students get together, they often talk about trends in art, music, or the theatre.
74.7	34.2	Most students have considerable interest in round tables, panel meetings, or other formal discussions.

(Numbers are percentages of "True" responses.)

Insofar as a theory has developed around instruments of this type, it is that the personality can be described in terms of "needs"—for change, achievement, affiliation, etc.—and the situation can be described in terms of "presses" to behave in certain ways. A "press" might include formal demands from the figures in authority, subtle demands contained in the expectations of the student group, and opportunities to receive reward and attention for acts of a certain kind. There is some evidence of a statistical trend for students of a certain kind to seek an environment of a certain kind, and some hints (e.g., McKeachie *et al.*, 1966) that students learn more from a classroom environment that matches its "press" to their "needs." But studies of this sort are still at an exploratory level.

Item-sampling designs. The investigations using CUES can profitably adopt a kind of testing that has been uncommon—the item-sampling design. Whereas the conventional notion of a standardized test is one in which every subject confronts the same items, in item sampling each subject faces a random sample

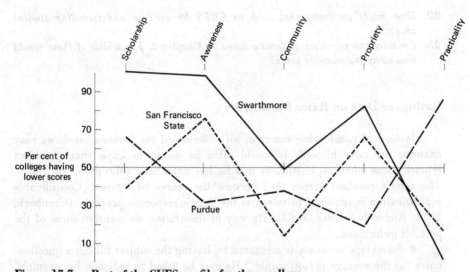

Figure 17.7. Part of the CUES profile for three colleges.
The scores can be briefly characterized as follows: Scholarship, competitive academic-intel-
lectual emphasis; Awareness, concern for human and aesthetic problems apart from course
work; Community, cohesiveness and warmth among students; Propriety, mannerliness, con-
ventionality, and considerateness; Practicality, emphasis on practically useful learning. *CUES
manual, 1963.*

from the whole collection of items. Practically, this usually means dividing the
pool of items into a number of subsets that require the same amount of time,
and administering different subsets to different examinees. Thus, if one has
200 questions on college environment, he can divide them into five subsets, so
that no one subject marks more than 40 of them. This greatly shortens time
for information gathering, yet there is no important loss in the quality of the
information.

The reason for the efficiency of the item-sampling design is that in studies
of environments one wishes to draw conclusions about the situation of the group,
not of the individual. The design also serves in evaluating the effects of curricula, where (again) a summary for the group is of greatest importance. The
score obtained for the group is supposed to represent both a population of persons resembling the present sample and a universe of items like those entering
the test. When we employ item sampling we sample as many persons from the
population as in the conventional design, but a far larger sample of items can
be administered in a given time; hence the conclusions better represent the
universe. Among 40 CUES items in a uniform-test design, one could include
about 8 on propriety; with item sampling one could use 40 different propriety
items. Item sampling is a new idea; some of the theory is laid out by Lord &
Novick (1968).

22. *How might an instrument such as CUES be used in understanding student unrest?*

23. *Consider the purposes of testing listed in Chapter 2. For which of these would item sampling possibly serve?*

Ratings as Data on Rater Personality

Instead of considering the rater an observer of the persons rated, we may examine the rater himself. It would often be useful to know that a subject typically sees others as hostile, or that he has unrealistic conceptions of others. The rater's constant errors thus become the center of interest. Considerable sophistication is required to interpret the rater's responses properly (Cronbach, 1958; Richards & Cline, 1963). By way of illustration we mention three of the possible techniques.

● Stereotype accuracy is measured by having the subject fill out a questionnaire "as the average person would." He may be asked to indicate, for example, the percentage of male college graduates who respond "L" to each SVIB item, or, more simply, to select the most popular response. This could be scored in a manner like that of Kuder's OIS. There is ample evidence that individuals are not equally skilled in this task, but there is very little evidence about the relation of this type of "social intelligence" to other behavior.

One might, in vocational guidance, ask the man who says he wants to study engineering to fill out OIS as the typical engineer would, i.e., ask him to fake. Discrepancies between his stereotype and the actual key would bring to light his misconceptions about the vocation.

● Perceived similarity between valued and disvalued associates. Fiedler (1967) has asked subjects to fill out questionnaires so as to describe particular colleagues or subordinates that they regard favorably or unfavorably. His findings are complex, but they suggest that most often the effective leader is one who gives markedly different descriptions of high- and low-rated associates, i.e., who does not claim that all his associates are fine people.

● The Role Concept Repertory Test. In this procedure (G. Kelly, 1955), the subject is given a list of about twenty roles, of which the following are representative:

Your wife or present girl friend
Your mother
A person with whom you have worked who was easy to get along with
A girl you did not like when you were in high school
The person whom you would most like to be of help to (or whom you feel most sorry for)

The subject names a person who fills each role for him. The examiner then selects three of the persons and asks, "In what *important way* are two of them alike but different from the third?" If the response is superficial ("These two are tall") the examiner asks for some further similarity. A useful response might be, "These two are self-confident and this one is shy." The subject has then stated a bipolar scale along which he perceives people to differ. The procedure is continued until many scales have been elicited and applied to the significant others. Later research has modified the technique in many complicated ways. More attention has been paid to the complexity of the person's system for describing others than to the particular configurations he reports. Recent work is covered in Bannister and Mair (1968) and Bonarius (1965); see also Fancher's study (p. 560).

Kelly's approach provides an alternative to conventional trait psychology. Instead of trying to describe how the subject relates to people in general, Kelly examines what he has to say about the particular people he has to deal with. The psychologist is thus in a position to account for some of the variation in response from one interpersonal situation to another. In this respect, the method is comparable to the Osgood-Luria analysis of Eve. Mischel (1968), while taking a generally behavioristic line and arguing that a trait psychology is worthless as a guide to the therapist, urges that observation of behavior be combined with the Kelly type of phenomenology, on the ground that the person's way of interpreting his world is a potent force in self-regulation. For purposes of therapy, we would want to know how the client construes tasks and settings as well as persons.

24. *What does Figure 17.2 suggest about the belief systems of the two raters?*
25. *Does a procedure like Kelly's have any advantage over an interview?*

Observation of Behavior Samples

Self-reports, and judgments by peers and supervisors, are haphazard composites of observations. The rater did not see the individual in all situations, and selective recall also operates. Systematic observations can give a more accurate description of typical behavior. A distinction must be made between observations intended to be a representative sample of behavior and observations in a standard situation. The former estimates typical behavior from situations occurring in daily life; the situations may and usually will differ for different persons. The later observes every subject's reaction to a fixed situation.

Field observations—observations of the subject under his normal circumstances—are relatively easy to carry out and for some studies are more suitable than standardized observations. Many investigators feel that it is impossible to know personality unless we watch the subject as he reacts to the conditions most significant for him. Different stimuli are significant for different people. Standard situations are perhaps not as likely to elicit the important behavior patterns as are the normal (dissimilar) conditions under which the subjects live. The difficulty lies in seeing enough of the person's normal behavior, and in obtaining dependable records.

Problems of Sampling and Consistency of Behavior

The best way to summarize the typical behavior of a subject—employee, student, or patient—is to observe him in normal situations. If he does not know that we are watching, we obtain a truthful picture, limited only by our skill as observers and our persistence. This is our usual basis for judging associates and friends. Observation, however, is subject to sampling errors and observer errors.

To know the "typical" behavior of an individual, we must know how he usually acts in a particular situation. But situations change from day to day and from moment to moment. If we observe the attentiveness of an employee before lunch, we get a different impression than we get in midafternoon. If we observe cheerfulness or politeness when he is worried, our impression may be unfair. The only way to estimate typical behavior moderately well is to study the subject on many occasions, all sampled from the same universe. Since this is expensive one must compromise between validity and economy.

Inference about individual differences is difficult because one can never truly observe two individuals "in the same situation." Even when the situation is externally constant, previous conditions affect behavior. When Jimmy fidgets more than John in the classroom, one is likely to infer that Jimmy is "restless," "nervous," or "jumpy." If the impression is confirmed by repeated observations, this difference seems to be fundamental. But if Jimmy usually comes to school without breakfast, if he expects to be criticized by the teacher for poor work, or if he is large for the chairs provided, the difference in activity may tell nothing about the boys' basic restlessness. In fact, if conditions were reversed, Johnny might be more restless than Jimmy is now. Observations show how people typically act under their present conditions.

One of the best approaches to precise comparison is *time sampling*. A time sample is a set schedule of observations planned in advance. The schedule is randomized so that each subject is seen under comparable conditions. To study social contacts of preschool children, for example, a schedule of 1-minute observations may be drawn up. After the observer watches a child for 1 minute, noting all social interaction, he writes a full record. Children are watched in a predetermined order, different from day to day. Each child was observed an equal number of times during the first 5 minutes of the free-play hour, during the second 5 minutes, and on so. With well-distributed time samples the cumulative picture is likely to be far more typical than an equal amount of evidence obtained in a few longer observations. Moreover, errors of memory are reduced, as the observer can make full notes during or just after observing. Time samples are especially suitable for recording facts that can be expressed numerically (e.g., number of social contacts), but the data can also sustain judgmental interpretations. Observer-to-observer correlations, following extended sampling of children's behavior in a day camp, were 0.88 to 0.94 for the following attributes, among others: instigation of physical aggression, parallel play with peers, withdrawal from the social environment, affection-seeking, attempts to master gross motor tasks (Virginia Crandall, 1966).

At best, a summary of time samples jumbles different responses together. Responses the observer counts as the same may have quite different meanings, and situations that appear similar to him may evoke unlike responses. Newcomb (1929) observed boys in a summer camp, making daily records of cooperation in after-meal work, fighting with other boys, persistence, etc. When these day-to-day records were studied, most boys were found to be inconsistent. As Newcomb pointed out, situations are only superficially alike. Johnny is much more likely to fight a boy he thinks he can hold his own against than another boy who seems tougher. Johnny's actions, inconsistent from an observer's frame of reference, is highly consistent to Johnny. Correlations were computed between frequencies of actions supposed to represent single traits—showing off, dominance, etc. Responses grouped within one of the supposed traits correlated little higher than obviously dissimilar responses. Sears (1963, p. 35) showed that a concept of "dependence" in preschool children unwisely combines important specifics. When he separately scored actions such as staying near the adult, touching the adult, seeking reassurance, etc., the correlations between these kinds of supposedly dependent behavior ranged from -0.24 to 0.37. One kind of dependency does not imply another kind. The problem is reduced with narrower categories. But even when they become absurdly narrow—for example, dominance over Jimmy in an argument about the baseball umpire's decision—there is still inconsistency.

Conclusions formed in one situation—even on the basis of many cumulated observations—are valid only for that situation. Inference as to how a person would act in another situation is warranted only when responses under the two conditions have been shown to be correlated, or when observation yields so much understanding of his underlying personality structure (his stimulus equivalences) that we can see what a new situation means to him.

The extreme variation in performance is illustrated by a study of navigators. The student was taken on a mission on which his task was continually to compute his air speed by dead reckoning. Four separate legs were run, and the accuracy of his report of air speed for the leg was recorded. The score for each mission had a split-half reliability of 0.77; this is an indication of leg-to-leg consistency under unchanging conditions, with the same plane, etc. A day-to-day correlation was also computed; it was 0.00! (Carter & Dudek, 1947). Differences in score were determined almost entirely by transient conditions (e.g., wind) rather than by the individual's ability.

Despite these dramatic examples of zero and even negative correlations between observations of the same trait, observations can give meaningful summaries if an adequate sample is collected. Any one observation is like a one-item test. Observing on many days, in many circumstances, can give a highly dependable summary score. That is to say, one such score will agree with another, collected on another series of days. We cannot predict what Johnny will do tomorrow, but we can identify significant trends. Even if single observations correlate only 0.10, observations in ten situations ought to correlate 0.50 with a second set of ten observations; and 30 observations brings the correlation to 0.75. Short observations are generally advisable. Six 5-minute observations on different children—repeated on 12 days—uses the observer's time much better than observing one child for 30 consecutive minutes on each of two days. A generalizability study has to be carried out to determine just how many observations are required for a given purpose.

One can design the observation technique so as to capture a good deal of the variation associated with situations. Caldwell's "ecological" system (1969) conceives of behavior in terms of descriptive clauses. Each clause has three elements: the subject, who does something; the predicate, or action; and the object, toward whom the action is directed. In addition, there are qualifying adverbs, such as "intensely" or "imitatively." For each element a set of categories is listed, in the light of the purposes of the investigation. For a preschool observation there are nine kinds of subject: the child under study, a female in a supervisory role, etc. The observer, or coder of a videotape record, etc., encodes any single act by a string of numbers. Teacher-praises-John's-finger-painting becomes 24301—2 for female supervisor, 43 for approval, 0 for the case under study, and 1 for a verbal interaction ("verbally"). The data can be cross-tabulated complexly to identify changes in John's experiences and reactions as he deals with various kinds of persons, or they may be tabulated to study the teacher's actions toward various children.

26. *Why might an unfair picture of a child's behavior be obtained if he were always observed during the first 5 minutes of the play period and never during the second five minutes?*

27. *As a criterion in selection research, would it be better to test every flier with repeated landings on the same day or with a similar number of landings spread over several days?*

Observer Error and Its Reduction

An observer notices some happenings and ignores others. This is unavoidable, since any activity has too many aspects for the mind to attend to all at once. Especially in social situations, the complexity of interaction prevents exhaustive reporting. Random omissions would be unimportant, but observers make systematic errors, overemphasizing some types of happenings and failing to report others.

Viewing the identical scene, observers give widely different reports. The following reports were written by four observers, each of whom saw the same motion-picture scene of about 10 minutes' duration. The film was shown twice without sound. The film sequence, taken in the classroom and on the playground, showed several activities that revealed much of Robert's personality. The observers were directed to note everything they could about one boy, Robert, and were told to use parentheses to set apart inferences or interpretations. Numbers in these accounts, referring to scenes in the film, have been inserted to aid comparison.

Observer A: (2) Robert reads word by word, using finger to follow place. (4) Observes girl in box with much preoccupation. (5) During singing, he in general doesn't participate too actively. Interest is part of time centered elsewhere. Appears to respond most actively to sections of song involving action. Has tendency for seemingly meaningless movement. Twitching of fingers, aimless thrusts with arms.

Observer B: (2) Looked at camera upon entering (seemed perplexed and interested). Smiled at camera. (2) Reads (with apparent interest and with a fair degree of facility). (3) Active in roughhouse play with girls. (4) Upon being kicked (unintentionally) by one girl he responded (angrily). (5) Talked with girl sitting next to him between singing periods. Participated in singing. (At times appeared enthusiastic.) Didn't always sing with others. (6) Participated in a dispute in a game with others (appeared to stand up for his own rights). Aggressive behavior toward another boy. Turned pockets inside out while talking to teacher and other students. (7) Put on overshoes without assistance. Climbed to top of ladder rungs. Tried to get rung which was occupied by a girl but since she didn't give in, contented himself with another place.

Observer C: (1) Smiles into camera (curious). When group breaks up, he makes nervous gestures, throws arm out into air. (2) Attention to reading lesson. Reads with serious look on his face, has to use line marker. (3) Chases girls, teases. (4) Girl kicks when he puts hand on her leg. Robert makes face at her. (5) Singing. Sits with mouth open, knocks knees together, scratches leg, puts fingers in mouth (seems to have several nervous habits, though not emotionally overwrought or self-conscious). (6) In a dispute over parchesi, he stands up for his rights. (7) Short dispute because he wants rung on jungle gym.

Observer D: (2) Uses guide to follow words, reads slowly, fairly forced and with careful formation of sounds (perhaps unsure of self and fearful of mistakes). (3) Perhaps slightly aggressive as evidenced by pushing younger child to side when moving from a position to another. Plays with other children with obvious enjoyment, smiles, runs, seems especially associated with girls. This is noticeable in games and in seating in singing. (5) Takes little interest in singing, fidgets, moves hands and legs (perhaps shy and nervous). Seems in song to be unfamiliar with words of main part, and shows disinterest by fidgeting and twisting around. Not until chorus is reached does he pick up interest. His especial friend seems to be a particular girl, as he is always seated by her.

Every observer is more sensitive to some types of behavior than others. How does he regard nailbiting, failure to look one in the eye, or profanity? If he considers these significant, he will note them and base his impression on them. Another observer might give greatest attention to voice modulation, careful use of grammar, or friendliness of conversation. Ideally, an observer would detect every revealing act, but when looking for one thing he necessarily overlooks something else.

Observers interpret what they see. When they make an interpretation, they tend to overlook facts that do not fit the interpretation, and may even invent facts (but not deliberately) to complete the event as interpreted.

Systematic recording. Do factory workers attend to their work? A time record can note the exact moments when they are at work, and the time spent in looking around, obtaining tools, and visiting. The causes of distractions can be noted. Such records for different workers and departments can be analyzed both for judging the workers and for planning rest periods or improved tool distribution. (But this may invade privacy to an objectionable degree.)

Child development has been studied through records of social contacts, play activities, speech, and other objectively defined actions (Barker, Kounin, & Wright, 1943, pp. 509 ff.). Precise and objective reports are especially useful for measuring changes.

If behavior is too varied for direct tabulation, it may be possible to define categories in which the observer can tabulate each incident as it occurs. Bales (1951) categorized social interaction in small groups. Twelve categories are defined, including:

Shows solidarity, raises other's status, gives help, reward.

Shows tension release, jokes, laughs, shows satisfaction.

Asks for orientation, information, repetition, confirmation.

Disagrees, shows passive rejection, formality, withholds help.

The observer tallies responses moment by moment. Noting who makes each remark and its approximate time, he can keep a full record of the interplay of thought and emotion. An "interaction recorder" with a motor-driven tape has been designed to facilitate recording. Later analysis can trace the emergence of conflict and other group processes.

Anecdotal records. Objective counts and tabulations are well suited to research, but of limited value for individual guidance. Anecdotal records escape— as in the case of the Stones—the bleakness of quantitative reports. The observer is free to note any action that appears significant, rather than having to concentrate on the same traits for everyone. Often the anecdotes report incidents noted by a teacher or supervisor in daily contacts.

In an anecdotal record, the observer describes exactly what he observed, keeping interpretation and fact as separate as he can. The record is made promptly, to eliminate errors of recall. Cumulated over a period of time, the incidents provide a richer picture of behavior than any other equally simple technique. The following are typical anecdotal reports:

Paul, after projecting the film for the class, took it back to the office (where I happened to be) to rewind. He is not very skilled, and missed his timing, so that much of the film cascaded onto the floor instead of going onto the takeup reel. John came up just then and said something sarcastic about Paul's clumsiness. Paul gave no answer, but kept on at work with no change of manner and a stolid face. Richard, who had been watching Paul, turned on John, told him to "shut up and give Paul a chance," and muttered something about "some of these kids make me sick." (Paul seems to suppress emotion; he certainly heard John's very unpleasant tone.)

Joan spent the entire science period wandering from group to group instead of helping Rose as she was expected to. She interrupted many of the others, telling them they were doing the work wrong. She asked a lot of (foolish) questions ("Does filter paper make certain things go through or just keep certain things out?") and was teased a good deal by the boys. By the time Rose was finished she returned; Rose was quite angry, but they made up and Joan helped put things away. But on her first trip to the storeroom she stayed to plate a gold ring with mercury, while Rose made repeated trips with the equipment.

The reporter has two responsibilities: he must select incidents worth reporting, and he must be objective. Both incidents characteristic of the person and striking exceptions to his normal conduct are helpful. The typical incidents provide a more individualized picture than the hackneyed trait names that would otherwise be used—friendly, showing initiative, rude, and so on. Exceptional actions are rarely reported in ratings and general impressions, but they too are significant. A single incident showing interest in the company's welfare from a man known as a troublemaker, or a sign of enthusiasm for learning on the part of a boy who rebels against school, may be the key to a new and successful treatment. The observer must weed out value judgments and interpretations, attempting to report the exact occurrences, including significant preceding events and environmental conditions. One can never report "everything" about the incident. The reporter selects for his record the facts he considers relevant.

Single anecdotes tell little. As anecdotes accumulate, however, they fill in a picture of the person's habits. If a particular response is typical, it will recur. An effective method of determining personality characteristics is to search through the anecdotes about the individual to detect repetitions. A summary based on these recurring patterns usually requires confirmation by further directed observation.

28. *What do you think really happened in scene (4)? Which observer came closest to adequate reporting of it?*

29. *Which of the numbered scenes appears to give the most significant information about Robert? How many of the observers reported that information?*

30. *Did the observers of the film about Robert succeed in identifying and marking all their judgments and hypotheses?*

31. *Do the observers of the film about Robert ever disagree, or are the differences entirely due to omissions and oversights?*

32. *A clinical psychologist asks a parent how well his 6-year-old child gets along with other children. Illustrate how each of the following errors might operate:*
   a. *The observer has not observed an adequate sample for judging typical behavior.*
   b. *The observer notices events that fit his preconceived notions.*
   c. *The observer is likely to note the behaviors he considers significant and to ignore others of equal importance.*
   d. *The observer may give a faulty interpretation to an event.*

33. *What advantages and disadvantages would a checklist or schedule have for each of the following purposes, compared to a one-paragraph descriptive report?*
   a. *A social agency wishes its visitor to report the condition of homes of its clients, including furnishings, conveniences, and neatness.*
   b. *A department store sends shoppers to be served by its clerks and to observe their procedure and manner.*
   c. *A state requires an observation of the applicant's driving before issuing a license to drive.*

SUGGESTED READINGS

Biber, Barbara E., & others. Recording spontaneous behaviors. *Life and ways of the seven-year-old.* New York: Basic Books, 1952. Pp. 33–53.

An account of procedures used in 10-minute schoolroom observations, together with illustrative anecdotal records and evidence of observer reliability.

Gronlund, Norman E. Validity of sociometric results. *Sociometry in the classroom.* New York: Harper & Row, 1959. Pp. 158–188.

A review of studies shows how sociometric choices of school children relate to observed behavior, teacher opinions, and adjustment.

Lindzey, Gardner, and Byrne, Donn. Measurement of social choice and interpersonal attractiveness. In G. Lindzey and E. Aronson (Eds.), *Handbook of social psychology,* Vol. II. Cambridge, Mass.: Addison-Wesley, 1968. Pp. 452–455.

A comprehensive summary of the major sociometric techniques. Includes reports of correlations between sociometric evidence and other measures of personality.

Prescott, Daniel A. Interpreting behavior. *The child in the educative process.* New York: McGraw-Hill, 1957. Pp. 99–150.

Anecdotal records collected on one boy throughout a school year are compared to show consistencies and deviations from his normal pattern. The discussion shows how teachers form and test hypotheses when they use such records as a case-study technique. Several other chapters in the book also give useful information on the collection of anecdotal information.

Taylor, James B. Rating scales as measures of clinical judgment: a method for increasing scale reliability and sensitivity. *Educational and Psychological Measurement,* 1968, 28, 747–766.

A review of problems in previous rating scales, a proposal for a new kind of anchored procedure, and a demonstration of its value in clinical work.

Tuddenham, Read D. Studies in reputation: II. The diagnosis of social adjustment. *Psychological Monographs,* 1952, 66, No. 1.

Reports on school children obtained by the nomination technique can be used for personality analysis. Five illustrative records are interpreted.

Weick, K. E. Systematic observational methods. In G. Lindzey and E. Aronson (Eds.), *Handbook of social psychology.* Vol. II. Cambridge, Mass.: Addison-Wesley, 1968. Pp. 357–451.

An encyclopaedic account of problems in observation and means for overcoming them. Emphasis is placed on techniques for studying social interaction.

18

Performance Tests of Personality

We now come to one of the least organized, least complete, but most active areas of research in differential psychology. Performance tests of personality have a long history; they entered even into Binet's earliest attempts to find out how the bright differ from the dull. To stretch the point, one might even use modern concepts to argue that the slow reactions of the astronomer Kinnebrook (see p. 197) were expressing a play-it-safe style, and hence that Bessel's studies of differences in reaction time were really studies of personality.

The evolution of performance tests was set back by a premature attempt to use the tests practically. During the first half of this century, validation studies destroyed ill-founded hopes for one technique after another, and interest in the whole approach waned. The results, even when illuminating for theory, often disappointed the investigator by undermining the interpretation with which he had confidently begun. For example, the excellent Hartshorne-May procedures for observing actions related to character were virtually abandoned when the data persuaded these workers that character is not unified and that, therefore, one cannot "measure character." In this and similar instances, modern research is reopening supposedly settled questions. Performance tests of personality now play a large role in research on the development, social psychology, motivations, and regulating systems of normals. A somewhat different subset of the tests are equally important in the study of disturbed patients.

A measuring procedure will have lasting use only if developed through long and careful validation. The instrument constructed on a hunch is likely to be unreliable, perhaps hard to score, very likely to be interpreted in terms of a single trait even though the determiners of performance are many. When the basic hunch has some validity, continued self-critical research can shape an observing procedure that does get sound and interpretable data. Although persistent research on a single type of measure has been rare, a number of continued programs are now bearing fruit.

Even in these studies, the investigator all too commonly concentrates on a single measuring procedure, perhaps one no other investigator has used. As we have said several times, a construct interpretation is hard to defend when research employs only a single indicator, as a single measure can be given conflicting interpretations. Quite commonly a personality test is left in whatever form the inspiration of its creator gave it. Consequently, as the Murphys (1960, p. 341) have said, many of the tests "are still essentially 'sonnets' or 'essays' in the literary style of individual psychologists." Each of these creators has his faithful disciples who carry on a conversation with each other rather than with the whole of psychology.

When the theory of intelligence was confused and primitive in the first quarter of the century, Binet's scale provided a common starting point, conceptual and methodological, for all workers. Out of this exchange of views came a much clearer theory regarding the nature and growth of ability. Such an advance can happen in the personality area, but only slowly, as no one construct will be as central as Binet's.

There is no construct and no performance test of salient importance in the personality field. Worse than that, there are thousands of candidate tests: R. B. Cattell's laboratory alone measures 21 supposed factors by using 412 performance-test procedures and deriving 2366 scores from them (Cattell & Warburton, 1967). This book can describe only enough tests to show the range of approaches. Among the performance tests this chapter describes projective tests, and also returns to the subject of inferences about personality from ability tests; there is no sharp distinction between the classes of tests. This chapter stresses performance tests as quantitative measuring instruments. Such tests are also used for impressionistic assessment, being integrated with other data into a portrait or evaluation of the whole person; the validity of integrative assessment is the topic of Chapter 19.

We may contrast the performance test with the time-sampling method of observation. The limitations of time sampling come from its high cost and from the fact that scores depend upon the situations in which the subject happens to be observed. What the subject is trying to do is under no experimental control. It has been the great dream of personality testers to get quantitative reports that directly summarize behavior rather than biased impressions, and that compare individuals in a *standard* situation.

A performance test is an observation of what the person does (not just of "how well" he does) in a standard task. The task is designed to elicit a particular type of response. One trait of great interest, for example, is the control and expression of aggression. It is difficult to judge this by observing the daily life of most subjects, because a person is only occasionally in an aggression-provoking situation. Therefore, testers have developed standardized procedures for annoying the subject, such as administering a standard interview and condemning the opinions the person voices. How a subject reacts may be more revealing than several hours of observation in uncontrolled circumstances. The purpose of such testing is concealed; hence the tester is ethically required to follow it by a frank conversation that explains the deception and allows the subject to discharge his feelings. Even with this safeguard, some psychologists consider the procedure ethically indefensible (Kelman, 1967). A slightly different style of performance test arranges special circumstances in an everyday context. For example, to get good evidence of readiness to act aggressively, classes of boys were led during their sports period to play a game for which facilities were so limited that only half of them could play at any one time. The frequency of observable aggression was much higher than in normal time-sampling (Winder & Wiggins, 1964).

Galton once compared psychological testing to the geologist's "sinking shafts at critical points" to obtain samples of significant material. Ratings return surface impressions. The time sample sinks its shaft entirely at random. But the performance test provokes exhibitions of significant behavior. The usual features of such a test are as follows:

● Standardization. The stimulus situation is highly controlled, reproducible, and applicable in a nearly uniform manner to all subjects.

● Disguise. The subject is led to believe that one characteristic is being tested while the observer is actually observing some other aspect of performance. In effect, a definite task is set. For example, "Pick the funniest jokes in this collection." This inquiry may be disguised as a study of the jokes, purporting not to be a measure of the individual. And the score is based on the type of joke the subject picks (e.g., hostile), not on whether he picks the ones usually considered funny.

● Specificity of concern. The investigator is interested in one or more distinctly labeled traits. The hypothesized trait is much more sharply conceptualized than the good, strong, active dimensions that predominate in self ratings; sometimes the construct is narrowed to a very limited kind of situation.

● Multivariate data. The observer makes records of the subject's method of performance, rather than noting only the amount performed.

An example is the Operational Stress technique. To assess whether a man entering pilot training can resist pressure, the candidate is subjected to stress-producing stimuli during an apparatus test. The apparatus has controls (pedal, throttle, stick, and various levers) that the man resets as signal lights change. The time required to react to each signal is recorded electrically. The examinee is told that he will be observed by a concealed observer "just as a checkpilot will rate you in flying." Administration is standardized: 1 minute of rest and anticipation, 1 minute of directions regarding signals and controls, and three short test periods. In each period, the examinee is given increasingly reproving "stress directions" while he is busily moving levers. In test period C, the pattern of lights changes six times, at intervals of about 15 seconds, while the examiner is delivering the following speech in an urgent manner: "Don't make lights flicker on and off. Be steady. . . . Quit making errors. You aren't moving fast enough. . . . More speed. . . . Hurry and stop the clock. . . . Last chance. . . . Set controls quickly. . . . You are still making errors." The concealed observer, meanwhile, makes extensive ratings of manner and reaction to criticism. Objective clock scores are also recorded (Guilford, 1947, pp. 660–664; Melton, 1947, pp. 811–814).

The test observation reveals characteristics infrequent in normal activities— bravery, reaction to frustration, dishonesty, etc. Second, desire to make a good impression does not invalidate the test. In fact, the subject anxious to make a good impression reveals himself. It is necessary, however, to take this motivation into account in interpretation. Third, the performance test comes closer than other techniques to comparing subjects under identical conditions.

Performance tests vary greatly in design. The test may be a strictly psychometric instrument measuring one narrowly defined construct such as persistence in routine work. It may yield scores on persistence and cautiousness and tempo simultaneously. It may be a basis for evaluation of the person's total life-style. It may be a worksample of a specific prospective assignment, or a cross section of behavior without reference to any single assignment.

The tasks range from highly structured to almost totally unstructured. A situation is structured if it has for all subjects a definite meaning. An unstructured situation presents so few cues or has so little pattern that he can give it almost any meaning. The strange sound in the night is unstructured. Is it the wind? a burglar? a cat? The interpretation one makes is strongly influenced by his interests, by fears conscious and unconscious, and, of course, by knowledge. In a structured situation, the subject knows exactly what he is expected to do and how he is expected to do it. In the unstructured situation, he guides himself. The more ambiguous the situation, the more opportunity there is for individual interpretation both of the stimuli and the task. As an extremely unstructured situation, one investigator simply turned the subject loose in a studio equipped with all types of art media and materials, with little more instruction than "You may do anything you like with these." Both actions and products were evaluated.

Highly structured tasks are excellent for measuring ability just because they force everyone to try the same thing. Projective tasks, at the opposite extreme, provide little structure. The projective test is so named because it permits the subject to project into the situation his unconscious thoughts, wishes, and fears. The householder who interprets the creak in the dark as a burglar may be more anxious than a man who interprets the same stimulus as a natural phenomenon and goes back to sleep.

There is no obvious classification to be used in organizing this chapter. Whatever categories we adopt to sort performance tests, there is some investigator whose work cuts across them. Indeed, any single test fits various descriptions. The Binet is an ability test; it is a chance to observe impulsiveness and other traits under standard conditions; and it is a projective test—e.g., when antisocial content of responses is noted. We shall organize the chapter primarily according to types of behavior investigated.

A few methodological distinctions will be a useful preliminary. Here is one possible category system:

A. *Given with maximum-performance directions.* The subject is given an explicit task which he is led to construe as an ability test on which he should do well. In his eyes, the task calls for his maximum performance.

 Aa. *Direct ability measure.* The test is scored along the lines indicated in the directions to the subject. That is, the examiner defines maximum performance just as the subject does. Examples: the Operational Stress clock score; the old Downey measure of self-control in which the subject is told to write his name as slowly as he can; EFT; the Stroop Color-Word Test (p. 625). The interpretation of the score usually goes beyond a statement of competence; to consider a low Porteus score as a sign of impulsiveness is to go beyond "ability" measurement.

 Ab. *Vehicle for observation of style or associations.* The test is used as a vehicle for observing traits other than maximum performance, such as emotional upset in the Operational Stress test. The subject may or may not realize what the examiner is observing. Even when he does realize, he cannot reasonably try to do anything other than maximize the performance the directions called for. A second example is where the examiner interprets the nature of the errors made in Block Design as an indicator of intellectual style.

 Ac. *Disguised.* An example is the cheating test (p. 615), in which the child is told to show how well he can do some task, and is given a chance to increase his score by cheating. The directions are camouflage. The examiner is not interested in the performance the subject is told to maximize. If the subject knew this he might display some other quality, even at the expense of a good "ability" score.

B. *Given without explicit instructions to do well.* The subject may be given an assignment, but only in general terms, with an indication that "there are no right answers." The situation may be set up like a field observation, perhaps with the observer behind a one-way mirror; the subject may believe that he is entirely free to do what he wishes.

This is not a rigorous system. A test such as TAT (p. 651) has a little of every quality in it. The subject is asked to make up a story about a picture, with the understanding that no two people produce the same story; in this respect it seems to fit the B category. But it is usually also understood to be a test of imagination, and that fits the A category. Imaginativeness is observed (Aa), but much more weight is given to the character of responses (e.g., content of response to a picture on an authority theme); that emphasis is of type Ab.

Type A tests do a reasonably good job of standardizing mental set and motivation. In some disguised procedures of types Ab and Ac, however, the experimenter must interpret his data in full awareness that the subjects are onto his game and the validity of the method is compromised. For example, conformity procedures test whether a subject will give a sensible response when others around him (perhaps voices played into the testing booth from a tape) have put forward an answer he cannot believe:

(Q.) "What per cent of Americans go to church every Sunday?"

(A.—heard from others before he states his own belief) "92 per cent."

Stricker, Messick, and Jackson (1967) questioned adolescents after they had been through such a procedure. Roughly 60 per cent suspected the purpose of what had been presented as a straight-forward measure of opinions. Specimen comment: "[I think the purpose was] to see if we would conform with the ridiculous average answers and if they influenced us any." Interestingly, the suspicious boys are those who fake-good on questionnaires, and the suspicious girls are naysayers on questionnaires. Nowadays, a "naive subject" is hard to find.

We cannot point to any one "official" version of a performance test; rarely is there a manual collating data for any such test. The Cattell-Warburton catalog might ultimately standardize test procedures, but one writer in this field is rarely able to persuade a majority of investigators to adopt precisely his procedure for a test. McClelland (1957, p. 53) is right to say: "To a very considerable extent, the disagreement among theoretical psychologists in the field of personality arises from the fact that they are dealing with different data to start with and cannot use each other's concepts." This also means that a summary statement regarding any category of tests or any trait is likely to oversimplify.

1. *In each of the following enterprises, would it be preferable to employ observations in natural conditions, or standardized observations where conditions are fixed in advance and identical for all subjects?*
    a. *The telephone company wishes to rate its operators on courtesy and clarity of speech. It is able to tap conversations and make recordings.*
    b. *Navy personnel are to be screened for tendency to panic under conditions of extreme noise, as in amphibious landings.*
    c. *An investigator wishes to study the habitual recklessness of 7-year-old boys in climbing and jumping.*
2. *To what extent may each of the following be considered an unstructured stimulus?*
    a. *A teacher, during an examination, glances up from her desk and barely observes a hasty movement of one boy who is pulling his hand into his lap from the aisle.*
    b. *In duplicate bridge, the same set of hands is played at every table.*
    c. *A questionnaire is designed to obtain information about age, income, education, etc. All possible answers are anticipated and presented on the blank in multiple-choice form.*
3. *To what extent is each of the following unstructured? If the test is at all unstructured, discuss whether that is an advantage or a disadvantage.*
    a. *Stanford-Binet test, Memory for Sentences.*

    b. *Wechsler Comprehension test.*

    c. *A test of addition presents in random order the combinations up to 9 + 9, the pupil being directed to do as many items as he can in the time allowed.*

    d. *In the Porteus test (Figure 2.1), the subject is to solve a maze. The time it takes him to trace the correct path with his pencil is scored.*

4. *Classify the following as A or B, and, if A, in the subcategories.*

    a. *The continuous addition test asks the subject to add a row of one-digit numbers, going as far as he can in 1 minute. Then he immediately starts a new row. There are 15 rows. Interpretation is based on the shape of the work curve; e.g., on whether amount completed fluctuates from minute to minute, whether there is a drop after the first few minutes, etc.*

    b. *The Winder-Wiggins measure of aggression on the sports field.*

    c. *The Wallach drawing measure of constrictedness of graphic expression (p. 563).*

    d. *A preschool child is asked to learn to assemble a wooden gasoline station. The teacher shows him what to do, but does a number of things not included in the oral directions and not essential to the task—for example, storing the box under the table before proceeding, laying all the pumps side by side in parallel at the outset, etc. The number of these incidental acts copied by the child when his turn comes is taken as a measure of dependency.*

5. *Classify the following tests as well as you can in terms of the categories outlined above.*

    a. *The tendency of a person to "repress" certain threatening ideas is measured by exposing words in a tachistoscope. Any one word is exposed very briefly and then again at increasing exposures until the person reads it. Into a list of neutral words are mixed a number of words related to sex, aggression, or some other possibly threatening topic. The score is the difference in exposure required between neutral and loaded words.*

    b. *Persistence is measured by determining how long a person remains at work on a college final examination when he may leave as early as he chooses.*

    c. *An "in-basket" test presents a person with an array of information about a job he is supposed to fill: the community, the organization he works for, his associates, his responsibilities, etc. Then (under some time pressure) he is to work through the correspondence, memos, etc., in his basket, disposing of each by a referral, a direct reply or instruction to his staff, or by disregarding it. His performance is judged in terms of the soundness of his judgment, what priorities he assigns, and what style (e.g., buck-passing, tendency to "call a meeting," etc.) he displays.*

Character

The Character Education Inquiry

This section deals with observations of surface traits that have a direct interpretation: honesty, persistence, etc. While one can look behind the data to the underlying personality—Why was Javert persistent in the extreme? Was his zeal pathological?—the scores have significance simply as behavior samples.

The Character Education Inquiry of Hartshorne and May (1928, 1929, 1930) was a remarkable extended effort to evaluate personality of school children by strictly quantitative and objective methods. "Typical behavior" involving character cannot be extensively observed in everyday life, and self-reports are surely distorted. Valid appraisal requires that we observe response to temptation when the person believes he can violate standards without detection. Hartshorne and May had strictly a research aim; data were not used to make decisions about the pupils.

Honesty in a situation involving prestige was tested by a supposed ability test. The child was asked to place marks in small circles while keeping his eyes closed. It was impossible to do well. Many children turned in "successful performances" that could have been obtained only by opening their eyes.

Honesty with money was tested by arranging an arithmetic lesson in which each pupil had to use a boxful of coins. The box provided for each pupil was secretly identified. At the end of the lesson each pupil carried his own box to a pile in front of the room. Unaware that boxes could be identified, many pupils took advantage of the opportunity to keep some money.

Maller (J. McV. Hunt, 1944) tells us that the Hartshorne-May findings on character led one national agency working with youth to revise its program completely, because the study showed that those who had received most recognition in the agency's character-building activities were on the average *most* likely to cheat. This is not hard to explain when we consider that striving for recognition in competition, and working hard on a puzzle, may stem from the same basic feeling of inadequacy.

Motivation to put forth effort has been of particular interest because it is thought of as the link between aptitude and achievement. The employer, the teacher, the clinician, and all other users of tests wish they could predict whether a person's behavior will bear out the promise shown in tests of ability. Many investigators have explored possible performance tests. Hartshorne and May tested how long children persist as a task becomes difficult. Pupils read a story which builds to a climax: "Again the terrible piercing shriek of the whistle screamed at them. Charles could see the frightened face of the engineer. . . ." Here the examiner tells them that if they wish to learn the ending they must read the difficult printed material that follows:

CHARLESLIFTEDLUCILLETOHISBACK"PUTYOURARMSTIGHT
AROUNDMYNECKANDHOLDON

. . . .

NoWhoWTogETBaCkoNthETREStle.HoWTOBRingTHaTTErrIFIED
BURDeNOFACHiLDuPtO

. . . .

fiN ALly 'tAp-taP'C AME' ARHYTH Month e ' BriD GeruNNing' fee Tfee
TéomING

The pupil separates each word with a vertical mark as he deciphers it; the amount deciphered is an index of persistent effort (Hartshorne & May, 1928, p. 292). The ambiguity of single tests is nicely illustrated by this task. Does it measure interest in adventure stories? compulsiveness in following directions? tolerance for annoyance? enjoyment of an intellectual challenge? or mostly reading skill and fluid ability?

Derivatives of the Hartshorne-May procedures are used today, e.g., in research concerned with the influence of models and of persuasion. Thus Bandura and Whalen (1966) arranged for children to win coins in a game, and gave them the option of depositing some of their winnings in a box as a contribution to orphans. Child models, coached to drop in some of their winnings, were used with some subjects; their action stimulated other children to do the same. (For the tester, this is a reminder that what a subject does in a performance test will be altered if he can observe what other subjects are doing. These influences are probably especially strong in character tests.)

6. *Class the Hartshorne-May tests as Aa, Ab, etc.*
7. *If Bill does better than Fred on the circle-dotting test of honesty, what conclusions can be drawn about Bill's character?*
8. *Joe is a known delinquent, having gotten into trouble together with a gang of boys for several minor thefts and disturbances. How can you explain the fact that he does well on all the tests of honesty, cooperation, and generosity?*
9. *Analyze the story-completion test of persistence, identifying all the external conditions which might cause one 5th-grader to earn a higher score than another.*
10. *Children from homes with low socioeconomic status cheat more on achievement tests than other children: $r = 0.49$ (Hartshorne & May, 1928). How safe is it to conclude that these children are more likely to violate other standards of good conduct?*

Moral-Conflict Problems

Verbal tests of moral judgment share characteristics of general-ability tests, self-report, and projective techniques. The stimulus material is usually a story in which the central figure is torn between courses of action serving different ends, or commits an act that violates some standard of conduct. The question may take such forms as, "What should he do? Why?" "What would *you* do?" or "How do you think he felt?" Or the subject may be asked simply to complete the story. Such methods have been used by Hartshorne and May, by Binet, by Piaget, and many others. While moral judgment is of interest in itself, it is also an indicator of mental ability. When such items are used in a mental test they usually have a conventional answer; when the aim is to study moral concepts, each item must pose a dilemma.

In most of these procedures, there is no disguise; the subject can clearly see that a moral problem is being posed. In a typical Piaget procedure, two children are described; the subject is to decide whose behavior is more open to condemnation, and explain. Here the issue is honesty (Piaget, 1932, p. 119) :

Alfred meets a little friend of his who is very poor. This friend tells him that he has had no dinner that day because there was nothing to eat in his home. Then Alfred goes into a baker's shop, and as he has no money, he waits till the baker's back is turned and steals a roll. Then he runs out and gives the roll to his friend.

Henrietta goes into a shop. She sees a pretty piece of ribbon on a table and thinks to herself that it would look very nice on her dress. So while the shop lady's back is turned, she steals the ribbon and runs away at once.

Young children's responses show a failure to grasp what the adult sees as the crucial difference. Some of them censure Alfred more because rolls are costlier than ribbon, or the roll is bigger; the criterion is damage done, without regard to justification. The older child is ready to credit the boy with a good motive, while criticizing the act.

Piaget elaborated data such as this into a theory of the sequential development of moral judgment comparable to his theory of intellectual development; indeed, he sees the two developmental processes as similar and intertwined. A summary of the theory, and an evaluation in terms of relatively recent work, is offered by Kohlberg (1964). It is evident that one could develop a "moral intellect" scale comparable to that of Binet for general ability. Moral development, according to Kohlberg, correlates 0.31 with IQ; it is more closely related to age and experience than to mental age.

The usual problems of validity are intensified here. It is unclear, especially with children, whether the subject is being asked to display righteousness, intelligence, or honest feelings. While writers rarely suggest that the answers indicate what the child really would do if he were placed in a conflict like that described, this leap can easily be made by the unwary interpreter. The techniques are appropriate to study intellectual development and socialization. Every finding linking such responses to antecedent conditions (e.g., to parent attitudes) paves the way to better explanatory constructs.

Pittel and Mendelsohn (1966) provide a historical review and critique of the procedures in this class (dating back to 1894). They note certain faults or hazards that have appeared with discomforting frequency. Many procedures assess knowledge of approved standards, not the individual's own attitude. "Right" responses are usually determined by current social norms; this is scarcely a basis for inferring moral judgment or conscience. Questions often ask about abstractions such as "stealing" rather than about specific acts under specific conditions. Mitigating factors are then left out of account; "the subject is asked to do something in the test situation which he would never do in real life." There is poor coverage of the areas in which morality can be demonstrated; theft receives a good deal more attention than malicious gossip.

Pittel and Mendelsohn favor an attempt to study the subject's own perception and evaluation of realistic conflict problems. What issues is he aware of? What sympathies does he express? How strong is his defense or condemnation of an act? These questions can be investigated independent of and prior to the comparison of the subject's verdict with that of current social rules.

11. *The question asked in Piaget's research, conducted in Switzerland, was "Ces enfants, sont ils la même chose vilain?" The translator appends this comment:*
    "While . . . we have translated vilain by 'naughty,' the reader should note that the English word has an exclusively authoritarian ring which the French has not. Children can only be naughty in reference to grown-ups. Indeed, the word is so powerful a weapon in the hands of adult constraint that its use in any verbal experiments in English would probably give appreciably different results from those based on the word vilain." (Elsewhere, she equates vilain with "horrid.")
    What changes in response might come from alternative translations in American experiments?

Problems of Design and Validity

With the example of character tests before us, we can discuss the evaluation of performance measures. The ultimate contribution of a procedure depends primarily on whether a theoretical explanation for it can be worked out, but that takes a long time. A theoretical advance suggests ways to refine the test, and an improvement in the test gets data that suggests ways to refine the theory. Examining a new procedure in its primitive form, one cannot say whether it will ultimately make a contribution.

Certain types of statistical research enter into the evaluation and improvement of nearly all performance tests. An ideal performance test of personality would satisfy the standards implied by this list of questions (though how close a test should come to the ideal depends on the use intended).

• Does the test obtain an accurate measure of performance averaged over the universe of tasks like this, and over all occasions within this period of the subject's life?

• Are the scores stable over a reasonable period of time?

• Is there convergence between the scores and those from other tasks that appraise the same trait?

• Can the scores be explained in part by traits other than the one stressed in the interpretation? In particular, does ability influence the score? The desired answer is "No"—if "Yes," can a statistical correction be made? Does the corrected score satisfy the questions above?

• Are the score interpretations consistent with field observations, case histories, etc.?

Consistency over Forms and Trials

The performance test is likely to be less accurate than other procedures. The test is often brief. Among the character tests described above, the entire box-of-coins tests consists of a single item that the subject passes or fails. The cheating-on-circles test has many "items," in the sense that we could count how many small circles have been dotted, but the decision to open one's eyes and cheat is a single decision. The whole test is really a single "item"—i.e., only one critical act determines the score. This probably accounts for the low magnitude of many correlations between performance tests. Some of the tests may be highly valid, within the limits imposed by this inadequacy of sampling.

Sampling of occasions is inadequate. An event such as a regular school examination alters anxiety, motivation to achieve, and hostility, etc., and alters scores on performance tests of personality given the same day. Scores may also vary with the personality, sex, age, etc., of the examiner.

To estimate the magnitude of such inconsistencies requires a generalizability study with, as a minimum, two forms of the test given on two days, preferably by examiners who convey different impressions. Split-half analysis of a single test does not give enough information. Nor are two tests given in succession necessarily equivalent; the experience of taking the personality test can alter retest performance, probably to a greater degree than in other tests. In one study a laboratory conformity procedure was administered; a week or so later there was a second test, with a lower degree of pressure to conform. Some conformers shifted to nonconformity on the second test. The ones who did not change, the confirmed conformers, had personalities markedly different from those who conformed on the first day only. The one-shot test was not a good measure (Steiner & Vannoy, 1966).

A stability study requires two well-separated testings, usually with alternate forms, each form being given first to half the subjects. For cheating tests there were retest correlations of 0.75 over 6 months and 0.37 between early adolescence and adulthood (Hartshorne & May, 1928, II, 88–89; V. Jones, 1946). We expect character to change, hence these results are satisfactory. Moreover, they suggest that the cheating test is reasonably accurate.

12. *What types of error in character tests do split-half correlations ignore?*
13. *For which performance tests of character would administration of half-tests on 2 days, a week apart, give adequate data on generalizability?*
14. *What would be gained, in a study of child development, by administering a moral-judgment test to each child in a class on a different day?*

Generalization Over Tasks

The trait mentioned in test interpretation is ordinarily broad. We discuss "cheating," not "cheating in a test of two-digit multiplication." To sustain the broad interpretation we must find correlations of reasonable size between measures of cheating in various school subjects and cheating in tasks not related to school. To sustain a still-broader interpretation in terms of "good character," cheating scores must correlate with scores on honesty with money, etc.

Each task has its specific elements. A general measure has to be built up by combining several tasks, each containing the same common element along with different specifics. Preferably, these tasks would be administered on different days. Hartshorne and May (1930) established that a general trait cannot be measured by one or two specific samples. Although each deception test was generalizable over forms and time, tasks correlated little with each other. The correlation between cheating on a classroom test and on the Circles test was only 0.50 even after correction for sampling errors. While the correlations are positive and support the idea of a weak general-honesty factor (Burton, 1963), they contradict the notion that honesty is unified. Furthermore, honesty, cooperation, and so on intercorrelated only about 0.25, making untenable the view that a generalized "good character" accounts for desirable actions. Whatever "general factor" there may be in character has small influence on any one type of behavior.

Likewise for persistence (Thornton, 1939; MacArthur, 1955). MacArthur obtained 21 measures on English schoolboys, all the tests being presumed to have something to do with persistence. Intercorrelations were largely insignificant, though some were in the range of 0.50 to 0.60. The general factor accounted for only 14 per cent of test performance. Combining eight scores could provide a meaningful measure of general persistence with a coefficient of generalizability of 0.79. MacArthur also found four group factors. One factor linked tests on which the pupil had a chance to see if his classmates were still hard at work (in contrast to those for which each had to set his own standards). This he called "social suggestibility in situations demanding persistence." Reputation measures formed a second group factor. Other factors were for persistence on intellectual tasks and persistence on physical tasks. Persistence is to a large degree situational.

Accepting this, we remind the reader that in a sense every performance test is a single "item," a single sample of behavior. The correlations between Stanford-Binet items in a single age group rarely exceed 0.25, and within a single test such as Wechsler Comprehension correlations are no higher. One could easily defend the view that character is just as consistent as mental ability, though it takes longer to arrange the scene to obtain one observation on character.

The investigator needs to know how stable scores are, over situations and over time. When personality is conceived in terms of broad traits such as "dominance," a measure that is not generalizable is irrelevant. What is the good of observing that Mary tends to boss the other 2nd-graders when they are planning a playlet, if that is not characteristic of her behavior in other activities? For the trait-theorist, this can at best make up one element in a battery of measures that, taken together, provide a global measure of dominance. Such a composite measure is generalizable; that is, one broad sample agrees with another. One can do interesting research on, for example, the home background of high and low scorers. But the score gives little insight into the individual, nor does it tell us when to expect the person to show dominant behavior.

A performance measure does not have to be highly generalizable or unchangeable to be useful. A well-designed performance measure is used perhaps more profitably to investigate variability within the person. If we set up five situations in which Mary might show dominance, her change from situation to situation may tell us a great deal. The requirement is that performance be generalizable over other situations of the same narrow type. One interprets, not a broad trait of "dominance," but a narrow trait such as "dominance over peers in a nonacademic task when no adult is participating." The very fact that her performance in such settings is consistently different from her performance elsewhere is significant. The same reasoning is employed when a person makes up stories to fit various pictures, and, upon encountering a picture with a sexual theme, uncharacteristically makes false starts, becomes incoherent, and finally produces a bland, stereotyped story. The conclusion that sex is a conflict area for him cannot be taken seriously unless we know that behavior of this kind *is* generalizable over pictures of the same sort, on various testings. A third example of capitalizing on the variability of performance measures is the study of drug effects. Changes in the level of scores and in ranks of individuals are meaningful if similar changes are observed when the same drug is administered on another occasion. What one wants, as a minimum, is a measure that shows respectable consistency from one application to another when there has been no intervening attempt to change the person.

The term *experimental analysis of behavior* is applied to much current research of this kind (Bachrach, 1962; Krasner & Ullman, 1965). The essential tactic is to vary stimulus conditions and record precisely the responses of the subject, in the Skinnerian manner. Changes from the base level during a session indicate that the experimenter has applied a significant stimulus. Such reproducible measures are particularly valuable for comparing behavior after therapeutic intervention against pretreatment behavior. One must, as usual, be cautious in interpreting change on any single indicator; it is much better to have consistent evidence from two or more superficially different tests.

This approach has affinities to the idiographic conception of the personality discussed earlier (p. 562) and to the analysis of the subject as perceiver (p. 598). (See Mischel, 1968, and D. R. Peterson, 1968.) Just as George Kelly and his followers concern themselves with the subject's perception of significant others in his life, so experimenters concerned with interpersonal behavior look at each significant figure as a distinctive stimulus. It becomes important to appraise the child's response to his mother's commands, not his obedience or submissiveness in general. But generalization is still intended—not over stimulus persons, but over commands of different types, when the child is in various moods. The argument of the behavior analyst is not that personality has no consistency, but that the classes over which one generalizes must be constructed to fit observations on the individual. This kind of thinking is central to clinical treatment and, in one form or other, has always been. Freud derived general personality theory from idiographic analyses, and very likely some of the experimental analysts will. Past research with performance measures, however, has almost always been framed in terms of the nomothetic, broad-trait model.

Control for Ability and Other Competing Constructs

One tends to think of a personality trait as independent of ability, but the two interpenetrate in perplexing ways. The child who can do his schoolwork does not need to cheat; does his failure to cheat imply honesty? One should always be aware of the possibility that ability accounts for score differences, and sometimes it makes sense to adjust scores so as to remove the ability effect.

Thus one might pretest children on arithmetic to form, say, five ability groups, and give each group a test that causes its members considerable difficulty. Then all children are given some incentive to cheat. With or without this procedure, the research worker ought to make a separate analysis at each ability level. Cheating by a student with a good school record has a different and probably more pathological significance than cheating by an inept student; likewise for anxiety, drive to excel, etc. Separate analyses by ability level have rarely been made; this may account for many negative or contradictory results.

Sometimes statistical corrections are suggested. One might take the difference between the child's moral-judgment score and the average score of children with the same MA. (A regression line is used for this.)

Age groups have to be treated separately. Sex also conditions the significance of many performance-test scores. Hence the investigator has to establish the meaning of his test for cases of each age and sex.

When a personality test confounds a trait with other variables—and this is nearly inevitable—one wants to be sure that the *independent portion* is accurately measured and stable. How much of the 6-month stability of cheating scores results because low achievement is stable, so that the same children have an incentive to cheat? Such questions have not been examined.

15. *It has been suggested that the general factor running through honesty tests may be an indication, not of honesty, but of willingness to accept risk of detection and punishment. Is it possible to design unambiguous tests so as to settle this issue?*

16. *If 9-year-old boys are sorted out on MA and moral judgment by dividing at the medians, what personalities would you expect in the High-High, Low-Low, High-Low, and Low-High groups?*

17. *A boy and girl, each with age 12, IQ 14, score the same on a test of judgment regarding aggressive conflicts. Do their scores have the same meaning?*

Perception

Many investigators have suggested a link between personality and simple perceptual processes. They may emphasize underlying biochemical and neural processes not under voluntary control, or ways in which the perceiver deliberately copes with his environment, or differences in sensitivity presumed to reflect unconscious emotional defenses. These views lead investigators in very different directions, and there is little coherent, well-supported theory. There is, however, ample evidence that perception, even in the psychophysical laboratory, expresses personality.

Psychophysiological Measures

If the organism is an information-processing system, simple perceptual tests will identify some of its operating characteristics. These tests are analogous to the test performed by an electronic technician when he puts a perfect sine-wave signal into an amplifier and examines the distorted signal the speaker puts out. This gives the unique "signature" of that particular system. Flicker fusion and apparent movement are examples of similar signatures of the human perceptual system.

When a person views a light flashed on and off electronically (strobotac), he reports flicker at low rates of interruption. At high rates (e.g., the 60-per-second interruption of the usual light bulb), no interruption or flicker is noticed. As the tester increases the rate gradually, the subject reports when he no longer sees flicker. The "fusion threshold" can be precisely measured and individual differences are large.

When two lights, side by side, are flashed alternately in quick succession, the light appears to jump back and forth. This apparent-movement phenomenon is the basis for the traveling light patterns in electrical signs. In apparent movement, as in flicker fusion, the nervous system integrates stimulation into a pattern. One can vary the dark period between flashes. As the interval is reduced there is a threshold at which apparent movement first appears and a second threshold where it disappears—beyond which point the subject sees two steady lights. The separation of these thresholds, i.e., the range of intervals that permit an impression of movement, is much wider for some subjects than others.

The flicker threshold, it has been suggested, indicates the ability of the nervous system to register details of incoming stimulation. For Halstead (1951), fusion

represents a dramatic change in consciousness for the subject. For once he reaches the rate at which separate flashes . . . fuse for him, he cannot tell the unsteady light from a steady one. He has broken with physical reality. The rate is much higher in our normal individuals than in our frontal brain-injured patients. It is as if the mental engine were running in the brain-injured, but running on inadequate power. It fails at the first little hill. . . . It seems clear that the test reflects an important aspect of cerebral metabolism.

Cattell interprets fusion threshold as showing speed of neural processes (those who fuse only at high frequencies having greater "nervous alertness"). His factor analyses relate high thresholds also to impulsive, uncritical reaction, to restlessness, to the ability to perceive rapidly, and to eagerness. He claims that, even though mediated physiologically, the threshold is established by learning. It is, he says, of practical use as a predictor of "active behaviors" including piloting of aircraft (Cattell & Warburton, 1967, pp. 198, 478). As in the case of Guilford's system, we must remain skeptical of these interpretations; factor analysis cannot alone establish validity claims.

There is a good deal of support for using measures of physiological functioning to study changes in physiology that may be relevant to the person's behavior. Flicker-fusion measures help to diagnose brain damage, and serve as one of many dependent variables in experiments on drugs. There is not much support, however, for the view that these internal regulating mechanisms explain the temperament or social reactions of normal persons. Averill and Opton (1968, p. 285) state:

It appears unlikely that normal variations in personality are greatly dependent upon gross constitutional differences. . . . The normal human nervous system has the capacity and the plasticity of accommodate quite diverse personality developments. Constitutional differences may serve as predisposing factors toward, or set biological limits on, the development of certain personality characteristics; but the normal personality is much less the expression of such physiological factors than it is the result of prior experience.

A number of measures of physiological state are used to assess changes in response to stimulation. Heartbeat, respiration, skin conductance, brain-wave patterns, and the like are related to emotional arousal and attentiveness. Investigators have thought in the past that the characteristic level of some of these variables might be an index to degree of chronic anxiety, emotional stability, or to other aspects of personality. In Cattell's laboratory, skin conductance ("psychogalvanic reflex") is measured during a resting, stabilizing period, and then during a sequence of stimuli (20 seconds apart) that starts as follows:

Card with words "frightful terror"
Picture of man and woman kissing
Experimenter drops metal can with tools inside, onto floor behind subject

It is said that inhibited persons are likely to show the greatest change in conductance. But the loadings of conductance measures on the *Inhibition* factor are

Phase 1. Read the words as rapidly as possible.

italic   roman   capitals   italic   capitals   roman   roman

italic   capitals   roman   capitals   roman   italic   roman   italic

Phase 2. Call off the type styles as rapidly as possible.

AAAAAA   *aaaaaa*   aaaaaa   AAAAAA   AAAAAA   *aaaaaa*   aaaaaa
AAAAAA   aaaaaa   *aaaaaa*   aaaaaa   *aaaaaa*   AAAAAA   aaaaaa

Phase 3. Read the words as rapidly as possible.

italic   ROMAN   *capitals*   ITALIC   ROMAN   capitals   *roman*

italic   *capitals*   italic   *roman*   *capitals*   ROMAN   ITALIC

Phase 4. Call off the type styles as rapidly as possible in the selection above.

Figure 18.1. Specimen lines from a test of typeface-word interference based on the pattern of the Stroop Color-Word Test.

around 0.20 (Cattell & Warburton, 1967, p. 471), which implies the merest trace of a connection.

Most investigators would now argue that individual differences in level of physiological functioning or even in amount of change are of anatomical rather than psychological significance. They would prefer to use physiological indices to compare the individual's response to various stimuli, to find out what commands his attention, what arouses him, etc. (Opton & Lazarus, 1967; Averill & Opton, 1968). A striking example of what can be done with this approach is a study by Freund (1963). A series of pictures, including unclothed males and females, were shown to subjects while physiological measures were taken. The pattern of change for men known to be homosexuals was markedly different from that of others.

18. *What legal and ethical problems arise in the use of a (hypothetical) physiological measure that distinguishes men known to have molested children sexually from others of similar age and education?*

19. *Does the measure of flicker fusion represent a behavioristic approach, a phenomenological approach, or neither?*

Structured Tests of Perceptual Ability

The tests in the following section, and several others appearing later in the chapter, are undisguised ability tests. The subject is given a clear job to do, and he presumably goes at it with no need to think about whether he is "revealing himself" or not. Yet, by indirect inference, the psychologist hopes to understand the subject's personality. The tests have been designed with the idea that a person who typically employs a certain "perceptual style" or "cognitive style" will do well while another person will be handicapped.

The ingenious Stroop Color-Word Test (CWT) may be taken as an example. The task calls for nothing but reading and color naming. There is pressure for speed, and the situation is made highly confusing. The subject's ability to shift mental set on demand, so as to perform efficiently, is surely of interest. Some psychologists regard CWT as a measure of a personality trait called "flexibility" or the like. The usual test employs pages printed in color; we have prepared an example using typeface instead of color for illustrative purposes (Figure 18.1.). In the color version, the successive, separately timed tasks have this form:

1. Read these words as fast as you can. The words ("blue," "yellow,". . .) are printed in black, so that there is no interference. This serves for warmup.
2. Name the colors of these symbols, in order, as fast as you can. The symbols are asterisks (* * *) printed in several colors. This is a baseline measure of color-naming.
3. Name the colors here, in order, as fast as you can. The sheet displays words printed in contradictory colors; the word "blue" in red or green ink, etc. Now the subject must overcome interference.

The score on task 3, corrected for speed of naming on task 2, is the significant measure.

Jensen and Rohwer (1966) review the literature on the Stroop test and express dissatisfaction with the research because investigators use different forms and different scoring schemes so that results are hard to compare. They list a large number of intriguing findings. For instance (Amster, 1965), subjects who name colors much faster than they read color names (task 2 vs. task 1) do about equally well at incidental and intentional learning, but those who do better at the reading task also do much better at intentional learning than incidental. With regard to the interference score based on task 3, they draw on many studies by various authors, some unpublished. On the whole, persons with good performance under the interference condition also do well on other intellectual tasks where there is stress, distraction, or strong motivation. They tend to be dominant, and, in marriage, the partner who scores well on task 3 tends to be the one who takes responsibility for various everyday operations of the family. There is no support for the hypothesis once held that those who resist interference are more stable or more persistent. They sum up in the following sentences:

"The Stroop measures certain highly stable characteristics of individuals. The psychological nature of these characteristics is not well understood. But the fact that various Stroop scores have shown significant, though nearly always quite low, relationships to a diverse host of other psychological variables which are often phenotypically very different from the Stroop task itself, suggests that whatever processes are tapped by the Stroop are of a very basic and broad significance. . . .

"Stroop processes seem to enter most strongly into the cognitive sphere, particularly where learning, tempo, and response competition are involved. . . . This factor [interference proneness] has considerable generality and is identifiable to some extent with classical interference effects in learning and retention. . . .

"Stroop processes are manifest rather sporadically and in complex ways in the personality domain. Some genuine relationships undoubtedly exist here, but their meaning is hardly decipherable from the present evidence." In other words, the process of building a valid interpretation of this stylistic measure as an aspect of personality has scarcely begun.

The most extensive work with stylistic tests of this kind is that of Witkin and his colleagues. Most of their tests ask the subject, "Which way is up?" He sits in a dark room, facing a luminous square frame that is tilted 28° from the vertical. Within the square is a rod, also luminous, that rotates when the subject operates a control switch. His task is to put the rod in a true up-and-down position. To do this, he must attend entirely to his own kinesthetic sense of the vertical. As in CWT, two sets of cues are in conflict. Actually, as Witkin now uses the Rod-and-Frame Test (RFT), there is an additional complication: the chair in which the subject sits is also tilted to one side, sometimes as the frame is tilted, sometimes in the opposite direction. Twenty-four trials constitute the full test. Tilting-Room-Tilting-Chair goes a step further. The chair is housed in a small chamber that can be tilted to either side. This time the subject operates with the lights on, but visual cues from the room are misleading. His task is to adjust controls to bring his chair to the vertical. The test in this form is called BAT—Body-Adjustment Test. Alternatively, the RAT form leaves the chair fixed at a tilt and requires that the room be rotated around the chair until the room position matches the gravitational upright. One crucial personality measure in the Witkin research is, surprisingly, the Embedded Figures Test, which we met on p. 240. According to Witkin, this measures the same quality of personality—"field-dependence"—as the postural tests. While Witkin uses forms of his own devising, there is evidence that the changes he introduced do not affect what the test measures (Jackson, Messick, & Myers, 1964).

Here again we face the question of generality, and Witkin *et al.* (1962, pp. 44–45) provide a good deal of evidence for various age groups:

> RAT with RFT: correlation for adults ranges 0.13 to 0.61, with a median of 0.37; for children, —.15 to 0.45, median 0.24.
> RAT with BAT: adults, —0.30 to 0.52, median 0.24; children —0.09 to 0.43, median 0.29.

RFT with BAT: adults, 0.11 to 0.55, median 0.39; children, 0.25 to 0.45, median, 0.35.

EFT with BAT or RFT: adults, 0.15 to 0.63, median 0.42[1]; children, 0.26 to 0.55, median 0.39.

EFT with RAT: adults, −0.16 to 0.56, median, 0.25; children, −0.11 to 0.38, median 0.24.

Each correlation is for a different sample, and those for adults are calculated separately within sexes. There is a clear tendency for men's correlations to be higher than those for women.

There is consistency, but there are puzzling variations. When tests supposed to measure the same thing correlate zero or even negatively in some groups, it is clear that no one task can be relied on. RAT, requiring adjustment *of* the field, is now thought to be psychologically different from the tasks that require analysis *within* the field. In his recent work, Witkin has employed the composite of BAT, RFT, and EFT as an index for the trait he wants to study, discarding RAT.

As for stability, the evidence from the available small samples is favorable enough. Over 3- to 4-year periods, beginning at age 10 or 14, the composite score has coefficients of 0.64 to 0.94, the higher figure being, of course, for the adolescents. Hence the Witkin measure has a stability comparable to that for specialized aptitude tests. There's the rub. The index correlates at least 0.50 with WISC Performance IQ, which we know to be quite stable. We are not told whether the information Witkin's score contains that is independent of IQ is stable, or whether the stability derives entirely from the mental-ability component of the Witkin tests. We classified EFT earlier as a measure of fluid ability, on the evidence, particularly, of its 0.80 correlation with Block Design. While BAT and RFT correlations with Block Design are lower (0.53 and 0.65), a large fraction of individual differences is accounted for by fluid ability. That is not to say that Witkin tests have *no* independent information. The difficulty is that studies have not isolated and validated the significance of the *independent* contribution of the less-conventional kind of test.

Interpretation of the ability-personality complex. Investigators who use these perceptual tasks to study personality take their ideas from several traditions, and there are differences among their working hypotheses. Witkin's thinking is indicated in the following extract and paraphrase from *Psychological differentiation* (Witkin *et al.*, 1962, pp. 1–22).

We found two decades ago that people differ in the way they orient themselves in space. The way each person orients himself is an expression of a preferred mode

[1] The correlation of EFT with RFT rises by a striking amount when nonlinear transformations are made of the scores (Barrett, Cabe, & Thornton, 1968). In effect, this means not only that the tests cohere better than Witkin's figures imply, but that Witkin has not found the best method of computing a composite index.

of perceiving that is linked to many areas of functioning. "Field-dependent" persons find it difficult to overcome the influence of the surrounding field or to separate an item from its context. They are likely to change their views to agree with an authority. They favor occupations calling for social contact.

Thus a seemingly narrow perceptual activity came to be seen as a manifestation of a style of life. The central element is the degree of "differentiation" or ability to keep things apart in experience. The field-dependent person displays a global, ill-articulated way of perceiving his social world. A high level of differentiation implies clear separation of what is identified as belonging to the self from what is external.

Witkin's associate Faterson (1962) adds some simpler language:

. . . a person with a well-developed sense of separate identity would have relatively less need for guidance and support from others; would show relatively greater "individuality". . . ; would maintain more firmly his orientation and direction in the face of outer pressures. . . .

She illustrates by referring to a 10-year-old who said he was sitting upright when his chair was tilted 30° from the vertical, in line with the walls of the tilted room. In an interview, asked, "What are you like?"; his reply was "Other people say I am nice."

Validity research often leads to puzzling inconsistencies and contradictions. Partly this is because hypotheses are vaguely stated, partly because no study bears down and examines a particular trait-complex with several measures, alongside several measures of alternative hypotheses. Self-report criteria are especially likely to be misused; the typical study is a shotgun investigation in which a dozen or more trait measures are correlated with the test being validated; chance alone guarantees that some significant-looking relation will emerge. With Witkin's measures, there has been a good deal of research having to do with dependency, independence, and self-direction or drive to achieve. As for dependency, several studies failed to produce the expected relation, and Witkin modified his claim by distinguishing "passive" dependency from "social" dependency, the latter supposedly being what low EFT scores reflect. But a criterion based on observations of social dependency correlated only −0.22 with EFT (Vaughn Crandall & Sinkeldam, 1964). There was a good correlation with observations on drive toward achievement and task persistence: 0.46, dropping a little (to 0.32) after age and IQ were partialled out. Related traits entered Pemberton's (1952) study with a questionnaire criterion. Among a large number of items, EFT had "significant" correlations with 29 of them, such as "I stay in the background," "I am not conventional," and "I am interested in physical science." The suggestion is that the test indicates self-centeredness or nonconformity. But in another study of students, Messick and Fritzky (1963) could not find a correlation of EFT with independence or unconventionality. While EFT and other Witkin measures seem frequently to have the personality correlates he suggests, the correlations are weak and undependable.

The big question is whether most of the results are simply a function of ability. EFT correlates highly with Rod and Frame and the other Witkin tests, but it also correlates highly with Block Design and other measures of fluid ability (D. Goodenough & Karp, 1961). The simplest interpretation of the Witkin data, taken as a whole, is that people who have high fluid ability—i.e., who use their minds efficiently—are distinctive in their attitudes, drawing styles, demands on themselves, etc.

The personality interpretation could be called superfluous. But recall that styles of response, resistance to distraction, etc., are an important part of what mental ability tests measure. Block Design and Number Series, like EFT, measure ability to overcome interference; they would not be problem-solving tests if the answer were not "hidden." How the person handles risky, challenging situations is an aspect of personality that leads to effective or ineffective intellectual work.

There is also evidence from many sources that some pupils excellent in crystallized abilities are highly constricted and have difficulty when they have no guaranteed technique for arriving at the answer authority will approve. If we were to apply a 2 × 2 design at any age, dividing persons on fluid (or field-independent or analytic) ability *and* on crystallized verbal ability, we would no doubt find four distinct styles. Witkin's research is not as useful as it should be because he analyzes groups contrasted only on fluid ability.

Before dropping this issue we may insert a word to rebut the critic who may want to call the *ability* interpretation of EFT, BD, etc., superfluous. Subjects earn poor scores because they allow themselves to become so confused that they cannot perform tasks that are, in their elements, very simple. Is the failure, then, truly one of "personal style?" Here our initial distinction helps. EFT is a test of maximum performance; the low-scoring subjects are doing the best they can. A "style" can be put aside when it is disfunctional. Since the Low-EFT subject seems unable to shift to an analytic "style," he is showing a deficiency in ability.

20. *Field-dependent college girls are less likely* (r = −0.54) *to marry than others in the next 3 years, according to a small study by Fliegel. How could Witkin justify this as consistent with his theory* (*Witkin* et al., *1962, p. 147*)? *Could a correlation of* plus *0.54 have been justified just as easily?*

21. *Discuss this statement: "A test presented to the subject as a test of ability should be regarded as a measure of ability if the subject knows what aspect of his performance will actually be scored, and as a measure of personality if he does not know."*

22. *Messick (1964) comments that labels for traits measured in performance tests usually hint that one end of the dimension is good and the other bad. He suggests that readers of the research might draw different conclusions if "flexibility vs. rigidity" were relabeled "confusion vs. control."*

   a. *Suggest ways of relabeling the following traits to reverse the implied value judgment: persistence, anxiety, compulsivity, field-independence.*

b. *Does the labeling of a trait represent a theory of adjustment, a widely held value system, or the investigator's bias?*

23. *It is stated that "independent" (high EFT) subjects do better than dependent persons on tests of creativity. Assuming that one has usable tests of creativity, outline a study that would show whether this result can be adequately explained by calling EFT a measure of fluid ability rather than independence.*

24. *High EFT subjects are less likely to classify nude paintings (from museums) as pornographic, according to Stuart (1966). Can this possibly be explained except by arguing that high EFT persons have a distinct personality?*

25. *If the CWT were given repeatedly, on 3 days, would you expect more valid indications of susceptibility to interference on the first run or the third?*

Complex Clinical Tests

The Bender test. Whereas the perceptual tests discussed above are highly focused, each getting a quantitative measure of a single aspect of personality, others are complex and multivariate. The Bender test, which we now examine, is from the subject's point of view a straightforward ability test.

The Bender Visual Motor Gestalt Test (Bender, 1938) displays figures with various patterns of organization, including those shown in Figure 18.2. The tester asks the subject to make a copy and observes his mode of attack and his success. Responses may differ in a hundred ways, which the tester attempts to observe, collate, and interpret. Scoring rules have been developed, but the clinician generally attempts a qualitative integration (see p. 668 where the record of Figure 18.3 is interpreted).

Performance may be treated statistically by observing "signs" that characterize some criterion group. Gobetz (1953) listed responses common among neurotics; for example: upward slope in reproducing rows of dots, incorrect number of wave crests, counting aloud during reproduction, figures crowded into half of page. Nineteen per cent of a crossvalidation group of neurotics showed nine or more of these signs, compared with 4 per cent of normals. Many signs reported by other authors as characteristic of neurotics did not differentiate in Gobetz' study. He concluded that the test can be helpful in screening, provided that other data are used to confirm any conclusion about the person. Others have sought to validate the widespread belief that the Bender can discriminate patients with brain damage from those whose disorders are emotional in origin (Hain, 1964; Kramer & Fenwick, 1966). The count of false alarms and misses is far too high for the Bender to be used alone as a classifying procedure (Billingslea, 1963; Tolor & Schulberg, 1963; Mosher & Smith, 1965).

With children, the Bender is fundamentally a test of ability. Koppitz (1964) has done considerable work with children in the age range 5 to 10 that supports the following statements. Counting response features characteristic of children who do well in school obtains a rough measure of mental ability. The low

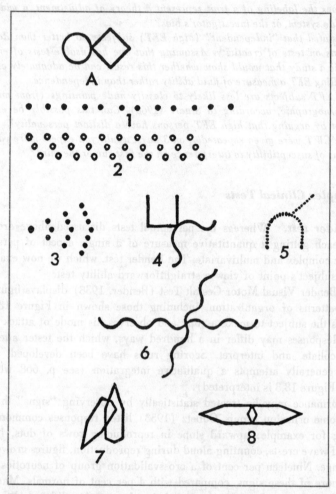

Figure 18.2.   Bender-Gestalt patterns to be copied.
*Copyright 1946, American Orthopsychiatric Association. Reproduced
by permission of Dr. Lauretta Bender and the American Orthopsychiatric Association.*

stability of Bender scores (0.60 over 4 months) limits the dependability of the
test. Even so, a score obtained at the start of grade 1 predicts school achievement
as late as the third grade, with *r* about 0.50. (Correlations of this score with
EFT, Matrices, and other such measures would, one suspects, be fairly large.)
Beyond grade 3, the abilities the Bender measures are ordinarily well developed;
an inferior performance suggests emotional interference or brain damage. A
second Koppitz score counts elements associated with emotional disturbance;

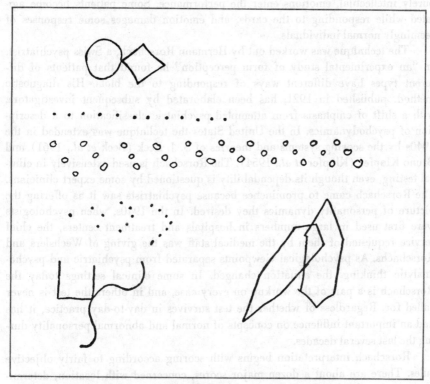

Figure 18.3.   Bender reproductions by a young male mental patient.
Shneidman, 1951, p. 228.

there is no crossvalidation for this scale. As to brain damage, the overlap of
brain-damaged and normal groups is considerable; poor Bender performance,
especially when a child appears normal or superior on conventional ability tests,
does signal the need to check on possible brain damage.

Perception of inkblots.   The Bender, like the Stroop or the flicker-fusion
task, is a test of mental efficiency. A simple, objective, literal task is set; any
perturbation of mental processes can impair the performance. In inkblot tests,
the stimulus has little structure, so that "reality" and "efficiency," play a much
smaller role. In the Rorschach, the subject is to tell what he sees in ten inkblots,
blots whose form is so irregular as to permit innumerable interpretations. The
blots are calculated to arouse emotional response with their bloody reds, ominous
blacks, and luminous grays, and with their forms suggestive of nursery animals,
overbearing giants, and sex organs. While the task as stated to the subject is

purely intellectual, emotions enter the performance. Some patients become agitated while responding to the cards, and emotion damages some responses of seemingly normal individuals.

The technique was worked out by Hermann Rorschach, a Swiss psychiatrist. In "an experimental study of form perception" he found that patients of different types have different ways of responding to the blots. His diagnostic method, published in 1921, has been elaborated by subsequent investigators, with a shift of emphasis from attempted psychiatric classification to a description of psychodynamics. In the United States the technique was extended in the 1940s by the scoring systems and theories of S. J. Beck (Beck *et al.*, 1961) and Bruno Klopfer (Klopfer *et al.*, 1954). The Rorschach is used extensively in clinical testing, even though its dependability is questioned by some expert clinicians. The Rorschach came to prominence because psychiatrists saw it as offering the picture of personality dynamics they desired. In the 1940s, when psychologists were first used in large numbers in hospitals and treatment centers, the chief service requested of them by the medical staff was the giving of Wechslers and Rorschachs. As psychological viewpoints separated from psychiatric and psychoanalytic thinking, the situation changed. In some clinical settings today the Rorschach is a part of the workup on every case, and in others the test is never called for. Regardless of whether the test survives in day-to-day practice, it has had an important influence on concepts of normal and abnormal personality during the last several decades.

Rorschach interpretation begins with scoring according to fairly objective rules. There are about a dozen major scores, concerned with location, determinants, and content. Location scores indicate whether the response uses the whole blot (W), commonly perceived subdivisions (D), or unusual details (Dd). The "determinants" are the shape, color, and shading of the blot which the subject takes into account. "Movement" (M), for example, is scored when the subject describes humans in motion, and CF when the response depends on both form and color, with color the more significant in determining the response. The scorer also notes how well the response fits the form of the blot, scoring form quality $+$ or $-$. Finally, the content score notes whether the response refers to persons (H), parts of persons (Hd), clothing (Cg), etc.

The scoring of four responses will illustrate the procedure. Card X is a mixture of brightly colored forms. Suppose that these four responses are given:

1. A big splashy print design for a summer dress.
2. Enlarged photograph of a snowflake [refers to a large irregularly shaped area].
3. Two little boys blowing bubbles. You just see them from the waist up.
4. Head of a rabbit.

The scoring of these responses (based on supplementary explanation obtained by inquiry) is as follows.

Response	Location	Determinant and form level	Content
1	W	CF+	Art, Cg
2	D	F—	Nature
3	D	M+	Hd
4	D	F+	Ad

Although scoring is systematic, interpretation is not.

The quality of responses indicates something both about the subject's intellectual level and about the care he puts into his performance. Much is made of the subject's control over his impulses and his emotional reactions. Rorschach movement responses are thought to represent imagination and creative impulses arising from within, and color responses are thought to represent emotional reactions to external stimuli. "Form" is equated with ability to take reality into account. A person who harmonizes form and movement is said to accept and use constructively his inner impulses; a person who rarely reports a movement response is regarded as lacking in imagination or as repressing it.

The interpretation is constructed through interrelated hypotheses about the internal forces and controls that lead to each type of response. Each of these hypotheses must ultimately be verified to make interpretation trustworthy. Successful experience with individual cases is the chief basis on which users defend the Rorschach method. There has been considerable formal research on the hypotheses, but the complexity of the problems posed by the technique has made comprehensive research exceedingly difficult (M. Ainsworth, 1954, pp. 405–500; Zubin, Eron, & Schumer, 1965, pp. 193–239). Sometimes the evidence is strikingly favorable, sometimes not.

Rorschach (1921; see 1942, p. 7) said that movement responses are indicative of personalities that "function more in the intellectual sphere, whose interests gravitate more towards their intrapsychic living rather than towards the world outside themselves." This interpretation was checked by Barron (1955), who employed a psychophysical technique to obtain an M score similar to Rorschach's but much more reliable. This score was compared with ratings made by clinical assessors using other data. Persons with strong M tendencies were described by the independent observers as inventive, having wide interests, introspective, concerned with self as object, valuing cognitive pursuits. The low-M subjects were described as practical, stubborn, preferring action to contemplation, and being inflexible in thought and action. This supports Rorschach's interpretation. Klopfer's use of M as a prime indicator of intelligence is questioned; there was no correlation between Barron's M score and objective tests of general ability or originality. To be sure, the psychologist assessors rated the high M's as more intelligent, but in view of the objective test results this implies that assessors are biased toward judging persons intelligent if they appear "thoughtful." This study would have been better if a 2 × 2 analysis had been employed (as in the studies of Gough and Wallach) to describe separately cases with High M-High IQ, High M-Low IQ, etc.

In another study, similar mixed confirmation of Rorschach theory is found. White-space (S) responses, i.e., interpretations of the space between the blots, are presumed to indicate oppositional tendencies. Bandura (1954) found a correlation of 0.35 between the S score and ratings of negativism. No support was found, however, for the hypothesis—equally significant in Rorschach lore—that S in high-M subjects implies self-criticism and in high-C subjects implies opposition to others. (See also D. Murray, 1957; Fonda, 1960).

Hundreds of additional studies could be cited, each dealing with one bit of Rorschach theory. The trend of the results (Holtzman, Iscoe, & Calvin, 1954; Rickers-Ovsiankina, 1960; Sarason, 1954; Zubin, Eron & Schumer, 1965; Holt, 1966) is this:

- About half of the experimental tests of Rorschach hypotheses give results consistent with clinical theory. The interpretation certainly has "validity greater than chance."

- These confirmations indicate rather modest relationships between Rorschach indicators and postulated traits. (Bandura's correlation of 0.35 is typical.) Many personality factors and abilities influence any one score, and no direct interpretation can be made with confidence. As Jensen (1964) points out in his review of Rorschach research, coefficients below 0.40 provide little support for clinical use of the test.

- Some aspects of the theory are definitely incorrect and should be revised. Some evidence of the adequacy of the test, with these limitations, for comprehensive clinical assessment will be considered in Chapter 19.

There have been attempts to use quantitative scores from the Rorschach either as trait measures or as empirical predictors. "Signs" of organic brain damage have been suggested, for example. Generally, these formulas prove valueless on crossvalidation, either showing no validity or having too high a false positive rate (A. J. Yates, 1954; Fisher, Gonda, & Little, 1955). Style measures (e.g., of approach and rigidity, p. 642 below) sometimes correlate with external criteria, but the correlations are too small to warrant use of the Rorschach as a quantitative measure.

Some investigators are continuing to develop interpretations that will tie the Rorschach to general personality theory. One of the best examples is Holt's attempt (1966) to study impulsive, wish-expressing responses, as cues to sexual and aggressive concerns. This has proved to be difficult; Holt's scoring manual has been through nearly a dozen revisions. He finds a number of interesting but scattered correlations with behavior observed on other tests, qualities inferred from clinical interviews, and performance in Peace Corps assignments. The correlations are not large enough to warrant decisions about individuals. Holt concludes that further work can develop the Rorschach into an important source of hypotheses about personality. "But," he adds, "no research is going to make it into a first cousin of the Stanford-Binet as a measuring instrument; it will remain almost as diffuse as it is broad, and inferences based on it will necessarily be more probabilistic than is implied in the usual concept of measurement."

The nearest to a psychometric version of the Rorschach is the Holtzman Inkblot Technique (Holtzman *et al.*, 1961; *Psych. Corp.*). Holtzman presents 45 blots (or 90 if two forms are used) and elicits one response to each blot. Rules yield scores for a number of characteristics such as Location (whole vs. detail), Space, Form Appropriateness, Pathognomic Verbalization, and Hostility. The test construction and standardization was carried out with a degree of attention to technical detail no other personality test can match. For example, precision printing was used to produce the collection of inkblots for large-scale tryout, before final items were selected. A more casual investigator would have used hand-painted blots for small tryouts to make the selection, trusting that the ultimate printed reproductions would have the same stimulating qualities. There are two excellently matched forms—a rarity among personality tests. There is even a system for computer scoring of the free responses, in which the computer makes use of a dictionary that tells how "bad thunderstorm," for example, is to be coded.

Holtzman hopes that his instrument will serve the original clinical purposes of the Rorschach with considerably greater precision, and that it will also advance research on personality. The evidence that has appeared so far is unpersuasive. In the first place, correlations between forms given a week apart are mixed: 0.81 for Location, 0.49 for Form Appropriateness, 0.59 for Hostility, for example. Perhaps the scores can be combined for use in clinical screening. A combination of scores designed to separate schizophrenics from normals correctly identified 89 per cent of the normals and 82 per cent of the schizophrenics (Moseley, 1962; base rate must be taken into account).

As to construct interpretations, we are told, for example, that there is no correlation of HIT anxiety with questionnaire anxiety or with interviewers' ratings. This is disturbing. We are told that HIT hostility correlates 0.50 with ratings of hostility by interviewers (Brown, Harkness, & Proctor, see Holtzman, 1968); this is astonishingly high, considering the errors in both measures. Replication and extension of such studies are needed. One can say that Holtzman scores have much the same meaning as Rorschach scores, and, because of their advantage in administration and scoring, open the way to much more adequate validation of inkblot hypotheses. The validation of HIT is only beginning, and only gradually will we learn which interpretations to rely on.

26. *Judging from Gobetz' signs, what traits does the Bender measure?*

27. *Compare the screening effectiveness of Gobetz' scoring system with that for the MMPI (pp. 538 f.).*

28. *Why might a "perfect" Rorschach accuracy score, 100 per cent F+, indicate a personality pattern undesirable for many situations?*

29. *Do the Rorschach scores related to quality of output reveal maximum ability or typical behavior? How does the Rorschach compare with the Binet test in that respect?*

30. *"Responses to ten inkblots, presented by one tester on one occasion, constitute too small a sample of behavior to measure any intellectual or emotional trait reliably." To what extent does Holtzman's instrument overcome this objection?*

31. *How satisfactory is the screening effectiveness of the Holtzman technique, in a population in which 5 per cent of those tested are expected to be schizophrenic?*

Styles in Problem Solving

There are alternative ways to proceed with any task: impulsively or cautiously, systematically or haphazardly, etc. Variation in style of response is sometimes a source of invalidity, if style is irrelevant to the investigator's interest. Yea-saying or nay-saying reduces validity when knowledge is measured by true-false questions and when a "yes"–"no" format is used to get self-reports on anxiety. The person's response bias, however, may reflect his general approach to the world. Cognitive theories of behavior and psychoanalytic theory—in the modern derivation known as "ego psychology"—emphasize the strategies by which man copes with unpleasant memories, threats, and obstacles. Acquiescence-when-in-doubt may be a person's characteristic coping mechanism. "Faking good" on a questionnaire can likewise be seen as a significant act of overt behavior; it does correlate with other indicators of a desire to ingratiate oneself (Crowne & Marlowe, 1964). Such interpretations treat even the questionnaire as a "performance test."

What at first glance are transient or trivial individual differences in test-taking turn out to have striking relationships with other behavior. In Chapter 3 we discussed the tendency of some persons to answer achievement-test items about which they are uncertain, and of other persons to play safe. Ziller (1957) got a reasonably exact measure of this tendency by administering an extremely hard information test, on which the students tested had reason to think good performance was expected. The score counted wrong answers as evidence of willingness to gamble, and omissions as evidence of caution. The students were then classified according to their stated vocational goals. The prospective salesmen, mechanical engineers, educators, and business-administration majors gambled freely; gambling was relatively rare among electrical and civil engineers, and lowest of all among those whose stated vocational choice was "undecided." The relations are not strong enough to suggest using a gambling measure in vocational guidance, but they have some relevance to a theory of career choice.

Porteus has had more success than any other investigator in capitalizing practically on stylistic measures, perhaps because of his persistence and flexibility in explicating the exact meaning of maze performance. Over the years he came to

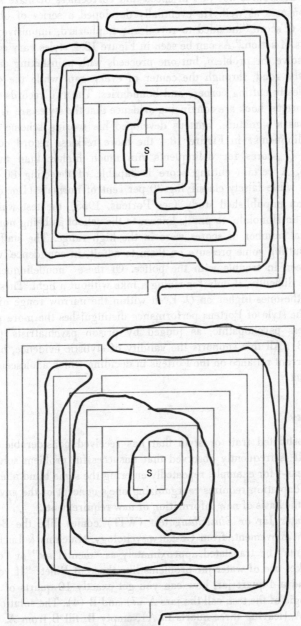

Figure 18.4. **Stylistic differences in maze performance of two girls.**
Porteus, 1965, p. 234.

distinguish differences not just in speed and correctness of maze solutions, but in meticulousness as well. He eventually developed a series of objective rules to obtain a Q score "intended to reveal any haphazard, impulsive, or overconfident habits of action." As can be seen in Figure 18.4, styles vary conspicuously. Both girls solve the problem, but one proceeds with painstaking care down the middle of the road, through the center of every gap, while the other swoops along, recklessly cutting corners and boundaries. The two records for each girl shown in Porteus' book are convincing evidence that the styles are as personalized and stable as a signature. Porteus developed his scoring scheme especially to identify delinquents; in Figure 18.4 the more reckless record comes from a delinquent. Q scores for delinquents run much higher than those of non-delinquents. A certain cutting score is capable of detecting 80 per cent of delinquents while falsely classifying 30 per cent of normals (Docter & Winder, 1954). In an unpublished study (see Porteus, 1965) the test was given in a ninth grade in Honolulu, to pupils known to the school as being nondelinquents. A substantial number of scores were in the high range. The staff interviewed 160 boys, putting some pressure on them to admit, in confidence, whether they had ever been in trouble with the police. Of these "nondelinquents," 48 admitted some difficulty, if only for riding a bike without a light. These boys were, in general, the ones higher on Q. Even within the narrow range of a group of criminals, the style of Porteus performance distinguishes the more psychopathic from the less psychopathic, as judged by prison psychiatrists (Schalling & Rosén, 1968). All this supports the validity of stylistic evidence, but of course does not warrant reliance on the Porteus in deciding which adolescents to suspect of misconduct.

Rigidity

One postulated trait or style that has received considerable attention is "rigidity." It is frequently observed that unsuccessful problem solvers cling to incorrect ideas—for example, repeatedly entering the same blind alley in a maze. Successful adaptation requires reorganizing one's concept of the environment or stimulus on the basis of new information or new requirements.

The Water Jar or *Einstellung* test (WJT) comes, like the Bender, EFT, and apparent movement, from Gestalt psychology (Luchins & Luchins, 1959). *Einstellung* may be translated approximately as "mental set" or "orientation." The test makes use of water-jar problems like those of Binet: "If you have a 7-quart jar and a 4-quart jar, how can you get exactly 10 quarts of water?" To follow the logic of the test, call the jars A (7) and B (4). The solution is: Fill A, fill B from A (leaving three quarts in A), empty B, fill B from A, fill A. Thus three quarts are obtained by the rule $(A - B)$, and the additional seven quarts from A; i.e., $(A-B) + A = 10$. The series of problems in a test might be as follows.

	Jars				
	A	B	C	To be obtained	Solution
Example:	7	4	—	10	A − B + A	
a.	21	127	3	100	B − A − 2C	
b.	14	163	25	99	B − A − 2C	
c.	18	43	10	5	B − A − 2C	
d.	9	42	6	21	B − A − 2C	
e.	20	59	4	31	B − A − 2C	
f.	23	49	3	20	B − A − 2C or A − C	Critical
g.	15	39	3	18	B − A − 2C or A + C	Critical
h.	28	76	3	25	A − C	Extinction
i.	18	48	4	22	B − A − 2C or A + C	Critical
j.	14	36	8	6	B − A − 2C or A − C	Critical

The subject may be given help in solving the first few problems. As he solves the string of problems *a* to *e* by applying a particular rule, he builds up a mental set to use that rule. "Critical" and "extinction" problems are then introduced. In a critical problem such as *f*, the "set" solution works but there is a much easier solution. In the extinction problem *h*, the set solution does not work; the flexible subject can find another simple rule. To score well the subject must attend to the immediate problem, discarding memories of the previous solutions.

A person poor on the WJT criticals is called "rigid"—seemingly a bad trait. Yet extracting a pattern from events and applying it in the future is an act of intelligence. *Not* to search for a new rule usually saves time. Only failure on the extinction trial clearly indicates dysfunctional rigidity. WJT behavior on critical trials (wherein the "set" solution works but is unnecessarily round-about) has different psychological properties and correlates from behavior on extinction trials (for which the "set" solution does not work). (See Adamson & Taylor, 1954; L. Ainsworth, 1958; Back, 1956). Witkin argues that his tests ought to correlate only with the extinction trial, and mentions data confirming this. (But this, like too many discussions of convergence among personality tests, does not say how strong the relation is; Witkin *et al.*, 1962, p. 77).

To summarize research on test-to-test consistency in the personality domain is next to impossible. For "rigidity" there have been a dozen papers summarizing correlations, and even the summaries disagree. Some conclude that there is a general trait of rigidity, some find three or four rigidity factors (never the same from study to study), and some argue that the very concept of rigidity is invalidated by the data. Levitt (1956) summarized more than thirty correlations of WJT with other alleged measures of rigidity and found that disagreements outnumbered significant correlations three to one. Investigators have been too quick to assign trait names to tests. Among the tests that have been claimed to measure rigidity are an anxiety questionnaire, a questionnaire measure of rigidity, the California F scale testing social attitudes, Wechsler Similarities, and mirror writing. To expect agreement among them reflects an unreasonably simple view of mental organization.

Luchins (1951), although he popularized the Water Jar test, is critical of those who try to measure an "amount" of rigidity. For him, both the test as an observation of a mental process and its meaning shift with conditions. Those who seek to measure an abstract trait underlying the test performance, he says,

err in assuming that every Einstellung solution to a test problem is brought about by the same psychological process—namely, rigidity of behavior . . . . Moreover, the alleged rigidity in solving the criticals is taken as an indication of rigidity in the respondent's personality or of rigidity in his ego-defense system. His behavior is rigid because he possesses rigidity. One is reminded of the outmoded belief that a thing burns because it has fire in it. . . . Rigidity of behavior is sought for in the respondent; it is considered as relatively independent of the field conditions under which the individual is operating.

. . . I do not think that there is anything inherently wrong with attempting to determine within a short period of time, a few hours of testing, the probability that an individual will shift his behavior in real life situations in order to meet changing circumstances. . . . At the present time the most fruitful approach seems to me to involve intensive observation of and experimentation with rigidity of behavior under various conditions, if possible suspending biases as to the nature of the behavior involved. . . . The aim should be to vary conditions systematically and to observe what happens. As a final step—and not as a first step as is so common today—one may be able to propose an explanation for such behavior.

Observations of Process

Whereas the test of rigidity is designed to bring a single trait to the surface, information on styles of work can come from observation during any complex performance—such as taking the Wechsler.

In giving Block Design, for example, the tester can observe method of attack and response to frustration. Better information is obtained by modifying the test and by specifying precisely what is to be observed. Goldner (1957) studied "whole-part approach" and rigidity. He used six tests: a modified Block Design test; the Arthur Stencil Design test, in which cutouts of various colors must be superimposed to form a specified pattern; Anagrams I, in which the subject builds numerous words from a set of letters; Anagrams II, requiring identification of a scrambled 10-letter word; the Rorschach blots; and a version of Unusual Uses: "What are possible different uses of a box?" Goldner developed scoring rules for each test.

For Unusual Uses the whole-part score was assigned according to whether the answer used the whole object ("Put things in the box") or broke it into parts ("Use it for firewood"). In Block Design, a "whole" attack is shown by the person who turns each block to the correct face before beginning assembly, and then assembles the pattern as a unit, paying attention to symmetry. A "part" approach is shown by starting at one corner and building up the pattern one block at a time. To bring out differences in approach, Goldner used irregular, nonsquare designs so as to make analysis of the pattern more difficult. He presented every design, whether it used 9 or 16 blocks, in the same size, so that the subject had to decide how many blocks to use. The "whole-approach" subject would count out his blocks at the start.

Goldner also judged rigidity. In Block Design, for example, rigidity was scored if the subject had difficulty in judging the correct number of blocks, retained the same attack after a failure without finishing a problem. In Unusual Uses, rigidity was identified with a tendency to give many logically similar uses ("as a tool box," "for mailing," "to pack things") whereas flexibility was identified with variety. This technique contrasts with the WJT measure of rigidity. In that simpler task the score reports a particular countable symptom. In Goldner's battery each score is a rating of an assumed mental process that can come to light in different ways. His complex tasks "spread out" performance so that mental process can be inferred.

Goldner found substantial support for the hypothesis of generality of the two traits observed. The results above the diagonal in Table 18.1 show that five of his six "whole-part" scores are correlated. Each test agrees substantially with the total of the other measures. Particularly striking is the correlation between tasks as dissimilar as Anagrams I and Stencil Design. Unusual Uses

Table 18.1. Generality among tests of problem-solving style[a]

	Inkblot	Unusual Uses	Anagrams I	Anagrams II	Stencil Design	Block Design	Total "whole-part" score minus particular test
Inkblot		.25	.40	.40	**.58**	.40	**.67**
Unusual Uses	**.42**		.00	−.02	−.02	.10	.08
Anagrams I	**.51**	.19		.25	**.53**	.36	**.48**
Anagrams II	.10	.25	−.30		.29	−.03	.27
Stencil Design	.17	.32	−.19	**.50**		**.62**	**.66**
Block Design	.26	.16	.00	.34	**.83**		**.48**
Total rigidity score minus particular test	**.54**	**.43**	.06	.30	**.58**	**.54**	

[a] Correlations above diagonal are for whole-part scores, those below diagonal for rigidity scores. Correlations in boldface are significant.

SOURCE: Goldner, 1957, p. 14.

is an exception; whole approach on this test either is unreliable or is a different trait from whole approach on the other tasks. Goldner's findings on rigidity are quite similar: five tasks have marked correlations with each other. This time, however, Anagrams I is independent.

32. *Which of Goldner's tests are most structured? Do they correlate more highly with each other than with unstructured tests?*

The In-Basket "Situational" Test

The in-basket procedure started as a device for selecting responsible men and choosing work assignments to fit their individual styles, but it now fills quite different functions. It is often used to train decision-makers; it can also be used to evaluate the effectiveness of such training. The procedure originated in the Island Story Test of the British civil service. Candidates (university graduates who had already passed conventional qualifying tests) were given a large amount of information about an island where, hypothetically, each was to serve as a government official. They were required to work out written plans for solving several complex local problems, some involving conflicting pressures (Vernon & Parry, 1949). Realistic tasks of this nature, and the even more lifelike group-performance tasks described below, are often referred to as "situational tests."

For an account of the interesting details of various in-basket procedures the reader should consult Frederiksen, Saunders, and Wand (1957); Hemphill, Griffiths, and Frederiksen (1962); and Lopez (1966). Drawing on the last-named source, we can give a brief account of a procedure developed for Sears Roebuck.

The candidate for appointment or promotion is told to assume that he has just been assigned to replace a store manager in Exville, who is out of action with a heart attack. It is Sunday; he must go to the store today and in three hours cope with problems on the manager's desk. He cannot reach other employees on Sunday, and, because he has a trip to make, anything postponed must await his return on Thursday. He receives a chart of the store organization and a personnel list. The basket contains 37 "items"—letters, memos, policy papers for review, forms to sign, etc.—realistically done up on Sears forms. (But familiarity with company practice gives no real advantage.) Having disposed of as many items as he can by decision, referral, or whatever, the man writes down his reason for each action.

Various scores are obtained, including productivity (number of items dealt with), depth or thoughtfulness of response, and sensitivity to human relations. Scorers may also write descriptive reports on the man's apparent style.

This kind of test has not been very satisfactory for assessing individuals, though some personnel departments are using it for this. It is expensive to give and score, and correlates appreciably with conventional verbal-educational measures. There is no clear basis for defining what responses are good. There is no assurance that style in the test situation—with its artificial constraints on time, information, and means of communication—is representative of the style the person will display in an actual job. The in-basket is a one-item test, even though the candidate makes many responses. Performance on one problem (Frederiksen, 1961) indicates very little about how the person will score on a second, independent in-basket task. At least among elite candidates, individual differences in style are hard to pin down. The literature that advocates use of the in-basket test in assessment seems to place undue emphasis on the attractiveness of the test. It looks like a fair, realistic sample of the job, and is fun to take. Unfortunately, validations against criteria are rarely well reported; relationships appear to be extremely modest—as would be expected from the apparent lack of generalizability over forms.

More and more, users have shifted away from assessment toward training. If the concrete in-basket materials, imbedded in a program of theoretical presentations and group discussion, can help a man evaluate and change his style, this is far more constructive than weeding him out. Moreover, an in-basket test at the end of training can show which recommendations have "gotten across" and which have not, thus guiding revision of the training.

33. *A General Electric validation of an in-basket score (summarized by Lopez, 1966, p. 107) gives the following data:*

High third on test	68% above average on criterion
Middle third on test	53% " " " "
Low third on test	37% " " " "

What would you guess the correlation to be in these data? Check the soundness of your estimate with the aid of Figure 5.3.

Summary Comments on Perceptual and Problem-Solving Tests

Behavior in groups and thematic projective techniques remain to be discussed, but they are sufficiently novel that before proceeding it is well to make some summary comments on the tests examined so far. There are three ways to interpret a structured performance test:

● The test can be regarded as a measure of one specific type of performance, defined only by the operations used in measuring. When such a test is used as dependent variable in a psychological experiment, any positive findings are likely to be of ultimate theoretical importance even though the test cannot at present be given a broad interpretation.

● It can be used to measure a broad trait. Because of the low correlations among tests of the same supposed trait, adequate measurement requires a composite of tasks, as in Witkin's studies. The problem is essentially one of assembling a collection of test *tasks* just as an ability test assembles items. Performance testing of a personality construct seems to require a "hodgepodge," such as Binet invented to measure intelligence when no single type of problem proved adequate. A good deal of testing time, spaced out over several periods, very likely must be invested to measure even one trait well.

● It can perhaps be used (alone or in a composite) to predict for practical purposes.

Comparisons of performance tests with socially important criteria have been few and unsystematic. As comprehensive as any evaluation program was the Air Force work, summarized by Melton (1947, pp. 848–849):

A continuing effort was made during the Aviation Psychology Program to obtain a test of the reaction of the candidate to emotion-producing stimuli, either directly through the application of such stimuli as distractions during the course of performance on some psychomotor task or indirectly through the measurement of muscular tension or other psychophysiological variables. . . . The available data do not support the hypothesis that additional validity for the prediction of success in elementary pilot training accrues to a test situation when verbal threats and other distractions, including presumably fear-producing stimuli, are administered.

Although the Operational Stress Test had validities of 0.20–0.30, it overlapped so much with ability tests that it made no useful contribution to prediction. Twenty years of further sporadic efforts seem not to have changed the picture.

Structured tests have been widely applied in clinical research. Differences between patients and normals or among patients of different types are difficult to interpret; diagnostic categories have uncertain psychological significance, and results can often be attributed to differences in cooperation and attention rather than to fundamental psychological processes. To be sure, many relations are reported; for example, discharge of schizophrenics from hospital is predicted by low flicker-fusion threshold. Burdock, Sutton, and Zubin (1958), reviewing such findings, complain that investigations have picked variables too unsystematically, have not distinguished conceptual from perceptual performances, and have failed to compare complex performances against "baseline" measures of physiological and neurological functioning. Hence the data add little to psychological knowledge or practice.

Work on stylistic variables has commanded the greatest amount of attention in the past decade. While one can find considerable basic psychological interest in the work of such authors as Witkin and Wallach, there has been nothing to suggest that measures of style are ready for practical use—except, perhaps, as a part of a full appraisal of the person. Even in-basket data, on style in a realistic context, seem unlikely to indicate much about style on the job.

Styles in Work Groups

Group Discussion

The Leaderless Group Discussion (LGD) extends systematic observation to social behavior. A group of persons, perhaps applying for the same job, are told to discuss a certain problem (e.g., how to increase movie attendance). Observers rate predetermined aspects of each member's performance. The LGD is unstructured: no rules of procedure are established, the topic is left largely undefined, and the group, being strangers to each other, have no initial friendship or dominance relations. During the discussion, however, social patterns are quickly built up, and the role the person plays is presumably similar to the role he is prone to adopt in natural groups.

The variables most commonly rated have to do with three traits: prominence, goal facilitation (efficiency, suggesting useful ideas), and sociability. Bass (1954) measures prominence by rating the following on a scale from "a great deal" to "not at all"):

> showed initiative
> was effective in saying what he wanted to say
> clearly defined or outlined the problems
> motivated others to participate
> influenced the other participants
> offered good solutions to the problem
> led the discussion

What the test chiefly measures, Bass says, is "tendency to initiate structure in an initially unstructured situation."

The effectiveness of LGD can be evaluated in several ways. Stability over trials is fairly high; with a week between tests, the correlations range from 0.75 to 0.90. Over longer time intervals or with radical changes in the type of problem, correlations drop to about 0.50. The test is measuring some consistent and general aspect of personality. Behavior in practical situations is no doubt determined by many forces other than personality (seniority, relative prestige, specifically relevant knowledge, etc.) but LGD scores nonetheless have striking predictive value. Bass and Coates (1952) compared LGD scores with ratings by superiors given as much as 9 months later and found correlations of 0.40 to 0.45. Arbous (1955) found a validity of 0.60 for LGD against rated promise of executives in training. Suitability for the British foreign service as rated after two years on duty was predicted (validity 0.33) by LGD at the time of selection (Vernon, 1950).

LGD illustrates the advantage that can be obtained from systematic observations. Social relations are important in personnel assignment, yet very difficult to judge validly from questionnaires, letters of recommendations, or interviews. LGD is an economical "worksample" of group behavior. It avoids much of the bias inherent in summary impressions. Army colonels' ratings of cadet potential were much poorer predictors of later merit ratings than were total scores recorded by these same colonels acting as observers for an LGD session (Bass, 1954).

No doubt LGD is "fakable." The applicant who wants to make a good impression surely will say more and try to lead. But this only increases the validity of the technique. If he lacks social skills his ineptness will be clear to the observer. If he "puts on a good show," he is likely to put on an equally good show on a job, where he is motivated to display the same skills.

Task Leadership

The Leaderless Group Discussion is one of a number of worksample techniques for measuring personality that originated in German and British military psychology. Psychologists selecting officers thought it necessary to observe complex behavior combining intellect, emotion, and habit.

One team-performance task devised by the Germans uses two pairs of shears linked by rods so that they must move in unison. While one shear is opening, the other is closing. Each subject operates one pair of shears, cutting a series of increasingly complex patterns from a sheet of paper. If one man goes directly and forcefully at his task, the shears of the other man move in a rhythm that makes accurate cutting almost impossible. By means of observation, automatic recording, and inspection of the product, the tester looks for evidence of initiative, dominance, and cooperation. In a group leadership test that OSS (forerunner of CIA) used to assess candidates for operational jobs, candidates were directed to move a heavy 8-foot log, and themselves, over two walls 10 feet high, 8 feet apart, and separated by an imaginary bottomless chasm. Observers noted which men showed initiative and leadership, how they directed others, how they accepted orders, and so on.

Perhaps the high point of fiendish ingenuity was the OSS construction test. The subject is assigned to build a 5-foot cube with a set of super-Tinkertoys. Poles and spools must be fitted together, and since the parts are too large to be managed by one man, two helpers are assigned. After giving directions, the tester ostentatiously clicks his stop watch and retreats. What the subject does not know is that his helpers are highly trained stumblebums. Kippy is negative, indolent, a drawback. Buster is an eager beaver, ready to do all manner of things, mostly wrong, and also primed to needle the candidate with personal criticism. This is reported as a typical dialogue (Anon., 1946):

> *Candidate:* Well, let's get going.
> *Buster:* What is it you want done, exactly? What do I do first?
> *Candidate:* Well, first put some corners together—let's see, make eight of these corners and be sure you pin them like this one.
> *Buster:* You mean we both make eight corners or just one of us?
> *Candidate:* You each make four of these, and hurry.
> *Kippy:* Whacha in, the Navy? You look like one of them curly-headed Navy boys all the girls are after.
> *Candidate:* Er, no, I'm not in anything.
> *Kippy:* Just a draft dodger, eh?

Candidate: Let's have less talk and more work. You build a square over here and you build one over there.

Kippy: Who are you talking to—him or me? Why don't you give us a number or something—call one of us number one and the other number two?

Candidate: I'm sorry. What's your name?

Buster: Mine's Buster and his is Kippy. What's yours?

Candidate: You can call me Slim.

Buster: Not with that shining head of yours. What do they call you, Baldy or Curly? Did you ever think of wearing a toupee?

Slim: Come on, get to work.

Kippy: He's sensitive about being bald.

Slim: Just let's get this thing finished. We haven't much more time. Hey, there, you, be careful. You knocked that pole out deliberately.

Kippy: Who, me? Now listen to me, you———, if this———thing had been built right from the beginning, the poles wouldn't come out. For———, they send a boy out here to do a man's job. . . .

Kippy and Buster are psychologists and are in a position to make an excellent report on the man's reaction. (The fact that they had served as Army privates, and that some of the candidates they were privileged to torment were generals out of uniform being considered for special assignment, set an untouchable record for job satisfaction among psychologists.)

Interpersonal Relations

The procedures described above are designed to investigate the personality of each single individual. The other persons in the group are in effect stimuli necessary to elicit the responses of interest. Groups can be assembled at random for that purpose. One might instead investigate existing groups of persons who regularly interact. While the occasion is randomly selected, the group itself is considered to be fixed. The observation has to be interpreted as evidence on the group as a unit, rather than as evidence on the participants as separate personalities.

Probably the widest application of such methods is in the study of the family. To study how mothers educate their children, women have been asked to teach the preschool child to copy a simple drawing by using the toy in which a marking stylus is driven by two controls, one turned by the mother and one turned by the child. Each knob controls movement in one direction, so that responsibility is divided. The observer notes indications of patience, criticism, use of praise, clarity of directions, and other variables that presumably enter the mother's everyday relations with the child (Hess & Shipman, 1965). Another method is to bring up a controversial subject, such as rules regulating an adolescent's social life, and ask the parents and child to try to reach agreement. This can be used either for research or as a lead in family counseling.

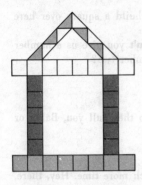

Figure 18.5.   Pattern to be constructed in Russell Sage Social Relations Test.
Original display in three colors.

Schooling ought to develop skill in interpersonal relations, and evaluation that confines itself to individual performance in seatwork is seriously incomplete. Information that could profitably be collected in, for example, comparing the effects of a programmed curriculum with those of a school program allowing much group activity is illustrated in the Russell Sage Social Relations Test. A set of snap-together plastic blocks is used, each child in the class being given at least one; the group is to construct a model of a figure. One of the figures appears in Figure 18.5. Directions (much abbreviated) are as follows:

In this test you are *supposed* to talk to each other, you are *supposed* to help each other, and you are *supposed* to work together. You do not, each one of you, get a score. Instead the whole class gets *one* score, and this score depends on how *fast* and how *well* you work the problems.

I want all of you to study the house to see if you can figure out some good ways the class can get together and build it. . . . Before you begin you can take as much time as you need to talk about it and to figure out a way in which the class can do it. I will not begin timing until you tell me that you are all ready to start.

The examiner tries to move the discussion forward without giving the class any ideas. The group discussion continues until there is a plan for action, after which the house is built; then the next problem, a bridge, is presented in the same way. A record is made of the way the group reacts in each phase (talking all at once, leaving it to a single leader to generate ideas, comparing alternatives, etc.) and of the adequacy of the ideas put forward in the planning phase (appointing a leader, having all the children bring up their pieces at once, etc.). Numerical ratings on several dimensions provide a summary, or the group may be fitted into a typology as "mature," "rollicking," "suppressed," etc. (See Damrin, 1959; the test was developed by ETS, but the original blocks, a toy in mass production, are no longer manufactured. Other kinds of blocks can no doubt be substituted.)

34. *Give reasons for each of the following recommendations by Bass regarding LGD technique.*

a. *Counts of actual behavior (e.g., new approaches suggested) should be sub-stituted for ratings of the subject's tendency to suggest new approaches.*
b. *Problems should be equally ambiguous to all participants.*
c. *Examinees tested in a group should all have the same rank.*
35. *Compare LGD and peer ratings as methods of assessing leadership potential.*
36. *A field performance test of an NCO's ability to lead his squad was developed by the Army as a criterion measure of proficiency. Why are some performance tests regarded as measures of personality and some as measures of proficiency?*

Thematic Projective Techniques

The Bender and Rorschach illustrate projective techniques in which the subject's style of handling a problem is the focus of attention. Those *stylistic* tests may be contrasted with *thematic* tests, in which the interpreter is especially concerned with the content of thoughts and fantasies. This distinction resembles that between trait questionnaires that focus on response tendencies, and techniques for studying stimulus meanings such as the Semantic Differential and the Role Concept Repertory test. The stylistic and thematic categories are not mutually exclusive. Obsessions show up in the Rorschach protocol, and one can observe intellectual style in the Thematic Apperception Test (TAT). But the stylistic tests generally yield rich stylistic information and are poor sources of thematic information. The thematic test comes nearer to examining "the whole person" at once than any other testing technique, seeking information on emotions, attitudes, and cognitive processes. In addition to TAT, the thematic category includes the Sentence Completion Test and doll-play observations.

The Thematic Apperception Test

The Thematic Apperception Test of H. A. Murray and his coworkers (1938) requires the subject to interpret a picture by telling a story—what is happening, what led up to the scene, and what will be the outcome. The responses are dictated by the constructs, experiences, conflicts, and wishes of the subject. Essentially the person projects himself into the scene, identifying with a character just as he vicariously takes the place of the actor when he sees a film. TAT consists of twenty pictures, different pictures being used for men and women. Since two 1-hour sessions are required for the full test, investigators ordinarily use selected cards. The subject is led to believe that his imagination is being tested.

Interpretation of protocols. The interpreter gives particular attention to the themes behind the plots. The stories may indicate a defeatist attitude, concern about overbearing authority figures, or preoccupation with sex. In addition to these aspects of response content, the interpreter considers the style: use of the whole picture rather than piecemeal attack, fluency, concern with accuracy in fitting the story to the picture, etc.

The interpreter looks at each story in turn, deriving hypotheses from the plot, the symbolism, and the style. The hypothesis from one story (e.g., "This man represses hostile feelings") is checked against subsequent stories. The interpreter must decide how much weight to give to each of many conflicting indications and must integrate the information on intellectual powers, emotional conflicts, and defense mechanisms.

Only a few illustrations of the impressionistic analysis can be given here. Card I of TAT shows a boy, perhaps 10 years old, looking at a violin lying on a flat surface. A girl, age 14, with a Binet IQ of 143, gives this story (Henry, 1956, p. 111):

> Right now the boy is looking at the violin. It looks like he might be kind of sad or mad because he has to play. Before he might have played ball with the other boys and his mother wouldn't let him. He had to go in and play. Looks like he might practice for a little while and then sneak out.

Henry, working from this and other stories, estimated her IQ at 140, commenting on how clearly the story "takes into account the basic stimulus demands of the picture" and goes on to "entirely relevant elaborations of good quality . . . [which] attribute motive and action to the characters."

Whereas this story led more to a study of process than of plot, the story of a 42-year-old clerk is interpreted thematically (p. 145):

> The story behind this is that this is the son of a very well-known, a very good musician and the father has probably died. The only thing the son has left is this violin which is undoubtedly a very good one and to the son, the violin is the father and the son sits there daydreaming of the time that he will understand the music and interpret it on the violin that his father had played.

Henry comments that the first sentence shows preoccupation with excellence and a conviction that to match the example is impossible. The man dreams only of things within himself, and takes no action to carry out his ambition.

In contrast to this rather direct interpretation of a plot as reflecting the teller's drives and style of behavior, another story shows the possibility of looking for symbolism. A recent immigrant, a man age 29, tells this story (Henry, p. 178):

> A young boy sitting in front of a violin spread out on white table, or white linen. It is not clear in the expression of the face if he thinks in glorification and admiration of that what the violin and music could hold for him or if he is bored and in disgust with the lesson he has to take and doesn't want.

Note, says Henry, the emphasis on conflicting alternatives: glorification or disgust, has to take and doesn't want. This personality "may well be marked by its attraction to opposites." The core of conflict appears to be sexual, the basic issue being whether woman can be

both the Madonna and the sexual object. . . . This is an instance of the use of the violin as a sexual symbol. The man is basically preoccupied with some strong emotional issue; hence he utilizes form details in a distorting manner [e.g., "violin spread out"]. . . . He feels impelled to make a formal heterosexual adjustment as well as a conventional social adjustment, even though both are somewhat forced and against his will.

These excerpts by no means represent the intricacy of a full interpretation in which stories are compared with each other and with background information about the subject. For examples of such full interpretations the reader is referred to Henry (1956) and Shneidman (1951). We should also emphasize that such interpretations as Henry makes are—if the psychologist is properly trained—extremely tentative. They are discarded unless there is supporting evidence elsewhere in the test and the subject's history. These illustrations do indicate the individuality TAT responses exhibit, and the variation in the interpreter's attack. At one moment he views the performance entirely as an intellectual effort; at another he treats the response as a symbolization of unconscious conflict. How he interprets each response depends upon the story and perhaps upon his own artistic impulses of the moment. Interpretation has been primarily qualitative and impressionistic, and no two interpreters proceed in the same way.

It is possible to develop objective scoring. There are dozens of variables whose strength can be observed in almost every TAT performance: perception of authority, reaction to extremely difficult tasks, originality, reliance on luck and magical intervention, etc. The themes themselves may be individualistic, but common elements can be tabulated. Scoring can look at the percentage of stories the outcomes of which is unhappy, the number of female characters seen as predatory, etc. Formal scoring most often emphasizes the "needs"—or, to use the better term recently suggested by McClelland, "concerns"—for achievement, affiliation, power, and other values. Some studies suggest that the original conception of projective tasks as unstructured should be revised; apparently the most significant information is elicited by pictures that are structured to suggest a particular emotion or conflict, though not so explicit that every subject tells the same story (Murstein, 1965).

Stability coefficients over 2 months are in the range from 0.60 to 0.90 for such scores as abasement themes, giving stories with positive outcomes, and presence of words referring to relief of tension. Scoring is imprecise and the strength of motive-arousal depends on the subject's most recent experiences. That holds down the coefficient. On the whole, it appears that TAT collects sufficient information to permit fairly accurate scoring of traits, if scoring keys are carefully developed toward that end. Harrison (1965) provides an excellent guide to the literature on TAT, citing some 700 studies.

Relation to overt behavior.   The difficult question is what TAT information means. It is too simple to say that the stories describe what the person does or would like to do. A preoccupation seen in the stories is not necessarily acted out. Skolnick (1966) found some correspondence between adolescent boys' power imagery in TAT and ratings by their peers of assuredness ($r = 0.33$). Likewise, for power imagery and observer-rated submissiveness, $r = -0.41$; for affiliation imagery and dependency, $r = 0.25$. There were not many such relations for boys, and even fewer for girls.

Frequency of behavioral aggression correlated with aggression themes in stories given by problem boys, and fear of punishment judged from overt behavior correlated with frequency of mention of punishment in stories. The trait configuration matters. Every one of the seven boys with high TAT aggression and low fear of punishment behaved very aggressively; only two out of nine with high TAT aggression and high fear of punishment acted aggressively (Mussen & Naylor, 1954). In another study, a score representing *inhibition* of aggression and denial of aggressive impulses correlated as strongly with aggressive action as did the TAT score on presence of aggressive plots (Skolnick, 1966). Olweus (1969) made a careful theoretical elaboration of the relations between aggressive tendencies and inhibitory tendencies seen in projective responses, and situational factors that elicit and inhibit aggression. He obtained strong evidence for his theoretical model: among boys whose tests showed little inhibition, strength of aggressive themes correlated around 0.55 with rated overt aggression; among high inhibitors, the correlation was about -0.50. A comparable result emerged when aggressive behavior of patients in a neuropsychiatric hospital was rated by attendants (Pittluck, 1950). Aggressive behavior went with aggressive TAT stories; but when the patient's stories muffled the aggression by introducing a plot justification or some other mechanism, he was much more likely to control his aggression in the ward. For a more complete review of this literature, see Zubin, Eron, and Schumer (1965, Chapter 9). To summarize: a particular sign (e.g., large number of aggressive themes) is meaningful only in the light of the subject's sex, level of education, cultural background, and other aspects of his TAT projective responses.

McClelland (1966, p. 479) puts the matter into perspective:

[TAT] is a sample of operant behavior, that is, thoughts. The term projective creates a kind of pseudoproblem by suggesting that we must study the relation between what a person's motives "really" are and what he "projects": a person "is" just as much what he says in response to a TAT card as he "is" anything else he does. And since when is fantasy not behavior? . . . Let us redefine the problem as a study of the relationship between thought and action. A TAT gives a sample of a person's thoughts. . . . When the problem is rephrased in this simple way, it almost becomes a pseudoproblem to ask: Are thoughts generally positively, negatively, or nonrelated to relevant actions? At least to me it has always seemed likely that it would depend on a lot of other variables. . . . If I wanted to prove [that] *nega-*

tive correlations between thought and action predominate, I think I could manage to get this result simply by sampling from a universe of performance responses in which the subject was operating under high stress. . . . That is, there is evidence that high stress lowers the performance *especially* of highly motivated people so that one could get a negative correlation in this way between, say, TAT *n* Ach and performance (italics added).

Among Skolnick's many findings, one more should be mentioned. When TAT was given to the subjects again in their late 30s, most scores correlated higher with adolescent behavior than the scores on the adolescent TAT did. The number of significant relations is large for males. Adult power imagery correlated 0.40 to 0.50 with adolescent popularity, prestige, and leadership. Adult affiliation imagery correlated *minus* 0.41 with late-adolescent talkativeness. Evidently one's developmental history leaves its mark on his fantasy productions—which was, of course, one of Freud's main points. But fantasy does not directly imply what one's behavior is now or will be in the future.

Transient states that affect TAT. McClelland's remarks (quoted above) emphasize how situational stresses and instigators influence the "criterion" side of test-to-behavior comparisons. These forces influence TAT performance as well, as was neatly demonstrated by Clark (1952). He gave TAT to college men after having presented a series of slides of nude females, on the pretext that rating their sexual attractiveness had something to do with studying relations of body-type to personality in a psychology course. (*This* deception by a psychological experimenter seems not to have aroused any complaint.) The control group, meanwhile, had been kept busy rating landscapes. On TAT, 66 per cent of the controls were high in sex imagery (above the median for both groups combined). Only 27 per cent of the experimentals' stories had that degree of sexual content. One might well conclude that taking sexual drives out for exercise reduces their intensity. But Clark destroys that interpretation by another experiment, essentially repeating the first one but in the context of a fraternity beer-party. The scores this time were: controls, 26 per cent above median; experimentals, 60! (The median itself was much higher than in the first experiment.) Clark's interpretation takes into account the experimental students' guilt over sexual arousal in the classroom; this served to inhibit sexual responses on TAT. One does not know how many sexual responses came to the subjects' minds in the first experiment and were suppressed.

The usual aim in personality measurement is to study traits rather than states; but as we said at the end of Chapter 16, research on experimental interventions requires sensitive, hence *unstable*, outcome measures. Thematic tests seem to have a sensitivity that enhances their validity as experimental measures, but perhaps makes them less trustworthy as trait indicators. Surely the most interesting of the studies is one on parachutists.

Figure 18.6. (*above and opposite page*) **Thematic pictures to measure reactions of parachutists.**
Fenz & Epstein, 1962. Pictures courtesy of the authors.

Fenz and Epstein (1962) prepared pictures having high, low, or no relevance to parachuting. (See Figure 18.6.) Members of a sport parachuting club were tested on the day when they were scheduled to jump, and also either two weeks before or two weeks after the jump (with a parallel set of pictures). The parachutists were much more aroused on the day of the jump. The skin conductance measure of Table 18.2 is a "sweaty palm" reaction; just showing a picture related to parachuting on the day of the jump produced a flash of tension. While stories produced on the day of the jump carry a positive message about parachuting (more so than on the nonjump day), many of these stories are so exaggerated that they suggested deliberate denial of fear; e.g., "He is not afraid at all, just looks that way because of the wind that is blowing in his face. He will have a wonderful jump. It will be great, just great!" This is only a sample of

the findings, all of which, just because they involve a more genuine stress than experimental research can provide, shed light on the way individuals cope with conflict.

Though thematic tests are sensitive to testing conditions, one gets better evidence on traits if he tests the person in a normal emotional state, on a day when he is not subject to examination or other stresses. This policy is not easy to carry out, especially in doing a workup on an incoming clinical patient who by definition is in a peculiar state of stress. A second suggestion is to test on several days, preferably with different testers.

TAT has been remarkably successful in improving the prediction of grades, according to Harrison's summary (1965, p. 582). There have been a number of correlations as high as 0.70. Perhaps TAT can enhance prediction over that derived from mental tests or past records, but prediction is probably not important enough to justify so costly a test. It would be useful to predict the kind

Table 18.2.   Galvanic skin response to thematic pictures as a function of the situation

Relevance of picture to parachuting	Mean response of nonparachutist controls	Mean response of parachutists	
		2 weeks from jump	On day of jump
None	1.0	0.7	1.1
Low	0.8	0.8	1.3
High	0.9	1.0	2.2

Source: Fenz and Epstein, 1962; see also Fenz, 1964.

of instruction (e.g., independent study, group discussion) a student would learn most from, but TAT research has not gone in that direction. The McKeachie research (see below) was aimed at theory, not practical procedure, and the effects found were weak.

In sum, except for LGD, no performance test has established practical correlates that now warrant using it alone, as a psychometric basis for decisions about personality. The ability tests—flicker fusion, EFT, Bender, etc.—are usable, but probably not as measures of "personality." One can make good use of a number of the techniques (character tests, WJT, Russell Sage, In-Basket) in educational evaluation.

37. *Harrison (1965) cites a number of studies in which TAT predicted success in some occupation (usually one wherein human relations are important). There is one study of seminarians, one of camp counselors, one of marriage counselors, etc. If these problems were important enough to study in the first place, why do you suppose there has been no confirming study in the decade since they were first reported?*

38. *Harrison (1965, p. 590) says that negative evidence on TAT should be given much less credence than positive evidence:*

   "Negative validity results . . . do not necessarily constitute damaging evidence, for the researchers may have employed improper methods of analysis in confounded designs against unreliable or otherwise inadequate criteria. . . . Positive results do demonstrate something, assuming that the work has been done honestly and that grievous errors have not been introduced into the design." What are the merits and demerits of this position? Is it pertinent only to projective tests?

39. *How many traits are mentioned in Henry's three interpretations?*

40. *Can one regard the frequency of punishment by authority in TAT stories as an indication of how often the subject is punished in life?*

41. *Harrison (1965, p. 577) warns of the risk that the psychologist will project himself and his "theoretical predilections" into a TAT interpretation, and goes on to say that "pathologizing is a common error." What does he mean?*

Measurement of Concern for Achievement

TAT, designed to cover the whole range of ideas and behavior, cannot cover any one topic thoroughly. While a person obsessed with independence conflicts may bring them into every story, most people reveal feelings about authority only on one or two cards. As the examples above show, any single picture is indefinite enough to bring out different types of information from different subjects. Flexibility that permits the subject to reveal almost any trait or theme prominent in his personality structure is an advantage in a free-ranging exploration of personality. It is a serious disadvantage when one wishes to answer a specific question.

Focused tests are designed to elicit thematic responses that bear on a single question. For example, Murphy and Likert (1938) carried out research on labor-management conflict with pictures of strikers in conflict with police, etc. A focused test for Air Force personnel was based on the hypothesis that outwardly directed aggression would be associated with tolerance for high centrifugal forces. The criterion was a measure of the force required to produce blackout in a human centrifuge. In the best-designed of several validation studies, the score from the thematic test classified 18 of 25 subjects correctly as having high or low tolerance (Silverman *et al.*, 1957).

The possibilities of the focused thematic test have been most thoroughly exploited by D. C. McClelland (1953), J. W. Atkinson (1958; 1966), and their associates. These investigators selected pictures intended to bring out attitudes regarding achievement. One such set shows a work situation (men at a machine), a study situation (boy at desk with book), a father-son picture, and a boy apparently daydreaming. Achievement motivation is credited whenever a story suggests competition with a standard: e.g.,

A worker is putting a hot plate of metal back in the oven with a pair of tongs in order to heat it up again. The gentleman beside him is a helper.

This is scored as implying concern for achievement because the reheating implies "desire to move ahead to the ultimate goal" (Atkinson, 1958, p. 722). Following Murray's tradition, the score was called "need for achievement" (or *n* Achievement)—but, as mentioned earlier, McClelland notes the dubious connotations of "need" and suggests that one think of "concern" for achievement. The concerned person "has achievement on his mind," we might say.

A second projective measure for the same purpose is the Test of Insight (by E. G. French; see Atkinson, 1958, pp. 242–248). A brief description of behavior is given; for example: "Bill always lets the 'other fellow' win." The subject is to provide an explanation. The test consists of twenty such items, ten in each form. The score is the number of times desire for achievement is mentioned as a motive.

Such projective measures presumably get at an aspect of personality other measures do not. As reported in McClelland (1955, pp. 414 ff.), de Charms *et al.* made up a questionnaire on desire to achieve. This correlated only 0.23 with the score from the thematic test. The subject who scores high on this questionnaire is concerned with conformity, defers to authority, and disapproves unsuccessful people, whereas a high thematic-test score is more often associated with striving and effectiveness. Scores on the French test correlate near zero with peer judgments of motivation to achieve (Atkinson, 1958, p. 247). French was able to show that the peer judgments of motivation depend heavily on observed success, and probably reflect ability rather than motivation. It is not entirely certain that other techniques cannot obtain the information evoked by the thematic test. Sherwood (1966) claims to have a questionnaire that does measure concern for achievement, and Carney (1966) finds high or low correlations between projectives and questionnaires, according to the test situation.

Construct validation. The thematic test is related to nontest behavior at a level significant for theory, if not for decisions. E. French and Thomas (1958) asked highly intelligent subjects to solve a difficult intellectual problem. The problem had several acceptable solutions. The group high on the thematic test worked, on the average, twice as long as the low scorers before giving up, and were much more successful in finding at least one solution. Among the Highs, performance correlated 0.36 with ability, but the correlation was zero for the Lows. Ability predicts poorly unless men are motivated to use that ability. (But cf. p. 549.)

Men who give achievement-oriented stories also are men who tend to be upward mobile, rising to a higher level of employment than their fathers had. (This finding is based on tests given to the men as adults; no truly predictive findings are at hand.) Achievement stories given in response to pictures of men on jobs unlike the subject's current work produced scores related to the criterion, while response to pictures of familiar work scenes had no such validity (Veroff, Feld, & Crockett, 1966). Evidently, the thematic test has to provide a stimulus for fantasy rather than for recall of experience. Another methodological point worth passing mention is the value of a statistical correction for verbal fluency; without the correction, long stories are likely to lead to undeserved high scores (Veroff *et al.*, 1960).

The work on the measurement of concern for achievement is perhaps the best example to date of a program of construct validation. The theory has been elaborated into a complex network of relations, taking into account the subject's ability, his present temporary state of arousal, and his basic pattern of motives. The theory emerged from the research, an amendment being made whenever an expectation was not confirmed. While alternative theories are emerging from other laboratories, most of the conceptualization that has emerged from the Atkinson and McClelland teams seems likely to survive. We can barely hint at the complexity of the theory by displaying a portion of the network and summarizing

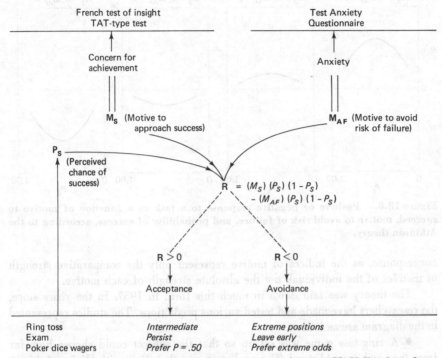

Figure 18.7. Portion of the theory developed by Atkinson, McClelland, and co-workers to interpret thematic measures of concern over achievement.

some of the work (from Atkinson & Feather, 1966). At the top and bottom of Figure 18.7 are two lines that separate off the observable indicators from the constructs used in building up the theory. For n Achievement the French test and the picture test supply moderately adequate measures; unfortunately, their intercorrelation is rather low—again, an argument for multiple-task measurement. A questionnaire developed by Sarason and others is generally used to measure anxiety in these studies.

The theory argues that concern for achievement expresses a motive to approach success and that anxiety is a motive to avoid failure. Experience has led to the complicated equation combining these two motives with P_S, the perceived difficulty of a task. A positive resultant R implies a readiness to work on a task, and a negative R implies avoidance of the task. The equation produces curves like those shown in Figure 18.8. Interest centers on the shapes of the curves rather than the precise numerical values. The argument is that a person with strong M_S is more likely to respond constructively to a task on which the chance of success is intermediate. One cannot say literally that an R_S of zero implies

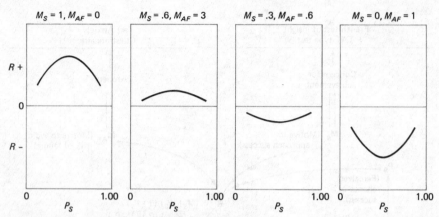

Figure 18.8.   Positive or negative response to a task as a function of motive to succeed, motive to avoid risk of failure, and probability of success, according to the Atkinson theory.

nonresponse, as the indices of motive represent only the comparative strength of motives of the individual, not the absolute strength of each motive.

The theory was laid down in much this form in 1957. In the years since, the researchers have made and tested various predictions. The studies represented in the diagram are as follows:

• A ring-toss game was set up so that the subject could choose how far from the peg he would stand. The prediction was that those with High *n* Achievement and Low anxiety (HL pattern) would prefer a moderate challenge intermediate risk, and that LH subjects would prefer to stand close or far away. While one is likely to miss the peg if he throws from far away, he is shielded from loss of self-esteem because he is attempting the near-impossible. The experiment confirmed the prediction.

• In a 3-hour course examination, it was predicted that HL subjects would work on the test longer than the average student. Eleven out of 15 of them did, compared with 3 out of 9 LH's.

• A dice game was devised in which the subject could choose his level of risk on each play—high, medium, or low. The prediction was that HL subjects would prefer medium risks. Instead, they chose bets very likely to win. The LH's—predicted to pick extreme bets, either very likely or very unlikely to win—chose bets unlikely to win, but for which winning had a generous payoff. As the theoretical prediction did not work out, the network had to be changed. It was suggested that the usual equation does not hold in a gambling situation, in which the subject's merit as a performer is not challenged. This modification generated further testable hypotheses (Raynor & Smith, 1966; Van der Meer, 1967). The current state of the theory is summarized by Feather (1968).

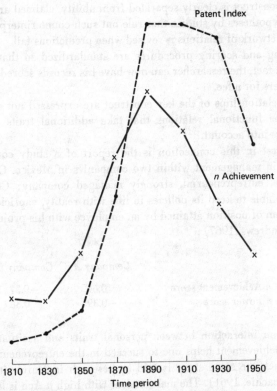

Patent Index

n Achievement

1810   1830   1850   1870   1890   1910   1930   1950
                        Time period

Figure 18.9. Comparison of patents, as an index of creative business effort, with emphasis on achievement themes in school readers, at various times in United States history.
The vertical scale is arbitrary. *McClelland, 1961, p. 150.*

Another line of work extends the theory to consider achievement motivation in a culture as a whole. There is evidence of regular relations between the prevalence of this motivation and the economic development of a country (e.g., Figure 18.9). An historical study cannot measure individuals, so investigators try to assess the prevalent motives from the themes represented in children's readers. Validation studies support the use of these as an indicator of the culture's concern for achievement. Katz (1967) has discussed how this motive is generated in the child, with particular reference to American minorities.

This program of research demonstrates a number of the features desirable in obtaining measures that are to be given a theoretic interpretation:

● More than one indicator of the construct is used, to rule out the effect of specific factors.

● The construct is clearly separated from ability, claimed ambition, and the other rival hypotheses by studies that rule out such counterinterpretations.

● The network of relations is revised when predictions fail.

● Testing and scoring procedures are standardized so that results can be replicated. In fact, the researcher can now have his records scored by McClelland-trained workers for a fee.

● The relationships of the key construct are expressed not as simple correlations but as functional relations that take additional traits and situational characteristics into account.

Of interest in this connection is the report of a study correlating scores with success in management within two companies in Mexico. Company A was a competitive, entrepreneurial, strongly managed company; Company B was feudalistic, unable to keep its policies in line with reality, capriciously managed. The correlation of position attained by an employee with his projective score was as follows (Andrews, 1967):

	Company A	Company B
n Achievement score	0.64	−0.37
n Power score	−0.39	0.38

Here we see an interaction between personal traits and a situational variable. Concern for achievement helps one to succeed in the entrepreneurial setting, not the other. Much the same story is told by research in University of Michigan classes (McKeachie, 1961). The male student with high n Ach is likely to do best in a classroom where the instructor is strongly task oriented, but not where the dominant tone is togetherness. (Recall also Domino's study, p. 550.)

Probably the greatest weakness of the work with n Achievement is the concentration on male college students and executives. There has been some work with women, with blue-collar workers, etc., but not enough to justify extension of the theory to them. There is evidence that the interpretative network for men does not apply to women (E. French & Lesser, 1964). For many personality measures, responses of the two sexes have to be interpreted differently, since scores often have different correlates for men and women, or boys and girls. Perhaps the development of the male is a more continuous phenomenon, with the emergence of a self-concept that is consistent from year to year. The girl-becoming-woman, however, shifts back and forth among the roles of student, worker, mate, and mother. The complexities of female personality have so far thwarted the theorist—but perhaps the difficulty arises because almost all persons constructing personality theories are males!

Although the focused projective test works well as a research variable when mean scores for groups are needed, scores of individuals are often undependable. Correlations between two picture sets or between testings separated by modest time intervals range from 0.85 down to some deplorable 0.15's. No investigator should undertake a study without a pilot study checking out the adequacy of his stimuli, his scoring rules, and his instructions to subjects.

SUGGESTED READINGS

Bass, Bernard M. The leaderless group discussion. *Psychological Bulletin*, 1954, *51*, 465–492.

A comprehensive account of evidence on the practical validity of LGD scores, together with an analysis of the personality and ability factors that lead to good LGD performance.

Levitt, Eugene E. The water-jar Einstellung test as a measure of rigidity. *Psychological Bulletin*, 1956, *53*, 347–370.

Levitt summarizes numerous investigations of the generality of this test. He shows that the same test takes on different psychological properties with only slight changes in design. Levitt's critique of the psychometric properties of WJT raises questions pertinent to nearly all performance tests.

McClelland, David C. The measurement of human motivation: an experimental approach. In *Proceedings, invitational conference on testing problems*, 1952. Princeton: ETS, 1953. Pp. 41–51. (Reprinted in Anastasi, 1966.)

Describes the early development of the picture test of motivation to achieve and reports studies extending the construct validation. In reading, note when McClelland is making a claim that a relationship is strong, and when he is only claiming that it is significantly different from zero.

Peterson, Donald R. Scientific, professional, and ethical issues. In *The clinical study of social behavior*. New York: Appleton-Century-Crofts, 1968. Pp. 221–238. See also pages 19–23, 32–35, and 138–141.

The summary chapter of a book which, taken as a whole, reflects a dispairing attitude regarding the possibility of arriving at valid generalizations about personality. Peterson sees behavior as so heavily conditioned by situational factors that he relies entirely on idiographic analysis. His previous research with MMPI and with factor analysis qualifies him as a critic of trait approaches.

Skolnick, Arlene. Motivational imagery and behavior over twenty years. McClelland, David C. Longitudinal trends in the relation of thought to action. Lazarus, Richard S. Story telling and the measurement of motivation: the direct versus substitutive controversy. *Journal of Consulting Psychology*, 1966, *30*, 463–487.

Skolnick reports extensive and carefully collected data comparing adolescent behavior with TAT scores in adolescence and in adulthood. While accepting her facts, McClelland and Lazarus raise basic questions about Skolnick's interpretation and about the meaning of fantasy productions. Lazarus in particular discusses the methodological problems in collecting thematic data. The papers are loaded with comments suggesting worthwhile further investigations.

Tyler, Leona E. Individual differences in cognitive style. In *The psychology of human differences* (3rd ed.). New York: Appleton-Century-Crofts, 1965. Pp. 210–235.

Tyler reviews the history of perceptual and stylistic tests from their earliest beginnings, including some of their European prototypes. She introduces briefly a great number of tests. Her account will seem more enthusiastic than our somewhat critical treatment. This is largely because she emphasizes the value of tests for group comparisons in research whereas we have asked about their usefulness in examining single individuals.

Witkin, H. A. The perception of the upright. *Scientific American*, February 1959, *200*, 50–70. (Reprinted in Jackson & Messick, 1967.)

A summary account of the Witkin procedures, theory, and findings regarding the so-called field-dependence dimension. Particularly to be noted is the argument that field-dependence may not imply maladjustment, but that it does imply what kind of maladjustment (if any) the person will develop.

Assessment of
Personality Dynamics

The psychometric tradition isolates separate dimensions within ability and personality, and represents the individual by assigning scores on those dimensions. Other testers follow a more artistic tradition in which tests are seen as just one procedure for gaining insight into a complexly organized system of needs, concepts, and perceptual attitudes. The impressionistic interpreter is not primarily concerned with arriving at quantitative scores on summarizing dimensions. He is concerned with the organization of processes within the individual. The impressionistic interpreter asks what "personality structure" could account for the observed facts—for the ways the subject perceives significant others in his life, for the discrepancies between his abilities on various tests, for the seeming differences between his fantasy concerns and his overt behavior, etc. Such a coherent picture could be of great potential value in dealing with a case, but its usefulness depends entirely upon its quality and completeness, and these in turn depend on the range of information available and the astuteness of the clinician's synthesis. The clinician's judgment makes full use of his psychological theory and his experience with other cases, but the final portrait he draws of the subject is an artistic reconciliation of diverse impressions.

Almost any psychological test, observation, or interview can be used as a basis for such a portrait. We have illustrated with many examples: Kirk's description of a type of underachiever (p. 505); Osgood and Luria's description of Eve from the Semantic Differential (p. 566); Henry's TAT interpretations (p. 652). These examples vary considerably in the extent to which the interpreter speculates. Henry's sketches range from an almost literal description of the young girl's reasoning methods to a symbolic translation of the story given by the immigrant man. As one further example which shows how freely a clinician may employ creative imagination, psychoanalytic theory, and even frank speculation, we may quote a Bender interpretation made by Max Hutt (Shneidman, 1951, pp. 227–233). Hutt first notes that the reproduced figures are arranged in the same sequence as in the original, the first six being aligned with the left margin, but that the last two drawings are fitted into the right half of the page.

Our first hunches then are: this individual has strong orderly, i.e., compulsive needs, tending towards a sort of compulsive ritual, but tries to deny them [the first drawing being displaced away from the margin and the examiner having noted that the man draws fast and unhesitatingly] . . . , and he is oppressed with some (probably) generalized feelings of anxiety and (more specifically) personal inadequacy (clings to the left margin and is "constrained" to use all of the space available to him on this one sheet). We raise the question for consideration, at once, "How strong and from what source is this anxiety and what is his defense?" We can speculate, from his use of space, that he attempts in some way to "bind" his anxiety, i.e., he cannot tolerate it for long or in large amounts, and that one of the features of this young adult's functioning is the need of control. . . . The super-ego is very strict.

Here Hutt has looked at the style of the man's performance, and then has tried to infer what inner tensions and defenses could generate such a style. As he says, these are hunches and speculations to be checked against other evidence in the protocol and against all other information about the patient. As in most "dynamic" interpretations, Hutt uses Freudian concepts of drives, conflict, and defenses.

As an example of more detailed analysis, consider Hutt's remarks on the subject's reproduction of the rows of circles (see Figure 18.3).

. . . the ten diagonal columns of circles [offer] further evidence of the marked variability which begins to appear to be characteristic of this "S." The examiner notes, "Checks number of rows (i.e., columns) about two-thirds through." We note that the angles of the columns of dots differ, becoming more obtuse (from the vertical) with a correction towards the end. The whole figure is exaggerated in the lateral plane. Together, these findings suggest a strong need to relate to people, but difficulty in establishing such relationships. The orientation of the first column is correct, so the variation in "angulation" is not a simple perceptual difficulty. "S" gets the number of columns correct, but varies *both* angulation and spacing. We have evidence, then, for the presence of considerable internal tension with an attempt at denial of its existence. How can we explain the apparent contradiction of the need for order and control with the speed and variability of performance?

Without giving further details of Hutt's reasoning about perceptual style, we quote a few of his conclusions for comparison with the opinions of the therapist. He uses all the following descriptions, in a context that explains how they were derived and with what degree of confidence: compulsive defenses not effective . . . acting out . . . regressive impulsivity breaks through . . . possibility of psychotic episodes . . . depressive reaction.

The interpretation of scraps and shreds of evidence is daring. Can one really know a person from the minor irregularities of his rows of dots? But if the interpretations of style seem bold, there are more startling things to come. From statements about defenses and controls, Hutt turns to the symbolism of the figures, following certain Freudian ideas about "masculine" and "feminine" designs:

[In the figure composed of an open square with a wave form at one corner] "S" has increased the vertical sides of the open square. . . . S's reaction to authority figures can now be inferred more completely: he is hostile to such figures, unable to express this hostility directly, and reacts either symbolically or impulsively. In line with the "acting out" hypothesis, the former is more likely. The curved portion of this figure is enlarged, flattened out in the middle and reveals an impulsive flourish at the upper end. Now we may speculate that S's major identification is with a female figure, but she is perceived as more masculine (i.e., dominant, aggressive) than feminine and is reacted to openly with antagonism. It is interesting that the upper portion of the curved figure extends well above its position on the stimulus card, and is at least as high up as the vertical lines. Here we may conjecture that S's mother (or surrogate) was stronger psychologically than his father, or at least seemed so to S, and that S would like to use his mother (or women) to defy his father (or men).

Such unscientific test interpretation is often severely criticized. In defense of the method, we may note that Hutt is able to give a detailed rationale for each of his inferences; he is by no means allowing his fantasy free rein. A much stronger defense is that his description of the patient agrees well with the clinical picture in the therapist's notes. Here is what the therapist (quoted by Shneidman, 1951, pp. 268–269) said:

He seemed suspicious, indecisive and unable to relax. . . . There seems to be considerable guilt in relation to his own hostility. He has established some defenses against this through obsession but these defenses are cracking and he fears that his hostile impulses might become so great that he would be unable to control them. . . . The patient seemed obsessed with thoughts about death, homicide, and suicide.

Word for word, we find confirmation of ineffectual defense through obsession, hostile impulses the subject fears to express, and so on. Remarks of the therapist support some of Hutt's most hazardous-seeming guesses: "The father seems to be a hazy person in the patient's life." "He talked of wishing to strangle his mother." "Had difficulty with authority figures." While the Bender analysis was not a perfect description, it yielded much better information about the depths of personality than one might expect from seemingly wild interpretations of a little task suitable for a child's drawing exercise.

Such striking successes give clinicians considerable right to feel confident in their methods and theory. At the same time, the clinical tests rarely satisfy the demand for systematic validation. If it was difficult to nail down the validity of score 4 (Pd) of MMPI, it is impossible to put into statistical form the evidence for such innumerable hypotheses as that enlargement of the Bender wave-form indicates a particular attitude toward one's mother. Validation is haphazard; we cannot guess what fraction of clinical descriptions work as well as this specimen.

Comprehensive interpretation of the person by means of a single complex test or a whole assortment of techniques is frequently called "assessment," to distinguish it from psychometric measurement. Assessment most commonly takes one of two forms. The first is clinical analysis, illustrated in the Hutt interpretation. The second is prediction of performance in a responsible job.

Personality assessment of normals grew out of the German military testing of the 1930s, the source of the team-performance tests mentioned earlier. In the hands of German testers, tests were regarded primarily as samples of character traits such as will power and rigidity. The techniques were adapted in Great Britain for War Office Selection Boards. When wartime conditions made it necessary to select officers from the ranks instead of relying on professionals from the upper classes, these boards took responsibilty for judging the ability and character of applicants for commissions. In the United States, Professor Henry Murray and his associates applied a large number of assessment techniques to Harvard students in the ground-breaking *Explorations in personality* (1938). During World War II, Murray was asked to select staff for the fore-runner of today's CIA (OSS Assessment Staff, 1948). In that program, use was made of group discussions, team-performance tests, stress interviews, observation at meals and social events, peer ratings, projective techniques, and structured tests of many types.

The principal features of assessment procedures are: use of a variety of techniques, primary reliance on observations in rather unstructured situations, and integration of information by experienced psychologists. No assessment program refuses to employ intelligence test scores or other relevant facts, but the emphasis remains upon quasiartistic synthesis rather than statistical combination.

Our chief concern in this chapter is to evaluate impressionistic assessment. Of the many validity studies, some penetrating and some superficial, we shall review several of the most solid.

Validation Studies

Attempts to Predict Job Performance

The original assessment programs in the military and intelligence services were not adequately validated, largely because candidates were scattered to far places and to diverse duties, so that criterion data were lacking. Perhaps the most meaningful figure is the report from the British Army that ratings of 500 officers in combat by their noncommissioned subordinates correlated 0.35 with Selection Board ratings. (This validity is corrected to apply to the entire range of candidates processed rather than the restricted group recommended for commissions—Vernon & Parry, 1949, p. 125.) These British studies also found that assessment may be seriously unreliable. One group of candidates was assessed separately by two boards, and the correlation between ratings was only 0.67. Reliabilities of 0.80 were achieved, however, by teams trained to use similar standards and procedures.

Assessment of British civil servants. Three-day "house-party" assessments of candidates for the British civil service were validated by Vernon (1950), who collected follow-up data on the men accepted. Though measurement of individual differences among such superior university graduates is extremely difficult, the validity coefficients were encouraging. Grades in a training course were predicted by final assessment rating with a validity of 0.82. For job-performance criteria the validities were 0.50–0.65.

Two hundred administrators were rated by superiors after a 2-year probationary period. Vernon gives 50 correlations of predictors with this criterion, and the predictors fall into two distinct groups. There are 27 validities for written ability tests; every coefficient is below 0.30, and the median is about 0.12. There are 19 correlations for ratings made by observers after performance tests or interviews; these correlations range from 0.26 to 0.49, the median being 0.41. Peer ratings had validities near 0.25. Evidently the impressionistic procedure identified aptitudes the pencil-and-paper tests did not.

It is important to note that in this successful study judges had "a clear and agreed conception of what they were selecting for, based on a thorough job analysis." The performance tests were for the most part job replicas of civil service paper work, committee tasks, and group discussions. Little use was made of personality theory. Projective tests, field observations, and stress interviews were absent or were given minimal attention by the raters.

The VA study of clinical psychologists. When the Veterans Administration began to support training of clinical psychologists in 1947, a program of selection research was directed by E. L. Kelly. Kelly's experienced team applied "every promising technique and procedure: objective, projective, subjective, clinical and quantitative" to 137 graduate students, in a 9 day assessment program. Supplementary groups were also tested. Criterion data collected from universities in 1950 included information on the trainee's ability as a therapist, as a diagnostician, and as a student of research methods. A decade later there was a second follow-up, but criterion data on skill in clinical work could not be obtained (Kelly & Goldberg, 1959).

During assessment, ratings had been made of general surface habits (e.g.,

Table 19.1. Selected validity coefficients for single predictors of competence in clinical psychology

	Criterion rating			
	Academic	Therapy	Diagnostic	Clinical competence
Miller Analogies (verbal ability)				
Guilford self-report questionnaires	**.47**	.02	**.24**	**.35**
S social extraversion	.06	**.22**	**.23**	.11
T thinking extraversion	.05	.09	.17	.19
Highest of 13 *r*'s	(.14)	(.22)	(.23)	(.19)
MMPI				
Highest of 9 *r*'s, regular scales	(.26)	(−.16)	(−.12)	(−.16)
Gough Psychologist key	.16	.15	**.22**	**.25**
Strong VIB				
Group I (creative-scientific)	**.26**	.06	.04	**.21**
Kriedt Clinical Psychologist key	.10	**.23**	**.23**	**.26**
Ratings from Bender-Gestalt	.15	.02	**.33**	**.32**
Ratings from TAT	.08	.16	**.24**	.15
Ratings from performance tests (pooled)	.19	.19	.02	**.24**
Self rating	**.25**	.20	.05	.00
Peer ratings	.13	**.28**	**.23**	**.25**

Boldface correlations are statistically signficant.
SOURCE: Kelly & Fiske, 1951, pp. 146 ff.

readiness to cooperate), underlying personality (e.g., characteristic intensity of inner emotional tension), and potential performance as a psychologist in various roles (e.g., group psychotherapy). Ratings were made by some persons who knew only the situational data, by some who knew only the interview, and by some who had access to various combinations of data; this procedure permitted comparison of techniques. Only a partial account of the hundreds of correlations can be given here.

Table 19.1 indicates how well single test scores or ratings based on them predicted certain important criterion ratings. The correlations, though frequently better than chance, are much too small for the predictors taken singly to be of substantial value in selection or guidance. The general ability test was much better than other methods for predicting academic performance, and also best for predicting rated clinical competence. The next best measure is peer ratings; these had some validity even for the criterion ratings of ability in diagnosis and therapy. The Bender-Gestalt rater did remarkably well on two of the criteria. Validities are lowered by the unreliability of criteria and by the fact that the trainees had already been screened to eliminate obviously unsuitable candidates.

Table 19.2. Validity of assessment ratings of trainees in clinical psychology

	Criterion rating			
Assessment rating	Academic	Therapy	Diagnosis	Clinical competence
Academic	.46	.09	.21	.45
Therapy	.24	.24	.29	.36
Diagnosis	.36	.14	.16	.32
Overall suitability for clinical psychology	.27	.18	.22	.38

SOURCE: Kelly & Fiske, 1951, p. 161.

Table 19.2 reports the overall validity for impressionistic assessments combining all sources of data. The correlations of 0.46 for academic prediction and 0.38 for clinical competence compare very favorably with the best that could be expected from a statistical combination of scores and ratings. The coefficients for diagnosis and therapy are lower, as in Table 19.1. This is to be explained partly by the inadequacy of those criteria. Probably an even more pertinent explanation is that the assessors, some of whom had no experience in analyzing personalities of graduate students and none of whom had studied the personality required in such roles as psychotherapist, were unable to make competent forecasts of these outcomes.

The third table indicates how much each part of the assessment program added to the final judgment. (Since this final judgment is based on only three assessors rather than the whole staff, the figures cannot be matched with those in Table 19.3.) Apparently, assessors did just as well when they had only the credentials file and objective test scores as they did with the addition of interviews and performance tests. This information, considered along with the modest validity coefficients for the performance tests taken alone (Table 19.1),

Table 19.3. Evidence on changes of validity with added information

	Criterion rating	
	Academic	Clinical competence
Credentials file plus objective tests (one rater)	.36	.37
Above plus autobiography, projectives (one rater)	.38	.40
Above plus interview (one rater)	.32	.37
All above information (conference of three raters)	.32	.42
Above plus performance tests (one rater)	.31	.39
Final pooled judgment of three raters	.33	.37

SOURCE: Kelly & Fiske, 1951, pp. 168–169.

does not encourage the use of performance observations, at least in the absence of a psychological job analysis.

Menninger study of psychiatrists.   A similar problem was investigated by Holt and Luborsky (1958) at the Menninger School of Psychiatry. Applicants were interviewed and evaluated by structured and projective tests. One principal criterion was the competence of the accepted man as judged during the residency that completed his training.

The original assessment employed the usual practice of asking an assessor to forecast success. This forecast was based on a judgment as to how well the person functioned in challenging situations. The results were in general unsatisfactory. The average validity for information from tests was 0.27, and that for interview assessments was 0.24. Even allowing for the fact that the correlations are based only on the restricted group whose members were accepted and finished training, these validities indicate a high rate of error.

Holt and Luborsky (1958, II, p. 139) examined whether some interviewers or test interpreters were markedly better than others, and although they did find differences, they conclude that the evidence

throws cold water on a frequently encountered suggestion for improving selection methods: "Find the interviewer who does the best job and have him teach the others how he does it." Even if one entertained the dubious assumption that an interviewer knows "how he does it," and is able to teach the helpful rather than the erroneous parts of his technique, there is still too little difference between the predictive performance of the best interviewer and those of the others to make such an endeavor worth while.

One comment by a test interpreter is particularly significant in pointing to a central difficulty in assessment: "Reviewing some predictions on which we erred, we were impressed with our correct assessment of many specific qualities and our inability to cast these up into proper balance so as to judge ability to develop skill as a psychiatrist" (Luborsky, 1954).

Predicting emotional difficulty in flying training.   Just as the Menninger data indicate that highly competent psychiatrists may make poor evaluations, predictions made by the best of projective testers are sometimes no better than guesses. Data on aviation cadets were collected prior to training. Some of the most prominent authorities on projective methods were later asked to distinguish the cadets who succeeded in flight training from those eliminated because they had developed overt personality disturbances (Holtzman & Sells, 1954). The judge was given the subject's responses to group forms of the inkblot, draw-a-person, and sentence-completion tests, a biographical inventory, and an inventory of psychosomatic complaints.

Each judge classified 20 cases. The mean number of correct classifications per judge was 10.2 compared with 10 expected by chance. Even when judges were unanimous in rating a case, accuracy was 56 per cent, scarcely better than the chance expectancy of 50. The results were not improved by counting only those judgments the clinician said he felt sure of.

Assessment of officer candidates. In contrast to the three preceding studies, in which ratings were made by highly qualified psychological assessors, men just graduated from Officer Candidate School were successful in assessing candidates for the school (Holmen *et al.*, 1956). Squads of ten applicants were observed for 2 weeks in an assessment center. There were four assessors, each a recent OCS graduate. Leadership exercises designed by psychologists as performance tests were administered by these officers. Data collected included ratings by the officers and by the other squad members, and self-report scores. Pass-fail records in OCS were the criterion.

For all men combined, average ratings by the assessors had a validity of 0.55, and peer ratings a validity of 0.58. Ratings based on specific performance tests generally had validities between 0.25 and 0.50. Self-report tests had essentially zero correlations with success. It was recommended that a 5-day version of the procedure be used for selection whenever a reasonably large supply of qualified applicants is available. Although the assessment is time consuming, the procedure provides training and orientation that helps in OCS, and therefore is economical.

IPAR study of Air Force officers. The Institute for Personality Assessment and Research was organized at the University of California by D. W. MacKinnon, one of the original OSS staff. Studies have been conducted on student, military, and professional groups, but the only full technical report is of an assessment of Air Force captains (MacKinnon *et al.*, 1958; Gough & Krauss, 1958; Barron *et al.*, 1958; Gough, 1958; MacKinnon, 1958; Woodworth & MacKinnon, 1958). This is an exceptionally good test of what assessment can and cannot do. An expert staff applied an enormous range of procedures to a large sample of men. Several criteria were later available. The staff had a reasonable understanding of the criterion task.

Pencil-and-paper tests (ability measures, personality and interest questionnaires, biographical data) were taken by captains eligible for promotion. One hundred of them were brought together in groups of 10 for "living-in" assessment. For 3 days, they lived with the psychologists, being interviewed, having a medical examination, taking projective tests, and being observed by the staff in informal contacts. In all, there were 233 "field test" (pencil-and-paper) scores and 398 scores or ratings from "living-in" assessment. These scores were compared with nine major criteria. More than 15,000 validity coefficients were calculated, some on subgroups.

Such a dragnet search for correlates of effectiveness is difficult to interpret.

Just by chance roughly 5 per cent of the predictors will show "significant" correlations with a criterion, and it is always possible to invent a plausible explanation for such a relation. The investigators, however, guarded against serious misinterpretation by confining interpretation to results appearing in several subsamples.

A second difficulty is the dubious validity of the criteria. Independent criteria of officer effectiveness correlated in the neighborhood of 0.30. Consequently, test validities cannot be expected to rise much beyond this level. Even the most valid assessment techniques cannot predict unstable criteria. The probable reasons for low agreement among criteria are the restricted range of ability in the group, and the different standards of judgment employed by various superiors.

For staff ratings in which a global assessment was attempted, all correlations with criteria of effectiveness were below 0.20. Three cluster-scores summarizing the assessment ratings had "disappointing" correlations with criteria of effectiveness (median 0.13). Whereas effectiveness was hard to predict, a criterion of success in interpersonal relations was predicted by assessment ratings, with validities in the range from 0.20 to 0.30. This is about as good as the criterion permits. The valid information came, not from test scores as such, but from staff appraisals. The person seen by the staff as tolerant, conforming, and relaxed was more often rated by his superior as having good relations with others. This interpersonal merit did not correlate with rated effectiveness. No psychometric measure gave consistent evidence of validity. In fact, out of 194 test variables not a single one correlated significantly with the officer effectiveness rating in three successive subsamples. Scattered correlations in the neighborhood of 0.30 promise a little predictive value in empirical keys based on successful performance (e.g., a CPI merit key based on responses of high achievers) and in self-ratings on adjustment. Rorschach and TAT were not at all promising.

Subsequent work at IPAR has concentrated on describing more and less successful groups in various fields (as in Helson's study, p. 587), and has dropped the attempts to evaluate single individuals.

Assessment of Bell System trainees. An assessment program to select potential executives for telephone companies processed men during the years 1957 to 1960; in 1965, criteria of advancement in responsibility became available (Bray & Grant, 1966). The assessment, requiring 3½ days, used situational tests, questionnaires, ability tests, and an interview. Each man was rated on his likelihood of moving up to a middle-management position. The assessment program appears to have been effective; the man for whom success in management was predicted rose to a middle-management position (by 1965) about four times as often as the man for whom the prediction was negative or doubtful.

Test scores reflecting education and scholastic aptitude correlated with a salary criterion, though not as well as did the rating of assessors. Personality questionnaires had no worthwhile relation to the criterion. The predictions by the assessors were influenced by the ability tests, an in-basket, LGD, and a situational "business game." It is clear that the situational tests made a worthwhile indirect contribution. It is not clear whether direct ratings made by observers in those separate situations would have predicted the criterion better or worse than the integrative impressions of the assessors did. The study confirms other evidence that information on likeability or social effectiveness is an important supplement to pencil-and-paper performance.

Another Bell System study, applying similar techniques to salesmen, supports global assessment using conventional and situational tests together with interviews (Bray & Campbell, 1968). The criterion was a rating of each salesman by an experienced team of specialists who accompanied him on a series of calls, rating his preparation and performance. This criterion was predicted with validity 0.51 by the assessors, whereas the weighted composite of conventional ability tests gave an R of only 0.33. Perhaps the most striking finding is that on-the-job ratings by supervisors and by trainers who worked with the men had little in common with the field-observation criterion; they also disagreed with the initial assessment. Among the men originally assessed as less than acceptable, only 23 per cent later satisfied the qualified observers of job performance (vs. 68 per cent of those assessed favorably). Of those the supervisors rated high on the job, only 47 per cent satisfied qualified observers; so did 44 per cent of the men that supervisors rated low. As Bray and Campbell point out, a researcher who relied on the criterion from supervisors would have concluded that the assessment was worthless.

Summary.   The foregoing studies include the major validations of global predictions to date. The most favorable results were obtained in OCS assessment, the Bell System studies, and British civil-service selection. The VA psychologist study showed about equal validities for psychometric prediction and for assessment based on those tests plus a credentials file; interviews and performance tests evidently added little. The initial Menninger study of psychiatrists (their later study remains to be discussed) was less successful, and the classification of emotional failures among pilots by projective tests had zero validity. Common elements in the more successful procedures may be noted:

  ● There is no evidence that psychological training gives the assessor an advantage. The best results occurred when officer candidates were rated by recent OCS graduates. The worst, as it happens, were obtained when the assessors were expert clinicians who, however, lacked specific experience with the types of candidates and criteria under study. The clinician's experience and theoretical background gives him confidence but seems not to make his judgments superior to those of the intelligent observer who knows the job requirements. This conclusion is supported by the usual validity of peer ratings.

• Performance tests that are very near to worksamples of the criterion task have considerable validity. These tests are directly interpreted without use of intervening personality theory and can be used by nonprofessional judges. Tests requiring the judge to infer the subject's personality structure and then to predict behavior are rarely helpful. Group performance tasks including LGD are likely to predict criteria reflecting acceptance by associates. They contribute much less when the criterion task calls for individual performance.

• The most important requirement for valid assessment is that the assessors understand the psychological requirements of the criterion task. The civil service and OCS assessors understood the ability requirements of the criterion task and made little effort at subtle psychological evaluation. The VA assessors and the Menninger assessors tried to match the candidates against mental pictures of the successful psychologist or psychiatrist. The IPAR assessors assumed, incorrectly, as the data later showed, that the requirements for effectiveness were the same for ground officers as for flying officers. These stereotypes had never been checked by controlled observation of successful performers. If such an "obvious" relation as that between spatial aptitude and success in geometry is contrary to the facts, it is not surprising that stereotypes concerning therapists prove false.

Impressionistic interpretations, then, often lack validity. The assessor must learn to distrust even the most compelling hunch until it has been independently verified. In Kelly's apt phrase, too many psychological techniques are used on the basis of nothing more than "faith validity."

The generally black picture painted above of psychologists' most ambitious efforts at assessment is not, however, the final answer. There is the difficult problem of reconciling the statistical evidence with the claimed "clinical validity" of assessment techniques. We need to identify the sources of error in assessment and to arrive, if possible, at a statement of the conditions under which they are or can be made profitable.

1. *When a group has been preselected before collection of validity data, correlations are reduced. In which of the assessment studies cited are the correlations based on groups more restricted than those that would usually be assessed?*

2. *In the OCS study, peer ratings were collected from nine men and assessment ratings from four judges. How is this fact relevant to the interpretation of the validity coefficients of 0.58 and 0.55, respectively?*

3. *In which studies did the criterion depend substantially upon ability to make a good impression upon and win the cooperation of peers?*

4. *In the VA study, TAT's were collected. An analysis (not part of the Kelly-Fiske report) found discouraging correspondence between TAT ratings of personality dimensions and observational evidence on those dimensions. Is the following complaint by Harrison (1965, p. 593), one of the original judges, a sound argument or a lame excuse?*

"Some of the staff members assigned to TAT assessment were by their own

*statement relatively inexperienced with the test and performed their duties with-
out confidence. Some of these were later replaced, but not before their appraisals
had been incorporated into the permanent pool of records. Moreover, all interpreters were required to fill out ratings for 31 personality traits for all examinees,
even though in most instances there were little or no relevant TAT data. . . .
Writeups in which the interpreters could state their conclusions in their own
terms were . . . disregarded [in the research analysis]."*

Sources of Error in Assessment

In order to understand the difficulties of assessment, we need to recognize
the steps involved in information gathering and inference. Figure 19.1 compares three types of personnel evaluation: inference based on dynamic interpretation, direct impressionistic evaluation from behavior samples, and psychometric prediction.

Let us begin with the right-hand column, which outlines the stages leading
to the criterion. Each box distinguishes one stage. Between boxes, the small
type lists some of the sources of error that preclude a perfect correspondence
among the findings at successive stages. Time intervenes between assessment
and criterion performance; changes in personality during this period reduce
the possibility of perfect assessment. Job performance (2b) depends not only
on personality but on the specific conditions of the individual's job. Given a
different superior or a different assignment, the man's performance might
change. The criterion 6d reflects performance (2b) indirectly, being affected by
the bias and incomplete observation of the supervisor. The sources of error in
the right-hand column imply that even with perfect information about personality
one could not predict job criteria perfectly.

The simplest assessment method is psychometric scoring of behavior and
application of a "cookbook" formula to arrive at a prediction (center column
of Figure 19.1). Reduction of behavior to scores discards some information.
The combining formula may introduce error if it was developed under conditions that do not apply perfectly to this new sample. Every stage from 1a to
6c and from 1a to 6d involves an additional opportunity for error. By this
analysis, there are seven places where error can lower the correlation between
prediction 6c and criterion 6d.

Impressionistic rating from observed behavior is illustrated in the OCS
study, in which value judgments were made directly, without intervening dynamic analysis of personality. Here again there are seven possible sources of
error between 6b and 6d. These may not all be damaging to the correlation if,
as in the OCS study, the bias of the raters resembles the bias of work supervisors.

Dynamic assessment, in the left-hand column, involves two added stages
of inference. The step from 3a to 4a is hazardous because personality constructs are poorly developed and poorly matched to test behavior. The step

from 4a to 5a involves equally undependable constructs about the nature of the criterion task and about how personality differences affect job behavior. The added links of hazardous inference make dynamic prediction far more prone to error than the more conservative predictions 6b and 6c.

This diagram leads to several suggestions for validation research and for the improvement of assessment. If criterion 6d is affected by errors, perhaps a better criterion could be obtained. A worksample of job behavior should correlate higher than the rating criterion with 5a and 3b. The psychologist may quite accurately predict a high degree of initiative, for example, and yet not be able to predict whether the man's (unknown) supervisor will evaluate that initiative favorably or unfavorably.

Even more important is the possibility of comparing the inferred personality structure (4a) with personality on the job (1b). It will be recalled that Luborsky was able, he said, to judge personalities accurately and yet was not able to judge whether the men would make good in psychiatry. If this type of claim is valid, then the weak links of the assessment chain are those linking personality to expected behavior. The generally low validity coefficients in studies attempting to pin down the worth of dynamic assessment indicate that something is wrong along the chain of inferences, but it may be that 4a corresponds excellently to 1b.

Validity of Clinical Descriptions

The validity of inferences about personality structure cannot be deduced from the assessment studies discussed above, in which descriptive inferences were not recorded in a form suitable for verification, and in which the criterion was an overall evaluation rather than a description. This evidence must come from studies in which inferences are compared with other descriptions of personality structure.

The literature contains a great many impressive case reports in which clinical analyses agree strikingly with other data on the individual. The Hutt case description, for example, corresponded very well with the therapist's case notes. Nearly every clinical tester can point to cases where projective techniques gave him insight into unique features of individuals, features so rare that they could not possibly be attributed to chance. George DeVos once analyzed the Rorschach record of a research worker he had never met and, in reporting on the inferred personality structure, commented, "This man ought to be an historian. He'd be completely happy down in Washington digging minute details out of the Lincoln archives" (these being a set of century-old documents that had just been opened to scholars). The man was a specialist in a field in which historical research is most uncommon—but he actually was in Washington at the time the analysis was made, extracting detailed information from 50-year-old files

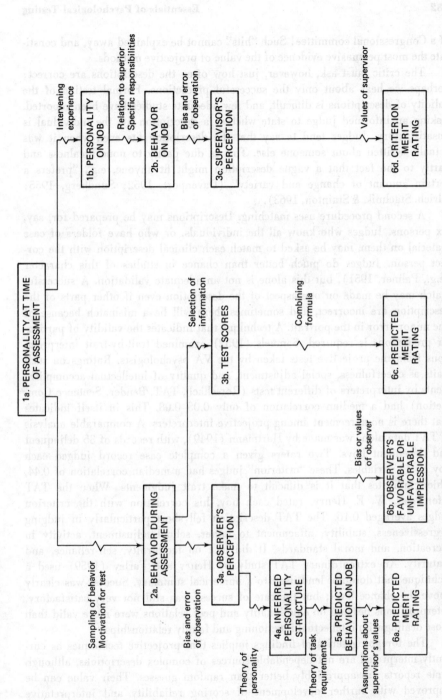

Figure 19.1. Stages in assessment and in criterion development.

of a Congressional committee! Such "hits" cannot be explained away, and constitute the most persuasive evidence of the value of projective methods.

The critic must ask, however, just how often the descriptions are correct; perhaps we hear about only the successful predictions. Formal testing of the validity of descriptions is difficult, and few adequate studies have been reported. Asking an informed judge to state whether a description fits the individual is unsatisfactory. Judges tend to say that the description fits even when it was actually written about someone else. This is due partly to noncriticalness and partly to the fact that a vague description might fit anyone, e.g., "prefers a certain amount of change and variety" (Davenport, 1952; Sundberg, 1955; Ulrich, Stachnik, & Stainton, 1963).

A second procedure uses matching. Descriptions may be prepared for, say, six persons. Judges who know all the individuals, or who have folders of case material on them, may be asked to match each clinical description with the correct person. Judges do much better than chance in studies of this character (e.g., Palmer, 1951), but this alone is not an adequate validation. A successful match may be made on one aspect of the description even if other parts of the description are incorrect, and sometimes there will be a mismatch because of one minor error in the portrait. A technique that indicates the validity of particular predictions is required. Samuels (1952) examined trait-by-trait interpretations from the projective tests taken by the VA psychologists. Ratings on such traits as cheerfulness, social adjustment, and quality of intellectual accomplishments by interpreters of different tests (Rorschach, TAT, Bender, Sentence Completion) had a median correlation of only 0.05–0.08. This in itself indicates that there is no agreement among projective interpreters. A comparable analysis of TAT data alone was made by Hartmann (1949), with records of 35 delinquent and dependent boys. Two raters given a complete case record judged each boy on 42 variables. These "criterion" judges had a median correlation of 0.44, which indicates that it is difficult to make trait judgments. When the TAT interpreter, W. E. Henry, rated each boy, his correlation with the criterion judges averaged 0.16. The TAT description fell short particularly in judging aggressiveness, stability, attachment to father, school adjustment, activity in recreation, and moral standards. It did best on taciturnity, self-reliance, and maturity. An extraordinary TAT study by Henry and Farley (1959) used a technique that does not lend itself to a numerical summary. Success was clearly above the chance level; but the rate of success was still not very satisfactory. Interpretations bearing on emotionality and peer relations were more valid than those dealing with intellectual functioning and family relationships.

The foregoing series of findings implies that projective techniques as currently interpreted are not dependable sources of complex descriptions, although some reports are appreciably better than random guesses. Their value can be improved with further development of scoring reliability and interpretative theory. No evidence is available on the adequacy of personality descriptions from observations in complex performance tests or in interviews.

Improving Assessment

Some critics conclude that projective methods and impressionistic assessment are indefensible, and that psychologists who depend on them are deluding themselves and those to whom they report. Confirmed believers in assessment methods, on the other hand, have at times rejected their critics as "methodological bluenoses" (Bellak, 1954) and even denied the relevance of such formal evidence as is available. This denial goes much too far; as R. R. Holt (1958), a proponent of clinical techniques, said at the height of the controversy: "If the issue were whether some clinicians have made themselves look foolish by claiming too much, then I should agree: these studies show that they have, and unhappily, brought discredit on clinical methods generally." Since the claims made in the past have frequently been discredited, any would-be assessor is responsible for presenting indisputable public evidence of the dependability of his judgment; vague claims regarding successful experience will not suffice.

On the other hand, the evidence does not demand abandonment of research on assessment. Personality testing has had a shorter history than ability testing. With personality as difficult to analyze as it is and with the available techniques all open to one serious objection or another, it is important to turn attention to how assessment techniques can be improved. It is equally necessary to understand just what function each procedure is best for. Many of the attacks on global approaches and many of the defensive arguments have been based on a misconception of their proper role.

Improving Test Interpretation

Projective tests and situational observations have been interpreted by means of whatever theory a particular interpreter adopts. Some TAT interpreters view the stories as samples of stable traits likely to be shown in overt behavior, some consider the test a measure of present state, and some consider the test a measure of unconscious and unexpressed drives. If interpretation of a test has not been stabilized, no one knows what the instrument—especially when checked by using additional indicators of the same construct—might do at its best. The whole conception of personality is undergoing substantial change (Mischel, 1968; D. R. Peterson, 1968).

Certain techniques—maybe all of them—have a built-in bias. Soskin (1954, 1959; see also Samuels, 1952) asked judges to indicate was a subject was likely to do in a situation. The situations were drawn from incidents in the subject's actual history. One group of judges responded knowing only the subject's age, sex, and social background. Other judges were given Rorschach and TAT records. Answers were scaled from 4.0 (implying excellent adjustment) to 1.0 (implying severe maladjustment). The median scale value of actions recorded in the life history was 2.5. Judges relying on general background data gave a favorable assessment (their predictions scaled at a median of 3.1). Judges relying on projective data were unfavorable (median, 2.0). Projective interpreters tended to misjudge the subject whenever his actual behavior showed good adaptation. In uncertain situations, they expected the worst.

This apparent bias toward psychopathology in Rorschach interpretations is implied also in Roe's work on eminent scientists, the Menninger psychiatrist study, and other investigations. Within any group of normal persons one encounters records that, considered by themselves, would seem to indicate gross emotional disturbance or psychopathology (Gallagher, 1955). As one Menninger assessor commented:

> The TAT usually exposed a man's weakest points, without giving compensatory signs of his strong ones. . . . To some extent the same thing is true of the Rorschach. . . . Latent conflicts show up in these tests much more plainly than the compensating strengths; . . . [it is necessary] to be very cautious in assuming that such *potential* liabilities are *actual* if they are not seen operating in much more direct fashion" (quoted by Holt & Luborsky, 1958, I, p. 246).

One reason for the bias is that projective theory was developed through the study of mental patients without appropriate control studies of normals. In more recent work, on normals and superior individuals, the emphasis has shifted to research on one construct at a time, so that the integration of normal personality is still little understood. A projective technique reveals drives and impulses, but it does not indicate clearly how they are controlled. Strong hostility is likely to be an unfavorable sign in a person tested by a clinic; in an executive, author, or school superintendent, the same force may be harnessed to creative and socially constructive activity. Until the tester is able to distinguish unchanneled from controlled forces, he must interpret damaging indications with caution. Ultimately, we may learn to identify control mechanisms through projective protocols as well as disruptive forces.

Projective and performance tests are not cross-sections of personality. On the contrary, they are observations in a specific situation, and one generalizes to future situations with considerable risk. Indeed, one can scarcely generalize even to another test. Giving four groups of judges four different sets of data, Goldberg & Werts (1966) found that the ratings of dependency, for example, correlated only 0.03 across techniques. No test is a measure of personality in isolation; it is a sample of social interaction with a certain other person (Schafer, 1954; Sarason, 1954). There is considerable risk when one generalizes to another social interaction.

"Blind analysis" is the custom in validation studies aimed at determining what can be done with a single test, but practical interpretation should be based on considerable background knowledge. Indeed, Holt and Luborsky (1958, p. 303) wisely recommend study of projective tests *only* along with intellectual tests and a case history.

If one could give only the Rorschach and TAT, it would be better to give no tests at all rather than spend time with so dubious a prospect of satisfactory results. Projective tests give valuable insights into personality, but the level of material from which they draw varies . . . from one case to another and its significance is . . . dependent on a framework of realistic knowledge about the person.

Semantic confusion is a difficulty that can be remedied only by improving personality theory. If the test interpreter uses words that mean different things to different people, he cannot hope that his interpretations will be confirmed or that they will be practically beneficial. Many of the key words in dynamic interpretations are highly ambiguous. Grayson and Tolman (1950) asked psychologists and psychiatrists to define such words as *bizarre* and *aggression*. Twenty-three of these clinicians defined the aggressive person as strong-active-bad; but for 21 of them it meant strong-active-good. As the authors said, "For the most part, the lack of verbal precision seems to stem from theoretical confusion in the face of the complexity and logical inconsistency of psychological phenomena."

Psychological Study of Treatment Situations

No psychometric tester would willingly introduce a selection plan without first validating his tests against criterion information, but the assessor has generally made blind predictions. The assessor has picked Army officers, civil servants, espionage agents, and fliers with no better standard than his hunches about the situations they would face. While one might excuse such presumptuousness on the grounds of wartime necessity, when men must be selected according to someone's best guess, prudence demands realistic job analysis and test tryout when circumstances permit. Nearly all the validations of assessment methods have examined the merit of "naïve clinical assessment," which Holt (1958) describes as follows:

The data used are primarily qualitative with no attempt at objectification; their processing is entirely a clinical and intuitive matter, and there is no prior study of the criterion or of the possible relation of the predictive data to it. Clinical judgment is at every step relied on not only as a way of integrating data to produce predictions, but also as an alternative to acquaintance with the facts.

Sound choice of psychometric methods and interpretations has, from the days of Wissler and Binet, depended upon thorough empirical follow-up; similar follow-up is even more essential in personality appraisal. Holt suggests the following as a "sophisticated" clinical method:

Qualitative data from such sources as interviews, life histories, and projective techniques are used as well as objective test facts and scores, but as much as possible of objectivity, organization, and scientific method are introduced into the planning, the gathering of data, and their analysis. All the refinements of design that the actuarial tradition has furnished are employed, including job analysis, pilot studies, item analysis, and successive cross-validations. Quantification and statistics are used wherever helpful, but the clinician himself is retained as one of the prime instruments, with an effort to make him as reliable and valid a data-processor as possible; and he makes the final organization of the data to yield a set of predictions tailored to each individual case.

This procedure was applied as well as possible in the second phase of the Menninger psychiatrist study. Naïve assessment, as described above, had been applied with mediocre success, validity being 0.24. In the "sophisticated study" the investigators examined enough successful and unsuccessful men to formulate a concept of the good psychiatrist. Specific clues in TAT and other data were identified, to provide an objective framework for judging the remaining cases. Despite this effort, scores or judgments based on a single projective test had poor validity. Predictive ratings based on all data had validities of 0.57 for one judge, 0.22 for the second (average, 0.40). Holt and Luborsky called the validities from the final study "impressive" and recommended application of refined assessment methods to the selection of psychiatrists. The issue appears still to be in doubt, however. The one coefficient of 0.57 is high, but it gives no assurance that the validity of judges would be consistently superior to the naïve predictions. Moreover, when a verbal IQ correlates 0.39 with the criterion, it is hard to believe that clinical judgments represent an improvement sufficient to justify the labor involved.

Every test represents performance in a highly specific situation, as we noted earlier; there is a counterpart problem with respect to the criterion. A criterion rating is generated by the interaction of a man and one set of duties. The psychiatrist who might do well with children will be rated a failure if he is unable to cope with hospitalized adults early in his practical training. An unfortunate first assignment or an incompatible first supervisor may develop feelings of incompetence and a bad reputation that prevent the man from reaching his potential. The psychoanalysis the student of psychiatry often undergoes is another significant but rather unpredictable feature of the situation. Assessment is rarely used to select men for uniform, well-defined jobs. The usual problem in executive appraisal or clinical evaluation is to judge how the individual will get along in an ill-defined or unspecified situation. Where many variable conditions intervene between prediction and follow-up, high validity cannot be hoped for.

Test data probably can predict success averaged over many *independent* situations. A statistical composite such as a college grade average is a "convergent phenomenon" (Langmuir, 1943; L. K. Frank, 1948). Experience in a single course may be unlucky, but the student has many independent chances to show what he can do. His average becomes more stable and easier to predict as more courses are added. All-round popularity is a similar convergent phenomenon. A person's standing varies from church to office to bowling team, but as more groups are added his average "seeks its level." A phenomenon is "divergent" if the successive events that cause it to develop are highly inter-related. In a landslide, one stone jars another, the two moving together dislodge others, and soon an irresistible stream of debris is pouring downhill at a certain point. This force is a sum of many separate movements, but not an average of independent events. Rather, every added stone amplifies the original move-ment; if the first stone had not moved, there would have been no landslide.

One cannot predict the divergent phenomenon. Possibilities can be identi-fied ("That hill looks loose enough to slide"), but what *will* occur can be pre-dicted only on the average over independent situations ("Landslides will cost the State road department x thousands of dollars"). The social scientist can predict how many women in a college class will marry, assuming that times do not change. He can predict much less well whether a particular woman will marry. To predict whether she will marry the man she met last night is foolhardy. Successes and failures do not average out in a continuing relationship; one quarrel may end all chance for compensating pleasant experience. Even with full day-to-day information, the fate of this possible marriage will be unpre-dictable for many months.

The assessor can reasonably hope to figure out how many men of a certain type will succeed in psychiatry. He can perhaps judge what any one man would do on the average if he could have ten independent careers in psychiatry. But one career is like a horse race; a delay in the starting gate, a jam on the track, one mistake by the rider—and the favorite loses. The psychiatrist has just one career, in one group, under one set of demands. If he establishes a good rela-tion with the significant figures in this environment, the beneficial consequences will rebound through his whole life. Yet that relation depends on chance events as much as on his stable personal qualities. As William James warned, psychology can establish general expectations but cannot hope to give biographies in advance.

5. *Show that each of these is the result of a divergent phenomenon:*
   a. *The ceremony was a moving emotional experience.*
   b. *Terry is cooperative, but no one can manage his brother Mike.*
   c. *Charles' interest in science is becoming focused on genetics.*
6. *How reasonable is it to try to predict each of the following?*
   a. *Will men of this type respond better to close supervision or to freedom?*
   b. *How will this man respond to close supervision?*
   c. *Will Mark like selling?*
   d. *Will Mark like this job as salesman?*
7. *Defend the statement: "After a certain point in its development, the divergent phenomenon becomes predictable." What sort of information is needed for this prediction?*

The Unique Functions of Assessment Procedures

In the writer's opinion, assessment techniques have been asked to do a job for which they are ill suited. It has been necessary to emphasize the extensive and discouraging negative results on clinical prediction, but there is a more positive evaluation to be made.

Three related features set assessment techniques apart from conventional psychometric methods:

- They provide information both on typical response patterns and on stimulus meanings.
- They cover a very large number of questions about the individual.
- They provide information about different questions for different individuals.

Coverage of stimulus meanings.   The psychometric approach is to confront the individual with carefully selected tasks that represent a criterion situation in some way. This description applied to proficiency tests, to aptitude tests, to questionnaires on typical performance, and to worksamples such as LGD. We saw that even impressionistic interpretation of such samples of behavior gave valid predictions for civil service and OCS. The essential assumption in this type of testing is that we can generalize from a sample of behavior to performance in *one class* of situations.

A person's behavior changes from situation to situation, however, and whenever one must understand the person as a whole, or must select treatments to fit him, sampling within one general class of situations does not give the information needed. One must begin to learn what situations mean for the subject. Much of the content of an interview deals with situational meanings: attitudes toward parents, former employers, school subjects, etc. The thematic projective tests elicit similar information, though in a more disguised and perhaps less censored form.

The Semantic Differential is the only psychometric technique designed to study meanings the person gives to significant others. Even this procedure, though structured and quantifiable, is interpreted impressionistically when a single individual is under study. Hence there is no psychometric technique for obtaining information about the subject's reactions to various persons and situations—unless one wishes to prepare dozens of questionnaires or Q sorts, each dealing with one person or situation. While research along the lines opened by Osgood, G. A. Kelly, and Endler and Hunt may lead to well-controlled psychometric techniques, at this time there is no alternative to some type of clinical assessment if we want attitudinal information covering a wide range of objects. It is unfortunate that there have been no controlled validation studies to show just how well such procedures as TAT and Semantic Differential identify significant belief systems. Virtually all systematic validation of impressionistic methods has examined their adequacy as measures of broad response tendencies.

In Chapter 6 we pointed to the bandwidth-fidelity dilemma. The attempt to cover many questions, some unique to the individual, calls for a wideband procedure. Extreme bandwidth is disadvantageous because the information becomes too unreliable for use, except in an interactive setting in which every statement is verified by subsequent observations. A narrowly focused inquiry, on the other hand, is appropriate only when there is one specific, all-important question to be answered, to which all testing effort should be devoted. While no rule can specify the ideal bandwidth for testing, we can point to conditions favoring greater bandwidth, or less:

● The first is the number and relative importance of decisions to be made. If an institution is concerned with a simple decision and only one outcome, it should concentrate on the information most relevant to that decision. (Example: a college wishing to admit students who will make good academic records, without regard to values, social or emotional adjustment, or probable post-college career.) If many outcomes or alternatives are to be considered, most types of information are needed and bandwidth must increase. Counseling, diagnosis, remedial teaching, and supervision of professional workers generally involve multifaceted decisions. The testing effort should be balanced to obtain relatively dependable information on the most important questions or those that are most likely to arise. It is better to ignore minor questions than to spread one's inquiry too thin (Cronbach & Gleser, 1965, pp. 104, 149).

● Bandwidth can be greatly increased when it is possible to confirm or reverse judgments at a later time. Lack of fidelity does no harm unless it leads to costly errors. Narrowband instruments are desired for making final, irreversible decisions about important matters (e.g., scholarship awards). The wideband technique, on the other hand, serves well as the first stage in a sequential measuring operation. As a first stage, the wideband test scans superficially a range of important variables, pointing out significant possibilities for further study. In this use the wideband procedure is used for *hypothesis formation*, not for final decisions.

Hypothesis formation is the proper function of the Strong blank, for example. It is not a highly valid basis for career choice. It is an inexpensive pencil-and-paper interview that gives an excellent preliminary mapping of the vocational field. Ease of administration, objective scoring, norms for students, and norms for the occupation make it superior to the unconstrained interview (which has even greater bandwidth). Having the test profile, the counselor uses a more focused interview to confirm high scores and to determine implications. Even this discussion should not lead to final decision. It is better to narrow the choice to two or three areas; these hypotheses can be tested by enrolling in suitable courses and by trying relevant summer jobs.

Comparable opportunities to confirm assessments or score interpretations exist in virtually every decision except selection. Fallible tests can suggest assignments for an employee, treatments for a patient, or teaching techniques for a student. Even if a test is little better than a guess, it has some value when there is no sounder basis for choice. Since trying out the hypothesis permits verification, and leads to a change when the hypothesis is disconfirmed, little has been lost. We may say, in sum, that the fallibility of wideband procedures does no harm unless the hypotheses and suggestions they offer are regarded as verified conclusions about the individual.

Impressionistic procedures, and psychometric procedures in clinical settings, are chiefly used for hypothesis formation. Clinicians bring a Rorschach interpretation or a Wechsler IQ to a case conference, during which it is considered along with other data, and this conference concludes that it is better to try one therapy than another. Only when the decision is irreversible—as when a surgical procedure is prescribed or when the patient once classified is forever left in the same pigeonhole—is this use of impressions and imperfectly valid scores dangerous; even then, they probably are no less valid than the other bases available for the decision. The most telling charge made against appraisals in clinical work is that they are not worth their considerable cost (Mischel, 1968, Chapter 5). And the most telling point made by their defender is that they may be the *only* way to answer crucial questions (Holt, 1969, esp. pp. 792–793).

In executive appraisal or school psychology, also, the recommendations of the tester are recommendations about experiments to be tried. Unfortunately, assessors (and psychometric testers) have far too often claimed that their methods give valid final conclusions. This has two bad consequences: nonpsychologists expect more than the assessor can deliver, and the psychologist tries to live up to his claim by giving one description or recommendation instead of outlining the reasonable alternatives.

Adaptation to the individual. Closely related to the foregoing comments are the advantages of assessment procedures for shaping the testing to the individual. The psychometric tester standardizes his test to answer a question presumed to be important for everyone. The impressionistic tester may vary the problems and topics covered by the testing to fit the individual. The psychometric tester tries to standardize every aspect of his measuring procedure, so that precisely the same information is obtained about each subject. The impressionistic tester wishes to obtain significant information regarding a particular individual, even if this means asking different questions of each person. The flexibly administered interview, the individualized description of significant others in George Kelly's procedure (p. 598), and the unstructured projective technique elicit idiosyncratic, personally significant responses for which there is no counterpart in psychometric methodology. These responses can only be interpreted impressionistically.

Meehl discusses such an interpretation made by the psychoanalyst Reik (1948, p. 263):

> Our session at this time took the following course. After a few sentences about the uneventful day, the patient fell into a long silence. She assured me that nothing was in her thoughts. Silence from me. After many minutes she complained about a

toothache. She told me that she had been to the dentist yesterday. He had given her an injection and then had pulled a wisdom tooth. The spot was hurting again. New and longer silence. She pointed to my bookcase in the corner and said, "There's a book standing on its head." Without the slightest hesitation and in a reproachful voice I said, "But why did you not tell me that you had had an abortion?"

How Reik made this correct inference from the patient's chain of associations and silences is not our concern here. The skill is compounded of theory, imagination, experience, and willingness to make (and verify or discard) rash guesses. The important point is that this interpretation, which might accelerate appreciably the therapy, could not possibly have been reached by formal testing. In the first place, such a procedure would be unlikely to touch upon the particular topic of abortion. Even if it did, there is no "trait" on which the response could be scored, unless one envisions keying the MMPI to distinguish ex-abortion patients from other women—and similarly for every other group of conceivable clinical interest. Secondly, the response cannot possibly be interpreted on a statistical base. How could one establish frequency tables to give the meaning of associations-about-a-dental-extraction-plus-silence-plus-observation-about-an-inverted-book? This is a unique datum to be interpreted by a creative act, here, by applying the psychoanalytic hypothesis that tooth extraction is a disguised symbol for birth. This example shows clinical interpretation in its purest form.

The interpreter must likewise deal with the unprecedented when he predicts response to a specific situation. "Should this child be sent back to his mother or placed in a foster home?" is a decision in which statistics cannot aid. No experience table can predict from IQ, anxiety level, or anything else whether he will adjust well to his mother. This can be estimated only from a study of her character, the child's character, and the precise home situation. The decision is likely to be wrong, but that is beside the point. The decision must be made, and insofar as psychological study of the child can improve the decision, the risk of error is reduced. In this case, impressionistic appraisal, together with psychological theory, is the best available basis for decision. All the "little" decisions that take place from minute to minute in therapy and teaching are similarly resistant to measurement and statistics. In these judgments, in which the psychometric tester would have nothing to say, hints from TAT or a case history may provide a lead.

The difference between psychometric and impressionistic assessment, we find, is not that the one uses multiple-choice questions and the other inkblots, or that the one is compulsively cautious, the other erratically overambitious. The two approaches are suited to different purposes. When clinical testers answer questions for which their methods and theory are badly suited, their answers are next to worthless and at best are costly beyond their value. When psychometric testers are faced with a clinical problem calling for understanding (e.g., What lies behind a given child's anxious withdrawal?), they are unable to give any answer at all. Each in his own proper province will surpass the other and each outside his province is nearly impotent. Assessment methods have earned a bad name for themselves by trying to compete with measurement on its own ground. In the absence of excellent research to guide the combination of information, the wideband technique should not be advanced as a means of predicting specific, recurring criteria. The precisely focused instrument, on the other hand, should not be exalted into the sole approved technique for gathering information. It is efficient only when the decision-maker asks the particular question for which the test has been validated. Even MCT must be interpreted impressionistically when one wants to explain a low score, or to predict performance in a new training program, or to predict in a population of persons on whom there has been no validation study (e.g., school dropouts).

An evolution from naturalistic to highly structured techniques is usual. Alfred Binet's exploration of intelligence began with impressionistic interpretations of imaginative performance. It was only after this study had suggested important components that he began to design the structured tests from which all later ability tests sprang. The personality questionnaire developed out of psychiatric observations of symptoms, and the interest questionnaire out of counseling interviews. Naturalistic observation is always the first step in science, followed by gradual structuring of the observations, and ultimately by definition of specific variables and quantitative measurement. Whenever the importance of some treatment and criterion becomes great enough to warrant quantitative measurement, formal psychometric procedures can be developed to measure them. The psychometric method can give refined and trustworthy answers to any recurrent question, better than pure, natural-history observation can. Successive stages of research eliminate sources of error.

This does not mean that impressionistic methods will or should ultimately disappear. There will always be unique problems to deal with and unique facts to interpret. Indeed, since every person is unique in certain ways, each case will present problems beyond the reach of standard interpretative formulas. Moreover, treatments will continually change, and judgments about assignment to the new treatments have to be made without waiting for years of follow-up research. Even the growth of psychometric testing creates a demand for greater and more skillful use of wideband techniques. As more and more specialized scales are developed, it becomes even more important to have suitable wideband procedures at the first stage to determine which psychometric scales are relevant to a given case. Psychometric and impressionistic testing procedures should supplement each other.

Here again we encounter the principle introduced early in this book: one cannot identify one group of tests as good and recommend it for exclusive use. For every type of decision and for every type of psychological information, there are many techniques and many specific instruments. The instruments differ in practicality, in the training required to use them, in the variety of information they obtain, and in fidelity. The instrument that works best for one tester will not be best for another tester making the same decision. Tests must be chosen by a highly qualified professional worker who has a thorough understanding of the institution and persons he serves.

All in all, psychological testing is an accomplishment its developers may well boast of. Errors of measurement and interpretation have been reduced year by year, and the significance of tests has been increased, until today all facets of American society feel the impact of the testing movement. The school, industry, governmental policy, and character-building agencies have all been aided by tests. Interpretations of test data are daily creating better lives, guiding a man into a suitable lifework, placing an adolescent under therapy that will avert mental disorder, detecting causes of a failure in school that could turn a child into a beaten individual. Methods are now available that, if used carefully by responsible interpreters, can unearth talents, and identify personality aberrations that would cause those talents to be wasted. Building on these techniques, we are in a better position to help people live happier lives.

SUGGESTED READINGS

Gordon, Leonard V. Clinical, psychometric, and work-sample approaches in the prediction of success in Peace Corps training. *Journal of Applied Psychology*, 1967, *51*, 111–119.

> A comparison of validities for four methods of prediction, one of which is impressionistic. Gives a good brief account of the assessment procedures.

Holt, R. R. The evaluation of personality assessment. In I. L. Janis (Ed.) *Personality: Dynamics, development, assessment.* New York: Harcourt, Brace, & World, 1969. Pp. 773–801.

> A sympathetic treatment of clinical, impressionistic assessment, combined with a sharp critique of the studies attempting to prove that actuarial formulas do what a clinician does, and do it better. Holt describes what a "sophisticated" and self-critical clinician will do, often under circumstances where no actuarial solution is practicable. Holt summarizes several of the major studies of assessment; the reader should note how his summaries differ from ours.

Lindzey, Gardner. Seer versus sign. *Journal of Experimental Research on Personality*, 1965, *1*, 17–26; comment by Meehl follows on pp. 27–32. See also comment by Goldberg (1968). (Lindzey paper only reprinted in Megargee, 1966.)

> The one study now available in which there is unmistakeable superiority for impressionistic over psychometric methods. TAT data were processed in both ways, in an attempt to discriminate homosexuals from others. Of particular importance is Lindzey's discussion of probable reasons for the clinician's success. Goldberg, it should be noted, challenges the Lindzey-Meehl reasoning.

Macfarlane, Jean W., and Tuddenham, Read D. Problems in the validation of projective techniques. In H. H. Anderson and G. L. Anderson (Eds.), *An introduction to projective techniques.* Englewood Cliffs, N.J.: Prentice-Hall, 1951. Pp. 26–54.

> An authoritative statement on the requirements of sound validation.

Meehl, Paul E. Wanted—a good cookbook. *American Psychologoist*, 1956, *11*, 263–272. (Reprinted in Jackson & Messick, 1967.)

> In an experiment, psychometric methods were devised for obtaining from the MMPI profile a clinical "description" that proved to be more highly related to the therapist's impression than the judgment of qualified clinicians.

Ruff, George E., and Levy, Edwin Z. Psychiatric evaluation of candidates for space flight. *American Journal of Psychiatry*, 1959, *116*, 385–391. (Reprinted in Flynn & Garber, 1967).

> Clinical assessment is used to select astronauts because there is no way to apply statistical methods to a large sample of candidates, some of whom ultimately fail on the job. This description of procedures lacks evidence on validity; could validity in this kind of selection for hazardous and responsible duty be evaluated systematically?

List of Publishers
and Test Distributors

American College Testing Program, P.O. Box 168, Iowa City, Iowa 52240

American Guidance Service, Inc., Publishers' Building, Circle Pines, Minn. 55014

California Test Bureau, Del Monte Research Park, Monterey, Calif. 93940 (*CTB*)

Consulting Psychologists Press, Inc., 577 College Ave., Palo Alto, Calif. 94306 (*CPP*)

Educational and Industrial Testing Service, P.O. Box 7234, San Diego, Calif. 92107 (*EITS*)

Educational Testing Service, Princeton, N.J. 08540 (*ETS*)

Grune & Stratton, Inc., 381 Park Ave. South, New York, N.Y. 10016.

Harcourt, Brace & World, Inc., 757 Third Ave., New York, N.Y. 10017 (*Harcourt*)

Houghton Mifflin Company, 110 Tremont St., Boston, Mass. 02107 (*Houghton*)

Institute for Personality and Ability Testing, 1602 Coronado Drive, Champaign, Ill., 61822 (*IPAT*)

Personnel Press, Inc., 20 Nassau St., Princeton, N.J. 08540

Psychological Corporation, The, 304 East 45th St., New York, N.Y. 10017 (*Psych. Corp.*)

Psychological Test Specialists, Box 1441, Missoula, Mont. 59804.

Research Psychologists Press, Goshen, N.Y. 10924.

Scholastic Testing Service, 480 Meyer Road, Bensenville, Ill. 60106.

Science Research Associates, Inc., 259 East Erie St., Chicago, Ill. 60624 (*SRA*)

Sheridan Psychological Services, P.O. Box 837, Beverly Hills, Calif. 90213

C. H. Stoelting Co., 424 North Homan Ave., Chicago, Ill. 60624

Western Psychological Services, 12035 Wilshire Blvd., Los Angeles, Calif. 90025

References and Index of Sources*

Adamson, R. E., & Taylor, D. W. Functional fixedness as related to elapsed time and set. *Journal of Experimental Psychology*, 1954, 47, 122–126. — 641

Adorno, T. W., *et al. The authoritarian personality.* New York: Harper & Row, 1950. — 9

Ainsworth, L. H. Rigidity, insecurity, and stress. *Journal of Abnormal and Social Psychology*, 1958, 56, 67–74. — 641

Ainsworth, M. D. Problems of validation. In B. Klopfer *et al.*, 1954. Pp. 405–500. — 635

Allport, G. W. *Personality: A psychological interpretation.* New York: Holt, Rinehart and Winston, 1937. — 561

Allport, G. W. Traits revisited. *American Psychologist*, 1966, 21, 1–10. — 525

American College Testing Program. *ACT Technical Report*, 1965 ed. Iowa City: ACTP, 1965. — 276

American College Testing Program. *College student profiles.* Iowa City: ACTP, 1967–1968. — 219

American Psychological Association. *Ethical standards of psychologists.* Washington: APA, 1953. — 18

American Psychological Association. *Standards for educational and psychological tests and manuals.* Washington, D.C.: APA, 1966. — 40, 108, 119 f., 150, 216

American Psychological Association. Ethical standards of psychologists. *American Psychologist*, 1968, 23, 357–361. — 17

Ames, L. B., & Walker, R. N. Prediction of later reading ability from kindergarten Rorschach and IQ scores. *Journal of Educational Psychology*, 1964, 55, 309–313. — 237

---

* For authors discussed without regard to particular works (e.g., Binet), see Index of Subjects. For tests (e.g., Strong Vocational Interest Blank) see Index of Subjects.

Amster, H. The relation between intentional and incidental concept learning as a function of type of multiple stimulation and cognitive style. *Journal of Personality and Social Psychology*, 1965, *1*, 217–223.   **626**

Anan'ev, B. G., & others. *Psychological science in the U.S.S.R.* Moscow: Academy of Pedagogical Sciences, 1960.   **306**

Anastasi, A. *Differential psychology*. (3rd ed.) New York: Macmillan, 1958.   **247, 266**

Anastasi, A. (Ed.) *Testing problems in perspective*. Washington, D. C.: American Council on Education, 1966.   **113, 451, 665**

Anastasi, A. Psychology, psychologists, and psychological testing. *American Psychologist*, 1967, *22*, 297–306.   **190, 307**

Anastasi, A. *Psychological testing*. (3rd ed.) New York: Macmillan, 1968. **15, 20, 193, 253**

Anastasi, A., & Drake, J. D. An empirical comparison of certain techniques for estimating the reliability of speeded tests. *Educational and Psychological Measurement*, 1954, *14*, 529–540.   **176**

Anderson, G. L. A comparison of the outcomes of instruction under two theories of learning. Unpublished doctoral dissertation, University of Minnesota, 1941.   **447**

Anderson, J. E. The limitations of infant and preschool tests in the measurement of intelligence. *Journal of Psychology*, 1939, *8*, 351–379.   **292**

Anderson, R. G. A note on the McAdory and Meier Art tests in counseling. *Educational and Psychological Measurement*, 1951, *11*, 81–86.   **402**

Andersson, B. E., & Nilsson, S. G. Studies in the reliability and validity of the critical-incident technique. *Journal of Applied Psychology*, 1964, *48*, 398–403.   **409**

Andrews, J. D. W. The achievement motive and advancement in two types of organizations. *Journal of Personality and Social Psychology*, 1967, *6*, 163–168.   **664**

Angoff, W. H. Scales with nonmeaningful origins and units of measurement. *Educational and Psychological Measurement*, 1962, *22*, 27–34.   **111, 112**

Angoff, W. H. Technical problems of obtaining equivalent scores on tests. *Journal of Educational Measurement*, 1964, *1*, 11–13.   **111**

Angoff, W. H. Units, scales, and norms. In R. L. Thorndike (Ed.), *Educational measurement*. Washington, D. C.: American Council on Education, 1970. (In press.)   **111**

Anon. A good man is hard to find. *Fortune*, 1946, *33*, 92–95 *et seq.*   **648**

Anon. Medical education in the United States and Canada. *Journal of the American Medical Association*, 1956, *161*, 1659.   **425**

Appell, M. J., Williams, C. M., & Fishell, K. N. Significant factors in placing mental retardates from a workshop situation. *Personnel and Guidance Journal*, 1962, *41*, 260–265.   **237**

Arbous, A. G. *Selection for industrial leadership*. London: Oxford University Press, 1955.   **647**

Ash, P. The implications of the Civil Rights Act of 1964 for psychological assessment in industry. *American Psychologist*, 1966, *21*, 797–803. **298, 440**

Atkinson, J. W. (Ed.) *Motives in fantasy, action and society*. Princeton, N.J.: Van Nostrand, 1958.   **79, 659 f.**

Atkinson, J. W., & Feather, N. (Eds.) *A theory of achievement motivation*. New York: Wiley, 1966.   **659 ff.**

Averill, J. R., & Opton, E. M., Jr. Psychophysiological assessment: Rationale and problems. In McReynolds, 1968a. Pp. 265–288.   **624, 625**

Ayres, L. P. *A scale for measuring the quality of handwriting of school children.* New York: Russell Sage Foundation, 1912.   79

Baas, M. L. Kuder interest patterns of psychologists. *Journal of Applied Psychology*, 1950, *34*, 115–117.   458

Bachrach, A. J. (Ed.) *Experimental foundations of clinical psychology.* New York: Basic Books, 1962.   621

Back, K. W. The Einstellung test and performance in factual interviewing. *Journal of Abnormal and Social Psychology*, 1956, *52*, 28–32.   641

Baldwin, A. L. The role of an "ability" construct in a theory of behavior. In McClelland *et al.*, 1958. Pp. 195–233.   42

Baldwin, A. L., Kalhorn, J., & Breese, F. H. Patterns of parent behavior. *Psychological Monographs*, 1945, *58*, No. 3.   580

Baldwin, A. L., Kalhorn, J., & Breese, F. H. The appraisal of parent behavior. *Psychological Monographs*, 1949, *63*, No. 4.   579 ff.

Bales, R. F. *Interaction process analysis.* Cambridge, Mass.: Addison-Wesley, 1951.   604

Baller, W. R., Charles, D. C., & Miller, E. L. Mid-life attainment of the mentally retarded: A longitudinal study. *Genetic Psychology Monographs*, 1967, *75*, 235–329.   236

Balma, M. J. The concept of synthetic validity. *Personnel Psychology*, 1959, *12*, 395–396.   445

Bandura, A. The Rorschach white space response and "oppositional" behavior. *Journal of Consulting Psychology*, 1954, *18*, 17–21.   636

Bandura, A., & Whalen, C. K. The influence of antecedent reinforcement and divergent modeling cues on patterns of self-regard. *Journal of Personality and Social Psychology*, 1966, *3*, 373–382.   616

Bannister, D., & Mair, J. M. M. *The evaluation of personal constructs.* New York: Academic Press, 1968.   599

Barclay, J. R. Sociometric choices and teacher ratings as predictors of school dropout. *Journal of School Psychology*, 1966, *4*, 40–44.   593

Barker, R. G., Kounin, J., & Wright, H. F. (Eds.) *Child behavior and development.* New York: McGraw-Hill, 1943.   604

Barnette, W. L. (Ed.) *Readings in psychological tests and measurements.* (2d ed.) Homewood, Ill.: Dorsey, 1968.   150, 519

Barratt, E. S. The relationship of the Progressive Matrices (1938) and the Columbia Mental Maturity Scale to the WISC. *Journal of Consulting Psychology*, 1956, *20*, 294–296.   271

Barrett, G. V., Cabe, P. A., & Thornton, C. L. Relation between Hidden Figure Test and Rod and Frame Test measures of perceptual style. *Educational and Psychological Measurement*, 1968, *28*, 549–550.   628

Barrett, R. S. Guide to using psychological tests. *Harvard Business Review*, 1963, *41*, No. 4, 133–146.   42

Barron, F. *Personal soundness in university graduate students.* Berkeley: University of California Press, 1954.   480, 573

Barron, F. Threshold for the perception of human movement in inkblots. *Journal of Consulting Psychology*, 1955, *19*, 33–38.   635

Barron, F. The psychology of creativity. In T. M. Newcomb (Ed.), *New directions in psychology: II.* New York: Holt, Rinehart and Winston, 1964. Pp. 1–134.   395

Barron, F., & others. An assessment study of Air Force officers. Part III:
    Assessment correlates of criteria of officer effectiveness. *WADC
    Technical Report* 58–91 (III), Wright Air Development Center,
    1958.   675
Bartlett, C. J., & Green, C. G. Clinical prediction: Does one sometimes
    know too much? *Journal of Counseling Psychology,* 1966, *13,*
    267–270.   442
Bass, B. M. The leaderless group discussion. *Psychological Bulletin,* 1954,
    51, 465–492.   647, 665
Bass, B. M. Social behavior and the Orientation Inventory: A review.
    Psychological Bulletin, 1967, *68,* 260–292.   558
Bass, B. M., & Coates, C. H. Forecasting officer potential using the
    leaderless group discussion. *Journal of Abnormal and Social
    Psychology,* 1952, *47,* 321–325.   647
Bass, B. M., & others. Self, interaction, and task orientation inventory
    scores associated with overt behavior and personal factors. *Educa-
    tional and Psychological Measurement,* 1963, *23,* 101–116.   558
Bauernfeind, R. H. *Building a school testing program.* (2nd ed.) Boston:
    Houghton Mifflin, 1969.   20, 193
Baughman, E. E., & Dahlstrom, W. G. *Negro and white children.* New
    York: Academic Press, 1968.   231, 284, 331
Bayley, N. Consistency and variability in the growth of intelligence from
    birth to eighteen. *Journal of Genetic Psychology,* 1949, *75,* 165–196.   231
Bayley, N. On the growth of intelligence. *American Psychologist,* 1955,
    10, 805–818.   229
Bayley, N. Data on the growth of intelligence between 16 and 21 years
    as measured by the Wechsler-Bellevue Scale. *Journal of Genetic
    Psychology,* 1957, *90,* 3–15.   231
Bayley, N. Comparisons of mental and motor test scores for ages 1–15
    months by sex, birth order, race, geographical location, and educa-
    tion of parents. *Child Development,* 1965, *36,* 379–411.   260
Bayley, N. *The two year old.* Durham, N.C.: Durham Education Improve-
    ment Program. Undated [1966 or 1967].   263
Bayley, N., & Schaefer, E. S. Correlations of maternal and child behaviors
    with the development of mental abilities: Data from the Berkeley
    Growth Study. *Monographs, Society for Research in Child Develop-
    ment,* 1964, *29,* No. 6.   232 f.
Beck, S. J., *et al. Rorschach's test: I. Basic processes.* New York: Grune &
    Stratton, 1961.   634
Becker, W. C. The Personality Inventory. In O. K. Buros (Ed.), *Sixth
    Mental Measurements Yearbook,* 1965. Pp. 156–157.   117
Becker, W. C., & Krug, R. S. A circumplex model for social behavior in
    children. *Child Development,* 1964, *35,* 371–396.   574, 577
Bellak, L. *The Thematic Apperception Test and the Children's Apper-
    ception Test in clinical use.* New York: Grune & Stratton, 1954.   683
Bellows, R. M. The status of selection and counseling techniques for
    dental students. *Journal of Consulting Psychology,* 1940, *4,* 10–16.   390
Bender, L. A visual motor gestalt test and its clinical use. *Research
    Monographs, American Orthopsychiatric Association,* 1938, No. 3.   631
Bennett, C. C. The drugs and I. In J. G. Miller & L. S. Uhr (Eds.), *Drugs
    and behavior.* New York: Wiley, 1960. Pp. 596–609.   42

Bennett, G. K., & Fear, R. K. Mechanical comprehension and dexterity. *Personnel Journal*, 1943, *22*, 12–17. **390**

Bennett, G. K., Seashore, H. G., & Wesman, A. G. *Counseling from profiles.* New York: Psychological Corporation, 1951. **103, 374 f., 382**

Berkowitz, B., & Green, R. F. Changes in intellect with age: I. Longitudinal study of Wechsler-Bellevue scores. *Journal of Genetic Psychology*, 1963, *103*, 3–21. **229**

Biber, B., & others. *Life and ways of the seven to eight year old.* New York: Basic Books, 1952. **76, 249, 606**

Billingslea, F. Y. The Bender Gestalt: A review and a perspective. *Psychological Bulletin*, 1963, *60*, 233–251. **631**

Bilodeau, E. A. *Acquisition of skill.* New York: Academic Press, 1966. **384**

Bingham, W. V. Expectancies. *Année Psychologique*, 1951, *50*, 549–555. (Reprinted in *Educational and Psychological Measurement*, 1953, *13*, 47–53.) **87**

Bixler, R. H., & Bixler, V. H. Test interpretation in vocational counseling. *Educational and Psychological Measurement*, 1946, *6*, 145–155. **379 f.**

Block, J. *The Q-sort method in personality assessment and psychiatric research.* Springfield, Ill.: Thomas, 1960. **585 ff.**

Block, J., & Peterson, P. Q-sort item analysis of a number of Strong Vocational Interest Blank Inventory Scales. *AFOERL Technical Memoranda* TM-55-9, 1955. **479**

Bonarius, J. C. Research in the personal construct theory of George A. Kelly. In B. A. Maher (Ed.), *Progress in Experimental Personality Research*, 1965, *2*, 1–46. **599**

Bond, E. A. *Tenth grade abilities and achievements.* New York: Teachers College, Columbia University, 1940. **237**

Bordin, E. S. A theory of vocational interests as dynamic phenomena. *Educational and Psychological Measurement*, 1943, *3*, 49–66. **472**

Bordin, E. S. Ethical responsibilities of instructors in testing courses. *Educational and Psychological Measurement*, 1951, *11*, 383–386. **379**

Bordin, E. S. Test selection and interpretation and Illustrations and problems. In *Psychological counseling.* (2nd ed.) New York: Appleton-Century-Crofts, 1968. Pp. 295–302. **382**

Bouchard, T. J., Jr. Current conceptions of intelligence and their implications for assessment. In McReynolds, 1968a. Pp. 14–33. **345**

Bowers, J. E. A study of the relationships among measures of productive thinking, intelligence, and ninth-grade achievement. Unpublished doctoral dissertation, University of Minnesota, 1966. **396**

Bradshaw, D. H. Stability of California Test of Mental Maturity IQ's from the second to the fourth grade. *Educational and Psychological Measurement*, 1964, *24*, 935–939. **287**

Bradway, K. P., & Thompson, C. W. Intelligence at adulthood: A twenty-five year follow-up. *Journal of Educational Psychology*, 1962, *53*, 1–14. **229, 263**

Bray, D. W., & Campbell, R. J. Selection of salesmen by means of an assessment center. *Journal of Applied Psychology*, 1968, *58*, 36–41. **676**

Bray, D. W., & Grant, D. L. The Assessment Center in the measurement of potential for business management. *Psychological Monographs*, 1966, *80*, No. 17. **676**

Brim, O. G., Jr., Neulinger, J., & Glass, D. C. *Experiences and attitudes*

of American adults concerning standardized intelligence tests. New
York: Russell Sage Foundation, 1965.   **300**

Brinkmann, E. H. Programmed instruction as a means of improving spatial
visualization. *Journal of Applied Psychology,* 1966, *50,* 179–184.   **361**

Brogden, H. E. A new coefficient: Application to biserial correlation and
to estimation of selective efficiency. *Psychometrika,* 1949, *14,*
169–182.   **429**

Brogden, H. E. Increased efficiency of selection resulting from replacement of a single predictor with several differential predictors.
Educational and Psychological Measurement, 1951, *11,* 173–196.   **446**

Brokaw, L. D. Technical school validity of the Airman Activity Inventory.
AFPTRC Development Report 56–109, 1956.   **475**

Bronson, W. C. Central orientations: A study of behavior organization
from childhood to adolescence. *Child Development,* 1966, *37,*
125–155.   **553, 574**

Brown, C. W., & Ghiselli, E. E. Prediction of labor turnover by aptitude
tests. *Journal of Applied Psychology,* 1953, *37,* 9–12.   **435**

Brown, E. W. Observing behavior during the intelligence test. In
E. Lerner & L. B. Murphy (Eds.), *Methods for the study of per-
sonality in young children. Monographs, Society for Research in
Child Development,* 1941, *6* (4), 268–283.   **225**

Brown, R. R. The time interval between test and retest in its relation to
the constancy of the intelligence quotient. *Journal of Educational
Psychology,* 1933, *24,* 81–96.   **233**

Burdock, E. I., Sutton, S., & Zubin, J. Personality and psychopathology.
Journal of Abnormal and Social Psychology, 1958, *56,* 18–30.   **646**

Burket, G. R. A study of reduced rank models for multiple prediction.
Psychometric Monographs, 1964, No. 12.   **434**

Buros, O. K. (Ed.) *The Mental Measurements Yearbooks.* Highland
Park, N.J.: Gryphon Press, 1941–1965 (irregular).   **117, 121, 190,
                                                                                     307**

Burt, C. The inheritance of mental ability. *American Psychologist,* 1958,
13, 1–15.   **331**

Burton, R. V. Generality of honesty reconsidered. *Psychological Review,*
1963, *70,* 481–499.   **620**

Butcher, H. J. *Human intelligence.* London: Methuen, 1968.   **352, 395**

Butcher, J. N. (Ed.) *MMPI: Research developments and clinical applica-
tions.* New York: McGraw-Hill, 1969.   **537**

Byrd, E. A study of validity and constancy of choice in a sociometric test.
Sociometry, 1951, *14,* 175–181.   **593**

Byrne, D., & Hamilton, M. L. (Eds.) *Personality research.* Englewood
Cliffs, N. J.: Prentice-Hall, 1966.   **383, 569**

Calandra, A. Angels on a pin. *Saturday Review,* Dec. 31, 1968, *51,* 60.   **405**

Caldwell, B. M. A new "approach" to behavior ecology. In J. M. Hill (Ed.)
Minnesota symposium on child psychology, 1969, *2,* 74–109.   **602**

Callis, R., Polmantier, P. C., & Roeber, E. C. *A casebook of counseling.*
New York: Appleton-Century-Crofts, 1955. Pp. 77–103.   **488**

Cameron, J., Livson, N., & Bayley, N. Infant vocalizations and their relationship to mature intelligence. *Science,* 1967, *157,* 331–333.   **258**

Campbell, D. P. The vocational interests of APA presidents. *American
Psychologist,* 1965, *20,* 636–644.   **466**

Campbell, D. P. The Minnesota Vocational Interest Inventory. *Personnel and Guidance Journal*, 1966, *44*, 854–858. (a)   467

Campbell, D. P. The 1966 revision of the Strong Vocational Interest Blank. *Personnel and Guidance Journal*, 1966, *44*, 744–749. (b)   460

Campbell, D. P. The stability of vocational interests within occupations over long time spans. *Personnel and Guidance Journal*, 1966, *44*, 1012–1019. (c)   462

Campbell, D. P. The Strong Vocational Interest Blank: 1927–1967. In McReynolds, 1968a. Pp. 105–130.   12, 13

Campbell, D. P., & others. A set of basic interest scales for the Strong Vocational Interest Blank for Men. *Journal of Applied Psychology*, December, 1968, *52*, No. 6, Part 2.   465

Campbell, D. T. A typology of tests, projective and otherwise. *Journal of Consulting Psychology*, 1957, *21*, 207–210.   492, 502

Campbell, D. T., & Fiske, D. W. Convergent and discriminant validation by the multitrait-multimethod matrix. *Psychological Bulletin*, 1959, *56*, 81–105.   296

Canning, L., *et al.* Permanence of vocational interests of high school boys. *Journal of Educational Psychology*, 1941, *32*, 481–494.   469

Cantoni, L. J. Guidance: 4 students 10 years later. *Clearing House*, 1954, *28*, 474–478.   289

Cantoni, L. J. High school tests and measurements as predictors of occupational status. *Journal of Applied Psychology*, 1955, *39*, 253–255.   287 ff.

Carney, R. E. The effect of situational variables on the measurement of achievement motivation. *Educational and Psychological Measurement*, 1966, *26*, 675–690.   660

Carroll, J. B. The prediction of success in intensive foreign language training. In R. Glaser (Ed.), *Training research and education*. New York: Wiley, 1965. Pp. 87–136.   295

Carter, L. F., & Dudek, F. J. The use of psychological techniques in measuring and critically analyzing navigators' flight performance. *Psychometrika*, 1947, *12*, 31–42.   601

Cattell, R. B. Theory of fluid and crystallized intelligence: A critical experiment. *Journal of Educational Psychology*, 1963, *54*, 1–22.   234

Cattell, R. B. (Ed.) *Handbook of multivariate experimental psychology.* Chicago: Rand McNally, 1966.   319

Cattell, R. B., & Warburton, F. W. *Objective personality and motivation tests.* Urbana: University of Illinois Press, 1967.   121, 524, 609, 624 f.

Cavanaugh, M. C., *et al.* Prediction from the Cattell Infant Intelligence Scale. *Journal of Consulting Psychology*, 1957, *21*, 33–37.   259

Champney, H., & Marshall, H. Optimal refinement of the rating scale. *Journal of Applied Psychology*, 1939, *23*, 323–331.   579

Charters, W. W., Jr. Social class and intelligence tests. In W. W. Charters, Jr. & N. L. Gage (Eds.), *Readings in the social psychology of education*. Englewood Cliffs, N. J.: Allyn and Bacon, 1963. Pp. 12–21.   305

Chase, C. I., & Ludlow, H. G. (Eds.) *Readings in educational and psychological measurement.* Boston: Houghton Mifflin, 1966.   383

Churchill, W. D., & Smith, S. E. The relationship of the 1960 revised Stanford-Binet Intelligence Scale to intelligence and achievement test scores over a three-year period. *Educational and Psychological Measurement*, 1966, *26*, 1015–1020.   237

Clark, K. E. *The vocational interests of nonprofessional men.* Minneapolis: University of Minnesota Press, 1961.   475

Clark, R. A. The projective measurement of experimentally induced levels of sexual motivation. *Journal of Experimental Psychology*, 1952, *44*, 391–399.   655

Cleary, T. A., & Hilton, T. I. Test bias: Prediction of grades of Negro and white students in integrated colleges. *Journal of Educational Measurement*, 1968, *5*, 115–124.   306

Coffman, W. E. A factor analysis of the Verbal section of the Scholastic Aptitude Test. *Research Bulletin* 66–30, Educational Testing Service, 1966.   333

Coleman, J. S., *et al. Equality of educational opportunity.* Washington, D. C.: Government Printing Office, 1966.   303 f.

College Entrance Examination Board. *46th annual report of the executive secretary.* New York: CEEB, 1946.   31

College Entrance Examination Board. A statement on personality testing. *College Board Review*, 1963, No. 51, 11–13.   549

College Entrance Examination Board. *College Freshman Profiles, 1967–1969.* New York: CEEB, 1967.   219

Combs, A. W., Soper, D. W., & Courson, C. C. The measurement of self concept and self report. *Educational and Psychological Measurement*, 1963, *33*, 493–500.   503

Conrad, H. S. The validity of personality ratings of nursery-school children. *Journal of Educational Psychology*, 1932, *23*, 671–680.   577

Conrad, H. S. *Statistical analysis for the Mechanical Knowledge Test.* Princeton, N. J.: College Entrance Examination Board, 1944.   146

Conrad, H. S. *A statistical evaluation of the Basic Classification Test battery (Form 1).* OSRD Report 4636. Washington, D. C.: Department of Commerce, 1946.   310 ff.

Conrad, H. S., & Satter, G. A. *The use of test scores and Qualification Card ratings in predicting success in electrician's mate school.* Washington, D. C.: Department of Commerce, 1945.   442

Conry, R., & Plant, W. T. WAIS and group predictions of an academic success criterion: High school and college. *Educational and Psychological Measurement*, 1965, *25*, 493–500.   236

Cooper, G. D., *et al.* The Porteus test and various measures of intelligence with southern Negro adolescents. *American Journal of Mental Deficiency*, 1967, *71*, 787–792.   237

Cottle, W. C. Card vs. booklet forms of the MMPI. *Journal of Applied Psychology*, 1950, *34*, 255–259.   532

Cowen, E. L., *et al.* The relation of anxiety in school children to school record, achievement, and behavioral measures. *Child Development*, 1965, *36*, 685–695.   554

Cox, C. M. *Genetic studies of genius: II. The early mental traits of three hundred geniuses.* Stanford, Calif.: Stanford University Press, 1926.   235

Crandall, Vaughn, J., & Sinkeldam, C. Children's dependent and achievement behaviors in social situations and their perceptual field dependence. *Journal of Personality*, 1964, *32*, 1–22.   629

Crandall, Virginia C. Personality characteristics and social and achievement behaviors associated with children's social desirability response tendencies. *Journal of Personality and Social Psychology*, 1966, *4*, 477–486.   **601**

Cronbach, L. J. Processes affecting scores on "understanding of others" and "assumed similarity." *Psychological Bulletin*, 1955, *52*, 177–193.   **442**

Cronbach, L. J. The two disciplines of scientific psychology. *American Psychologist*, 1957, *12*, 671–684.   **447**

Cronbach, L. J. Proposals leading to analytic treatment of social perception scores. In R. Tagiuri & L. Petrullo (Eds.), *Person perception and interpersonal behavior*. Stanford, Calif.: Stanford University Press, 1958. Pp. 353–379.   **576, 586, 598**

Cronbach, L. J. *Essentials of psychological testing*. (2nd ed.) New York: Harper & Row, 1960.   **330, 510**

Cronbach, L. J. *Educational psychology*. (2nd ed.) New York: Harcourt, Brace & World, 1964.   **348**

Cronbach, L. J. How can instruction be adapted to individual differences? In R. M. Gagné (Ed.), *Learning and individual differences*. Columbus, Ohio: Merrill, 1967. Pp. 23–39.   **447**

Cronbach, L. J. Heredity, environment, and educational policy. *Harvard Educational Review*, 1969, *39*, 338–347. (See Kagan *et al.*, 1969.)   **247**

Cronbach, L. J. Test validation. In R. L. Thorndike (Ed.), *Educational measurement*. Washington, D. C.: American Council on Education, 1970, in press.   **142, 149**

Cronbach, L. J., & Gleser, G. C. (Review of *The study of behavior*.) *Psychometrika*, 1954, *19*, 327–333.   **254**

Cronbach, L. J., & Gleser, G. C. The signal/noise ratio in the comparison of reliability coefficients. *Educational and Psychological Measurement*, 1964, *24*, 467–480.   **170**

Cronbach, L. J., & Gleser, G. C. *Psychological tests and personnel decisions*. (2nd ed.) Urbana: University of Illinois Press, 1965.   **24, 173, 180 f., 365, 441, 445, 586, 689**

Cronbach, L. J., Gleser, G. C., Nanda, H., & Rajaratnam, N. *The dependability of behavioral measurements*. New York: Wiley, 1970, in press.   **152, 162, 171, 343, 368**

Cronbach, L. J., & Meehl, P. E. Construct validity in psychological tests. *Psychological Bulletin*, 1955, *52*, 281–302.   **142, 554**

Cronbach, L. J., & Warrington, W. G. Efficiency of multiple-choice tests as a function of the spread of item difficulties. *Psychometrika*, 1952, *17*, 127–147.   **100**

Crosby, R. C., & Winsor, A. L. The validity of students' estimates of their own interests. *Journal of Applied Psychology*, 1941, *25*, 408–414.   **471**

Crowne, D. P., & Liverant, S. Conformity under varying conditions of personal commitment. *Journal of Abnormal and Social Psychology*, 1963, *66*, 547–555.   **518**

Crowne, D. P., & Marlowe, D. *The approval motive*. New York: Wiley, 1964.   **638**

Dahlstrom, W. G., & Welsh, G. S. *An MMPI handbook: A guide to use in clinical practice and research*. Minneapolis: University of Minnesota Press, 1960.   **530**

Dailey, J. T. A system for classifying public high schools. In J. C. Flanagan *et al.*, *Studies of the American high school*. Pittsburgh: University of Pittsburgh Press, 1962. Pp. 4–1 to 4–26.   **107, 112**

Damrin, D. E. The Russell Sage Social Relations Test: A technique for measuring group problem solving skills in elementary school children. *Journal of Experimental Education*, 1959, *28*, 85–99.   **650**

d'Andrade, R. G. Trait psychology and componential analysis. *American Anthropologist*, 1965, *67*, 215–228.   **575**

Darcy, N. T. The effect of bilingualism upon the measurement of the intelligence of children of preschool age. *Journal of Educational Psychology*, 1946, *37*, 21–44.   **239**

Darley, J. G. Tested maladjustment related to clinically diagnosed maladjustment. *Journal of Applied Psychology*, 1937, *21*, 632–642.   **540**

Darley, J. G., & Haganah, T. *Vocational interest measurement: Theory and practice*. Minneapolis: University of Minnesota Press, 1955.   **469, 471, 478, 479, 482, 488**

Dart, F. E., & Pradhan, P. L. Cross-cultural teaching of science. *Science*, 1967, *155*, 649–656.   **248**

Dauterman, W. L., & Suinn, R. M. *Stanford-Ohwaki-Kohs Tactile Block Design Intelligence Test for the Blind: Final report*. Washington, D.C.: Vocational Rehabilitation Administration, 1966.   **48**

Davenport, B. F. The semantic validity of TAT interpretations. *Journal of Consulting Psychology*, 1952, *16*, 171–175.   **682**

Davis, A. Socio-economic influences upon children's learning. *Understanding the Child*, 1951, *20*, 10–16.   **305**

Davis, P. C. A factor analysis of the Wechsler-Bellevue Scale. *Educational and Psychological Measurement*, 1956, *16*, 127–146.   **330**

DeHaan, R. F., & Havighurst, R. J. *Educating gifted children*. Chicago: University of Chicago Press, 1957.   **374**

Dennis, W. The performance of Hopi children on the Goodenough Draw-a-Man Test. *Journal of Comparative Psychology*, 1942, *34*, 341–348.   **253**

Dennis, W. Goodenough scores, art experience, and modernization. *Journal of Social Psychology*, 1966, *68*, 211–228.   **253**

Deutsch, M., *et al.* Guidelines for testing minority group children. *Journal of Social Issues* (Supplement), 1964, *22*, 129–145.   **307**

Dewey, J. *Experience and education*. New York: Macmillan, 1938.   **380**

Dicken, C. Good impression, social desirability, and acquiescence as suppressor variables. *Educational and Psychological Measurement*, 1963, *23*, 699–720.   **530**

di Finetti, B. Methods for discriminating levels of partial knowledge concerning a test item. *British Journal of Statistical Psychology*, 1967, *18*, 87–123.   **59**

Digman, J. M. Child behavior ratings: further evidence of a multiple-factor model of child personality. *Educational and Psychological Measurement*, 1965, *25*, 787–799.   **574**

Dillon, H. J. *Early school leavers—a major educational problem*. New York: National Child Labor Committee, 1949.   **219**

Dobbin, J. E., *et al.* (Reviews of the *Test standards*.) *Educational and Psychological Measurement*, 1966, *26*, 751–811.   **193**

Docter, R. F., & Winder, C. L. Delinquent *vs.* nondelinquent performance on the Porteus Qualitative Maze Test. *Journal of Consulting Psychology*, 1954, *18*, 71–73.   **640**

Domino, G. Differential predictions of academic achievement in conforming and independent settings. *Journal of Educational Psychology,* 1968, *59,* 256–260.   **550**

Doppelt, J. E., & Bennett, G. K. Testing job applicants from disadvantaged groups. *Test Service Bulletin,* 1967, No. 57. New York: Psychological Corporation.   **300, 307**

Drake, L. E., & Oetting, E. R. *An MMPI codebook for counselors.* Minneapolis: University of Minnesota Press, 1959.   **534**

Droege, R. C. Sex differences in aptitude maturation during high school. *Journal of Counseling Psychology,* 1967, *14,* 407–411.   **371**

DuBois, P. H. (Ed.). *The classification program.* Washington, D. C.: Government Printing Office, 1947.   **412, 426, 428, 431**

Duff, F. L. Item subtlety in personality inventory scales. *Journal of Consulting Psychology,* 1965, *29,* 565–570.   **532**

Duncan, A. K. Some comments on the Army General Classification Test. *Journal of Applied Psychology,* 1947, *31,* 143–149.   **51**

Dunham, J. L., Guilford, J. P., & Hoepfner, R. Abilities pertaining to classes and the learning of concepts. *Psychological Laboratory, University of Southern California, Reports,* 1966, No. 39.   **340, 342**

Dunnette, M. D. Vocational interest differences among engineers employed in different functions. *Journal of Applied Psychology,* 1957, *41,* 273–278.   **472 f.**

Dunnette, M. D. *Personnel selection and placement.* Belmont, Calif.: Wadsworth, 1967.   **429, 440, 450**

Dunnette, M. D., & Kirchner, W. K. Validation of psychological tests in industry. *Personnel Administration,* 1958, *21,* 20–27.   **408**

Dunnette, M. D., *et al.* A study of faking behavior on a forced-choice self-description checklist. *Personnel Psychology,* 1962, *15,* 13–24.   **497, 500**

Dvorak, B. J., Droege, R. C., & Seiler, K. New directions in U. S. Employment Service aptitude test research. *Personnel and Guidance Journal,* 1965, *44,* 136–140.   **359**

Ebel, R. L. Content standard test scores. *Educational and Psychological Measurement,* 1962, *22,* 15–25.   **85, 113**

Eber, H. W., & Cattell, R. B. Maximizing personality scale validities on the 16 PF by the computer synthesis service. *IPAT News.* Undated, unnumbered [1966].   **559**

Eells, K., *et al. Intelligence and cultural differences.* Chicago: University of Chicago Press, 1951.   **61, 286, 303, 305**

Emery, J. R., & Krumboltz, J. D. Standard versus individualized hierarchies in desensitization to reduce test anxiety. *Journal of Counseling Psychology,* 1967, *14,* 204–209.   **505**

Endler, N. S., & Hunt, J. McV. Sources of behavioral variance as measured by the S-R Inventory of Anxiousness. *Psychological Bulletin,* 1966, *65,* 336–346.   **561**

Endler, N. S., & Hunt, J. McV. Generalizability of contributions from sources of variance in S-R inventories of anxiousness. *Journal of Personality,* 1969, *37,* 1–24.   **561**

Endler, N. S., Hunt, J. McV., & Rosenstein, A. J. An S-R inventory of
anxiousness. *Psychological Monographs*, 1962, 76, No. 17.   **561**

Estes, B. W. Relationships between the Otis, 1960 Stanford-Binet and
WISC. *Journal of Clinical Psychology*, 1965, 21, 296–297.   **217**

Ewart, E., *et al.* A factor analysis of an industrial merit rating scale.
Journal of Applied Psychology, 1941, 25, 481–486.   **573**

Eysenck, H. J. *Dynamics of anxiety and hysteria.* London: Routledge &
Kegan Paul, 1957.   **215**

Eysenck, H. J. Comment on "The relation of neuroticism and extraversion to intelligence and educational attainment." *British Journal of
Educational Psychology*, 1963, 33, 192.   **524**

Eysenck, H. J. Extraversion and the acquisition of eyeblink and GSR
conditioned responses. *Psychological Bulletin*, 1965, 63, 258–270.   **516**

Eysenck, H. J. Personality and experimental psychology. *Bulletin, British
Psychological Society*, 1966, 19, 1–28.   **516**

Fahmy, M. *Initial exploring the Shilluk intelligence.* Cairo: Dar Misr
Printing Co., 1954.   **247**

Fancher, R. E., Jr. Explicit personality theories and accuracy of person
perception. *Journal of Personality*, 1966, 34, 252–261.   **560**

Fargo, G. A., *et al.* Comparability of group television and individual
administration of the Peabody Picture Vocabulary Test. *Journal of
Educational Psychology*, 1967, 58, 137–140.   **225**

Faterson, H. F. Articulateness of experience: An extension of the field
dependence-independence concept. In S. Messick & J. Ross (Eds.),
Measurement in personality and cognition. New York: Wiley, 1962.   **629**

Feather, N. T. Valence of success and failure in relation to task difficulty:
past research and recent progress. *Australian Journal of Psychology*,
1968, 20, 111–122.   **662**

Feder, D. D., & Baer, P. L. A comparison of test records and clinical
evaluations of personality adjustment. *Journal of Educational Psychology*, 1941, 32, 133–144.   **541**

Feifel, H. Qualitative differences in the vocabulary response of normals
and abnormals. *Genetic Psychological Monographs*, 1949, 39, 151–
206.   **249**

Feldman, M. J., & Corah, N. L. Social desirability and the forced-choice
method. *Journal of Consulting Psychology*, 1960, 24, 480–482.   **500**

Fenz, W. D. Conflict and stress as related to physiological activation and
sensory, perceptual, and cognitive functioning. *Psychological Monographs*, 1964, 78, No. 8.   **658**

Fenz, W. D., & Epstein, S. Measurement of approach-avoidance conflict
along a stimulus dimension by a thematic apperception test. *Journal
of Personality*, 1962, 30, 613–632.   **656 f., 658**

Fiedler, F. E. *A theory of leadership effectiveness.* New York: McGraw-
Hill, 1967.   **598**

Finley, C. J. (Book review.) *Educational and Psychological Measurement*, 1965, 25, 915–917.   **237**

Finley, C. J., Thompson, J. M., & Cognata, A. Stability of the California
Short Form Test of Mental Maturity in Grades 3, 5, and 7. *California Journal of Educational Research*, 1966, 17, 157–168.   **287**

Fisher, G. M., Kilman, B. A., & Shotwell, A. M. Comparability of intelligence quotients of mental defectives on the Wechsler Adult Intelligence Scale and the 1960 revision of the Stanford-Binet. *Journal of Consulting Psychology*, 1961, *25*, 192–195. **217**

Fisher, J., Gonda, T. A., & Little, K. B. The Rorschach and central nervous system pathology: A cross-validation study. *American Journal of Psychiatry*, 1955, *11*, 487–492. **636**

Fitts, P. M. German applied psychology during World War II. *American Psychologist*, 1946, *1*, 141–161. **33**

Flanagan, J. C. *Factor analysis in the study of personality*. Stanford, Calif.: Stanford University Press, 1935. **522**

Flanagan, J. C. The critical incidents technique. *Psychological Bulletin*, 1954, *51*, 327–358. **408**

Flanagan, J. C. The development of an index of examinee motivation. *Educational and Psychological Measurement*, 1955, *15*, 144–151. **61**

Fleishman, E. A. Dimensional analysis of psychomotor abilities. *Journal of Experimental Psychology*, 1954, *48*, 437–454. **385**

Fleishman, E. A. Psychomotor selection tests: Research and application in the United States Air Force. *Personnel Psychology*, 1956, *9*, 449–468. **385**

Fleishman, E. A. A comparative study of aptitude patterns in unskilled and skilled motor performances. *Journal of Applied Psychology*, 1957, *41*, 263–272. **392**

Fleishman, E. A. The description and prediction of perceptual-motor skill learning. In R. Glaser (Ed.) *Training research and education*. Pittsburgh: University of Pittsburgh Press, 1962. **405**

Fleishman, E. A. *The structure and measurement of physical fitness*. Englewood Cliffs, N. J.: Prentice-Hall, 1964. **386**

Fleishman, E. A. Human abilities and the acquisition of skill. In Bilodeau, 1966. Pp. 147–167. **384**

Fleishman, E. A. (Ed.) *Studies in personnel and industrial psychology*. Homewood, Ill.: Dorsey, 1967. **42, 450**

Fleishman, E. A., & Berniger, J. One way to reduce turnover. *Personnel*, 1960, *37*, 63–69. **450**

Fleishman, E. A., & Ellison, G. D. A factor analysis of five manipulative tests. *Journal of Applied Psychology*, 1962, *46*, 96–105. **391**

Fleishman, E. A., & Hempel, W. E., Jr. Changes in factor structure of a complex psychomotor test as a function of practice. *Psychometrika*, 1954, *19*, 239–252. **392**

Flynn, L., & Garber, H. (Eds.) *Assessing behavior*. Cambridge, Mass.: Addison-Wesley, 1967. **43, 193, 383, 694**

Fonda, C. P. The white space response. In Rickers-Ovsiankina, 1960. Pp. 80–105. **636**

Ford, A., et al. *The sonar pitch-memory test: A report on design standards*. San Diego: University of California Division of War Research, 1944. **164**

Frank, I. H. Psychological testimony in a courtroom. *American Psychologist*, 1956, *11*, 50–51. **186**

Frank, L. K. *Projective methods*. Springfield, Ill.: Thomas, 1948. **686**

Franks, C. M. Personality and eyeblink conditioning seven years later. *Acta Psychologica*, 1963, *31*, 295–312. **516**

Frederiksen, N. *Consistency of performance in simulated situations.* Princeton, N. J.: Educational Testing Service, 1961. **645**

Frederiksen, N., & Satter, G. A. The construction and validation of an arithmetical computation test. *Educational and Psychological Measurement*, 1953, *13*, 209–227. **315**

Frederiksen, N., Saunders, D. E., & Wand, B. The in-basket test. *Psychological Monographs*, 1957, *71*, No. 9. **644**

Freeberg, N. E. The Biographical Interest Blank as a predictor of student achievement: A review. *Psychological Reports*, 1967, *20*, 911–925. **549**

Freedman, M. H. A plea to professional psychologists. *American Psychologist*, 1965, *20*, 877–879. (a) **510**

Freedman, M. H. Testimony. *American Psychologist*, 1965, *20*, 923–931. (b) **510, 518**

French, E. G., & Lesser, G. S. Some characteristics of the achievement motive in women. *Journal of Abnormal and Social Psychology*, 1964, *68*, 119–128. **664**

French, E. G., & Thomas, F. H. The relation of achievement motivation to problem-solving effectiveness. *Journal of Abnormal and Social Psychology*, 1958, *56*, 45–48. **660**

French, J. W. The description of aptitude and achievement tests in terms of rotated factors. *Psychometric Monographs*, 1951, No. 5. **328**

French, J. W. Validation of new item types against four-year academic criteria. *Journal of Educational Psychology*, 1958, *49*, 67–76. **149**

French, J. W. *A machine search for moderator variables in massive data.* Princeton, N.J.: Educational Testing Service, 1961. **440**

French, J. W. Comparative prediction of success and satisfaction in high school curricula. *Research Bulletin 62–4.* Princeton, N. J.: Educational Testing Service, 1962. (a) **477**

French, J. W. Schools of thought in judging excellence of English themes. *Proceedings, Invitational Conference on Testing Problems,* 1961. Princeton: Educational Testing Service, 1962. Pp. 19–28. (b) **113**

French, J. W. Comparative prediction of college major-field grades by pure-factor aptitude, interest, and personality measures. *Educational and Psychological Measurement*, 1963, *23*, 767–774. **371, 477**

French, J. W. Comparative prediction of high-school grades by pure-factor aptitude, information, and personality measures. *Educational and Psychological Measurement*, 1964, *24*, 321–329. **371 f.**

French, J. W. The relationship of problem-solving styles to the factor composition of tests. *Educational and Psychological Measurement*, 1965, *25*, 9–28. **350**

French, J. W., & Dear, R. E. Effect of coaching on an aptitude test. *Educational and Psychological Measurement*, 1959, *19*, 319–330. **67**

Freund, K. A laboratory method for diagnosing predominance of homo- and hetero-erotic interest in the male. *Behavior Research and Therapy*, 1963, *1*, 85–93. **625**

Freyberg, P. S. Concept development in Piagetian terms in relation to school attainment. *Journal of Educational Psychology*, 1966, *57*, 164–168. **244**

Gagné, R. M. *The conditions of learning.* New York: Holt, Rinehart and Winston, 1966. **333**

Gallagher, J. J. Normality and projective techniques. *Journal of Abnormal and Social Psychology,* 1955, *50,* 259–264. **684**

Gallagher, J. J. Productive thinking. In M. L. Hoffman & L. W. Hoffman (Eds.), *Review of child development research.* Vol. I. New York: Russell Sage Foundation, 1964. Pp. 349–381. **400**

Galperin, P. R. Towards research on the mental development of the child. *International Journal of Psychology,* 1968, *3,* 257–272. **306**

Galton, F. *Hereditary Genius.* New York: Macmillan, 1869. **198, 394**

Gardner, J. W. *Excellence.* New York: Harper & Row, 1961. **302**

Gardner, R. C. Motivational variables in second-language acquisition. Unpublished doctoral dissertation, McGill University, 1960. **343**

Gardner, R. C., & Lambert, W. E. Language aptitude, intelligence, and second-language achievement. *Journal of Educational Psychology,* 1965, *56,* 191–199. **373**

Garman, G. D., & Uhr, L. An anxiety scale for the Strong Vocational Interest Inventory. *Journal of Applied Psychology,* 1958, *42,* 241–246. **480**

Garrett, H. E. *Testing for teachers.* New York: American Book, 1965. **237**

Garry, R. Individual differences in ability to fake vocational interests. *Journal of Applied Psychology,* 1953, *37,* 33–37. **500**

Gee, H. H., & Cowles, J. T. (Eds.) *The appraisal of applicants for medical schools.* Evanston, Ill.: Association of American Medical Colleges, 1957. **474, 478**

Gehman, I. H., & Matyas, R. P. Stability of the WISC and Binet tests. *Journal of Consulting Psychology,* 1956, *20,* 150–152. **231**

Gesell, A., & Amatruda, C. S. *Developmental diagnosis.* New York: Hoeber, 1947. **259**

Ghiselli, E. E. The prediction of predictability. *Educational and Psychological Measurement,* 1960, *20,* 3–8. **439**

Ghiselli, E. E. (Comment.) *Personnel Psychology,* 1964, *17,* 61–63. **440**

Ghiselli, E. E. *The validity of occupational aptitude tests.* New York: Wiley, 1966. **140, 188, 290 f., 364**

Ghiselli, E. E., & Barthol, R. P. The validity of personality inventories in the selection of employees. *Journal of Applied Psychology,* 1953, *37,* 18–20. **547**

Giannell, A. S., & Freeburne, C. M. The comparative validity of the WAIS and the Stanford-Binet with college freshmen. *Educational and Psychological Measurement,* 1963, *23,* 557–567. **236**

Gilberstadt, H., & Duker, J. *A handbook for clinical and actuarial MMPI interpretation.* Philadelphia: Saunders, 1965. **534**

Gilbert, H. B. On the IQ ban. *Teachers College Record,* 1966, *67,* 282–285. **302**

Gilliland, A. R., & Colgin, R. Norms, reliability, and forms of the MMPI. *Journal of Consulting Psychology,* 1951, *15,* 435–438. **532**

Gilmore, J. B., & Zigler, E. Birth order and social reinforcer effectiveness in children. *Child Development,* 1964, *35,* 193–200. **61**

Glaser, R. Instructional technology and the measurement of learning outcomes. *American Psychologist*, 1963, *18*, 510–522. **84**

Glaser, R., & Klaus, D. Proficiency measurement: Assessing human performance. In R. M. Gagné (Ed.), *Psychological principles in system development*. New York: Holt, Rinehart and Winston, 1962. Pp. 419–474. **149**

Glasser, A. J., & Zimmerman, I. L. *Clinical interpretation of the Wechsler Intelligence Scale for Children*. New York: Grune & Stratton, 1967. **250**

Gleser, G. C. Psychometric contributions to the assessment of patients. In D. H. Efron *et al.* (Eds.), *Psychopharmacology: Review of progress, 1957–1967*. Washington, D.C.: Government Printing Office, 1968. Pp. 1029–1037. **576, 578**

Gobetz, W. A quantification, standardization, and validation of the Bender-Gestalt test on normal and neurotic adults. *Psychological Monographs*, 1953, *67*, No. 6. **631**

Gobetz, W. Suggested personality implications of Kuder Preference Record (Vocational) scores. *Personnel and Guidance Journal*, 1964, *43*, 159–166. **478**

Goldberg, L. R. Seer over sign: The first good example? *Journal of Experimental Research on Personality*, 1968, *3*, 168–171. **693**

Goldberg, L. R. The search for configural relationships in personality assessment. *Multivariate Behavioral Research*, in press. **545**

Goldberg, L. R., & Hase, H. D. Strategies and tactics of personality inventory construction: an empirical investigation. *Multivariate Behavioral Research*, in press. **434**

Goldberg, L. R., & Rorer, L. G. Use of two different response modes and repeated testings to predict social conformity. *Journal of Personality and Social Psychology*, 1966, *3*, 28–37. **515**

Goldberg, L. R., & Werts, C. E. The reliability of clinicians' judgments: a multitrait-multimethod approach. *Journal of Consulting Psychology*, 1966, *30*, 199–206. **684**

Goldman, L. *Using tests in counseling*. New York: Appleton-Century-Crofts, 1961. **450**

Goldner, R. H. Individual differences in whole-part approach and flexibility-rigidity in problem solving. *Psychological Monographs*, 1957, *71*, No. 21. **642 f.**

Goldstein, M. J., & Jones, R. B. The relationships among word association test, objective personality test scores and ratings of clinical behavior in psychiatric patients. *Journal of Protective Techniques*, 1964, *28*, 271–279. **555**

Goodenough, D. R., & Karp, S. A. Field dependence and intellectual functioning. *Journal of Abnormal and Social Psychology*, 1961, *63*, 241–246. **240, 630**

Goodnow, J. J., & Bethon, G. Piaget's tasks: The effects of schooling and intelligence. *Child Development*, 1966, *37*, 573–582. **244 f., 271**

Gordon, L. V. Clinical, psychometric, and work-sample approaches in the prediction of success in Peace Corps training. *Journal of Applied Psychology*, 1967, *51*, 111–119. **693**

Gordon, L. V., & Medland, F. F. The cross-group stability of peer ratings of leadership potential. *Personnel Psychology*, 1965, *18*, 173–177. **593**

Gottschaldt, K. Über den Einfluss der Erfahrung auf die Wahrnehmung von Figuren. I: Über den Einfluss gehäufter Einprägung von Figuren auf ihre Sichtbarkeit in umfassenden Konfigurationen. *Psychologische Forschung,* 1926, *8,* 261–317. **240**

Gough, H. G. An assessment study of Air Force officers. Part IV: Predictability of a composite criterion of officer effectiveness. *WADC Technical Report* 58–91(IV), Wright Air Development Center, 1958. **675**

Gough, H. G. Academic achievement in high school as predicted from the California Psychological Inventory. *Journal of Educational Psychology,* 1964, *55,* 174–180. **549**

Gough, H. G. An interpreter's syllabus for the California Personality Inventory. In McReynolds, 1968a. Pp. 55–79. **564**

Gough, H. G., & Hall, W. B. Prediction of performance in medical school from the California Psychological Inventory. *Journal of Applied Psychology,* 1964, *48,* 218–226. **569**

Gough, H. G., & Krauss, I. An assessment study of Air Force officers. Part II: Description of the assessed sample. *WADC Technical Report* 58–91(II), Wright Air Development Center, 1958. **675**

Gough, H. G., Wenk, E. A., & Rozynko, V. A. Parole outcome as predicted from the CPI, the MMPI, and a base expectancy index. *Journal of Abnormal Psychology,* 1965, *70,* 432–441. **542**

Grayson, H. M., & Tolman, R. S. A semantic study of concepts of clinical psychologists and psychiatrists. *Journal of Abnormal and Social Psychology,* 1950, *45,* 216–231. **685**

Greenwald, A. G. Behavior change following a persuasive communication. *Journal of Personality,* 1965, *33,* 370–391. **501**

Gronlund, N. E. *Sociometry in the classroom.* New York: Harper & Row, 1959. **590, 592, 606**

Gronlund, N. E. *Readings in measurement and evaluation.* New York: Macmillan, 1968. **114, 150, 193, 683**

Grummon, D. Client-centered counseling. In B. Stefflre (Ed.), *Theories of counseling.* New York: McGraw-Hill, 1966. **378**

Guertin, W. H., *et al.* Research with the Wechsler Intelligence Scales for Adults: 1960–1965. *Psychological Bulletin,* 1966, *66,* 385–409. **251**

Guilford, J. P. (Ed.). *Printed classification tests.* Washington, D. C.: Government Printing Office, 1947. **324, 364, 411, 611**

Guilford, J. P. A revised structure of intellect. *Psychological Laboratory, University of Southern California, Reports,* 1957, No. 19. **342**

Guilford, J. P. A system of the psychomotor abilities. *American Journal of Psychology,* 1958, *71,* 164–174. **386**

Guilford, J. P. Progress in the discovery of intellectual factors. In C. W. Taylor (Ed.), *Widening horizons in creativity.* New York: Wiley, 1964. Pp. 261–297. (a) **399**

Guilford, J. P. Zero intercorrelations among tests of intellectual abilities. *Psychological Bulletin,* 1964, *61,* 401–404. (b) **331**

Guilford, J. P. Intellectual factors in productive thinking. In M. J. Aschner & C. E. Bish (Eds.), *Productive thinking in education.* Washington, D. C.: National Education Association, 1965. Pp. 5–20. **395, 405**

Guilford, J. P. Intelligence: 1965 model. *American Psychologist,* 1966, *21,* 20–25. **383**

Guilford, J. P. *The nature of human intelligence.* New York: McGraw-Hill, 1967. **335 ff., 345**

Guilford, J. P. Intelligence has three facets. *Science,* 1968, *160,* 615–620. **352**

Guilford, J. P. *Intelligence, creativity and their educational implications.* San Diego, Calif.: Educational and Industrial Testing Service, 1969. **339**

Guilford, J. P., Hoepfner, R., & Petersen, H. Predicting achievement in ninth-grade mathematics from measures of intellectual-aptitude factors. *Educational and Psychological Measurement,* 1965, *25,* 659–682. **449**

Guilford, J. P., Kettner, N. W., & Christensen, P. R. The nature of the general reasoning factor. *Psychological Review,* 1956, *63,* 169–172. **352**

Guion, R. M. *Personnel testing.* New York: McGraw-Hill, 1965. **292**

Guion, R. M., & Gottier, R. F. Validity of personality measures in personnel selection. *Personnel Psychology,* 1965, *18,* 135–164. **547**

Gulliksen, H. Louis Leon Thurstone, experimental and mathematical psychologist. *American Psychologist,* 1968, *23,* 786–800. **293**

Guthrie, G. M. Six MMPI diagnostic profile patterns. *Journal of Psychology,* 1950, *30,* 317–323. **544**

Guttman, L. A faceted definition of intelligence. *Scripta Hierosolymitana,* 1965, *14,* 166–181. (a) **282, 333**

Guttman, L. The structure of relations among intelligence tests. *Proceedings, Invitational Conference on Testing Problems, 1964.* Princeton, N. J.: Educational Testing Service, 1965. Pp. 25–36. (b) **282, 333**

Haan, N. Proposed model of ego functioning. *Psychological Monographs,* 1963, *77,* No. 8. **287**

Haganah, T. A normative study of the revised Strong Vocational Interest Blank for Men. Unpublished doctoral dissertation, University of Minnesota, 1953. **471**

Hain, J. D. The Bender-Gestalt test: A scoring method for identifying brain damage. *Journal of Consulting Psychology,* 1964, *28,* 34–40. **631**

Halpern, G., & Sasajima, M. Effectiveness of PSAT and SAT booklets: III. A description of the College Board Scholastic Aptitude Test. *Research Bulletin 66–16.* Princeton, N. J.: Educational Testing Service, 1966. **67**

Halstead, W. C. Biological intelligence. *Journal of Personality,* 1951, *20,* 118–130. **623**

Harari, H., & McDavid, J. W. Cultural influences on retention of logical and symbolic set. *Journal of Educational Psychology,* 1966, *57,* 18–22. **248**

Harker, J. S. Cross-validation of an IBM proof machine test battery. *Journal of Applied Psychology,* 1960, *44,* 237–240. **450**

Harman, H. *Modern factor analysis.* Chicago: University of Chicago Press, 1967. **319**

Harper, E. A. Discrimination between matched schizophrenics and normals by the Wechsler-Bellevue Scale. *Journal of Consulting Psychology,* 1950, *14,* 351–357. **251**

Harris, D. B. *Children's drawings as measures of intellectual maturity: A revision and extension of the Goodenough Draw-a-Man Test.* New York: Harcourt, Brace & World, 1963. **253 f.**

Harris, D. H. Questionnaire and interview in neuropsychiatric screening. *Journal of Applied Psychology*, 1945, *30*, 644–648. **540**

Harrison, R. Thematic apperception methods. In B. B. Wolman (Ed.), *Handbook of clinical psychology.* New York: McGraw-Hill, 1965. Pp. 562–620. **653, 657 f., 678**

Hartley, E. L., & Hartley, R. E. (Eds.) *Outside readings in psychology.* (2d ed.) New York: Crowell, 1958. **226**

Hartmann, A. A. An experimental examination of the Thematic Apperception Technique in clinical diagnosis. *Psychological Monographs*, 1949, *63*, No. 8. **682**

Hartshorne, H., & May, M. A. *Studies in deceit.* New York: Macmillan, 1928. **615 ff., 619**

Hartshorne, H., & May, M. A. *Studies in service and self-control.* New York: Macmillan, 1929. **590, 615**

Hartshorne, H., & May, M. A. *Studies in the organization of character.* New York: Macmillan, 1930. **615, 620**

Hathaway, S. R. MMPI: Professional use by professional people. *American Psychologist*, 1964, *19*, 204–210. **512**

Hathaway, S. R., & McKinley, J. C. A multiphasic personality schedule (Minnesota): III. The measurement of symptomatic depression. *Journal of Psychology*, 1942, *14*, 73–84. **539**

Hathaway, S. R., & Meehl, P. E. *An atlas for the clinical use of the MMPI.* Minneapolis: University of Minnesota Press, 1951. **534**

Hathaway, S. R., & Monachesi, E. D. (Eds.) *Analyzing and predicting juvenile delinquency with the MMPI.* Minneapolis: University of Minnesota Press, 1953. **532, 541**

Hays, W. L. *Statistics for psychologists.* New York: Holt, Rinehart and Winston, 1963. **158**

Heath, R. W. Curriculum, cognition, and educational measurement. *Educational and Psychological Measurement*, 1964, *24*, 239–253. **501**

Hebb, D. O. *The organization of behavior.* New York: Wiley, 1949. Pp. 274–303. **307**

Hebb, D. O., & Williams, K. A method of rating animal intelligence. *Journal of Genetic Psychology*, 1946, *34*, 59–65. **65**

Helson, R. Personality of women with imaginative and artistic interests. *Journal of Personality*, 1966, *34*, 1–25. **479**

Helson, R. Sex differences in creative style. *Journal of Personality*, 1967, *35*, 214–233. **587**

Hemphill, J. K., Griffiths, D. E., & Frederiksen, N. *Administrative performance and personality.* New York: Teachers College, Columbia University, 1962. **644**

Hemphill, J. K., & Sechrest, L. B. A comparison of three criteria of aircrew effectiveness in combat over Korea. *Journal of Applied Psychology*, 1952, *36*, 323–327. **574**

Henry, W. E. *The analysis of fantasy.* New York: Wiley, 1956. **652 f.**

Henry, W. E., & Farley, J. The validity of the Thematic Apperception Test in the study of adolescent personality. *Psychological Monographs*, 1959, *73*, No. 17. **682**

Herron, E. W. The Multiple Affect Adjective Check List: A critical analysis. *Journal of Clinical Psychology*, 1969, *25*, 46–53. **569**

Herzberg, F., & Bouton, A. A further study of the stability of the Kuder Preference Record. *Educational and Psychological Measurement*, 1954, *14*, 326–331.   469

Hess, R. D., & Bear, R. M. (Eds.) *Early education: Current theory, research, and practice.* Chicago: Aldine, 1968.   256, 307, 308

Hess, R. D., & Shipman, V. C. Early experience and the socialization of cognitive modes in children. *Child Development*, 1965, *36*, 869–886.   256, 649

Highland, R. W., & Berkshire, J. R. A methodological study of forced-choice performance ratings. *Research Bulletin* 51–9, USAF Human Resources Research Center, 1951.   588

Hills, J. R. Factor-analyzed abilities and success in college mathematics. *Educational and Psychological Measurement*, 1957, *17*, 615–622.   362

Hoepfner, R., & Guilford, J. P. Figural, symbolic, and semantic factors of creative potential in ninth-grade students. *Psychological Laboratory, University of Southern California Reports*, 1965, No. 35.   340

Hoepfner, R., Guilford, J. P., & Merrifield, P. R. A factor analysis of the symbolic-evaluation abilities. *Psychological Laboratory, University of Southern California, Reports*, 1964, No. 33.   340

Hofstee, W. K. B. Gedwongen-keuze persoonlijkheidstests. Mimeographed. Personnel division, Royal Dutch Navy, 1963.   500

Holland, J. L. *The psychology of vocational choice.* Waltham, Mass.: Blaisdell, 1966.   560

Holland, J. L., & Richards, J. M., Jr. Academic and nonacademic accomplishment: Correlated or uncorrelated? *Journal of Educational Psychology*, 1965, *45*, 165–174.   290

Holland, J. L., & Richards, J. M., Jr. The many faces of talent: A reply to Werts. *Journal of Educational Psychology*, 1967, *58*, 205–209.   290

Hollingworth, H. L. *Judging human character.* New York: Appleton-Century-Crofts, 1922.   573, 574

Holmen, M. G., *et al.* An assessment program for OCS applicants. *HumRRO Technical Report*, No. 26, 1956.   675

Holt, R. R. Clinical and statistical prediction: A reformulation and some new data. *Journal of Abnormal and Social Psychology*, 1958, *56*, 1–13.   683, 685

Holt, R. R. Individuality and generalization in the study of personality. *Journal of Personality*, 1962, *30*, 377–404.   569

Holt, R. R. Measuring libidinal and aggressive motives and their controls by means of the Rorschach test. In D. Levine (Ed.), *Nebraska Symposium on Motivation, 1966.* Lincoln: University of Nebraska Press, 1966. Pp. 1–48.   636

Holt, R. R. "Editor's foreword." In D. Rapaport, M. M. Gill, & R. Schafer, *Diagnostic psychological testing* (Revised ed.). New York: International Universities Press, 1968. Pp. 1–44.   545

Holt, R. R. The evaluation of personality assessment. In Janis, 1969. Pp. 773–801.   690, 693

Holt, R. R., & Luborsky, L. *Personality patterns of psychiatrists.* New York: Basic Books, 1958.   674, 684, 686

Holtzman, W. H. Holtzman Inkblot Technique. In A. I. Rabin (Ed.), *Projective techniques in personality assessment.* New York: Springer, 1968. Pp. 136–170.   637

Holtzman, W. H., Iscoe, I., & Calvin, A. D. Rorschach color responses and manifest anxiety in college women. *Journal of Consulting Psychology*, 1954, *18*, 317–324. **636**

Holtzman, W. H., & Sells, S. B. Prediction of flying success by clinical analysis of test protocols. *Journal of Abnormal and Social Psychology*, 1954, *49*, 485–490. **674**

Holtzman, W. H., & Young, R. K. Scales for measuring attitudes toward the Negro and toward organized religion. *Psychological Reports*, 1966, *18*, 31–34. **86**

Holtzman, W. H., *et al. Inkblot perception and personality: Holtzman Inkblot Technique.* Austin: University of Texas Press, 1961. **637**

Honzik, M. P., Macfarlane, J. W., & Allen, L. The stability of mental test performance between two and eighteen years. *Journal of Experimental Education*, 1948, *17*, 309–324. **232**

Horn, C. A., & Smith, L. F. The Horn Art Aptitude Inventory. *Journal of Applied Psychology*, 1945, *29*, 350–359. **400**

Horn, J. L., & Cattell, R. B. Refinement and test of the theory of fluid and crystallized intelligence. *Journal of Educational Psychology*, 1966, *57*, 253–276. **282**

Horn, J. L., & Cattell, R. B. Age differences in fluid and crystallized intelligence. *Acta Psychologica*, 1967, *26*, 107–129. **230**

Horst, P. *Factor analysis of data matrices.* New York: Holt, Rinehart and Winston, 1965. **319**

Hubbard, J. P. Programmed testing in the examinations of the National Board of Medical Examiners. *Proceedings, Invitational Conference on Testing Problems, 1963.* Princeton, N. J.: Educational Testing Service, 1964. Pp. 49–63. **444**

Hubbard, J. P., *et al.* An objective evaluation of clinical competence. *New England Journal of Medicine*, 1965, *272*, 1321–1328. **444**

Humphreys, L. G. The organization of human abilities. *American Psychologist*, 1962, *17*, 475–483. **352**

Humphreys, L. G. Critique of Cattell's "Theory of fluid and crystallized intelligence." *Journal of Educational Psychology*, 1967, *58*, 129–136. **282**

Humphreys, L. G. The fleeting nature of the prediction of college academic success. *Journal of Educational Psychology*, 1968, *59*, 375–380. **414**

Humphreys, L. G., Buxton, C. E., and Taylor, H. R. Steadiness and rifle marksmanship. *Journal of Applied Psychology*, 1936, *20*, 680–688. **388**

Hunt, J. McV. (Ed.) *Personality and the behavior disorders.* New York: Ronald Press, 1944. **615**

Hunt, J. McV. *Intelligence and experience.* New York: Ronald Press, 1961. **255**

Hunt, J. McV. Traditional personality theory in the light of recent evidence. *American Scientist*, 1965, *53*, 80–96. **561**

Hunt, W. A., & Stevenson, I. Psychological testing in military clinical psychology: II. Personality testing. *Psychological Review*, 1946, *53*, 107–115. **540**

Hutt, M. L. A clinical study of "consecutive" and "adaptive" testing with the revised Stanford-Binet. *Journal of Consulting Psychology*, 1947, *11*, 93–103. **212**

Hutton, J. B. A comparison of digit repetition scores on the WISC and the Revised Binet, Form L-M. *Journal of Clinical Psychology*, 1964, *20*, 364–366. **215**

Identification and guidance of able students. Washington, D. C.: American Association for the Advancement of Science, 1958.   **285**

Indiana Prediction Study. *Manual of Freshman class profiles for Indiana colleges.* Princeton, N. J.: College Entrance Examination Board, 1965.   **595**

Ingersoll, R. W., & Peters, H. J. Predictive indices of the GATB. *Personnel and Guidance Journal,* 1966, *44,* 931–937.   **361, 427**

Inhelder, B. The diagnosis of reasoning in the mentally retarded. New York: John Day, 1968.   **243**

Inhelder, B., & Matalon, B. The study of problem solving and thinking. In P. H. Mussen (Ed.), *Handbook of research methods in child development.* New York: Wiley, 1960. Pp. 421–455.   **243, 258, 266**

Jack, L. M. An experimental study of ascendant behavior in preschool children. *University of Iowa Studies on Child Welfare,* 1934, *9,* No. 3.   **574**

Jackson, D. N., & Messick, S. (Eds.) *Problems in human assessment.* New York: McGraw-Hill, 1967.   **20, 114, 150, 352, 451, 488, 666, 694**

Jackson, D. N., Messick, S. J., & Myers, C. T. The role of memory and color in group and individual embedded-figures measures of field-independence. *Educational and Psychological Measurement,* 1964, *24,* 177–192.   **627**

Janis, I. L. (Ed.) *Personality: Dynamics, development, assessment.* New York: Harcourt, Brace & World, 1969.   **690, 693**

Jarvik, L. F., Kallman, F. J., & Falex, A. Intellectual changes in aged twins. *Journal of Gerontology,* 1962, *17,* 289–294.   **229**

Jenkins, W. O. A review of leadership studies with particular reference to military problems. *Psychological Bulletin,* 1947, *44,* 54–79.   **574**

Jensen, A. R. The Rorschach Technique: A re-evaluation. *Acta Psychologica,* 1964, *22,* 60–77.   **636**

Jensen, A. R. Another look at culture-fair testing. *Proceedings, Western Invitational Conference on Testing Problems, 1968.* Princeton, N.J.: ETS, 1968. Pp. 50–104. (a)   **303**

Jensen, A. R. The culturally disadvantaged and the heredity-environment uncertainty. In J. Hellmuth (Ed.), *The culturally disadvantaged child.* Vol. II. Seattle, Wash.: Special Child Publications, 1968. Pp. 27–76. (b)   **294**

Jensen, A. R. Social class, race, and genetics: Implications for education. *American Educational Research Journal.* 1968, *5,* 1–42. (c)   **294**

Jensen, A. R. How much can we boost IQ and scholastic achievement? *Harvard Educational Review,* 1969, *39,* 1–123.   **247**

Jensen, A. R., & Rohwer, W. D., Jr. Syntactical mediation of serial and paired-associate learning as a function of age. *Child Development,* 1965, *36,* 601–608.   **293**

Jensen, A. R., & Rohwer, W. D., Jr. The Stroop Color-Word Test: A review. *Acta Psychologica,* 1966, *24,* 36–93.   **626**

Jones, F. E. Predictor variables for creativity in industrial science. *Journal of Applied Psychology,* 1964, *48,* 134–136.   **398**

Jones, L. V. Primary abilities in the Stanford-Binet, age 13. *Journal of Genetic Psychology,* 1954, *84,* 126–147.   **330**

Jones, V. A comparison of measures of honesty at early adolescence with honesty in adulthood—a follow-up study. *American Psychologist,* 1946, *1,* 261.   **619**

Kagan, J., & Freeman, M. Relation of childhood intelligence, maternal behaviors, and social class to behavior during adolescence. *Child Development,* 1963, *34,* 899–911.   **231**

Kagan, J., & Moss, H. A. *Birth to maturity.* New York: Wiley, 1962.   **553**

Kagan, J., *et al.* Infants' differential reactions to familiar and distorted faces. *Child Development,* 1966, *37,* 519–532.   **262**

Kagan, J., *et al.* Discussion: How much can we boost IQ and scholastic achievement? *Harvard Educational Review,* 1969, *39,* 273–356.   **247**

Kaiser, H. F., & Caffrey, J. Alpha factor analysis. *Psychometrika,* 1965, *30,* 1–14.   **319**

Kanfer, F., & Saslow, G. Behavior analysis: An alternative to diagnostic classification. *Archives of General Psychiatry,* 1965, *12,* 529–538.   **562**

Katz, I. Review of evidence relating to effects of desegregation on the intellectual performance of Negoes. *American Psychologist,* 1964, *19,* 381–398.   **76**

Katz, I. The socialization of academic motivation in minority group children. In D. Levine (Ed.), *Nebraska Symposium on Motivation, 1967.* Lincoln: University of Nebraska Press, 1967. Pp. 133–191.   **663**

Katz, I., Epps, E. G., & Axelson, L. J. Effect upon Negro digit-symbol performance of anticipated comparison with whites and with other Negroes, *Journal of Abnormal and Social Psychology,* 1964, *69,* 77–83.   **64**

Katz, I., Roberts, S. O., & Robinson, J. M. Effects of task difficulty, race of administrator, and instructions on Digit-Symbol performance of Negroes. *Journal of Personality and Social Psychology,* 1965, *2,* 53–59.   **64**

Kelly, E. L. Consistency of the adult personality. *American Psychologist,* 1955, *10,* 659–681.   **552**

Kelly, E. L. Alternative criteria in medical education and their correlates. *Proceedings, Invitational Conference on Testing Problems, 1963.* Princeton, N. J.: Educational Testing Service, 1964. Pp. 64–85.   **443, 451**

Kelly, E. L. *Assessment of human characteristics.* San Francisco: Brooks-Cole, 1967.   **20**

Kelly, E. L., & Fiske, D. W. *The prediction of performance in clinical psychology.* Ann Arbor: University of Michigan Press, 1951.   **475 f., 671 ff.**

Kelly, E. L., & Goldberg, L. R. Correlates of later performance and specialization in psychology. *Psychological Monographs,* 1959, *73,* No. 12.   **475, 671**

Kelly, G. A. (Ed.) *New methods in applied psychology.* College Park: University of Maryland, 1947.   **594**

Kelly, G. A. *The psychology of personal constructs.* Vol. I. New York: Norton, 1955.   **598**

Kelman, H. C. Human use of human subjects: The problem of deception in social psychological experiments. *Psychological Bulletin,* 1967, *67,* 1–11.   **511, 610**

Kennedy, W. A., & Lindner, R. S. A normative study of the Goodenough Draw-a-Man Test on Southeastern Negro elementary school children. *Child Development,* 1964, *35,* 33–62.   **110**

Kennedy, W. A., Van de Reit, V., & White, J. C. A normative sample of intelligence and achievement of Negro elementary school children in the southeastern United States. *Monographs, Society for Research in Child Development*, 1963, *28*, No. 6.   **110**

Kent, G. H. Suggestions for the next revision of the Binet-Simon Scale. *Psychological Record*, 1937, *1*, 409–433.   **142**

Kirk, B. A. Test versus academic performance in malfunctioning students. *Journal of Consulting Psychology*, 1952, *16*, 213–216.   **505**

Kirk, S. A. Amelioration of mental disabilities through psychodiagnostic and remedial procedures. In G. A. Jervis (Ed.), *Mental retardation*. Springfield, Ill.: Thomas, 1967. Pp. 186–219.   **20**

Kirkpatrick, J. J., *et al. Testing and fair employment*. New York: New York University Press, 1968.   **299, 301**

Klein, S., & Owens, W. A., Jr. Life history and ability correlates of mechanical ingenuity. *Research Bulletin* 65–18. Princeton, N. J.: Educational Testing Service, 1965.   **477**

Kleinmuntz, B. Identification of maladjusted college students. *Journal of Counseling Psychology*, 1960, *7*, 209–211.   **533**

Kleinmuntz, B. MMPI decision rules for the identification of college maladjustment: A digital computer approach. *Psychological Monographs*, 1963, *77*, No. 14.   **533 f.**

Kleinmuntz, B. *Personality measurement*. Homewood, Ill.: Dorsey Press, 1967.   **510**

Kleinmuntz, B. Personality test interpretation by computer and clinician. In J. Butcher, 1969. Pp. 67–104.   **533**

Klett, C. J. Assessing change in hospitalized psychiatric patients. In McReynolds, 1968a. Pp. 191–222.   **585**

Klopfer, B., *et al. Developments in the Rorschach technique*. Vol. I. Yonkers: World Book, 1954.   **634**

Knauft, E. G. Test validity over a seventeen-year period. *Journal of Applied Psychology*, 1955, *39*, 382–383.   **291**

Kohen-Raz, R. Scalogram analysis of some developmental sequences of infant behavior as measured by the Bayley Infant Scale of Mental Development. *Genetic Psychological Monographs*, 1967, *76*, 3–21.   **261**

Kohlberg, L. Development of moral character and moral ideology. In M. L. Hoffman & L. W. Hoffman (Eds.), *Review of child development research: I*. New York: Russell Sage Foundation, 1964. Pp. 383–431.   **617**

Kohs, S. C. *Intelligence measurement*. New York: Macmillan, 1923.   **48, 145**

Koppitz, E. M. *The Bender Gestalt test for young children*. New York: Grune & Stratton, 1964.   **631**

Koran, M. L. The effect of individual differences on observational learning in the acquisition of a teaching skill. Unpublished doctoral dissertation, Stanford University, 1969.   **448**

Kramer, E., & Fenwick, J. Differential diagnosis with the Bender-Gestalt test. *Journal of Projective Techniques*, 1966, *30*, 59–61.   **631**

Krasner, L., & Ullman, L. P. (Eds.) *Research in behavior modification*. New York: Holt, Rinehart and Winston, 1965. Pp. 211–228.   **621**

Krug, R. E. Some suggested approaches for test development and measurement. *Personnel Psychology*, 1966, *19*, 24–35.   **451**

Kurtz, A. K. Recent research on the selection of life insurance salesmen. *Journal of Applied Psychology*, 1941, *25*, 11–17.   **548**

Langmuir, I. Science, common sense, and decency. *Science*, 1943, *97*, 1–7.   **686**

Lasky, J. J., *et al.* Post-hospital adjustment as predicted by psychiatric patients and by their staffs. *Journal of Consulting Psychology*, 1959, *23*, 213–218.   **542, 593**

Lawson, D. E. Need for safeguarding the field of intelligence testing. *Journal of Educational Psychology*, 1944, *35*, 240–247.   **20**

Layton, W. L. *Counseling use of the Strong Vocational Interest Blank.* Minneapolis: University of Minnesota Press, 1958.   **481**

Lazarus, R. S. Story telling and the measurement of motivation: The direct versus substitutive controversy. *Journal of Consulting Psychology*, 1966, *30*, 483–487.   **665**

Lennon, R. T. The test manual as a medium of communication. In *Proceedings, Invitational Conference on Testing Problems, 1953.* Princeton, N. J.: Educational Testing Service, 1954. Pp. 90–94.   **185**

Lennon, R. T. Norms: 1963. In *Proceedings, Invitational Conference on Testing Problems, 1963.* Princeton, N. J.: Educational Testing Service, 1964. Pp. 13–22.   **105, 111, 113**

Levitt, E. E. The water-jar Einstellung test as a measure of rigidity. *Psychological Bulletin*, 1956, *53*, 347–370.   **641, 665**

Liberty, P. G., Jr., Burnstein, E., & Moulton, R. W. Concern with mastery and occupational attraction. *Journal of Personality*, 1966, *34*, 105–117.   **478**

Lindsley, O. R. Operant conditioning methods applied to research in chronic schizophrenia. *Psychiatric Research Reports*, 1965, *5*, 118–139.   **74**

Lindzey, G. (Ed.). *Handbook of social psychology.* Reading, Mass.: Addison-Wesley, 1954.   **592**

Lindzey, G. Seer versus sign. *Journal of Experimental Research on Personality*, 1965, *1*, 17–26.   **693**

Lindzey, G., & Aronson, E. (Eds.) *Handbook of social psychology,* Vol. II. (2nd ed.) Reading, Mass.: Addison-Wesley, 1968.   **606, 607**

Linn, R. L. Grade adjustments for prediction of academic performance: A review. *Journal of Educational Measurement*, 1966, *3*, 313–329.   **428**

Linn, R. L., Rock, D. A., & Cleary, T. A. The development and evaluation of several programmed testing methods. *Educational and Psychological Measurement*, 1969, *29*, 129–146.   **173**

Lipsett, L., & Wilson, J. W. Do "suitable" interests and mental ability lead to job satisfaction? *Educational and Psychological Measurement*, 1954, *14*, 373–380.   **474**

Lister, J. L., & McKenzie, D. H. A framework for the improvement of test interpretation in counseling. *Personnel and Guidance Journal*, 1965, *45*, 61–71.   **383**

Littell, W. M. The Wechsler Intelligence Scale for Children: Review of a decade of research. *Psychological Bulletin*, 1960, *57*, 132–156.   **217, 225**

Liverant, S. Intelligence: A concept in need of reexamination. *Journal of Consulting Psychology*, 1960, *24*, 101–110.   **248**

Locke, E. A., Zavala, A., & Fleishman, E. A. Studies of helicopter pilot performance: II. The analysis of task dimensions. *Human Factors,* 1965, 7, 285–302.   **352**

London, P., Conant, M., & Davison, G. C. More hypnosis in the un-hypnotizable: Effects of hypnosis and exhortation on rote learning. *Journal of Personality,* 1966, *34,* 71–79.   **62**

Long, L., & Perry, J. D. Academic achievement in engineering related to selection procedures and interests. *Journal of Applied Psychology,* 1953, *37,* 468–471.   **469**

Longstaff, H. P. Fakability of the Strong Interest Blank and the Kuder Preference Record. *Journal of Applied Psychology,* 1948, *32,* 360–369.   **497**

Lopez, F. M., Jr. *Evaluating executive decision making.* New York: American Management Association, 1966.   **645 f.**

Lord, F. M. The relation of the reliability of multiple-choice tests to the distribution of item difficulties. *Psychometrika,* 1952, *17,* 181–194.   **100**

Lord, F. M. Speeded tests and power tests—an empirical study of validities. *Research Bulletin 53–12, Educational Testing Service,* 1953.   **286**

Lord, F. M. Cutting scores and errors of measurement. *Psychometrika,* 1962, *27,* 19–30.   **438**

Lord, F. M., & Novick, M. *Statistical theory of mental test scores.* Reading, Mass.: Addison-Wesley, 1968.   **152, 157, 597**

Loretan, J. O. The decline and fall of group intelligence testing. *Teachers College Record,* 1965, *67,* 10–17.   **302**

Lorr, M., Klett, C. J., & McNair, D. M. *Syndromes of psychosis.* New York: Pergamon, 1963.   **532, 584**

Lorr, M., & McNair, D. M. Expansion of the interpersonal behavior circle. *Journal of Personality and Social Psychology,* 1965, *2,* 823–830.   **575**

Lovell, V. R. The human use of personality tests. *American Psychologist,* 1967, *22,* 383–393.   **519**

Lowell, F. E. A study of the variability of IQ's in retest. *Journal of Applied Psychology,* 1941, *25,* 341–356.   **233**

Luborsky, L. Selecting psychiatric residents: survey of the Topeka research. *Bulletin of the Menninger Clinic,* 1954, *18,* 252–259.   **674**

Luchins, A. S. On recent usage of the Einstellung-effect as a test of rigidity. *Journal of Consulting Psychology,* 1951, *15,* 89–94.   **642**

Luchins, A. S., & Luchins, E. H. *Rigidity of behavior.* Eugene: University of Oregon Books, 1959.   **640**

Lunneborg, C. E., & Lunneborg, P. W. EPPS patterns in the prediction of academic achievement. *Journal of Counseling Psychology,* 1967, *14,* 389–390. (a)   **440**

Lunneborg, C. E., & Lunneborg, P. W. Pattern prediction of academic success. *Educational and Psychological Measurement,* 1967, *27,* 945–952. (b)   **440**

Lyman, H. B. *Test scores and what they mean.* Englewood Cliffs, N. J.: Prentice-Hall, 1963.   **42, 113**

McArthur, C. Long-term validity of the Strong interest test in two subcultures. *Journal of Applied Psychology,* 1954, *38,* 346–353.   **474**

McArthur, C., & Stevens, L. B. The validation of expressed interests as compared with inventoried interests: A fourteen year follow-up. *Journal of Applied Psychology*, 1955, *39*, 184–189. **474**

MacArthur, R. S. An experimental investigation of persistence in secondary school boys. *Canadian Journal of Psychology*, 1955, *8*, 42–55. **620**

MacArthur, R. S., & Elley, W. B. The reduction of socioeconomic bias in intelligence testing. *British Journal of Educational Psychology*, 1963, *33*, 107–119. **273**

McCall, R. J. Face validity in the D scale of the MMPI. *Journal of Clinical Psychology*, 1958, *14*, 77–80. **532**

McCarthy, J. J., & Kirk, S. A. *Illinois Test of Psycholinguistic Abilities: Experimental edition.* Urbana: University of Illinois Press, 1961. **221**

McCarthy, J. J., & Olson, J. L. *Validity studies on the Illinois Test of Psycholinguistic Abilities.* Urbana: University of Illinois Press, 1964. **253**

McClelland, D. C. The measurement of human motivation: An experimental approach. In *Proceedings, Invitational Conference on Testing Problems, 1952.* Princeton, N. J.: Educational Testing Service, 1953. Pp. 41–51. **665**

McClelland, D. C. *Personality.* New York: Holt, Rinehart and Winston, 1957. **519, 613**

McClelland, D. C. *The achieving society.* Princeton, N. J.: Van Nostrand, 1961. **663**

McClelland, D. C. Longitudinal trends in the relation of thought to action. *Journal of Consulting Psychology*, 1966, *30*, 479–482. **654, 665**

McClelland, D. C. (Ed.) *Studies in motivation.* New York: Appleton-Century-Crofts, 1955. **660**

McClelland, D. C., *et al. The achievement motive.* New York: Appleton-Century-Crofts, 1953. **659**

McClelland, D. C., *et al. Talent and society.* Princeton, N. J.: Van Nostrand, 1958. **42**

McCormick, E. J., Cunningham, J. W., & Thornton, G. C. The prediction of job requirements by a structured job analysis procedure. *Personnel Psychology*, 1967, *20*, 431–440. **409**

Macfarlane, J. W., Allen, L., & Honzik, M. P. *A developmental study of the behavior problems of normal children between twenty-one months and fourteen years.* Berkeley: University of California Press, 1954. **553**

Macfarlane, J. W., & Tuddenham, R. D. Problems in the validation of projective techniques. In H. H. Anderson & G. L. Anderson (Eds.), *An introduction to projective techniques.* Englewood Cliffs, N. J.: Prentice-Hall, 1951. Pp. 26–54. **693**

McHugh, G. Changes in IQ at the public school kindergarten level. *Psychological Monographs*, 1943, *55*, No. 2. **263**

McKeachie, W. J. Motivation, teaching methods, and college learning. In M. R. Jones (Ed.), *Nebraska Symposium on Motivation, 1961.* Lincoln: University of Nebraska Press, 1961. Pp. 111–146. **664**

McKeachie, W. J., *et al.* Student affiliation motives, teacher warmth, and academic achievement. *Journal of Personality and Social Psychology*, 1966, *4*, 457–461. **596**

McKinley, J. C., Hathaway, S. R., & Meehl, P. E. The MMPI. VI. The K Scale. *Journal of Consulting Psychology*, 1948, *12*, 20–31. **530**

MacKinnon, D. W. An assessment study of Air Force officers. Part V: Summary and applications. *WADC Technical Report* 58–91 (V), Wright Air Development Center, 1958.   675

MacKinnon, D. W., *et al.* An assessment study of Air Force officers. Part I: Design of the study and description of the variables. *WADC Technical Report* 58–91 (I), Wright Air Development Center, 1958.   675

McLain, G. A. Personnel testing and the EEOC. *Personnel Journal*, 1967, 46, 448–452.   299

McNemar, Q. (Book review.) *Journal of Abnormal and Social Psychology*, 1952, 47, 857–860.   416

McNemar, Q. Lost: Our intelligence? Why? *American Psychologist*, 1964, 9, 871–882.   341, 372, 383

McNemar, Q. *Psychological statistics.* (4th ed.) New York: Wiley, 1969.   158

McReynolds, P. The asessment of anxiety: A survey of available techniques. In McReynolds, 1968a. Pp. 244–264. (b)   568

McReynolds, P. (Ed.) *Advances in psychological assessment.* Vol. I. Palo Alto: Science and Behavior Books, 1968. (a)   698, 701
                                                                         720, 724

Madden, J. M., & Bottenberg, R. A. Use of an all possible combination solution of certain multiple regression problems. *Journal of Applied Psychology*, 1963, 47, 365–366.   434

Magaret, A., & Thompson, C. W. Differential test responses of normal, superior, and mentally deficient subjects. *Journal of Abnormal and Social Psychology*, 1950, 45, 163–167.   220

Mallinson, G. G., & Crumbine, W. M. An investigation of the stability of interests of high school students. *Journal of Educational Research*, 1952, 45, 369–383.   469

Mandler, G., & Sarason, S. B. A study of anxiety and learning. *Journal of Abnormal and Social Psychology*, 1952, 47, 166–173.   65

Marks, P. A., & Seeman, W. *The actuarial description of personality: An atlas for use with the MMPI.* Baltimore: Williams & Wilkins, 1963. 528, 531, 535

Marting, E. (Ed.) *AMA Book of Management Forms.* New York: American Management Association, 1967.   578

Masling, J. M. The effects of warm and cold interaction on the administration and scoring of an intelligence test. *Journal of Consulting Psychology*, 1959, 23, 336–341.   211

Maslow, A. P. Issues and strategies in employment of the disadvantaged, *Proceedings, Invitational Conference on Testing Problems, 1968.* Princeton, N.J.: Educational Testing Service, 1969. Pp. 123–141.   299

Massey, J. O. *WISC scoring criteria.* Palo Alto, Calif.: Consulting Psychologists Press, 1964.   211

Matthews, E., & Tiedeman, D. V. Attitudes toward career and marriage and the development of life style in young women. *Journal of Counseling Psychology*, 1964, 11, 375–384.   470

Mays, R. J. Relationships between length of acquaintance and nature of trait rated and agreement between raters. *AFPTRC Research Bulletin* 54–55, 1954.   573

Meehl, P. E. The dynamics of "structured" personality tests. *Journal of Clinical Psychology*, 1945, 1, 296–303.   519

Meehl, P. E. MMPI: Research results for counselors. Unpublished lecture, VA hospital, Fort Snelling, Minnesota, 1951.   534

Meehl, P. E. *Clinical vs. statistical prediction.* Minneapolis: University of Minnesota Press, 1954. — 442

Meehl, P. E. Clinical versus actuarial prediction. In *Proceedings, Invitational Conference on Testing Problems, 1955.* Princeton, N. J.: Educational Testing Service, 1956. Pp. 136–141. (a) — 544 f.

Meehl, P. E. Wanted—a good cookbook. *American Psychologist,* 1956, *11,* 263–272. (b) — 535, 694

Meehl, P. E. A comparison of clinicians with five statistical methods of identifying psychotic MMPI profiles. *Journal of Counseling Psychology,* 1959, *6,* 102–109. — 544

Meehl, P. E., & Hathaway, S. R. The K factor as a suppressor variable in the MMPI. *Journal of Applied Psychology,* 1946, *30,* 525–564. — 529

Meehl, P. E., & Rosen, A. Antecedent probability and the efficiency of psychometric signs, patterns or cutting scores. *Psychological Bulletin,* 1955, *52,* 194–216. — 446, 539

Megargee, E. I. *Research in clinical assessment.* New York: Harper & Row, 1966. — 693

Mehrens, W. A., & Ebel, R. L. (Eds.) *Principles of educational and psychological measurement.* Chicago: Rand McNally, 1967. — 113

Melton, A. W. (Ed.) *Apparatus tests.* Washington, D. C.: Government Printing Office, 1947. — 42, 51, 387, 390, 391, 611, 646

Messick, S. Personality measurement and college performance. *Proceedings, Invitational Conference on Testing Problems, 1963.* Princeton, N. J.: Educational Testing Service, 1964. Pp. 110–129. — 630

Messick, S., & Fritzky, F. J. Dimensions of analytic attitude in cognition and personality. *Journal of Personality,* 1963, *31,* 346–370. — 629

Meyers, C. E., Attwell, A. A., & Orpet, R. E. Prediction of fifth-grade achievement from kindergarten test and rating data. *Educational and Psychological Measurement,* 1968, *28,* 457–463. — 289

Mischel, W. Predicting the success of Peace Corps Volunteers in Nigeria. *Journal of Personality and Social Psychology,* 1965, *1,* 510–517. — 515

Mischel, W. *Personality and assessment.* New York: Wiley, 1968. — 257, 517, 561, 562, 569, 599, 621, 683, 690

Mitchell, M. B. The revised Stanford-Binet for university students. *Journal of Educational Research,* 1943, *36,* 507–511. — 237

Moely, B. E., & others. Production deficiency in young children's clustered recall. *Developmental Psychology,* 1969, *1,* 26–34. — 293

Mollenkopf, W. G. Time limits and the behavior of test takers. *Educational and Psychological Measurement,* 1960, *20,* 223–230. — 77

Monachesi, E. D., & Hathaway, S. R. The personality of delinquents. In J. Butcher, 1969. Pp. 207–219. — 541 f.

Monroe, W. S. (Ed.) *Encyclopedia of educational research.* (2d ed.) New York: Macmillan, 1941. — 257

Moore, H. *Experience with employment tests.* New York: National Industrial Conference Board, 1941. — 547

Moreno, J. L. *Who shall survive?* Washington, D. C.: Nervous and Mental Diseases Publishing Company, 1934. — 590

Moriarty, A. Coping mechanisms of preschool children in response to intelligence test demands. *Genetic Psychology Monographs,* 1961, *64,* 3–128. — 263, 266

Morsh, J. E. Job analysis in the United States Air Force. *Personnel Psychology*, 1964, *17*, 7–17.   **410**

Morsh, J. E., & Schmid, J., Jr. Supervisory judgment as a criterion of airman performance. *AFPTRC Development Report* 56–56, 1956.   **574**

Moseley, E. C. *Psychodiagnosis based on multivariate analysis of the Holtzman Inkblot Technique.* Unpublished doctoral dissertation. University of Texas, Austin, 1962.   **637**

Mosher, D. L., & Smith, J. P. The usefulness of two scoring systems for the Bender Gestalt Test for identifying brain damage. *Journal of Consulting Psychology*, 1965, *29*, 530–536.   **631**

Mosier, C. I. A critical examination of the concepts of face validity. *Educational and Psychological Measurement*, 1947, 7, 191–205.   **184**

Moss, J. Measuring creative abilities in junior high school industrial arts. Monograph No. 2, American Council on Industrial Arts Teacher Education, 1966.   **397**

Moss, J., Jr., & Duenk, L. G. Estimating the concurrent validity of the Minnesota Tests of Creative Thinking. *American Educational Research Journal*, 1967, *4*, 387–396.   **397**

Mugaas, H. D., & Hester, R. The development of an equation for identifying the interests of carpenters. *Educational and Psychological Measurement*, 1952, *12*, 408–414.   **458**

Mumpower, D. L. The fallacy of the short form. *Journal of Clinical Psychology*, 1964, *20*, 111–113.   **225**

Munday, L. Predicting college grades using ACT data. *Educational and Psychological Measurement*, 1967, *27*, 401–406.   **289**

Murphy, G., & Likert, R. *Public opinion and the individual.* New York: Harper & Row, 1938.   **659**

Murphy, L., & Murphy, G. Hermann Rorschach and personality research. In Rickers-Ovsiankina, 1960. Pp. 341–357.   **609**

Murray, D. C. An investigation of the Rorschach white space response in an extratensive experience balance as a measure of outwardly directed opposition. *Journal of Projective Techniques*, 1957, *21*, 40–53.   **636**

Murray, H. A., *et al. Explorations in personality.* New York: Oxford University Press, 1938.   **651, 670**

Murstein, B. I. New thoughts about ambiguity and the TAT. *Journal of Projective Techniques*, 1965, *29*, 219–225.   **653**

Murstein, B. I., & Leipold, W. D. The role of learning and motor abilities in the Wechsler-Bellevue Digit Symbol subtest. *Educational and Psychological Measurement*, 1961, *21*, 103–112.   **210**

Mussen, P. H., & Naylor, H. K. The relationships between overt and fantasy aggression. *Journal of Abnormal and Social Psychology*, 1954, *49*, 235–240.   **654**

Nanda, H. Factor analytic techniques for interbattery comparison and their application to some psychometric problems. Unpublished doctoral dissertation, Stanford University, 1967.   **368**

National Industrial Conference Board. Employee rating. *Studies in Personnel Policy*, No. 39. New York: the Board, 1942.   **578**

National Retail Merchants Association. *Appraising retail executive and employee performance.* New York: the Association, 1968.   **578**

Navran, L., & Stauffacher, J. C. Social desirability as a factor in Edwards Personality Preference Schedule performance. *Journal of Consulting Psychology*, 1954, *18*, 442. **500**

Nettler, G. Test burning in Texas. *American Psychologist*, 1959, *14*, 682–683. **510**

Newcomb, T. M. *The consistency of certain extrovert-introvert behavior patterns in 51 problem boys.* New York: Teachers College, Columbia University, 1929. **601**

Newman, F. B., & Jones, H. E. The adolescent in social groups. *Applied Psychological Monographs*, 1946, No. 9. **590**

Newman, S. H., Howell, M. A., & Cliff, N. The analysis and prediction of a practical examination in dentistry. *Educational and Psychological Measurement*, 1959, *19*, 557–568. **451**

Nihara, K., *et al.* A factor analysis of the semantic-evaluation abilities. *Psychological Laboratory, University of Southern California, Reports*, 1964, No. 32. **340**

Norman, W. T. Personality measurement, faking, and detection: An assessment method for use in personnel selection. *Journal of Applied Psychology*, 1963, *47*, 225–241. **501**

Norman, W. T., & Goldberg, L. R. Raters, ratees, and randomness in personality structure. *Journal of Personality and Social Psychology*, 1966, *4*, 681–691. **575**

Nummenmaa, T. Factors of level and speed of intelligence. *Acta Academiae Paedagogicae Jyvaskylaensis*, *18*, 1960. **286**

Oaks, W. W., Scheink, P. A., & Husted, F. L. Objective evaluation of a method of assessing student performance in a clinical clerkship. *Journal of Medical Education*, 1969, *44*, 207–213. **580**

O'Bryan, K. G., & MacArthur, R. S. Reversibility, intelligence, and creativity in nine-year-old boys. *Child Development*, 1969, *40*, 33–45. **244**

Oden, M. H. The fulfillment of promise: 40-year follow-up of the Terman gifted group. *Genetic Psychology Monographs*, 1968, 77, No. 1, 3–93. **235, 394**

Ohlsen, M. M. (Comment.) *Journal of Counseling Psychology*, 1963, *10*, 134–135. **381**

Olsen, I. A., & Jordheim, G. D. Use of WAIS in a student counseling center. *Personnel and Guidance Journal*, 1964, *42*, 500–503. **236**

Olson, G. M., *et al.* Long-term correlates of children's-learning and problem-solving behavior. *Journal of Educational Psychology*, 1968, 59, 227–232. **293**

Olweus, D. *Prediction of aggression.* Stockholm: Scandinavian Test Corporation, 1969. **654**

Ombredane, A., Robaye, F., & Plumail, H. Résultats d'une application répétée du matrix-couleur à une population de Noirs Congolais. *Bulletin, Centre d'Études et Recherches Psychotechniques*, 1956, 6, 129–147. **272**

Opton, E. M., Jr., & Lazarus, R. S. Personality determinants of psychophysiological response to stress: A theoretical analysis and an experiment. *Journal of Personality and Social Psychology*, 1967, 6, 291–303. **625**

Ortar, G. R. The transfer of psychological diagnostic measures from one culture to another. *Acta Psychologica*, 1963, *21*, 218–230. **301**

Osborne, R. T., & Gregor, A. J. The heritability of visualization, perceptual speed, and spatial orientation. *Perceptual and Motor Skills*, 1966, 23, 379–390.   **363**

Osburn, H. G., Lubin, A., Loeffler, J. C., & Tye, V. M. The relative validity of forced choice and single stimulus description items. *Educational and Psychological Measurement*, 1954, 14, 407–417.   **501**

Osgood, C. E., & Luria, Z. A blind analysis of a case of multiple personality using the Semantic Differential. *Journal of Abnormal and Social Psychology*, 1954, 49, 579–591.   **566 f.**

Osgood, C. E., Suci, G. J., & Tannenbaum, P. H. *The measurement of meaning*. Urbana: University of Illinois Press, 1957.   **565**

OSS Assessment Staff. *Assessment of men*. New York: Holt, Rinehart and Winston, 1948.   **670**

O'Sullivan, M., Guilford, J. P., & de Mille, R. Measurement of social intelligence. *Psychological Laboratory, University of Southern California, Reports*, 1965, No. 34.   **340, 344**

Otis, J. L. The prediction of success in power sewing machine operating. *Journal of Applied Psychology*, 1938, 22, 350–366.   **386 f.**

Otis, J. L. Psychological espionage. Unpublished address, American Psychological Association, 1957.   **510**

Owens, W. A. Age and mental abilities: A second adult follow-up. *Journal of Educational Psychology*, 1966, 57, 311–325.   **229, 233, 287**

Palmer, J. O. A dual approach to Rorschach validation: A methodological study. *Psychological Monographs*, 1951, 65, No. 8.   **682**

Parker, J. The relationship of self report to inferred self concept. *Educational and Psychological Measurement*, 1966, 26, 691–700.   **503**

Parkinson, C. N. *Parkinson's law*. Boston: Houghton Mifflin, 1957.   **20**

Paterson, D. G., *et al. Minnesota Mechanical Ability Tests*. Minneapolis: University of Minnesota Press, 1930.   **426**

Patterson, C. H. *The Wechsler-Bellevue scales: A guide for counselors*. Springfield, Ill.: Thomas, 1953.   **251**

Patterson, G. R., & Bechtel, G. G. Formulating the situational environment in relation to states and traits. In R. B. Cattell (Ed.), *Handbook of modern personality study*. Chicago: Aldine, in press.   **243**

Paul, G. L., & Eriksen, C. W. Effects of test anxiety on "real-life" examinations. *Journal of Personality*, 1964, 32, 480–494.   **549**

Payne, D. A., & McMorris, R. F. (Eds.) *Educational and psychological measurement*. Waltham, Mass.: Blaisdell, 1967.   **43, 307**

Peak, H. Problems of objective observation. In L. Festinger & D. Katz (Eds.), *Research methods in the behavioral sciences*. New York: Holt, Rinehart and Winston, 1953. Pp. 243–299.   **149**

Pearson, J. S., *et al.* Further experience with the automated Minnesota Multiphasic Personality Inventory. *Mayo Clinic Proceedings*, 1964, 39, 823–829.   **536**

Pemberton, C. The closure factors related to other cognitive processes. *Psychometrika*, 1952, 17, 267–288.   **629**

Perry, D. K. Validities of three interest keys for U. S. Navy yeomen. *Journal of Applied Psychology*, 1955, 39, 134–138.   **473**

Perry, D. K. Evaluation of tests for improvement of programmer trainee

selection. *SDC Technical memorandum 3570*, System Development
Corporation, 1967. 421

Perry, D. K., & Cannon, W. M. Vocational interests of female computer
programmers. *Journal of Applied Psychology*, 1968, *52*, 31–35. 488

Personnel classification tests. War Department Technical Manual 12–260.
Washington, D. C.: War Department, 1946. 88

Persons, S. (Ed.) *Evolutionary thought in America.* New Haven, Conn.:
Yale University Press, 1950. 202

Peters, R., & Campbell, J. T. Diagnosis of training needs of B-29 mechanics from supervisory ratings and self-ratings. *AFPTRC Technical Memorandum* 55–12, 1955. 574

Peterson, D. A. *Factor analysis of the new United States Navy Basic
Classification Battery.* Princeton, N. J.: College Entrance Examination Board, 1943. 314

Peterson, D. A., & Wallace, S. R. Validation and revision of a test in
use. *Journal of Applied Psychology*, 1966, *50*, 13–17. 431

Peterson, D. R. Scope and generality of verbally defined personality
factors. *Psychological Review*, 1965, *72*, 48–59. 524

Peterson, D. R. *The clinical study of social behavior.* New York: Appleton-Century-Crofts, 1968. 546, 621,
665, 683

Piaget, J. *The moral judgment of the child.* London: Routledge & Kegan
Paul, 1932. 617

Piaget, J., & Inhelder, B. *The child's conception of space.* London: Routledge & Kegan Paul, 1956. 347 ff., 361

Pintner, R., *et al.* Supplementary guide for the Revised Stanford-Binet
Scale (Form L). *Applied Psychological Monographs*, 1944, No. 3. 215

Pittel, S. M., & Mendelsohn, G. A. Measurement of moral values: A
review and critique. *Psychological Bulletin*, 1966, *66*, 22–35. 617

Pittluck, P. The relation between aggressive fantasy and overt behavior.
Unpublished doctoral dissertation, Yale University, 1950. 654

Plant, W. T. Mental ability scores of freshmen in a California state college. *California Journal of Educational Research*, 1958, *9*, 72–73. 219

Pollaczek, P. P. A study of malingering on the CVS abbreviated individual intelligence scale. *Journal of Clinical Psychology*, 1952, *8*,
75-81. 61

Porteus, S. D. *The Porteus maze test and intelligence.* Palo Alto, Calif.:
Pacific Books, 1950. 239

Porteus, S. D. *Porteus maze test—fifty years application.* Palo Alto,
Calif.: Pacific Books, 1965. 42, 254,
639, 640

Prescott, D. A. *The child in the educative process.* New York: McGraw-
Hill, 1957. 606

Preston, C. E. Psychological testing with Northwest Coast Alaskan Eskimos. *Genetic Psychology Monographs*, 1964, *96*, 323–419. 65

Preston, H. O. *The development of a procedure for evaluating officers in
the United States Air Force.* Pittsburgh: American Institute for
Research, 1948. 409

Privacy and behavioral research. Washington, D. C.: Government Printing Office, 1967. 514

Rabin, A. I. Diagnostic use of intelligence tests. In B. B. Wolman (Ed.),
   Handbook of clinical psychology. New York: McGraw-Hill, 1965.
   Pp. 477–497.   **250**
Rajaratnam, N., Cronbach, L. J., & Gleser, G. C. Generalizability of strati-
   fied-parallel tests. *Psychometrika*, 1965, *30*, 39–56.   **177**
Rapaport, D. *Diagnostic psychological testing*. Vol. I. Chicago: Year Book
   Publishers, 1945.   **250**
Raynor, J. O., & Smith, C. P. Achievement-related motives and risk-
   taking in games of skill and chance. *Journal of Personality*, 1966,
   36, 16–31.   **662**
Reed, J. C. The relationship between the primary mental abilities and
   reading achievement at given developmental levels. *American Psy-
   chologist*, 1958, *13*, 324.   **373**
Reik, T. *Listening with the third ear*. New York: Farrar, Straus &
   Giroux, 1948.   **690**
Remmers, H. H., *et al*. (Eds.) *Growth, teaching, and learning*. New
   York: Harper & Row, 1957.   **173**
Rice, J. A., & Brown, L. F. Validity of the Peabody Picture Vocabulary
   Test in a sample of low IQ children. *American Journal of Mental
   Deficiency*, 1967, *71*, 602–603.   **254**
Richards, J. M., Jr., & Cline, V. B. Accuracy components in person per-
   ception scores and the scoring system as an artifact in investigations
   of the generality of judging ability. *Psychological Reports*, 1963,
   12, 363–373.   **598**
Richards, T. W. Mental test performance as a reflection of the child's
   current life situation: A methodological study. *Child Development*,
   1951, *22*, 221–233.   **226**
Rickers-Ovsiankina, M. (Ed.) *Rorschach psychology*. New York: Wiley,
   1960.   **636**
Roadman, H. C. An industrial use of peer ratings. *Journal of Applied
   Psychology*, 1964, *48*, 211–214.   **593**
Robeck, M. C., & Wilson, J. A. R. Comparison of Binet and the Kinder-
   garten Evaluation of Learning Potential. *Educational and Psycho-
   logical Measurement*, 1964, *24*, 393–397.   **264**
Roe, Anne. *The making of a scientist*. New York: Dodd, Mead, 1952.   **478, 480**
Roe, Anne. A psychological study of eminent psychologists and anthro-
   pologists, and a comparison with biological and physical scientists.
   Psychological Monographs, 1953, *67*, No. 2.   **480**
Roe, Anne. Early determinants of vocational choice. *Journal of Counsel-
   ing Psychology*, 1957, *4*, 212–217.   **478**
Roe, Anne, & Siegelman, M. *The origin of interests*. Washington, D. C.:
   American Personnel and Guidance Association, 1964.   **478**
Roe, Anne, *et al*. Studies of occupational histories: Part I. Job changes
   and the classification of occupations. *Journal of Counseling Psy-
   chology*, 1966, *13*, 387–393.   **465**
Roe, Arnold. An adaptive decision structure for educational systems.
   Report No. 63–63. Los Angeles: Department of Engineering, Uni-
   versity of California, 1963.   **415**
Roethlisberger, F., & Dickson, W. J. *Management and the worker*. Cambridge, Mass.: Harvard University Press, 1939.   **490**
Rogers, C. R. Psychometric tests and client-centered counseling. *Educa-
   tional and Psychological Measurement*, 1946, *6*, 139–144.   **377**

Rogers, C. R. Toward a science of the person. In T. W. Wann (Ed.), 1964. Pp. 109–133. **378**

Rogow, A. A. *James Forrestal: A study of personality, politics, and policy.* New York: Macmillan, 1963. **513**

Rohwer, W. D., Jr. Learning, race, and school success. *Journal of Research and Development in Education,* in press. **294**

Rorschach, H. *Psychodiagnostics.* P. Lemkau & B. Kronenberg (trans.) (2nd ed.) Bern: Huber, 1942. **635**

Rosen, A. Development of MMPI scales based on a reference group of psychiatric patients. *Psychological Monographs,* 1966, *70,* No. 8. **544**

Rosenbaum, B. L. Are psychological tests perishables? *Personnel Journal,* 1967, *46,* 576–579. **118**

Rosenberg, N. Stability and maturation of Kuder interest patterns during high school. *Educational and Psychological Measurement,* 1953, *13,* 449–458. **469**

Rosenthal, R. *Experimenter effects in behavioral research.* New York: Appleton-Century-Crofts, 1966. **61, 72**

Rosenthal, R., & Jacobson, L. *Pygmalion in the classroom.* New York: Holt, Rinehart and Winston, 1968. **302**

Rotter, J. B. Generalized expectancies for internal versus external control of reinforcement. *Psychological Monographs,* 1966, *80,* No. 1. **517**

Ruch, F. L., & Ruch, W. W. The *K* factor as a (validity) suppressor variable in predicting success in selling. *Journal of Applied Psychology,* 1967, *51,* 201–204. **530**

Ruff, G. E. [& Levy, E. Z.] Psychiatric evaluation of candidates for space flight. *American Journal of Psychiatry,* 1959, *116,* 385–391. **694**

Rulon, P. J., & Schweiker, R. F. *Validation of a nonverbal test of military trainability.* Harvard University: Graduate School of Education, 1953. **294 f.**

Rundquist, E. A. Item and response characteristics in attitude and personality meaurement. *Psychological Bulletin,* 1966, *66,* 166–177. **499**

Rust, M. M. The effect of resistance on intelligence scores of young children. *Child Development Monographs,* 1931, No. 6. **263**

Ryan, T. A., & Johnson, B. R. Interest scores in the selection of salesmen and servicemen: Occupational vs. ability-group scoring keys. *Journal of Applied Psychology,* 1942, *26,* 543–562. **476**

Samuels, H. The validity of personality-trait ratings based on projective techniques. *Psychological Monographs,* 1952, *66,* No. 5. **682, 683**

Saltz, E., Reece, M., & Ager, J. Studies of forced-choice methodology: Individual differences in social desirability. *Educational and Psychological Measurement,* 1962, *22,* 365–370. **500**

Sarason, S. B. *The clinical interaction with special reference to the Rorschach.* New York: Harper & Row, 1954. **636, 684**

Sarason, S. B., *et al.* A test anxiety scale for children. *Child Development,* 1958, *29,* 105–115. **62**

Sarason, S. B., Mandler, G., & Craighill, P. G. The effect of differential instructions on anxiety and learning. *Journal of Abnormal and Social Psychology,* 1952, *47,* 561–565. **62 f.**

Sarbin, T. R. A contribution to the study of actuarial and individual methods of prediction. *American Journal of Sociology,* 1943, *48,* 593–602. **442**

Sattler, J. M. Analysis of the functions of the 1960 Stanford-Binet Intelligence Scale, Form L-M. *Journal of Clinical Psychology*, 1965, *21*, 173–179.   **214**

Savage, R. D. (Ed.) *Readings in clinical psychology*. Oxford: Pergamon, 1966.   **77**

Schafer, R. *The clinical application of psychological tests*. New York: International Universities Press, 1948.   **250 f.**

Schafer, R. *Psychoanalytic interpretation in Rorschach testing*. New York: Grune & Stratton, 1954.   **70–73, 77, 117, 684**

Schaie, K. W., & Strother, C. R. A cross-sequential study of age changes in cognitive behavior. *Psychological Bulletin*, 1968, *70*, 671–680.   **230, 397**

Schalling, D., & Rosén, A.-S. Porteus maze differences between psychopathic and non-psychopathic criminals. *British Journal of Social and Clinical Psychology*, 1968, *7*, 224–228.   **640**

Schiele, B. C., & Brozek, J. "Experimental neurosis" resulting from semi-starvation in man. *Psychosomatic Medicine*, 1948, *10*, 31–50.   **570**

Schlesinger, I. M., & Guttman, L. Smallest space analysis of intelligence and achievement tests. *Psychological Bulletin*, 1969, *71*, 95–100.   **282**

Schrader, W. B. Validierungsuntersuchungen und Normen als Hilfsmittel bei der Interpretation von Testwerten. In K. Ingenkamp & T. Marsolek (Eds.) *Möglichkeit und Grenzen der Testanwendung in der Schule*. Weinheim: Beltz, 1968. Pp. 987–1002.   **136**

Schuchman, H. Evaluating the educability of the severely mentally retarded child. *Psychological Monographs*, 1960, *74*, No. 14.   **245**

Schwartz, P. A. Adapting tests to the cultural setting. *Educational and Psychological Measurement*, 1963, *23*, 673–686.   **301**

Scrimshaw, N. S. Infant malnutrition and adult learning. *Saturday Review*, Mar. 16, 1968, *51*, 64–66, 84.   **252**

Sears, R. R. Dependency motivation. In M. R. Jones (Ed.), *Nebraska Symposium on Motivation*. Lincoln: University of Nebraska Press, 1963. Pp. 25–64.   **601**

Seashore, H. G. Methods of expressing test scores. *Test Service Bulletin*, No. 45. New York: Psychological Corporation, 1955.   **114**

Seashore, H. G., & Ricks, J. H., Jr. Norms must be relevant. *Test Service Bulletin*, No. 39. New York: Psychological Corporation, 1950.   **108**

Seeman, W. "Subtlety" in structured tests. *Journal of Consulting Psychology*, 1952, *16*, 278–283.   **500**

Semans, H. H., Holy, T. C., & Gunigan, L. H. A study of the June 1955 graduates of public high school in certain California counties. *California Schools*, 1956, *27*, 417–430.   **219**

Sessions, F. Q. An analyis of the predictive value of the Pre-Engineering Ability Test. *Journal of Applied Psychology*, 1955, *39*, 119–122.   **422**

Shannon, C., & Weaver, W. *The mathematical theory of communication*. Urbana, Ill.: University of Illinois Press, 1949.   **180**

Shapiro, M. B. Experimental method in the psychological description of the individual psychiatric patient. *International Journal of Social Psychiatry*, 1957, *3*, 89–103.   **56, 77**

Sherman, J. A. Problem of sex differences in space perception and aspects of intellectual functioning. *Psychological Review*, 1967, *74*, 290–299.   **360**

Sherwood, J. J. Self-report and projective measures of achievement and affiliation. *Journal of Consulting Psychology*, 1966, *30*, No. 4.   **660**

Shneidman, E. S. (Ed.) *Thematic test analysis.* New York: Grune &
Stratton, 1951.   **633, 653, 668 f.**

Shuford, E. H., Jr., Massengill, H. E., & Albert, A. Admissible probability measurement procedures. *Psychometrika,* 1966, *31,* 125–145.   **59**

Silverman, A. J., Cohen, S. I., Zuidema, G. D., & Lazar, C. S. Prediction
of physiological stress tolerance from projective tests. *Journal of
Projective Techniques,* 1957, *21,* 189–193.   **659**

Simpson, R. H. The specific meanings of certain terms indicating different
degrees of frequency. *Quarterly Journal of Speech,* 1944, *30,*
328–330.   **494 f.**

Skinner, B. F., Solomon, H. C., & Lindsley, O. R. A new method for the
experimental analysis of the behavior of psychotic patients. *Journal
of Nervous and Mental Disease,* 1954, *120,* 403–406.   **74**

Skolnick, A. Motivational imagery and behavior. *Journal of Consulting
Psychology,* 1966, *30,* 463–478.   **654, 665**

Slakter, M. J. Generality of risk-taking on objective examinations. *Educational and Psychological Measurement,* 1969, *29,* 115–128.   **58**

Smedslund, J. The acquisition of conservation of substance and weight in
children. *Scandinavian Journal of Psychology,* 1961, *2,* 1–10, 71–84,
85–87, 153–160, 203–210.   **244**

Smedslund, J. Psychological diagnostics. *Psychological Bulletin,* 1969,
71, 237–248.   **244**

Smith, M. B. An analysis of two measures of "authoritarianism" among
Peace Corps teachers. *Journal of Personality,* 1965, *33,* 513–535.   **547**

Smith, P. C., & Kendall, L. M. Retranslation of expectations: An approach
to the construction of unambiguous anchors for rating scales.
Journal of Applied Psychology, 1963, *47,* 149–155.   **584**

Snow, R. E., & Elashoff, J. D. *Pygmalion revisited.* Unpublished manu-
script.   **302**

Sontag, L. W., Baker, C. T., & Nelson, V. L. Mental growth and personality development: A longitudinal study. *Monographs, Society for
Research in Child Development,* 1958, *23,* No. 2.   **233**

Soskin, W. F. Bias in postdiction from projective tests. *Journal of Abnormal and Social Psychology,* 1954, *49,* 69–74.   **683**

Soskin, W. F. The influence of four types of data on diagnostic conceptualization in psychological testing. *Journal of Abnormal and Social
Psychology,* 1959, *58,* 69–78.   **683**

Spence, K. W. A theory of emotionally based drive (D) and its relation
to performance in simple learning situations. *American Psychologist,* 1958, *13,* 131–141.   **530**

Spence, K. W., & Spence, J. T. Relation of eyelid conditioning to manifest anxiety, extraversion, and rigidity. *Journal of Abnormal and
Social Psychology,* 1964, *68,* 144–149.   **516**

Spielberger, C. D. (Ed.) *Anxiety and behavior.* New York: Academic
Press, 1966.   **516, 549**

Staff, Division on Child Development, American Council on Education.
Helping teachers understand children. Washington, D. Č.: American
Council on Education, 1945.   **591**

Stanley, J. C. Reliability. In R. L. Thorndike (Ed.), *Educational measurement.* Washington, D.C.: American Council on Education, 1970.
(In press.)   **152**

Starch, D., & Elliot, E. C. Reliability of grading high school work in English. *School Review*, 1912, *20*, 442–457. 78

Starch, D. & Elliot, E. C. Reliability of grading high school work in mathematics. *School Review*, 1913, *21*, 254–259. 78

Statistical studies of selective service testing, 1951–1953. Princeton, N. J.: Educational Testing Service, 1955. 106

Steiner, I. D., & Vannoy, J. S. Personality correlates of two types of conformity behavior. *Journal of Personality and Social Psychology*, 1966, *4*, 307–315. 619

Stephenson, W. *The study of behavior.* Chicago: Univerity of Chicago Press, 1953. 585

Stern, G. G. The measurement of psychological characteristics of students and learning environments. In S. Messick & J. Ross (Eds.), *Measurement in personality and cognition.* New York: Wiley, 1962. Pp. 27–68. 596

Sternberg, J. An analytical study of a selection interview procedure. Unpublished master's thesis, Syracuse University, 1950. 576

Stevens, S. S. (Ed.) *Handbook of experimental psychology.* New York: Wiley, 1951. 393

Stevenson, H. W., & Odom, R. D. Interrelationships in children's learning. *Child Development*, 1965, *36*, 7–19. 292

Stewart, E. E. The stability of the SAT-Verbal score scale. *Research Bulletin* 66–37. Princeton, N. J.: Educational Testing Service, 1966. 97

Stewart, L. H., & Roberts, J. P. The relationship of Kuder profiles to remaining in a teachers college and to occupational choice. *Educational and Psychological Measurement*, 1955, *15*, 416–421. 477

Stice, G., & Eckstrom, R. B. High-school attrition. *Research Bulletin* 64–53. Princeton, N. J.: Educational Testing Service, 1964. 218

Stockford, L., & Bissell, H. W. Factors involved in establishing a merit rating scale. *Personnel*, 1949, *26*, 94–116. 574

Stott, L. H., & Ball, R. S. Infant and preschool mental tests: Review and evaluation. *Monographs, Society for Research in Child Development*, 1965, *30*, No. 3. 259 ff., 266

Strauss, A. A. Enriching the interpretation of the Stanford-Binet test. *Journal of Exceptional Children*, 1941, *7*, 260–264. 249

Stricker, L. J. Compulsivity as a moderator variable. *Journal of Applied Psychology*, 1966, *50*, 331–335. 440

Stricker, L. J., Messick, S., & Jackson, D. N. Suspicion of deception: Implications for conformity research. *Journal of Personality and Social Psychology*, 1967, *5*, 379–389. 613

Strodtbeck, F. L. The hidden curriculum in the middle-class home. In J. D. Krumboltz (Ed.), *Learning and the educational process.* Chicago: Rand McNally, 1965. Pp. 91–111. 256

Strong, E. K., Jr. *Vocational interests of men and women.* Stanford, Calif.: Stanford University Press, 1943. 429, 466, 472, 475, 477

Strong, E. K., Jr. Vocational interests of accountants. *Journal of Applied Psychology*, 1949, *33*, 474–481. 462

Strong, E. K., Jr. *Vocational interests 18 years after college.* Minneapolis: University of Minnesota Press, 1955. 137, 469, 477

Stuart, I. R. Field dependency, authoritarianism and perception of the human figure. *Journal of Social Psychology*, 1966, *66*, 209–214. 631

Stuit, D. B. (Ed.) *Personnel research and test development in the Bureau of Naval Personnel*. Princeton, N. J.: Princeton University Press, 1947. **414**

Sullivan, P. L., & Welsh, G. S. A technique for objective configural analysis of MMPI profiles. *Journal of Consulting Psychology*, 1952, *16*, 383–388. **544**

Sundberg, N. D. The acceptability of "fake" versus "bona fide" personality test interpretations. *Journal of Abnormal and Social Psychology*, 1955, *50*, 145–147. **682**

Super, D. E. (Ed.) *The use of multifactor tests in guidance*. Washington, D. C.: American Personnel and Guidance Association, 1958. **376**

Super, D. E., & Crites, J. O. *Appraising vocational fitness*. (2d ed.) New York: Harper & Row, 1962. **364, 463, 470, 471, 488**

Swets, J. A., & Feurzig, W. Computer-aided instruction. *Science*, 1965, *150*, 572–576. **75**

Taft, R. Extraversion, neuroticism, and expressive behavior: An application of Wallach's moderator effect to handwriting analysis. *Journal of Personality*, 1967, *35*, 570–584. **564**

Taylor, J. A. The relationship of anxiety to the conditioned eyelid response. *Journal of Experimental Psychology*, 1951, *41*, 81–92. **531**

Taylor, J. B. Rating scales as measures of clinical judgment: A method for increasing scale reliability and sensitivity. *Educational and Psychological Measurement*, 1968, *28*, 747–766. **584, 607**

Tenopyr, M., Guilford, J. P., & Hoepfner, R. A factor analysis of symbolic-memory abilities. *Psychological Laboratory, University of Southern California, Reports*, 1966, No. 38. **340**

Terman, L. M. *The measurement of intelligence*. Boston: Houghton Mifflin, 1916. **200 f.**

Terman, L. M. The discovery and encouragement of exceptional talent. *American Psychologist*, 1954, *9*, 221–230. **226, 235**

Terman, L. M., & Merrill, M. A. *Measuring intelligence*. Boston: Houghton Mifflin, 1960. **55, 79, 211 ff., 219, 224**

Terwilliger, J. S. Representation of vocational interests on an absolute scale. Unpublished master's thesis, University of Illinois, 1960. **487**

Thigpen, C. H., & Cleckley, H. A case of multiple personality. *Journal of Abnormal and Social Psychology*, 1953, *49*, 135–151. **566**

Thigpen, C. H., & Cleckley, H. *The three faces of Eve*. New York: McGraw-Hill, 1957. **566**

Thorndike, R. L. *Personnel selection*. New York: Wiley, 1949. **175**

Thorndike, R. L. *The concept of overachievement*. New York: Teachers College, Columbia University, 1963. (a) **87**

Thorndike, R. L. The prediction of vocational success. *Vocational Guidance Quarterly*, 1963, *11*, 179–187. (b) **383**

Thorndike, R. L. Some methodological issues in the study of creativity. In *Proceedings, Invitational Conference on Testing Problems, 1962*. Princeton: ETS, 1963. Pp. 40–54. (c) **395 f.**

Thorndike, R. L. Educational decisions and human assessment. *Teachers College Record*, 1964, *66*, 103–112. **43**

Thorndike, R. L., & Hagen, E. *Measurement and evaluation in psychology and education.* (3rd ed.) New York: Wiley, 1969.   **368**

Thornton, G. G., & McCormick, E. J. *The experimental use of dimensions of worker-oriented job variables in determining job requirements.* Lafayette, Ind.: Occupational Research Center, Purdue University, 1964.   **409**

Thornton, G. R. A factor analysis of tests designed to measure persistence. *Psychological Monographs,* 1939, *51,* No. 3.   **620**

Thurstone, L. L. Primary mental abilities. *Psychometric Monographs,* 1938. No. 1.   **326**

Tiffin, J., & McCormick, E. J. *Industrial psychology.* (5th ed.) Englewood Cliffs, N. J.: Prentice-Hall, 1965.   **451**

Tolor, A., & Schulberg, H. C. *An evaluation of the Bender-Gestalt Test.* Springfield, Ill.: Thomas, 1963.   **631**

Torrance, E. P., & Hansen, E. The question-asking behavior of highly creative and less creative basic business teachers identified by a paper-and-pencil test. *Psychological Reports,* 1965, *17,* 815–818.   **397**

Torrance, E. P., & Ziller, R. C. Risk and life experience: Development of a scale for measuring risk-taking tendencies. *AFPTRC Research Bulletin* 57–23, 1957.   **58**

Towbin, A. P. Psychological testing from end to means. *Journal of Projective Techniques,* 1964, *28,* 86–91.   **77**

Training Aids Section, Ninth Naval District Headquarters, Great Lakes, Ill. A comparative study of verbalized and projected pictorial tests in gunnery. Unpublished, 1945.   **147**

Trattner, M. H. Comparison of three methods of assembling aptitude test batteries. *Personnel Psychology,* 1963, *16,* 221–232.   **434**

Treat, K. Tests for garment machine operators. *Personnel Journal,* 1929, *8,* 19–28.   **390**

Trinkhaus, W. K. The permanence of vocational interests of college freshmen. *Educational and Psychological Measurement,* 1954, *14,* 641–646.   **469**

Tucker, L. R. An inter-battery method of factor analysis. *Psychometrika,* 1958, *23,* 111–136.   **319**

Tucker, L. R. Experiments in multimode factor analysis. *Proceedings, Invitational Conference on Testing Problems, 1964.* Princeton, N. J.: Educational Testing Service, 1965. Pp. 46–57.   **319**

Tuddenham, R. D. Soldier intelligence in World Wars I and II. *American Psychologist,* 1948, *3,* 54–56.   **229**

Tuddenham, R. D. Studies in reputation: II. The diagnosis of social adjustment. *Psychological Monographs,* 1952, *66,* No. 1.   **607**

Tuddenham, R. D. The nature and measurement of intelligence. In L. Postman (Ed.), *Psychology in the making.* New York: Knopf, 1962. Pp. 469–525.   **350**

Tupes, E. C. Relationships between behavior trait ratings by peers and later officer performance of USAF Officer Candidate School graduates. *AFPTRC Research Bulletin* 57–125, 1957.   **593**

Tupes, E. C., & Christal, R. E. Recurrent personality factors based on trait ratings. *USAF ASD Technical Report,* 1961, No. 61–97.   **574**

Turnbull, W. W. (Test review.) In Buros, 1965. Pp. 766–767.   **307**

Tutton, M. E. Stability of adolescent vocational interests. *Vocational Guidance Quarterly,* 1955, *3,* 78–80.   **469**

Tyler, L. E. Antecedents of two varities of vocational interests. *Genetic Psychology Monographs*, 1964, *70*, 177–277. **469**

Tyler, L. E. *The psychology of human differences.* (3rd ed.) New York: Appleton-Century-Crofts, 1965. **247, 666**

Tyler, R. W. *Constructing achievement tests.* Columbus: Ohio State University, 1934. **31**

Ullmann, C. A. *Identification of maladjusted school children.* Washington, D. C.: U. S. Public Health Service, 1952. **554**

Ullmann, C. A. Teachers, peers, and tests as predictors of adjustment. *Journal of Educational Psychology*, 1957, *48*, 257–267. **570**

Ulrich, R. E., Stachnik, T. J., & Stainton, N. R. Student acceptance of generalized personality interpretations. *Psychological Reports*, 1963, *13*, 831–834. **682**

Underwood, B. J., & Richardson, J. Some verbal materials for the study of concept formation. *Psychological Bulletin*, 1956, *53*, 84–95. **27**

USES. Development of USES Aptitude Test Battery for mounter. *Technical Report* S-8, 1967. (a) **436**

USES. Summary of occupational validity on the General Aptitude Test Battery. *Test Research Report* No. 17, 1967. (b) **363**

USES. Development of a nonreading edition of the General Aptitude Test Battery. *Test Research Report* No. 23, 1968. (a) **359**

USES. Modernization of USES Dictation Test and Spelling Test. *Test Research Report* No. 22, 1968. (b) **110**

Uzgiris, I. C., & Hunt, J. McV. Toward ordinal scales of psychological development in infancy. Unpublished data. **261**

Van der Meer, H. C. Decision making: Need for achievement and probability preference under chance and skill orientations. *Acta Psychologica*, 1967, *26*, 353–372. **662**

Vernon, P. E. The validation of civil service selection board procedures. *Occupational Psychology*, 1950, *24*, 75–95. **647, 671**

Vernon, P. E. *Personality assessment.* London: Methuen, 1964. Pp. 179–200. **519**

Vernon, P. E. Ability factors and environmental influences. *American Psychologist*, 1965, *20*, 723–733. **331**

Vernon, P. E. Intelligence and cultural environment. London: Methuen, 1969. **343**

Vernon, P. E., & Parry, J. B. *Personnel selection in the British forces.* London: University of London Press, 1949. **271, 364, 644, 671**

Veroff, J., Feld, S., & Crockett, H. Explorations into the effects of picture cues on thematic apperceptive expression of achievement motivation. *Journal of Personality and Social Psychology*, 1966, *3*, 171–181. **660**

Veroff, J., *et al.* The use of thematic apperception to assess motivation in a nationwide interview survey. *Psychological Monographs*, 1960, *74*, No. 12. **660**

Vigotsky, L. S. *Thought and language.* New York: Wiley, 1962. **245**

Walker, R. E., Hunt, W. A., & Schwartz, M. L. The difficulty of WAIS Comprehension scoring. *Journal of Clinical Psychology*, 1965, *21*, 427–429. **211**

Wallace, J. An abilities conception of personality: Some implications for personality measurement. *American Psychologist*, 1966, *21*, 132–138.   549

Wallace, P., Kissinger, B., & Reynolds, B. Testing of minority group applicants for employment. *Equal Employment Opportunity Commission, Research Report*, March, 1966.   299

Wallach, M. A., & Gahm, R. C. Personality functions of graphic construction and expansiveness. *Journal of Personality*, 1960, *28*, 73–88.   564

Wallach, M. A., & Kogan, N. *Modes of thinking in young children*. New York: Holt, Rinehart and Winston, 1965.   395

Wallach, M. A., *et al.* Contradiction between overt and projective personality indicators as a function of defensiveness. *Psychological Monographs*, 1962, *76*, No. 1.   563

Wann, T. W. (Ed.) *Behaviorism and phenomenology*. Chicago: University of Chicago Press, 1964. Pp. 109–133.   520

Ward, C. H., *et al.* The psychiatric nomenclature: Reasons for diagnostic disagreement. *Archives of General Psychiatry*, 1962, *7*, 198–205.   533

Watts, K. P. Intelligence test performance from 11 to 18. *British Journal of Educational Psychology*, 1968, *28*, 112–119.   287

Wechsler, D. *The measurement and appraisal of adult intelligence.* (4th ed.) Baltimore: Williams & Wilkins, 1958.   228

Wechsler, D., & Jaros, E. Schizophrenic patterns on the WISC. *Journal of Clinical Psychology*, 1965, *21*, 288–291.   250

Weick, K. E. Systematic observational methods. In Lindzey & Aronson, 1968.   607

Welsh, G. S., & Dahlstrom, G. W. *Basic readings on the MMPI in psychology and medicine*. Minneapolis: University of Minnesota Press, 1956.   537, 570

Werner, E., & Bayley, N. The reliability of Bayley's revised scale of mental and motor development during the first year of life. *Child Development*, 1966, *37*, 39–50.   260

Wesman, A. G. Faking personality test scores in a simulated employment situation. *Journal of Applied Psychology*, 1952, *36*, 112–113. (a)   496, 498

Wesman, A. G. Reliability and confidence. *Test Service Bulletin*, No. 44. New York: Psychological Corporation, 1952. (b)   193

Westin, A. F. *Privacy and freedom*. New York: Atheneum, 1967.   501, 510

White, S. H. Some educated guesses about cognitive development in the pre-school years. In Hess & Bear, 1968. Pp. 203–214.   308

Wiener, D. N. Subtle and obvious keys for the MMPI. *Journal of Consulting Psychology*, 1948, *12*, 164–170.   500

Wiener, G. The effect of distrust on some aspects of intelligence test behavior. *Journal of Consulting Psychology*, 1957, *21*, 127–130.   62

Wiggins, J. S. Personality structure. *Annual Review of Psychology*, 1968, *19*, 293–330.   499

Wiggins, N. Individual viewpoints of social desirability. *Psychological Bulletin*, 1966, *66*, 68–77.   500

Willemin, L. P., Mellinger, J. J., & Karcher, E. K., Jr. Identifying fighters for combat. *Personnel Research Branch, Technical Research Report* 1112, 1958.   416

Williams, P. A., Kirk, B. A., & Frank, A. C. New men's SVIB: A comparison with the old. *Journal of Counseling Psychology,* . 1968, *15*, 287–294.   463

Wilson, D. P. *My six convicts.* New York: Holt, Rinehart and Winston, 1951. **16, 71**

Wilson, J. A. R., & Robeck, M. C. A comparison of the Kindergarten Evaluation of Learning Potential (KELP), readiness, mental maturity, achievement, and ratings by first grade teachers. *Educational and Psychological Measurement,* 1964, *24,* 409–414. **264**

Wilson, J. W., & Carpenter, K. E. The need for restandardizing altered tests. *American Psychologist,* 1948, *3,* 172 f. **112**

Wilson, R. N., & Kaiser, H. E. A comparison of similar scales on the SVIB and the Kuder, Form DD. *Journal of Counseling Psychology,* 1968, *15,* 468–470. **471**

Winder, C. L., & Wiggins, J. S. Social reputation and social behavior: A further validation of the peer nomination theory. *Journal of Abnormal and Social Psychology,* 1964, *68,* 441–448. **610**

Winkler, R. C., & Mathews, T. S. How employees feel about personality tests. *Personnel Journal,* 1967, *46,* 490–492. **512**

Wissler, C. *The correlation of mental and physical tests.* New York: Columbia University, 1901. **198**

Witkin, H. A. The perception of the upright. *Scientific American,* Feb., 1959, *200,* 50–70. **666**

Witkin, H. A., *et al. Personality through perception: An experimental and clinical study.* New York: Harper & Row, 1954. **240**

Witkin, H. A., *et al. Psychological differentiation.* New York: Wiley, 1962. **240, 627–630**

Witkin, H. A., *et al.* Cognitive patterning in mildly retarded boys. *Child Development,* 1966, *37,* 301–306. **226, 240–242**

Wodtke, K. H. Some data on the reliability and validity of creativity tests at the elementary school level. *Educational and Psychological Measurement,* 1964, *24,* 399–408. **397**

Wohl, J. Traditional and contemporary views of psychological testing. *Journal of Projective Techniques,* 1963, *27,* 359–365. **43**

Wolfle, D. *America's resources of specialized talent.* New York: Harper & Row, 1954. **218**

Wolfle, D. Diversity of talent. *American Psychologist,* 1960, *15,* 535–545. **373**

Womer, F. B. *Test norms, their use and interpretation.* Washington, D. C.: National Association of Secondary School Principals, 1965. **114**

Woodrow, H. The ability to learn. *Psychological Review,* 1946, *53,* 147–158. **292**

Woodworth, D. G., & MacKinnon, D. W. The use of trait ratings in an assessment of 100 Air Force captains. *WADC Technical Note 58–64.* Wright Air Development Center, 1958. **675**

Wylie, R. *The self-concept.* Lincoln, Neb.: University of Nebraska Press, 1961. **551, 552, 586**

Yamamoto, K. Creative writing and school achievement. *School and Society,* 1963, *91,* 307–308. **397**

Yamamoto, K. Creativity—a blind man's report on the elephant. *Journal of Counseling Psychology,* 1965, *12,* 428–434. (a) **405**

Yamamoto, K. Effects of restriction of range and test unreliability on correlations between measures of intelligence and creative thinking. *British Journal of Educational Psychology,* 1965, *35,* 300–305. (b) **396**

Yates, A., *et al.* Symposium of the effects of coaching and practice in intelligence tests. *British Journal of Educational Psychology*, 1953, *23*, 147–162; 1954, *24*, 1–8, 57–63. 67

Yates, A. J. The validity of some psychological tests of brain damage. *Psychological Bulletin*, 1954, *51*, 359–379. 636

Yerkes, R. M. (Ed.) Psychological examining in the United States Army. *Memoirs of the National Academy of Sciences*, 1921, No. 15. 205

Yinger, J. M. *Toward a field theory of behavior.* New York: McGraw-Hill, 1965. 561

Yoakum, C. S., & Yerkes, R. M. *Army mental tests.* New York: Holt, Rinehart and Winston, 1920. 204

Yonge, G. D. Certain consequences of applying the *K* factor to MMPI scores. *Educational and Psychological Measurement*, 1966, *26*, 887–893. 530

Young, M. The rise of the meritocracy, 1870–2033. London: Thames and Hudson, 1958. 226

Zavala, A. Development of the forced-choice rating scale technique. *Psychological Review*, 1965, *63*, 117–124. 588

Zeaman, D., & House, B. J. The relation of IQ and learning. In R. M. Gagné (Ed.), *Learning and individual differences.* Columbus, Ohio: Merrill, 1967. Pp. 192–212. 266

Zigler, E., & Butterfield, E. C. Motivational aspects of changes in IQ test performance of culturally deprived nursery school children. *Child Development*, 1968, *39*, 1–14. 215, 263

Ziller, R. C. Vocational choice and utility for risk. *Journal of Counseling Psychology*, 1957, *4*, 61–64. 638

Zubin, J., Eron, L. D., & Schumer, F. *An experimental approach to projective techniques.* New York: Wiley, 1965. 635, 636, 654

Zytowski, D. G. Relationship of equivalent scales on three interest inventories. *Personnel and Guidance Journal*, 1968, *47*, 44–49. 471

Index

Index*

* For particular instruments, see list under Tests and techniques, specific